PIPES AND ACTIONS
SOME ORGAN BUILDERS IN THE MIDLANDS
AND BEYOND

St. Mary's Church, Warwick.
Courtesy of Nicholson & Co. Photo by Dennis Thurlow

PIPES AND ACTIONS

Some Organ Builders in the Midlands and beyond

by

LAURENCE ELVIN

F.S.A., F.R.Hist.S., F.R.S.A., F.I.M.I.T.

Foreword by

ROY MASSEY

D. Mus., F.R.C.O.(C.H.M.), F.R.S.C.M., A.D.C.M., A.R.C.M.

And a Message by

H.R.H. THE PRINCE OF WALES

Published by
LAURENCE ELVIN
10 ALMOND AVENUE, SWANPOOL, LINCOLN

TO THE MEMORY OF

W. C. JONES

Distinguished voicer and a great gentleman

'Organs are like human beings; some are good, some are bad, and many are quite temperamental. I have played on some that are like friends when I first met them and others seem to fight me the minute I touch the keys. I don't think I have ever found two organs which are exactly alike. They have individuality and even when I get used to them, they have fits of obstinacy and temper.'

Organs I have met   The Autobiography of Edwin H. Lemare

'There is nothing to it. You only have to hit the right notes at the right time and the instrument plays itself.'

J. S. Bach (1685–1750)   From *The Bach Family*, Geiringer, 1954

ISBN 0–9500049–8–7

Designed by Christopher Bagot and Laurence Elvin

Printed in Great Britain by H. Charlesworth & Co., Huddersfield

Contents

Foreword

by Roy Massey D.MUS., F.R.C.O. (C.H.M.), F.R.S.C.M., A.D.C.M., A.R.C.M.

Organist and Master of the Choristers, Hereford Cathedral

IT gives me great pleasure to write a few words of introduction to Laurence Elvin's latest book which describes some of my favourite organ builders in the Midlands and beyond. For too long some of these firms have been largely unrecorded in the annals of organ literature and a survey of them is long overdue.

Last year, it was my pleasure to give the opening recital on the superb Nicholson rebuild of the organ in Birmingham Cathedral. The association of the Nicholson firm with the Cathedral organ, beginning in 1894 with their work on the 1715 Schwarbrick organ in its wonderful case, has continued through two major restorations until the present day, and this faithfulness to the Worcester/Malvern firm over a long period is repeated in countless churches and chapels throughout the Midland area where they have been building fine organs since the early nineteenth century. As a Midlander born and bred, and someone whose working life has rarely taken him far from the Malvern Hills, it has fallen to my lot over the years to be associated with many Nicholson organs both large and small, and I have enjoyed the privilege of playing opening recitals on several of their major installations in the area. From the splendours of the Birmingham Oratory, Holy Trinity, Stratford-on-Avon and St Mary's, Warwick, down to the superbly restored John Nicholson one-manual of *c.*1845 at Bishop's Frome and the beautifully cased two-manual of 1993 at Lugwardine in Herefordshire, their work has been of the same consistently high standard. They are an honoured name in the Midlands and I am delighted that Laurence Elvin has described their history in such detail.

But, of course, he doesn't stop there. For many years, beginning in my early youth as an avid organ enthusiast on a bicycle, I have discovered not only Nicholson organs in these parts, but many others by less familiar builders, often of beautiful quality. I have always particularly admired the singing tone of the instruments by Porritt of Leicester and Nicholson and Lord of Walsall. I also found solidly built, if slightly unimaginative work horses by Banfield of Birmingham, Ebrall of Camp Hill, W. J. Bird of Harborne, Conacher of Huddersfield, and the exotic stop keys of John Compton also attracted my youthful attention both in church and cinema. Laurence Elvin takes in all these firms in his survey and also includes West Country and Northern worthies from further afield, many of whom have produced work of considerable distinction. Neither does he forget the younger generation of organ builders who are so splendidly keeping the flag flying.

Throughout his long life, Laurence Elvin has realised that beauty can often be found in unexpected places and in unfashionable areas, and this latest survey is typical of his approach. It is beautifully written, superbly illustrated, meticulously researched and full of wondrous nuggets of information expressed in readable, entertaining style, all enriched with many a personal anecdote culled from a lifetime of interest in the King of Instruments. His other contributions to the literature of the organ are well known and have already taken their place among the classics of the genre, though he tells me that this may well be his last extended work. If this is so, I am doubly honoured to be writing this Foreword.

It is a cause for rejoicing that the Classical emphasis of the 1960s, which so fascinated both organists and organ builders, has largely been replaced by a heightened awareness of the achievements of our native school of organ builders and a renewed interest in the history of the English organ. These days, I believe, exports of organs from these shores outnumber imports from the Continent and, although one must never underestimate the importance of what has been learnt from our Continental brethren over the centuries, it is re-assuring that we are once again employing our own stop nomenclature and 'Open Diapason' and 'Open Wood' are no longer unfashionable terms!

For over half a century, Laurence Elvin has encouraged us to appraise and appreciate the English organ, and all makers, players and lovers of the instrument in this country and beyond, owe him a great debt of gratitude for this, his latest work.

Hereford, 14th January, 1994

A Message

ST. JAMES'S PALACE

Laurence Elvin's scholarly research into our splendid tradition of organ building gives us a better appreciation of the exceptional work of English master organ builders which still, thank goodness, survives in many churches and halls throughout the country.

These magnificent instruments, many of which are, inevitably, under threat from lack of funds for repair, serve not only to maintain the glorious tradition of church music - but also as a lasting testament to the ingenuity and sheer quality of British craftsmanship.

Preface

THIS book was intended to be part of *Family Enterprise*, published in 1986, but circumstances dictated otherwise, which was just as well, for a great deal has happened in the organ world during the past eight years which otherwise would have gone unrecorded.

Inevitably, once again some of this book is autobiographical; it has provided the opportunity to record my experiences in the Midlands, the West Country, Merseyside and London. Moreover, it has been possible to deal in depth with the once eminent firm of The John Compton Organ Company and to a lesser extent, Nicholson of Worcester, builders of fine organs since 1841. The life and work of John Nicholson merits a more thorough approach than has been possible here, and this is in hand by Jim Berrow; likewise, that well-known Yorkshireman, James Jepson Binns, whose sterling work is now receiving appreciation, which is long overdue. Nicholas Plumley has undertaken the history of J. W. Walker & Sons, while Hill & Son has occupied a number of years of patient and extremely thorough research on the part of the Revd. B. B. Edmonds, whose fount of knowledge is always readily available to the serious worker. Much has been written about Father Willis at various times and in various publications, but I do feel that an appraisal of his grandson's work, Henry Willis III, is overdue. It has given me particular pleasure to touch very briefly on the work of this great man. The fascinating book by Charles Callahan, *The American Classic Organ. A history in letters*, has given us a 'taster' of his ideals, but there is much more to be said.

It is hoped that this book will provide an adequate appreciation of the work of a wide spectrum of firms, all of whom have made, and are making, a contribution to the art of organ building in this country, which has long been the home of craftsmen, who are second to none, throughout the English speaking world and the Continent. This opinion I hold to most strongly; we are now in the midst of a 'topsy turvy' world of organ building, where those (of whom I am proud to be a member) are labelled as 'fuddy duddys' who are strongly opposed to the importation of instruments from the Continent. I will not repeat my opinions regarding this, which were fully expressed in my last book: *The Story of some North Country Organ Builders*, but I do bring forward a number of points, which *should* give us cause for great concern, particularly the organ builders in this country who love their craft and at the same time have a living to earn. Some seventeen years spent as Organ Adviser to the Diocese of Lincoln have opened my eyes to the real problems facing our town and village places of worship and the outlook for the future is far from re-assuring. Depleted congregations mean that a greater burden is placed on the faithful few; finances are strained to the utmost limit, for the Diocesan quotas have been increased and our magnificent churches (Medieval and Victorian) in some of our villages require extensive restoration and there just isn't the money. From personal experience I am aware of the great concern of our caring Bishop, The Right Revd. Robert Hardy—who has visited many of them—and returned home determined that something must be done. I have seen village churches closed, not only in Lincolnshire but elsewhere, having been declared redundant; the nonconformists have similar problems, and I learn with sadness, the closure of one after another village chapel. This leads me to the inevitable problem of redundant organs—*BIOS Journal* never fails to produce a list—where do they all go? The grapevine tells me that some places of worship have great difficulty in disposing of them.

A further problem is the change in pattern of worship in some of our churches where organs have little or no place. In my own city, I have seen a magnificent three-manual Jardine stand silent for a number of years until eventually destroyed. It is not the only one. Another mainstream nonconformist church known to me was recently considering the possibility of replacing a fine two-manual instrument by a once famous Yorkshire firm, which only required restoration at a very reasonable cost. It was felt that an electronic would be much more suitable to accompany hymns, "to keep the young people". His Royal Highness, The Prince of Wales, has shown his care for the fabric of our churches, as well as 'Music in Country Churches' of which he is Patron; we need to take the strongest possible line on the care of our organs. The slogan I wish to put forward most strongly is: *'Buy British'* instead of spending vast sums of money on Continental instruments which many of us regard as totally unsuitable for accompanying English liturgical worship, or for that matter, concert performances. To quote Henry Willis III in his contribution to the *Journal of the Incorporated Society of Organ Builders* for May 1963, entitled 'The Baroque Revival'; 'What we want in this country are not instruments capable only of rendering organ music of the Bach and pre-Bach era, but that of *every* period and to that end we should, indeed must, include all the charm of early periods, with the developments of later days used in correct perspective'. Henry Willis was a much travelled man, with a wide experience of Continental organs and contemporary organ builders there, a number of whom were his personal friends. Enough has now been said here to show that English organ builders will need all the support that can be mustered in future years.

Finally—where have all the correspondents gone in the columns of our organ and musical journals, who once battled for and against the organ building of their day, in which John Compton and Henry Willis took part? We learned so much from their different points of view; they were amusing too, adding spice to our reading. I would urge our organ lovers to enter the 'field of battle' once again—we have no shortage of very able writers—who could also help by writing to the ecclesiastical press, as well as local newspapers, where the occasion merited intervention on organs in our churches and chapels. To quote the uncrowned King—Edward VIII, when Prince of Wales— *'Something must be done'*.

Tone production has always been an absorbing interest and I have enjoyed many discussions with various organ builders, whose ideals and views have been of great value and taught me much. I find that in some quarters today, there is a tendency to loudness and tone of a brittle nature, particularly in the reeds. A theory I put forward to one of our leading voicers was that our ears have been battered by every conceivable noise possible, from radio, television, discos and the like; it is impossible to find quiet in any public place and I wonder whether subconsciously we have been compelled to attune to this (for myself with great difficulty, for my hearing is still very acute), with a result that a particular voicer here and there reflects this in his voicing. Our discussion resulted in his agreeing that I might have a point! In a lifetime's study of organs and in particular, those of Father Willis in his early, middle and late periods, I am most emphatic in saying that he achieved great brilliance at times, which created an exciting ensemble of absolute cohesion, without hardness, shriek or over loudness.

Tonal design and tone production have been a matter for discussion (sometimes heated) during the whole of this century and changes in thinking have been most marked in the past two decades or so. One's individual likes and dislikes lead inevitably to bias on the part of some, but there are certain rules which must be adhered to. For example, I recently came across a specification of a two-manual instrument for a nonconformist church, with a plethora of mixtures, one reed and two stopped flutes, there being no quiet tonal colour to provide warmth and mystery, for voluntaries, anthems and concerts. The inclusion of a salicional or mild viola would have made all the difference. How on earth can one provide the necessary atmosphere for worship with such a specification? This leads me to express my opinion most emphatically, that there should be less thought given to theorising and more to the practical considerations involved for the particular situation. In writing this Preface, I came across the following statement by Henry Willis III in his advertisement for *Musical Opinion* in December 1936. It gives us much food for thought.

> 'Organs are for playing music upon. An artist may produce an instrument which is truly musical, yet its ensemble is weary and unrefreshing. On the other hand, he may create an ensemble which is striking, but with individual voices sacrificed to that end.'

Whilst thinking of bias, I am conscious of the fact that in this age of enlightenment, some reviewer may castigate me for my enthusiasm for John Compton's use of extension. Let me make it clear, that not all of his instruments were equally successful (particularly the smaller jobs), but to quote three, Downside Abbey; St Luke's Chelsea; and St Bride's, Fleet Street, I am not alone in saying that they were masterpieces. As I was penning these observations, I had the opportunity of examining minutely (both at the console and up in the chambers) Compton's *magnum opus* at Downside Abbey. Here, I marvelled not only at the ingenuity of planning in a difficult site, but the artistry and skill of designer and voicer at producing the most glorious sound imaginable. Mr Roger Taylor, curator of the organ who, with many years of experience, is conversant with every inch of this remarkable instrument, is in complete agreement with my views.

One of the encouraging features of organ building today is the increase of true conservation in dealing with some of our great Victorian and Edwardian treasures (quite apart from earlier historic work). Instead of rebuilding, every care has been taken to restore them to the state they were in on leaving the factory for their destination. This work has entailed study, skill and time which has inevitably involved high cost to the customer, but how rewarding it has been to deal with masterpieces by builders such as Binns, Harrison, Hill, Lewis and Father Willis, giving them a new lease of life for many more years without any alterations to the original work whatsoever. So successful has this become, that it is hoped it will be possible to give greater attention to this branch of organ building as the years go by. We have lost some magnificent instruments in the past, for reasons which are well known without repeating them here. It is my hope that when the time eventually comes for renewal of the best examples of John Compton, that his skill, together with that of his partner, J. I. Taylor, will not be forgotten. In their case, I refer of course to design and tone and not to the original system of electric action, which, when worn out, is best replaced by Solid State.

In conclusion, what has given me particular pleasure is to draw attention to the enterprise of youth, in establishing their own firms and in each case achieving great success in their own particular sphere. I feel certain that His Royal Highness, The Prince of Wales, will be greatly heartened by their enthusiasm and hard work in establishing businesses which are highly thought of by musicians who are acquainted with them.

Laurence Elvin, Lincoln, December 1994

Acknowledgements

I am honoured that H. R. H. The Prince of Wales has contributed a Message and thank him most warmly for his gracious contribution to this book. It could not be more apposite for today, when churches are experiencing great difficulties due to depleted congregations and lack of funds. When Prince Charles was a cadet at the Royal Air Force College, Cranwell, he used to pay informal visits to a number of churches in the county where he would have ample opportunity of seeing some examples of organs sadly needing care and attention. His great interest in architecture led him to Boston 'Stump' which was undergoing extensive restoration. This so impressed him that he supported the appeal and visited this great church on 23rd November, 1988, to see the results of ten years work of restoration. After meeting official representatives of the town and area organisations, he climbed the scaffolding to the nave roof to see work in progress at close quarters. He then examined the many features of the interior of this magnificent church as well as having a word with each one of the 120 guests who had worked so hard for the restoration appeal. In my capacity as Diocesan Organ Adviser, being responsible for over-seeing the reconstruction of the organ by Harrison & Harrison, I was standing next to David Wright, the organist, in whose work the Prince showed great interest. The Prince requested that some music be played as he concluded his visitation—altogether a most informal and happy occasion which I shall always remember. The Prince's Trusts, from the Prince's Youth Business Trust to his Business Leaders' Forum—altogether, some eight in number—have done invaluable work. Now, on the twenty-fifth anniversary of his investiture as Prince of Wales, his deep love for architecture has led him to found the Prince of Wales's Institute of Architecture. It will be a centre of teaching and research to encourage 'public awareness and public concern about how to conserve the fabric and hold on to the spirit of the past, while at the same time building for the present and the future'. This has led to the publication of a new magazine, *Perspectives in Architecture*, which has been widely acclaimed. His many interests include: Music in Country Churches, of which he is Patron.

My good friend Dr. Roy Massey, F.R.C.O.(C.H.M.), F.R.S.C.M., A.D.C.M., A.R.C.M., Organist and Master of the Choristers, Hereford Cathedral, contributed the Foreword to my book, *Family Enterprise: Some North Country Organ Builders*. In the midst of an extremely busy life music making, which is carried out with distinction, combined with a friendly warmth of personality, he is in great demand far beyond his own confines at Hereford. I am honoured and grateful to him that he has been able yet again to contribute a Foreword which gives me cause for great pride.

During the writing of this book, new friendships have been forged, and I find it difficult adequately to thank the various organ builders who have gone to endless trouble to supply me with valuable information as well as to many others who have taken great interest as the story has developed. Dennis Thurlow, Chairman of Nicholson & Co., has been a mine of information regarding his firm's history, as has been Mrs Winifred Lambert, widow of Stanley Lambert, who was proprietor of the firm for many years. The history of the John Compton Organ Co., from its humble beginnings in Nottingham, to worldwide fame in London, has generated great interest, bringing to light records and reviving memories of life at this happy establishment in London. Alastair Rushworth, Managing Director of Rushworth & Dreaper Ltd., must have been sorely tried at times answering my enquiries from Compton's records, now in his firm's possession, as well as those regarding the work of his own company. The following former employees of Comptons have been generous in sharing their knowledge. They include J. Saxon Aldred, Derek Batten, J. A. Crutchley, the late Frank Hancock, Michael Mason and Ivor Norridge (Scottish Representative of Rushworth & Dreaper). As the story moves further North, the history of Conachers has been brought to life by the efforts of Philip Wood, his son David and its present owner, John Sinclair Willis, son of Henry Willis IV, whose friendly personality and enthusiasm has been a great tonic, particularly when the going was hard. Moving north-west, Liverpool has developed into a more detailed story than was intended, but one which I trust readers will find as fascinating as I have. To this end, Bruce Buchanan, Ian Frost, David Wells and Henry Willis IV have been generous with their knowledge and the unearthing of little-known photographs. I recall, with gratitude, the memory of Henry Willis III, who almost up to the time of his death, was generous with his knowledge of his firm's work. Finally, as the northern limit of this story is reached, my good friend Miss Margaret L. Wilkinson has entered enthusiastically into the history and personalities of her very clever and highly respected family and to her I say a very warm thank you. We have corresponded since 1966 and by the time this manuscript was ready for the printer, we had met at long last at her lovely home in Kendal.

One of the very many pleasurable contacts has been 'phone conversations with the veteran organ builder, Mr Herbert Norman, formerly Managing Director of Hill and Son & Norman & Beard Ltd. At the age of almost 91, he retains a phenomenal memory of the past as well as a keen interest in current organ building. His reminiscences have been invaluable. My thanks are also due to the following organ builders for so kindly sharing their knowledge with me. Mr Dick Barker, Mr H. A. Benyon, Mr E. A. Cawston, Mr David Clegg and Mr J. R. M. Pilling (Makin Organs Ltd.), Mr Andrew Cooper, Mr William Drake, Mr Michael Farley, Mr Frank Fowler, Mr Lance Foy, Mr Harold Gilbert (Bishop & Son, Ipswich), Hawkins of Lichfield, Hill & Son and Norman & Beard Ltd., Mr Peter Hopps (Harrison & Harrison Ltd.), Jardine Church Organs, The Johnson Organ Co., Kimber Allen Ltd., Mr Maurice Merrell (Bishop & Son), Mr J. H. Poyser, A. J. & L. Taylor Ltd., Mr Roger D. Taylor, Mr Mark Venning (Managing Director, Harrison & Harrison Ltd.), Mr Jonathan Wallace, Mr David Wells, R. A. Williams (Birmingham) Ltd., Mr Philip and David Wood (Wood of Huddersfield Ltd.), Mr Peter Wood and Mr Roy Young. Mrs Elizabeth Buckle (F. J. Rogers Ltd.) not only gave me a warm welcome, but initiated me into the many facets of pipe-making at her very busy business in Leeds.

The history of Lloyd and Roger Yates would have been impossible without the enthusiastic co-operation of his son, Mr Thomas Yates, who went through his father's vast accumulation of records and photographs as well as the late Mr John Holmes of Monasterevan, North Ireland, who died tragically in a road accident in December 1993. A personal friend of Mr Roger Yates, in common with myself, he shared many reminiscences of Roger's activities. John Holmes was a distinguished engineer and in demand throughout Ireland for advice where church organs were concerned; he will be greatly missed.

The following long list of individuals and libraries shows the extent of assistance received and to all I wish to record my thanks. The Revd. David Baker, Mr David Bell, Mr W. Neville Blakey, Mr & Mrs G. Brightman, Business Design Associates Bristol, The Revd. Anthony Clayton, Mr Ted Crampton, Mr N. Crown, Mr C. R. A. Davies (photography), my cousin, Dr. D. J. Drew, the Revd. Donald M. Eadie, my son Andrew and daughter Judith, the Revd. B. B. Edmonds, Miss Belinda Harley (Assistant Private Secretary to H. R. H. The Prince of Wales), Mr R. J. C. Hill, Mr H. W. Hinton, Mr Richard Hird, Mr Ian R. Hunt, Mr Michael Johnson, Dr. P. P. Keith, Mrs Mavis Knight, Mr Terence Lake, Mr D. R. Lane, the Revd. J. Barry Lumley, Mr Brian Martin, Dr. Philip Marshall, Sally McKeown, Mr Colin Menzies, Mr G. Merrick, Dom Andrew Moore (Downside Abbey), Mr Tony Moss, Mr Bernard Millett, Mr W. Davies Owens, Mr Douglas Pearman, Mr J. Portbury, Mr E. G. Robertson, Mr J. B. Rogers, Dr. Michael Sayer, Selfridges, London, Mr Arthur Starke, Mrs Winifred Stone (daughter of W. C. Jones), Mr N. H. Tasker, Mr J. S. G. Taylor, the Revd. Henry Thorold, Professor Ian Tracey, Mr Arthur Trafford, Mr J. H. Tuddenham, Miss Natalie Vella, Mr L. C. Whiteley, Mr David Wickens, the Revd. Stephen J. Wild, Dr. David Wyld.

The Local Studies and reference libraries of Bath, Birmingham, Bristol, Chester, Hereford & Worcester, Huddersfield, Hull, Leicester, Lincoln, Newark, Nottinghamshire, Redruth, Stockport and Walsall.

I have been fortunate to enlist the interest and expertise of Mr Christopher J. Bagot, B.A. HONS, Creative Director of Chapter One, Chorley, Lancashire, who has collaborated with me in design and has been responsible for the typesetting throughout, and my thanks are due to him for creating this handsome production. With his practical knowledge of organ building and as a musician—former Organist of the Catholic Cathedral, Lancaster—a firm friendship has developed, which I greatly value.

I am also indebted to C. V. Middleton & Son of Lincoln, the local branch of Supersnaps and Kall Kwik, for the care they have taken in photography and the copying of old documents.

Once again, it gives me great pleasure to express my appreciation to my friend Claire Armitage (née Smith) for her sensitive drawing on the jacket. Drawn specially for this book in 1988, it indicates the length of time since this project was first envisaged.

I owe a great debt of gratitude to my wife for her valuable work in proof reading and encouragement in the production of this, my seventh book, and the Trustees of the Marc Fitch Fund for their generous assistance over a period of twenty-six years in providing a guarantee towards the production of each of my volumes on organ building.

Lastly, I wish to thank my friends Canon Peter Fluck (until April 1994, Vicar of St. Botolph's Church, Boston) and the Revd. A. J. G. Walker, M.A., Minister of St. Andrew's with Newland United Reformed Church, Lincoln, for their interest, encouragement and much else besides.

If by mischance some have been ommitted from this list of acknowledgements, will they please accept my sincere thanks for any contribution they have made to this study.

The illustration on the title page is a copy of the drawing by the distinguished architect Caröe, of a case intended for the Parish Church of Barrow-on-Soar, which was never added.

CHAPTER I

Nicholson of Worcester

IN the year 1840, John Nicholson, eldest son of Richard Nicholson, organ builder of Rochdale, decided, at the age of twenty-five, to establish a business in Worcester. For a short time (from *c.*1838) he had been organ building on his own account in Moor Street, Rochdale, having previously worked with his father at Redcross Street, but he felt the need to expand and Worcester seemed to be an ideal centre with splendid opportunities in the county and beyond. It was a wise move and from the date of commencement in humble premises in the city and shortly afterwards in a cottage and stable in Palace Yard, in the shadow of the cathedral, he never looked back.

NICHOLSON,

CHURCH, CHAMBER,

AND

BARREL ORGAN BUILDER,

(FROM ROCHDALE),

Begs leave to acquaint the Nobility, Clergy, and Gentry of Worcester and its Neighbourhood, that he has taken extensive premises in New Street, where every branch of the above business will be carried on under his own immediate inspection, and most respectfully solicits their patronage and support.

———

Residence—Greenhill Terrace.
Manufacto·y—New Street, near the Old Greyhound.

From *Bentley's History, Gazetteer, Directory & Statistics of Worcester* for 1840

Here he gathered together a small staff who shared his enthusiasm and passion for perfection and the name of 'Nicholson' was not long in gaining a reputation for high quality of workmanship, which laid the basis for a century and a half of successful organ building, which, under successive ownership, has never deviated from the ideals of its founder.

An original John Nicholson organ of 1840, enlarged in 1896, is still in existence in the Countess of Huntingdon Hall, Worcester, formerly the Countess of Huntingdon's chapel, erected in 1804 and enlarged in 1815. This instrument has been most sensitively restored from a derelict condition by the present Nicholson firm and now proudly stands in the beautifully refurbished former chapel, now the Concert Hall for the new Elgar School of Music. Its lovely, singing quality of tone tells us most clearly about the ideals and capabilities of its maker.

I

COUNTESS OF HUNTINGDON HALL, WORCESTER 1840, 1896

2 manuals: CC to F, 54 notes   Pedal: CCC to F, 30 notes

Courtesy of Dennis Thurlow

GREAT ORGAN	ft		
		Open Flute	2
Open Diapason	8	Oboe	8
Stopt Diapason	8	*Tremulant*	
Principal	4		
Twelfth	2⅔	**PEDAL ORGAN**	
Fifteenth	2	Bourdon	16
Mixture	III	Principal	8
Trumpet	8	Choral Bass	4

SWELL ORGAN		COUPLERS	
Open Diapason	8	Swell to Great Swell to Pedal Great to Pedal	
Salicional	8		
Voix Celeste (tenor C)	8	Mechanical action to manuals and drawstops	
Principal	4	Pneumatic action to pedals (the Choral Bass being	
Clarabella	4	partly derived from the Principal)	

Another very early contract carried out by Nicholson was for Christ Church, Cheltenham, in 1840 but unfortunately no record of its specification is available. Alfred Hunter of Clapham built an entirely new instrument in 1895. Nicholson & Co. of Malvern, under the direction of the then proprietor, Mr Stanley Lambert, completely rebuilt it in 1957–58 with detached console and electric action and I had the pleasure of reviewing this glorious instrument in the September 1965 issue of *Musical Opinion*.

A two-manual organ dating from *c.*1840, with John Nicholson's name recorded on paper behind glass, is to be found in Mount Bures Church. It was rebuilt, or more correctly restored, in 1936, for there are no signs of alteration.

MOUNT BURES CHURCH *c.*1840

2 manuals: CC to G, 56 notes   Pedal: CCC to CC, 25 notes

GREAT ORGAN

	ft
Open Diapason	8
Keraulophon	8
Stopped Diapason Treble	8
Stopped Diapason Bass	8
Principal	4
Wald Flute	4
Fifteenth	2

SWELL ORGAN

Swell Dulciana	8
Swell Stopped Diapason	8
Swell Viol di Gamba	8
Swell Dulciana Octave	4
Swell Oboe	8

PEDAL ORGAN

Bourdon	16

COUPLERS

Swell to Great   Great to Pedal
Pedal CCC to CC permanently coupled to Swell
Ratchet swell pedal   Straight pedal board
Ornate case with gilded pipes

Coming to *c.*1845, at Croxton Kerrial Church, Leics., there is another example of John Nicholson's early work, to the following specification:

CROXTON KERRIAL CHURCH, LEICESTERSHIRE *c.*1845

GREAT ORGAN

	ft
Open Diapason	8
Stopped Diapason	8
Stopped Bass	8
Dulciana	8
Principal	4
Twelfth	2⅔
Fifteenth	2
Mixture	II

SWELL ORGAN

Bourdon	16
Open Diapason	8
Stopped Diapason	8
Principal	4
Cornopean	8
Oboe	8

PEDAL ORGAN

Bourdon	16

ACCESSORIES

Swell to Great   3 Composition Pedals

Great compass: GG—f³   Tenor C Swell (keys to GG)
The Swell Organ was added in 1855
Radiating and concave pedals (added 1953)
Ivory stop heads on square rods
Keys not overhanging

I spent an interesting hour here in 1992; the instrument can only be described as a gem, with a fine, bright, clear sound and is treasured by the authorities there who promote concerts from time to time which attract much interest. It is understood that the organ originally stood in Barton Road Methodist Church, Gloucester. It replaced one by Abbott & Smith at Croxton of 1889. It is now situated at the west end of the north aisle.

Only ten years after his establishment in Worcester, Nicholson was consulted about building a new organ at Malvern Priory Church to replace the two-manual organ built by Samuel Green, with additional work by Elliot, which had been sold to the trustees of the United Methodist Church at Dudley Port. The new organ was opened on October 24th, 1850, and was situated at the west end of the church. It contained the following stops:

3

THE PRIORY CHURCH, MALVERN 1850

GREAT ORGAN	ft		
Large Open Diapason	8	Stopped Diapason	8
Small Open Diapason	8	Flute	4
Stopped Diapason	8	Principal	4
Keraulophon	8	Doublette	2
Wald flöte	4	Sesquialtera (prepared)	
Principal	4	Cornopean	8
Twelfth	2⅔	Oboe	8
Fifteenth	2	Clarion	4
Sesquialtera	III		
Mixture (prepared)		PEDAL ORGAN	
Trombone (prepared)		Double Open Diapason	16
Clarion (prepared)		Principal	8
		Fifteenth	4
SWELL ORGAN		Sesquialtera (prepared)	
		Posaune (prepared)	
Bourdon	16		
Open Diapason	8	COUPLERS	

Swell to Great   Great to Pedal   Swell to Pedal

John Nicholson was called in again in 1862 to remove his organ to the position the present instrument by Rushworth & Dreaper now occupies—under the arch of the south transept. It was enlarged into a three-manual organ by the addition of a Choir division of nine stops together with new stops to the Great, Swell and Pedal, which resulted in a very comprehensive tonal scheme. Finally, between 1879–80, a new Solo Organ was added and the whole of the action converted to pneumatic lever, which resulted in the following specification:

THE PRIORY CHURCH, MALVERN 1879–80

4 manuals: CC to G, 56 notes   Pedal: CCC to F, 30 notes

GREAT ORGAN	ft		
Bourdon	16	Clarabella	8
Large Open Diapason	8	Viol di gamba	8
Small Open Diapason	8	Stopped Flute	4
Stopped Diapason	8	Harmonic Flute	4
Principal	4	Principal	4
Wald Flöte	4	Piccolo	2
Twelfth	2⅔	Cremona	8
Fifteenth	2		
Sesquialtera	III	SOLO ORGAN	
Mixture	II	Dulciana	8
Trumpet	8	Vox Angelica	8
Clarion	4	Clarabella	8
		Harmonic Flute	4
SWELL ORGAN		Orchestral Oboe	8
Bourdon	16	Vox Humana	8
Open Diapason	8	Tuba	8
Stopped Diapason	8	Tremulant	
Harmonic Flute	4		
Principal	4	PEDAL ORGAN	
Doublette (2 ranks from tenor C)	II	Open Diapason	16
Sesquialtera	III	Violone (prepared)	–
Cornopean	8	Bourdon	16
Oboe	8	Stopped Flute	8
Clarion	4	Principal	8
		Fifteenth	4
CHOIR ORGAN		Mixture	V
Dulciana	8	Trombone	16
Stopped Diapason	8		

COUPLERS

Swell to Great   Choir to Great   Solo to Great
Swell Octave   Swell to Choir   Solo Octave
Pedal Octave   Choir to Pedal   Great to Pedal
Swell to Pedal   Solo to Pedal

ACCESSORIES

4 Composition Pedals to Great Organ
(acting also on pedals)
3 Composition Pedals to Swell and Choir Organs
Reversible pedal to Great to Pedal coupler

This organ remained unaltered until 1927 when Rushworth & Dreaper built a new instrument which included some sixteen stops which were re-arranged and revoiced and nine others which were partially retained. Thus ended a connection with the Nicholson firm extending over a period of 77 years.

In 1854, John Nicholson was commissioned to build an organ for the Music Hall, Worcester, the specification, taken from 'Hopkins and Rimbault', 1st edition, and erroneously titled 'Shire Hall 1844', being as follows:

THE MUSIC HALL, WORCESTER 1854

GREAT ORGAN

	ft
Great Diapason (metal throughout)	16
Open Diapason	8
Small Open Diapason	8
Gamba	8
Bourdon	8
Quint	5⅓
Octave	4
Gemshorn	4
Wald Flute	4
Twelfth	2⅔
Fifteenth	2
Tierce	1⅗
Mixture	V
Posaune	8
Clarion	4
Spare Slider	

SWELL ORGAN

Great Diapason (open throughout)	16
Open Diapason	8
Gamba	8
Stopped Diapason	8
Keraulophon	8
Octave	4
Gambette	4
Wald Flute	4
Super Octave	2
Mixture	V
Trombone	16
Cornopean	8
Hautboy	8
Clarionette	8
Clarion	4
Spare Slider	

CHOIR ORGAN

Open Diapason	8
Viol di Gamba	8
Dulciana	8
Clarabella	8
Stopped Diapason	8
Harmonic Flute	4
Dulcet	4
Suabe Flute	4
Octave Flute	2
Echo Cornet	V
Trumpet	8
Spare Slider	

PEDAL ORGAN

Great Diapason (wood)	32
Open Diapason	16
Small Open Diapason (wood)	16
Dulciana (metal)	16
Violon	16
Bourdon	16
Quint (stopped)	10⅔
Principal	8
Bass Flute	8
Fifteenth	4
Mixture	III
Posaune	16

COUPLERS & ACCESSORIES

Swell to Great   Swell to Choir   Choir to Great
Great to Pedal   Choir to Pedal   Swell to Pedal
Pedal Octave   Swell Octave
Pedal Organ "off" or "on"
Sforzando pedal   Tremulant Swell
Pneumatic Lever Attachment
10 Composition Pedals

The tonal design was very forward looking for its time and placed its builder as very much ahead of some of his contemporaries. David Wickens contributed valuable information regarding this instrument in *BIOS Reporter* Vol.13, No.4 (October 1989). Sufficient to say here, that this organ was severely damaged in a storm and in 1879 Nicholson built a second one which was smaller in scope, using the best of the 1854 material. This was destroyed when the hall was gutted by fire in 1881. A new building was erected and named the Public Hall and Nicholson built a new four-manual for this in 1884.

In 1861, Nicholson was particularly proud to receive the prestigious contract for a new organ in his home county of Lancashire; this was for Manchester Cathedral and was built to the following specification which, as far as is known, was drawn up by the builder. It was situated at the east end of the north aisle. Three years after the installation of a new four-manual instrument by William Hill & Son in 1874, Nicholson's organ was removed to Holy Trinity Church, Bolton. It is understood that Jardines rebuilt it in 1905, replacing the tierce and larigot from the Great, by a harmonic flute. On the Choir, a gamba 4 was replaced by a voix celeste and a krummhorn by a clarion. The construction of the Manchester Cathedral organ must have taxed the workshops in Palace Yard to the utmost and it is possible that the extensions to these premises were carried out to accommodate the larger work secured by John Nicholson.

As this chapter was being written, Holy Trinity Church, Bolton, was made redundant and after prolonged negotiations, the John Nicholson organ, which happily remained intact, was acquired to form the basis for a new one to be built by the Nicholson firm for Portsmouth Cathedral. It is good news indeed that this has been made possible, due to a generous benefactor.

HOLY TRINITY CHURCH, BOLTON 1861, 1874

GREAT ORGAN

	ft
Bourdon	16
Large Open Diapason	8
Small Open Diapason	8
Stopped Diapason	8
Gamba	8
Stopped Flute	4
Principal	4
Gemshorn	4
Twelfth	2⅔
Fifteenth	2
Larigot	1⅓
Tierce	1⅗
Full Mixture 19·22·26	III
Mixture 26·29	II
Trumpet	8
Clarion	4

Oboe	8
Clarion	4

CHOIR ORGAN

Enclosed

Stopped Diapason	8
Clarabella	8
Viol di Gamba	8
Dulciana	8
Gamba	4
Stopped Flute	4
Piccolo	2
Krummhorn (tenor C)	8

Unenclosed

Solo Flute (tenor C)	4
Solo Ophicleide	8

SWELL ORGAN

Bourdon	16
Open Diapason	8
Stopped Diapason	8
Gamba	8
Gemshorn	4
Flute	4
Fifteenth	2
Sesquialtera 17·19·22	III
Cornopean	8

PEDAL ORGAN

Open Diapason	16
Bourdon	16
Violone	16
Principal	8
Trombone	16

COUPLERS

Swell to Great	Great to Pedal	Swell to Pedal
Swell to Choir	Choir to Great	Choir to Pedal

In the same year, John Nicholson obtained the order for an organ at Sansome Walk Chapel, Worcester. This is recorded in *The Musical Standard* for 1861, as follows:

SANSOME WALK CHAPEL, WORCESTER 1861

2 manuals: Great, CC to G, 56 notes; Swell, C to G 44 notes   Pedal: CCC to C, 25 notes

WORCESTER.— We have received an account of an organ built for Sansome Walk Chapel, by Mr Nicholson, of this city. He has produced, says a local writer, although on a small scale, one of the best specimens of his craft with which we are acquainted. The following are the details of the instrument:—

GREAT ORGAN

	ft
Open Diapason	8
Viol di Gamba	8
Stopped Diapason Treble	8
Stopped Diapason Bass	8
Principal	4
Flute	4
Fifteenth	2
Sesquialtera	III
Spare slide for Trumpet	8

SWELL ORGAN

Bourdon	16
Open Diapason	8

Stopped Diapason	8
Principal	4
Spare slide for Flute	4
Piccolo	2
Cornopean	8

PEDAL ORGAN

Bourdon	16

COUPLERS

Swell to Great   Great to Pedal

The case is of Gothic outline, painted oak and
varnished, relieved with blue and gold, the pipes
in front being diapered

An important contract in 1872 was a new organ built for Pershore Abbey, and this lasted for nearly seventy years until J. W. Walker & Sons built a new instrument using a number of Nicholson's stops after complete re-scaling and revoicing.

PERSHORE ABBEY 1872

GREAT ORGAN

	ft
Bourdon	16
Open Diapason Nº 1	8
Open Diapason Nº 2	8
Stopped Diapason	8
Bell Diapason	8
Principal	4
Twelfth	2⅔
Fifteenth	2
Sesquialtera	III
Trumpet	8

SWELL ORGAN

Bourdon	16
Open Diapason	8
Lieblich Gedackt	8
Bell Diapason	8
Gamba	8
Principal	4
Harmonic Flute	4
Piccolo	2
Mixture	III

Cornopean	8
Oboe	8

CHOIR ORGAN

Dulciana	8
Gamba	8
Stopped Diapason Treble	8
Stopped Diapason Bass	8
Gemshorn	4
Flute	4
Clarinet	8

PEDAL ORGAN

Open Diapason (wood)	16
Bourdon	16
Principal	8
Trombone	16

COUPLERS

Swell to Great   Great to Pedal   Swell to Pedal
Choir to Pedal   Octave to Swell   Octave to Pedal

Tracker Action   Hand Blowing

Two instruments built during the 1870s are recorded in *The Musical Standard* for 24th February, 1877 (Rushock, Worcester) and August 4th, 1877 (Wellingborough).

RUSHOCK PARISH CHURCH, WORCESTER 1877

2 manuals: CC to G, 56 notes   Pedal: CCC to F, 30 notes

RUSHOCK, WORCESTER.— A small but sufficiently powerful and sweet-toned instrument has been erected by Mr Nicholson, of Worcester, in the parish church of Rushock. The organ is on the left (north) side, and at the entrance to the chancel. Upon the front is a text, the pipes are illuminated with good effect, and the case is also decorated with fitting taste. The specification of the organ is as follows:—

GREAT ORGAN	ft
Open Diapason	8
Viol di Gamba	8
Stopped Diapason Bass	8
Clarabella	8
Principal	4
Flute	4
Fifteenth	2

SWELL ORGAN	
Bourdon	16
Spitzflute	8

Lieblich Gedact	8
Principal	4
Oboe	8

PEDAL ORGAN	
Bourdon	16

COUPLERS

Swell to Great   Great to Pedal

3 Composition pedals to the Great Organ
2 octaves and a half of radiating German pedals

WELLINGBOROUGH PARISH CHURCH 1877

GREAT ORGAN	ft
Bourdon	16
Large Open Diapason	8
Small Open Diapason	8
Keraulophon	8
Clarabella	8
Principal	4
Harmonic Flute	4
Twelfth	2⅔
Fifteenth	2
Sesquialtera	IV
Trumpet	8

SWELL ORGAN	
Bourdon	16
Spitz Flute	8
Salicional	8
Lieblich Gedact	8
Principal	4
Harmonic Flute	4
Mixture	III
Cornopean	8
Oboe	8
Clarion	4

CHOIR ORGAN	
Dulciana	8
Stopped Diapason	8
Vox Celeste	8
Gemshorn	4
Wald Flute	4
Piccolo	2
Clarionet	8

PEDAL ORGAN	
Open Diapason	16
Bourdon	16
Principal	8
Stopped Flute	8

COUPLERS

Choir to Pedal   Great to Pedal   Swell to Pedal
Swell to Choir   Swell to Great
Tremulant   Octave pedals

3 Composition pedals each to Swell and Great Organs
One and a half octaves of radiating and concave pedals

There are two fronts to the organ,
facing south and west.
The case is of oak, with spotted metal pipes.

C. W. Perkins, organist of Birmingham Town Hall (1887–1923) was organist of Wretham Road Church, Handsworth, Birmingham, in 1876, and he engaged John Nicholson to rebuild the organ there to an agreed specification:

WRETHAM ROAD CHURCH, HANDSWORTH 1876

3 manuals: CC to G, 56 notes   Pedal: CCC to F, 30 notes

GREAT ORGAN	ft
Open Diapason	8
Viol di Gamba	8
Clarabella	8
Principal	4
Wald Flute	4
Twelfth	2⅔
Fifteenth	2
Sesquialtera	III
Trumpet	8

SWELL ORGAN	
Bourdon and Double Dulciana	16
Open Diapason	8
Salicional	8
Lieblich Gedacht	8
Principal	4
Piccolo	2
Mixture	III
Cornopean	8
Oboe	8

8

CHOIR ORGAN		PEDAL ORGAN	
Keraulophon	8	Open Diapason	16
Dulciana	8	Bourdon	16
Stopped Diapason	8		
Flute	4	6 couplers and 8 composition pedals	
Cremona	8		

In 1877, the Revd. Sir F. A. Gore-Ouseley, BART, M.A., MUS. DOC., drew up a specification for a new organ for Holy Trinity Church, North Malvern, and the work was given to John Nicholson. Opened on January 15th, 1878, by W. Haynes, organist of the Priory Church, Malvern, the specification was as follows:

HOLY TRINITY CHURCH, NORTH MALVERN 1878

GREAT ORGAN			
	ft	Piccolo (prepared for)	2
		Mixture	III
Bourdon	16	Cornopean	8
Open Diapason Large	8	Oboe	8
Open Diapason Small	8	Clarion (prepared for)	4
Clarabella	8		
Keraulophon	8	CHOIR ORGAN	
Principal	4	Dulciana	8
Harmonic Flute	4	Voix Celeste	8
Twelfth (prepared for)	2⅔	Lieblich Gedact	8
Fifteenth	2	Wald Flute	4
Mixture	III	Gemshorn	4
Trumpet	8	Cremona	8

SWELL ORGAN		PEDAL ORGAN	
Bourdon	16	Open Diapason	16
Horn Diapason	8	Bourdon	16
Salicional	8	Principal	8
Lieblich Gedact	8	Flute (prepared for)	8
Harmonic Flute	4		
Gemshorn	4	7 couplers	

The presence of the voix celeste on the Choir Organ, instead of its usual home on the Swell, will be noted and one wonders what was the thinking behind this.

Master organ builders of the past have seldom been known to retire; they were dedicated to their craft and preferred to work on, although there were exceptions. Six years before his death in 1886, at the age of 71, John Nicholson was busy planning and working on the reconstruction of the organ at Malvern Priory; he was then 65 and during the past forty years had built up a team of skilled and dedicated craftsmen and enlarged his workshop to cope with the large organs which had come his way.

John Nicholson's last organ was built for Twyning Parish Church, near Tewkesbury; on his death in 1886, the business passed into the hands of William Haynes, who was organist of Malvern Priory Church and the owner of a music shop and concert hall—St Cecilia's Hall, adjacent to the Priory Churchyard. By this time, the original cottage and stable had developed into a substantial block of buildings; a lofty erecting shop was now added and the practical side of the business was placed in the hands of Nicholson's foreman, Mr J. Waldron, who had been with him for many years. Thus began a second phase in the history of the firm, which had a number of loyal and skilled workmen who were determined to carry on the traditions of careful and perfect work, regardless of other considerations, a tradition passed on from father to son. In 1890, Haynes was succeeded by Mr A. H. Whinfield, who was formerly musical director at the Royal Victoria Institute for the Blind, Melbourne, Australia, and organist at Christ Church, Brunswick, Melbourne. He was organist also at the Parish Church, Claines, Worcester, from 1898 until his death.

It is worthwhile to look back on some other outstanding contracts carried out since John Nicholson commenced his business in 1841.

9

Upton-on-Severn Parish Church	1850	Barmouth, St John's Church	1891
Worcester, St John's Church	1865	Rugby, Lower School	1892
Pershore Abbey	1872	Birmingham and Midland Institute	1894
Balliol College, Oxford	1874	Castle Freke, Ireland	1897
Warwick Grammar School	1886	Bangor, St Mary's Church	1899

Before we leave the era of the firm's founder, his signature on an apprentice's indenture, is not without interest. The date is 1860.

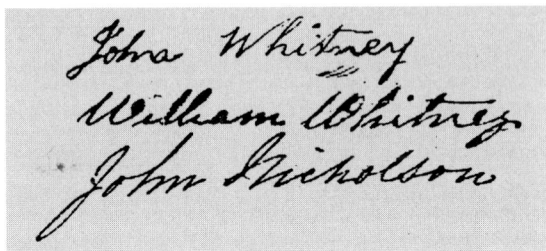

Nicholson appears to have done little or no advertising in local directories during his career; the Worcester City Library kindly carried out a thorough check of their very complete stock, but it was not until 1890 that the newly formed company advertised in *Bennett's Business Directory* for that year:

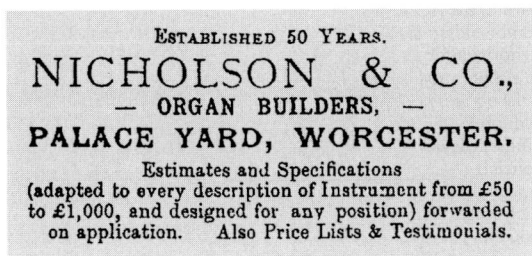

ESTABLISHED 50 YEARS.

NICHOLSON & CO.,
— ORGAN BUILDERS, —
PALACE YARD, WORCESTER.

Estimates and Specifications
(adapted to every description of Instrument from £50
to £1,000, and designed for any position) forwarded
on application. Also Price Lists & Testimonials.

The Musical Standard and *The Choir* catered for organ builders' news in John Nicholson's day, and he made full use of their facilities. As accounts of new organ openings were considered as news items, it seems certain that no charge was made for their insertion; for the historian, they are an invaluable source of information as to what was going on in the organ world. When *Musical Opinion* came upon the scene, its major concern was the musical instrument trade—in fact, its full title was *Musical Opinion and Music Trade Review*.

The organ for the Lecture Theatre of the Midland Institute, Birmingham (1894), was a large three-manual, clothed in a handsome oak case to the design of Messrs. Martin & Chamberlain, to harmonise with its surroundings. Its specification was as follows:

THE MIDLAND INSTITUTE, BIRMINGHAM 1894

3 manuals: CC to A, 58 notes   Pedal: CCC to F, 30 notes

GREAT ORGAN

	ft		
Double Open Diapason	16	Principal	4
Large Open Diapason	8	Harmonic Flute	4
Small Open Diapason	8	Twelfth	2⅔
Keraulophon (grooved bass)	8	Fifteenth	2
Clarabella and Stopped Bass	8	Mixture	III
		Trumpet	8

SWELL ORGAN

Bourdon	16	Lieblich Gedact	8
Open Diapason	8	Hohl Flöte (prepared for)	4
Salicional	8	Flauto Traverso	4
Gamba	8	Piccolo	2
Rohr Flöte	8		
Voix Celeste	8	*enclosed*	
Principal	4	Orchestral Oboe	8
Wald Flöte	4	Clarionet	8
Harmonic Piccolo	2		
Mixture (prepared for)	III	**PEDAL ORGAN**	
Double Oboe (prepared for)	16	Open Diapason	16
Cornopean	8	Bourdon	16
Oboe	8	Violone	16
		Violoncello	8

CHOIR ORGAN

Dolce	8
Gamba	8

6 couplers, 10 Composition pedals
Tremulant

Nicholson & Co's improved tubular-pneumatic action to manuals, couplers and pedals on 4 ins. wind, with large French feeder, driven by electric motor (by Messrs Crompton & Co, London) to supply reservoir and bellows for the instrument which is voiced on 3 ins. wind. "The organ is particularly well adapted for giving first class tuition to students" (*The Musical Standard*, Sept 29th, 1894).

It was later rebuilt by the firm in 1924 during Stanley Lambert's ownership; Billy Jones was responsible for the reeds and it was considered to be one of the finest instruments in Birmingham. It was one of which I had personal experience, forming the subject of an article in *Musical Opinion* for January 1944. It has since been rebuilt by another firm.

A glance through an old organ scrap book compiled at the turn of the present century brought to light details of a three-manual organ at Claines Church near Worcester built by Nicholsons at that time (1903). It shows the muddled thinking in those days in the design of an organ for a small space where height was also limited. Its tonal design certainly was not in keeping with the outlook of the firm and it would appear that, faced with a difficult situation, they were influenced to some extent by Hope-Jones. The absence of mechanical blowing will be noted and one can but conjecture the effort required by two blowers to supply sufficient wind for action and pipes. I cannot imagine a more uninteresting and ineffective instrument to play, but it was built at a time when several builders were dabbling with Hope-Jones' methods and I cannot feel that Nicholsons were entirely happy with the result.

CLAINES CHURCH, WORCESTER 1903

3 manuals: CC to C, 61 notes   Pedal: CCC to F, 30 notes

GREAT ORGAN

	ft	CHOIR ORGAN	*ft*
Bourdon	16	Open Diapason	8
Large Open Diapason	8	Stopped Diapason	8
Small Open Diapason	8	Dulciana	8
Clarabella and Stopped Bass	8	Voix Celestes	8
Principal	4	Flute	4

SWELL ORGAN

		PEDAL ORGAN	
Bourdon	16	Harmonic Bass	32
Violin Diapason	8	Open Diapason	16
Stopped Diapason	8	Large Bourdon	16
Gambette	4	Small Bourdon	16
Clarionet	8	Bass Flute	8
Cornopean	8		

COUPLERS	ACCESSORIES
Swell to Pedal Great to Pedal Choir to Pedal	10 Pneumatic Pistons to Pedal and Couplers
Great Super Swell Sub to Great	3 Pneumatic Pistons to Great and Couplers
Swell Unison to Great Swell Super to Great	4 Pneumatic Pistons to Swell & Couplers
Choir Sub to Great Choir Unison to Great	3 Pneumatic Pistons to Choir and Couplers
Choir Super to Great	*Tremulant* by Rocking Tablet
Swell Sub Octave Swell Super Octave	2 foot pedals connected with
Choir Sub Octave to Great Choir Unison to Swell	MESSRS. NICHOLSON & CO'S
Choir Super to Swell Choir Super Octave	PATENT STOP KEY & SPECIAL COMBINATION ACTION
Swell Unison to Choir	Detached Console Tubular-pneumatic Action

On the death of A. H. Whinfield in 1916, Francis Waldron, who had been his partner for some time, became proprietor. It was a difficult time for organ builders for many of their craftsmen became engaged in the war effort; those at Nicholsons were requisitioned for the construction of aeroplanes. On the cessation of hostilities, the arrears of building and repair work in the world of organ building almost overwhelmed the firm and the altered conditions of finance necessitated the re-organisation of the business. In 1921 it was converted into a private limited company with Francis Waldron as managing director. He was joined on the board by two local gentlemen—Henry Hughes and Philip Leicester and, more importantly, from the practical standpoint, two highly-skilled practical organ builders—W. C. Jones, the distinguished voicer, and A. W. Taylor, who was appointed works manager. The latter's experience of all forms of action, particularly electric, enabled the company to handle successfully the latest developments in organ construction. There was a skilled staff of experienced workmen, some of whom had been with the firm all their lives and there was a determination by all concerned to maintain the high standards set by the founder. During the 1920s, Nicholsons set a high standard of design, layout and cabinet making of their consoles, with ivory drawstops on panels, which not only made them handsome to look at, but (like the Harrison console) easy to play; one knew where everything would be situated on sitting down for the first time and felt immediately at home. This standard never waivered throughout the years. In the June 1929 issue of *Musical Opinion*, a full-page advertisement included an illustration of such a console and stated: 'Visitors to the Nicholson Organ Works within the last month have seen in the course of construction the following organs: two-manual Tracker, three-manual Pneumatic, three-manual Electric, four-manual Pneumatic.' Furthermore, they offered customers for their consideration: 'All-Electric Action, Pistons instantly adjustable at Keyboard, Inclined Manuals, "Tracker" touch (electric or pneumatic)'. Such features at this time brought them to the fore. Over the years I was to play many instruments, both large and small, built by Nicholsons; it was a joy to sit down at the console and one could be guaranteed beautiful organ tone, produced from impeccably finished pipework.

One of the highlights of Nicholson's work in the 1920s was the reconstruction of the Hill organ at the Church of The Messiah, Birmingham, in 1923. This fine building (which alas was demolished some years ago) was built between 1860–62 on arches over the Birmingham ship canal to the designs of the architect J. J. Bateman in the Decorated style. To quote Nikolas Pevsner: 'This large Gothic building reflects the importance of the Unitarians in Birmingham in the second half of the nineteenth century under the leadership of the Chamberlain and Nettlefold families'. It had a tower with truncated spire and the interior consisted of a great rectangle under a high pitched roof with a big west gallery. The foundation of this church, one of the great centres of Unitarianism, goes back to 1692 when the first Meeting House was built. This was rebuilt in Moor Street in 1732 and due to the continued growth of the congregation, The Church of the Messiah was built. Nicholson's first connection with an organ here was c1870 when they were called in to reconstruct an organ by Halmshaw built for the new church ready for its opening. The congregation was a wealthy one and in 1882 it was decided to have an entirely new instrument from the factory of William Hill & Son at a cost of £1571-3-8d. Dr. A. G. Hill designed a simple Gothic case in keeping with the building and the tonal scheme drawn up by Mr W. Astley Langston, the organist of the church, was a comprehensive one with 38 speaking stops spread over three manuals and pedal. By 1923, the mechanical action of this instrument was in a very worn condition and so it was decided to completely rebuild and enlarge it, to a scheme drawn up by J. Gilbert Mills, the organist of the church in collaboration with Nicholsons. The whole of the pipework was re-voiced; several new stops were added and a new console with tubular-pneumatic action was installed. A new Choir box was added in 1929 and four years later a tuba on 11 ins. wind was inserted and extended to form a new Pedal trombone. The great open no.1 and super octave were also revoiced.

The outstanding success of this instrument, undoubtedly was due to the close collaboration of Gilbert Mills, the Nicholson firm and W. C. Jones, their voicer, who worked as one to create an instrument of outstanding tonal beauty on a wind pressure of 3¼ ins. throughout except for the tuba (added in 1933) and trombone. I shall never forget the effect of this glorious organ; I can hear it as I write! and few have made such an impression on me in a lifetime of listening. It had a diapason chorus of the most natural, singing quality of tone, silvery and bright and of perfect blending qualities. It is utterly impossible to convey by mere words the superlative effect of the brilliant, splashy reeds; impeccably finished, undoubtedly they were some of the finest stops that ever left the hands of Billy Jones and he was justly proud of them, while the tributes paid by some of our leading builders gave this modest man particular pleasure. Quiet stops of exquisite tonality were there aplenty; to hear Gilbert Mills demonstrate his beloved organ was a rare experience indeed; it was his great pride and joy and it was a sad day in 1973 when the church had to close, for the building was falling down, and thus this fine Hill/Nicholson instrument had to be removed. It affected Gilbert deeply, but he was a very positive person and immediately set to work to design a one-manual instrument for the new church at Five Ways. This was built to accommodate some 80 people and the organ had 'to fit into a kind of lethal chamber' as Gilbert described it to me! He re-designed the Choir Organ, replacing the vox humana and clarinet with a nazard and mixture 19·22. The old Swell bourdon in 16, 8, 4ft pitch formed the Pedal Organ. In a letter to me dated 14th May, 1974, he commented: 'However, it sounds very beautiful and you can keep your Electronics when such glorious pipework can be utilised'.

CHURCH OF THE MESSIAH, BIRMINGHAM 1923

3 manuals: CC to A, 58 notes   Pedal: CCC to F, 30 notes

GREAT ORGAN

	ft
Open Diapason	16
Open Diapason N° 1	8
Open Diapason N° 2	8
Claribel Flute	8
Octave	4
Hohl Flöte	4
Octave Quint	2⅔
Super Octave	2
Sesquialtera	III
Harmonic Trumpet	8

SWELL ORGAN

Bourdon	16
Geigen Diapason	8
Stopped Flute	8
Salicional	8
Voix Celeste	8
Echo Dulciana	8
Principal	4
Lieblich Flöte	4
Fifteenth	2
Cornet	III
Double Trumpet	16
Trumpet	8
Oboe	8
Clarion	4
Tremulant	

SWELL ORGAN

Open Diapason	8
Rohr Flöte	8
Viol di Gamba	8
Flauto Dolce	8
Harmonic Flute	4
Salicet	4
Dulcet	2
enclosed	
Clarinet	8
Vox Humana	8
Tremulant	

PEDAL ORGAN

Sub Bass	32
Open Diapason	16
Violone	16
Bourdon	16
Geigen	16
Violoncello	8
Trombone	16

COUPLERS

Swell to Great Sub Octave   Swell to Great
Swell to Great Octave   Choir to Great Sub Octave
Choir to Great   Choir Octave to Great
Swell Sub Octave   Swell Unison Off   Swell Octave
Swell to Choir Sub Octave   Swell to Choir
Swell to Choir Octave   Choir Sub Octave
Choir Unison Off   Choir Octave   Choir to Pedal
Pedal Octave   Great to Pedal   Swell to Pedal

13

ACCESSORIES

6 Thumb Pistons each to Great and Swell Organs   4 Thumb Pistons to Choir Organ
1 Reversible Thumb Piston to Great to Pedal   1 Reversible Pedal to Great to Pedal
1 Reversible Thumb Piston to Swell to Great   6 Composition Pedals to Pedal Organ
One knob, 'Pedal to Great Pistons'   Balanced Crescendo Pedals to Swell and Choir Organs
Tubular-pneumatic Action   Blowing by an Electric Motor and Discus Blower

The Church of The Messiah must have been unique in Unitarianism, for psalms and canticles to full Cathedral settings such as those by Stanford, Vaughan Williams, Walmisley, Walford Davies, Bairstow and others were sung by a choir of nine singers, to full professional standard while the anthems ranged from Tallis, Farrant, Blow, Purcell, Bach, Holst, Elgar, Dyson and other modern composers.

How can one pay adequate tribute to Gilbert Mills, who, when the Church of The Messiah closed, became organist at the Parish Church, Broadway, where he spent some eighteen years of happy retirement, if one can thus describe his still busy life, which continued almost to the end. He greatly enjoyed his Spurden Rutt organ and embellished the services in his own inimitable manner. He never let increasing age or pain from rheumatism diminish his zest for life and of course music in particular. He was the most lovable of men and kindness itself, a tremendous character, a great wit and a brilliant musician with a deep knowledge of organ building, seeking only the best, for he had no use for second-rate work and could be outspoken when necessary. There was no malice in Gilbert however and his friends were legion. After evening service at The Church of The Messiah, although living at Harborne at the time, he would drive to Broadway and there at the pub, with congenial friends, which more often than not, included Tommy North, Organist of Walsall Town Hall, they would enjoy a pint or two of the best! I cannot do better than quote from Anthony Lucas of Tetbury who contributed an appreciation in *The Cinema Organ Journal* for June 1982.

> 'I expect that few C.O.S. Members noticed (and fewer still remember) that Gilbert Mills died on June 14th at 88. He was a frequent broadcaster in the 20s and 30s from Birmingham Town Hall, The Church of The Messiah, Birmingham, Walsall Town Hall and numerous other organs in the Midlands. Apart from his expertise as a concert organist, he was a skilled extemporiser, to whom it was a pleasure to listen. Many church councils in the Midlands have reason to be grateful to him for his unstinted advice on an organ rebuild. Perhaps the best known example of his work as a consultant was the Compton organ in Wolverhampton Civic Hall. He was a great admirer of Compton's work. He saw the hey-day of the romantic organ and revelled in the flexibility of the large electro-pneumatic organs being built up to the beginning of the war. After the war, 'extension' became a dirty word and the so-called classical organ became the fashion. Gilbert Mills judged all organs by the simple criteria of whether or not he could play an Anglican church service on them. If he could, then they were organs. If he could not, then they were squeak boxes...'

My own memories of Gilbert (who became a close friend) are many; I am proud to be able to record some of his many achievements and to have known him was a rare privilege for which I shall always be thankful.

My contact with organs in the Birmingham area ceased after my marriage in 1938; we had only been married for a year when war broke out and 1940 saw me setting off for Blackpool to do my initial training in the R.A.F. (commonly known as 'square bashing'). There, I was fortunate enough to make the acquaintance of the organ in Rawcliffe Street Methodist Church, Blackpool, which so impressed me that I contributed an article on the organs and music of this beautiful Methodist Church, which appeared in *The Choir* for April 1941. It must have been one of the first instruments to have been built by the newly formed limited company of Nicholson & Co., in 1921. Moreover, W. C. Jones, who was then a working director, was responsible for the reed voicing and most probably some of the flue work too.

The tonal scheme of this instrument is typical of many built at that time, with a mixture conspicuous by its absence. Due to the artistry of its builders however, the organ sounded larger than it really was, for there was liveliness in the trebles of the diapasons and the upper work, with brilliance and fire in the trumpet; all the quiet stops were exquisitely voiced and the tonal finish of every stop—immaculate. In short, it could be described as a thoroughly musical instrument for the accompaniment of church worship. Its resources were fully exploited at the opening recitals by Dr. Wood, then organist of St John's Church, Blackpool, Mr Gatty Sellars and that great and kindly man, Harry Goss Custard, of Liverpool Cathedral. It was a matter of much sadness to me to learn that this beautiful church with its fine musical tradition was demolished some years ago.

RAWCLIFFE STREET WESLEYAN CHAPEL, BLACKPOOL 1921

3 manuals: CC to C, 61 notes   Pedal: CCC to F, 30 notes

GREAT ORGAN

	ft
Double Diapason	16
Large Open Diapason	8
Small Open Diapason	8
Clarabella	8
Principal	4
Harmonic Flute	4
Fifteenth	2

SWELL ORGAN

Open Diapason	8
Rohr Flute	8
Salicional	8
Voix Celeste	8
Geigen Principal	4
Harmonic Piccolo	2
Trumpet	8
Oboe	8
Tremulant	

CHOIR ORGAN

Claribel Flute	8
Gamba	8
Dulciana	8
Flauto Traverso	4

Corno di Bassetto	8
Tremulant	

PEDAL ORGAN

Open Diapason	16
Bourdon	16
Dolce Bass	16
Flute Bass	8

COUPLERS

Swell Sub Octave to Great   Swell Octave to Great
Swell to Great   Swell Sub Octave   Swell Octave
Swell to Choir   Great to Pedal
Swell to Pedal   Choir to Pedal

ACCESSORIES

4 Thumb Pistons each to Swell, Great and Pedal
duplicated by Toe Pistons
1 Reversible Pedal to Great to Pedal

WIND PRESSURES

Great, Choir and Pedal Organs: 3½ ins.
Swell Organ: 4 ins.

It is interesting to note the list of shareholders when the company was formed in 1921:

Henry Hughes	10 shares
Philip Lester	1 share
Samuel Southall of Worcester, Solicitor	10 shares
Edward Frederick Bulmer, Cyder Maker, Hereford	10 shares
Hubert Leicester, Agnes Leicester	each 10 shares
Philip Leicester (Secretary)	10 shares
W. C. Jones	100 shares

During the 1930s and beyond, Nicholsons designed and built several two-manual instruments of outstanding tonal beauty which undoubtedly brought them more important work from a wide area. Their tonal designs would be thought dreadfully old fashioned in some quarters today, but every instrument had great beauty of tone; to use a favourite expression of the late Sir George Thalben-Ball; they were 'musical' and were admirable for the accompaniment of church worship. Each of the following organs were well known to me; they exhibited the same tonal features as the Blackpool organ, and each one gave me much pleasure.

CANNON STREET MEMORIAL BAPTIST CHURCH
SOHO ROAD, BIRMINGHAM 1930

3 manuals: CC to C, 61 notes   Pedal: CCC to F, 30 notes

GREAT ORGAN

	ft
Contra Dulciana	16
Open Diapason	8
Claribel Flute	8
Dulciana (ext 16ft)	8
Principal	4
Harmonic Flute	4

SWELL ORGAN

Violin Diapason	8
Lieblich Gedact	8
Gamba	8

Viola	4
Trumpet	8
Tremulant	

PEDAL ORGAN

Bourdon	16
Contra Dulciana (from Great)	16
Flute	8
Dulciana	8

7 couplers, 14 pistons
Pneumatic Action   4 ins. wind pressure (pipework)
Detached Oak console: ivory drawstops, ebony panels

SANDON ROAD METHODIST CHURCH, BIRMINGHAM 1937

2 manuals: CC to C, 61 notes   Pedal: CCC to F, 30 notes

The organ, which was originally built by Nicholson and Co. in 1894, had been reconstructed and enlarged. The scheme included a new detached stop-key console and electric action, and the provision of several new stops. The console is situated on the south side of the nave. The specification of the organ was drawn up in consultation with the organist of the church, Mr W. T. Burden, L.T.C.L., and the instrument was dedicated on 18th December, 1937.

GREAT ORGAN

	ft
Lieblich Bourdon	16
Open Diapason N° 1	8
Open Diapason N° 2	8
Clarabella	8
Dulciana	8
Principal	4
Twelfth	2⅔
Fifteenth	2

SWELL ORGAN

Open Diapason	8
Lieblich Gedackt	8
Salicional	8
Voix Celeste	8
Salicet	4
Piccolo	2
Mixture	II
Cornopean	8
Oboe	8
Tremulant	

PEDAL ORGAN

Acoustic Bass	32
Open Diapason	16
Bourdon	16
Lieblich Bourdon	16
Bass Flute	8

COUPLERS

Great to Pedal   Swell to Pedal   Swell to Great
Swell Octave to Great   Swell Sub Octave to Great
Swell Octave   Swell Sub Octave
Swell Unison Off   Double Touch Canceller

ACCESSORIES

4 Thumb Pistons each to Great, Swell and Pedal
1 Reversible Thumb Piston to Great to Pedal
4 Toe Pistons to Great and Pedal (duplicating)
4 Toe Pistons to Swell (duplicating)
1 Reversible Toe Piston to Great to Pedal

Balanced Swell Pedal   Electro-pneumatic Action
"Discus" Electric Blower and Generator

To return to 1930, an important contract was carried out at Manchester College, Oxford. Harold Spicer was another who thought highly of Nicholson's work and he was responsible for drawing up the specification of the rebuild and enlargement of the two-manual instrument by Gray & Davison in 1893.

MANCHESTER COLLEGE, OXFORD 1930

3 manuals: CC to C, 61 notes   Pedal: CCC to F, 30 notes

The specification of the new organ was drawn up by the college organist, Mr Harold W. Spicer, in consultation with the organ builders. The original organ, a two-manual of 23 stops, was built in 1893 by Messrs. Gray & Davison. The new organ incorporates the best of the original pipework, but has been entirely re-designed and enlarged, consisting now of three complete manuals, with 40 speaking stops and 20 couplers.

GREAT ORGAN

	ft
Bourdon	16
Open Diapason Nº 1	8
Open Diapason Nº 2	8
Claribel Flute	8
Dolce	8
Harmonic Flute	4
Principal	4
Twelfth	2⅔
Fifteenth	2
Tuba Minor (from Choir)	8

SWELL ORGAN

Lieblich Bourdon	16
Open Diapason	8
Lieblich Gedackt	8
Salicional	8
Voix Celeste	8
Gemshorn	4
Fifteenth	2
Mixture 17·19·22	III
Oboe	8
Tremulant	
Contra Fagotto	16
Trumpet	8
Clarion (harmonic trebles)	4

CHOIR ORGAN

Viol di Gamba	8
Rohr Flute	8
Viole d'Orchestre	8
Viole Celeste	8
Dulciana	8
Hohl Flute	4
Viola	4
Clarinet	8
Tremulant	
Tuba Minor (harmonic trebles)	8

PEDAL ORGAN

Contrabass (acoustic)	32
Open Diapason	16
Bourdon	16
Echo Bass	16
Octave	8
Flute	8
Contra Fagotto	16
Ophicleide	16
Tuba	8

ACCESSORIES

20 Couplers   2 Combination Couplers
20 Combination Pistons instantly adjustable by
means of Single Locking Piston
7 Reversible Pistons

WIND PRESSURES

Great Organ, Pedal Organ and Swell Flues: 3 ins.
Swell Reeds: 5 ins.   Choir Organ: 3½ ins.
Tuba: 7 ins.   Action: 8 ins.

A LIST OF NOTABLE ORGANS BUILT BETWEEN 1901—31

Stockport, St Peter's Church	1901	Hereford, St Peter's Church	1919
Toddington Manor, Gloucs.	1903	Porthcawl, All Saints' Church	1920
Brasted Parish Church	1905	Blackpool, Wesleyan Church	1921
Wellingborough Parish Church	1906	St Briavel's Parish Church	1922
Eastbourne Parish Church	1908	Gorseinon, St Catherine's Church	1923
Wandsworth, St Mary Magdelene	1908	Birmingham, Midland Institute	1924
Bordighera (Italy), English Church	1909	Leominster Priory	1925
Birmingham, The Oratory	1910	Willaston, Christ Church	1926
Wallasey, St Nicholas' Church	1911	King's Heath, All Saints' Church	1927
Bromsgrove School	1912	Ellesmere Parish Church	1928
Southampton, St Mark's Church	1914	Birmingham Cathedral	1929
Barmouth, C. M. Church	1916	Oxford, Manchester College	1930
Purton Parish Church	1918	Bourton-on-the-Hill Parish Church	1931

Despite the high quality of the firm's work from 1921 onwards (or perhaps because of it!) financially it was not a success and ten years later it was taken over by J. W. Walker & Sons Ltd. It must be remembered that the aftermath of the Great War brought many difficulties to business in general and during this period a number of organ builders ceased to trade or were taken over by the larger firms, one or two of whom retained a tuning and maintenance base to serve a large area. Shortly after 1931, the factory in Palace Yard was disposed of as Worcester Corporation required the premises for street widening purposes. Small premises in Bromwich Lane were taken and a few employees were engaged in tuning, maintenance work and repairs, trading still under the Nicholson name. To those who appreciated the sterling worth of the Nicholson organ it seemed that the great days were over, but it was not to be so. A new and tremendously successful era commenced with the appointment as general manager of a highly accomplished young man, Mr Stanley E. Lambert, whose reminiscences, written for me before his death, I am privileged to reproduce.

> "My own experience in organ building started in the summer of 1918 when I went as an apprentice at the works of Wm. Hill & Son in York Road, Camden Town, and I was probably one of the last apprentices during the time that Dr. Arthur Hill was head of the firm. They had, of course, amalgamated in 1916 with Norman & Beard's but only Mr Wales Beard, who was in the offices, was there. All the old employees who were too old for war service were there from the Hill staff and I stayed with Hill, Norman & Beard Ltd. until 1926 after spending nearly two years in charge of the completion and alterations to the organ at Glyndebourne. Quite by chance I went into theatre work playing a cinema organ. This was a 3-manual concert organ, not extended, and with slider soundboards, one of about three of similar type which were built and installed before the extension organ became popular. I was then working on the tonal side and the organ was due to be opened on the Monday. A well known local organist was scheduled to give the opening Recital and recitals for the rest of the week. Unfortunately, he made rather a hash of the first recital, not being used to the type of console, and he did not give any more recitals after the first opening. The directors were in difficulty but, having heard me play during the time we were installing the organ, they asked me if I would help them out for the rest of the week, which I did. Eventually I was asked if I would take over the appointment which I also agreed to and I stayed in cinema work for two or three years but, with the advent of talkies, I lost interest in just playing popular numbers on the organ.
>
> During the accompaniment of silent films one had the opportunity of playing all types of organ and orchestral music and it was a marvellous experience which I never regretted doing. I played in a number of theatres in London and the provinces and, during this time I demonstrated an organ for R. Spurden Rutt who was then starting to go in for building cinema organs. I obtained three orders for him in consequence of which he asked me to join him as assistant to develop the electrical side and I did this for about four years, spread over a period between 1928 and 1935 when I went to Worcester on behalf of J. W. Walker & Sons. It was hard work trying to pull round the Nicholson Company, which I did do eventually and even before the war we were getting a considerable amount of work although trading conditions were very bad with the effects of the depression period. During the war I kept the firm going with a small staff and maintenance work and also had to manage an engineering company engaged on aircraft work."

Not only was Stanley Lambert an organ builder of great ability, versatile, setting the highest standards in workmanship and materials, but was blessed with a friendly and understanding personality which made him many friends in the world of music. He had the added advantage of being an accomplished organist. Distinguished musicians such as Dr. Willis Grant, Professor of Music at the University of Bristol, Roy Massey (now MUS.DOC.) and Gilbert Mills, to mention but three, became his friends and advised a number of churches to employ Nicholsons. He gathered together a skilled staff, who, once interested in his ideals, co-operated wholeheartedly with him. It was a very busy and happy 'shop' which was immediately apparent when I visited it in 1961.

In 1951, Stanley Lambert bought the Walker Company's shares and became sole proprietor. In the following year a small works in Cromwell Road, Malvern, were taken in order to make electrical parts such as relays, switches and solenoids because of difficulties in obtaining supplies. Finally, in 1957, the Worcester premises were given up and the firm moved to its present home in Quest Hills Road, Malvern.

There was much to be done in the immediate post-war years, the major task being the re-installation of the four-manual organ in St Philip's Cathedral, Birmingham. During the war, it had been removed to safety at Pershore Abbey while the air raids were at their height; the staff often wondered whether the removal would be completed, particularly when the roof of the nave was burnt out by incendiary bombs. The work of re-installation was completed in 1948 and included new electro-pneumatic action, some re-voicing and tonal improvements in consultation with Dr. Willis Grant, then organist and choirmaster of the Cathedral, who had been appointed in 1936, coming from Lincoln Cathedral where he had been assistant to Dr. Gordon Slater since 1931.

Stanley Lambert had the good fortune to have W. C. Jones to finish the reedwork in the Cathedral, which he had voiced for the 1929–30 rebuild, and on 3rd October, 1948, in a letter to him, Billy had this to say:

> 'Birmingham. In the main I am satisfied in what I have been able to do, but there has been deterioration generally owing to the conditions which the pipework of the organ suffered... however, Dr. Grant is immensely pleased with all you have done and for the time being, with effective tuning as required, the organ should give good service.'

Dr. Willis Grant was a versatile and brilliant musician, moreover he was friendly and approachable and was blessed with a great sense of humour. He was the youngest MUS.DOC. in the country, (Durham University at the age of 27) and until 1958 made a distinguished contribution to music in Birmingham, not only at the Cathedral, but as conductor of the Birmingham Bach Society from 1950–55, and lecturer for the Extra-Mural Department of the University of Birmingham, as well as other work. In 1958 he left Birmingham Cathedral to take up the appointment of Professor of Music at Bristol University which he held until 1972. His death in 1981 at the age of seventy-four was a great loss to the world of music, not only in this country, but overseas too, where he examined in no less than eleven countries.

One of the very finest examples of the firm's larger organs of the 1924 and 1949 eras is at Leominster Priory. It is an impressive sight in this noble church which is unique among the great churches of our land in that it has three parallel naves as well as a north aisle. The fine chancel case of 1739 was enlarged by adding a new front to the west side in the style of the old, when the new organ was built in 1924 to a specification drawn up by Dr. J. C. Bridge, organist of Chester Cathedral. It was not an exciting scheme, being typical of many three-manual instruments of the 1920s, but it was of superb tone and contained some magnificent low and high pressure reeds by W. C. Jones, whose association with the firm in those days undoubtedly helped to enhance their already high reputation. In 1949, the tonal scheme was enlarged, the action electrified and a detached console placed some fifty feet away from the organ. The organist, Edward R. Carlos, F.R.C.O., drew up the specification and the re-opening recital was given by Dr. J. Dykes Bower, M.A., F.R.C.O.

In summing up the tonal effect of this most beautiful instrument, I cannot do better than quote from my article in the August 1955 issue of *Musical Opinion*.

> 'What strikes the listener on hearing the instrument from down the church before examining its tonal contents in greater detail at the console? First, the perfect balance of each department and the organ as a whole; full organ fits the church like a glove and in prolonged use it never becomes oppressive. Everything speaks so naturally, yet the organ fills this spacious church with ease and is adequate for any demands made upon it. It has dignity, yet it has clarity; is most thrilling in its choruses and provides the listener with a real emotional experience.'

LEOMINSTER PRIORY 1925

3 manuals: CC to C, 61 notes   Pedal: CCC to F, 30 notes

GREAT ORGAN

	ft
Double Diapason (new metal bass)	16
Open Diapason N° 1	8
Open Diapason N° 2	8
Hohl Flute	8
Principal	4
Harmonic Flute	4
Fifteenth	2
Mixture 12·19·22 (new)	III
Tromba	8

SWELL ORGAN

Open Diapason	8
Stopped Diapason	8
Echo Gamba	8
Voix Célestes	8
Gemshorn	4
Fifteenth	2
Mixture 17·19·22 (new)	III
Double Trumpet (new)	16
Cornopean	8
Oboe	8
Clarion (new)	4
Tremulant	

CHOIR ORGAN

Open Diapason	8
Viol d'orchestre (new)	8
Dulciana	8
Claribel Flute	8
Unda Maris (new)	8
Wald Flute	4
Clarinet	8
Tremulant	
Tromba (from Great)	8

PEDAL ORGAN

Harmonic Bass	32
Open Diapason	16
Violone (new, from Great)	16
Bourdon	16
Dulciana (new)	16
Octave	8
Bass Flute	8
Double Trumpet (from Swell)	16
Trombone (from Great)	16
Tromba (from Great)	8

COUPLERS

Swell Octave   Swell Sub Octave   Swell to Great
Swell to Choir   Choir to Great   Choir Octave
Choir Sub Octave   Choir to Pedal   Great to Pedal
Swell to Pedal   Great Combinations to Pedal

ACCESSORIES

19 Thumb Pistons   14 Toe Pistons

WIND PRESSURES

Great flues: 3½ ins.   Swell Organ: 4½ ins.
Choir and Pedal Organs: 3¾ ins.
Great reed and Pedal trombone: 8 ins
Electro-pneumatic Action: 8 ins.

A second four-manual rebuild was carried out by Nicholsons at All Saints' Church, Cheltenham, in 1953. William Hill & Son built the original organ (a three-manual) in 1887; it had 43 stops with the Great Organ divided into transept and chancel sections with Barker Lever action to the various departments. The chancel division came from the Hill organ in Worcester Cathedral which Hope-Jones was rebuilding. Additions were made from time to time, which included a Choir tuba, Pedal trombone and Great tromba. The work in 1953 comprised a complete reconstruction with electric action and a new four-manual console. The following is the specification of this fine, versatile instrument:

ALL SAINTS' CHURCH, CHELTENHAM 1953

4 manuals: CC to C, 61 notes   Pedal: CCC to F, 30 notes

GREAT ORGAN

	ft
Double Open Diapason	16
Open Diapason	8
Gemshorn	8
Stopped Diapason	8
Octave	4
Octave Quint	2⅔
Super Octave	2
Sesquialtera 17·19·22	III
Tromba (heavy pressure)	8

SWELL ORGAN

Bourdon	16
Open Diapason	8
Hohl Flute	8
Salicional	8
Vox Angelica	8
Wald Flute	4
Octave	4
Twelfth	2⅔
Fifteenth	2
Mixture 19·22·26	III

Oboe	8	Clarinet	8
Double Trumpet	16	Orchestral Oboe	8
Trumpet	8	Tuba (heavy pressure)	8
Clarion	4	Tromba (from Great)	8
Tremulant		*Tremulant*	

CHOIR ORGAN		PEDAL ORGAN	
Gedeckt	16	Double Diapason	32
Open Diapason	8	Open Diapason	16
Gedeckt	8	Violone	16
Spitz Flute	8	Bourdon	16
Gemshorn	4	Gedeckt (from Choir)	16
Gedeckt	4	Quint	10⅔
Twelfth	2⅔	'Cello	8
Fifteenth	2	Octave Wood	8
		Bass Flute	8
SOLO ORGAN		Gedeckt (from Choir)	8
Open Diapason	8	Gedeckt (from Choir)	4
Gamba	8	Trombone (heavy pressure)	16
Hohl Flute	8		
Viola	4	ACCESSORIES	
Suabe Flute	4	20 Couplers 23 Double Touch Thumb Pistons	
Harmonic Gemshorn	2	6 Reversible Thumb Pistons 15 Toe Pistons	

I had been in touch with Stanley Lambert by correspondence since the 1940's. After that we corresponded from time to time when he was invariably helpful and interested in articles I was writing for *The Choir* and *Musical Opinion*. Billy Jones had spoken to me in glowing terms of his work and advised me to pay him a visit at Malvern and this I did in 1961. Armed with my half-plate Thornton Pickard camera, amongst other photographs taken I was able to get a splendid shot of the new four-manual console for Clitheroe Parish Church which was opened in 1961; this was later used in his leaflet describing the instrument as well as in advertisements in *Musical Opinion*. I was greatly impressed by the design of this handsome console and its superb cabinet work (common to all his consoles). Materials in use throughout the factory were of the finest—even mahogany for building frames etc—in short, nothing but the best satisfied him whether visible or not in his instruments. Fine tonal finishing too was common to all and in this, his close friend W. C. Jones rejoiced, for he had no use for second best—neither had that fine musician Gilbert Mills. In those days, the collaboration of these three resulted in some magnificent instruments, both large and small, being built.

The Clitheroe Parish Church rebuild of the 1913 J. J. Binns organ made a tremendous impression in Lancashire. A Clitheroe Parish Church Organ Society was formed by the organist, Charles Myers, and a number of distinguished players gave recitals from time to time. Fernando Germani opened it on September 19th, 1961 and thereafter, Roger Fisher (Chester Cathedral) Alwyn Surplice (Winchester Cathedral) Richard Lloyd (Hereford Cathedral), Gillian Weir, Dr. George Thalben-Ball and others, played to enthusiastic audiences. A recital of music and a battle of the organs was held on 21st February, 1968, in aid of the Royal College of Organists Centenary Appeal. On this occasion, a three-manual Compton electronic organ was used in the 'battle' and a good time was had by all!

On the occasion of my visit to Malvern, Mrs Winifred Lambert, Stanley's devoted wife, made me immediately at home. Conversation flowed freely; we all had much in common, including the music of Elgar. For eleven years they were joint secretaries of the Elgar Society which gave them immense pleasure in their very busy lives. How they accomplished this I know not, for Mrs Lambert acted as her husband's secretary for many years, typing estimates, correspondence, etc. Stanley (who was organist and choirmaster at Elgar's Church, St George's Catholic Church, Worcester), told me that it was more than likely that the young Elgar had earned a few pence, note holding for Nicholson's tuners. In what little time he had, Stanley Lambert was a very competent oil painter.

In 1961 he collaborated with me in the rebuild of the fine old Forster & Andrews organ of 1874 in the Catholic church of St Peter, Scarborough, where I was acting as consultant. This was carried out with great skill and sensitivity for the original work and it is always a pleasure to call in there and renew acquaintance with it when in Scarborough.

In September 1965 I contributed an article on The Organ at Christ Church, Cheltenham, for *Musical Opinion*. John Nicholson had built an organ here, *c.*1840, which was replaced by a new one by Alfred Hunter in 1895. Nicholsons rebuilt it in 1958 and so great was the interest that no less than 1300 people were present at the opening recital on All Saints' Day, 1958, and a similarly large congregation gathered to hear Fernando Germani on the 11th November, 1958.

To sum up the tonal effect of what is a truly outstanding instrument, I quote from my article and would add that the opinions expressed I strongly adhere to today.

'Much has been written about the clarity and vitality of the neo-classical organ. Here is an instrument designed with no marked leaning to either the romantic or classical schools, but steering a middle course. Heavy pressure reed work has not been frowned upon, yet no one listening to the glorious ensemble with an impartial ear can deny that it has absolute clarity without, however, the hardness and shriek that appears to have captivated the ears of some of our present-day organists. It is the writer's experience that as one grows older and perhaps more critical, fewer contemporary instruments stir one's emotions as do such works of art as the organs in the Cathedrals of Lincoln, Salisbury, St Paul's or Beverley Minster to mention but four of our greatest treasures. (Today, I would add those at Durham, Bristol and Liverpool Cathedrals, to name a further three!). The organ under review is an exception. The tingling stream of brilliance poured out by the Great Organ flue chorus, together with the angry fire of the reed work, has not been achieved by accident but only by the patient and skilful work of a master voicer and tonal finisher.'

CHRIST CHURCH, CHELTENHAM 1958

4 manuals: CC to C, 61 notes   Pedal: CCC to G, 32 notes

GREAT ORGAN	ft	CHOIR ORGAN	
		Contra Dulciana	16
Double Open Diapason	16	Lieblich Gedeckt	8
Open Diapason Nº 1	8	Dulciana	8
Open Diapason Nº 2	8	Spitz Flute	8
Stopped Diapason	8	Dulcet	4
Quint	5⅓	Gemshorn	4
Geigen Octave	4	Nason Flute	4
Principal	4	Flageolet	2
Twelfth	2⅔	Sesquialtera 12·17	II
Fifteenth	2	Quartane 19·22	II
Tierce	1⅗		
Mixture 19·22·26	III	SOLO ORGAN	
Posaune	8	†Contra Viol	16
		Claribel Flute	8
SWELL ORGAN		Viol	8
Open Diapason	8	Viol Celeste	8
Gamba	8	Harmonic Flute	4
Salicional	8	†Double Clarinet	16
Lieblich Gedeckt	8	Clarinet	8
Vox Angelica	8	Tuba Mirabilis	8
Wald Flute	4	*Tremulant*	
Principal	4		
Twelfth	2⅔	PEDAL ORGAN	
Fifteenth	2	Sub Bourdon	32
Mixture 19·22	II	Open Wood	16
Double Trumpet	16	Bourdon	16
Trumpet	8	Violone	16
Clarion	4	Dulciana (from Choir)	16
Tremulant		†Viol Bass (from Solo)	16

Bourdon Quint	10⅔
Cello	8
Bass Flute	8
Octave Wood	8
Dulcet (from Choir)	8
Viol (from Solo)	8
Cello Quint	5⅓
Viola	4
†Mixture 12·17·19·22	IV
†Clarinet (from Solo)	16
Trombone	16
Clarion	8

ACCESSORIES

18 Couplers   18 Foot Pistons   32 Thumb Pistons

WIND PRESSURES

Great flues: 3½ ins.   Great reed: 6 ins.
Swell flues: 4 ins.   Swell reeds: 6 ins.
Choir Organ: 3½ ins.   Solo flues: 6 ins.
Solo tuba: 10 ins   Pedal flues: 4 ins.
Pedal reeds: 6½ ins.

† indicates stops prepared for

A new organ, incorporating some pipework by W. J. Bird & Son of Birmingham, was built in 1953 for the then King's Norton Congregational Church, Birmingham. It had this specification:

KING'S NORTON CONGREGATIONAL CHURCH, BIRMINGHAM 1953

2 manuals: CC to C, 61 notes   Pedal: CCC to F, 30 notes

GREAT ORGAN

	ft
Open Diapason	8
Viola	8
Dulciana	8
Clarabella	8
Principal	4
Fifteenth	2

SWELL ORGAN

Open Diapason	8
Lieblich Gedeckt	8
Gamba	8

Voix Celestes	8
Gemshorn	4
Closed Horn	8
Tremulant	

PEDAL ORGAN

Harmonic Bass	32
Bourdon	16
Bass Flute	8

7 Couplers   14 Pistons
Electric action, detached stop-key console

Modern purists would have little use for the tonal scheme, but the important point to make is that it fulfilled the requirements of Free Church worship admirably; a Swell mixture would have been ideal, but no doubt there were good reasons why it could not be included. Stanley Lambert, in common with J. I. Taylor of Comptons, had a gift for 'sizing up' the potentialities of a building and then deciding on the voicing treatment that was most suitable. In his small organs he invariably created a 'big' organ effect in miniature, where the tonal result is out of all proportion to the number of ranks employed. S. E. L. was a skilful and sensitive voicer and devoted a great deal of time to fine tonal finishing; I recollect W. C. J. speaking to me on a number of occasions of his high regard for his work in this direction.

An instrument which gave me great pleasure to write up for *The Choir* was the 1953 rebuild of the organ by Walcker of Germany, in the Methodist Central Hall, Birmingham. Originally built by this firm for the old Central Hall in 1898, it was moved to the new building in 1903 by them when several stops were added. The action was tubular-pneumatic and the console was typical of the then German practice, with 'blind' thumb pistons and manual couplers all controlled by thumb pistons with indicators. Nicholsons provided new electric action, a new drawstop console, several new stops and some revoicing and re-arrangement of the mixture work in 1953. Alas, the building was closed some time ago and while this book was in preparation, its future, together with the organ, was uncertain.

Two large instruments built towards the end of Stanley Lambert's career were those in the great hall of the University of Bristol (1966) and St Edmundsbury Cathedral 1970—Bristol was the brain child of Dr. Willis Grant, who demonstrated it to me with great pride, soon after it was built. There are four manual divisions, the Choir and Solo Organs sharing the lower keyboard. It has a most exciting sound with a trompette of almost 'tearing' brilliance and splash! St Edmundsbury Cathedral showed how far Stanley Lambert's tonal thinking had developed during his career; both instruments merit Gilbert Mills'

METHODIST CENTRAL HALL, BIRMINGHAM 1953

3 manuals: CC to A, 58 notes   Pedal: CCC to G, 32 notes

GREAT ORGAN	ft	CHOIR ORGAN	
Bourdon	16	Contra Violon	16
Open Diapason N° 1	8	Flauto Traverso	8
Open Diapason N° 2	8	Lieblich Gedeckt	8
†Geigen	8	†Viola	8
Double Flute	8	Dulciana	8
Octave	4	Suabe Flute	4
Harmonic Flute	4	Piccolo	2
†Twelfth	2⅔	†Echo Cornet 12·15·17	III
Fifteenth	2	Clarinet	8
Mixture 12·15·19·22	IV	†Tuba	8
Trumpet	8		
Tuba (from Choir)	8	PEDAL ORGAN	

SWELL ORGAN		PEDAL ORGAN	
		†Resultant Bass	32
Contra Violon	16	Open Diapason	16
Open Diapason	8	Violon	16
Claribel Flute	8	Sub Bass	16
Echo Gamba	8	Bourdon	16
Voix Celestes	8	Quint Bass	10⅔
Violon Principal	4	Flute	8
Flageolet	2	Violoncello	8
Mixture 15·19·22	III	†Quintade	4
Contra Fagotto	16	†Fagotto (from Swell)	16
Cornopean	8	Trombone	16
Oboe	8		
†Clarion	4		

14 Couplers   41 Pistons
Electric action   Drawstop console
† indicates new stops inserted in 1953

appreciation of him in a letter to me dated 21st August, 1976, where he says: 'He is a great artist, has many superb organs to his credit and is well worthy of honourable mention'.

In 1974, owing to continued ill health, Stanley Lambert had to give up work after directing the Nicholson company for some 39 years and this was quite a blow to him. He was, however, happy that it was to be in good hands and was sure that the new owners, with their skill and experience, would ensure that Nicholson organs would continue to give pleasure for many years to come.

He listed for me some of his most important contracts and pointed out that 'over 39 years a considerable number of two-manual organs and other rebuilds of larger ones had been carried out'.

Sadly, his retirement was only too short; years of hard work in a number of directions had taken its toll and he died in March 1978 at the age of 73. He was survived by his wife and son, Philip, both of whom had been directors of the Nicholson firm. Mrs Winifred Lambert, with her wide interests, including antiquarian book-binding, has shown the greatest interest in the compilation of this story, while Dennis Thurlow, chairman and tonal adviser of the present Nicholson firm, visits her from time to time to keep her up to date with the firm's progress which she greatly appreciates.

SOME ORGANS BUILT OR REBUILT DURING THE MANAGEMENT OF STANLEY E. LAMBERT

Four-manual organs

Birmingham, St Philip's Cathedral
Birmingham, St Chad's Cathedral
Leicester, St Margaret's Church
Cheltenham, All Saints' Church

Cheltenham, Christ Church
Oxford, St Clement's Church
Clitheroe Parish Church
St Edmundsbury Cathedral

Some three-manual organs of note

Leominster Priory Church	Worcester, St Andrew's Church
Edgbaston, St Augustine's Church	Hereford, Belmont Abbey
Edgbaston, St George's Church	Worcester, St George's Church
Birmingham, Midland Institute	Babbacombe, All Saints' Church
Sparkbrook, St Agatha's Church	Plymouth, King Street Methodist
Birmingham, Central Hall	Oundle School Chapel
Bristol University, Great Hall	Sheffield, Ranmoor Parish Church
Cheltenham, Holy Trinity Church	Bristol, Parish Church of St Stephen

Stanley Lambert was held in high regard by his fellow master organ builders. He was a Fellow of the Incorporated Society of Organ Builders and lectured on 'Planning the Organ' at the Society's meeting in September 1957.

Stanley Lambert's decision to sell the business to which he had devoted so much hard work and expertise was a hard one, but the blow was softened by the decision of Dennis Thurlow and Raymond Todd to purchase the company, for both were highly experienced and anxious to carry on the great traditions of Nicholsons.

Dennis Thurlow had joined the staff of J. W. Walker & Sons Ltd. as an apprentice when Reginald H. Walker was a director. This was during the early part of World War II when only old men and young boys were allowed to work on organs. Fred Eagle, Walker's voicer, taught him tuning and voicing and eventually he had his own tuning round which included St George's Chapel, Windsor Castle. Tuning was carried out on alternate Saturdays and after his work there the young Dennis had to report back to Frederick Rothwell on the state of the action. It will be remembered that Rothwell had built the organ with two consoles, Walkers being responsible for the pipework, the whole being the brain child of Sir Walford Davies. All the Christian Science churches came within the tuning orbit as well as the organ in St Margaret's, Westminster, the private chapel in Windsor Castle (now alas no more after the great fire of 1992). The years 1945–48 were spent in the army and after his war service years were over he was responsible for tuning organs in Lubeck, being the only organ tuner in the British Army of Occupation on the Rhine. This period provided him with valuable experience in studying German tone production, then back at Walkers between 1948–49 he had his first experience of tonal finishing at Cricklewood and St Mary's Church, Oxford. Subsequent instruments of importance included the prestigious contracts at University College, Oxford; The City Temple, London; Brompton Oratory; Paisley Abbey; Ampleforth Abbey; Liverpool Metropolitan Cathedral (two instruments); St Patrick's Cathedral, Dublin; All Saints' Church, Clifton, Bristol; Armagh Cathedral; St Cuthbert's Edinburgh; York Minster; Whitworth Hall, Manchester, as well as various jobs in Holland and Germany, also the U.S.A.

By then, Dennis Thurlow had arrived and was a name to conjure with in the organ building world. He eventually left Walkers and rented part of Pennell's and Sharpe's factory at Brandon where he helped Robert Pennells to develop organ components, at the same time making Solid State on his kitchen table! his wife carrying out the secretarial duties. As if this was not enough, he formed 'Radnor Recordings' in collaboration with E. J. Creese and D. C. Simpson; they made professional recordings and were audio consultants and suppliers of audio equipment, working from 2 Ridge Way Industrial Estate, Iver, Bucks. He also founded Dennis F. Thurlow Ltd., (Church Organs), P.O. Box 20, Brandon, Suffolk, advertising two models of one-manual extension organs, a two-manual and pedal extension organ, a one- and two-manual mechanical action organ and a portable organ with mechanical action.

In 1974, together with Raymond Todd who had 27 years experience with Rushworth & Dreaper Ltd., J. W. Walker & Sons Ltd., and Hill Norman & Beard Ltd., they purchased the well-known Yorkshire firm of Laycock & Bannister, of Crosshills, Keighley. Three months later, Stanley Lambert approached Dennis Thurlow with a view to taking over the Nicholson company, with a result that he and his partner 'took the plunge' and for a time Dennis Thurlow ran his business at Keighley and commuted to Malvern. Due to the ever-growing demand for Nicholson's work, it became essential for Dennis to make his base at Malvern and since then, to say that his life has been lived to the full is an understatement! His first job was to finish the organ commenced by Stanley Lambert at St Edmundsbury Cathedral and thereafter, one important contract after another was received by the newly constituted firm.

In *Musical Opinion* for October 1975, a full-page advertisement was taken; this invited organists and organ lovers to an open day at the Malvern factory on 25th October. This listed no less than twenty-nine contracts in hand as well as naming their senior staff comprising: R. J. Todd, Managing Director, D. F. Thurlow, Voicing and Tonal Director, K. L. Jones M.A., Design and Drawing Director, R. A. Kitchenor, Works Manager, J. M. Heard, Solid State and Circuitry Design and W. Barrow, Metal Pipe-making Administrator. It was a formidable team indeed; since then there have been several changes in personnel, but D. Thurlow and Raymond Todd remained in sole control of the company with a skilled staff of some 24 organ builders.

I first met Dennis Thurlow in 1972 when he was engaged in the final tonal finishing of the magnificent Cousans rebuild of the Norman & Beard organ in Grantham Parish Church, due to the illness of the late Charles Besson who shared the flue voicing with J. W. Tye and was a Director of the Cousans firm. I was fortunate enough to spend many hours in his company, both at the organ and at home in Lincoln, and thus began another valued friendship which continues to this day. His great knowledge of tonal matters and skill in the final finishing, which was as meticulous as that of W. C. Jones was very evident at Grantham. One has only to hear such instruments as the Metropolitan Cathedral of Christ the King at Liverpool, voiced and finished by him when he was with Walkers, to realise the calibre of one whom I regard as one of the great organ builders of our time. Each Nicholson organ since 1974, whether large or small, bears the hallmark of his genius and it is very satisfying to record that the Nicholson firm has been able to uphold the highest standards throughout the long period of its history. The voicing staff at Malvern includes a link with W. C. Jones, in the person of Arthur Jones who was brought up at J. W. Walker's factory at Ruislip, where he received tuition from W. Goodey (flues) and W. C. Jones (reeds). He now works with some of the tools belonging to the latter which were deposited with Stanley Lambert at Malvern, when W. C. J. finally retired.

In their new work, Nicholsons prefer to build instruments with tracker action and tonally akin to that of Nicholsons and Walkers in the mid-nineteenth century. Some examples of these are to be found at the Golf Church, Madrid; Bishop's Frome Parish Church; St Oswald's Church, Flamborough; The Church of the Cowley Fathers, Oxford; St Mary's Catholic Church, Paisley; St Joseph's Church, Keighley; Church of the Holy Carpenter, Kowloon, Hong Kong and St Peter's Lutheran Church, Baldwin, U.S.A.

The tonal scheme of the instrument at Golf Church, Madrid, appeals to me and seems ideal for a twelve stop instrument. I recall a distinguished Cathedral organist (now retired) discussing a small two-manual instrument with me which he described as pleasant and ideal for the playing of Bach's trio-sonatas, but lacking in sensitivity. I knew exactly what he meant, for although this organ was not in the same bracket as some of the tonally bleak schemes created today on strictly historical lines, with only stopped flutes representing quiet tonal colours on a two-manual scheme, but having an abundance of upper work, the atmosphere (which is so essential for service accompaniment and the rendering of all periods of organ

GOLF CHURCH, MADRID, SPAIN 1989

2 manuals: CC to C, 61 notes   Pedal: CCC to G, 32 notes

GREAT ORGAN	ft		
Principal	8	Quincena	2
Flauta	8	Oboe	16
Octave	4	*Tremulant*	
Flautin	2	PEDAL ORGAN	
Sessquialtera	II	Bordon	16
		Principal	8
SWELL ORGAN		COUPLERS	
Flautado	8	Swell to Great Swell to Pedal Great to Pedal	
Salicional	8	Mechanical key and drawstop action	
Principal	4		

Golf Church, Madrid, Spain. Courtesy of Nicholson & Co

music) is just not there. At the Golf Church a quiet salicional and a 16ft oboe provide that essential variety of tone and I can well imagine the versatility of this organ at which I am sure I should feel thoroughly at home.

Another versatile scheme for a two-manual instrument with tracker action to the manuals was built for St Mary's Church, Welwyn. It incorporates pipework from two Hill organs. The tonal scheme was drawn up by Dennis Thurlow in conjunction with the church and Eric Park, the Diocesan Organ Adviser.

ST MARY'S CHURCH, WELWYN

GREAT ORGAN		SWELL ORGAN	
	ft		
Open Diapason	8	Salicional	8
Stopped Diapason	8	Voix Celeste	8
Principal	4	Gedeckt	8
Open Flute	4	Gemshorn	4
Fifteenth	2	Principal	2
Block Flute	2	Spitz Quint	1⅓
Fourniture	IV	Plein Jeu	IV
Sesquialtera	II	Contra Oboe	16
Trumpet	8	Cornopean	8
		Tremulant	

27

PEDAL ORGAN

Open Diapason	16	Octave Flute	4
Bourdon	16	Mixture	II
Principal	8	Trombone	16
Bass Flute	8		
Fifteenth	4	4 Couplers 8-level Capture system for pistons	

Nicholsons take great pride in the authentic restoration of fine instruments of the Victorian period. Two examples, each a masterpiece in its own way, are the Aberdeen Music Hall (Father Willis) and West Bromwich Town Hall (Forster & Andrews, 1878, with additions in 1888).

I am privileged to quote from a letter dated 28th November, 1983, from Dennis Thurlow on behalf of Nicholsons to The Town Clerk, Metropolitan Borough of Sandwell, West Bromwich, relating to the Town Hall organ, which reads as follows:

'In the *Illustrated London News* during 1875, it was reported that at a banquet given by Mr Reuben Farley in the West Bromwich Town Hall, a Mr Brogden promised an organ for the Town Hall as he had already done in 1872 at Wednesbury. It was six years later on 11th May, 1878, that the flags were on the West Bromwich Town Hall to celebrate the opening of the Grand Organ. The instrument, now 106 years old, has fortunately escaped the vandalism of fashion and speaks with the same clarity, intensity and fullness of tone that marked its pedigree over one hundred years ago—only dirt prevents the pipes speaking correctly...

The tone of the diapasons on this organ are full, both with power and starting transients, due in different amounts to the following factors: (1) metal, (2) scale, (3) width of mouth and (4) voicing. It is these factors which were different from the other English organ builders contemporary with Forster & Andrews, that made their instruments, including West Bromwich Town Hall, unique... Sometime during the years 1862–1870 the flue voicer Herr Vogel, employed by Schulze, joined the Hull company and it is without doubt that this man, who had voiced Doncaster Parish Church, was responsible for the tonal scheme and voicing of the instrument in your Town Hall. Once again, the writer can verify the wide mouths, scaling etc of Doncaster Parish Church, having been responsible for the tonal finishing of this organ during the 1950's and having inspected the instrument and pipes closely in West Bromwich Town Hall, can state without fear of contradiction that they are identical in tonal planning and voicing to the Doncaster organ.'

Nicholsons strongly recommended that apart from replacing damaged areas of the mixture stops and repairing broken pipes, no change whatsoever should be made to the pipework of the organ 'so retaining the unique Schulze/Forster & Andrews linkage'. Furthermore, it was also stressed that no alteration be made to the action in any way with the happy result that the work was carried out in 1984, no effort being spared to place the instrument in first class condition for many years to come. The case also received treatment at the hands of the decorator responsible for re-furbishing the hall. Framework and the main panels are in white; with smaller panels in an attractive shade of green; the pipes are dark green stencilled in gold, the whole looking very impressive in this fine Victorian hall. It is most encouraging that the authorities pursued a strict policy of conservation and they are to be congratulated on the result.

WEST BROMWICH TOWN HALL 1984

3 manuals: CC to C, 61 notes   Pedal: CCC to F, 30 notes

GREAT ORGAN

	ft		
		Principal	4
		Waldflöte	4
Double Open Diapason	16	Twelfth	2⅔
Open Diapason	8	Fifteenth	2
Gamba	8	Mixture	IV
Hohlflöte	8	Posaune	8

28

SWELL ORGAN

Lieblich Bordun	16	Dulciana	8
Open Diapason	8	Celestina	4
Stopped Diapason	8	Flautino Harmonique	2
Salicional	8		
Voix Célestes	8		
Principal	4		
Harmonic Piccolo	2		
Mixture	III		
Oboe	8		
Vox Humana	8		
Horn	8		
Clarion	4		
Tremulant			

PEDAL ORGAN

Open Diapason	16
Bourdon	16
Violon	16
Quint	10⅔
Principal	8
Trombone	16

SOLO/ECHO ORGAN

Orchestral Flute	8
Orchestral Oboe	8
Orchestral Clarionet	8
Bombarde (unenclosed)	8
Lieblich Gedact	8

COUPLERS

Swell to Great   Solo to Great
Swell Sub Octave   Swell to Solo   Swell to Pedal
Great to Pedal   Solo to Pedal

Barker Lever action to Great; Tubular-pneumatic
action to Swell, Solo/Echo and Pedal Organs
Mechanical drawstop action

Regarding the rebuild of The Oratory organ, Birmingham, in 1987, Roy Massey, in a letter to Dennis Thurlow, spoke of 'how overwhelmingly beautiful' he found it. 'It was always a fine old bus, but you have drawn out to the full, the latent tonal beauty of the pipework and your new material enhances most vividly the character of its splendid ensembles. The whole enterprise was a triumph… There is practically nothing in the Birmingham area which can touch it for tonal beauty and much of this is because of your astonishing sensitivity and expertise in handling old pipework and blending and balancing new stuff to go with it…'

The Oratory was Cardinal Newman's Church and the following is the specification of the Nicholson organ of 1910:

THE ORATORY, BIRMINGHAM 1910

GREAT ORGAN

	ft
Double Open Diapason	16
Large Open Diapason	8
Medium Open Diapason	8
Small Open Diapason	8
Clarabella	8
Corno Flute	8
Principal	4
Rohr Flute	4
Fifteenth	2
Trumpet	8

SWELL ORGAN

Contra Gamba	16
Bourdon (from Choir)	16
Open Diapason	8
Stopped Diapason	8
Viol d'Orchestre	8
Violes Celestes	8
Salicional	8
Geigen Principal	4
Fifteenth	2
Mixture	IV
Double Trumpet	16
Cornopean	8
Oboe	8

CHOIR ORGAN

Bourdon	16
Gamba	8
Dulciana	8
Lieblich Gedact	8
Harmonic Flute	4
Gambette	4
Piccolo	2
Solo Clarabella	8
Clarionet	8
Tremulant	

PEDAL ORGAN

Double Open Diapason	32
Large Open Diapason (wood)	16
Small Open Diapason (wood)	16
Open Diapason (metal)	16
Violone	16
Large Bourdon	16
Small Bourdon (from Choir)	16
Bass Flute	8
Double Trumpet (from Swell)	16

ACCESSORIES

15 Couplers   45 Pistons
Provision is made for the addition of a further 14 stops

THE ORATORY, BIRMINGHAM 1987

GREAT ORGAN

	ft
Double Open Diapason	16
Open Diapason Nº 1	8
Open Diapason Nº 2	8
†Open Diapason Nº 3	8
Corno Flute	8
†Stopped Diapason	8
Principal	4
Hohl Flute	4
Twelfth	2⅔
Fifteenth	2
†Mixture	III-IV
Tromba	8

SWELL ORGAN

†Contra Gamba	16
†Open Diapason	8
Stopped Diapason	8
Viol d'Orchestre	8
Salicional	8
Voix Celeste	8
Principal	4
Rohr Flute	4
Fifteenth	2
†Mixture	IV
Double Trumpet	16
Cornopean	8
Oboe	8
†Clarion	4
†Tremulant	

CHOIR ORGAN

Lieblich Bourdon	16
†Open Diapason	8
Viola da Gamba	8
Lieblich Gedeckt	8
†Unda Maris	8
†Stopped Flute	4
†Nazard	2⅔
Piccolo	2
†Tierce	1⅗
Clarinet	8
†Tremulant	
Tuba (unenclosed, from Solo)	

SOLO ORGAN

Cantabile Diapason	8
Echo Gedeckt	8
Dulciana	8
Gemshorn	4
†Flautina	2
†Tuba	8

PEDAL ORGAN

Double Open Wood	32
Open Wood Nº 1	16
Open Wood Nº 2	16
Open Diapason	16
Violone	16
Bourdon	16
Echo Bourdon (from Swell)	16
†Bass Quint	10⅔
Octave Wood	8
†Principal	8
Bass Flute	8
†Fifteenth	4
†Ophicleide	16
Trombone (from Swell)	16
†Bombarde	8
Clarion	4

† new pipework 1987

Nicholsons have been associated with the organ at Birmingham Cathedral for a century, for in 1894 they were instructed to rebuild the Schwarbrick/England organ to the following specification:

BIRMINGHAM CATHEDRAL 1894

"The following is a description of the organ now reconstructed and enlarged by Messrs. Nicholson & Co. of Worcester, at a cost of about £800; the specification having been prepared by Dr. Swinnerton Heap and Mr R. Yates Mander (organist). The present alterations have been found necessary owing to the rapid strides made in organ building and the obsolete character of the mechanism of the old instrument."

GREAT ORGAN

	ft
Bourdon	16
Large Open Diapason	8
Small Open Diapason	8
Gamba	8
Stopped Diapason	8
Harmonic Flute	4
Principal	4
Twelfth	2⅔
Fifteenth	2
Mixture	–
Trumpet	8
Clarion	4

SWELL ORGAN

Bourdon	16
Open Diapason	8
Violin Diapason	8

Lieblich Gedact	8	Flute	4
Salicional	8	Gemshorn	4
Voix Célestes	8	Cremona	8
Principal	4	PEDAL ORGAN	
Suabe Flute	4		
Piccolo	2	Open Diapason	16
Mixture	–	Bourdon	16
Cornopean	8	Bass Flute	8
Oboe	8	Violone	16
Tremulant		Contra Fagotto	16

CHOIR ORGAN

COUPLERS

Open Diapason	8
Dulciana	8
Stopped Diapason	8
Clarabella	8

Swell to Great Swell Octave Swell to Choir
Choir to Great Great to Pedal Swell to Pedal
Choir to Pedal Super Octave on Pedal open

This instrument gave splendid service for over thirty years until 1930 when it was decided to completely rebuild and modernise it to a scheme drawn up by Mr F. Dunnill, F.R.C.O., the organist and choirmaster of the Cathedral, in collaboration with Mr Arthur Priestley of Nicholson & Co (Worcester) Ltd. The action and handsome new console was a joy, the latter (like those of Harrison & Harrison) setting a standard for many years to come. 'Billy' Jones did some of his finest reed voicing here and the whole instrument was of great beauty—fitting the church like a glove. This then is the instrument I knew well during the mid 1930s; a visit to Birmingham was never complete without calling in at the Cathedral where I had the privilege of playing it at any convenient time. Then came the war, and in 1940 under conditions of great difficulty and danger it was dismantled and stored in a safe place.

BIRMINGHAM CATHEDRAL 1930

4 manuals: CC to C, 61 notes   Pedal: CCC to F, 30 notes

The organ stands on a gallery on the north side of the chancel, with original case intact. It is played from a console situated in the choir, the casework of which is of oak (wax polished) to match the original case. The action is tubular-pneumatic throughout. The chorus reeds are all mitred and hooded, and fitted with harmonic trebles. The reeds throughout are new. Inclined keyboards are fitted, with "tracker" touch, and drawknobs and pistons are of ivory, the jambs being arranged at an angle of 45° to the keyboards. The organ is blown by electric motor and "Discus" blower; there are ten separate reservoirs for the flues and reeds of each department and for the action.

GREAT ORGAN

	ft		
		Lieblich Gedackt	8
		Voix Célestes	8
Double Open Diapason	16	Principal	4
Open Diapason N° 1	8	Harmonic Flute	4
Open Diapason N° 2	8	Fifteenth	2
Hohl Flöte	8	Mixture	III
Stopped Diapason	8	Contra Fagotto	16
Principal	4	Cornopean	8
Suabe Flute	4	Oboe	8
Twelfth	2⅔	*Tremulant*	
Fifteenth	2		
Mixture	III	**CHOIR ORGAN**	
Trumpet	8		
Clarion	4	Open Diapason	8
		Dulciana	8
SWELL ORGAN		Stopped Diapason	8
		Clarabella	8
Bourdon	16	Gemshorn	4
Open Diapason	8	Flute	4
Salicional	8	Clarinet	8

SOLO ORGAN

Concert Flute	8
Viole d'Orchestre	8
Violes Célestes	8
Vox Humana	8
Cor Anglais	8
Orchestral Oboe	8
Tuba	8
Tremulant	

PEDAL ORGAN

Double Diapason	32
Open Wood	16
Open Metal	16
Bourdon	16
Violone	16
Echo Bourdon	16
Octave	8
Flute	8
Trombone	16
Contra Fagotto	16

COUPLERS

Swell Sub Octave   Swell Unison Off   Swell Octave
Solo Sub Octave   Solo Unison Off   Solo Octave
Swell Sub Octave to Great   Swell to Great
Swell Octave to Great   Solo Sub Octave to Great
Solo to Great   Solo Octave to Great
Swell to Choir   Choir to Great   Solo to Swell
Great to Pedal   Swell to Pedal   Choir to Pedal
Solo to Pedal   Swell Octave to Pedal
Solo Octave to Pedal

ACCESSORIES

22 Thumb Pistons   5 Toe Pistons
6 Reversible Pistons   1 Combination Piston

WIND PRESSURES

Great, Swell and Choir flues: 3 ins.
Great and Swell reeds: 4½ ins.
Solo flues and reeds: 7 ins.
Pedal: 3½ ins.   Action: 7½ and 9 ins.

At Birmingham Cathedral in 1993, a comprehensive, skilful and most sensitive rebuild was carried out by the present Nicholson firm, the opening recital being given by Dr. Roy Massey, Organist and Master of the Choristers, Hereford Cathedral, since 1974; previously he had held the same position at Birmingham Cathedral, to which he had been appointed in 1968. His musicianship, friendly personality and expertise where organs are concerned have all contributed to his outstanding achievements in the world of music. At Birmingham, he was also Organist to the City of Birmingham Choir and Director of Music at King Edward's School, Birmingham. His many other appointments have included Warden of the Royal School of Church Music 1965–68, Conductor of the Croydon Bach Society 1966–68, Special Commissioner of the Royal School of Church Music 1964–, Conductor of the Hereford Choral Society 1974, Adviser on organs to the Dioceses of Birmingham and Hereford 1974, Member of the Council and Examiner of the R.C.O. 1970—just a few of his activities, including recital work and the prestigious task of hosting the Three Choirs Festival every third year at Hereford as well as training the Hereford contingent for their contribution to the great event at Gloucester and Worcester. We first met when he was organist at St Alban's, Conybere Street, Birmingham, from 1953–60; since then his friendship and interest in my own sphere of organ building, has been a constant inspiration and finally—to listen to his broadcast Evensongs from Hereford Cathedral is a *must*!

BIRMINGHAM CATHEDRAL 1993

GREAT ORGAN

	ft
Double Diapason	16
Open Diapason N° 1	8
Open Diapason N° 2	8
Stopped Diapason	8
Principal	4
Octave	4
Chimney Flute	4
Twelfth	2⅔
Fifteenth	2
Tierce	1⅗
Fourniture	IV
Mixture (Quint)	III

Trumpet	8
Clarion	4
Tremulant	
3 Couplers	

SWELL ORGAN

Bourdon	16
Open Diapason	8
Lieblich Gedeckt	8
Salicional	8
Voix Celestes	8
Principal	4
Harmonic Flute	4

Fifteenth	2	Harmonic Flute	8
Recorder	2	Concert Flute	4
Sesquialtera	II	Cor Anglais	8
Plein Jeu	IV	Clarinet	8
Contra Fagotto	16	Orchestral Oboe	8
Cornopean	8	*Tremulant*	
Oboe	8	Tuba Minor	8
Clarion	4	Trompeta Real	8
Tremulant		3 Octave Couplers	
3 Octave Couplers			
Solo to Swell		PEDAL ORGAN	

CHOIR ORGAN

		Sub Bass	32
Open Diapason	8	Open Diapason (metal)	16
Stopped Diapason	8	Major Bass	16
Dulciana	8	Violone (wood)	16
Gemshorn	4	Bourdon	16
Flute	4	Echo Bourdon (from Swell)	16
Fifteenth	2	Principal	8
Larigot	1⅓	Bass Flute	8
Mixture	III	Fifteenth	4
Tremulant		Octave Flute	4
Trompeta Real (from Solo)	8	Mixture	IV
2 Couplers		Fagotto (from Swell)	16
		Ophicleide	16
SOLO ORGAN		Trombone (wood)	16
		Trumpet	8
Viole d'Orchestre	8	4 Couplers	
Violes Celestes	8		

Dr. Massey has spoken to me in glowing terms of the reconstructed organ which in every way has met his exceedingly high standards. Not only is the instrument of outstanding beauty and versatility, but the case after restoration and re-gilding is now glowing with life and has been enhanced by the addition of gallery casework. Dating from *c.*1730, it has seen service in various churches over the centuries; in its present home 'it fits miraculously'. This rebuild has been generally acclaimed as yet another triumph for the Nicholson firm; for myself I can only express my delight at the enhancement of an organ which has always been (as was that at the Church of The Messiah) very special to me.

Their work in the rebuilding and restoration of large instruments has included the Parish Church of St Alphege, Solihull; Newcastle Anglican Cathedral; The Collegiate Church of St Mary, Warwick; Tettenhall College Wolverhampton; Dornoch Cathedral; Ludlow Parish Church; Wellington Church, Glasgow; St Giles' Church Oxford; Bridlington Priory Church; Peel Cathedral (I.O.M.); St Michael's Church, Highgate, and Stratford upon Avon Parish Church.

Two examples may be cited of rebuilds of three-manual instruments built to unimaginative schemes of their period, which have been completely transformed by careful planning together with skill and artistry in voicing and tonal finishing in the building.

ST MICHAEL'S, HIGHGATE 1985

GREAT ORGAN

		SWELL ORGAN	
	ft		
Double Open Diapason	16	Open Diapason	8
Open Diapason	8	Lieblich Gedeckt	8
Stopped Flute	8	Salicional	8
†Viola	8	Voix Celeste	8
Octave	4	Principal	4
Wald Flute	4	†Flute	4
Twelfth	2⅔	Fifteenth	2
†Fifteenth	2	†Plein Jeu	IV-V
†Fourniture	III-IV	Contra Fagotto	16
Trumpet	8	Oboe	8
		Cornopean	8
		Clarion	4

CHOIR ORGAN

†Gedeckt	8
Dulciana	8
†Principal	4
†Open Flute	4
†Nazard	2⅔
†Gemshorn	2
†Tierce	1⅗
†Larigot	1⅓
Clarinet	8
Tuba (unenclosed)	8
Tuba	4

PEDAL ORGAN

Sub Bass (partly acoustic)	32
Open Wood	16
Violone	16
Bourdon	16
†Principal	8
Bass Flute	8
†Fifteenth	4
Octave Flute	4
Fagotto (from Swell)	16

Ophicleide (from Choir)	16
Posaune	8

COUPLERS

Choir to Pedal Great to Pedal Swell to Pedal
Swell Octave to Pedal Swell to Choir
Choir to Great Swell to Great Swell Octave
Swell Sub Octave Swell Unison Off
2 Combination Couplers

ACCESSORIES

22 Thumb Pistons 18 Toe Pistons
8 Reversible Pistons Setter Piston

WIND PRESSURES

Great and Swell Organs: 3½ ins.
Choir Organ: 2¾ ins. Pedal Organ: 4 ins.
Tuba/Ophicleide: 6½ ins. Action: 5 ins.

Pitch: 523 at 64°
† new pipework 1985

Courtesy of Nicholson & Co

St Michael's, Highgate, was completed in 1985 to a specification drawn up by Alan K. Gray, the organist of the church, and proved most successful. To quote from Mr Gray's booklet on the history of the organ: 'Supported by the Nicholson team of carpenter, electrician, metal-hand, designer and builders, the Tonal Director, Dennis Thurlow, has achieved a resourceful instrument which is an exciting example of modern tonal design. It is able to accompany the liturgy and festivals of the church, together with school and choral society occasions. On such an instrument, music of any period can be made to sound artistically convincing'.

The other is at the Parish Church of St Mary, Monmouth (1991), which also proved most successful and includes a sub-bass 32ft, the lowest twelve notes of which are electronic. New pipes are of spotted metal and the transmission and capture piston system —solid state TMS 9000.

In the September 1992 issue of the *Organists' Review*, Nicholsons announced the re-organisation of their tonal department by appointing Guy Russell (who had been assistant to Dennis Thurlow for the past fourteen years) as tonal director of the firm. In addition they were appointing a gifted young man to their voicing staff to assist Mr Russell. Dennis Thurlow became Chairman, consultant and tonal adviser to the firm in Malvern and with their associate company in the United States. Known as Design Integrity Associates (which is quite independent of the firm), it consists of four active members and six representatives, in the States. Based in Hartford, Conn., it is directed by Professor John Rose, to promote Nicholson organs. This arrangement is proving most successful; the instruments concerned are sold direct to the Association, not to the customers and at the time of writing five orders have been completed or booked for the U.S.A.

In 1994, Mr R. J. Todd left the company and in his place Mr A. D. Moyes, B.SC., C.ENG., was appointed Managing Director. With a skilled staff of twenty-four and a full order book, Nicholsons look forward to the future with justifiable confidence and pride.

Portsmouth Cathedral, 1994. Courtesy of Dennis Thurlow

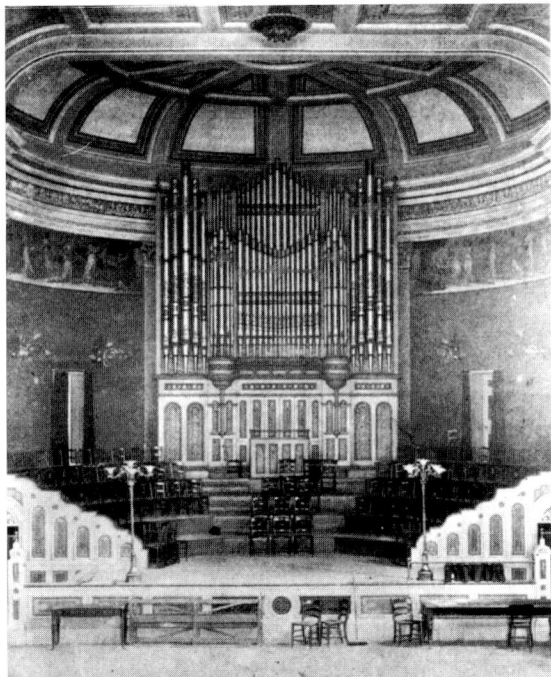

above left
John Nicholson, 1815–1886

above right
The Music Hall, Worcester

left
Croxton Kerrial Church, Leics.
Photo by the Author

below
Croxton Kerrial, the console.
Photo by the Author

above
Birmingham Cathedral, the 1930 console.
Photo by J. Parkes Foy, Worcester
right
All Saints' Church, Cheltenham, 1953
below
J. Gilbert Mills at the organ, Church of the
Messiah, Birmingham. Photo by the Author

right
Re-opening of the Elgar
Birthplace, 1967.
Standing left to right:
1st, Herbert Howells;
3rd, Mrs Winifred Lambert;
4th, Stanley E. Lambert.
Courtesy of Michael Dowty

below
West Bromwich Town Hall.
Courtesy of Nicholson & Co

above
Dennis Thurlow. Courtesy of the
Birmingham Post and Mail

left
Pinner Parish Church, West London.
Courtesy of Nicholson & Co

below
Birmingham Oratory, the console.
Courtesy of Nicholson & Co

CHAPTER II

The John Compton Organ Company

JOHN COMPTON, organ builder, inventor, musician and a great gentleman, has been described as a visionary. I find it difficult to give an adequate account of the countless achievements of this remarkable man, but have been fortunate in being able to draw on material contributed by others during the past sixty years or so, letters I have preserved from him and my acquaintance with a number of instruments built by his firm from its early days in Nottingham.

Born in the hamlet of Newton Burgoland, near Measham, Leics., he was educated at King Edward School, Birmingham, where he became head boy. Here he devoted his leisure to piano and organ practice, composition and scientific experiment. He was determined to became an organ builder and on leaving school at the age of seventeen he was apprenticed to Halmshaw & Sons of Birmingham. After six years with them, he was fully qualified in all departments and for a short time joined C. Lloyd & Co. of Nottingham who by then were resting on their laurels and somewhat in a rut. The go-ahead young Compton tried to interest them in the increased use of tubular and electric actions as well as more adventurous tonal schemes, but although he did not succeed, he gained valuable experience of all sorts of organs, for Lloyds had a wide tuning connection. In a letter to me dated 13th September, 1950, he said: 'I never worked in their factory except on voicing and finishing work'. In order to widen his experience he joined Brindley & Foster of Sheffield, travelling many thousands of miles for them in the capacity of voicer, tuner and finisher. This provided him with knowledge of a variety of firms' work, while he gained many friends with leading musicians of the day.

The urge to set up in business for himself led him to form a partnership with James Frederick Musson and premises were taken at 164½ Woodborough Road, Nottingham. It is interesting to record that Robert Hope-Jones visited him in 1901 in the hope of enlisting his services as manager of one of his factories, but he was too late, for Musson & Compton had contracted to build an extension organ for All Souls' Church, Radford, Nottingham. This was of sufficient importance for *Musical Opinion* to commission no less an authority than James I. Wedgwood, F.R.HIST.S. to contribute an article describing in depth its many unique features, for the May 1903 issue of that journal:

ALL SOULS' CHURCH, RADFORD, NOTTINGHAM 1903

'There has recently been opened at the above church an organ which must undoubtedly rank as one of the most interesting in England, and which, in the opinion of many, places the builders in the front rank of the building firms of the country. It is the first instrument by Messrs. Musson & Compton of Nottingham. When completed, the specification will be:—

GREAT ORGAN		SWELL ORGAN	
CC to C (61 notes)		CC to C (73 notes: extra octave)	
	ft	Contra Viola (extension)	16
Contra Tibia	16	Viole d'Orchestre (pure tin)	8
Tibia Minor (very large scale; cubical treble)	8	Octave Viole (extension)	4
Diapason (very heavy special metal, with		Diapason (special metal, with frein	
leathered lips)	8	harmonique)	8
†Keraulophon	8	Hohl Flöte (mahogany)	8
†Principal	4	Contra Tuba (extension: full length tubes)	16
Octaves		Tuba (harmonic; double-length tubes from	
		4ft C; heavier wind pressure and heavy	
		special metal)	8
		†Oboe	8
		Octaves	

CHOIR ORGAN
CC to C (61 notes, in the swell box)

†Quintatön	16
Salicional (finest spotted metal; 50% tin)	8
Lieblich Gedackt (finest spotted metal; 50% tin)	8
†Viole d'Orchestre (from Swell)	8
Viole Celeste (finest spotted metal; 50% tin)	8
†Flauto Traverso	4
†Orchestral Clarionet	8
†Octaves	

PEDAL ORGAN
CC to F (30 notes)

†Acoustic Contra Violone (Quintatön 32ft)	32
†Great Bass	16
Bourdon (from Great)	16
Flute Bass (from Great)	8
Tuba Bass (from Swell)	16

COUPLERS

Swell Unison to Great   Swell Octave to Great
† Choir Unison to Great   † Choir Octave to Great
† Swell to Choir   Swell to Pedal   Great to Pedal
† Choir to Pedal

WIND PRESSURES

Action and Tuba: 8 ins.
Great, Swell and Choir flue work: 4 ins.
Engine bellows: 12 ins.

'The Choir Organ and those stops marked † are only prepared for. The Choir viole celeste, however is at present in the Swell (in the place of the oboe) and the salicional and the lieblich gedackt are likewise in the Great. The organ is blown by a hydraulic engine supplied by Mr Swanton. The pedal board is of the pattern formerly adopted by the R.C.O., but possesses black sharps. Solid ivory stop keys, situated over the manuals, are employed instead of the more usual (but comparatively clumsy) stop knobs.

The action was tubular-pneumatic and the windchests were sliderless, single lift reservoirs with springs instead of weights, are used throughout the organ, it being absolutely impossible to disturb the wind supply even to the most delicate high note—a feature also due to the very liberal use of the trunks etc... I may commence by saying that this is undoubtedly the most effective organ for its size I have ever heard; and further, that it is much superior to many organs with more than twice the number of stops which I heard... The builders, I imagine, must be congratulated on having produced an unique organ, quite amply justifying the somewhat original specification. The instrument—their first *magnum opus*—will amply repay a pilgrimage to Nottingham, if only to hear the diapason, which I am able to commend unreservedly. I need hardly say that the workmanship throughout is above the average. Small sized pneumatic tubing is used. The organ was opened by Mr Liddle (organist, Southwell Minster) and built under the supervision of Mr F. Wyatt F.R.C.O.'

In his early days, Compton was influenced to a limited extent by the work of Hope-Jones, although he had reservations about some of it. There was the inevitable correspondence in the August and September issues of *Musical Opinion* for 1903 regarding the use of extension, sliderless chests and leathered lips for diapasons, all of which gave the writers anxiety! and to which John Compton gave a spirited reply. He quoted R. W. Liddle as saying that 'he had played church and cathedral organs with 40–50 stops which were not a jot more effective'. He also informed readers that the actual construction of the instrument was almost entirely carried out by Mr T. Musson, 'the part for which I was responsible (the tonal design and voicing) being of comparatively small importance'. Right to the end of his life, with many triumphs to look back on with justifiable pride, he retained an endearing modesty. Even in those early days of extension and its use, there was considerable correspondence for and against, and again in the 1920s, when Compton always found time to reply in spirited and informative letters.

John Compton himself relates his experiences in voicing the pipes for his first church organ (where, is not stated) in a letter to *Musical Opinion* for August 1945:

'Half a century ago I was experimenting with what I believed to be an improved organ stop. In my small workshop I made and re-made, voiced and re-voiced the pipes until I could improve them no more. Then, in 1901, I spent many weeks in making and voicing an entirely new rank of these pipes for my first church organ. It was not only the pleasantest stop in the organ, it was by far the best of its kind I ever made or voiced and it was admired and imitated by English, French and American organ builders and quoted in their writings.

This stop was of large scaled wooden pipes very lightly blown. It had low mouths and its very pure and serene tone resembled in some measure that of some of the gentle, old English stopped diapasons. And no doubt it might have survived if I had been content to label it so simply. But instead of this, I called it Tibia Minor—a fatal error that I did not realise until I revisited the church a few days ago. Then I was told that the organ had fallen into the hands of strangers who had undertaken to "improve" it. "Tibia!" said they, "this is no Tibia!" "We'll make a real Tibia of it!" And so they did, according to their notion of what a tibia should be. They chopped off its ears, carved up its mouths, and plastered its lips with leather and by these and various other well-known means, they converted it into a passable imitation of the sort of tibia one finds in some theatre organs—a loud, hooting abomination without the slightest trace of the delicate beauty that was once there.

This incident is trivial and of no interest or importance to anyone but myself and the owners of the organ, but it will serve to introduce what else I have to say.'

He went on to cite examples of Victorian organs by builders such as Hill, Lewis, Walker and Willis that had suffered 'irreparable damage at the hands of irresponsible "improvers" during the last few decades', and went on to say that 'there remains still here and there a good and well preserved example of Victorian and earlier English organ building craft, that has been carefully guarded and is still more or less in its pristine state. Let us see to it that it is not ruined either by the ignorance of its trustees, or by the incapacity of their employees'.

The year 1903 proved a very busy one for the partnership; *Musical Opinion* contained specifications of what were 'straight' instruments:

EMMANUEL CHURCH, NOTTINGHAM 1903

NOTTINGHAM.— The specification of the organ erected by Messrs. Musson & Compton at Emmanuel Church was drawn up by Mr Edward U. Ireland in consultation with the builders. The diapasons are of extremely heavy special metal with leathered lips. The other pipes are of the finest spotted metal (fifty per cent. tin) and varnished hardwood. There are two wind pressures, the light wind being stored in weightless bellows. Stops:—

GREAT ORGAN	ft
Rohr Bourdon	16
Open Diapason	8
Open Diapason	8
Tibia Minor	8
Principal	4
Wald Flöte	4
Twelfth	2⅔
Fifteenth	2

SWELL ORGAN	
Lieblich Bourdon	16
Diapason Phonon	8
Viola da Gamba	8
Hohl Flöte	8
Geigen Principal	4
Mixture	III
Cornopean (harmonic)	8
Oboe	8
Tremulant	

CHOIR ORGAN	
Contra Viola	16
Dulciana	8
Viole d'amour	8
Lieblich Gedackt	8
Flauto Traverso	4
Piccolo	2
Orchestral Clarionet	8

PEDAL ORGAN	
Open Diapason	16
Violone	16
Sub-bass	16
Flute Bass	8

COMBINATION TOUCHES

3 to Great   3 to Swell

Balanced crescendo pedal to Great and ditto to Swell.
3 Pedal Organ controllers, one to each manual,
providing an appropriate pedal bass for any
combination.

43

UNITED METHODIST FREE CHURCH, STAPLEFORD 1903

STAPLEFORD.— Specification of the organ erected in United Methodist Free Church by Messrs. Musson & Compton under the superintendence of Mr F. Wyatt, F.R.C.O., who also gave the opening recital:—

GREAT ORGAN

	ft		
		Hohl Flöte	8
Open Diapason	8	Quintadena	4
Dulciana	8	*Tremulant*	
Tibia Minor	8	PEDAL ORGAN	
Lieblich Flöte	4	Sub-bass	16

SWELL ORGAN

		COUPLERS	
Viole d'orchestre	8	Great to Pedal Swell to Pedal	
Salicional	8	Swell to Great Swell Octave	

The city of Nottingham was fortunate in the number of discerning church musicians in its midst at this time. By 1904, Musson & Compton had already gained the confidence of some, with a result that they received an order for their first four-manual organ for St Mary Magdalene's Church, Hucknall Torkard, the following details of which are reproduced from *Musical Opinion*.

It will be noted that extension was only used for the Great 16ft diapason and solo tubas; furthermore, tubular-pneumatic action was still in use. One can picture the zealous young Compton anxious to design a perfectly reliable electric action, working away into the early hours while his partner was abed, for he did not share John's enthusiasm for the use of 'electrics'!

In the absence of any records of the firm in its early years it has not been possible to trace many examples of their work. Publicity was given to several in the columns of *Musical Opinion* and *The Organist and Choirmaster* while the late H. S. V. Shapley's county lists have yielded one or two. Years ago I found a two-manual Musson & Compton of 1904 at Bingham Methodist Church, Notts; this was a rebuild of a Brindley & Foster of 1875. At St Mary Magdalene's Church, Hucknall Torkard, the partners built a two-manual instrument in 1904, and a two-manual at Albert Street Baptist Chapel, Stapleford, in the following year, was Compton's own work.

ST MARY MAGDELENE, HUCKNALL TORKARD 1903

HUCKNALL TORKARD.— On June 2nd, the dedication of the new organ at the Church of St Mary Magdelene took place, Mr Wolstenholme giving two recitals. The programs follow:— Funeral March from Sonata N° 6 (Op.26), Beethoven. Prelude and Fugue in C minor, Bach. Meditation in E flat, Faulkes. Bénédiction Nuptiale, Hollins. Toccata in C, D'Evry. Preludes in A flat and F, and Minuet in B flat, Wolstenholme. Improvisation. Dead March in Saul, Handel. First Sonata, Mendelssohn. Andante Cantabile in D, Hopkins. Fugue à la Gigue, Bach. Barcarolle, Cantilène in A flat, and Minuet and Trio, Wolstenholme. Improvisation. The organ is from the factory of Messrs. Musson & Compton, and contains the following stops:—

GREAT ORGAN

	ft		
		Fifteenth	2
Double Open Diapason (ext.)	16	Mixture	IV
Major Diapason	8	SWELL ORGAN	
Open Diapason	8		
Tibia Minor	8	Lieblich Bourdon	16
Principal	4	Diapason Phonon	8
Wald Flöte	4	Viol da Gamba	8
Twelfth	2⅔	Vox Angelica	8

44

Voix Céleste (tenor C)	8	Tuba	8
Hohl Flöte	8	Tuba Clarion (ext.)	4
Geigen Principal	4	*Tremulant*	
Harmonic Piccolo	2		
Mixture	IV	PEDAL ORGAN	
Contra Fagotto	16	Contra Bourdon	16
Cornopean (harmonic)	8	Major Bass	16
Oboe	8	Violone Bass	16
Vox Humana	8	Bourdon	16
Clarion	4	Principal	8
Tremulant		Flute Bass	8
		Tuba Bass (from Solo)	16

CHOIR ORGAN

Salicional	8
Dolce	8
Lieblich Gedackt	8
Flauto Traverso	4
Dulcet	4
Clarionet	8

COUPLERS

Great to Pedal Swell to Pedal Choir to Pedal
Solo to Pedal Swell to Great Choir to Great
Solo to Great Swell to Choir Choir Octave
Choir Sub Octave Swell Octave

15 combination touches and 9 combination pistons
4 Pedal Organ controllers

SOLO ORGAN

Harmonic Flute	8
Orchestral Flute	8
Orchestral Oboe	8
Contra Tuba (ext.)	16

Blown by 2 hydraulic engines
Tubular-pneumatic action throughout

The partnership lasted some three years, but it was not without its difficulties for John Compton adopted a firm stand on his ideals of electric action, total enclosure and the extension principle with which Musson was not in complete agreement. Musson finally decided to go his own way and moved to Huddersfield where he was appointed manager of Peter Conacher & Co. Sadly, his stay there was cut short by his death on 10th June, 1905, resulting from a fall from the crane doorway of the third storey of the works. A native of Nottingham and a well-known racing cyclist in his spare time, he was only thirty-six years of age and had been at Conacher's just under a year.

After the dissolution of the partnership, John Compton continued to work alone from the factory at Woodborough Road; then, on Guy Fawkes Day, 1906, disaster struck when a stray rocket set fire to the timber yard; this spread to the building which was then completely destroyed. Nothing daunted, Compton removed to premises near his old home at Measham, where, assisted by his Nottingham staff and some new ones, he developed the extension system and was busily engaged in idyllic surroundings.

'His voicing room was surrounded by a garden, the machine shop abutted on a spinney and for a cableway on which to make the cables for his electric organs, he used in the summer months a derelict and grass grown portion of an ancient turn-pike. In this sylvan retreat, Compton and his happy band of enthusiasts worked for several years.' His work attracted considerable interest beyond Nottingham and district, with a result that testimonials were received from G. T. Pattman F.R.C.O., Wm. Wolstenolme, MUS.BAC. (OXON), R. P. Elliot of New York and James I. Wedgwood, author of '*The Dictionary of Organ Stops*'. By 1911, he was trading under the name of The Extension Organ Company with H. S. Mills as partner. His notepaper bore the heading Artis Est Celare Artem ('the Art is to conceal the art').

In 1906, John Compton was instructed to rebuild and enlarge the three-manual organ in Selby Abbey, last rebuilt by Brindley in 1868. The following comprehensive specification shows Compton's tonal policy at that time in the design of a large instrument, incorporating older work, without any manual extension or total enclosure. The introduction of a diapason phonon and tibia shows the influence of Hope-Jones which persisted for a time, but as time went on, such stops were discarded in his church work. Alas, before it could be finally completed, a disastrous fire destroyed the organ and much of the building on 19th October, 1906. When the Abbey was completely restored, William Hill & Son built a new four-manual instrument.

SELBY ABBEY 1906

4 manuals: CC to C, 61 notes   Pedal: CCC to F, 30 notes

GREAT ORGAN

	ft
Double Open Diapason	16
Bourdon	16
Diapason Phonon	8
Open Diapason	8
Open Diapason	8
Tibia Minor	8
Suabe Flute	8
Principal	4
Harmonic Flute	4
Twelfth	2⅔
Fifteenth	2
Mixture	IV
Tromba	8

SWELL ORGAN

Bourdon	16
Open Diapason	8
Vox Angelica	8
Viole d'Orchestre	8
Viole Céleste (2 ranks)	8
Rohr Gedakt	8
Principal	4
Fifteenth	2
Mixture	III
Contra Fagotto	16
Horn	8
Cornopean	8
Oboe	8
Clarion	4
Tremulant	

CHOIR ORGAN

Quintaton	16
Viola da Gamba	8
Dolce	8
Lieblich Gedakt	8
Lieblich Flute	4
Piccolo	2
Clarinet	8

SOLO ORGAN

Harmonic Flute	8
Harmonic Flute	4
Orchestral Oboe	8
Vox Humana	8
Tuba	8
Tremulant	

PEDAL ORGAN

Gravissima	64
Double Open Diapason	32
Open Wood	16
Open Metal	16
Open Diapason (from Great)	16
Sub-bass	16
Bourdon (from Swell)	16
Quint	12
Principal	8
Violoncello	8
Flute	8
Contra Trombone	32
Trombone	16
Fagotto (from Swell)	16

COUPLERS

Swell to Great   Solo to Great   Choir to Great
Swell Sub Octave   Swell Super Octave
Swell to Choir   Solo Sub Octave
Solo Super Octave   Choir to Pedal   Great to Pedal
Swell to Pedal   Solo to Pedal

ACCESSORIES

8 pistons each to Great and Swell Organs
4 pistons each to Choir and Solo Organs
1 adjustable piston to each manual division
8 toe pistons each to Great and Swell.

WIND PRESSURES

Great: 4½ ins. and 7 ins.   Swell: 5 ins. and 8 ins.
Choir: 4 ins.   Pedal: 4 ins., 8 ins. and 20 ins.
Solo: 8 ins. and 20 ins.

Detached stop key console. Electric and tubular-pneumatic action. Kinetic blower.

Had Compton's organ remained it would have been his 'flagship'; as it was few heard it in its practically finished state. One who did, however, was J. I. Wedgwood, whose comments were recorded in a long letter to *Musical Opinion* in the January 1907 issue. He summed up what he had heard in the course of several visits during the finishing stages of the instrument and it is clear that he was greatly impressed. He made particular mention of the following stops and it is clear that he was an admirer of the Hope-Jones type of tone introduced at Selby. 'The tone of the 32ft open diapason was magnificent and what is more, the 32ft tone could be pitched right down to the lowest note… Turning next to the Great organ diapasons I am told that their effect was simply superb. That such was the case I can readily image from what I heard of them on the voicing machine. The large diapason phonon presented all the characteristics which go to render the leathered diapason so immensely fine a basis for the true organ tone. The solidity and the volume of tone were truly remarkable. Voiced on heavy pressure it furnished an excellent instance of what can be accomplished by the heavy pressure methods of treatment and the tone gave no indication of being forced or wearisome… the third diapason, an old stop which had been leathered—and which was rather softly winded—was a delightful quality partaking more of the quiet, smooth cantabile type of tone… the second diapason was brilliant in character. It was not overdone to the extent of the Schulze style of stop… The tibia I also heard; so I can well imagine that it sounded as magnificently effective in the general tonal scheme as this special stop of Mr Compton's always does.' How opinions have changed in the past eighty-six years. (The tibia—to which stop was he referring?)

No less an authority than G. T. Pattman, organist of Glasgow Cathedral, who presided at the organ on the first Sunday after its opening, supported Wedgwood's 'appreciation' in a letter to *Musical Opinion* for the February issue, 1907. 'It was as Mr Wedgwood truly says: "a remarkable specimen of artistic organ building", full, rich and sonorous, yet not noisy, not harsh and certainly not either screamy or blatant… The tuba was not at all like a magnified trumpet, as many tubas are, but had a magnificent, thick, smooth tone perhaps almost like the tone of a French horn in the orchestra, but more powerful… Unfortunately the mechanism was in an unfinished state, so I was unable to form an opinion as to what it would be like when completely regulated etc. But the touch of both manuals and pedal was delightful, so was the quick response to everything.' He did express the opinion however that 'the usual plan of stop handles would be better, because so many stop keys in a long line are apt to be confusing'.

The following specifications from 1907–1910 are revealing, for they show that Compton had not yet rid himself entirely of Hope-Jones' influence in the design of his tonal schemes.

ST PETER'S SCHOOL CHAPEL, YORK 1907

GREAT ORGAN

	ft
Bourdon	16
Open Diapason	8
Open Diapason	8
Dulciana	8
Stopped Diapason	8
Principal	4
Harmonic Flute	4
Twelfth	2⅔
Fifteenth	2

SWELL ORGAN

Quintatön	16
Diapason Phonon	8
Viol d'orchestre	8
Viole Céleste	II
Tibia Minor	8
Principal	4
Mixture	II

Harmonic Trumpet	8
Oboe	8

PEDAL ORGAN

Acoustic Bass	32
Open Diapason	16
Bourdon	16
Flute	8
Posaune	16

COUPLERS

Great to Pedal   Swell to Pedal   Swell to Great
Swell to Great Sub   Swell to Great Super
Swell Sub Octave   Swell Super Octave
4 pedal pistons each to Great and Swell Organs
Pedal piston *Tremulant* to Swell

The pedal controllers provide, when required, an appropriate pedal bass for any combination of manual stops and couplers.

WESLEYAN CHURCH, LAUNCESTON 1909

GREAT ORGAN

	ft
Double Open Diapason (ext. Open N° 2)	16
Contra Tibia (ext. Tibia Minor)	16
Open Diapason N° 1	8
Open Diapason N° 2	8
Tibia Minor	8
Principal (ext. Open N° 2)	4
Octave Tibia (ext. Tibia Minor)	4
Fifteenth	2
Tuba Sonora (heavy wind)	8
Tuba Clarion (ext. Sonora)	4

SWELL ORGAN

Diapason Phonon (heavy wind)	16
Hohl Flöte	8
Viole d'orchestre	8
Violes Célestes	II
Principal	4
Harmonic Trumpet	8
Oboe	8

CHOIR ORGAN

Salicional	8
Quintadena	8

47

Lieblich Gedackt	8
Flauto Traverso	4
Orchestral Clarinet	8
Tuba Sonora (from Great)	8
Tuba Clarion (from Great)	4

PEDAL ORGAN

Double Open Diapason	32
Open Diapason (ext.)	16
Small Open Diapason (from Great)	16
Bourdon (from Great)	16
Flute (from Great)	8
Tuba Profunda (ext. Sonora)	16

COUPLERS

Great to Pedal   Swell to Pedal   Choir to Pedal
Swell Sub   Swell Super   Swell Sub to Great
Swell to Great   Swell Super to Great   Choir Sub
Choir Super   Swell Sub to Choir
Swell to Choir   Swell Super to Choir
4 Pedal pistons to Great, 3 to Swell, 2 to Choir
Tremulant to Swell   *Tremulant* to Choir

Pedal Organ controllers, automatically preparing
when required, appropriate pedal bass for any
combination of manual stops and couplers, leaving
the pedal stops at all times free for independent use.

HOLDENHURST ROAD METHODIST CHURCH, BOURNEMOUTH 1909

GREAT ORGAN

	ft
Double Open Diapason	16
Open Diapason Nº 1	8
Open Diapason Nº 2	8
Open Diapason Nº 3	8
Stopped Diapason	8
Flute (Swell)	8
Octave	4
Principal	4
Stopped Flute	4
Super Octave	2
Cornet	IV
Trumpet (Swell)	8
Vibrato	

SWELL ORGAN

Contra Viola	16
Open Diapason (Great)	8
Viola da Gamba	8
Flute	8
Voix Célestes	8
Krummhorn (synthetic)	8
Kinura (synthetic)	8
Viola	4
Octave Flute	4
Piccolo	2

Mixture	III
Trombone	16
Trumpet	8
Clarion	4
Tremulant	
Vibrato	

PEDAL ORGAN

Acoustic Contra Bass	32
Sub Bass	32
Diaphone	16
Open Wood	16
Echo Violone	16
Bourdon	16
Bass Flute	8
Trombone	16

COUPLERS

Great to Pedal   Swell to Pedal   Swell to Great
4 double touch pistons each to Great and Pedal
and to Swell and Pedal

1 piston to Great to Pedal, 1 to Swell to Pedal
Balanced pedals to Swell and Great chambers
Balanced general crescendo pedal

The church was demolished in 1974: the organ was sold

WESTBOURNE WESLEYAN CHURCH, BOURNEMOUTH 1910

GREAT ORGAN

	ft
Rohr Bourdon	16
Open Diapason	8
Open Diapason	8
Tibia Minor	8
Principal	4
Tuba Sonora	8

SWELL ORGAN

Diapason Phonon	8
Viole d'orchestre	8
Viole Céleste	II

Hohl Flöte (open throughout)	8
Quintadena	4
Harmonic Trumpet	8
Oboe	8

CHOIR ORGAN

Salicional	8
Dolce	8
Lieblich Gedackt	8
Flauto Traverso	4
Orchestral Clarionet	8

PEDAL ORGAN	
Acoustic Bass	32
Open Diapason	16
Subbass	16
Bourdon	16
Flute	8
Tuba Profunda	16

COUPLERS

Great to Pedal   Swell to Pedal   Choir to Pedal
Swell to Great   Swell Sub   Swell Super
Great to Choir   Swell to Choir
3 pedal pistons each to Swell and Great Organs

Pedal controllers providing, when required,
an appropriate pedal bass for any combination of
manual stops and couplers.

In 1912, James Martin White of Balruddery who had shown the greatest interest in the work of Compton, gave him the order to restore the Thynne Hope-Jones organ at his home which resulted in him becoming a shareholder and director of the newly formed company John Compton Ltd. which was in need of capital to expand. It was decided to return to Nottingham where a disused church (a 'tin tabernacle') was purchased and re-fitted, on Castle Boulevard. After the firm's removal to London in 1919 this building was used for a variety of purposes; it was standing in 1990 but by the time I was hoping to photograph it in 1991 it had gone.

The Organist and Choirmaster for April 15th, 1914, contained the adjoining advertisement for Compton's work.

In 1940, just before joining the RAF, I was fortunate to examine the organ in Shakespeare Street Methodist Church, Nottingham, built by John Compton Ltd. in 1914, an article on which appeared in *The Choir* for December of that year. It was an interesting experience for it exemplified the principles laid down by John Compton at that stage of his career. Both manuals and pedal were totally enclosed; extension was used throughout, while the action was pneumatic to the electric relays inside the organ, this method being used owing to there being no satisfactory system of key contacts available at that time. (A similar system was used by the firm in their organ for Trinity Methodist Church, Leamington, in 1910.) The electric relays were of pioneer Compton design and up to that time were the most compact and successful of their type. The action to the windchest was electro-pneumatic, the magnets being designed just before the Shakespeare Street organ was opened. They were so successful that Comptons used them until 1924. The drawstop and piston action was pneumatic. The two swell chambers were placed immediately in front of each other, the Swell at the back, with shutters at the top of the box, and the Great in the front, with shutters to the top and front of the box.

SHAKESPEARE STREET METHODIST CHURCH, NOTTINGHAM 1914

2 manuals: CC to C, 61 notes   Pedal: CCC to F, 30 notes

GREAT ORGAN

	ft
Bourdon	16
Open Diapason Nº 1	8
Open Diapason Nº 2	8
Salicional	8
Stopped Diapason	8
Salicet	4
Flute	4
Principal	4
Mixture	II
Trumpet	8

SWELL ORGAN

Contra Viola	16
Viola	8
Open Flute	8
Strings	8
Strings	4
Viola	4
Flute	4
Piccolo	2

Mixture	II
Trombone	16
Trumpet	8
Clarion	4
Trumpet 2nd touch	8
Tremulant	

PEDAL ORGAN

Open Bass	16
Bourdon	16
Contra Viola (Swell)	16
Quint	10⅔
Flute	8
Trombone (Swell)	16

COUPLERS

3 couplers   6 pistons and appropriate pedal piston
(coloured red), each to Swell and Great.
3 general foot pistons
Balanced pedals to Swell and Great Organs
Electric blowing

There were eight basic ranks of pipes extended to the following pitches:

GREAT ORGAN	SWELL ORGAN
Open Diapason Nº 1 8ft (16ft to Pedal)	Viola 16, 8, 4, 2, 2⅔ft
Open Diapason Nº 2 16, 8, 4ft	Strings 8, 4ft
Salicional 8, 4, 2, 2⅔ft	Open Flute 8, 4, 2ft
Stopped Diapason 8, 4ft (16, 10⅔ft to Pedal)	Trombone 16, 8, 4ft

The organ was opened by Bernard Johnson, the City Organist, and on that occasion the pistons were not in working order, owing to the difficulty in obtaining tubing due to the outbreak of war, so that much of the stop changing was done by the young J. I. Taylor, who later was to become Technical Director of the firm. A week later, the piston action was complete for Dr. Alfred Hollins' recital.

The extension was carried out with skill and artistry; with the exception of the Swell viol and trumpet ranks which were voiced by J. I. Taylor, the whole of the voicing was by John Compton. Tonally the instrument exhibited the ideals of the firm in its early days some of which were considerably modified over the years. The Great flue chorus was based upon the second diapason, for the number one was a large stop with leathered lips, but it had its uses when used alone and sounded far better down the church than at the console. Full Great without it was a sparkling chorus; the salicional virtually was a dulciana, but the flutes were somewhat dull in tone. The basis of the Swell flue chorus was the viola, the scale of which was one of the smallest in the country—shades of Hope-Jones! It did, however, combine well with the open flute to form a geigen timbre; the strings were very beautiful, but the crowning glory were the three magnificent trumpets and so the full Swell was a thrilling ensemble when heard down the church. The Pedal Organ was very telling and altogether, despite the need for a major overhaul and the modernisation of the action, the instrument gave a good account of itself for general service accompaniment. The building still stands, but it is now a Jewish Synagogue, the organ having been sold.

During the First World War, John Compton and J. I. Taylor took turns in accompanying the worship Sunday by Sunday while the organist was on active service. Then, Jimmy Taylor (as he was always known to a countless number of friends) joined the Royal Flying Corps and his place was taken by James Harper, who, by 1940, was organist at the early Compton organ in Emmanuel Church, Nottingham.

How Jimmy Taylor came to join the Compton firm is best related by Ted Crampton: 'At the turn of the century, John Compton had established his works in Woodborough Road and was installing an organ in a church where the verger was a Mr Taylor. His schoolboy son, James, used to run errands for the busy organ builder and in due course he became almost a son to John Compton (who never married). Apprenticed in the art of organ building, he played a vital part in the firm's rapid expansion. John Compton wrote of him later: 'For many years past the chief responsibility of this firm has fallen on the ever willing shoulders of my faithful and affectionate friend and colleague, J. I. Taylor—not only a superb musician— but equally gifted on the mechanical side, where he has invented and put into practice some very ingenious and practical contrivances of stop control... He has never spared himself in time and effort if it is in his power to render service to anybody—proprietors, organists, managers or employees'. We shall hear much about J. I. Taylor as this story unfolds.

An instrument bearing a distinct resemblance to those designed by Hope-Jones, was built by Compton for Emmanuel Church, New Park Street, Leicester, in 1905, to the following specification:

EMMANUEL CHURCH, NEW PARK STREET, LEICESTER 1905
Manuals: CC to C, 61 notes   Pedal: CCC to F, 30 notes

GREAT ORGAN	ft	ORCHESTRAL ORGAN (within the swell chamber)	
Contra Tibia	16	Viol d'orchestre	8
Diapason Phonon	8	Viol Célestes (to gamut G)	8
Tibia Minor	8	Lieblich Gedact	8
Dolce	8	Orchestral Flute	4
Principal	4	Orchestral Clarinet	8
Tibia	4		
Tuba Sonora	8	PEDAL ORGAN	
		Contra Bourdon	32
SWELL ORGAN		Tibia Bass	16
		Sub Bass	16
Open Diapason	8	Flute Bass	8
Harmonic Flute	8	Tuba Profunda	16
Quintadena	4		
Cornopean	8	12 Couplers Electric Action	

It seems more than likely that Compton carried out some form of war work in his Nottingham workshop. The only organ work of any importance done during 1914–18 appears to be a rebuild of the two-manual Lloyd instrument in St Stephen's Church, Nottingham, in 1915.

A year after the conclusion of hostilities, John Compton, with the encouragement of his partner, decided to make London his base, for the business of the distinguished Belgian organ builder, August Gern, which had been established in 1866 was for sale, together with the premises at Turnham Green Terrace, Chiswick, W.1 which he had occupied since removal from Boundary Road, Notting Hill, in 1906. Part of the sale agreement was that Compton should complete the rebuilding of the organ in the Italian Church of St Peter, Hatton Garden, upon which Gern had been engaged. I came across a leaflet pasted in an old scrapbook which had come into my possession whilst this chapter was being written, and this gave the specification and the programme of the organ recital given by 'James I. Taylor Esq. of Nottingham'. Just how much work was done by Compton is not clear—but the work of reconstruction included a new console together with tubular-pneumatic action. All the original pipework was retained.

The Chiswick organ works soon became a hive of activity, both John Compton and J. I. Taylor were forward thinking engineers and a production line of standard components was introduced.

I well remember the factory, for I paid several visits during the years 1928–29; it was a most efficient and highly organised establishment, while a friendly atmosphere permeated the whole. No matter how busy they were, Jimmy Taylor and his staff were only too ready to show a young organ enthusiast everything that was going on; my one regret was that I was never fortunate enough to meet John Compton.

ST PETER'S ITALIAN CHURCH, HATTON GARDEN

GREAT ORGAN	ft
Double Diapason	16
Bourdon	16
Open Diapason	8
Stopped Diapason	8
Harmonic Flute	8
Viol de Gamba	8
Prestant	4
Octave Flute	4
Fifteenth	2
Mixture	III,IV
Cornet	II,II,IV,V
Bombarde	16
Trumpet	8

SWELL ORGAN	
Double Diapason	16
Open Diapason	8
Lieblich Gedact	8
Gemshorn	8
Voix Céleste	8
Echo Flute	4
Melephon	4
Twelfth	2⅔
Piccolo	2
Piccolo	1
Vox Humana	8
Oboe & Bassoon	8
Harmonic Trumpet	8
Tremulant	

CHOIR ORGAN	
Lieblich Gedact	16
Bourdon	8
Rohr Flute	8
Dulciana	8
Viola	8
Fulgara	4
Harmonic Flute	4
Clarinette	8

SOLO ORGAN	
Hohl Flute	8
Violon	8
Orchestral Flute	4
Orchestral Oboe	8
Tromba	8

PEDAL ORGAN	
Open Flute	32
Sub Bass	16
Open Diapason	16
Sub Bass	8
Bass Flute	8
Tubasson	16
Tubasson	8

COUPLERS

Swell Octave   Swell Sub Octave   Swell to Choir
Choir to Pedal   Solo to Great   Solo to Pedal
Swell to Pedal   Swell to Great   Great to Pedal

It is worthwhile to look at an extract from *The Complete Organ Recitalist* by Herbert Westerby, Chapter IV, 'The Organ of the Future' by John Compton. Published in 1927, he made one of his typically thoughtful contributions to this fascinating book, the first paragraph which reads as follows:

> 'Were I to take the example of some writers I might prophesy that the organ of the future— of ten or a hundred years hence—would be pretty much the same kind of instrument that I am planning and building nowadays; with electric mechanism, plenty of mutation and mixture work, wind pressures up to 50 or 100 inches, multiple concrete swell chambers, diaphonic basses and all the paraphernalia of the ultra-efficient organ of today. But, frankly, I do not believe anything of the kind. The whole art of organ building is now in the crucible, and it is impossible to predict the course of its development, or the permanence of any recrystallising that may occur in the near future; but it is quite safe to say that many features which today are considered essential to a well designed instrument will 'ere long be looked upon as monstrous and archaic.'

Prophetic words indeed and I often conjecture on what lines he would have been thinking and working if he was alive today. To put the record straight, he never used wind pressures approaching 50 or 100 inches.

Not only were John Compton and Jimmy Taylor men of outstanding calibre in their craft, but both had a great capacity for friendship. J. I. T. was a most outgoing personality, while J. C. was more retiring in manner; both were highly respected and quickly made contacts with some of the leading musicians of the time; other London firms certainly knew they were about! They soon made their presence felt amongst them and were highly respected by their competitors. Both men were skilled in the art of publicity and the advertisement columns of *Musical Opinion* in particular constantly drew attention to their achievements.

The writing of this chapter would have been immeasurably more difficult had it not been for their full-page advertisements which appeared more and more regularly each month as one important contract after another came their way.

They took a full-page advertisement in *The Dictionary of Organs and Organists* (2nd Edition, 1921) which made somewhat exaggerated claims particularly with regard to tuning.

The specification of the organ in the parish church of Stowmarket rebuilt during 1922 shows the minimal use of extension there.

THE PARISH CHURCH, STOWMARKET 1922

GREAT ORGAN

	ft
Bourdon	16
Large Open Diapason	8
Small Open Diapason	8
Major Flute (partly from Open Bass)	8
Hohl Flöte	8
Flauto Dolce	8
Quint	5⅓
Principal	4
Rohr Flöte	4
Flautina	2
Mixture	II
Corno di Bassetto	8
Harmonic Tromba	8

SWELL ORGAN

Violoncello	8
Salicional	8
Voix Célestes (tenor C)	8
Stopped Diapason	8
Harmonic Flute	4
Harmonic Piccolo	2
Mixture	II
Oboe	8
Double Trumpet	16
Trumpet	8
Clarion	4
Vibrato	

PEDAL ORGAN

Acoustic Bass (resultant)	32
Open Bass	16
Bourdon (from Great)	16
Octave (from Open Bass)	8
Twelfth & Fifteenth (from Open Bass and Great Bourdon)	5⅓, 4
Trombone	16
Echo Trombone (from Swell)	16

5 Couplers 1 reversible piston Swell to Great
6 combination pistons to each manual

Electro-pneumatic action Discus Blower

A Hope-Jones organ in St John's Church, Bognor. was re-modelled in 1922; its specification was published in *Musical Opinion* for November of that year:

BOGNOR.—Mr. John Compton has re-modelled the Hope-Jones organ in St. John's Church. The specification now stands as follows :—

PEDAL.		GREAT.		SWELL.	
Acoustic bass	..32	BContra flute	..16	Lieblich bordun	..16
Major bass ..	..16	Open diapason 1 ..	8	Violin diapason	.. 8
(prepared for)		Open diapason 2 ..	8	Salicional	.. 8
Sub-bass ..	..16	BHarmonic flute ..	8	Voix célestes	.. 8
Bourdon ..	..16	Principal ..	4	Hohl flöte	.. 8
(swell)		BOctave diapason..	4	Gemshorn ..	.. 4
Flute.. ..	.. 8	Bass oct. from pedal.		Mixture.	3 ranks
ATromba ..	..16	BTwelfth. ..	2⅔	Oboe ..	.. 8
(swell)		BFlautina ..	2	Octave.	
Great to pedal.		Mixture ..	4 ranks	AContra tromba	..16
Swell to pedal.		(prepared for)		ATromba ..	.. 8
Choir to pedal.		Posaune ..	8	AOctave tromba	.. 4
Solo to pedal.		Swell to great. ..		Tremulant.	
SOLO.		Solo to great.			
BHarmonic flute ..	8				
BOctave flute ..	4			CHOIR.	
BFlautina ..	.. 2			Viola di gamba	.. 8
(above from great)				Flauto dolce	.. 8
AContra tromba	..16			Lieblich flöte	.. 4
ATromba ..	.. 8			Corno di bassetto..	8
AOctave tromba ..	4	Manuals CC to C.		Octave.	
(above from swell)		Pedal CCC to F.		Swell to choir.	
Tuba ..	.. 8			Solo to choir.	
Orchestral oboe ..	8	Eletric pneumatic.			
Viole d'orchestre ..	8				
Violes célestes ..	8			Combination pedals.	
(last 4 prepared for)				4 to great. 4 to swell	

A Extended rank 85 pipes, metal, on heavy wind pressure.
B Extended rank 85 pipes, wood and metal.

About 1914, A. H. Midgley, M.I.E.E., a brilliant scientist and engineer, made the acquaintance of John Compton. A friendship developed which eventually led to the building of a four-manual chamber organ in his residence at Uxbridge between 1921–22. Strictly speaking it only consisted of two manual divisions, for the Great organ was duplicated on the Solo keyboard and the Swell on the Choir. It had a detached console in the drawing room and was Midgley's pride and joy; it attracted a number of well-known musicians and soon became known as the finest residence organ in the country.

CHAMBER ORGAN, PRIVATE RESIDENCE, UXBRIDGE 1922

4 manuals: CC to C, 61 notes   Pedal: CCC to G, 32 notes

GREAT ORGAN
(duplicated on "Solo" manual)

	ft
Contra Open Diapason	16
Contra Dulciana	16
Large Open Diapason	8
Small Open Diapason	8
Dulciana	8
Tibia Minor	8
Hohl Flute	8
Quint	5⅓
Principal	4
Dulcet	4
Octave Flute	4
Dulcet Fifteenth	2
Piccolo	2
Cornet 10·12·14·15	IV
Sesquialtera 17·19·21·22	IV
Double Clarinet	16
Clarinet	8
Contra Tuba	16
Tuba	8
Tuba Clarion	4

SWELL ORGAN
(duplicated on "Choir" manual)

Contra Viola	16
Bourdon	16
Violoncello	8
Viole	8
Muted Strings	8
Lieblich Gedackt	8
Octave Violin	4
Octave Strings	4
Lieblich Flute	4
Flautina	2
Twelfth	2⅔
Mixture 12·15	II

Bassoon	16
Oboe	8
Vox Humana	8
Trombone	16
Trumpet	8
Clarion	4

PEDAL ORGAN

Acoustic Contrabass	32
Sub Bass	32
Contra Bass	16
Sub Bass	16
Bourdon	16
Violone	16
Octave	8
Violoncello	8
Flute	8
Echo Flute	8
Contra Trombone	32
Trombone	16
Bassoon	16
Clarinet	16
Tuba Bass	16
Tuba	8
Tuba Tenor	4

COUPLERS

Great to Pedal   Swell to Pedal   Choir to Pedal
Solo to Pedal   Choir to Great   Swell to Great
Solo to Swell   Solo to Choir

ACCESSORIES

8 combination pistons to each manual
6 combination pedals   4 pistons to pedal couplers
Sustainer on Choir manual   2 *Tremulants*
3 balanced swell pedals   1 crescendo pedal

Mr Bruce Buchanan, Director & Archivist at Messrs. J. W. Walker & Sons Ltd., kindly placed on loan material relating to Midgley's important experiments in the development of a satisfactory electronic organ, while in the September 1938 issue of *Musical Opinion*, A. M. Midgley, son of A. H. M., provided interesting details relating to his father's work; this was covered by Patents Nos. 454720, 454783, 464863, 482284, 487220 and 489695. His first patent registered for the production of synthetic electronic tone was introduced in 1931 and from this, an elementary system developed. This patent was offered to Compton, but he showed no interest in it at that time. It should be stated here, that on 6th February, 1925, The John Compton Organ Co. was re-constructed; it consisted of Compton, Midgley, together with J. H. P. and

Reginald Walker, the Walker firm agreeing to supply general organ building components when the newly constituted firm was very busy. From about 1931–32, against his previous inclination, Compton became aware of the possibilities of electronics and employed a talented engineer, Leslie Bourn, to go further into the matter. Their first patent was granted during 1931 which was remarkably similar to Midgley's. Although both consulted each other at the time, an uneasy relationship developed between Midgley and Compton which eventually led to the parting of the ways—this was in 1937.

The patent was offered to Walkers and in the March issue of *The Musical Times*, the Midgley-Walker Pipeless Organ, with two manuals and pedals was introduced to the musical world, the press being invited to hear 'the latest product of inventive skill'. The March issue of *Musical Opinion* also contained an advertisement for this instrument. What is particularly interesting in this brief saga into the field of electronics was an advertisement in *Musical Opinion* for September 1939 by Midgley Electronic Instruments Ltd., of Dukes Road, Western Avenue, London W3, advertising the Midgley Electronic Organ, with 31 speaking stops and 4 mutation stops for the individual organist to build his own tone colour. The price for a standard console was £550, with sound cabinets additional as required. There was an illustration of an installation at the Perwale Park Free Church, Greenford. A year later, war came and whether the firm survived afterwards is not known.

Bourn continued his electronic explorations at Comptons, which resulted in one improvement after another.

At this time, voicing and tonal finishing was in the hands of John Compton, although whether he was responsible for reedwork is not known; it is likely that these came from the trade and it has led me to wonder whether W. C. Jones was responsible for some. In the many conversations I had with him, I was unable to glean much of his activities at this period of his career. Technical planning and development was the responsibility of J. I. Taylor. A brilliant technician and possessing an innovative mind, he shared the vision of John Compton and together they were responsible for one invention after another. No situation was too difficult for J. I. Taylor, whose mind immediately set to work on the problem and solutions were found of great originality, which seemed almost impossible in theory, but in practice—they worked. As this chapter unfolds it will be seen how Comptons soon became a name to be reckoned with, for one important contract after another came their way, and more often than not with the most incredible difficulties in siting and acoustics which exercised the fertile mind of J. I. Taylor to the full. Today, 'extension' is a dirty word, yet no one should under estimate its success at the hands of Comptons who created some magnificent instruments in what sometimes were almost impossible situations. It has been my privilege over the years to examine several such sites for myself and I have marvelled at the way they were tackled and the artistic result which evolved from the combination of voicers and technicians.

The instrument which undoubtedly set the seal for their future success in the ecclesiastical world was the four-manual in the Liberal Jewish Synagogue, St John's Wood, built in 1926. This was fully described by Gilbert Benham in an article in *The Organ* for April 1926, from which we learn that it was totally enclosed in two very large Swell chambers placed 'behind a very massive walnut screen between the pillars of which, swell shutters open into the building'. Additional shutters on the top of the chambers directed the tone upwards into the choir gallery, the ceiling of which formed a curved reflector, ensuring that the tone was thrown well into the building. Both sets of shutters could be operated independently. The degree of extension employed is not mentioned, but attention was drawn to the patented cubes or acoustic chests which generated the tone of the 32ft sub-bass, and the contra baryphone, which was 'identical with that of an orthodox 32ft reed'; it was a compound stop and every pipe was a stopped pipe. This magnificent instrument created a tremendous amount of interest in its day; sadly, during the war it received bomb damage, but was rebuilt with a new drawstop console in 1951, and later, even more sadly, removed altogether, being replaced by an electronic instrument, when it became necessary to reconstruct the building.

This specification was published in *Musical Opinion* for April 1925; it must have been an advance copy, for the works records show the completion of the instrument in 1926. This is the tonal scheme as it was after the post-war restoration. It is followed by an analysis of the ranks:

SPECIFICATION OF THE COMPTON ORGAN

IN THE

LIBERAL JEWISH SYNAGOGUE

Restored by the original builders, after damage to it by enemy action.

Four Manuals : CC to C, 61 notes.

Pedalboard : CCC to G, 32 notes.

PEDAL ORGAN

1.	Subbass	32 ft.
2.	Major Bass	16 ft.
3.	Minor Bass	16 ft.
4.	Bourdon	16 ft.
5.	Dulciana	16 ft.
6.	Echo Violone	16 ft.
7.	Quint	10-2/3 ft.
8.	Octave	8 ft.
9.	Flute	8 ft.
10.	Dulciana	8 ft.
11.	Super Quint	5-1/3 ft.
12.	Octave Flute	4 ft.
13.	Super Octave	4 ft.
14.	Contra Baryphone	32 ft.
15.	Baryphone	16 ft.
16.	Trombone	16 ft.
17.	Bombarde	16 ft.
18.	Tuba	8 ft.
19.	Tuba	4 ft.

   i. Choir to Pedal
   ii. Great to Pedal
   iii. Swell to Pedal
   iv. Solo to Pedal

Four toe-pistons for Pedal Organ.

One reverser toe-piston for Great to Pedal Coupler.

One toe-piston for the Choir Sustainer.

One toe-piston for the Solo Sustainer.

CHOIR ORGAN

1.	Double Dulciana	16 ft.
2.	Lieblich Bordun	16 ft.
3.	Open Diapason	8 ft.
4.	Dulciana	8 ft.
5.	Unda Maris	8 ft.
6.	Vox Angelica	8 ft.
7.	Lieblich Gedeckt	8 ft.
8.	Dulcet Quint	5-1/3 ft.
9.	Octave	4 ft.
10.	Dulcet Principal	4 ft.
11.	Vox Angelica	4 ft.
12.	Lieblich Flöte	4 ft.
13.	Stopped Twelfth	2-2/3 ft.
14.	Dulcet Fifteenth	2 ft.
15.	Flautino	2 ft.
16.	Acuta	15, 19, 22
17.	Krummhorn	16 ft.
18.	Clarinet	8 ft.
19.	Syntheton	8 ft.
20.	Kinura	8 ft.
21.	Tromba (Great)	8 ft.

   i. Choir Tremulant
   ii. Sustainer
   iii. Pedal to Choir
   iv. Swell to Choir
   v. Solo to Choir

Six double-touch thumb-pistons for Choir and Pedal.

One thumb-piston for Choir to Pedal.

GREAT ORGAN

1.	Sub Diapason	16 ft.
2.	Bourdon	16 ft.
3.	First Diapason	8 ft.
4.	Second Diapason	8 ft.
5.	Third Diapason	8 ft.
6.	Hohl Flöte	8 ft.
7.	Gedeckt	8 ft.
8.	Quint	5-1/3 ft.
9.	Octave	4 ft.
10.	Principal	4 ft.

11.	Flute	4 ft.
12.	Super Quint	2-2/3 ft.
13.	Super Octave	2 ft.
14.	Fifteenth	2 ft.
15.	Cornet	17, 19, 21, 22
16.	Contra Tromba	16 ft.
17.	Tromba	8 ft.
18.	Octave Tromba	4 ft.
19.	Solo Tuba	8 ft.

    i.   Solo to Great
    ii. Swell to Great
    iii. Choir to Great

Six double-touch thumb-pistons for Great and Pedal.

One thumb-piston for Great to Pedal Coupler.

One reverser thumb-piston for Swell to Great Coupler.

SWELL ORGAN

1.	Contra Viola	16 ft.
2.	Open Diapason	8 ft.
3.	Viole	8 ft.
4.	Harmonic Flute	8 ft.
5.	Violes Celestes	8 ft.
6.	Harmonic Flute	4 ft.
7.	Viola	4 ft.
8.	Octave	4 ft.
9.	Viol Fifteenth	2 ft.
10.	Cymbale	12, 15, 19, 22
11.	Contra Oboe (Tenor C)	16 ft.
12.	Oboe	8 ft.
13.	Octave Oboe	4 ft.
14.	Trombone	16 ft.
15.	Trumpet	8 ft.
16.	Clarion	4 ft.

    i. Swell Tremulant
    ii. Solo to Swell

Six double-touch thumb-pistons for Swell and Pedal.

One thumb-piston for Swell to Pedal Coupler.

SOLO ORGAN

1.	Violes Celestes	16 ft.
2.	Cello (synthetic)	8 ft.
3.	Violes Celestes	8 ft.
4.	Harmonic Flute	8 ft.
5.	Quintaton	8 ft.
6.	Harmonic Flute	4 ft.
7.	Celestina	4 ft.
8.	Harmonic Piccolo	2 ft.
9.	Quartane	19, 22
10.	Bassoon (Tenor C)	16 ft.
11.	Orchestral Oboe	8 ft.
12.	Vox Humana	8 ft.
13.	Musette	4 ft.
14.	Vox Humana	4 ft.
15.	Bombarde	16 ft.
16.	Trumpet	8 ft.
17.	Tuba	8 ft.
18.	Tromba	8 ft.
19.	Tromba Quint	5-1/3 ft.
20.	Tuba Clarion	4 ft.

    i. Solo Sustainer
    ii. Front shutters coupled

Six double-touch pistons for Solo and Pedal.

One thumb-piston for Solo to Pedal Coupler.

GENERAL ACCESSORIES

Two balanced swell-pedals, with indicators.

Balanced crescendo-pedal, with indicator.

General canceller.

Switchboard for piston adjustment.

Push-button starter to blowing apparatus.

CHAMBER ONE

Diapason I	Pedal 16 8 4 Great 8
Diapason Ia	Great 4
Diapason II	Pedal 16 10⅔ Great 16 8 4 2 1
Diapason III	Pedal 5⅓ Choir 8 4 Great 8 5⅓ 2⅔ 2
Hohl Flöte	Pedal 6⅖ 4⁴⁄₇ Great 16 8 4
Gedeckt	Choir 16 8 5⅓ 4 2⅔ 2 Great 8
Dulciana	Pedal 16 8 Choir 16 8 5⅓ 4 2⅔ 2 1⅓ 1 Great 2⅔ 1⅓
Vox Angelica	Choir 8 4
Unda Maris	Choir 8
Harmonics IVrks.	Pedal 32 16 Choir 16 8 Great 8
Tromba	Choir 8 Great 16 8 4 Solo 8 5⅓
Tuba	Pedal 16 8 4 Great 8 Solo 16 8 4

CHAMBER TWO

Subbass and Harmonic Flute	Pedal 32 16 8 4 Swell 8 4 Solo 8 4 2⅔ 2 1⅓ 1
Viola	Pedal 16 Swell 16 8 4 2⅔ 2 1⅓ 1 Solo 8
Diapason	Swell 8 4 2 Solo 8
Violes Célestes	Swell 8 Solo 16 8 4
Horn	Swell 16 8 4
Trumpet	Pedal 16 Swell 16 8 4 Solo 8
Orchestral Oboe	Solo 16 8 4
Vox Humana	Solo 8 4

MIXTURES AND SYNTHETICS

Harmonics	17 21 23 25
Acuta	15 19 22
Cornet	12 15 17 19 21 22 23 25
Cymbale	12 15 19 22
Quartane	19 22
Quintaton	1 12

One of the instruments which established the firm's reputation as builders of fine church organs as well as those for cinemas, was the instrument for St Osmund's Church, Parkstone, in 1931. It had to be versatile in design for Anglo-Catholic worship; money was scarce, as well as space, so that the use of extension and a limited amount of duplexing was essential. The natural choice was Comptons, who devised the following most comprehensive specification:

ST OSMUND'S CHURCH, PARKSTONE 1931

3 manuals: CC to C, 61 notes   Pedal: CCC to G, 32 notes

GREAT ORGAN

	ft		
Double Open Diapason	16	Dulcet	4
Bourdon	16	Open Flute	4
First Diapason	8	Twelfth	2⅔
Second Diapason	8	Fifteenth	2
Open Flute	8	Super Octave	2
Gedeckt	8	Cornet	V
Dulciana	8	Tromba	8
Octave	4	Octave Tromba	4

SWELL ORGAN

Contra Viola	16
Second Diapason	8
Viole da Gamba	8
Open Flute	8
Dulciana	8
Viola	4
Open Flute	4
Quint	2⅔
Doublette	2
Larigot	1⅓
Octavin	1
Bassoon	16
Hautboy	8
Hautboy	4
Trombone	16
Trumpet	8
Clarion	4

CHOIR ORGAN

Bourdon	16
Double Dulciana	16
Gedeckt	8
Viola da Gamba	8
Dulciana	8
Vox Angelica	8
Lieblich Flöte	4
Dulcet	4
Vox Angelica	4
Nazard	2⅔
Twelfth	2⅔
Flautina	2
Dulcet Fifteenth	2
Tierce	1⅗
Nineteenth	1⅓
Twenty-second	1
Clarinet	8
Musette	8
Hautboy	8
Hautboy	4

BOMBARDE ORGAN
(on the lowest manual)

Sub Diapason	16
First Diapason	8
Octave Diapason	4
Plein Jeu	V
Double Tromba	16
Tromba	8
Octave Tromba	4
Trombone	16
Trumpet	8
Clarion	4

PEDAL ORGAN

Sub Bourdon	32
Sub Quint	21⅓
Sub Bass	16
Bourdon	16
Open Wood	16
Great Bass	16
Stopped Quint	10⅔
Flute	8
Echo Flute	8
Octave Wood	8
Super Octave	4
Harmonics of 32ft 1·5·8·10·12·14·15·16·17	IX
Cornet 8·12·15·19·22	V
Bombarde	16
Trombone	16
Tromba	8

COUPLERS

Great to Pedal   Swell to Pedal   Choir to Pedal
Swell to Choir   Swell to Great   Choir to Great

The Choir clarinet and musette are synthetic stops

Features of interest are the use of diaphones to extend the Great first diapason down to form the Pedal great bass 16ft. The harmonics 32ft is made of bourdon pipes designed to produce a 32ft reed effect when added to such other stops as would normally be combined with such a register. To quote Francis Burgess in his very informative article in *The Organ*, No. 45; 'Its success is sufficient to justify it and no student of organ matters should henceforward consider his education complete until he has tested it'.

Mechanical features are the plentiful provision of adjustable pistons; there are nine to the Choir Organ and six each to Swell and Great Organs. Second touch brings on a suitable pedal, the four general pistons operating likewise. There are six toe pistons to the Pedal, while four adjustable master pistons can be tied to any combination of ordinary pistons. Each manual has a manual to pedal coupler 'with a second touch which adjusts the pedal basses to anything which happens to be playing on that manual at the moment, whether drawn by hand or otherwise'. Finally, there is second touch cancelling to the stop keys. Little wonder that an instrument with an outlook so advanced attracted the interest of many, and without doubt, spread the fame of Compton far and wide. To quote Francis Burgess: 'This modest instrument is unbelievably magnificent in every respect. It is a standing tribute to the artistic and mechanical genius of Mr Compton who built it…' I am happy to say that the organ has had excellent maintenance and is still going strong after sixty years or so of service.

The 1920s saw the introduction of the cinema organ in ever increasing numbers and there was great rivalry between Wurlitzer of America, Comptons and Hill, Norman & Beard Ltd. At the old works of the latter firm on York Way, I recall seeing rows of cinema organ consoles in various stages of construction, while at Compton's premises at that time (late 1920s) they were also fully engaged. As early as 1908, Compton built his first Theatre organ for the Palace Cinema, Tamworth; J. I. Taylor opened it, and with six ranks of pipes, it was played from the console of a Harper electric piano. In his works during 1914 he had a demonstration organ built which included a 'toy counter', but I do not know what happened to it. What few cinema organs there were until the great boom of the '20s and '30s comprised straight instruments of church design plus a set of tubular bells; they were built by Thomas S. Jones of London and known as The Saint Cecilia Pipe Organ, but there may have been one or two by other firms. I recall a St Cecilia model, with tracker action, at the Corn Exchange Cinema, Lincoln; it was in a gallery on one side of the screen and on the opposite side there was a small orchestra of three or four players. For ten years, from 1920–1931, Wharton Trevitt played regularly at 'The Exchange' at a weekly wage of £3-15-0 per week!

Comptons saw the potential of the cinema organ and once under way they became money spinners. Their first major instrument was installed in the Exchange Cinema, Northampton, in 1920; it had thirty-three ranks of pipes, only five of which were extended. A year later, their first true unit organ was built for the County Cinema, Sutton, and then, in 1923, the 17 rank 109 stop four-manual organ for Shepherd's Bush Pavilion made a tremendous impression in the cinema world and for a time became their 'flagship'. In design, it was more of a concert organ; Gilbert Benham wrote a thoughtful and eulogistical account of this instrument in *The Organ* for April 1924; situated in two small cement chambers under the stage, it was a triumph for John Compton, J. I. Taylor, and their skilled staff. A full toy counter was added in 1927, and during 1931 a more modern console on a lift, together with new relay action and a tibia rank. A flying bomb which landed back stage destroyed this fine instrument during the war. It was but one of many and great must have been the sadness at the Compton factory where many hours of planning and hard work had gone into the theatre organ which gave so much pleasure to large audiences throughout the land.

SHEPHERD'S BUSH PAVILION 1923

GREAT ORGAN

	ft
Double Open Diapason	16
Contra Flute	16
Diaphonic Diapason	8
Open Diapason	8
Salicional	8
Tibia Minor	8
Open Flute	8
Quint	5⅓
Principal	4
Octave Tibia	4
Flute	4
Piccolo	2
Rausch Quint	2⅔, 2
Cornet	V
Ballad Horn	16
Horn	8
Clarinet	8
Ophicleide	16
Tromba	8
Octave Tromba	4
Solo Tuba	8

SWELL ORGAN

Violone	16
Sub Strings	16
Violoncello	8
Violes Célestes	II

Muted Strings	II
Zauberflöte	8
Quintatön	8
Gambette	4
Octave Strings	4
Flauto d'amore	4
Flautina	2
Ottavina	II
Cymbale	IV
Synthetic Baryphon	16
Synthetic Krumhorn	8
Syntheton	8
Oboe	8
Vox Humana	16
Vox Humana	8
Vox Humana	4
Trombone	16
Trumpet	8
Clarion	4

ORCHESTRAL ORGAN

Contra Tibia	16
Contra Salicional	16
Open Diapason	8
Tibia	8
Salicional	8
Open Flute	8

Flute	4	Quartane	II
Salicet	4	Synthetic Krumhorn	8
Twelfth	2⅔	Vox Humana	8
Fifteenth	2	Contra Fagotto	16
Piccolo	2	Oboe	8
Acuta	III	Octave Oboe	4
Corno di Bassetto	16	Trombone	16
Clarinet	8	Trumpet	8
Horn	8	Clarion	4
Waldhorn	4	Tuba	8
Ophicleide	16	Xylophone	8
Tromba	8	Xylophone	4
Tromba	4	Chimes	8
Xylophone	8		
Chimes	8		
Xylophone	8		

COUPLERS

Great to Pedal   Swell to Pedal   Solo to Pedal
Orchestral to Pedal   Solo to Orchestral
Swell to Orchestral   Sustainer to Orchestral
Solo to Great   Swell to Great   Orchestral to Great
Sustainer to Solo   Solo to Swell

SOLO ORGAN

Violons Célestes	16
Bourdon	16
'Cello	8
Violes Célestes	8
Muted Strings	8
Zauberflöte	8
Quintatön	8
Gambette	4
Celestina	4
Flauto d'amour	4
Flautina	2

ACCESSORIES

2 *Tremulants*   3 swell pedals   Crescendo pedal
Drum pedal   Thunder pedal   2 sustainer pedals
8 pistons to each manual   4 pedal control pistons
4 pedal control pedals   3 comb. pedals to pedal
8 pistons in key cheeks
4 indicators for swell and crescendo pedals

Speed was essential to cope with the influx of orders for cinemas; I recall one of the voicing rooms at Comptons where, as each pipe was voiced, it was passed to a van driver and placed on a large baker's tray and it was not long before a complete stop was on its way to location where it was finally finished and balanced. Construction wise, erection was made easy by the manufacture of standard parts, technical drawings for the site foreman and careful organisation and with all-night working, the cinema concerned soon had its mighty organ! More than one record in the time of erection was made by the Compton staff who became used to irregular hours and working nights. In the heyday of the cinema organ during the 1930s the income gained was of tremendous help to the two London firms while it lasted. In the case of Comptons, constant experimentation certainly swallowed up money, but bore fruit in many ways, particularly in the field of electronics in later years.

My first experience of a Compton cinema organ at close quarters was a visit to Manchester Cathedral and thence to the Regal Cinema, Altrincham, with Willis Grant, then assistant organist at Lincoln Cathedral. He not only was a most talented musician, a brilliant recitalist and a fine teacher, but also a character with a northern sense of humour, having been born in Bolton. We struck up a good friendship and one Sunday, with Dr. Slater's reluctant acquiescence, he took the day off and we went to Manchester Cathedral for Evensong, sitting at the console with that great musician and character with an impish sense of humour— Norman Cocker. These were the days when the railway service was such that a visit to Manchester and back, with ample time to spare, was easily accomplished on a Sunday. Norman Cocker's accompaniment of the service was a sheer joy—enlivened by some most cunning tricks! including playing the choir out to a masterly improvisation which included several popular tunes of the day which appeared and disappeared so quickly in the general texture, that the listener down below would have the greatest difficulty in spotting them. We then flew off at great speed to the Regal Cinema, Altrincham, where Cocker was also organist and had the pleasure of sitting with him at the console before we dashed back to Manchester to catch our train home. It was an unforgettable experience to hear the transition from Cathedral organist to cinema playing of the highest order, and thus commenced a contact with Norman Cocker which continued for many years.

The Regal Cinema, which accommodated 2,000 persons, was opened on 13th May, 1931; the organ had eleven units; tromba, trumpet, clarinet, vox humana, orchestral oboe, tibia, flute, diapason, cello, celeste and salicional. It has been described as a 'quality instrument'; tragically the organ and cinema were destroyed by fire on 6th January, 1956.

The Cathedral organ was partially destroyed in the blitz on Manchester, but nothing daunted Norman and he cobbled together what could be salvaged, and using the four-manual console, Harrisons put together a highly effective two-manual instrument to accompany the services for the duration of the war. In a letter to me dated 9th November, 1943, he outlined his plans for the future as follows:

'As for the future organ equipment—three organs and five consoles…! I fear that must wait, for it is far too big a scheme for a short letter. In time it will be published in all its glory, but it has been ordered many months ago by the Dean & Chapter; so we now await the end of this silly war with impatience.

Comptons and Harrisons together are working out details at their end and I am busy daily doing some re-designing and improving in the matter of console layouts. In brief, there are two main organs: one in the chancel for the accompaniment in the choir, in all its multifarious musical jobs, and the other in the tower arch at the west end and for organ recital and big congregational use. The third is in a projected Lady chapel, east, and it will be purely electronic.

Both main organs will be extensional throughout, 44 ranks in the nave and 33 in the chancel, exclusive of 5 tonal percussions and of a GRAND CHOEUR section in the nave (which is a straight 26 rank chorus up to the 32nd harmonic ¼' including most of the 'odd' partials above the neuvieme… eg. onzième, trezième, quatorzième etc).

Comptons are the responsible party and will guide the work generally. As to which firm will do what is their affair, but of course, all extensional work vital to the choruses will be done by Compton, there will be lots for Harrisons to do nevertheless.

The chancel organ will be totally enclosed. The nave organ will have four unenclosed departments: Great, Bombarde (a second Great), Grand Choeur and Positif, together with enclosed Swell, Choir and Solo and 12 enclosed Pedal stops. The master console has close on 400 stops and the chancel console nearly 200. A two-manual console playing part of the Chancel organ goes into the Military chapel and with a two-manual console to the Lady chapel and the old Harrison 1934 console, for the benefit of the conservative player, tucked away west to play such parts of the nave organ as its stopknobs indicate; there you have it all in a nutshell.'

In the July 1943 issue of *Musical Opinion* it was announced that 'Manchester Cathedral is to have a new organ, which is to be the joint production of Messrs. Harrison & Harrison and the John Compton Organ Company'.

This grandiose scheme proved to be but a pipe-dream. In 1948, Norman Cocker collaborated with Harrison & Harrison in the design of a four-manual instrument of 100 speaking stops. He lived to see the erection of the Choir and Solo organs which were ready for the Christmas services in 1952 and which he exploited to the full in his usual masterly manner. Sadly, he died suddenly in the latter part of 1953, after a successful and highly active life which he enjoyed to the full. The remainder of the organ was installed in stages and Geraint Jones gave the opening recital on 27th February, 1957.

Reginald Foort thought highly of Compton's cinema organ work. In his book *The Cinema Organ* (1st edition), the firm inserted an advertisement which included a testimonial from Foort, dated 10th November, 1930, when he was Solo Organist at the New Victoria Theatre. This reads as follows:

'For the past six weeks I have had the wonderful pleasure of playing your superb organ at The New Victoria and I want to let you know exactly what I think about it. The quality of tone of various units is, individually and collectively magnificent; the swell shutter control is the most efficient I have ever experienced, the volume of the full organ being extremely impressive; the organ is, indeed capable of reproducing the effect of a Symphony Orchestra, a Cathedral

Organ or a Dance band at will. *I have at last found the perfect Theatre Organ, it is the finest I have ever played.* I find the action not only as responsive and 'snappy' as anyone could wish but it is absolutely reliable and free from trouble. The various drums, cymbals, glockenspiel, carillon etc and, indeed all the effects are, without exception, really amazing, your exclusive Compton patents, especially the double-touch stop key cancelling mechanism, are invaluable and an immense help in handling the organ which is certainly the most comfortable from this point of view I have ever played. You will be interested to hear that after my first broadcast on the new organ, the BBC were kind enough to telephone me to say that they considered it *the finest Cinema Organ broadcast they had ever put out.* As you know, this is the first time I have ever accepted an engagement on an all-British organ, and I must say that I am absolutely delighted and fascinated with it. Reginald Foort, F.R.C.O.'

Musical Opinion for November 1929 reported news of the firm's progress in their 'Minor Notes' column: 'The John Compton Organ Co. Ltd., inform us that they have recently acquired additional premises at their Chiswick works. Their factory is, and has been for the last eighteen months, working at high pressure to cope with the large number of orders, and the new premises provide a much needed means of enlarging the productive capacity of the firm. The company has recently rebuilt the Hope-Jones organs at the parish churches of Warwick and Sutton Coldfield. The former is now a very effective four-manual instrument and the latter a three-manual of some thirty-five speaking stops… The Bournemouth Pavilion organ is proving a great attraction and large audiences are the rule at the bi-weekly recitals of pure organ music, given by Mr Philip Dore, the municipal organist'.

In the June 1930 issue of *Musical Opinion,* the Compton advertisement announced that 'twenty-three Compton organs are at present under construction, including a large four-manual instrument for Downside Abbey'. On my first visit to the Turnham Green Terrace works it seemed very clear to me that with the rapid development of the business, new and more spacious premises would shortly become essential. To cope with their large order book additional premises had been taken at Chiswick and Park Royal, but with three separate units of floor space, production cannot have been easy. Accordingly, at the beginning of 1930, it was decided to concentrate all the constructional operations of the company under one roof, and so an extensive site was purchased. Plans (including a drawing) were unveiled in a second advertisement in *Musical Opinion* during 1930 which gave the following information:

'The new building, of which Mr F. E. Simpkins is the architect, has been very carefully designed for the purposes for which it is to be used. The various departments have been so arranged that the ten thousand and one operations which have to be performed in the construction of an organ can follow each other with perfectly ordered progress. The front part of the building contains an ample series of offices, drafting rooms, board room, telephone exchange, etc. Beyond this is the experimental laboratory where the newly invented mechanisms and their tonal devices are developed and thoroughly tested for long periods before being employed in Compton organs. In the next section of the building is the metal pipe shop leading to a suite of voicing rooms, each furnished with two electric voicing machines and a movable key-board. The engineering department is one of the largest and most interesting departments in the factory. Here are made all the electric mechanisms and many other components. A particularly up to date feature is the die-casting plant, which produces with absolute precision all the thousands of beautifully moulded parts which are to be seen in the modern Compton organ. Centrally placed in the building is the assembling shop, with a floor area of about eight thousand square feet and at the rear end are the woodworking mill, store rooms and other departments. The Compton Company propose shortly to extend to all organists and other interested persons to visit the new building and see for themselves the whole process of designing and building the Compton organ.'

As I remember it, I would say that this was the largest and most highly organised factory in the country at that time. Eventually, every component of an organ was manufactured there, except the keyboards.

Later, in a separate building there was an engineering department which manufactured caravans and juke boxes.

On August 16th, 1930, some members of The Organ Club paid a visit to the new factory and were welcomed by Mr John Compton who, together with his colleague Mr J. I. Taylor and the company secretary, Mr J. W. Byron, acted as guides through every department of the factory which was in full operation. They were immensely impressed by all they saw, but in particular the complete set of machinery for producing all the small units which go to make up an electric action. Tea was provided, and before leaving, the visitors were presented with souvenir literature and an ashtray made with a specially designed die in the bakelite press.

The opportunity to build a true concert organ upon which all classes of music could be played came with the award of the contract for the organ in the newly built Bournemouth Pavilion in 1929. The outstanding success that Comptons achieved was most ably described in full, by H. Stubington, F.R.C.O., A.R.C.M., in the July 1929 issue of *The Organ*; that the instrument has survived to this day, having received some restoration in recent years, is a testimony to its success in meeting the needs of any type of music. I shall never forget hearing a broadcast recital for the first time, through earphones in Beckenham Cottage Hospital, soon after its opening—I had just had my tonsils out and the sheer brilliance of Philip Dore's playing and the magnificence of the tone banished the soreness of throat for at least half an hour! and thereafter I listened whenever possible to broadcast recitals from the Pavilion. I have never had the good fortune to hear it 'in the flesh', but the fact that it has been preserved, gives me enormous pleasure. In a letter to me dated 17th May, 1950, J. I. Taylor (who was then chairman and technical director of the company) had this to say:

> 'The Solo concert flute and corno di bassetto were added in 1934 when the stage end of the Pavilion was altered and a revolving stage fitted, but otherwise the specification is as it was when installed in 1929.
>
> I don't know whether you have been inside the chambers but they are among the most curious we have ever had to deal with. The space in which the organ is installed came about almost by accident, as it only occurred because it was thought advisable to build out two curved features to help the acoustics of the hall. Not only was the space generally very restricted, but on the left-hand side where the Swell and Solo are accommodated, the total depth from front to back is less than 5ft owing to a ventilation duct which cuts across the corner of the chamber. The organ was accordingly built in four storeys. On the right hand side in the lower storey is the blowing apparatus and relays which are actually below the level of the auditorium. At auditorium level are the wind regulators and the softer stops of the Choir Organ. On the next level the strings, second diapason and tuba horn and on the top level the large diapason, harmonic flute and bombarde. The shutters are on the top of the chamber and the tone is reflected into the hall by the curved ceiling. A similar arrangement was adopted on the left side which contains the Swell, Solo and Percussion departments, except that in this case the work is disposed in three storeys, there being no relays or blowing apparatus on that side. The pressures in the organ are 6 ins., 10 ins. and 20 ins. The contra tibia 32ft and 16ft are cylindrical diaphones and the Pedal diaphone one of the ordinary conical type.'

What a situation facing an organ builder, but the ingenuity of Comptons knew no bounds; they were specialists in achieving the 'impossible' and in the case of the Pavilion organ with its remarkable tonal design, (with a mixture scheme described by H. Stubington as 'more audacious than has ever been attempted before'), they produced 'a very special' instrument which will always be a memorial to the genius of J. C. and J. I. T. and their devoted team of craftsmen. Happily, preservation rather than desecration has entered the organ scene within the last year or two; so that as long as funds can be found for its maintenance in these difficult times, I see no reason why it should not remain for many years ahead.

THE ORGAN

BUILT FOR

THE PAVILION, BOURNEMOUTH,

FOUR MANUALS. Compass CC to C, 61 notes.

PEDALBOARD, Compass CCC to G, 32 notes.

The whole organ is enclosed in two expression chambers (A & B)
and constructed on the extension principle.

PEDAL ORGAN (A & B):

Contra Tibia	32 ft.
Baryphone	32 ft.
Diaphone	16 ft.
Tibia	16 ft.
Violone	16 ft.
Baryphone	16 ft.
Bourdon	16 ft.
Octave	8 ft.
Tibia	8 ft.
Geigen	8 ft.
Bass Flute	8 ft.
Celli	8 ft.
Celli	4 ft.
Tibia	4 ft.
Octave Flute	4 ft.
Pleinjeu	VIII ranks
Contra Bombarde	32 ft.
Bombarde	16 ft.
Trombone	16 ft.
Fagotto	16 ft.
Bombarde	8 ft.
Horn	8 ft.
Bassoon	8 ft.
Bass Drum Tap p.	

Choir to Pedal	Great to Pedal
Swell to Pedal	Solo to Pedal

CHOIR ORGAN (A):

Violone	16 ft.
Violes Celestes	16 ft.
Bourdon	16 ft.
Contra Salicional	16 ft.
Open Diapason	8 ft.
Violoncello	8 ft.
Celestes	8 ft.
Stopped Diapason	8 ft.
Salicional	8 ft.
Viola	4 ft.
Celestina	4 ft.
Stopped Flute	4 ft.
Salicet	4 ft.
Stopped Twelfth	2-2/3 ft.
Flautino	2 ft.
Salicetina	2 ft.
Acuta	III ranks
Krummhorn	16 ft.
Clarinet	8 ft.
Syntheton	IV
Chimes	
Xylophone	4 ft.
Chrysoglott	4 ft.

Sustainer	Swell to Choir
Solo to Choir	Bombarde to Choir

GREAT ORGAN (A):

Double Open Diapason	16 ft.
Violone	16 ft.
Bourdon	16 ft.
Diaphonic Diapason	8 ft.
Open Diapason	8 ft.
Violoncello	8 ft.
Salicional	8 ft.
Harmonic Flute	8 ft.
Stopped Diapason	8 ft.
Quint	5-1/3 ft.
Octave	4 ft.
Viola	4 ft.
Harmonic Flute	4 ft.
Stopped Flute	4 ft.
Octave Quint	2-2/3 ft.
Twelfth	2-2/3 ft.
Superoctave	2 ft.
Fifteenth	2 ft.
Flautino	2 ft.
Cornet	XI ranks

Pleinjeu	IX ranks
Double Horn	16 ft.
Bombarde	8 ft.
Tuba Horn	8 ft.
Octave Bombarde	4 ft.
Octave Horn	4 ft.

Swell to Great   Solo to Great

SWELL ORGAN (B) :

Contra Viole	16 ft.
Open Diapason	8 ft.
Concert Flute	8 ft.
Viole	8 ft.
Strings	8 ft.
Octave	4 ft.
Violin	4 ft.
Concert Flute	4 ft.
Viole Twelfth	2-2/3 ft.
Flute Twelfth	2-2/3 ft.
Fifteenth	2 ft.
Piccolo	2 ft.
Larigot	1-1/3 ft.
Trombone	16 ft.
Chalumeau	16 ft.
Trumpet	8 ft.
Corno di Bassetto	8 ft.
Orchestral Oboe	8 ft.
Vox Humana	8 ft.
Clarion	4 ft.
Tibia	8 ft.
Chrysoglott	8 ft.
Chrysoglott	4 ft.
Chrysoglott	2-2/3 ft.

Solo to Swell

SOLO ORGAN (B) :

Contra Tibia	16 ft.
Sub Diapason	16 ft. T.C.
Strings	16 ft. T.C.
Tibia	8 ft.
Open Diapason	8 ft.
Viole	8 ft.
Strings	8 ft.
Concert Flute	8 ft.
Tibia	4 ft.
Strings	4 ft.
Nazard	2-2/3 ft.
Ocarina	2 ft.
Viole Fifteenth	2 ft.
Tierce	1-3/5 ft.
Fagotto	16 ft.
Vox Humana	16 ft. T.C.

Trumpet	8 ft.
Corno di Bassetto	8 ft.
Orchestral Oboe	8 ft.
Vox Humana	8 ft.
Octave Oboe	4 ft.
Vox Humana	4 ft.
Chimes	
Xylophone	4 ft.
Carillon	4 ft.
Glockenspiel	2 ft.
Sleigh Bells	2 ft.

Repeater   Sustainer
Bombarde to Solo

BOMBARDE (A) :

Diaphone	16 ft.
Diaphonic Diapason	8 ft.
Octave Diapason	4 ft.
Gross Cornet	VI ranks
Contra Flute	16 ft.
Harmonic Flute	8 ft.
Harmonic Flute	4 ft.
Flageolet	2 ft.
Violes Celestes	16 ft.
Violes Celestes	8 ft.
Violes Celestes	4 ft.
Contra Bombarde	16 ft.
Bombarde	8 ft.
Tuba Horn	8 ft.
Octave Bombarde	4 ft.
Octave Horn	4 ft.
Chimes	
Xylophone	4 ft.
Glockenspiel	2 ft.
Sleigh Bells	2 ft.

Sustainer

TREMULANTS :

Diapason I : Flute; Horn
Diapason II : Cello; Celestes
Stopped Flute : Salicional; Harmonics
Tibia
Diapason III : Viole; Trumpet
Vox; Oboe; Strings; Flute; Corno
Vibraphone

SECOND TOUCH COUPLERS :

Bombarde to Pedal
Bombarde to Choir
Bombarde to Great
Bombarde to Swell
Bombarde to Solo

ー

PEDAL TRAPS—SECOND TOUCH:

Bass Drum Tap
Bass Drum Roll
Cymbal Roll
Cymbal Crash
Triangle Tap
Tolling Bell
Traps to First Touch

MANUAL TRAPS:

Snare Drum Roll
Snare Drum Tap
Tom Tom
Castanets
Tambourine
Chinese Block
Sand Block
Sleigh Bells
Traps on Choir
Traps on Swell

SPECIAL EFFECTS:

Bass Drum Roll
Cymbal Roll
Grand Crash
Syren
Steamboat Whistle
Fire Bell
Whistle
Aeroplane
Surf
Bird I
Bird II
Auto Horn
Triangle Tap
Door Bell

VENTILS, ETC.:

Pedal to Great Toe-Pistons

Pedal to Swell Toe-Pistons

Traps and Effects Silent

Twelve ventils controlling whole organ

CONTROLS:

Balanced Pedal for Chamber A Shutters

Balanced Pedal for Chamber B Shutters

Balanced Pedal for Stop Crescendo

Eleven Toe-Pistons for Pedal Stops and Special Effects

One Sustainer on Toe-Piston

Eight thumb pistons to each manual

Four thumb pistons to Bombarde Organ

One Pedal Controller to each Manual

All the above thumb pistons have suitable basses on second touch, and are instantly adjustable at the console.

The John Compton Organ Company, Ltd.,
Minerva Road, North Acton, London, N.W.10.

In 1931, Compton's introduced their Miniatura Organ; this was brought to the notice of the musical world in a full page illustrated advertisement in *Musical Opinion* in March of that year which stated that:

'We have received so many enquiries for an inexpensive but thoroughly effective small organ that we have designed the "Compton Miniatura". The Miniatura is designed on the extension principle and possesses a complete tonal scheme and perfect electric action. The Miniatura is self contained with silent electric blower which can be connected to a lighting or heating point. Its dimensions are: Height 8ft 4ins., Width 7ft 6ins., Depth 5ft 6ins., including detachable pedalboard. It costs £575 delivered and erected within 100 miles of London. Demonstrations at our works by appointment.'

The casework was of oak, with an attractive grille front; it was an immediate success and other firms were quick to introduce their own 'model' organs, chief of which were Walkers and Rushworths.

Specifications

Manuals: CC to C4, 61 notes
Pedals: CCC to G, 32 notes

MINIATURA III

PEDAL ORGAN			SWELL ORGAN		
1. Subbass	16 ft.		11. Contra flute	16 ft.
2. Flute	8 ft.		12. Diapason	8 ft.
			13. Gemshorn	8 ft.
GREAT ORGAN			14. Hohlflöte	8 ft.
3. Tenoroon	16 ft.		15. Gemshorn	4 ft.
4. Diapason	8 ft.		16. Flute	4 ft.
5. Gemshorn	8 ft.		17. Nasard	2-2/3 ft.
6. Hohlflöte	8 ft.		18. Flautino	2 ft.
7. Octave	4 ft.		19. Tremulant	—
8. Gemshorn	4 ft.			
9. Octave quint	2-2/3 ft.		**ACCESSORIES**	
10. Superoctave	2 ft.		Balanced swell pedal.	

COUPLERS

20. Great to Pedal
21. Swell to Pedal

Balanced cresendo pedal acting on Great and Pedal stops.
Three pistons to Great.
Three pistons to Solo.
Two pistons to Pedal couplers.

Dimensions are as follows:
   III Width 9 ft. 2 in. Depth 6 ft. 0 in. (including pedalboard) Height 10 ft. 0in.

MINIATURA II

PEDAL ORGAN			SWELL ORGAN		
1. Bourdon	16 ft.		8. Open Diapason	8 ft.
2. Flute	8 ft.		9. Rohr Gedeckt	8 ft.
			10. Flute	4 ft.
GREAT ORGAN			11. Piccolo	2 ft.
3. Bourdon	16 ft.			
4. Open Diapason	8 ft.		**COUPLERS**	
5. Rohr Gedeckt	8 ft.		12. Great to Pedal	
6. Principal	4 ft.		13. Swell to Pedal	
7. Fifteenth	2 ft.		Balanced Swell Pedal.	

Dimensions are as follows:
   II Width 7 ft. 1 in. Depth 6 ft. 0 in. (including pedalboard) Height 10 ft. 0 in.

MINIATURA MODEL II
Wind Pressure 3½   Pitch 523.25

Table 1   Open Diapason, Haskel Bass

	Note:	Scale:	Cut-up:
	CC	$4\frac{7}{8}$	$1\frac{1}{4}$ bare
	B	3	$\frac{22}{32}$
	ten.C	$3\frac{1}{8}$	$\frac{13}{16}$
	mid. C	$1\frac{7}{8}$	$\frac{15}{22}$
	treb. C	$1\frac{3}{32}$	$\frac{9}{32}$
	c^1	$\frac{21}{32}$	$\frac{5}{32}$
	c^2	$\frac{13}{32}$	$\frac{5}{64}$
	c^3	$\frac{7}{32}$	$\frac{3}{64}$

½" diameter of tube above slide.
Scale of inside tube CC, 3½"; B, 2⅛".
²⁄₉" mouth.

Table 2   Rohr Gedact

Length:	Note:	Scale:	Cut-up:
8' 2"	CCC	6"	3"
4' 5"	BB open pipes cut up		$\frac{1}{4}$"
4' $1\frac{1}{4}$"	CC	$3\frac{15}{16}$"	2" (bare)
2' $1\frac{1}{4}$"	C	$2\frac{9}{16}$"	$1\frac{5}{32}$" †
1' $1\frac{3}{8}$"	C	$1\frac{15}{32}$"	$\frac{21}{32}$"
$6\frac{3}{4}$"	C	$\frac{59}{64}$"	$\frac{25}{64}$"
$3\frac{11}{16}$"	C	$\frac{37}{64}$"	$\frac{13}{64}$"
2"	C	$\frac{3}{8}$"	$\frac{7}{64}$"
$1\frac{7}{16}$"	C	$\frac{15}{64}$"	$\frac{1}{16}$"
$\frac{3}{4}$"	C	$\frac{7}{64}$"	$\frac{1}{32}$" (bare)

† From G below 1ft C, increase by one note
to 1' C, then decrease from F to C above.

MINIATURA MODEL III
Wind Pressure 3½

Table 3   Open Diapason

Length:	Note:	Scale:	Cut-up:
8'	C	$4\frac{7}{8}$"	$1\frac{1}{4}$"(bare)
	B	3"	$\frac{27}{32}$"
4'	C	$3\frac{1}{8}$"	$\frac{13}{16}$"
2'	C	$1\frac{7}{8}$"	$\frac{15}{32}$"
1'	C	$1\frac{3}{32}$"	$\frac{9}{32}$"
6"	C	$\frac{21}{32}$"	$\frac{5}{32}$"
3"	C	$\frac{13}{32}$"	$\frac{5}{64}$"
$1\frac{1}{2}$"	C	$\frac{13}{64}$"	——

Table 4   Gemshorn

Length:	Note:	Scale:	Cut-up:
8'	CC	3.16"	$\frac{9}{16}$"
	B	1.96"	$\frac{11}{32}$" (full)
4'	C	1.86"	$\frac{11}{32}$"
2'	C	1.19"	$\frac{1}{4}$" (full)
1'	C	.75"	$\frac{5}{32}$"
6"	C	.47"	$\frac{3}{32}$"
3"	C	.30"	cut-up $\frac{1}{5}$ of pipe
$1\frac{1}{2}$"	C	.19"	
$\frac{3}{4}$"	C	.12"	

Lowest 12 pipes stopped and bevelled half.
Tapered pipes to the top of the 8'; ⅓ taper.

Table 5   Hohl Flute

Length:	Note:	Scale:	Cut-up:
16'	CCC	6"	3"
8'	CC	$3\frac{15}{16}$"	$1\frac{7}{8}$"
8'	B	$2\frac{11}{16}$"	$1\frac{5}{32}$"
4'	C	$2\frac{5}{8}$"	$1\frac{5}{8}$" (full)
2'	C	$1\frac{9}{16}$"	$\frac{5}{8}$"
1'	C	$\frac{31}{32}$"	$\frac{3}{8}$"
6"	C	$\frac{9}{32}$"	$\frac{3}{16}$"
3"	C	$\frac{3}{8}$"	$\frac{7}{64}$"
$1\frac{1}{2}$"	C	$\frac{7}{32}$"	$\frac{1}{16}$" (bare)
$\frac{3}{4}$"	C	$\frac{9}{64}$"	$\frac{1}{16}$" (full)

Eared up to 6" C. The cut-up should 'run on'
to ¼ from the scale.
Metal bourdon, stopped flute bass,
Haskel open bass, stopped gemshorn bass.

It is through the kindness of Mr Ivor Norridge,
that I am able to record the scales and cut-up of
the ranks used in the Miniatura Models II and III.
To the uninitiated, it will be seen how meticulous
the tonal director and voicer must be in order to
achieve the desired results.

In 1935, yet another two models were launched and announced to the public in *Musical Opinion* for March of that year.

COMPTON "MINIATURA" ORGANS

The great success of the original "MINIATURA" has induced its builders to design a still smaller instrument to meet the requirements of very small Churches and other buildings, and for practice purposes. The new "Miniatura" is available in two specifications, as follows :—

MINIATURA "A"

PEDAL ORGAN — FEET
1. Bourdon 16
2. Flute 8
3. Great to pedal
4. Swell to pedal

GREAT ORGAN
5. Bourdon 16
6. Open diapason 8
7. Rohr gedeckt 8
8. Principal 4
9. Fifteenth 2

SWELL ORGAN
10. Open diapason 8
11. Rohr gedeckt 8
12. Flute 4
13. Piccolo 2
    Balanced Swell Pedal

MINIATURA "A" will effectively lead a congregation of 150 voices, and may be tonally amplified to do much more.

MINIATURA "B"

PEDAL ORGAN — FEET
1. Bourdon 16
2. Flute 8
3. Flute 4
4. Great to pedal
5. Solo to pedal

GREAT ORGAN
6. Salicional 8
7. Stopped diapason 8
8. Salicet 4
9. Twelfth (middle C) 2⅔
10. Fifteenth 2

SOLO ORGAN
11. Bourdon 16
12. Salicional 8
13. Stopped diapason 8
14. Salicet 4
15. Flute 4
16. Nazard (middle C) 2⅔
17. Flautino 2
    Balanced Swell Pedal

MINIATURA "B" has been designed specially for the practice and performance of polyphonic organ music. It is more quietly voiced than Miniatura "A" and is therefore more suitable for practice rooms and private residences.

Miniatura "A" **PRICES** *Miniatura "B"*

£450   £465

These prices include electric blowing apparatus, oak case-work and organ bench, and erection within 100 miles of London. A detached console can be provided at a small additional charge.

Compton Organs are the best in the World

THE JOHN COMPTON ORGAN CO. LIMITED

Chase Road, North Acton, London, N.W.10

Telephone—Willesden 6666   *Nearest Station—North Acton, Central London Railway*

Thirty-two years later, a further 'model' organ known as The Compton Augmentum was brought out, but I gather that it was not a success. A list of organs built by the firm which terminates in 1963 gives two Augmentum organs in stock and a special enclosed model which went to a location in Nitts Hill. It will be noted from the reproduction of the firm's leaflet that the manual pipework was entirely 'straight'. Whether any further Augmentums were built in the last eight years trading of the company is not known, but I would say that it is doubtful.

Comptons added yet another 'Model' organ to their range—'the Cecilian'—which was an up-dated version of the short compass Positive Organ introduced by Casson, and further improved by Cousans of Lincoln and R. Spurden Rutt. Compton's was entirely mobile, with unenclosed pipework; part of the firm's leaflet is reproduced, which is interesting, for until Alastair Rushworth kindly sent me a copy, I had not been aware of its existence. My bound volumes of *Musical Opinion,* which go back to 1928, contain no advertisement from the firm as to its introduction. It appears to have been introduced in 1959 when three were built for stock. Classically voiced, they were useful as temporary organs during rebuilding operations or the installation of new ones. In all, six were built; it is believed that one went to Harlaxton Manor, Lincs. where it remained for a time, but I have been unable to trace where the remainder found a home.

In the 1930s the new factory became a highly efficient unit, which, as more and more orders flowed in for churches and cinemas, further space was provided. I cannot do better than quote from the reminiscences of former members of staff, all of whom have spoken with enthusiasm of their life there and have provided a detailed picture of what eventually became the most highly organised organ building factory in the country. What memories they recall to me, for I was a frequent visitor there in the 1930s. Frank A. Hancock recalls the administration: 'John Compton, overall boss, idealist and perfect gentleman. J. J. Broad, Managing Director (Finance)—a very nice person. J. I. Taylor, Technical Director, later Managing Director. J. Byron, Secretary. E. Broad (son of J. J.) became Managing Director in the last few years of the firm. H. Brown, Works Manager and H. Earle, General Foreman. All administrative staff took a great interest in the members of the working staff even to the lowest apprentice. We were made to feel part of a family; a friendly discipline was maintained throughout. An incident comes to mind; I went for an interview one Saturday morning in July 1934, age fourteen, feeling very scared waiting in the front reception to see H. Brown, the Works Manager. The boss, in his white apron, passing by inquired the reason I was there; very scared I told him; he then said there was nothing to worry about and took me in himself to see the Works Manager. He also said that if I joined the firm I would be very happy there ... I certainly was for thirty-one years! Just an example of the splendid way the firm was run'.

Once, a prominent organist quoted that one always had the impression that one never bought an organ from Comptons, but was allowed to keep it (at a price!) provided it was played and treated properly, as the staff always considered it to be one of their jobs.

Another example of kindness that comes to mind. In the 1920s, T. Bartlett walked from Deal to London looking for work; he collapsed in the works from hunger and exhaustion; after being brought round and fed, he was interviewed. It was discovered that he had been 'sacked' as a timekeeper at the Deal Gas Works. The firm decided it needed a timekeeper and took him on; it was found that he had no accommodation and his shoes were worn so thin they only had paper soles inside them to cover the holes. Shoes and lodgings were found for him; at a later date he was helped to bring his wife to London and stayed with the firm for some forty-five years until his retirement.

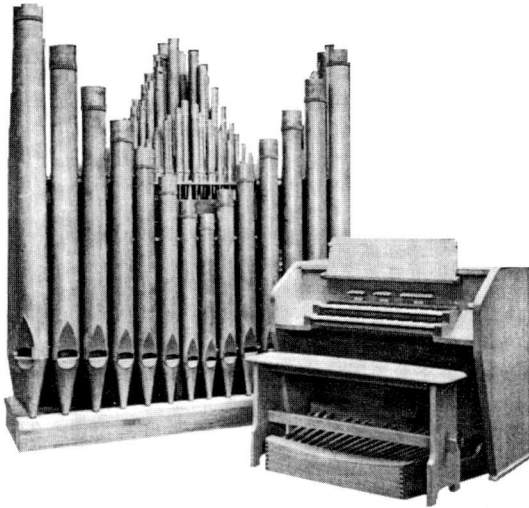

Specification of the

COMPTON 'CECILIAN'

One Manual compass FF to F, 49 notes with automatic Pedal-bass operating in lowest octave-and-a-half.

1.	Pedal-bass	16 ft.
2.	Salicional	8 ,,
3.	Stopped Flute . . .	8 ,,
4.	Salicet	4 ,,
5.	Flute	4 ,,
6.	Nazard	2-2/3 ,,
7.	Fifteenth	2 ,,
8.	Piccolo	2 ,,

The overall dimensions are :—

WIDTH : 5 ft.

DEPTH : 2 ft. 3 ins. plus $4\frac{1}{2}''$ when keyboard is drawn out.

Including stool and organist, 4ft. 6 ins.

HEIGHT : 7 ft. 3 ins.

The complete weight is not more than 4 cwt., and the instrument is readily movable on its own castored platform.

The integral electric blowing-plant is operated by an $\frac{1}{8}$ h.p. motor.

SOME DETAILS OF THE FIRM AT CHASE ROAD, 1934 ONWARDS

Voicing Shops (pre-war).— Cliff Hawtin, *head voicer*. F. Bond, *flue voicer*. S. Day, *reed voicer*. S. Laurie, *general finisher*. G. Farrer, *reeds* (later joined Peter Conacher & Co. F. Hancock, A. Simms, D. Turnpenny, *apprentices*.

Voicing Shops (post-war).— Cliff Hawtin, later *managing director* (left *c*.1963). J. Degens, *flue voicer*. F. Hancock, *reed voicer* and *general organ builder*. W. C. Jones (for a short period to train). F. Hancock. D. Lichfield, G. Carrington, S. Aldred, M. Mason, I. Norridge, *apprentices*. Ian Bell (later joined N. P. Mander Ltd.).

Metal Shop (pre-war).— W. Long, *foreman*. F. Skinner, S. Sanderson, E. Atkins, J. Paterson, *pipemakers*. Various *apprentices*.

Metal Shop (post-war).— W. Long, *foreman*. F. Skinner, later *foreman*. S. Sanderson, E. Atkins, M. Hancock. Various *apprentices*.

Console Shop (pre-war).— W. Greenacre, *chargehand*. E. Rippin, L. Griffin. Various *apprentices*, including F. Hancock in 1934.

Console Shop (post-war).— E. Rippin, *chargehand*. F. Huggett (later *works superintendent*). R. Skingle (started as an *apprentice*). L. Latham (when busy also *general organ builder* and for short periods in *voicing*, later in *drawing office*).

Cable Shop (pre-war).— J. Pollard, *foreman*. W. Knight, F. Adams, S. Hawes, D. Byron, R. Skinner, A. Gillingham. Various apprentices.

Cable Shop (post-war).— J. Pollard (later *managing director*). W. Knight, D. Byron, D. Bartlett, D. Batten. Various apprentices.

Experimental Shop, Electronics etc.— L. Bourne, founded Compton Electronics, later *director* after the war when electronics took off. W. Fair, Bourne's *assistant*, developed some of the ideas and made them work.

Engineers' Department.— E. Hirst, *foreman*. W. Clarke (solo cello expert), became post-war *manager*. S. Bell, *toolmaker* (made moulds for bakelite stop-keys etc.). W. Wheller, H. Humphreys, S. Worrall, made various works such as relay selectors, stop-keys etc. F. Eagle, *engraving* (believed to have helped with the design of machine), later in electronic maintenance and post-war tuning rep. in Bournemouth area. F. James, *apprentice* to S. Bull and later, after the war, took over the *toolmaking*. This department grew very large during the war and for some time after.

Relays.— Under H. Earle and J. Pollard. Pre-war and post war, E. Betts, H. Jermy, R. Muir and G. Morris, all *general organ builders* specialising in making relays and selectors.

Maintenance.— R. Puch, *chargehand* until 1937. W. Grinstead, E. Massey, J. Calvert, R. Gillingham, all based at London. W. Barnes (East coast), J. Ivey (a very good man), Birmingham, Midlands and North Wales. C. Dunn (Liverpool). F. Holdens, F. Geiger (London, Scotland). M. Ireson (London, Belfast).

Drawing Office.— Pre-war: F. Mitchell *organs*, P. Mullins *engineering*. Post-war, C. F. Crutchley *c*.1947–*c*.1961. F. George, L. Latham, S. Aldred (as part of apprenticeship).

Mill.— W. Perriman, *chargehand*. J. Hawkins, pre-war *apprentice*, post-war *chargehand*, plus four others.

L. Spurling, A. Priestley, Mr Bond, *sales*. John W. Byron *secretary*. Dr. George Thalben-Ball, *consultant*.

General Organ Builders.— Alfred Hawes, Charles Benall, Len Bowden, Eric Broad (*c*.1936-J. J. Broad's son), Harold Brown *works manager*, Reg Cochran *works superintendent*, Dick Coffin *swell fronts and general organ builder*, Ernie Crisp *swell pedals*, "Tiny Davis" *percussions and store-keeper*, Bert Earle *works foreman*, Bill Fletcher *traps*, Ronald Gough *pedalboards*, Len Haws, Fred Huggett *general organ builder*, later *works superintendent*, Sid Osmond, Bob Parsons, Wally Sargeant *apprentice* in the 1930s), Bill Spinks *reservoirs, regulators, general organ builder*, Albert Tuffs *general organ builder*, Jack Wardrop *traps*.

A formidable list indeed, and according to Frank Hancock, there may be others who have slipped his memory. There were upwards of one hundred in the main building and in the engineering department a number of female workers were employed on electric action components, including coil winding for chest magnets and stop-key tablets, etc. The engineering company also manufactured the plastic moulding for the stop-key units, stop tablets, illuminated stop tablets, drawstops, chest magnets, cup motors, relays, thumb and toe pistons, etc.

Derek Batten, now Managing Director of Solid State Logic, recalls: 'I spent twenty years with the Compton Company, starting in 1944, when I was a tuner's assistant travelling regularly to the south-west, covering Southampton, Bournemouth and Torbay down to Penzance. I then (after National Service) spent some time in the electrical shop, then went into the electronic department, testing and installing Electrones.I spent six years (1952–1958) in Scotland, then returned to London until 1964, when the pipe organ side ceased and Rushworths purchased the tuning connection and I joined them at that time. The Compton Engineering Company manufactured all electrical and mechanical organ parts for pipe organs and electrones as well as carrying out contracts from non-organ building companies for such things as aircraft parts, caravans, etc'.

Saxon Aldred, who now has his own business at Redbourn, Herts., and has spent a most interesting life in organ building since he left school at the age of seventeen in 1948 to join Comptons, where he remained until 1960, has vivid memories of life at Chase Road: 'My first job was in the console shop with Ted Rippin (later of Grant, Degens & Rippin). Then, after a time, I went as a tuner's boy with Frank Geiger who had been the resident tuner for Henry Willis & Sons Ltd. at Birmingham Town Hall for G. D. Cunningham… We tuned all the BBC organs at two-weekly intervals and other famous Compton organs around London including many cinema organs. Then, after persistent badgering, I was transferred to the voicing shop. F. G. did not want to part with me because I was doing all the tuning while he was sitting at the keys! In the voicing shop I was one of the team under Johnny Degens, a very fine voicer and an especially nice man. I started off by being a sweeper and tea boy! Then elevated to slotting and preparing basses, then preparing whole stops for J. D. who was very particular and painstaking over the smallest details. Johnny Degens was head voicer working on flue stops. Frank Hancock was second in command and worked on reeds. We had recently been trained by Billy Jones, the famous reed voicer, who had gone independent. Then there was Doug Litchfield, the head apprentice, who worked in the centre voicing room; for the most part, Doug did his own preparing. After his National Service he came back to Comptons but did not last long and left to take up other employment. Gerald Carrington, Ivor Norridge and I were left in the voicing shop. I took over the centre room and started off by re-voicing stops for rebuilds, cleanings and overhauls, etc. Then I became chief voicer for the small standard jobs like Miniaturas (2 and 3 ranks) and 4 rank jobs, leaving J. D. to concentrate on the big jobs. It was a very busy time and more or less every pipe from Hull City Hall passed through my hands, together with Wakefield Cathedral and Bridlington Priory, to mention just three big jobs we tackled at that time.

I remember on one occasion I came into my voicing room and found the tuning rank behind my voicing machine had been "messed about with"! I was very angry and eventually found out that Mr Compton himself had been in the night before, experimenting with an unequal temperament tuning. For the next month or so this became a regular occurrence and I regret not questioning him further about his thoughts on unequal temperament tuning. It is interesting that as early as 1953, John Compton was experimenting with unequal tuning, which was not to become generally known about for another twenty years.

After my National Service, I went back to Comptons and I noticed the drive and togetherness of the firm was beginning to diminish. I was also making friends with Charlie Crutchley (George Crutchley's father) and I spent half my time in the drawing office and half in the voicing shop. I helped quite a lot with the drawings for St Bride's, Fleet Street, and in the voicing shop helped J. D. with the voicing. Gradually I did more and more work in the drawing office working with Charlie Crutchley; again, he was a very fine man and taught me a great deal, especially concerning the "maths" of organ design. He would never use the rule of thumb—everything had to be worked out mathematically! When Charlie Crutchley left the firm in 1959, due to economies, it left Saxon Aldred on a wage of £12-10s a week responsible for the design and installation of all the new organs Comptons were producing. Fred George [the other member of the drawing office staff] was an experienced general organ builder and was responsible for the setting out of rebuilds and all old work. We were working on St Mary-le-Boltons, West Kensington (1959). Fred George was working on the rebuild of the old organ at St Nicholas Parish Church, Great Yarmouth, whilst I was designing the new organ for St Mary-le-Boltons.

With Charlie Crutchley I had attended the first ever International Congress of Organ Builders in Amsterdam during 1957. That week was my organ building 'Road to Damascus'. My eyes and ears were opened to the wonderful sounds of the historical classical organs in Haarlem and elsewhere. It was the inspiration of that first I.S.O.B. Congress that inspired the design of the new organ for St Mary-le-Boltons… Another spin off of the 1957 I.S.O.B. Congress was in my voicing techniques and the effect of nicking on the quality of tone of the pipe. At St Mary-le-Boltons, J. D. used reduced nicking'.

Without exception, all those who have been in touch with me regarding their employment at Comptons, have spoken of the 'happy family spirit' which permeated the whole factory. For myself, I recall Frank Geiger, a Lincoln man, who was apprenticed to Cousans, Sons & Co. of that city. From them he went to Henry Willis & Sons Ltd. as a provincial tuner; I met him at Lincoln Cathedral during my early teens and thereafter, when free, held down for him when he came to tune at the Cathedral. He was an enthusiast and I learned a great deal from him, ranging from the technicalities of organ building to the current gossip! His last years were spent as provincial tuner for Comptons, and we met again at St Swithin's Church, Lincoln, where he was 'touching up' the Compton organ for a recital to be given by Dr. Melville Cook in the evening. Frank, as usual, wanted to chat, and Melville wanted to rehearse. On Frank Geiger's retirement he came back to live in Lincoln—still full of enthusiasm for the old days—and on odd occasions our paths crossed when he usually imparted some news of interest—a great character in every way.

Musical Opinion for January 1937, devoted space to a report on 'The Compton Dinner, when more than 170 technicians and craftsmen of the John Compton Organ Co. Ltd., Willesden, NW, were entertained at dinner by the directors on December 17th. Mr J. J. Broad, who presided, read a telegram from Mr John Compton (who was unwell) at Palermo, sending his greetings and best wishes… Mr Broad said that the year just ended had been one of the most successful in the company's long record. The Compton business was today, the largest and most successful of its kind in Europe, notwithstanding that they had to face competition at home and from the United States of America and from the Continent. They did not feel worried on that account. Others came: others went: but Compton remained. Mr J. I. Taylor (Technical Director), in a tribute to the staff, said that 1936 was a record year. The number of installations included two Cathedral organs and four broadcasting instruments…There was also the magnificent instrument for the new Civic Centre at Southampton, to be opened in January. It was a fact that the Compton works had never yet failed to "open" an organ by the time given in the contract'.

The organ at St Mary Magdalene's Church, Paddington, occupies a particularly interesting spot in the fascinating history of the firm. L. S. Barnard, in his usual scholarly article in *The Organ* for October 1952, tells us that in 1905, John Compton and his young assistant, J. I. Taylor, walked into the church in order to examine the instrument with a view to rebuilding it. They were approached by one Alfred Hunter who was on the same errand! "So you're John Compton" he said; he had obviously heard of the progress of the young builder from Nottingham and was most considerate: they had a long journey home he said, they should be the first to look at 'the old rattletrap' and he would come back another day. A fine gesture from one who had made his name and in his dealings was a true gentleman. Neither builders obtained the contract, which was awarded to Lindsay Garrard, who went bankrupt before the work was completed, and it is believed that the church authorities made direct payments to his workmen to complete it. Another rebuild was carried out by Phipps of Oxford, but by 1932, the instrument was in a derelict state. Once more John Compton entered the scene and this time he too was a notable organ builder. A scheme was drawn up by the well-known organist of the church, Douglas Coates, for a new instrument using some pipework from the old organ after re-scaling and revoicing. Totally enclosed in two chambers one above the other on the south side of the church, the detached luminous stop console was on the north side, the player facing west. The following tonal scheme was created from the ranks as shown:

ST MARY MAGDELENE'S CHURCH, PADDINGTON 1932

Enclosed in the lower chamber—	pipes
First Diapason	61
Second Diapason	97
Third Diapason	85
Melodic Diapason	61
Stopped Diapason	85
Flauto Traverso	61
Viola da Gamba	61
Dulciana	61
Viola Céleste	56
Vox Angelica	49
Nasard	61
Flauto Piccolo	61
Tierce	61
Clarinet	61

	pipes
Tromba	85
Posaune	73
Enclosed in the upper chamber—	
Open Diapason	73
Salicional	109
Rohr Gedeckt	85
Voix Célestes	66
Octave	73
Trumpet	73
Hautboy	73
Fagottone	85
Unenclosed—	
Sub Bass and Open Wood	44
Bourdon and Flute	44

SPECIFICATION

GREAT ORGAN *Lower chamber*

	ft
Double Diapason	16
Bourdon	16
First Diapason	8
Second Diapason	8
Third Diapason	8
Stopped Diapason	8
Flauto Traverso	8
Quint	5⅓
Principal	4
Octave	4
Flute	4
Twelfth	2⅔
Superoctave	2
Fifteenth	2
Plein Jeu	VI
Contra Posaune	16
Tromba	8
Posaune	8
Clarion	4

SWELL ORGAN *Upper chamber*

Salicional	16
Diapason	8
Salicional	8
Voix Célestes	8
Rohr Gedeckt	8
Octave	4
Salicet	4
Rohr Flöte	4
Fifteenth	2
Cymbale	IV
Fagottone	16
Trumpet	8
Fagotto	8
Hautboy	8
Clarion	4

CHOIR ORGAN *Lower chamber*

Diapason	8
Melodic Diapason	8
Viola da Gamba	8
Dulciana	8

Vox Angelica	8
Viola Céleste	8
Stopped Diapason	8
Principal	4
Flute	4
Nasard	2⅔
Flauto Piccolo	2
Tierce	1⅗
Clarinet	8
Trombone	16
Tromba	8

CHOIR ORGAN *Upper chamber*

Salicional	16
Rohr Bordun	16
Salicional	8
Rohr Gedeckt	8
Salicet	4
Rohr Flöte	4
Fifteenth	2
Kleine Flöte	2
Acuta	III
Fagottone	16
Fagotto	8
Clarion	4

PEDAL ORGAN

Sub Bass	32
Open Wood	16
Contra Basso	16
Salicional	16
Bourdon	16
Octave	8
Salicional	8
Flute	8
Flute Octave	4
Harmonics	VI
Trombone	16
Fagottone	16
Tromba	8
Fagotto	8

COUPLERS & ACCESSORIES

Choir to Pedal   Great to Pedal   Swell to Pedal   Choir Sub Octave   Choir Octave   Choir Unison Off
Great to Choir   Swell to Choir   Swell to Great   Swell Sub Octave   Swell Unison Off
2 *Tremulants*   2 Sustainers   2 Balanced Swell Pedals (with indicators)   Balanced Crescendo Pedal (with indicator)
10 Double Touch Pistons to Choir & Pedal Organs   8 Double Touch Pistons to Great & Pedal Organs
8 Double Touch Pistons to Swell & Pedal Organs   3 Double Touch Pistons to Pedal Couplers
3 Reversing Pistons   4 General Pistons   1 Piston "Doubles Off"   16 Toe Pistons
Switch to disconnect 2nd touch cancellers   General Cancel   Discus Blower with 7 h.p. motor and generator

Not having heard the organ for myself, but knowing the superlative qualities of the Downside organ and that at St Luke's, Chelsea, I can imagine the grandeur, scintillating brilliance of the flue chorus, the splendour of the reeds and the great beauty of the many quiet registers. Were the reeds the work of W.C. Jones one wonders. I cannot do better than sum up the characteristics of the instrument by quoting from L. S. Barnard's article: 'Whenever I have heard it, I have been struck by some fresh aspect of it; general impressions of the balance and grandeur of the main ensembles remain constant, but there is always some fresh detail of colour or piquancy to claim the attention… The instrument and others like it convince me that the current Baroque bias has got rather out of hand and all sense of proportion has been lost by the more volatile protagonists; it seems to me to combine the virtues of the classical organ with the best of modern practice. The results are of importance; the means are not…' and as an example of the latter he quotes the high wind pressures of flues and reeds. He sums up thus: 'Perhaps the ideals of the designer and the skill of the voicer are of more importance in the final result than a reading on a wind pressure gauge'. I could not agree more.

In June 1932, Comptons announced a series of advertisements in *Musical Opinion* explaining briefly 'the broad principles governing their work and some of the minutiae of design and construction which distinguish it'. They went on to say that 'the methods employed by this company are fundamentally different from those of any other organ builders and include, *inter alia*:

1   A thoroughly scientific and efficient system of electric mechanism, first used in the Compton organs more than a quarter of a century ago.
2   The development on strictly scientific and logical lines, of the extension principle of tonal design, introduced in the Compton Organs in 1902.
3   The principle of complete expressive control, exemplified in the organs built by John Compton in 1908 and used as a normal feature of his organs since that date.
4   Many tonal and mechanical excellencies found only in the Compton organs'.

The July 1932 issue dealt with the Electric Mechanism, from which one learned that 'the reliability of the action is assisted by the use of bakelite mouldings of great accuracy and dielectric efficiency which are unaffected by atmospheric variations… all contacts are of specially hardened silver and are so durable that they have been known to outwear the ⅛" key ivories standard in the Compton consoles…' In August 1932 it was stated that 'every stop has its own windchest and every pipe its own magnet and windvalve. This system permits the utmost flexibility in the use of the pipes and the planning of the organ to suit the space available. The contact and coupling mechanisms are operated without the aid of pneumatic apparatus of any kind and are compact, reliable and made with the greatest precision in metal or bakelite… In the past five years, over one hundred and fifty Compton organs have been built, all equipped with electric mechanism manufactured in the Compton works'.

In the early 1930s it was essential for the firm to get over the message of *artistic* extension and so in *Musical Opinion* for September 1932, and thereafter, for the next two issues, they explained the extension system in detail, summarising its advantages in the November issue as follows:

1   The provision of a complete ensemble with an appropriate variety of mutations, doubles and pedal basses at moderate cost.
2   A great saving of space, with increased accessibility to the soundboards, pipework and mechanism.

3   The enclosure of all speaking stops, so that every stop can be used in several degrees of power, giving expressive control to the whole ensemble.

4   The permanent silence of all mechanism and the protection of all interior parts from dust.

5   The perfect tonal balance assured by finely regulated registers, without recourse to octave couplers.

6   The enduring pitch of the whole instrument, due to a constant temperature throughout.

7   The maintenance of the best traditions of British organ workmanship, with a perfect action wedded to perfect control.

The Compton Church Organ was the first to embody the extension system in the production of traditional organ tone. It was the first to make true organ tone flexible and entirely expressive. The Compton Church Organ has long since passed out of its experimental stage. Its enduring beauty and ingenuity have placed it in a position of commanding pre-eminence among discriminating organ lovers.

The Compton Church Organ is produced under ideal conditions in works that are unique in the organ building industry. You are cordially invited to inspect the recently enlarged Compton works where there is much to interest you.

Many a convert was made after a visit to this highly organised factory, where, more often than not there was a demonstration model to hear, with 'Jimmy' Taylor at hand to conjure magical sounds from it, while occasionally John Compton himself would make an appearance.

The new organ for Downside Abbey was a landmark in the firm's history, for it set the whole organ world agog; it received acclaim from many leading musicians of the day, with a result that one important contract after another for Cathedrals and great churches was received with jubilation at the Chase Road works. The late Dom Gregory Murray's broadcast recitals revealed the great beauty of this truly remarkable organ, the effect of which I feel quite unable adequately to describe. From first hearing it on the radio, it has taken me exactly sixty years to hear it 'in the flesh' in the summer of 1991, when my son Andrew, who lives but a few miles away, took me over to Downside to High Mass and afterwards to play the organ myself. Ever since, it has been engraved in my mind as 'The Downside Experience' and in conversation since, with organ builders and musicians, I have found that they too have shared it. Arriving a minute or two late, we heard outside that great hymn of Charles Wesley's, *Love Divine all Love's Excelling* sung to the tune *Hyfrydol*, and on entering the building were in time to hear verses two and three sung by a vast congregation of monks, boys from the Abbey School, parents and Catholics from the district around, led by a thrilling and imaginative organ accompaniment. Plainchant was not sung, this being reserved for weekdays when it is part of the daily Office, sung by the monks in choir.

The service provided an ideal opportunity to hear many of the features of this famous instrument, which attracted tremendous interest when it was built and still does—who could fail to be inspired by the whole tonal spectrum which of course is enhanced by the splendid acoustics of the building. Although time was limited I was able to explore many of the tonal possibilities from no less than 142 registers, from the console itself. This is situated close to the north transept, the player sitting with his back to the choir, the tone reaching one from the south transept gallery behind its carved oak screen designed by Sir Giles Gilbert Scott. One marvels at the planning of the pipework in a gallery of limited depth, although its width is more helpful. Three expression chambers of cement and stone are completely roofed with swell shutters of pine, three inches thick, above which there is a light screen of dustproof fabric. The Great and Choir organs, with their respective pedal basses, occupy Chamber A, Swell and Solo together with their pedal stops are in Chamber B, while the tubas are in a smaller chamber which has shutters in front as well as on top. Wind is supplied by a large Rockingham plant which incorporates a reservoir and this feeds the wind to pressure regulators at the bottom of each windchest. The action is the original which works promptly and silently; in 1984, the main cable was replaced and by the time this book is in print, the console will have been re-furbished with Solid State capture system and other work, the luminous stops being retained.

I must confess that I have never felt completely comfortable at luminous stop consoles, the arrangement of the stop names in families is confusing and I miss the normal arrangement of drawstops in columns of two. In addition, the lamps do burn out occasionally and this makes for difficulties, which one must be careful in touch, particularly where double touch cancelling is fitted. The drawstop consoles of Comptons are the acme of comfort, but it is clearly a matter of personal preference. Maintenance is carried out most efficiently and enthusiastically by the organ builder Mr Roger D. Taylor, an ex-Rushworth man, who runs his own business from Burrington near Bristol. He has been responsible for the Solid State capture system. Due to his kindness I am able to show the derivation of each stop from its parent rank, which, to the best of my knowledge has not before been published.

After hearing Downside during High Mass, the voluntary afterwards and listening to it from the console, I can but marvel at the artistry and expertise that has created such a superb ensemble and wherever one hears it—nave or transepts—its balance cannot be faulted. The flue work speaks naturally and builds up gradually to a scintillating brilliance; several individual ensembles are possible while the whole is adequate for any demands made upon it without the slightest sense of the tone being forced. The reedwork is fiery and varied in timbre, showing the greatest skill in voicing and finishing while the innumerable quiet tonal colours are of great beauty. Total enclosure means endless flexibility in playing in services or recitals; and I recall as if they were but yesterday, the unforgettable broadcast recitals of Dom Gregory Murray which thrilled the organ world sixty years ago! Here I was hearing for myself a unique instrument and it proved an emotional experience, which I gather has been felt by several musicians and organ builders with whom I have discussed it. I am thankful that no attempt has been made to alter it in any way—long may it remain as a memorial to the genius of John Compton and J. I. Taylor, its creators. Dr. Philip Marshall, Organist and Master of the Choristers, Lincoln Cathedral from 1966–1986, recalls a well-known musician congratulating John Compton after the opening recital and receiving the reply: 'A penny whistle would sound glorious in these acoustics'.

Let us look at some of the testimonials from our leading musicians of the 1930s taken from the firm's advertisement in the April and May 1933 issue of *Musical Opinion*.

Sir Walter G. Alcock, M.V.O., MUS.DOC.
'I was delighted with the organ at Downside and it seems incredible to me that so much variety can be secured from comparatively few pipes. The voicing in every department is perfect'.

Sir Edward C. Bairstow, MUS.DOC.
'The organ at Downside Abbey upon which I also played is still more remarkable. With Mr Compton's ingenious system of extensions, a large four-manual organ has been made with endless variety and beauty of tone colour, but with wonderful economy in the number of pipes and consequently in the space taken up by the organ.'

Monsieur Joseph Bonnet, St Eustache, Paris
'I am absolutely delighted with the new organ at Downside Abbey. The tone is marvellous in its nobility, grandeur and charm. This instrument possesses an infinite variety of tone colour.'
[The opening recital was given by him on 16th February 1931]

Sir Richard R. Terry, MUS.DOC. OXON.
'The tone is perfectly beautiful, both in the individual stops and in the building up of the combinations. I was delighted to find how entirely you are justified by results.'

Reginald Goss–Custard, MUS.B., F.R.C.O.
'It is wonderful… it is seldom that one can go to an organ and come away without any criticism, but I had none to make.'

On the occasion of my visit to Downside, I had hoped to meet Dom Gregory Murray, but it was not to be. He occupied his usual stall in the Choir, but I gathered he was not in the best of health; later he took to his bed and sadly, passed away in January 1992. One of the world's leading authorities on plainchant, he was a Fellow of the Royal College of Organists, and a composer of music for congregational singing in the Mass when the Roman Catholic Church switched to a vernacular liturgy in the 1960s. His *People's Mass*, written in the 1950s, was followed by *A New People's Mass* in 1975. (This is sung at Choral Eucharist in Lincoln Cathedral from time to time.) His quiet, sensitive accompaniment to plainchant, sung daily by the monks, was an inspiration, as were his improvisations as the monks entered and left the building, which left an organ builder of my acquaintance close to tears when he was there to maintain the instrument. After his first broadcast recital of the Compton organ, it proved so popular that a permanent radio link was installed in the Abbey and for no less than seventeen months he gave a recital weekly.

The *Daily Telegraph* published an appreciative and informative obituary, together with a portrait, in their issue dated 1st February, 1992. In it the writer had this to say: 'Although Dom Gregory disapproved of plainchant for congregations, he continued to accompany his brethren's singing of the *opus dei* on a miniature electric [sic] organ, providing quick improvisations that were not without humour'.

DOWNSIDE ABBEY 1931

There are 140 registers derived from the following 30 ranks.
(The numbers shown are those assigned to the ranks in the departmental stop-lists)

Great & Choir Organs *Chamber A*		Swell & Solo Organs *Chamber B*	
1	Posaune	10	Trumpet
2	Tromba	11	Hautboy
3	Diapason I	12	Horn
4	Diapason II	13	Gamba
5	Diapason III	14	Geigen
6	Diapason IV	15	Strings
7	Salicional	16	Violone
8	Hohl Flute	17	Diapason
9	Flauto Traverso	18	Stopped Flute
20	Clarinet	19	Harmonic Flute
21	Tierce	27	Tuba
22	Gedeckt	28	Harmonics
23	Dulciana	29	Oboe
24	Vox Angelica		
25	Celeste		
26	Gemshorn		
30	Diaphone		

The Tuba rank (27) is enclosed
in a separate swell box

GREAT ORGAN

Stop	ft	Unit					
Clarion	4	1	Posaune	3rd Diapason	8	… …	
Posaune	8		… …	Double Diapason	16	… …	
Contra Posaune	16		… …	Fifteenth	2	7	Salicional
Tromba	8	2	Tromba	Salicet	4	… …	
Cymbale Conique	VII	7	Salicional 2, 1	Salicional	8	… …	
		26	Gemshorn 2⅔, 2, 1⅓, 1, ⅓	Salicional	16	… …	
				Octave	4	4	Diapason II
Plein Jeu	VIII	3	Diapason I, 4	2nd Diapason	8	… …	
		4	Diapason II, 2, 1	Flute	4	8	Hohl Flute
		5	Diapason III, 2, 1	Hohl Flute	8	… …	
		6	Diapason IV, 5⅓, 2⅔, 1⅓, ⅔	Double Flute	16	… …	
		26	Gemshorn, 8, 4				
Twelfth	2⅔	6	Diapason IV	Cymbale Conique breaks at:— F(42), A(47), F(54), A(59)			
Fifth	5⅓		… …				
4th Diapason	8		… …	Plein Jeu breaks at:—			
Superoctave	2	5	Diapason III	G(45) and C(50)			
Principal	4		… …				

CHOIR ORGAN

Stop	ft	Unit	
Posaune	8	1	Posaune
Petite Cymbale	VI	5	Diapason III, 4
		7	Salicional 2⅔, 2, 1⅓, 1
		26	Gemshorn 2
Clarinet	8	20	Clarinet
Krumhorn	16		… … …
Flautino	2	9	Flauto Traverso
Nazard	2⅔		… … …
Open Flute	4		… … …
Flauto Traverso	8		… … …
Musette	8	23	Dulciana 8, 4, 2⅔
		21	Tierce 1⅗
Tierce	1⅗	21	Tierce 1⅗
Lieblich Flute	4	22	Gedeckt
Gedect	8		… … …
Lieblich Bourdon	16		… … …
Acuta	III	23	Dulciana 2, 1⅓, 1
Dulcet	2		… … …
Dulcet Twelfth	2⅔		… … …
Dulcet	4		… … …
Dulciana	8		… … …
Double Dulciana	16		… … …
Vox Angelica	4	24	Vox Angelica
Vox Angelica	8		… … …
Voix Celestes	8	25	Voix Celetes
Salicional	8	7	Salicional
Prestant	4	6	Diapason IV
Gemshorn	2	26	Gemshorn
Gemshorn	4		… … …
Gemshorn	8		… … …
Open Diapason	8	5	Diapason III
Melodic Diapason	8	26	Gemshorn
		7	Salicional

Petite Cymbale breaks at F(31)
Acuta breaks back one octave at C(49)

SWELL ORGAN

Stop	ft	Unit	
Clarion	4	10	Trumpet
Trumpet	8		… … …
Trombone	16		… … …
Octave Hautboy	4	11	Hautboy
Hautboy	8		… … …
Bassoon	16		… … …
Horn	8	12	Horn
Cymbale	V	14	Geigen 2⅔, 2, 1⅗
		16	Violoncello 2, 1
		13	Gamba 2⅔, 1⅗
Larigot	1⅓	13	Gamba
Quinte	2⅔		… … …
Octavin	1		… … …
Doublette	2		… … …
Viola	4		… … …
Viola da Gamba	8		… … …
Geigen Octave	4	14	Geigen
Geigen	8		… … …
Strings	8	15	Strings
Violoncello	8	16	Violoncello

Violone	16	16	Violoncello
Open Diapason	8	17	Open Diapason
Stopped Octave	4	18	Stopped Diapason
Stopped Diapason	8		… … …
Flute	8	19	Flute

Cymbale breaks at:—
F(42), C(49), F(54)

SOLO ORGAN

Stop	ft	Unit	
Tuba	8	27	Tuba
Octave Horn	4	12	Horn
Horn	8		… … …
Double Horn	16		… … …
Kalophone	8	13	Gamba 8
		28	Harmonics 8
Basset Horn	8	28	Harmonics 8
		18	Stopt Flute 2⅔
Baryphone	16	16	Violone
		19	Flute 8, 4, 5⅓
		28	Harmonics
Oboe	8	29	Oboe
Quartane	II		
Stopt Twelfth	2⅔	18	Stopped Diapason
Stopped Diapason	8		… … …
Bourdon	16		… … …
Piccolo	2	19	Flute
Flute	4		… … …
Flute	8		… … …
Celestina	2	15	Strings
Strings	4		… … …
Strings	8		… … …
Strings	16		… … …
Violin	4	16	Violoncello
Violoncello	8		… … …
Violone	16		… … …

PEDAL ORGAN

Stop	ft	Unit	
Krumhorn	16	20	Clarinet
Trombone	16	10	Trumpet
Tuba	4	27	Tuba
Tuba	8		… … …
Tuba	16		… … …
Posaune	16	1	Posaune
Bassoon	16	11	Hautboy
Baryphone	16	16	Violone
Baryphone	32	19	Flute 8, 4, 5⅓
		28	Harmonics
Bass Cornet	VII	3	Diap. I 8, 4, 2
		4	Diap. II 5⅓, 2⅔
		21	Tierce 1⅗
Fifteenth	4	8	Hohl Flute
Octave	8		… … …
Principal	8	4	Diapason II
Contrabass	16	5	Diapason III
Open Diapason	16	3	Diapason I
Great Bass	16	29	Major Flute
Great Bass	32	29	Major Flute
		30	Diaphone
Twelfth	2⅔	22	Gedeckt

84

	ft	Unit	
Fifth	5⅓	22	Gedeckt
Gedeckt	8		... ...
Lieblich bourdon	16		... ...
Octave Flute	4	19	Flute
Flute	8		... ...
Subbass	16		... ...
Subbass	32		... ...
Dulciana	16	23	Dulciana
Salicional	8	7	Salicional
Salicional	16		... ...
Violoncello	8	16	Violoncello
Violone	16		... ...

BOMBARDE ORGAN

Stop	ft	Unit	
Tuba Clarion	4	27	Tuba
Tuba	8		... ...
Octave Tromba	4	2	Tromba
Tromba	8		... ...
Contra Tromba	16		... ...
Sesquialtera	VII	5	Diap. III 4, 2
		6	Diap. IV 8, 5⅓, 2
		21	Tierce 1⅗, 1⅓

		ft	Unit	
Grand Cornet	XII	4	Diap. II 8, 4, 2, 1⅓, 1
		1	Posaune 16, 8, 5⅓ 4, 2⅔, 2
Octave Diapason		4	3	Diapason I
Open Diapason		8		... ...
Sub Diapason		16		... ...
Dulciana		8	23	Dulciana
Major Flute		8	29	Major Flute
Vox Angelica		8	24	Vox Angelica

Sesquialtera:— no breaks
Grand Cornet:— no breaks

WIND PRESSURES

Choir: 6 ins.
Great Flue work: 6 ins. and 8 ins.   Reeds: 12 ins.
Swell Flue work: 6 ins. and 8 ins.
Light Reeds 6 ins., Chorus Reeds 8 ins.
Solo: 8 ins. and 11 ins., Horn 15 ins., Tuba 20 ins.
Pedal Flue work: 6 ins.,
Reeds 8 ins., 10 ins., 12 ins and 20 ins.
Diaphones: 20 ins.

SPECIFICATION

GREAT ORGAN

	ft
Double Diapason	16
Contra Salicional	16
Contra Hohl Flöte	16
First Diapason	8
Second Diapason	8
Third Diapason	8
Fourth Diapason	8
Salicional	8
Hohl Flöte	8
Flauto Traverso	8
Fifth	5⅓
Octave	4
Principal	4
Salicet	4
Flute	4
Twelfth	2⅔
Superoctave	2
Fifteenth	2
Plein Jeu 1·5·8·10·12·15·17·19·22	IX–XIII
Cymbale Conique 12·15·19·22·26·29	VII–IX
Contra Posaune	16
Posaune	8
Tromba	8
Clarion	4

SWELL ORGAN

	ft
Violone	16
Open Diapason	8
Geigen Principal	8
Violoncello	8
Viola da Gamba	8
Strings II ranks	8
Stopped Diapason	8
Harmonic Flute	8
Geigen Octave	4
Viola	4
Nason	4
†Quinte	2⅔
†Doublette	2
†Larigot	1⅓
†Octavin	1
Cymbale 8·12·15·19·22	V–X
Trombone	16
Bassoon	16
Trumpet	8
Horn	8
Hautboy	8
Clarion	4
Octave Hautboy	4

† = Echo Cymbale IV

CHOIR ORGAN

	ft
Double Dulciana	16
Lieblich Bourdon	16
Open Diapason	8
Melodic Diapason	8
Gemshorn	8
Dulciana	8
Vox Angelica	8
Salicional	8
Voix Célestes	8
Flauto Traverso	8
Lieblich Gedeckt	8
Prestant	4
Gemshorn	4
Dulcet	4
Vox Angelica	4

Open Flute	4
Lieblich Flöte	4
Nazard	2⅔
Dulcet Twelfth	2⅔
Dulcet Fifteenth	2
Flautino	2
Gemshorn	2
Tierce	1⅗
Acuta 15·19·22	III
Petite Cymbale 12·15·19·22	IV–V
Krummhorn	16
Clarinet	8
Musette	8
Posaune	8

SOLO ORGAN

Violone	16
Strings II ranks	16
Bourdon	16
Violoncello	8
Strings II ranks	8
Stopped Diapason	8
Harmonic Flute	8
Violin	4
Strings II ranks	4
Harmonic Flute	4
Stopped Twelfth	2⅔
Harmonic Piccolo	2
Celestina	2
Quartane	II
Baryphone	16
Double Horn	16
Basset Horn	8
Kalophone	8
Orchestral Oboe	8
Horn	8
Tuba	8
Octave Horn	4

BOMBARDE ORGAN
(floating)

Sub Diapason	16
Open Diapason	8
Great Flute	8
Octave Diapason	4
Sesquialtera 1·5·8·10·12·15·17	VII
Grand Cornet de Bombardes	XII–XIV
Sub-unison, 1·5·8·10·12·14·15·16·17·19·22	
Contra Tromba	16
Tromba	8
Tuba	8
Tuba Clarion	4
†Dulciana	8
†Vox Angelica	8
†Gedeckt	4
† = included for the sake of general utility	

PEDAL ORGAN

Great Bass	32
Sub Bass	32
Great Bass	16
Open Diapason	16
Contra Bass	16
Violone	16
Salicional	16
Dulciana	16
Sub Bass	16
Bourdon	16
Fifth	10⅔
Octave	8
Principal	8
Violoncello	8
Salicional	8
Flute	8
Gedeckt	8
Twelfth	5⅓
Fifteenth	4
Octave Flute	4
Bass Cornet 12·15·17·19·22·24	VI
Baryphone	32
Baryphone	16
Bassoon	16
Krummhorn	16
Trombone	16
Posaune	16
Bass Tuba	16
Tuba	8
Tuba Clarion	4

COUPLERS

Swell to Great   Solo to Great   Bombarde to Great
Bombarde to Great (second touch)
Solo to Swell   Bombarde to Swell
Pedal to Choir   Great to Choir   Swell to Choir
Solo to Choir   Bombarde to Choir
Solo to Choir (second touch)
Bombarde to Solo   Choir to Pedal
Great to Pedal   Swell to Pedal
Solo to Pedal   Bombarde to Pedal

ACCESSORIES

Sustainer to Choir
Sustainer to Solo
Tremulant to Dulciana
Tremulant to Choir flutes
Tremulant to Clarinet
Tremulant to Harmonic Flutes & Hautboy
Tremulant to Viola da Gamba & Stopped Diapason
Tremulant to Orchestral Oboe

8 double touch pistons each to Solo, Swell, Great
and Choir Organs
3 double touch pistons to Bombarde Organ
1 double touch piston to each manual
(*pp* pedal and coupler)
1 piston cancelling the entire organ

3 balanced swell pedals with indicators
10 double touch toe pistons
1 crescendo pedal controlling Great & Pedal Organs,
with indicator.

In the December 1932 and January 1933 issues of *Musical Opinion*, the firm published the following letters from Fred Dunhill, organist of Birmingham Cathedral, T. W. North (Walsall Town Hall), William F. Horden (St Paul's, Lozells, Birmingham) and J. Gilbert Mills (Church of The Messiah, Birmingham) all of whom were not only brilliant musicians, but acknowledged authorities on organ tone; moreover, they were quite unbiased, owing no allegiance to any particular firm.

'Dear Sirs,
In view of the recent statements appearing in the musical press regarding the question of 'Extension and Totally Enclosed Organs', we the undersigned have journeyed to Downside to judge for ourselves the merits or de-merits of the scheme. We are of unanimous opinion that the organ in this Abbey is the most magnificent instrument that it has ever been our privilege to play and hear. We can now well understand why the BBC have decided to install a "totally enclosed" instrument, for without a doubt this is the organ of the future. We offer you our hearty and most sincere congratulations on this masterpiece.'

With the exception of Comptons, the organ of the future remained unenclosed (with one or two exceptions). Opinions were strongly and lengthily expressed in the columns of *Musical Opinion*, *The Organ* and to a lesser extent *The Musical Times* in those days, on the merits or de-merits of extension alone, together with other aspects of organ building too numerous to mention. They make fascinating reading, for organ builders, musicians, and 'fans' battled away, which makes one wonder how on earth they found the time! Somehow the excitement has gone from the correspondence columns of musical journals today, and there are few who seem concerned enough to do battle over contentious issues.

In researching this chapter, it was heartening to learn that the Compton organ in St Luke's Church, Chelsea, built in 1931, was still giving excellent service, being well maintained and this revived memories of a visit to hear the organ demonstrated by J. I. Taylor in company with Gilbert Benham, not long after it was completed. He taught me a great deal in those impressionable days of my youth, including the development of a critical ear, what to look and listen for in assessing an organ, and the importance of being open-minded, avoiding any bias towards the work of one particular builder. A number of Jimmy Taylor's contemporaries have, without exception, spoken to me concerning the many qualities of this remarkable and kindly man and all have commented they will never forget his extemporisation. Every feature of this instrument was demonstrated, so that the many combinations appeared and disappeared into the stonework! being replaced by yet more magic and introduced with such subtlety that one was left enthralled. A modest man, I shall always remember sitting under the dome at St Paul's Cathedral in the 1930s listening to the concluding voluntary, in company with Gilbert Benham. J. I. T. came up to us when it was over and obviously moved as we were, said 'there's no organ quite like it in the world, I wish our firm could build anything half as fine'. Back to Chelsea, where I had tried to take in everything, bearing in mind that it was built on the extension system. I can hear it now—the sheer beauty and variety of the quiet registers; the unforced nobility of the diapasons, the streaming brilliance or glitter, call it what you will, of the upper work, together with the richness and brilliance of the Swell and Great reeds— contrasted in timbre yet not excessively developed in either direction. A former voicer for Comptons told me that 'Billy Jones' was responsible for the reeds at Chelsea—is there any wonder that they are so magnificent? Total enclosure made the organ so very flexible and how J. I. T. mixed his tonal colours, all with the greatest of ease, creating such beauty that I can recall it as if it were but yesterday.

I had been told that J. I. T. could make the most wretched organ sound beautiful! When the last chord had sounded, Gilbert spoke with great appreciation of the organ, but qualified it by commenting 'but Jimmy, don't you think all out, it's a little too much?' The disarming reply was: 'Well Gilbert, you needn't use it all you know'! and he was right, for it was merely a matter of holding back the opening of the Swell shutters a fraction. I recall a visit to Compton's works with Gilbert Benham and Gilbert Mills; the latter thought highly of the firm's work and if ever anyone was fastidious it was Gilbert. We were shown with pride the plastic imitation ivory stop knobs, manufactured in the factory—Gilbert, who had been imbibing his favourite 'tipple' before we caught up with him, turned to us with a wide grin saying: 'They're made with dried milk you know'!

ST LUKE'S CHURCH, CHELSEA 1931

Disposition of ranks and stop scheme

GREAT ORGAN

Rank	Pitch
Diapason I	8
Diapason II	16, 4
Diapason III	8, 2
Violone	16, 8
Harmonic Flute	8
Posaune I	8
Posaune II	16, 4
Salicional I (from Choir)	8, 2⅔, 2
Salicional II (from Choir)	4
Stopt Diapason (from Choir)	16, 8, 5⅓, 4
Tromba (from Bombarde)	8
Diaphonic Horn (from Bombarde)	8

SWELL ORGAN

Geigen I	8, 2
Geigen II	4
Viola da Gamba	16, 8, 4, 2⅔, 2, 1⅓, 1
Viola Celeste	8, 4
Rohr Gedact	16, 8, 4, 2
Trumpet I	8
Trumpet II	4
Hautboy	16, 8, 4
Orchestral Oboe	16, 8

CHOIR ORGAN

Salicional I	16, 4, 1⅓, 1
Salicional II	8, 2⅔, 2
Vox Angelica (2 ranks)	8, 4
Stopt Diapason	8, 4, 2⅔, 2

Clarinet	16, 8
Diapason I (from Great)	8
Diapason III (from Great)	4
Violone (from Great)	8

BOMBARDE ORGAN

Diaphonic Horn	16, 8
Tromba	8, 4
Diapason I (from Great)	8
Diapason III (from Great)	4
Posaune I (from Great)	16
Posaune II (from Great)	8
Trumpet I (from Swell)	8
Trumpet II (from Swell)	16, 4

PEDAL ORGAN

Open Wood	32, 16, 8, 4
Open Diapason	16
Subbass (lowest 24)	32, 16, 8, 4
Posaune (lowest 24)	32, 16
Tromba (lowest 12)	16, 8
Salicional (from Choir)	16
Clarinet (from Choir)	16
Diaphonic Horn (from Bombarde)	16
Violone (from Great)	16, 8
Gedeckt (from Swell)	16, 8
Trumpet (from Swell)	16
Hautboy (from Swell)	16, 8
Orchestral Oboe (from Swell)	16

SPECIFICATION

GREAT ORGAN

	ft
Double Open Diapason	16
Violone	16
Bourdon	16
Diaphonic Horn	8
Open Diapason I	8
Open Diapason II	8
Salicional	8
Violoncello	8
Harmonic Flute	8
Stopped Diapason	8
Stopped Quint	5⅓
Octave	4
Salicet	4
Harmonic Flute	4
Twelfth	2⅔
Superoctave	2
Fifteenth	2
Petite Cymbale	IV
Plein Jeu	IV–VIII
Contra Posaune	16
Tromba	8
Posaune	8
Clarion	4

SWELL ORGAN

Contra Viola (tenor C)	16
Rohr Bordun	16
Geigen	8
Viola da Gamba	8
Viola Celeste	8
Gedeckt	8
Geigen Octave	4
Viola	4
Violino Celeste	4
Flute	4
Fifteenth	2
Kleine Flöte	2

Cymbale	III–IV		Open Wood	16
Contra Hautboy	16		Open Metal	16
Bassoon	16		Contra Bass	16
Trumpet	8		Violone	16
Hautboy	8		Salicional	16
Orchestral Hautboy	8		Sub Bass	16
Clarion	4		Bourdon	16
Hautboy Clarion	4		Octave Wood	8

CHOIR ORGAN

			Violoncello	8
			Flute	8
Contra Salicional	16		Gedeckt	8
Open Diapason	8		Fifteenth (wood)	4
Violoncello	8		Flute	4
Salicional	8		Fourniture	V
Vox Angelica II	8		Contra Posaune	32
Stopped Diapason	8		Trombone	16
Octave	4		Posaune	16
Salicet	4		Trumpet	16
Vox Angelica	4		Clarinet Bass	16
Stopped Flute	4		Hautboy Bass	16
Twelfth	2⅔		Bassoon	16
Nazard	2⅔		Tromba	8
Fifteenth	2		Hautboy	8
Flauto Piccolo	2			
Nineteenth	1⅓			
Twenty Second	1			
Double Clarinet	16			
Clarinet	8			

COUPLERS

Great to Pedal   Swell to Pedal   Choir to Pedal
Great to Choir   Swell to Choir   Choir Sustainer
Swell to Great   Swell Sustainer

BOMBARDE ORGAN
(on Choir manual)

Diaphonic Horn	16	
Diaphonic Horn	8	
Diapason I	8	
Octave Diapason	4	
Fourniture	VI	
Contra Posaune	16	
Posaune	8	
Tromba	8	
Clarion	4	
Double Trumpet	16	
Trumpet	8	
Clarion	4	

ACCESSORIES

2 balanced expression pedals (with indicators)
Balanced crescendo pedal (with indicator)
10 double touch pistons to Bombarde Organ
10 double touch pistons to Choir Organ
8 double touch pistons each to Great Organ
8 double touch pistons each to Swell Organ
4 toe pistons each to Pedal Organ
4 toe pistons each to Swell Organ
3 double touch pistons to pedal couplers
3 reversible pistons each to manual couplers
and to pedal couplers
1 piston to take off all doubles
1 general cancel piston   2 *Tremulants*

PEDAL ORGAN

Double Open Wood	32	
Sub Bass	32	

Electric motor, blower and generator

The Church of St Edmund, Lombard Street, in the City of London, had a musical history going as far back, it is thought, to Renatus Harris. His instrument was rebuilt in 1833 by J. C. Bishop; then in 1880 it was enlarged and modernised by Eustace Ingram; then along came Lewis & Co. who rebuilt it in 1893. On 7th July, 1917, it was hit by a bomb during an enemy air raid, which did considerable damage and for two years it was out of commission until Harrison & Harrison placed it in working order, at the same time revoicing the pipework and adding an octave coupler to the Swell. At that time the organ was placed on the floor of the church, but when Comptons were instructed to build a new organ in 1932, it went back to its old home in the gallery, with the exception of two ranks of pedal pipes, which remained on the floor. The main portion of the organ was enclosed in two expression chambers 'masked by one of the historic fronts'. Francis Burgess in his article in *The Organ* (July 1933) tells us that most of the historic pipes were placed on the Choir Organ. He also comments on the 'luxury of a tempered dulciana twelfth (by extension) and the untempered nazard, which, like the untempered tierce and septieme is unextended'.

ST EDMUND'S CHURCH, LOMBARD STREET, LONDON 1932

Disposition of ranks and stop scheme

GREAT ORGAN

Chamber I

Rank	Pitch
First Diapason	8
Second Diapason	16, 8, 4
Fourth Diapason	8, 2⅔, 2
Zauberflöte	16, 8, 5⅓, 4
Tromba	8, 4
Dulciana	from Choir

SWELL ORGAN

Chamber II

Third Diapason	8, 4
Viola da Gamba	16 (t.c.), 8, 4, 2⅔, 2, 1⅓, 1
Violes Celestes	(t.c.) 8, 4
Rohr Flöte	8, 4
Oboe	16, 8
Vox Humana	8
Trumpet	8, 4

CHOIR ORGAN

Chamber I

Dulciana	16, 8, 4, 2⅔, 2, 1⅓, 1
Lieblich Gedackt	8

Hohl Flöte	8
Salicional	8
Vox Angelica	(t.c.) 8
Nazard	2⅔
Tierce	1⅗
Septième	1⅟₇
Clarinet	8
Second Diapason (from Great)	8
Fourth Diapason (from Great	4
Zauberflöte (from Great)	16, 8, 4, 2
Tromba (from Great)	8

PEDAL ORGAN

† *unenclosed*

†Bourdon	32, 16, 8
†Open Wood	16, 8
Trombone (20 from Great)	16
Second Diapason (from Great)	16
Dulciana (from Choir)	16
Zauberflöte (from Great)	8, 4
Oboe (from Swell)	16

SPECIFICATION

GREAT ORGAN

	ft
Double Open Diapason	16
Bourdon	16
Large Open Diapason	8
Medium Open Diapason	8
Small Open Diapason	8
Dulciana	8
Zauberflöte	8
Stopped Quint	5⅓
Octave	4
Stopped Flute	4
Twelfth	2⅔
Fifteenth	2
Plein Jeu	IV
Tromba	8
Octave Tromba	4
Swell to Great	

SWELL ORGAN

	ft
Contra Viola	16
Open Diapason	8
Viola da Gamba	8
Violes Célestes	8
Rohr Flöte	8
Octave	4
Viola	4
Violes Célestes	4
Octave Flute	4
Fifteenth	2
Cymbale	IV
Contra Hautboy	16
Hautboy	8
Trumpet	8
Clarion	4
Vox Humana	8
Tremulant	

CHOIR ORGAN

Contra Dulciana	16
Bourdon	16
Open Diapason II	8
Salicional	8
Dulciana	8
Vox Angelica (tenor C)	8
Hohl Flöte	8
Zauberflöte	8
Gedackt	8
Principal	4
Dulcet	4
Stopped Flute	4
Quint	2⅔
Nazard	2⅔
Doublette	2
Flageolette	2
Tierce	1⅗

Larigot	$1\frac{1}{3}$	Bourdon	16
Septième	$1\frac{1}{7}$	Echo Bass	16
Octavin	1	Octave Wood	8
Clarinet	8	Octave Bourdon	8
Tremulant		Flute	8
Tromba	8	Octave Flute	4
Swell to Choir		Harmonics	VI
Great to Choir		Trombone	16
PEDAL ORGAN		Hautboy	16
		Choir to Pedal	
Contra Bourdon	32	*Great to Pedal*	
Open Wood	16	*Swell to Pedal*	
Contra Bass	16		

In 1932, the BBC were giving careful consideration to the installation of an organ for their new concert hall and after consulting various distinguished musicians, who had to consider the very difficult situation (in fact it was an almost impossible one), the contract was given to Comptons. The firm announced the impending completion of the work in the March 1933 issue of *Musical Opinion* and in July, an account appeared of the opening recital given by three of our most distinguished players, Sir Walter Alcock, Mr G. T. Thalben-Ball and Mr G. D. Cunningham. To quote the report: 'We were much struck by the beauty of tone of many of the quieter stops and the full organ is most thrilling, in fact almost too much so in the restricted space of the concert hall. However, it must be borne in mind that this organ has been designed and built for broadcasting purposes and not for the limited audience that can be accommodated in the hall itself'.

John Compton gave a thorough and illuminating account of the instrument in the August issue of *Musical Opinion*, accompanied by his portrait, and one of J. I. Taylor seated at the console with its illuminated stop heads. In view of the considerable correspondence which had appeared on the merits and de-merits of the extension system, Compton gave a masterly account of the thinking behind the employment of this system as well as details of the scientific experiments which were conducted on site, to ensure its success. He summed up by saying, with his usual modesty, 'It must not be thought from this that I regard the BBC organ as perfect, but I am confident that, had the organ been built on 'straight' lines, the result would have been a much smaller and considerably less effective instrument. It was only by the use of the extension system that a really complete four-manual concert organ scheme could have been devised'.

Filson Young, in an article entitled 'The Wonderful New Organ That is Being Built for Broadcasting House' in *The Radio Times* for October 21st, 1932, had this to say: 'I am one among the many who have been converted, by one visit to a Compton organ, from being on vague general principles, an opponent of the Extension and Total Enclosure systems, to being a complete believer in their power to more than double the resources of an organ containing any given number of pipes. From the moment of that conversion I studied each new church organ as it appeared from the hands of Mr Compton. What chiefly attracts me in these instruments is the genius of Mr Compton's voicing which he adapts with marvellous skill to exigencies of space and position. I doubt whether these could ever be a greater test of his powers in this direction than is afforded by the chamber provided in the concert hall at Broadcasting House. It is virtually a great cupboard, deeply recessed in the end wall of the building, of no regular shape, full of corners and angles, representing simply the space which was left over when all kinds of building exigencies had been provided for. Fifty years ago, any organ builder of repute would have declined even to attempt to put an organ of the size required into such a chamber, and an organ built on the old system simply could not breathe there, let alone be heard'. In *The Radio Times* for June 9th, 1933, Filson Young had this to say after the inauguration of the organ, ...'it has been a delight to sit at the finished console and put into actuality the effects that had hitherto only existed on paper and in imagination, and to find them more than fulfilling one's dreams of the ideal broadcasting organ'.

It is many years since the organ has been used for broadcast recitals, but it is still in use, having been well maintained and Solid State piston action fitted. It is occasionally heard in private concerts (which are not broadcast) and is recorded from time to time for inclusion in such programmes as 'The Organist Entertains'. On 20th June, 1993, Colin Goulden, Past President of The Organ Club arranged a concert to celebrate the 60th anniversary of its inauguration, when five young musicians played organ and piano music. It is good to know that the instrument has not been allowed to become silent.

THE BBC CONCERT HALL
BROADCASTING HOUSE, LONDON 1932
4 manuals: CC to C, 61 notes   Pedal: CCC to G, 32 notes

GREAT ORGAN

	ft
Double Diapason	16
First Diapason	8
Second Diapason	8
Gemshorn	8
Salicional	8
Stopped Diapason	8
Octave	4
Gemshorn Octave	4
Zauberflöte	4
Twelfth	2⅔
Superoctave	2
Fifteenth	2
Plein Jeu 12·15·19·22	IV
Petite Cymbale 19·22·26·29	IV
Contra Tromba	16
Tromba	8
Horn	8
Tromba Octave	4

SWELL ORGAN

Contra Viola	16
Geigen	8
Viola da Gamba	8
Vox Angelica	8
Rohr Gedeckt	8
Geigen Octave	4
Viola	4
Vox Angelica	4
Gedeckt Octave	4
Superoctave	2
Sifflöte	2
Cornet 15·19·22	III
Cymbale 22·26·29	III
Double Hautboy	16
Hautboy	8
Hautboy Clarion	4
Trumpet	8
Clarion	4
Tremulant	

CHOIR ORGAN

Violone	16
Double Dulciana	16
Lieblich Bourdon	16
Violoncello	8
Viola Acuta	8
Viola Célestes	8
Dulciana	8
Flauto Traverso	8
Lieblich Gedeckt	8
Echo Flute	8

Violino	4
Dulcet	4
Flauto Traverso	4
Lieblich Flöte	4
Echo Flute	4
Dulcet Twelfth	2⅔
Dulcet Fifteenth	2
Echo Cornet 17·19·22	III
Nazard	2⅔
Kleine Flöte	2
Tierce	1⅗
Septième	1⅐
Neuvième	⁸⁄₉
Double Clarinet	16
Clarinet	8
Oboe	8
Vox Humana	8
Musette	4
Tuba Mirabilis	8
Sustainer	
Tremulant	

PEDAL ORGAN

Subbass	32
Subbass (wood)	16
Diapason (metal)	16
Contrabass (metal)	16
Violone	16
Dulciana	16
Viola da Gamba	16
Octave	8
Violoncello	8
Dulciana	8
Flute	8
Gedeckt	8
Flute Octave	4
Fourniture 12·15·17·19·22	V
Bass Hautboy	16
Hautboy	8
Bass Clarinet	16
Clarinet	8
Contra Trombone	32
Trombone	16
Ophicleide	16
Tuba	8

SOLO ORGAN
(mostly by extension from Choir, Great & Swell)

Contra Viola	16
Contra Viola Céleste	16
Violoncello	8
Viola Acuta	8

Viola Céleste	8	Viola da Gamba	8
Dulciana	8	Vox Angelica	8
Flauto Traverso	8	Cor de Nuit	8
Viola Ottava	4	Quintaten	4
Viola Ottava Céleste	4	Double Trumpet	16
Flauto Traverso	4	Trumpet	8
Flauto Piccolo	2	*Sustainer*	
Fagotto	16		
Clarinet	8		
Oboe	8		
Vox Humana	8		
Vox Humana	4		
Basset Horn (compound)	8		
Kalophone (compound)	8		
Tuba Mirabilis	8		
Tuba Clarion	4		
First Diapason	8		
Zauberflöte	8		
Concert Flute	8		
Stopped Flute	4		
Cornet 12·15·19·22	IV		
Double Horn	16		
Horn	8		
Octave Horn	4		
Contra Tromba	16		
Tromba	8		
Tromba Ottava	4		

COUPLERS

Great to Pedal   Swell to Pedal   Choir to Pedal
Solo to Pedal   Pedal to Choir   Swell to Choir
Solo to Choir   Great to Choir   Choir to Great
Solo to Great, second touch   Solo to Swell
Swell to Great   Solo to Great

ACCESSORIES

3 interchangeable expression pedals, with indicators
Crescendo pedal, with indicator
10 double touch combination pistons to each manual
8 general pistons
1 automatic pedal control to each manual
12 reverser pistons for pedal couplers
5 toe pistons each to Swell, Great and Pedal Organs

Total number of pipes: 2,362
The whole is controlled from a moveable console
connected with the organ chamber by a flexible cable

The success of this instrument for broadcasting led the BBC to place an order with Comptons for a three-manual organ for their Maida Vale Studios. *Musical Opinion* (March 1936) announced that 'it will be used for accompanying the complete BBC chorus and the large symphony orchestra of one hundred and fifteen players… It is also intended for use in oratorio works of the largest dimensions and it will take its place as a solo instrument in organ concerto music'. Early in February it had been announced that the BBC had decided to install a four-manual Compton organ in St George's Hall. News of Compton's success at Broadcasting House had reached the A.V.R.O. Broadcasting Station at Hilversum, Holland, with a result that they ordered a four-manual concert organ and a three-manual church organ in the Dutch style. As if this wasn't enough for the time being their order books became swollen by the demand for a four-manual organ with two consoles for Southampton Civic Centre and a four-manual instrument for Wolverhampton Town Hall. There was much other work in hand or proposed, of a smaller nature too. All in all, some thirteen new instruments were under construction by October 1936.

St George's Hall, Langham Place, was originally a theatre and the home of Maskelyn and Devant, the famous magicians. I was taken by my uncle to see their shows as a lad and ever since then I have been a devotee of magic, or as it more correctly termed, illusion. When the Maskelyn productions ceased, the building was taken over by the BBC and until its destruction by enemy bombing during the war, broadcasts of cinema organ music were a regular and popular feature of radio.

The organ in St George's Hall was the first instrument of its type in the country to be designed and built exclusively for broadcasting; it all arose from the tremendous popularity of the first broadcasts from the Shepherd's Bush Pavilion and the New Gallery Kinema and to quote Reginal Foort's comments in a booklet which was on sale for a shilling! 'it has been an unqualified success. As it is not merely an ordinary cinema organ, but is also a very fine and complete concert organ; in addition to its immense popularity as a solo instrument, it has proved its worth by being used to enhance practically every type of show produced by Variety and Music Production Departments'.

It had four manuals, 23 units of pipes, together with the Compton Patent Electrone, a Steinway grand piano playable from the console, some 260 stops and 1,780 pipes. The units comprised tuba magna, tuba horn, trumpet, English horn; two diapasons, large wood and small metal tibia clausas, vox humana, clarinet, krumet, orchestral oboe, kinura, cello, cello celestes (2 ranks), gamba, violin, violin celeste, strings

(2 ranks), salicional, solo concert flute, hohl flute, stopped flute. To quote Reginal Foort, 'the stage, which, by the way, is as big as the entire auditorium, has been permanently thrown open to make a magnificent broadcasting studio, several of the front stalls have been removed to provide space for a large orchestra, and a sound-proof control cubicle has been installed on one side of the stage through the glass windows, of which the engineers and balance and control experts can observe everything taking place in the hall. The circle was formerly of the old fashioned type running along both sides of the theatre right up to the proscenium arch, but now the two ends of the horse-shoe have been converted into organ swell-boxes to hold all the organ pipes, drums, bells, etc'. The tone of the Electrone was projected through a large loud speaker near the roof of the hall.

Sadly, this magnificent instrument and the hall were destroyed during the blitz. Happily, the large three-manual organ built by Comptons in 1936 for the BBC Maida Vale Studios, to accompany the complete BBC Chorus and the Symphony Orchestra of 115 players, escaped damage and is still in use.

The organ at the church of St Stephen, Coleman Street, built in 1933, was not one of the largest of City of London churches, being but 70ft long, 35ft wide and 24ft high and acoustically completely 'dead'. It was the second of the firm's organs in the City of London and despite the unhelpful acoustics, the results exceeded all expectations; the organ attracted a considerable amount of attention and soon became known as one of the finest of the City's modern church instruments.

Occupying the west gallery and retaining its former case with the addition of side extensions, the new luminous stop console was sited at the south east corner of the church so that the organist was in sight of the altar and in touch with the singers. With the exception of four stops from the former organ (last rebuilt by Thomas S. Jones & Son in 1907), the pipework was entirely new; Great and Choir Organs were enclosed in one box, the Swell in another. The open wood, lying on the gallery, was duophoned to give twelve notes from six pipes and the lowest twelve of the 32ft sub bass were obtained by a Compton Cube measuring 10ft by 1½ft by 2½ft.

It was my privilege to examine this organ during 1933, and eight years later, in 1941 (when it had been destroyed during the blitz), I contributed an article to *The Choir* in March of that year. I was greatly impressed by the beauty of the diapason chorus and the thrilling effect of the many superb chorus reeds. The exquisite quiet effects possible were innumerable, whilst a particularly impressive feature of the organ was the weight and depth of the pedal department, despite the fact that it was made up of only one independent rank, two downward extensions of manual stops and four duplicated ranks from the manuals, for purpose of variety. Another feature of this fine instrument was the augmentation of the Choir Organ by the accompanimental stops from the Swell division.

The organ attracted a considerable amount of attention and soon became known as one of the city's modern church instruments. Recitals were regularly given throughout the year, by such distinguished organists as Dr. Stanley Marchant, Mr G. D. Cunningham, Dr G. T. Thalben-Ball, Mr Reginald Goss Custard and many others.

From an advertisement in 1939

THE COMPTON UNIT ORGAN

IN

ST. GEORGE'S HALL, LANGHAM PLACE, W.I.

FOUR MANUALS, CC to C, 61 notes.
PEDALS, - CCC to G, 32 notes.

PEDAL ORGAN.

1.	Acoustic Contrabass	32 ft.
2.	Tuba magna	16 ft.
3.	Tuba horn	16 ft.
4.	Diaphone	16 ft.
5.	Trombone	16 ft.
6.	Tibia clausa	16 ft.
7.	Bourdon	16 ft.
8.	Gamba	16 ft.
9.	Tuba magna	8 ft.
10.	English horn	8 ft.
11.	Tuba horn	8 ft.
12.	Octave	8 ft.
13.	Trumpet	8 ft.
14.	Tibia clausa	8 ft.
15.	Diapason	8 ft.
16.	Tibia minor	8 ft.
17.	Gamba	8 ft.
18.	Cello	8 ft.
19.	Violin	8 ft.
20.	Flute	8 ft.
21.	Diapason	4 ft.
22.	Tibia clausa	4 ft.
23.	Octave cello	4 ft.
24.	Piano	16 ft.
25.	Piano	8 ft.
26.	Bass drum tap F.	
27.	Bass drum tap P.	
28.	Gong drum tap.	
29.	Drum roll.	
30.	Snare drum roll.	
31.	Cymbal tap.	
32.	Cymbal crash.	
33.	Triangle.	
34.	Effects to second touch.	
35.	Accompaniment to pedal.	
36.	Great to pedal.	
37.	Solo to pedal.	
38.	Orchestral to pedal.	
39.	Orchestral octave to pedal.	

ACCOMPANIMENT.

1.	Vox humana, T.C.	16 ft.
2.	Contra gamba	16 ft.
3.	Contra viola, T.C.	16 ft.
4.	Bourdon	16 ft.

Accompaniment—continued.

5.	English horn	8 ft.
6.	Trumpet	8 ft.
7.	Tuba horn	8 ft.
8.	Diaphonic diapason	8 ft.
9.	Diapason	8 ft.
10.	Tibia minor	8 ft.
11.	Vox humana	8 ft.
12.	Clarinet	8 ft.
13.	Kinura	8 ft.
14.	Gamba	8 ft.
15.	Violin	8 ft.
16.	Strings, II ranks	8 ft.
17.	Salicional	8 ft.
18.	Hohl flute	8 ft.
19.	Stopped flute	8 ft.
20.	Tuba horn	4 ft.
21.	Diapason	4 ft.
22.	Tibia	4 ft.
23.	Vox humana	4 ft.
24.	Gambette	4 ft.
25.	Violin	4 ft.
26.	Strings II ranks	4 ft.
27.	Salicet	4 ft.
28.	Hohl flute	4 ft.
29.	Stopped flute	4 ft.
30.	Stopped twelfth	2⅔ ft.
31.	Salicet twelfth	2⅔ ft.
32.	Violin	2 ft.
33.	Salicet	2 ft.
34.	Flautino	2 ft.
35.	Tierce	1⅗ ft.
36.	Acuta III ranks.	
37.	Quartane II ranks.	
38.	Marimba harp (49 notes)	8 ft.
39.	Vibraphone } Compton Electronic Patent.	8 ft.
40.	Vibraphone }	4 ft.
41.	Piano	8 ft.
42.	Piano	4 ft.
43.	Snare drum.	
44.	Block.	
45.	Castanets.	
46.	Tambourine.	
47.	Sleighbells.	
48.	Tomtom.	
49.	Sandblock.	

Accompaniment—*continued.*

50. Choke cymbal.
51. Brushed cymbal.
52. Bird whistle.
53. Effects on second touch.
54. Great to Accompaniment.
55. Solo to Accompaniment.
56. Orchestral to accompaniment.
57. Tuba　　　second touch 8 ft.
58. English horn　　,,　　,,　　8 ft.
59. Tibia clausa　　,,　　,,　　8 ft.
60. Tibia clausa　　,,　　,,　　4 ft.
61. Great to Accompaniment
　　　　　　second touch 8 ft.
62. Great to Accompaniment
　　　　　　second touch 4 ft.

GREAT ORGAN.

1. Trombone | 16 ft.
2. Contra tuba | 16 ft.
3. Diaphone | 16 ft.
4. Diapason | 16 ft.
5. Contra tibia | 16 ft.
6. Gamba | 16 ft.
7. Tuba magna | 8 ft.
8. English horn | 8 ft.
9. Trumpet | 8 ft.
10. Tuba | 8 ft.
11. Diaphonic diapason | 8 ft.
12. Diapason | 8 ft.
13. Tibia clausa | 8 ft.
14. Tibia minor | 8 ft.
15. Oboe | 8 ft.
16. Krumet | 8 ft.
17. Gamba | 8 ft.
18. Violin | 8 ft.
19. Salicional | 8 ft.
20. Cello | 8 ft.
21. Strings, II ranks | 8 ft.
22. Hohl flute | 8 ft.
23. Stopped flute | 8 ft.
24. Quint | 5⅓ ft.
25. Tuba Magna | 4 ft.
26. English horn | 4 ft.
27. Trumpet | 4 ft.
28. Tuba horn | 4 ft.
29. Octave | 4 ft.
30. Diapason | 4 ft.
31. Tibia clausa | 4 ft.
32. Gambette | 4 ft.
33. Violin | 4 ft.
34. Hohl flute | 4 ft.
35. Twelfth | 2⅔ ft.
36. Ocarina | 2 ft.
37. Fifteenth | 2 ft.
38. Gambette | 2 ft.
39. Cornet IV ranks.

Great Organ—*continued.*

40. Cymbale IV ranks.
41. Marimba harp (49 notes) 8 ft.
42. Vibraphone　　　　　　8 ft.
43. Chimes (25 notes) } *Electronic Compton Patent.*
44. Carillon (25 notes) }
45. Piano | 16 ft.
46. Piano | 8 ft.
47. Piano | 4 ft.
48. Great octave.
49. Solo to great.
50. Orchestral to great.
51. Accompaniment effects to great
52. Tuba horn second touch 16 ft.
53. Trumpet　　,,　　,,　　8 ft.
54. Tibia minor　　,,　　,,　　8 ft.
55. Tibia minor　　,,　　,,　　4 ft.
56. Solo to great　,,　　,,　　16 ft.
57. Solo to great　,,　　,,　　8 ft.
58. Solo to great　,,　　,,　　4 ft.
59. Accompaniment effects to great

SOLO ORGAN.

1. Trombone | 16 ft.
2. Tibia clausa | 16 ft.
3. Clarinet, T.C. | 16 ft.
4. Cello, T.C. | 16 ft.
5. English horn | 8 ft.
6. Trumpet | 8 ft.
7. Tuba horn | 8 ft.
8. Tibia clausa | 8 ft.
9. Tibia minor | 8 ft.
10. Vox humana | 8 ft.
11. Clarinet | 8 ft.
12. Oboe | 8 ft.
13. Krumet | 8 ft.
14. Kinura | 8 ft.
15. Cello | 8 ft.
16. Strings, II ranks | 8 ft.
17. Concert flute | 8 ft.
18. Trumpet | 4 ft.
19. Tuba horn | 4 ft.
20. Tibia clausa | 4 ft.
21. Tibia minor | 4 ft.
22. Vox humana | 4 ft.
23. Oboe | 4 ft.
24. Cello | 4 ft.
25. Concert flute | 4 ft.
26. Tibia twelfth | 2⅔ ft.
27. Flute twelfth | 2⅔ ft.
28. Ocarina | 2 ft.
29. Piccolo | 2 ft.
30. Cello fifteenth | 2 ft.
31. Tibia tierce | 1⅗ ft.
32. Flute tierce | 1⅗ ft.
33. Cymbale III ranks.

Solo Organ—*continued.*

34.	Xylophone	(42 notes)	4 ft.
35.	Glockenspiel	,,	4 ft.
36.	Orchestral bells	,,	4 ft.
37.	Piano		8 ft.
38.	Marimba		8 ft.
39.	Sonnettes.		
40.	Sub-octave.		
41.	Octave.		
42.	Unison off.		
43.	Orchestral to solo.		

ORCHESTRAL.

1.	Tuba Magna	16 ft.
2.	Trombone	16 ft.
3.	Tuba horn	16 ft.
4.	Tibia clausa	16 ft.
5.	Diapason	16 ft.
6.	Bassoon	16 ft.
7.	Cello	16 ft.
8.	Tuba magna	8 ft.
9.	English horn	8 ft.
10.	Trumpet	8 ft.
11.	Tuba horn	8 ft.
12.	Diaphonic diapason	8 ft.
13.	Diapason	8 ft.
14.	Tibia clausa	8 ft.
15.	Tibia minor	8 ft.
16.	Vox humana	8 ft.
17.	Clarinet	8 ft.
18.	Oboe	8 ft.
19.	Krumet	8 ft.
20.	Kinura	8 ft.
21.	Gamba	8 ft.
22.	Violin	8 ft.
23.	Strings, II ranks	8 ft.
24.	Cello	8 ft.
25.	Celestes	8 ft.
26.	Concert flute	8 ft.
27.	Hohl flute	8 ft.
28.	Tuba magna	4 ft.
29.	Trumpet	4 ft.
30.	Tuba horn	4 ft.
31.	Diapason	4 ft.
32.	Tibia clausa	4 ft.
33.	Tibia minor	4 ft.
34.	Cello	4 ft.
35.	Tibia twelfth	2⅔ ft.
36.	Ocarina	2 ft.
37.	Piccolo	2 ft.
38.	Tierce	1⅗ ft.
39.	Piano	8 ft.
40.	Marimba	8 ft.
41.	Marimba	4 ft.

Orchestral—*continued.*

42.	Melotone		8 ft.
43.	Melotone		4 ft.
44.	Melo twelfth		2⅔ ft.
45.	Melotone		2 ft.
46.	Melo Tierce		1⅗ ft.
47.	Cor anglais		8 ft.
48.	Krummhorn		8 ft.
49.	Vibrato		
50.	Echo control I.		
51.	Echo control II.		
52.	Chimes		
53.	Carillon		
54.	Sub octave		
55.	Octave		
56.	Unison off		

(items 42–53 braced: Electronic Compton Patent.)

EFFECTS.

Operated by switches or pistons from
sliding tray at left of keyboards.

1. Bird whistles.
2. Autohorn (electric).
3. Autohorn (wind).
4. Cymbal roll.
5. Drum roll.
6. Steamboat syren.
7. Railway whistle.
8. Surf.
9. Fire bell.
10. Police whistle.
11. Crockery smash.
12. Three Chinese gourds.

ACCESSORIES.

Twelve double touch pistons to
Accompaniment.

Twelve double touch pistons to Great.

Twelve double touch pistons to Solo.

Twelve double touch pistons to
Orchestral.

Six double touch pistons to Pedal.

Six general pistons operating all stops,
couplers and tremulants.

Toe pistons for Solo sustainer.

Toe piston for Orchestral sustainer.

Three balanced expression levers.

One balanced crescendo pedal, operating stops of great, solo and pedal in
appropriate sequence from pp to ff.

One graduated sforzando pedal operating stops of great, solo, and pedal
departments.

One double touch pedal operating snare
drum on first touch and bass drum
and cymbal on second touch.

One setter toe piston, enabling all
piston combinations to be set from
the keyboard by the Compton
patent mechanism.

Compton's advertising was constant and highly organised. During May-June 1934 the series of organ recitals held at the factory attracted tremendous interest as will be seen from this account in *Musical Opinion* for June 1934.

ORGAN RECITALS AT COMPTON WORKS

THE series of organ recitals arranged by the John Compton Organ Co. Ltd., to take place at their works at North Acton on Tuesday evenings in May and June had a successful send-off on May 15th, when the initial recital was given by Mr G. D. Cunningham, City Organist of Birmingham. For the purpose of these recitals, the company erected a modern two-manual organ in the console shop, which was crowded by a large, and as events proved, enthusiastic audience, the members of which came from from all parts of the country. The specification of the organ is as follows.—

GREAT ORGAN

	ft
Double Diapason	16
Bourdon	16
First Diapason	8
Second Diapason	8
Third Diapason	8
Harmonic Flute	8
Stopped Flute	8
Salicional (from Swell)	8
Octave	4
Harmonic Flute	4
Stopped Flute	4
Salicet (from Swell)	4
Quint	5⅓
Twelfth	2⅔
Fifteenth	2
Flautina	2
Cymbale 19·22·26·29	IV
Plein Jeu 12·15·19·22	IV
Double Clarinet	16
Clarinet	8
Posaune	8
Clarion	4
Posaune (2nd touch)	8

SWELL ORGAN

Contra Viole	16
Contra Salicional	16
Diapason	8
Viola da Gamba	8
Flauto Traverso	8
Salicional	8
Vox Angelica (tenor C)	8
Melodic Diapason	8
Strings, 2 ranks	8
Principal	4
Viola	4
Flute	4
Salicet	4
Vox Angelica	4
Twelfth	2⅔

Fifteenth	2
Cymbale 15·19·22	III
Acuta 19·22	II
Trombone	16
Trumpet	8
Clarion	4

PEDAL ORGAN

Sub Bass	32
Diapason	16
Bourdon	16
Stopped Flute	16
Salicional	16
Octave	8
Bourdon	8
Stopped Flute	8
Salicional	8
Octave Flute	4
Twelfth & Fifteenth	II
Acoustic Posaune	32
Posaune	16
Trombone	16
Posaune	8

COUPLERS

Great to Pedal   Swell to Pedal   Swell to Great

ACCESSORIES

8 double touch combination pistons each
to Great and Swell Organs
Double touch thumb pistons Great to Pedal
and Swell to Pedal
4 toe pistons each to Great, Swell and Pedal Organs
Reversible toe pistons Great to Pedal, Swell to Pedal
Reversible thumb pistons Swell to Great,
Great to Pedal, Swell to Pedal   4 general pistons
2 balanced expression pedals
1 balanced crescendo pedal
Luminous stop control. Double touch cancellers to all
stops, with switch to render inactive if desired.
General canceller by thumb piston

It may be mentioned that the Compton Organ Co. have received over 1,400 applications for tickets of admission, a number considerably in excess of the accommodation available; and in order to meet the demand for further invitations it is possible that another series of recitals will be arranged later on. Many of the visitors availed themselves of the opportunity to inspect the works; and as a number of organs were in various stages of construction, the inspection proved of exceptional interest. Mr J. J. Broad, managing director, mentioned that, much to the great regret of everyone, Mr Compton was unable to be present on account of illness, but that he hoped to be able to attend subsequent recitals.

Mr Cunningham rendered his programme from memory. His playing was full of beauty, interest and that fine restraint associated with the work of a great artist. He used the enclosed Great Organ with thrilling results and displayed to the full the many tonal excellencies of the instrument, which is built on the extension principle. An unusually high level of performance is expected of Mr Cunningham, but the brilliantly clean playing of the Dupré Prelude and Fugue in G minor, the reverent beauty of the "Gerontius" Prelude, and the satisfying solidity of the Bach "Wedge" were (even for so great a player) exceptional examples of artistry.'

An organ which attracted considerable interest in the early 1930s was that built for the Priory Church of St Benedict, Ealing, in 1935. It was situated in a chamber over the south-west porch of the church, the tone entering the building through an unglazed window in the south aisle and another in the south-east chapel. The 32ft sub-bass was placed horizontally under a table in the chapel, while the luminous stop-head console stood in the south aisle. Some of the stops of octave and sub-octave pitch were derived by the extension of unison stops, but the more important ones (for example the 16ft and 4ft principals, the mixture work and the octave posaune of the Great Organ) were not so derived. The Pedal contra bass was diaphonic. Wind pressures ranged from 4 ins. to 12 ins. Here was another fine example of Compton's artistry destined, sadly, for but a limited life; it was destroyed during the blitz and after the war, Rushworth & Dreaper built a new two-manual instrument on neo-classical lines.

PRIORY CHURCH OF ST BENEDICT, EALING 1935

3 manuals: CC to C, 61 notes   Pedal: CCC to G, 32 notes

GREAT ORGAN

	ft
Principal	16
Bourdon	16
Diapason	8
Principal	8
Dulciana	8
Hohl Flöte	8
Quint	5⅓
Principal	4
Salicet	4
Flute	4
Twelfth	2⅔
Super Octave	2
Fifteenth	2
Cymbale 19·22	II–IV
Posaune (harmonic from treble C)	8
Posaune Octave	4

SWELL ORGAN

Contra Viola	16
Diapason	8
Viola da Gamba	8
Flauto Traverso	8
Viola	4
Flauto Traverso	4
Flageolet	2
Cymbale 15·19·22	III
Hautboy	8
Trombone	16
Trumpet	8
Clarion	4
Sustainer	
Tremulant	

CHOIR ORGAN

Contra Dulciana	16
Bourdon	16
Principal	8
Salicional	8
Dulciana	8
Vox Angelica	8
Hohl Flöte	8
Lieblich Gedeckt	8
Salicet	4

Dulcet	4	Bourdon		16
Vox Angelica	8	Echo Bass		16
Flute	4	Octave		8
Lieblich Flöte	4	Dulciana		8
Twelfth	2⅔	Flute		8
Fifteenth	2	Flute Octave		4
Flautino	2	Fourniture 12·15·19·22		IV
Acuta 15·19·22	III	Harmonics 5·8·10·14		IV
Double Clarinet	16	Posaune		16
Clarinet	8	Trombone		16
		Posaune		8

BOMBARDE ORGAN
(on Choir manual)

Diapason	8
Plein Jeu 5·8·12·15·19·22	VI–VIII
Cymbale 19·22·26·29	IV–VIII
Contra Posaune	16
Posaune (harmonic from mid. C)	8
Posaune Octave	4
Trombone	16
Trumpet	8
Clarion	4
Sustainer	
Tremulant	

PEDAL ORGAN

Subbass	32
Contra Bass	16
Principal	16

COUPLERS

Great to Pedal Swell to Pedal Choir to Pedal
Great to Choir Swell to Choir Swell to Great

ACCESSORIES

2 balanced expression pedals with indicators
Balanced crescendo pedal with indicator
9 double touch combnation pistons to Choir
and Pedal Organs
6 double touch combination pistons each to
Great, Swell and Pedal Organs
3 toe pistons to Pedal Organ 4 general pistons
3 pistons to Pedal couplers
Reversible toe pistons to Great to Pedal
and Swell to Great
General cancel piston 2 toe pistons to sustainers
All combination pistons are instantly adjustable.

In my own city of Lincoln I had the opportunity of seeing the erection of the 'Compton' in the then Savoy Cinema; this was between 1935–1936 and it included one of the early 'Melotones' which greatly intrigued me. After the war, the authorities at St Swithin's Church nearby, decided at long last to replace their worn out Gray & Davison organ which had really reached the end of its usefulness. The two Walter brothers (Vicar and Curate respectively) made the church a centre for musical activities which featured the organ from time to time. Several estimates were sought and on hearing Comptons were to build an extension organ, great was the anticipation of local musicians from the Cathedral organist downwards as well as the local organ builder, R. A. Cousans, then head of Cousans Sons & Co., who had hoped to build a 'straight' organ which would be smaller in scope, due to limitations of funds. Again, I was able to see the various stages in its erection, but to judge the organ from the stop-key console is quite impossible, for it is situated in the chamber itself on the north side of the chancel where the organist is quite out of touch with his choir, aurally and visually. The firm designed a pleasant case of oak to replace the ugly pipe-rack of the former organ, which was a blot in this magnificent church designed by Fowler of Louth. The great day came for the opening recital and I recall being very pleasantly surprised by what had been achieved from the extension of 17 ranks to provide 56 stops. Not so R. A. Cousans, however, who was anti-extension in outlook, though he admitted there was some splendidly voiced individual ranks! Today, the instrument is badly in need of a thorough renovation and I understand that action troubles are the result of years of fumes affecting the magnets from incense used in what is a church of the Anglo-Catholic tradition. Like many a large city centre church, it is only kept alive by a devoted few; it is unthinkable that it should ever be made redundant. The instrument is enclosed in two swell chambers and consists of the following basic ranks (912 pipes, extended to form 56 speaking stops):

Great Organ Chamber: First diapason, 85 pipes (lowest octave diaphonic). Second diapason, 97 pipes. Sub bass and stopped diapason, 98 pipes. Dulciana (lowest octave stopped metal), 97 pipes. Vox angelica, 61 pipes. Trombone & tromba, 85 pipes.
Swell Organ Chamber: viola, 85 pipes. viola céleste, 61 pipes. Harmonic flute, 85 pipes. Trumpet, 85 pipes. Hautboy, 73 pipes.

Specification of the

COMPTON ORGAN

IN

ST. SWITHIN'S CHURCH, LINCOLN

Three Manuals : CC to C, 61 notes
Pedals : CCC to G, 32 notes

PEDAL ORGAN

1. Subbass		32 ft.
Actual pitch to EEEE		
2. Open Bass		16 ft.
3. Violone		16 ft.
4. Subbass		16 ft.
5. Echo Bass		16 ft.
6. Flute		8 ft.
7. Flute		4 ft.
8. Trombone		16 ft.
9. Double Trumpet		16 ft.
10. Tromba		8 ft.

i. Choir to Pedal
ii. Great to Pedal
iii. Swell to Pedal

GREAT ORGAN

1. Sub Diapason		16 ft.
2. First Diapason		8 ft.
3. Second Diapason		8 ft.
4. Stopped Diapason		8 ft.
5. Dulciana		8 ft.
6. Octave		4 ft.
7. Stopped Flute		4 ft.
8. Twelfth		2-2/3 ft.
9. Fifteenth		2 ft.
10. Mixture III ranks		
11. Tromba		8 ft.
12. Octave Tromba		4 ft.

iv. Swell to Great

SWELL ORGAN

1. Contra Viola (T.C.)	16 ft.
2. Harmonic Flute	8 ft.
3. Viola	8 ft.
4. Viola Celeste	8 ft.
5. Harmonic Flute	4 ft.
6. Viola	4 ft.
7. Piccolo	2 ft.
8. Cymbale III ranks	
9. Double Trumpet	16 ft.
10. Trumpet	8 ft.
11. Hautboy	8 ft.
12. Clarion	4 ft.

v. Tremulant

CHOIR ORGAN

1. Contra Dulciana	16 ft.	
2. Second Diapason	8 ft.	
3. Stopped Diapason	8 ft.	
4. Dulciana	8 ft.	
5. Vox Angelica (T.C.)	8 ft.	
6. Stopped Flute	4 ft.	In Great Chamber
7. Dulcet	4 ft.	
8. Vox Angelica	4 ft.	
9. Dulcet Twelfth	2-2/3 ft.	
10. Flautino	2 ft.	
11. Dulcet Fifteenth	2 ft.	
12. Acuta III ranks		
13. Krumhorn	8 ft.	
14. Tromba	8 ft.	
15. Octave Tromba	4 ft.	
16. Viola	8 ft.	
17. Harmonic Flute	8 ft.	
18. Octave Viola	4 ft.	In Swell Chamber
19. Harmonic Flute	4 ft.	
20. Contra Hautboy	16 ft.	
21. Hautboy	8 ft.	
22. Octave Hautboy	4 ft.	

vi. Great to Choir
vii. Swell to Choir

ACCESSORIES

Six double touch combination pistons to Choir Organ.
Six double touch combination pistons to Great Organ.
Six double touch combination pistons to Swell Organ.
Three double touch combination pistons to Pedal Couplers.

Six toe pistons to Pedal Organ.
Reversible toe piston to Great to Pedal.
Two balanced swell pedals } with indicators
One balanced crescendo pedal }
Second touch cancellor to stopkeys, with optional switch.
General cancel piston.
Push button starter to blowing apparatus.

The organ is enclosed in two swell chambers and is designed on the Compton Extension principle

Southampton Civic Centre (1936) is a dual-purpose organ comprising a very comprehensive scheme for recitals and concert use playable from a four-manual luminous stop console, together with stops, percussion and 'traps' suitable for recitals of light music, dancing etc—in short, a typical theatre organ which has its own stop-key console. The instrument is accommodated in four chambers masked by grilles, situated over the stage about 40ft above the floor. This most ambitious project was a major undertaking with much ingenious electrical mechanism. How much easier it would have been if Solid State had been available in those days. A comprehensive article by Frances Burgess appeared in *The Organ*, for July 1937.

THE
CONCERT ORGAN
IN
SOUTHAMPTON CIVIC CENTRE
ASSEMBLY HALL.

SPECIFICATION

OF THE

CONCERT ORGAN

IN

SOUTHAMPTON CIVIC CENTRE ASSEMBLY HALL.

FIRST CONSOLE.

4 MANUALS   CC to C, 6l notes.

PEDALS   -   CCC to G, 32 notes.

PEDAL ORGAN.

1.	Contra Bass	...	...	...	32 ft.
2.	Contra Bourdon	...	..	...	32 ft.
3.	Contra Bass	...	...	...	16 ft.
4.	Violone	...	...	...	16 ft.
5.	Sub Bass	...	...	...	16 ft.
6.	Diapason	...	...	...	16 ft.
7.	Salicional	...	...	...	16 ft.
8.	Bourdon	...	...	...	16 ft.
9.	Octave	...	...	...	8 ft.
10.	Salicional	...	...	...	8 ft.
11.	Stopped Octave	...	...	...	8 ft.
12.	Flute	...	...	...	8 ft.
13.	Octave Flute	...	...	...	4 ft.
14.	Fourniture IV ranks				
15.	Contra Posaune	...	...	...	32 ft.
16.	Posaune	...	...	...	16 ft.
17.	Fagottone	...	...	...	16 ft.
18.	Cor Anglais	...	...	...	16 ft.
19.	Tuba	...	...	...	16 ft.
20.	Trombone	...	...	...	16 ft.
21.	Clarinet	...	...	...	16 ft.
22.	Tuba	...	...	...	8 ft.
23.	Tromba	...	...	...	8 ft.
24.	Clarinet	...	...	...	8 ft.
25.	Tuba	...	...	...	4 ft.

GREAT ORGAN.

1.	Double Diapason	... ...	16 ft.
2.	Bourdon ...	... ...	16 ft.
3.	First Diapason	... ...	8 ft.
4.	Second Diapason	... ...	8 ft.
5.	Third Diapason	... ...	8 ft.
6.	Fourth Diapason	... ...	8 ft.
7.	Stopped Diapason	... ...	8 ft.
8.	Hohl Flute ...	... ...	8 ft.
9.	Quint ...	... ...	5-1/3 ft.
10.	Octave ...	... ...	4 ft.
11.	Principal ...	... ...	4 ft.
12.	Flute ...	... ...	4 ft.
13.	Twelfth ...	... ...	2-2/3 ft.
14.	Super Octave ...	... ...	2 ft.
15.	Fifteenth ...	... ...	2 ft.
16.	Pleinjeu, IV ranks.		
17.	Cymbale, IV ranks.		
18.	Cornet, IV ranks.		
19.	Contra Posaune	... ...	16 ft.
20.	Posaune ...	... ...	8 ft.
21.	Tromba ...	... ...	8 ft.
22.	Clarion ...	... ...	4 ft.

SWELL ORGAN

1.	Contra Viola ...	... ...	16 ft.
2.	Geigen ...	... ...	8 ft.
3.	Viola da Gamba	... ...	8 ft.
4.	Flauto Traverso	... ...	8 ft.
5.	Rohr Flöte ...	... ...	8 ft.
6.	Voix Céleste ...	... ...	8 ft.
7.	Viola ...	... ...	4 ft.
8.	Octave Geigen	... ...	4 ft.
9.	Flauto Traverso	... ...	4 ft.
10.	Celestina ...	... ...	4 ft.
11.	Twelfth ...	... ...	2-2/3 ft.
12.	Fifteenth ...	... ...	2 ft.
13.	Flageolet ...	... ...	2 ft.
14.	Fourniture, IV ranks.		
15.	Cymbale, IV ranks.		
16.	19th and 22nd, II ranks.		
17.	Fagottone ...	... ...	16 ft.
18.	Fagotto ...	... ...	8 ft.
19.	Trumpet ...	... ...	8 ft.
20.	Horn ...	... ...	8 ft.
21.	Hautboy ...	... ...	8 ft.
22.	Clarion ...	... ...	4 ft.
23.	Tremulant.		

CHOIR ORGAN

1.	Contra Salicional	... ...	16 ft.
2.	Lieblich Bourdon	... ...	16 ft.
3.	Diapason ...	... ...	8 ft.
4.	Gemshorn ...	... ...	8 ft.
5.	Salicional ...	... ...	8 ft.
6.	Lieblich Gedeckt	... ...	8 ft.
7.	Stopped Diapason	... ...	8 ft.
8.	Vox Angelica ...	... ...	8 ft.
9.	Octave ...	... ...	4 ft.
10.	Salicet ...	... ...	4 ft.
11.	Lieblich Flöte	... ...	4 ft.
12.	Gemshorn ...	... ...	4 ft.
13.	Vox Angelica ...	... ...	4 ft.
14.	Nazard ...	... ...	2-2/3 ft.
15.	Twelfth ...	... ...	2-2/3 ft.
16.	Flautino ...	... ...	2 ft.
17.	Fifteenth ...	... .	2 ft.
18.	Super Octave ...	... ...	2 ft.
19.	Harmonics, III ranks.		
20.	Acuta, III ranks.		
21.	Cor Anglais ...	... ...	16 ft.
22.	Cor Anglais ...	... ...	8 ft.
23.	Posaune (Great)	... ...	8 ft.
24.	Horn (Swell) ...	... ...	8 ft.
25.	Celesta ...	... ...	4 ft.
26.	Tremulant.		

SOLO ORGAN

1.	Violone ...	... ...	16 ft.
2.	Violoncello ...	... ...	8 ft.
3.	Strings, II ranks	... ...	8 ft.
4.	Harmonic Flute	... ...	8 ft.
5.	Viole ...	... ...	8 ft.
6.	Viole Celeste ...	... ...	8 ft.
7.	Harmonic Flute	... ...	4 ft.
8.	Violina ...	... ...	4 ft.
9.	Viole Celeste ...	... ...	4 ft.
10.	Harmonic Piccolo	... ...	2 ft.
11.	Double Clarinet	... ...	16 ft.
12.	Orchestral Oboe	... ...	8 ft.
13.	Vox Humana ...	... ...	8 ft.
14.	Clarinet ...	... ...	8 ft.
15.	Harmonic Trumpet	... ...	8 ft.
16.	Tuba ...	... ...	8 ft.
17.	Carillon.		
18.	Chimes.		
19.	Tremulant.		

BOMBARDE ORGAN (playable from Choir keyboard)

1. Diapason ... ... 8 ft.
2. Pleinjeu, VIII ranks.
3. Cymbale, IV ranks.
4. Fourniture, IV ranks.
5. Contra Posaune ... ... 16 ft.
6. Fagottone ... ... 16 ft.
7. Tromba ... ... 8 ft.
8. Trumpet ... ... 8 ft.
9. Tuba ... ... 8 ft.
10. Octave Tromba ... ... 4 ft.
11. Clarion ... ... 4 ft.
12. Cornet de Bombardes, VI ranks.

COUPLERS.

Choir to Pedal.   Solo to Choir.   Swell to Great.
Solo to Pedal.   Great to Choir.   Solo to Swell.
Great to Pedal.   Swell to Choir.   Solo to Great.
Swell to Pedal.

ACCESSORIES

Eight General Pistons operating all stops and couplers.
Eight double touch thumb pistons to Choir.
Eight double touch thumb pistons to Great.
Eight double touch thumb pistons to Swell.
Eight double touch thumb pistons to Solo.
    All the above adjustable at the Keyboard by Compton patent mechanism.
Four double touch pistons to Pedal Couplers, second touch giving suitable Pedal bass to any manual combination.
Ten reversible pistons to manual and pedal couplers,
Swell pedals interchangeable as desired.
One "doubles off" piston.
General cancel piston.
Four toe pistons to Pedal Organ.
Four toe pistons to Great Organ.
Four toe pistons to Swell Organ.
One toe piston to Swell to Great (reversible).
One toe piston to Great to Pedal (reversible).
Two toe pistons to sustainers on Choir and Solo.
One toe piston for setting piston combinations.
Two spare toe pistons.
Four switches to couple pedal basses to second touch of manual pistons as desired.
Three balanced swell pedals with indicators.
One General crescendo pedal acting on Stops of Great, Swell and Pedal Organs.

Stop control by Compton patent luminous heads.

Wind pressure 6" to 25", provided by 15 h.p. Discus blower.

Compton's new factory, Chase Road, North Acton, London NW10, 1930

One of the largest and best-known London cinemas, The Odeon, Leicester Square, fortunately retains its five-manual Compton organ of 1937, which is in regular use; moreover, the interest is so great that special organ concerts are held from time to time which attract a large audience of cinema organ 'buffs'. The site was formerly occupied by the Alhambra Theatre and before that, the Royal Panopticon of Arts and Sciences was there and it contained a Hill organ of 1853 which was fitted with drums—arguably the first of its kind.

Opened in October 1937, the organ has sixteen units (in all, some 17 ranks of pipes) together with the Compton Electrone, which provided four additional tone colours, chimes, carillon and marimba. There are five manuals, the fifth being a coupler manual. It also has a full range of percussions and effects; all in all there are 152 speaking stops. The units consist of tuba, posaune, trumpet, French horn, diapason, geigen, tibia, vox humana, clarinet, krummet, gamba, violin, strings (two ranks), salicional, concert flute and stopped flute. A number of these are extended down to provide pedal basses so that a variety of tone is available on the pedals. The pipes are in two stone chambers under the stage, the Swell shutters opening into the orchestra pit—a typically difficult site—which Comptons always tackled successfully. Two loud-speakers were used for the Electrone—one beneath the stage and the other at the back of the auditorium; these were controlled by two switches at the console. A full account of this very popular instrument, which contains some superbly voiced pipework, was contributed to *Musical Opinion* (January 1939) by J. E. Wright.

THE ODEON CINEMA, LEICESTER SQUARE 1937

5 manuals: CC to C, 61 notes   Pedal: CCC to G, 32 notes

GREAT ORGAN

	ft		
Tuba	16	Posaune	8
Posaune	16	Trumpet	8
Diaphone	16	French Horn	8
Geigen (tenor C)	16	Diapason	8
Tibia	16	Geigen	8
Gamba (tenor C)	16	Tibia	8
Tuba	8	Vox Humana	8

Clarinet	8
Crummet	8
Gamba	8
Violin	8
Strings	8
Salicional	8
Concert Flute	8
Stopped Flute	8
Tuba	4
Posaune	4
Trumpet	4
Quint	5⅓
Octave	4
Geigen	4
Tibia	4
Gambette	4
Violin	4
Concert Flute	4
Stopped Flute	4
Tibia Twelfth	2⅔
Flute Twelfth	2⅔
Twelfth	2⅔
Ocarina	2
Flautino	2
Fifteenth	2
Cornet	IV
Solo to Great	
Bombarde to Great	
Traps to Great	

SOLO ORGAN

Trumpet (tenor C)	16
Tibia	16
Gamba (tenor C)	16
Vox Humana (tenor C)	16
Tuba	8
Posaune	8
Trumpet	8
French Horn	8
Diapason	8
Geigen	8
Tibia Clausa	8
Vox Humana	8
Clarinet	8
Krummet	8
Gamba	8
Violin	8
Strings, 2 ranks	8
Salicional	8
Concert Flute	8
Stopped Flute	8
Trumpet	4
Tibia	4
Geigen	4
Gamba	4
Violin	4
Strings	4
Salicional	4
Concert Flute	4
Stopped Flute	4
Tibia Twelfth	2⅔
Ocarina	2
Piccolo	2
Quartane	III
Tierce	1⅗

Xylophone	8
Glockenspiel	4
Orchestral Bells	
Vibraphone	8
Vibraphone	4
Sub Octave	
Octave	

BOMBARDE ORGAN

Tuba	16
Posaune	16
Trumpet	16
Tuba	8
Posaune	8
Trumpet	8
French Horn	8
Tibia	8
Vox Humana	8
Krummet	8
Tuba	4
Posaune	4
Trumpet	4
Xylophone	4
Glockenspiel	4
Orchestra Bells	4
Schalmei (synthetic)	16
Sub Octave	
Octave	
Melophone	8
Melophone	4
Melophone	2⅔
Melophone	2
Tierce	1⅗
Krummhorn	8
Cor Anglais	8
Musette	8
Vibrato	
(last 9 by Compton patent method)	
Chimes	
Carillon	
Echo Control	

ACCOMPANIMENT ORGAN

Vox Humana (tenor C)	16
Bourdon	16
Contra Viola (tenor C)	16
Salicional	16
Tuba	8
Posaune	8
Trumpet	8
French Horn	8
Diapason	8
Geigen	8
Tibia Clausa	8
Vox Humana	8
Clarinet	8
Krummet	8
Gamba	8
Violin	8
Strings, 2 ranks	8
Salicional	8
Stopped Flute	8
Concert Flute	8
Tuba	4

Posaune	4
Tibia	4
Vox Humana	4
Geigen	4
Gambette	4
Viola	4
Strings	4
Salicet	4
Concert Flute	4
Stopped Flute	4
Nazard	2⅔
Twelfth	2⅔
Piccolo	2
Fifteenth	2
Acuta	III
Marimba	8
Marimba	4
(last 2 from Electrone)	
Snare Drum	
Block	
Castanets	
Tambourine	
Sleigh Bells	
Choke Cymbal	
Tom-tom	
Sand Block	
Solo to Accompaniment 8ft	

2nd touch.—
Solo to Accompaniment 8ft
Great to Accompaniment 4ft

Tuba	8
Tibia Clausa	8
Tibia	8
Krummet	4

MANUAL V

Great to Manual V	8
Great to Manual V	4
Solo to Manual V	16
Solo to Manual V	8
Solo to Manual V	4
Bombarde to Manual V	16
Bombarde to Manual V	8
Bombarde to Manual V	4
Vibraphone	

EFFECTS

by stop-keys.—
Auto Horn
Cymbal Roll
Drum Roll
Boat Whistle
Train Whistle
Aeroplane
Syren

by foot pistons.—
Surf
Slapstick
Grand Crash
Bird Whistle
Telephone Bell

PEDAL ORGAN

Sub Bass	32
Acoustic Bass	32
Tuba Bass	16
Posaune	16
Diaphone	16
Tibia Bass	16
French Horn	16
Bourdon	16
Salicional	16
Tuba	8
Posaune	8
Trumpet	8
Octave	8
Tibia	8
French Horn	8
Flute	8
Salicional	8
Strings, 2 ranks	8
Cello	8
Clarinet	8
Tibia	4
Bass Drum *p*	
Bass Drum *f*	
Snare Drum	
Cymbal	
Crash Cymbal	
Triangle	
Accompaniment to Pedal	
Great to Pedal	
Solo to Pedal	
Bombarde to Pedal 8ft	
Bombarde to Pedal 4ft	
Effects to 2nd Touch	

ACCESSORIES

10 double touch pistons each to Great, Solo
and Accompaniment   4 pistons to Pedal couplers
8 double touch pistons to Bombarde
2 balanced swell pedals
1 balanced crescendo pedal with indicator
4 combination pistons to Pedal
2 sustainer pistons   6 tremulants
Ventils to all units and effects
Stop-key for vibraphone control
Switches for Electrone loudspeakers
Second touch cancelling device to all speaking stops

The Electrone was the result of many years experiment at the Compton factory by Leslie E. A. Bourn, and was based on his original invention. In a letter to *Musical Opinion* in September 1937, John Compton discussed the development of what was named 'The Electrone' which, he stated, would soon be ready for the market; it was first introduced to the public in January 1938, but more about the electronic side of the business will follow later in this narrative. Reginal Whitworth was possibly the first author to describe the new product also in *Musical Opinion* for September 1937.

Although Compton's work in this field was streets ahead of any other firm at that time, I cannot say that I was impressed by the general ensemble, although there were some convincing quiet registers. In those days there were a large number of stops produced from a single set of generators. There have been vast developments since then, as will be seen at the end of this chapter, resulting in some downright opposition, a grudging acceptance, or great enthusiasm on the part of some musicians for the work of our leading manufacturers. It cannot be disputed that John Compton and his team led the way in those early days of electronics—the result of many and costly experiments which must have drained the company's finances at times. They were particularly proud to have one of their instruments installed at the Royal Festival Hall during the time the Harrison & Harrison organ was being built.

Amongst ten organs under construction in 1937 were three four-manual instruments: the rebuild of the four-manual Forster & Andrews organ for Holy Trinity Church, Hull; the Nicholson & Lord in Walsall Town Hall, and a new four-manual for Wolverhampton Civic Centre.

The organ for Wolverhampton Civic Centre was yet another prestigious civic contract during 1938. Costing around £6,000 (a goodly sum in those days), it was designed by John Compton with the collaboration of Gilbert Mills. They were faced with what seemed to be another very difficult site, which was to house a four-manual organ in a chamber some 12 feet high by approximately 12 feet in depth. Furthermore, the chamber (which is divided into two swell boxes) is above the roof of the hall; this did not daunt Comptons for they had wide experience in the siting of cinema organs. The tone reaches the auditorium via a grille in the acoustic hood, travelling some fourteen feet before reaching listeners. Six inch wind pressure was necessary for the Great diapasons and the whole of the Swell organ, with eight inches for the Solo organ except the tuba which is twenty inches. On the Solo organ is an electrophonic apparatus providing the effects of large solo flutes, solo reeds, chimes and reverberation. It will be noticed from the specification that there is less extension employed here than was usual, which leads me to wonder whether this was due to the influence of Gilbert Mills. The Borough Organist, Arnold Richardson, exploited this magnificent instrument to the full in his regular recitals which attracted large audiences; during 1946, a series of recitals on Sunday evenings were advertised in *The Musical Times* which proved very successful.

THE CIVIC HALL, WOLVERHAMPTON 1938

Disposition of ranks and stop scheme

CHAMBER ONE			CHAMBER TWO		
Rank	*Feet*	*Pipes*	*Rank*	*Feet*	*Pipes*
Sub Bass	32	62	Contra Viola	16	85
Contra Bass	16	56	Geigen	8	61
Bombarde	16	56	Voix Célestes	4	49
Contra Salicional	16	109	Rohr Flöte	8	61
Gemshorn	8	61	Geigen Octave	4	61
Vox Angelica	4	49	Fifteenth	2	61
Lieblich Gedeckt	16	97	Mixture	IV	244
Claribel Flute	8	61	Double Trumpet	16	85
Flauto Traverso	4	61	Trumpet	8	61
Nasard	2⅔	61	Hautboy	8	61
Tierce	1⅗	61	Violoncello	8	61
Double Open Diapason	16	97	Viole Céleste	8	61
First Diapason	8	61	Harmonic Flute	8	61
Second Diapason	8	61	Harmonic Flute	4	61
Stopped Diapason	8	61	Clarinet	8	61
Octave	4	61	Orchestral Oboe	8	61
Twelfth	2⅔	61	Tuba	8	73
Super Octave	2	61			
Fourniture	IV	244			
Harmonics	V	364			
Contra Posaune	16	85			
Tromba	8	61			
Horn	8	61	Total number of pipes: 3,219		

SPECIFICATION

GREAT ORGAN

	ft
Double Open Diapason	16
Open Diapason I	8
Open Diapason II	8
Open Diapason III	8
Stopped Diapason	8
Octave	4
Principal	4
Twelfth	2⅔
Fifteenth	2
Superoctave	2
Fourniture 19·22·26·29	IV
Harmonics 17·21·23·25	IV
Contra Posaune	16
Tromba	8
Horn	8
Clarion	4
Acuta 19·22	II
Horn	8
Posaune	8
Tuba	8
Krummhorn (compound)	8
Vibraphone	4

SOLO ORGAN

Violoncello	8
Viole Céleste	8
Harmonic Flute	8
Harmonic Flute	4
Clarinet	8
Orchestral Oboe	8
Tuba	8
Tuba Clarion	4
Trumpet	8

SWELL ORGAN

Violone	16
Geigen	8
Viola da Gamba	8
Viole Céleste (tenor C)	8
Rohr Flöte	8
Geigen Octave	4
Viola	4
Fifteenth	2
Mixture 12·15·19·22	IV
Double Trumpet	16
Trumpet	8
Hautboy	8
Clarion	4

CHOIR ORGAN

Contra Salicional	16
Bourdon	16
Open Diapason	8
Gemshorn	8
Salicional	8
Vox Angelica (tenor C)	8
Claribel Flute	8
Lieblich Gedeckt	8
Salicet	4
Flauto Traverso	4
Lieblich Flöte	4
Nazard	2⅔
Twelfth	2⅔
Flautino	2
Fifteenth	2
Tierce	1⅗

PEDAL ORGAN

Sub Bass	32
Contra Bass	16
Open Bass	16
Salicional Bass	16
Violone	16
Sub Bass	16
Bourdon	16
Quint	10⅔
Octave	8
Salicional	8
Flute	8
Twelfth	5⅓
Fifteenth	4
Flute	4
Fourniture	IV
Harmonics	32
Harmonics	16
Bombarde	16
Posaune	16
Trumpet	16
Bombarde	8
Posaune	8
Bombarde	4

In addition to normal couplers and accessories, there is an electrophonic apparatus providing, inter alia, the effects of large solo flutes, solo reeds, chimes and reverberation.

The wind pressures are from 6 to 20 ins., and the whole organ is enclosed in two expression chambers

At Holy Trinity Hull, Forster & Andrews had been responsible for five rebuilds (1845, 1855, 1876, 1900 and 1908). The distinguished organist, Norman Strafford, was very fond of this instrument, describing it to me as 'perhaps in its ensemble akin to the finest French work, but possessing an individuality all its own'.

When it became necessary to carry out a major reconstruction of the instrument in 1938, Norman Strafford was faced with some hard thinking. In correspondence with me, it was clear that he had a great affection for this grand old giant which had been developed over the years by Forster & Andrews, ever since they had taken it in hand in 1845, some two years after their establishment in Hull. In his comprehensive article in *The Organ* (No.74, p. 73), describing the Compton rebuild, he had this to say: 'Tonally the F. & A. instrument was not adequate for the spacious building, which on occasions of civic services had seated a congregation of nearly four thousand people. On such occasions, full organ sounded like a distant full swell. Though the interior of the organ had been ingeniously planned, there was not sufficient room for the vast amount of material which was crowded into the case. The Great Organ was buried under the huge swell box and solo box, whose louvres opened on to each other with only the width of a passage board between the boxes…'

Mr G. D. Cunningham was called in; he and Norman Strafford evolved a scheme comprising the electrification of the action and the removal of the Swell Organ 'to a corresponding position over the existing screen under the south arch of the tower in a new case, together with additional new stops'. J. I. Taylor, in collaboration with the aforementioned, evolved the following scheme which embraced some extension.

The new pipework included: viol d'orchestre, tuba, tuba clarion and the extension to CC of the Choir corno di bassetto; on the Swell, the viola da gamba, trumpet, clarion and the extension of the contra fagotto; Great, bourdon, first diapason, cymbale, together with the extension of the second diapason and double trumpet, the latter being revoiced as a posaune. The Choir Organ received a new open diapason, dulciana (109 notes) gemshorn and tierce, and the pedal, sub bass, contra bass, bombarde and the extension of the existing stops to eight and four feet pitch. W. C. Jones was responsible for voicing the reeds and this explains their magnificence. To quote Norman Strafford, writing in *The Musical Times* for March 1944, (for it is over 40 years since I played this instrument): 'Apart from complete success with which this new work has been grafted on to the old, the supreme tonal achievement of this reconstruction is undoubtedly the manner in which the old registers have been re-vitalised, so that their characteristic voices are heard to advantage in any part of the building. Their capacity to blend, too, has been so developed that now almost fantastic combinations will yield quite musical results… Sombre dignity or electrifying brilliance is available as required… it is possible to stimulate successfully characteristic German, French or English ensembles as occasion demands. Incidentally, the church has many foreign visitors, Hull being the third port in the country; and from this interest many have shown their expressions of admiration. This instrument will play a not unimportant part abroad in further developing respect for English organ building. To hear this superb instrument once is to experience a thrill; to know it intimately is to be warmed by an ever increasing admiration for the tonal artistry and inventive genius of Mr John Compton and his staff'.

CHURCH OF THE HOLY TRINITY, HULL 1938

Manual compass: CC to C, 61 notes   Pedal: CCC to G, 32 notes

GREAT ORGAN

	ft
Double Open Diapason	16
Bourdon	16
First Diapason	8
Second Diapason	8
Third Diapason	8
Harmonic Claribel	8
Gamba	8
Stopped Diapason	8
Dulciana (from Choir)	8
Quint	5⅓
Octave	4
Principal	4
Wald Flöte	4
Dulcet (from Choir)	4

Twelfth	2⅔
Fifteenth	2
Superoctave	2
Mixture 17·19·21♭·22	IV
Cymbale 26·29	II
Contra Posaune	16
Tromba	8
Posaune	8
Clarion	4

SWELL ORGAN

Bourdon	16
Geigen	8
Viola da Gamba	8
Rohr Flöte	8

Salicional	8
Voix Céleste	8
Vox Angelica	8
Geigen Octave	4
Hohl Flöte	4
Fifteenth	2
Mixture	III
Sesquialtera 12·17	II
Contra Fagotto	16
Horn	8
Trumpet	8
Fagotto	8
Hautboy	8
Clarion	4
Tremulant to reeds	
Tremulant to flues	

CHOIR ORGAN

Double Dulciana	16
Bourdon	16
Open Diapason	8
Bell Gamba	8
Dulciana	8
Lieblich Gedeckt	8
Gemshorn	4
Dulcet	4
Lieblich Flöte	4
Twelfth	2⅔
Nazard	2⅔
Fifteenth	2
Piccolo	2
Tierce	1⅗
Acuta	II
Contra Fagotto (from Swell)	16
Fagotto (from Swell)	8
Clarinet (from Solo)	8
Tremulant	

SOLO ORGAN

Clarabella	8
Viole d'orchestre	8
Viole Céleste	8
Concert Flute	4
Double Clarinet	16
Orchestral Oboe	8
Clarinet	8
Vox Humana	8
Tuba	8
Tuba Clarion	4
Tremulant to light wind	

PEDAL ORGAN

Sub Bass	32
Open Wood	16
Contra Bass	16
Open Metal (from Great)	16
Violone	16
Bourdon	16
Dulciana (from Choir)	16
Echo Bourdon (from Swell)	16
Quint	10⅔
Principal	8
Octave Wood	8
Flute	8
Dolce	8
Quint	5⅓
Prestant	4
Flute	4
Fourniture	VI
Contra Trombone	32
Bombarde	16
Trombone	16
Posaune (from Great)	16
Fagotto (from Swell)	16
Bass Clarinet	16
Trumpet	8
Bassoon (from Swell)	8
Clarinet (from Solo)	8

BOMBARDE DIVISION

Double Diapason	16
Diapason	8
Octave	4
Fourniture	IV
Cymbale	IV
Contra Posaune	16
Posaune	8
Tuba	8
Tuba Clarion	4

COUPLERS

Choir to Pedal   Great to Pedal   Swell to Pedal
Swell Octave to Pedal   Solo to Pedal
Solo Octave to Pedal   Pedal Octave
Swell to Choir   Solo to Choir   Choir to Great
Swell to Great   Solo to Great   Solo to Swell
Swell Sub Octave   Swell Octave   Swell Unison Off
Solo Unison Off   Solo Octave
Sustainers, 1 to Solo, 1 to Choir
A full complement of adjustable pistons with
double touch to those on the manuals.

During the war, Hull suffered tremendously from the blitz. After two nights of exceptionally heavy air attack, Norman Strafford carried out the most minute examination of the organ and found everything was working perfectly. He wrote to the Compton firm saying: 'That such a large instrument involving so much finely adjusted electric action could come through such a tremendous ordeal and remain in perfect working order is as amazing as it is almost incredible. May I again offer you my congratulations, thanks and a further expression of my admiration of the glorious instrument you built for us at Holy Trinity, Hull'. A tribute, together with a photograph of the luminous stop console, appeared in the firm's advertisement in *The Musical Times* in March 1944.

The fame of the organ at Downside Abbey had spread far and wide and undoubtedly led to Comptons securing no less than twelve contracts for Cathedrals in England, Scotland, Wales and Ireland. These were

Bangor (1954); Millport, Isle of Cumbrae (1935); Mullingar, Ireland (1936); Salford Cathedral (1938); Tuam, Galway (1936); Derby (1939); Kilkenny (1939); Ripon (new electric action, 1950); Wakefield (1951); Londonderry (1955–56); Cardiff, St David's Cathedral (1957) and Southwark, St George's Cathedral (1958).

Bangor was a rebuild of the Hill organ of 1897, which preserved much of the old work largely as before; other stops were re-scaled and revoiced while there was a certain amount of extension introduced.

Of the others, the organ for the Roman Catholic Cathedral of St John, Salford, Manchester, was particularly interesting. The pipes were located in the chamber of the north side aisle. To quote the paragraph in *Musical Opinion* for August 1938: 'No direct sound reaches the building, the tone being transferred to the east and west ends of the Cathedral, by a special microphone, amplifier and sound distributing system. There are two consoles placed in the east behind the high altar and in the west gallery respectively, near to the tone distributors and either source of sound may be operated from each console separately or simultaneously'.

Mullingar Cathedral (1936) was entirely extension; there were two organs (west end and east) and the whole conception was the work of J. I. Taylor, who designed and directed its tonal finishing. The main organ, with its three-manual console and 10 h.p. Rockingham blower, was located on the west gallery of the Cathedral behind a screen of oak and bronze designed by the architects, W. H. Byrne & Sons, of Dublin. The Sanctuary organ was placed in a lofty position near the east end of the building with its movable console about fifty feet away on the opposite side. A paragraph in *Musical Opinion* for October 1936 records that 'By means of an ingenious electrical system of stop control, either or both organs can be played from each console, so that if it were to be desired, the west organist can play the sanctuary organ while the sanctuary organist can play the west organ...' The east organ was blown by a small 1 h.p. Rockingham blower; it comprised 255 pipes, and the west 1,288 pipes; stop-keys were used for each console. According to *Musical Opinion*: 'Concerning the west organ, a famous Irish musician has already recorded his opinion that it is unquestionably the finest and most brilliant church organ in Ireland'.

Tuam Cathedral, Galway (1936), was a three-manual with a Bombarde division played from the Choir. The accessories included double-touch pistons giving suitable pedal stops on second touch, together with a sustainer to the Swell organ. Kilkenny (1939) was a three-manual rebuild with 47 speaking stops and a full complement of double touch pistons.

In the summer of 1939, the authorities of Church House, Westminster, commissioned Comptons to build a large three-manual organ for the Assembly Hall of their new building, then under construction, to the designs of two notable architects, Sir Herbert Baker, R.A., and A. T. Scott, F.R.I.B.A.. By June 1940, the firm's advertisement in *Musical Opinion* announced that it was then in course of erection, and by July the specification appeared in print. It proved to be a most interesting scheme, being a combination of pipework for Great, Swell, Choir and part of the Pedal, together with electronic tone production for the Solo division, which was playable from the Choir manual, together with the remainder of the Pedal. The organ was opened on June 10th, 1940, and consisted of the following stops:

CHURCH HOUSE, WESTMINSTER 1939

GREAT ORGAN	ft	SWELL ORGAN	
		Contra Viola	16
Double Open Diapason	16	Open Diapason	8
Open Diapason I	8	Viola	8
Open Diapason II	8	Céleste	8
Dulciana	8	Harmonic Flute	8
Stopped Diapason	8	Viola	4
Octave	4	Céleste	4
Dulcet	4	Octave Flute	4
Superoctave	2	Fifteenth	2
Mixture	IV	Cymbale	III
Tromba	8	Fagotto	16

Trumpet	8	Wald Flöte	8
Fagotto	8	Unda Maris, 2 ranks	8
Clarion	4	Dolce	8
Tremulant		Tibia	4
		Flute	4
CHOIR ORGAN		Nazard	2⅔
Contra Dulciana	16	Flautino	2
Bourdon	16	Cor Anglais	16
Open Diapason	8	Clarinet	8
Dulciana	8	Kalophone	8
Stopped Diapason	8	French Horn	8
Dulcet	4	*Vibrato*	
Stopped Flute	4		
Twelfth	2⅔	**PEDAL ORGAN**	
Fifteenth	2	Sub Bass	32
Acuta	II	Great Bass	16
Bassoon	16	Contra Bass	16
Orchestral Oboe	8	Violone	16
Tromba	8	Dulciana	16
Octave Tromba	4	Bourdon	16
Sustainer		Octave	8
Tremulant		Flute	8
		Flute	4
SOLO ORGAN		Harmonics of	32
(on Choir manual)		Trombone	16
Contra Tibia	16	Baryphone	16
Tibia	8	Fagotto	16
Diapason	8	Tromba	8

I clearly recall J. I. Taylor taking me to hear this instrument shortly after its opening. I was greatly impressed by the pipe division and intrigued by the electronic Solo organ, but cannot recall any critical assessment of the latter, of which Jimmy Taylor was very proud, for by that time his firm had made great developments in the new field of electronic tone production. The life of this instrument was but short, for it was destroyed in a bombing raid.

A year previous to the installation of the Church House organ, Comptons had built a combined pipe and electronic instrument for the Great Yarmouth Methodist Mission. As far as I am aware, these are the only two church instruments built on this system. Happily it is still in existence and working well after work was carried out some two years ago.

GREAT YARMOUTH METHODIST MISSION 1938

GREAT ORGAN				
	ft		
Double Open Diapason	16	Vox Angelica	8
Open Diapason I	8	Viola	4
Open Diapason II	8	Lieblich Flöte	4
Hohl Flöte	8	Cymbale	III
Salicional	8	Trombone	16
Octave	4	Trumpet	8
Hohl Flöte	4	Clarion	4
Twelfth	2⅔	*Tremulant*	
Fifteenth	2	*Sustainer*	
Tuba	8		
		CHOIR ORGAN	
SWELL ORGAN		Contra Salicional	16
		Viola da Gamba	8
Contra Viola	16	Open Diapason II	8
Viola	8	Hohl Flöte	8
Lieblich Gedackt	8	Salicional	8
Salicional	8		

Vox Angelica	8	Melotwelfth	2⅔
Lieblich Gedackt	8	Melo	2
Hohl Flöte	4	Clarinet	8
Salicet	4	Oboe	8
Vox Angelica	4	Musette	8
Twelfth	2⅔	Carillon	
Salicetina	2	Chimes	
Tuba	8	Vibraphone	
Clarion	4	*Echo Control*	
Tremulant		*Vibrato*	
Sustainer			

ELECTROPHONIC

Melotone	8
Melotone	4

COUPLERS

Great to Choir   Swell to Choir   Sub Octave
Octave   Unison Off   Choir to Pedal
Great to Pedal   Swell to Pedal   Swell to Great

The rebuild of the organ in Derby Cathedral, completed by the end of 1939, was the last great undertaking carried out by Comptons before war started in earnest. It was not an entirely problem free contract, as many pipes from the old organ had to be incorporated, which meant that some ranks had to be partly re-made. In all, some 1,535 pipes were used again and each stop received the most careful re-scaling and re-voicing. Space too was limited in the west gallery; all pipework except the Pedal open wood and its extensions, together with the 32 ft polyphone, were enclosed in two swell chambers. The detached console was placed by the choir stalls at the east end and was of the luminous stop-head type.

Dr George Thalben-Ball gave the opening recital on December 6th, 1939, when he played the following programme:

> Fantasia in G, Bach. Air with Variations, Michael Festing. Fantasia and Fugue in G, Parry. Andante in F, Dussek. Two Chorale Preludes: 'Adorn thyself, O dear soul', Paul Krause; 'Now thank we all our God', Karg-Elert. Air and Allegro, John Stanley. Fantasia and Fugue on B.A.C.H., Liszt. Chanson, Shippen Barnes. Air Varie, Duruflé. Elfes, Bonnet. Finale (Suite), Dupré

The organ attracted considerable interest in the Derby, Leicester and Nottingham area, and G. Heath Gracie, MUS.B., F.R.C.O. (organist between 1933–58) was very proud of it, displaying its many fine features to the full in his accompaniment to the services and in recitals. In the early part of the war, I spent a most interesting evening in his company and came away most impressed by what I had heard, although it did not give me the really outstanding thrill experienced at St Luke's, Chelsea. Over thirty years were to elapse before I heard it again, when, in 1973, the new two-manual Cousans organ was built in the Retro-Choir. I must confess that I did not warm to the sound of the Compton as a whole, quite as much as in 1940, and came to the conclusion that the bright, crystal clear voice of the Retro-Choir organ was more to my liking!

The war years saw the Compton organisation devoted entirely to war work, organ maintenance being kept to the minimum. John Compton was in Italy and in the March 1943 issue of *Musical Opinion* it was reported that Mr John Compton had reached London in good health after three years exile. He should have returned [from Italy] in the Spring of 1940, but his state of health made it impossible. A cause had been found for the trouble, but the Italian declaration of war came before the cure was completed. 'Mr Compton spent 2½ years fairly pleasantly in a delightful part of Italy where he had the use of five church organs and in addition was able to conduct a valuable series of experiments. He contributed two articles to *Musical Opinion* for June and August, 1943, entitled: 'Tales of the Sangro Valley' and one on 'An old Sicilian Organ' in the December 1945 issue.

DERBY CATHEDRAL

MANUAL COMPASS   CC to C, 61 notes.

PEDAL COMPASS - CCC to G, 32 notes.

PEDAL ORGAN

1.	Subbass	(to EEEE)	32 ft.
2.	Open Wood		16 ft.
3.	Diaphone		16 ft.
4.	Contra Bass		16 ft.
5.	Bourdon		16 ft.
6.	Echo Bourdon		16 ft.
7.	Dulciana	(Choir)	16 ft.
8.	Octave Wood		8 ft.
9.	Flute		8 ft.
10.	Dulciana	(Choir)	8 ft.
11.	Super Octave Wood		4 ft.
12.	Octave Flute		4 ft.
13.	Contra Trombone		32 ft.
	(Compound Bass)		
14.	Fourniture IV ranks.		
15.	Trombone		16 ft.
16.	Posaune	(Great)	16 ft.
17.	Fagotto	(Swell)	16 ft.
18.	Clarinet	(prepared) (Solo)	16 ft.
19.	Tromba		8 ft.
20.	Clarion		4 ft.

I.   Choir to Pedal.

II. Great to Pedal.

III. Swell to Pedal.

IV. Solo to Pedal.

V.   Solo Octave to Pedal.

CHOIR ORGAN

1.	Contra Dulciana		16 ft.
2.	Open Diapason		8 ft.
3.	Gemshorn		8 ft.
4.	Hohlflöte		8 ft.
5.	Dulciana		8 ft.
6.	Vox Angelica		8 ft.
7.	Lieblich Gedeckt		8 ft.
8.	Dulcet		4 ft.
9.	Open Flute		4 ft.
10.	Stopped Flute		4 ft.
11.	Twelfth		2-2/3 ft.
12.	Nazard		2-2/3 ft.
13.	Fifteenth		2 ft.
14.	Flautino		2 ft.
15.	Tierce		1-3/5 ft.
16.	Acuta, II ranks.		
17.	Double Clarinet		16 ft.
18.	Clarinet	(from Solo)	8 ft.
19.	Orchestral Oboe		8 ft.

VI.   Unison off.

VII. Suboctave.

VIII. Octave.

IX.   Great to Choir.

X.   Swell to Choir.

XI.   Solo to Choir.

XII. Tremulant.

XIII. Sustainer.

The John Compton Organ Company, Limited.

BOMBARDE ORGAN (on Choir Manual)
(mainly from Great)

1.	First Diapason	4 ft.
2.	Octave Diapason	4 ft.
3.	Pleinjeu V ranks.	
4.	Cymbale II-VIII ranks.	
5.	Contra Posaune	16 ft.
6.	Posaune	8 ft.
7.	Tromba	8 ft.
8.	Clarion	4 ft.
9.	Tuba	8 ft.

GREAT ORGAN

1.	Double Open Diapason	16 ft.
2.	First Diapason	8 ft.
3.	Second Diapason	8 ft.
4.	Third Diapason	8 ft.
5.	Hohlflöte	8 ft.
6	Dulciana	8 ft.
7.	First Octave	4 ft.
8.	Second Octave	4 ft.
9.	Twelfth	2-2/3 ft.
10.	First Fifteenth	2 ft.
11.	Second Fifteenth	2 ft.
12.	Cymbale, II-IV ranks.	
13.	Pleinju, II-VI ranks.	
14.	Contra Posaune	16 ft.
15.	Posaune	8 ft.
16.	Clarion	4 ft.
XIV.	Swell to Great.	
XV.	Solo to Great.	

SWELL ORGAN

1.	Bourdon	16 ft.
2.	Open Diapason	8 ft.
3.	Salicional	8 ft.
4.	Voix Celestes (*Tenor C*)	8 ft.
5.	Stopped Diapason	8 ft.
6.	Principal	4 ft.
7.	Waldflöte	4 ft.
8.	Flageolet	2 ft.
9.	Cymbale, IV ranks.	
10.	Contra Fagotto	16 ft.
11.	Trumpet	8 ft.
12.	Fagotto	8 ft.

SWELL ORGAN—*continued.*

13.	Hautboy	8 ft.
14.	Clarion	4 ft.
XVI.	Suboctave.	
XVII.	Octave.	
XVIII.	Unison off.	
XIX.	Tremulant.	
XX.	Solo to Swell.	

SOLO ORGAN

1.	Viole d'Orchestre	8 ft.
2.	Violes Celestes (*to Gamut G*)	8 ft.
3.	Concert Flute	8 ft.
4.	Viola	4 ft.
5.	Violes Celestes	4 ft.
6.	Harmonic Flute	4 ft.
7.	Viole Fifteenth	2 ft.
8.	Harmonic Piccolo	2 ft.
9.	Bassoon (*Tenor C*)	16 ft.
10.	Clarinet	8 ft.
11.	Orchestral Oboe	8 ft.
12.	Tuba	8 ft.
13.	Tuba Clarion	4 ft.
XXI.	Tremulant.	
XXII.	Sustainer.	

ACCESSORIES

Detached and movable console.
Three balanced expression pedals.
One balanced crescendo pedal.
Eight combination pistons to each manual, adjustable at the console.
Four toe pistons to Pedal organ, adjustable at the console.
Four toe pistons to Great organ, duplicating thumb pistons Nos. 1, 3, 5, 7.
Four toe pistons to Swell organ, duplicating thumb pistons Nos. 2, 4, 6, 8.
Four general pistons, adjustable at the console.
Four pistons controlling pedal couplers, cancelling on second touch.
Four reversing pistons operating Great to Pedal.
Four reversing pistons operating Swell to Pedal.
Four reversing pistons operating Solo to Pedal.
Four reversing pistons operating Swell to Great.
Pedal control piston to Great, Swell and Choir manuals, furnishing appropriate pedal basses for manual combinations.
One "Tremulants off" piston.
One "doubles off" piston.
One "General cancel" piston.
One "Pedal cancel" toe piston.
Electric motor, blower and generator.

The Great, Choir and Pedal organs (excepting only the Pedal Open Wood and its derivations), are enclosed in a general swell chamber.
The Swell and Solo organs are enclosed in separate swell boxes.

The John Compton Organ Company, Limited.

Comptons were able to announce in the April 1947 issue of *Musical Opinion* that: 'Transition in the Compton organisation from war work to organ building has now been accomplished. With spacious factories, capable and enthusiastic craftsmen, complete modern plant in all departments and many orders in hand, we look forward to increasing production during 1947. The Compton Miniatura and the new Compton Electrone will be exhibited at the British Industries Fair at Olympia from May 6 to May 16.' In the issue for August 1947 it was announced that: 'The Compton Electrone can now be heard and inspected by appointment'.

The Electrone was featured in a full-page advertisement in *Musical Opinion* for September 1948. It showed a traditional stop-key console and the subject matter summarised its features as follows:

> To make exaggerated claims for pipeless electronic organs is as much a mistake as to underestimate their undoubted merits. We do neither : we state with authority and emphasis that the COMPTON ELECTRONE resembles its more orthodox progenitor, the pipe organ, in its console management. Keys, pedals, stops, pistons and swell pedals are in customary positions and act as in a pipe organ.
> If you need an instrument more organ-like than anything else of its kind, capable of supporting a choir and congregation, with a large variety and range of tone, at relatively low first cost and withal, in a ridiculously small space, you must hear the

COMPTON ELECTRONE

An Electrone is being installed at Worcester Cathedral
for the Three Choirs Festival this month

When Philip Selfe (former works manager for Bishop & Son, where he had learned his trade) joined Forster & Andrews of Hull as manager in 1897, he little thought that one day he would become sole owner, and by 1911 build one of the largest and finest concert hall organs in the country—that at Hull City Hall, in 1911. Selfe was a man of extraordinary ability; he was a skilful planner and had a marked architectural taste. He was a very able and facile draughtsman and would have as many as six separate drawing boards going at one time, each with a particular view or aspect of the organ in question. He would move from one to the other, setting out everything on the comparatively large scale of one inch to the foot, finally linking the drawings to present a very graphic and quickly grasped layout which paid attention to the most minute detail. As organ builder case designers go, he had an exceptionally high standard and a marked individual characteristic in his designs, that of the Hull City Hall being outstanding. He invariably carved a small elephant somewhere on his cases and this motif was to be found on the console of the City Hall organ. I well remember seeing him on one or two occasions during my teenage years at the factory of Hill, Norman & Beard Ltd., whose technical staff he joined when John Christie purchased Forster & Andrews in 1924.

The Hull City Hall contract was a prestigious one; it had four manuals, 125 stops, 5,505 pipes and a detached console. Norman Cocker, who knew the instrument well, commented: 'It is not a concert hall organ at all, but it is one of the most ravishing Cathedral organs imaginable; it has dynamic force, flexibility, immense variety, seemingly endless and glorious colour and certainly possesses distinction, but it lacks one thing— the power to get across the footlights, all because it is too delicately toned and too fastidiously voiced'. He also spoke of its meticulous regulation, the living and distinct individuality of each stop and the ravishing tone of the Solo stops. Of the organ as a whole he said: 'In the presence of an audience, the whole instrument just fails to make one sit up and take notice, although one cannot fail to sit up very erectly and take minute notice of its undoubted glories when in communion with it in private. A shade more courage, Mr Selfe, and a lot more showmanship and your name would have gone down in posterity'.

The organ was badly damaged during the air raids on Hull in World War II; Norman Strafford was engaged as consultant to the Corporation and chose the very firm who could give it 'the power to get it across the footlights', The John Compton Organ Co., who completely reconstructed and enlarged it with the greatest skill and artistry. I shall always remember the thrilling experience of hearing every facet of this truly exciting concert organ from its detached luminous stop console. Due to the kindness of Mr Peter Goodman, the City Organist, I was able to spend most of the afternoon there, before re-adjusting my mind to talk about the history of Forster & Andrews to the local Organists' Association. Comptons had the highest praise for the superb quality of the pipework and its voicing, the fine workmanship throughout and the masterly layout and general spaciousness. It is still possible to hear a number of stops much as Selfe left them and without exception they possess great beauty of tone. In brief, the instrument was enlarged by the addition of a new Positif division, the duplication of some manual reeds on to the Pedal, the addition of the Great cymbal, together with a rank of tibias in the Solo box. The console, with luminous stop control, was placed on a movable platform; two Discus blowers supplied wind at pressures ranging from 3½ to 20 inches.

The opening recital was given on 27th April, 1951, by Norman Strafford and Fernando Germani. The music lovers of this great city and district flocked to hear their City Hall organ restored to life after the terrible batterings, received by homes, factories and churches during the war. They were thrilled by what they heard and the Corporation of Hull was encouraged by their support to hold recitals, moreover, to maintain the instrument. In the 1970s, humidifiers were installed and by 1985, action problems necessitated a programme of rehabilitation being embarked upon, together with the provision of drawstops to replace the luminous stop heads, and the installation of a new eight-level capture system from Solid State Logic, together with additional registration aids. Between 1989–90, all pipework was cleaned and regulated, slider seals were fitted to all soundboards, old leatherwork was replaced and wind leaks were sealed. The console was placed in a fixed position at the top of the stage. All this work was carried out with enthusiasm and skill by Rushworth & Dreaper Ltd. and the re-opening recital was given by David Liddle on 17th September, 1991. The City Council is to be congratulated on embarking on such a scheme during a difficult financial period. The consultants were Canon Geoffrey Hunter (Diocesan Organ Adviser), Roger Andrews, Joint Organ Curator and Dr. Ken Essex-Crosby. The post of City Organist held so long with distinction by Peter Goodman was abolished in 1991, his last recital being given on 8th May. Since then, recitals have been given by visiting players.

THE CITY HALL, HULL
FORSTER & ANDREWS ORGAN 1911

GREAT ORGAN	ft	SWELL ORGAN	
Double Open Diapason	16	Contra Gamba	16
Bourdon	16	Quintaton	16
Open Diapason	8	Open Diapason	8
Open Diapason	8	Geigen Principal	8
Open Diapason	8	Rohrflöte	8
Doppelflöte	8	Salicional	8
Claribel Flute	8	Viol d'Orchestre	8
Stopped Diapason	8	Voix Célestes, 2 ranks	8
Dolce	8	Waldflöte	4
Quint	5⅓	Gemshorn	4
Principal	4	Twelfth	2⅔
Harmonic Flute	4	Flageolet	2
Octave Diapason	4	Fifteenth	2
Twelfth	2⅔	Mixture	II
Harmonic Piccolo	2	Mixture	III
Fifteenth	2	Double Tromba	16
Mixture	III	Bassoon	16
Mixture	IV	Horn	8
Double Trumpet	16	Trumpet	8
Tromba (harmonic)	8	Oboe	8
Clarion	4	Musette	8
		Vox Humana	8
		Clarion	4

CHOIR ORGAN

Lieblich Bourdon	16
Open Diapason	8
Hohlflöte	8
Lieblich Gedact	8
Unda Maris	8
Dulciana	8
Voix Célestes	8
Viol d'Orchestre	8
Geigen Principal	4
Flauto Traverso	4
Harmonic Piccolo	2
Dulciana Mixture	III
Bass Clarinet	16
Corno di Bassetto	8
Cor Anglais	8
Celesta (Mustel, mechanical action)	8

SOLO ORGAN

Gamba	8
Harmonic Flute	8
String Gamba	8
Célestes, 2 ranks	8
Doppelflöte	4
Octave Violin	4
Harmonic Flageolet	2
Krummhorn	16
Orchestral Oboe	8
Orchestral Clarinet	8
Orchestral Trumpet	8
Double Tuba	16
Tuba	8
Tuba Clarion	4
Tubular Bells	
Steel Bars	

PEDAL ORGAN

Gravissima	64
Double Open Diapason	32
Open Diapason	16
Contra Bass	16
Violone	16
Sub Bass	16
Soft Bass	16
Contra Gamba	16
Principal	8
Octave	8
Cello	8

Flute	8
Fifteenth	4
Mixture	III
Contra Bombarde	32
Trombone	16
Trumpet	8
Bass Drums (repeat each octave)	
Timpani (repeat each octave)	

COUPLERS

Solo to Great   Swell to Great   Choir to Great
Great to Pedals   Solo Octave to Great
Solo Sub Octave to Great   Swell Octave to Great
Swell Sub Octave to Great   Choir Octave to Great
Choir Sub Octave to Great   Swell Octave
Swell Sub Octave   Swell Unsion Off   Solo to Swell
Swell to Pedal   Choir Octave   Choir Sub Octave
Choir Unison Off   Swell to Choir   Solo to Choir
Solo Octave to Choir   Swell Octave to Choir
Swell Sub Octave to Choir   Choir to Pedal
Solo Octave   Solo Sub Octave   Solo to Pedal
Solo Unison Off

WIND PRESSURES

Great Organ: 3 reservoirs, 3½, 4½ & 6 ins.
Swell Organ: 3 reservoirs, 3½ and 6 ins.
Choir Organ: 2 reservoirs, 3½ ins.
Solo Organ: 3 reservoirs, 4½ and 12 ins.
Tubular-pneumatic action: 3 reservoirs, 6 ins.
Wind is supplied by a Discus blower

SUMMARY

Pedal Organ: 19 stops, 392 pipes
Choir Organ: 16 stops, 1,013 pipes
Great Organ: 21 stops, 1,586 pipes
Swell Organ: 23 stops, 1,623 pipes
Solo Organ: 16 stops, 891 pipes
30 couplers
Total stops: 125
Total number of pipes: 5,505

19 other movements
35 combination pistons and pedals

The total cost of the instrument: £4,892

I have to record that, in a lifetime's experience of Compton's work, my one disappointment was their rebuild of the Harrison & Harrison organ in the Bull Ring, Birmingham, of 1913, with additions in 1926, leaving some sixteen registers to be added, but which were never inserted. This was an organ of great magnificence—and how I loved it! for I had the freedom of the console whenever I cared to look in. It was 'Harrison' at their very best—need I say more? In 1953, it was decided to reconstruct it and remove it to the north transept from its original position in a chamber on the north side of the chancel. Tonally, a number of additions were made and the former Choir/Solo organ became two separate manuals. A total of 67 speaking stops spread over four manuals and pedal were provided, as against forty-five in the Harrison organ. I venture to say that as far as the main ensemble is concerned, the Harrison 'character' did not re-emerge in the reconstructed instrument.

After six post war years of organ building, Comptons had made amazing progress in what was a difficult period for industry as a whole. They drew attention to their achievements in this advertisement reproduced from the January 1954 issue of *Musical Opinion*.

St Eugene's Cathedral, Londonderry was an 11 rank extension organ completed in 1956 to the following specification.

CATHEDRAL CHURCH OF ST EUGENE, LONDONDERRY 1956
3 manuals: CC to C, 61 notes   Pedal: CCC to G, 32 notes

Great Chamber.— 6 ranks
Open Diapason I, Open Diapason II, Stopped Diapason, Dulciana, Vox Angelica, Tromba

Swell Chamber.— 5 ranks
Harmonic Flute, Viola, Viola Céleste, Trumpet, Hautboy

GREAT ORGAN

	ft
Sub Diapason	16
First Diapason	8
Second Diapason	8
Stopped Diapason	8
Dulciana	8
Octave	4
Stopped Flute	4
Twelfth	2⅔
Fifteenth	2
Mixture	III
Tromba	8
Octave Tromba	4

SWELL ORGAN

Contra Viola	16
Harmonic Flute	8
Viola	8
Viola Céleste	8
Harmonic Flute	4
Viola	4
Piccolo	2
Cymbale	III
Double Trumpet	16
Trumpet	8
Hautboy	8
Clarion	4
Tremulant	

CHOIR ORGAN
(Section enclosed in Great Chamber)

Contra Dulciana	16
Second Diapason	8
Stopped Diapason	8
Dulciana	8
Vox Angelica	8
Stopped Flute	4
Dulcet	4
Vox Angelica	4
Dulcet Twelfth	2⅔
Flautino	2
Dulcet Fifteenth	2
Acuta	III
Krumhorn	8
Tromba	8
Octave Tromba	4
Tremulant	

CHOIR ORGAN
(Section enclosed in Swell Chamber)

Viola	8
Harmonic Flute	8
Octave Viola	4
Harmonic Flute	4
Contra Hautboy (tenor C)	16
Hautboy	8
Octave Hautboy	4

PEDAL ORGAN

Sub Bass (Pentaphone)	32
Open Diapason (Diaphone)	16
Violone	16
Sub Bass (Polyphone)	16
Echo Bass	16
Flute	8
Flute	4
Trombone	16
Double Trumpet	16
Tromba	8

ACCESSORIES

6 couplers
Pedal to Great pistons, 2nd touch
Pedal to Choir pistons, 2 touch
Pedal to Swell pistons, 2nd touch
6 thumb pistons to each manual
1 controller piston to each manual
1 general cancel piston
6 Pedal toe pistons   6 ventil switches
1 canceller switch
2 balanced swell pedals   1 general crescendo pedal
Detached stop-key console

NB.— The lowest octave of the sub bass 32ft is a Pentaphonic pipe—the lowest 5 notes, CCCC–EEEE speaking the same note. The 16ft bottom octave of the sub bass is a Polyphone system of six pipes giving 12 notes, CCC–BB, each pipe speaking 2 notes chromatically. The Choir krumhorn 8ft is a synthetic stop derived largely from the stopped diapason 8ft plus nazard 2⅔ with an added soft tierce 1⅗ taken from the angelica or dulciana.

The five-manual organ in Wakefield Cathedral was described in full by Reginald Whitworth in *The Organ*, No. 128. Last rebuilt by Abbott & Smith of Leeds, in 1902, and incorporating pipework by Gray (1804), Booth of Wakefield (1837, 1864 and 1867), Alfred Kirkland (1829) and Hill (1892), Comptons carried out a most difficult rebuild in 1951 which called for all the ingenuity for which they were well known. The tonal scheme was drawn up by the builders in consultation with Reginald Whitworth and Dr. Percy G. Saunders, F.R.C.O., organist of the Cathedral. The Swell and Choir Organs were completely 'straight' and the whole instrument enclosed, with the exception of the Pedal 32 ft polyphone, bourdon, open wood and tuba units. The Compton diaphone was used for the Pedal contra bass, whilst the bass cornet formed the Compton synthetic 32 ft reed. All the 8ft stops on the manuals, 16ft stops on the Pedal and the 32 ft polyphone were fitted with second-touch cancellation. 'A slight additional draw against a strong spring cancelled (by actual withdrawal) any stops of the department concerned which might at the moment be drawn.' This instrument has since been rebuilt most successfully by Wood of Huddersfield.

What undoubtedly was the finest entirely new church organ built by Comptons since their masterpiece at Downside Abbey in 1931, is the instrument in St Bride's Church, Fleet Street, which was taken into use in 1957. During the years of my retirement, I have rarely missed a broadcast of Choral Evensong from St Bride's and have never ceased to wonder at the sheer magnificence of its ensemble or the beauty of its many quiet tonal colours. No less an authority than Gordon Reynolds contributed an article for *The Organ* (April 1960) describing every facet of the instrument with an expertise and literary style which in my opinion has been unequalled in the long history of that periodical. It has been a great disappointment to me that I have been unable to hear it 'in the flesh', but the possession of a first-class radio has given me a very adequate impression of some of the vast possibilities of a most remarkable instrument. The design and ingenuity in its construction, the superb materials employed and the artistry in its voicing and tonal finishing have been commented on by those who have examined it. I have discussed it at length with several former employees of Comptons who (as they have said to me) were privileged to work on it; there was an enthusiasm and team spirit here which is vividly recalled today and I am sure will never be forgotten. To quote Gordon Reynolds: 'Nothing was too much trouble and no one doubted the final result. It is a great joy to record that when this magnificent team finally heard what they had created, they found that they had constructed a masterpiece which surprised even themselves'.

ST BRIDE'S CHURCH, FLEET STREET, LONDON 1957

4 manuals: CC to C, 61 notes   Pedal: CCC to G, 32 notes

GREAT ORGAN	ft	SWELL ORGAN	ft
Double Open Diapason	16	Contra Salicional	16
Bourdon	16	Open Diapason	8
First Diapason	8	Lieblich Gedeckt	8
Second Diapason	8	Salicional	8
Third Diapason	8	Voix Céleste	8
Hohl FLute	8	Principal	4
Stopped Diapason	8	Zauberflöte	4
Octave	4	Salicet	4
Principal	4	Fifteenth	2
Stopped Flute	4	Cornet 15·19·22	III
Twelfth	2⅔	Mixture 12·15·17	III
Fifteenth	2	Contra Hautboy	16
Super Octave	2	Trumpet	8
Mixture 17·19·22	III	Hautboy	8
Cymbal 15·19·22	III	Clarion	4
Contra Posaune	16	*Tremulant*	
Tromba	8	*Suboctave*	
Posaune	8	*Octave*	
Clarion	4	*Solo to Swell*	
Swell to Great			
Solo to Great			
Choir to Great			

POSITIVE ORGAN

	ft
Principal	8
Nason Flute	8
Octave	4
Nachthorn	4
Koppel Flute	2
Terz	$1\frac{3}{5}$
Larigot	$1\frac{1}{3}$
Zimbel 22·26·29	III
Positive on Choir	
Positive on Great	

CHOIR ORGAN

Double Dulciana	16
Geigen	8
Claribel	8
Dulciana	8
Vox Angelica	8
Gemshorn	4
Flauto Traverso	4
Dulcet Twelfth	$2\frac{2}{3}$
Nazard	$2\frac{2}{3}$
Flautino	2
Tierce	$1\frac{3}{5}$
Acuta 15·19·22	III
Tremulant	
Sub Octave	
Octave	
Swell to Choir	
Solo to Choir	
Double Clarinet (from Solo)	16
Clarinet (from Solo)	8
Contra Posaune (from Great)	16
Tromba (from Great)	8
Posaune (from Great)	8
Clarion (from Great)	4
Tuba (from Solo)	8

SOLO ORGAN

Harmonic Flute	8
Viol d'orchestre	8
Viol Céleste	8
Concert Flute	4
Piccolo	2
Double Clarinet	16
Orchestral Oboe	8
French Horn	8
Clarinet	8
Tremulant	
Sub Octave	
Octave	
Unison Off	
Tuba (unenclosed)	8
Tuba Clarion (unenclosed)	4

PEDAL ORGAN

Subbass	32
Contrabass	16
Open Diapason (from Great)	16
Bourdon (from Great)	16
Salicional (from Swell)	16
Dulciana (from Choir)	16
Octave	8
Stopped Octave	8
Flute (from Great)	8
Salicional (from Swell)	8
Superoctave	4
Major Flute	4
Flute (from Great)	4
Mixture (from Great)	IV
Grand Cornet	VI
Bombarde	16
Posaune (from Great)	16
Hautboy (from Swell)	16
Double Horn (from Solo)	16
Clarinet (from Solo)	16
Tuba	8
Posaune (from Great)	8
Clarinet (from Solo)	8
Clarion (from Great)	4
Choir to Pedal	
Great to Pedal	
Swell to Pedal	
Solo to Pedal	
Solo Octave to Pedal	

Gordon Reynolds sums up a fascinating story by saying, 'This is the greatest organ Compton's have yet built and takes its place among the greatest in the land. It is, of course, in itself the finest memorial J. I. Taylor could have and we are thankful that he was able to enjoy it as long as he did. As soon as the organ was completed, he was invested as a Liveryman of the Guild [Guild of St Bride] and immediately offered himself as Assistant Organist. He was already serving in this capacity when he was presented to H. M. The Queen at the Rededication Service. It was his turn to play for the day's services on Low Sunday, 1958, but he died on Easter Day. It is a moving thought that while the trumpets sounded on the other side, the grand instrument which was the triumph of his life, proclaimed the Resurrection'.

Knowing J. I. T. as I did, I am sure that in quiet moments spent in looking back to the humble beginnings of John Compton and himself at Nottingham, he marvelled at what they had achieved in their lifetime.

The death of J. I. Taylor was not only a great blow to Comptons, but to the musical world in this country; he was the friend of everyone who came into contact with him, his advice was sought by many and was readily given, while his musicianship was of the highest order. He had been associated with John

Compton for the whole of his working life; they were close friends and in their professional lives worked 'as one'. No matter what challenges the firm had to face in the building of a new organ (and there were many), Jimmy Taylor found a solution, for he combined both tonal and mechanical expertise to a remarkable degree. In his outlook, he was far-seeing, in his management of a large working force he was a 'father figure'; in return, he expected loyalty and enthusiasm from his staff, and there could have been no happier organ works than that at Chase Road. It was a privilege to know him and I treasure in my memory his many kindnesses to me as a young man and later, as well as his generous but sincere comments passed about my writings on not only his own firm's work, but that of other builders too. *Musical Opinion* for May 1958 contained a page devoted to 'Some Appreciations', some of which I quote. Harold Helman spoke of his remarkable gifts for improvisation 'both from the purely musical standpoint and also for displaying all the possibilities of any instrument, large or small, old or new'.

His competitor and friend, Henry Willis III, was generous in his resumé of J. I. T.'s career; they were poles apart in tonal design and thinking, yet each recognised in the other great qualities born of a love for the 'King of Instruments'. He recalled J. I. Taylor's birth in Nottingham (1892), his joining John Compton in 1905 at the age of seventeen, thereafter becoming 'a whole-hearted disciple of John Compton's theories and practice…' His 'contribution to the art of organ building took the form of many inventions, among which are named the all-electric piston setter relay; he developed the luminous stop-control and its associated reversing mechanism and many other ingenious electrical devices; all noted for simplicity in design combined with reliability in operation… Now for the man himself—Taylor was of short, somewhat stocky build, and the immediate impression given to all who met him, was of a man of equable and genial temperament to whom one at once felt to have an attractive personality. I first met him in 1919 and at once received that impression, and a firm and lasting impression followed, not marred by some pronounced differences in opinion upon professional matters, notably the use of manual extension! In 1937, Taylor was elected to the Executive Board of the Federation of Master Organ Builders and to the Chairmanship in 1951, following the loss of "Reggie" Walker, a position which he filled with dignity and efficiency, was elected a Vice-President in 1952, elected as an original Fellow of the Incorporated Society of Organ Builders in 1947 and a member of the Council; he made a notable contribution to the proceedings of the Society in administration, lectures and masterly contributions to the discussions following lectures; brain-trust and similar activities of the Society—for example, his talk on "Electric Actions, Past and Present and Future" given to the Society on 28th September, 1949, was a masterly survey of a highly technical subject and was recorded in the Society's *Journal*, Vol. 1 No. 2 of June 1951… "Jimmy Taylor" has passed from us but his memory and achievements will remain in the hearts and minds of all who knew him'.

Finally, Charles F. Waters, who had last seen and heard J. I. Taylor 'extemporising with his customary fluency' just before Easter, at St Bride's, Fleet Street. He commented: 'How often are passages to be met in orchestral music which seem ideally suited to a particular instrument or ensemble, even inspired by it! In Mr Taylor's extemporisation one could hear outlines for distinctive solo registers, sparkling textures for flutes, chords for diapasons and so on: all so appropriate as the registration changed. His playing was not merely a means for showing off an organ, however, for it was distinguished by neatness of construction and execution and colour of tonality and harmonisation'.

The rebuilding after war damage of St George's Catholic Cathedral, Southwark, carried out between 1953–58 to the design of Mr Romilly B. Craze, F.R.I.B.A., provided Comptons with a splendid opportunity to build an entirely new organ for this fine resonant building. J. C. Bishop had built a three-manual organ for the original building in 1848; it was then known as the Catholic Cathedral, St George's Fields. A full description of this is to be found in the author's book: *Bishop & Son, Organ Builders, The Story of J.C. Bishop and his successors* (1984). It was rebuilt by Bishop & Son in 1907, with a detached console and pneumatic action, all the old pipework being used again wherever possible. Henry Willis & Sons Ltd. built a fine three-manual instrument to replace it during the 1930s; it had an enclosed Mutation section in the apse, the Choir Organ being virtually a Solo division. The wind pressure for both flues and reeds was 3½ inches, except for the tuba/trombone on 12 inches.

In 1958, Comptons designed a three-manual organ comprising 19 ranks extended to provide 71 speaking stops. It is situated in a chamber above the Lady Chapel which is east of the south transept, the tone being directed westwards into the nave and north to the chancel. The choir stalls are in the retro-choir behind the high altar, with the console in front of the east window. Between the console and the back of the high altar there is a raised platform for the conductor, so that he and the organist are dependent on a mirror to keep in touch with what is happening in the sanctuary. I am indebted to E. W. Gallagher's most informative article in *The Organ* (No. 153) for details of disposition of the pipework. 'With the exception of the sub bass and tuba ranks, all the pipework is enclosed within two swell boxes. That containing the Swell Organ is at the front of the chamber, with horizontal shutters facing west and vertical shutters on the south side which open backwards to direct the sound to the choir; at the back is the box containing the Great and Choir stops, about five feet higher, with horizontal shutters opening over the top of the other box and into the nave and vertical shutters on the south side, but this time opening forward. Immediately behind the chancel grille work frontage stands the tuba-bombarde. The pipes of the sub-bass rank are variously disposed; some from the 8ft portion form the west front with the smaller ones behind; the polyphoned 16ft and 32ft pipes are placed near the tuba and Swell Organ box respectively. The net result of all this is that, despite the severe spatial restrictions imposed by the limited dimensions of the chamber, not only is every pipe easily accessible for tuning and maintenance, but the sound gets out to an extent which would hardly seem possible from such a position. Perhaps still more interesting, the balance is consistent in all parts of the building... For more effective dynamic control in a somewhat unusual lay-out, the builders have provided stop-knobs which link the swell pedals with the nave and chancel shutters separately', thus 'allowing for subtleties of gradation which would otherwise be un-attainable; furthermore, it does much to mitigate the awkwardness of the respective positions of organ and console.' I would like to pay tribute to the writings of E. W. Gallagher, which were thorough, informative in every way and unbiased, being a valuable source of reference for information on the organs of his day. This fine example of Compton's work receives thoughtful and sensitive treatment at the hands of this author; one could wish that there were more of his calibre writing today.

The Compton firm's records show the disposition of the pipe ranks as supplied to Gallagher for his article, together with the complete tonal scheme.

ST GEORGE'S CATHEDRAL, SOUTHWARK 1953–58

3 manuals: CC to C, 61 notes   Pedal: CCC to G, 32 notes

SWELL BOX ONE

Rank		Pipes	Pressure
A	First Diapason	73	8
B	Second Diapason	97	8
C	Third Diapason	109	6
D	Gemshorn	61	6
E	Dulciana	121	6
F	Vox Angelica	77	6
G	Hohl Flute	73	6
H	Stopped Diapason	97	6
I	Fourniture 5·12·19	85	6
J	Fourniture 8·15·22	85	6
K	Posaune	85	8

UNENCLOSED

Rank		Pipes	Pressure
L	Bombarde & Tuba	85	12
M	Sub Bass	51	6

SWELL BOX TWO

Rank		Pipes	Pressure
N	Geigen	85	6
O	Harmonic Flute	85	6
P	Viola	109	6
Q	Voix Céleste	49	6
R	Hautboy	73	6
S	Trumpet	73	6

Total pipes.— 1,573

GREAT ORGAN

	ft
Double Open Diapason B	16
Bourdon H	16
First Diapason A	8
Second Diapason B	8

Third Diapason C	8
Dulciana E	8
Stopped Diapason H	8
Octave B	4
Principal C	4

Open Flute G	4
Twelfth C	2⅔
Fifteenth B	2
Cymbal 15·19·22 C	III
Fourniture 12·15·19·22 I, J	IV
Contra Posaune K	16
Posaune K	8
Clarion K	4

SWELL ORGAN

★Contra Viola P	16
Geigen Diapason N	8
Harmonic Flute O	8
†Viola da Gamba P	8
†Voix Céleste (tenor C) Q	8
Geigen Octave N	4
Harmonic Flute O	4
†Viola P	4
Nazard O	2⅔
Fifteenth N	2
Piccolo O	2
†Cymbal 15·19·22 P	III
Contra Hautboy R	16
Hautboy R	8
Trumpet S	8
Clarion S	4
Tremulant	

CHOIR ORGAN

★Double Dulciana	16
Open Diapason C	8
†Gemshorn D	8
Dulciana E	8
Vox Angelica (tenor C) F	8
Hohl Flute G	8
Principal C	4
Dulcet E	4
Stopped Flute H	4
Dulcet Twelfth E	2⅔
Nazard H	2⅔
Dulcet Fifteenth E	2
Flautino H	2
Tierce F	1⅗
Krumhorn (synthetic, various)	8
Contra Posaune K	16
Posaune K	8
Tuba L	8
Tuba Clarion L	4
Tremulant	

PEDAL ORGAN

§Sub Bass M	32
•Contra Bass A	16
Open Metal B	16
★Contra Viola P	16
Sub Bass M	16
Bourdon H	16
★Echo Bass E	16
Octave B	8
Stopped Octave H	8
Flute M	8
Octave Flute M	4
Mixture 12·15·19·22 I, J	IV
Harmonics (various)	32
Bombarde L	16
Posaune K	16
Hautboy R	16
Tuba L	8
Posaune H	8
Clarion L	4

COUPLERS, ETC.

Choir to Pedal Great to Pedal Swell to Pedal
Swell Octave to Pedal   Choir to Great
Swell to Choir Swell to Great
Pedal combinations to Great pistons
Chancel shutters "on"
Nave shutters "on"

Double touch thumb pistons.—
8 each to Choir and Pedal, Great and Pedal,
Swell and Pedal, Pedal couplers.
4 general

Reversible thumb pistons.—
Swell to Great, Swell to Choir, Choir to Great

Double touch toe pistons.—
8 each to Pedal and Great, Swell and Pedal

Reversible toe pistons.—
Great to Pedal, general cancel, 2nd touch cancel
and wind ventils.

★ Lowest 12 haskelled   • Lowest 12 diaphonic
† Spotted metal

§ CCCC–DDDD drone;
EEEE–BB polyphonic,
CC upwards, heavy stopped metal.

Saxon Aldred tells me that the tonal finishing in the Cathedral had to be carried out throughout the night, due to the constant noise from passing trains during the day.

Compton's expertise in the construction of versatile and impressive instruments in extremely difficult situations, such as the BBC Concert Hall and Bournemouth Pavilion, made them the obvious choice for the building of large concert organs in the similar situations existing at the Guildhall, Portsmouth, Southampton Civic Centre, Wimbledon Town Hall and Wolverhampton Town Hall.

The Portsmouth organ (1959) contains twenty ranks which total one thousand six hundred and sixteen pipes. It is enclosed in three overhead chambers at the rear of the stage, one of which houses the blowers, supplying wind ranging from 6 to 15 ins. pressure; the other two, the pipes, windchests, etc. The drawstop console is on a movable platform and can be placed in any position on the stage. The cover illustration from Compton's own specification leaflet is reproduced overleaf.

THE NEW ORGAN

IN

THE GUILDHALL, PORTSMOUTH

Built 1959 by

THE JOHN COMPTON ORGAN COMPANY, LTD.,

CHASE ROAD : NORTH ACTON : LONDON, N.W.10

Telephone: ELGar 6666 (4 lines)

One encouraging feature of current thinking in the organ world in this country is the desire to preserve some of the outstanding examples of Victorian and Edwardian organ building, without tonal embellishment. To this end, Harrison & Harrison have devoted much thought and expertise to the restoration of the Lewis organs in Southwark Cathedral and Melbourne Town Hall as well as the Binns organ in The Albert Hall, Nottingham, for which they deserve hearty congratulations. Likewise, N. P. Mander Ltd. have been equally successful in re-creating the Hill sound at Birmingham Town Hall, and the rehabilitation of the Hill organ in Eton College Chapel, together with the Walker in Bristol Cathedral, in both cases retaining the tubular-pneumatic action. I am sure that these will not be isolated examples and where it is practicable there will be others in the future. All this poses the question, whether complete rebuilds and enlargements of the Lewis organ in Ilkley Parish Church, as well as the Forster & Andrews instrument in St George's Church, Stockport, would have been carried out had they been done today. Or—to put it another way—were those responsible for advising and carrying out the work at these three churches, right to do what they did? It is a very difficult question to answer and like much that goes on in the realm of organs, no matter what age we are in—it is largely a matter of opinion. It is dangerous to be too dogmatic, but most of us are liable at some time or other to be guilty of this.

At Ilkley, the T. C. Lewis organ of 1882, which was in need of reconstruction by 1943, came under the scrutiny of Col. George Dixon, T.D., M.A., of St Bees and Mr A. E. Pickett of Ilkley. Subsequently after the war, Reginald Whitworth, M.B.E. and A. E. Pickett finalised a scheme based on the original discussions with Col. Dixon, in consultation with the John Compton Organ Co. Ltd. The scheme provided for the extension of six manual ranks, viz: geigen, dulciana, viola, tromba, fagotto and clarinet. The whole of the original spotted metal and wood Lewis pipework, with minor exceptions, was incorporated in the reconstructed instrument. A detached all-electric stop-knob console was sited in the south east nave. Carved English oak cases to the north aisle and chancel fronts were carried out by that well-known Yorkshire wood carver, Robert Thompson of Kilburn (whose showrooms I had the pleasure of visiting in 1993) to designs by J. Stuart Syme, F.S.A., F.R.I.B.A., of Messrs. Brierly, Syme & Leckenby, of York. The organ was rebuilt with the customary Compton artistry and efficiency but in the light of current thinking, I would unhesitatingly comment that Lewis's original tonal scheme would have been best left alone.

In 1980, Messrs Rushworth & Dreaper entirely rebuilt the Compton organ at Stockport, discarding the old four-manual console with its luminous stop heads, and providing one of three manuals with normal draw-stop control. Tonally, most of the additional Compton stops were discarded and the tonal scheme was revised to provide an instrument more in keeping with the spirit of the old, but with six new ranks of pipes to give some modernisation in tonal colour.

John Compton died in 1957, and his passing was deeply felt by all members of the firm's staff. *Musical Opinion* for July 1957 carried the following obituary:

THE LATE JOHN COMPTON

'British organ building has suffered a severe loss in the passing, last April, of Mr John Compton at the age of 83. Founder, for many years Managing Director and latterly President of the John Compton Organ Company, he was a great artist in his craft, unusually modest and unassuming in personality, a loyal friend and a true gentleman. His genius for effective organ design is apparent in many notable instruments, including those at Downside Abbey, St Luke's Chelsea, the BBC Concert Hall and Maida Vale Studio organs; Derby Cathedral, Bridlington Priory; Christchurch Priory and many others where difficulties of space required special tonal methods and ingenuity of planning. A pioneer of reliable electric organ control which he adopted as standard in 1910, he was described by a famous American organ builder as "thinking years ahead". Never complacent, he was always devising new ideas and looking to the future. Even when detained as a prisoner of war in Italy, he occupied himself with experiments in tone and mixture design which have had valuable results. He was a most accomplished organist and had a wonderful gift for improvisation. It was a real joy to hear him demonstrate an organ, for he had an uncanny gift for using every tone quality and combination in exactly the right way. He was beloved by his colleagues and the entire staff for his courage, his courtesy and helpfulness, and he was never heard to speak disparagingly of any other organ builder. He bore repeated periods of ill health with great fortitude and that he reached so advanced an age is some consideration to those who are privileged to carry on the work he so ably began, fifty-six years ago.'

It seems undisputably clear that more patents were applied for by John Compton, and later in the name of The John Compton Organ Co. Ltd., than by any other builder. John Compton's applications numbered some twenty-five, those of the firm (an important contribution being made by J. I. Taylor)—some forty-seven. Some of the titles are vague to say the least and it is assumed that those relating to electrical musical instruments refer to Electronic Organs, and in the development of this form of tone production, Leslie Bourn played a very important part. *The Complete Organ Recitalist* by Herbert Westerby (*Musical Opinion*, 1927) lists the patents granted to John Compton from 1916–1927; those who wish to investigate further from the Patents Office can do so if patience, time and money warrant the exercise! Richard Blake, in Part ix, p.5, of Westerby's compilation 'British Organ Inventions' lists the following.—

January 1916	Electric stop control for automatic organs
	Electric selector device for roll-played two and three-manual organs
June 1920	Electric expressive touch mechanism
April 1921	Electro-pneumatic extension relay.
	A method of making organs dust-proof and protecting them from rapid change of temperature
June 1921	Diaphone wind chest with flexible wall to destroy harmful resonance
July 1921	Another expressive touch mechanism
October 1921	Electro-pneumatic windchest
May 1922	An electric "reverberator" for conferring the quality of resonance upon non-resonant buildings
	An electro-pneumatic switch
June 1924	An electrophonic organ
April 1925	Acoustic cubes

J. I. Taylor obtained a patent in October 1921 for 'An electro-pneumatic valve seat' while A. H. Midgley was awarded a patent in May 1921 for an 'Electro-pneumatic swell shutter machine' and in June 1922 for an 'Electro-pneumatic valve unit for extension organs.'

Even as early as the mid nineteen-twenties, John Compton and Leslie Bourn were experimenting with the production of electronic tone and by 1935 they produced the Melotone. *Theatre Organ World: The Organist Entertained* (1946, republished 1972) describes this as follows: 'Used alone or in combination with pipe ranks, it furnishes tone colours otherwise unobtainable. Expression is given by the normal use of the swell pedal and by means of the echo control, the tone can be made to die away gradually thus permitting realistic chimes and vibraphone effects'. I heard and saw one of the very first examples in the organ built for the Savoy Cinema, Lincoln, in 1935, where during its construction I learned a great deal about the design and construction of a cinema organ. I was particularly impressed by the 'Melotone' which greatly added to the resources of the instrument. Reverting to 1933, the Compton 'Solo Cello' unit was demonstrated at Compton's factory, but it did not find favour with organists and no more than a dozen units were manufactured. Ted Crampton, the well-known authority on the cinema organ, gives details of the apparatus, together with a photograph, in *Cinema Organ*, the journal of the Cinema Organ Society, Vol. XXXV, No. 154, Autumn 1987.

Ever ingenious, right to the end of his life, John Compton will be remembered by his 'Cube' and 'Polyphone Bass', both of which were invaluable where the firm was presented with an almost impossible situation for the building of an organ. Such problems were a challenge to John Compton and J. I. Taylor and they resorted to many ingenious devices to overcome what appeared to be insurmountable difficulties, such as the BBC Concert Hall and Bournemouth Pavilion, to mention but two. Reginald Whitworth in his book *The Electric Organ* (Musical Opinion, 1948), provides a sectional drawing of the 'remarkable patent cube bass pipes' from which, given suitable conditions, John Compton obtained 'a very fine 32ft stop, each cube providing several distinct notes. The tone produced by these cubes is very fundamental, not unlike that of a 32ft contra bourdon in quality, and entirely free from the distressing harmonics emitted by some contra bourdons'. A full technical description together with the drawing is to be found on pages 186 and 189 of *The Electric Organ*. Another ingenious invention was the Polyphone Bass, by which eight notes of the 32ft octave from EEEE to BBBB were obtained from one pipe. Briefly described, 'the speaking portion of the apparatus consists of a contra bourdon pipe of very generous scale, mounted on a windchest and giving the note BBBB. Fixed upon the back (or one side) of this pipe are seven chambers numbered one to seven, each communicating with the interior of the main pipe by a large rectangular hole governed by a suitable valve. When these valves are opened, their carefully proportioned chambers are added to the interior capacity of the pipe, each chamber in succession (from 1–7) lowering the pitch one semitone from AAAA to EEEE. It will of course be understood that as each chamber is added by opening its valve, the valves of the chambers for any note higher in the scale must be kept open. Hence it follows that the pipe + chamber 1 = AAAA ; + chambers 1 and 2 = AAAA; or + 1, 2, 3, 4, 5, 6 and 7 = EEEE. The pipe and each chamber can be separately tuned by their stoppers...' A detailed drawing of the Polyphone is to be found on page 188 of *The Electric Organ* together with a full description on page 190.

The Polyphone bass was also used to give 12 notes from 6 pipes, in the lowest octave. Through the kindness of Mr Ivor Norridge, I am able to provide the following measurements of this stop.

Note	Scale	Cut-up	Overall length	Length to centre of hole	Thickness of timber	Tuning length of tube under mitre
C	8" × 5¾"	3¹⁄₁₆"	8' 1"	7' 1"	⅞"	14"
D	7½" × 5⅜"	3⅝"	7' 2½"	6' 3½"	⅞"	11"
E	6¹⁵⁄₁₆" × 5³⁄₁₆"	3⅜"	6' 4½"	5' 6⁵⁄₁₆"	¾"	9"
F#	6⁷⁄₁₆" × 4¹³⁄₁₆"	3¼"	5' 8¼"	4' 10½"	¾"	7½"
G#	6⅛" × 4⁹⁄₁₆"	3"	5' ½"	4' 3⅜"	¾"	5½"
A#	5⁹⁄₁₆" × 4¼"	2¾"	4' 5½"	3' 7"	¾"	4¼"

Clifford Hawtin contributed a most interesting and informative article entitled: Polyphone Pipes in the *Journal of the Incorporated Society of Organ Builders*, Vol. 1, No. 4, July 1952. From it we learn that the Cube Polyphone, to give it its full title, 'consists of a perfect cube with a mouth cut on one of its sides, and a row of holes or slots on another. The slots are uncovered by pallets attached to motors and sharpen the pitch in the same way as the finger holes on an Ocarina. The CCCC requires a cube of approximately 4ft x 4ft x 4ft and can produce as many as 10 notes. The tone is very fundamental and completely devoid of harmonics, but the effect when used with quiet celestes or angelica combinations is very beautiful. Unfortunately, owing to the pure tone produced, this pipe is not only fundamental, but temperamental, and requires excellent acoustic conditions to give its best results'.

Concerning the Polyphone Bass, patented in 1932, he has this to say: 'These pipes are quite effective over a range of eight notes and can be relied upon to give consistent results in almost any type of building, provided they are in an open position. Good examples can be heard in a number of London organs and at Bridlington Priory, Holy Trinity, Hull and the new Wakefield Cathedral organ'.

During the preparation of this book, a master organ builder with a wide experience of other firms' work, told me that Compton's electric action led the way in its day, for the excellence of its design and manufacture. John Compton had used electrics since 1909; he consistently strove for perfection and was extremely innovative. For cinema organs it had to be 100% reliable in every way; they not only were worked hard six or seven days a week, but more often than not they were sited in difficult and at times the most incredible positions. One of the secrets of success of the Compton action was the manufacture of every part in their engineering section after the new factory was opened.

Both John Compton and Henry Willis III were concerned in the development of the perfect touch, in which they were most successful. G. A. Crutchley, with his wide experience of actions, contributed a detailed article with drawings entitled 'Tracker' or 'Toggle touch' Actions, for the Autumn 1978 issue of *The Journal of the Incorporated Society of Organ Builders*, in which he mentioned the work of a number of our leading firms in this direction. As early as 1911, Compton had introduced a 'toggle touch'. We learn that: 'A few years before their unfortunate closure, the John Compton Company developed a top resistance action, which was only used in two or three organs. I understand it had much teething troubles and was not very popular with the craftsmen involved in its manufacture. However, the idea was excellent, as it allowed the easy removal of the key if required. It was a modification of their 'Shepherd's Crook' spring on a balance key, which is so widely used nowadays. Whilst on the subject of actions, a feature of the Compton cinema and concert hall organs was the sustainer, which causes 'any note or notes struck on the keyboard concerned to continue to sound' until the sustainer was shut off.

Today, we take for granted a full complement of ordinary and general pistons, all instantly adjustable from a master piston in the key slip; in the 1930s they were a standard feature in the majority of Compton consoles. J. I. Taylor was the patentee for the adjustable piston actions, and possibly introduced double touch also.

Luminous stop-heads were not to everyone's liking, particularly their non-traditional arrangement on the jambs. I cannot do better than quote from the letter from Arthur Priestley (then a director of Comptons) in the June 1959 issue of *Musical Opinion*.

> 'The first Compton drawknob console was for the residence organ at Uxbridge, ordered by Mr Midgley in 1920, and the next was for the four-manual in the Liberal Jewish Synagogue at St John's Wood, in 1926. Apart from these, all Compton organs were equipped with stop-keys until the Downside Abbey four-manual of 1931, when luminous control first appeared. Holy Trinity, Hull, Derby Cathedral, Southampton Civic Centre, St Luke's Chelsea, St, Benedict's Priory, Ealing, the BBC Studios at Broadcasting House and Maida Vale, all embodied this system, but it was sufficiently dearer than either drawknobs or stop-keys for only 'the special cases' to justify its use. One of the last pre-war luminous consoles was built for East St Nicholas' Church, Aberdeen. Since the war, only three Compton consoles of this kind have been made: at Canons Park, Edgware (the so-called Handel organ), at Holbeach Parish Church [Lincs.] and at Hull City Hall...'

Arthur Priestley was probably not aware of the drawstop console at Shakespeare Methodist Church, Nottingham (1914), mentioned earlier in this narrative and even it may not have been the first.

Reginald Whitworth, in his *The Electric Organ* has this to say: 'Mr John Compton informs me that the luminous stop control was invented by him in 1917 when models were made of the action and though used in similar form by the Estey firm [America], he did not use the idea until it was incorporated in the now famous organ in Downside Abbey in 1931'. A complete description of the mechanism is to be found in *The Electric Organ*, pp.79–81.

One disadvantage of this method of stop control was the failure of the tiny lamp after prolonged use, whilst it was difficult for a blind organist to master the system. When Dr. Alfred Hollins visited the States on a recital tour, fears were expressed about how he would cope with Estey's luminous stops. Nothing daunted this remarkable man; he ascertained whether the stop was on by the slight warmth generated by the lamp—if it was off the stop-head was cold!

In his article, Notes on the Diaphone (*The Organ* No. 9, July 1932), John Compton commences thus: 'None of the Hope-Jones tonal innovations has been more misjudged than the Diaphone. This ponderous stop however, is much more highly esteemed by the organist who uses it, than by the organ builder whose business it is to tune it'. He goes on to point out its advantages and disadvantages and then tells us how the organ builder can avoid the defects which have prevented the more popular employment of this valuable means of tone production; which usually has a harmonic development equal or superior to a robust violone or Schulze contrabass (but with immensely greater power) and therefore its pitch is very much more definite and its stride more aggressive than that of the 'Pedal open, wood or metal'. Readers are advised by Compton to consult Wedgwood's *Dictionary of Organ Stops* if they wish to have constructional details of this stop. He points out the importance of a suitable windchest, vibrator mechanism and the form of the resonator, which latter to some extent determines the tonal character. The organ in the Shepherd's Bush Pavilion is quoted where 'resonators of several distinct forms' are used to provide a 16ft diaphonic diapason, a 32ft diaphonic sub-bass and a 16ft diaphonic salicional. Finally, he points out that 'diaphones are very accommodating in several ways. They may be mitred with impunity, a fact which makes them especially useful for situations where there is not sufficient height for long flue pipes'. Thus, Cinema organs usually included some form of diaphone, while their use in Compton's civic hall and church organs is denoted in the specification. Reginald Whitworth's book, *The Electric Organ* (pp.191–193), gives a technical description with drawings of this interesting stop, and he comments: 'great technical knowledge and skill enter into the construction of the diaphone today'.

The successful provision of synthetic tone colours was the result of constant experiment by John Compton and in this field he achieved some remarkable results. Downside Abbey organ contains some very successful stops, ranging from the Pedal 32ft baryphone of stopped flue pipes of various pitches, to the intriguing melodic diapason and musette on the Choir, together with the kalophone and basset horn on the Solo—all of which are compound stops based on stopped flue pipes with the addition of mutation ranks in various pitches. The ingenuity involved in producing them from pipes already existing in the organ is a source of wonder to all who hear them. Compound stops may be found in most of the major work of the Compton firm.

In pre-war days, an organ crawl with that indefatigable writer on organs, Gilbert Benham, often included a visit to the church of St Alban the Martyr, Holborn, where he had the use of the organ. It was my great joy to revel in the tonal architecture of the glorious four-manual Father Willis, which was certainly an example of all that is best in organ building.

Alas, this famous church was totally destroyed during the war; plans were immediately put in hand to rebuild after the cessation of hostilities, but it was not until 1961 that the present fine building was completed. Comptons were chosen to carry out the work in consultation with Arnold Richardson, a former Organist and Master of the Choristers at St Albans—a brilliant recitalist and Civic organist at Wolverhampton Town Hall.

The new organ, which was installed in the early part of 1961, marked a new departure from the usual practice of the firm in that only the Swell and Choir organs were enclosed and that only one rank on each manual was extended. Tonally, it was conceived as a traditional English organ with no leanings towards the 'classical' revival. It was voiced on bold lines, some consider rather too much so, in view of its open position. It has not been possible to hear it for myself, and for a detailed and unbiassed account of its tonal features, readers should consult E. W. Gallagher's article in *The Organ*, No.169, July 1963.

It is interesting to note that this copy of *The Organ* contains a striking advertisement (overleaf) which is worth illustrating in this narrative for it shows how important the electronic side of the business had become, whilst the flamboyant design work certainly drew attention to the subject matter.

From time to time, Comptons carried out straight rebuilds (ie. without manual extension). Some of these were St Catherine's, Philbeach Gardens, London (1963); Cooke Centenary Presbyterian Church, Belfast (1956); St Mary's Church, Hitchin; St Laurence's Church, Upminster; St Barnabas, Linthorpe (a rebuild in 1954 of a Hope-Jones organ, later rebuilt by Bishop & Son), St Ignatius' Church, Stamford Hill, London N15 (1961); St Catherine's College, Cambridge (tonal alterations, 1962).

They had wide overseas connections for both pipe and electronic organs, which included South Africa, New Zealand, Sudan, Holland, Australia, South America, Oslo and Nigeria.

After the death of J. I. Taylor, Clifford Hawtin took charge of the technical side of the firm, while the Broad family gave financial support. The artistic direction of J. I. Taylor was sorely missed; there was no

COMPTON PIPE ORGANS LTD

is now incorporated in

RUSHWORTH & DREAPER LTD

RUSHWORTH & DREAPER announce that as The John Compton Organ Co. are in future to engage solely in the design and manufacture of Electric Organs, they have taken over all the Compton Pipe Organ business including their tuning and maintenance contracts, together with all pipe organ stock, equipment and spare parts.

Rushworth & Dreaper are pleased to be able to state that the majority of the Compton tuning staff are joining them.

All concerned will now have the additional benefit of local service from the Rushworth & Dreaper headquarters in Liverpool and their many representatives and branches at London, Birmingham, Bristol, Leeds, Kendal, Eastbourne; and in Scotland—Edinburgh, Glasgow, Dundee and Aberdeen.

one to 'take on his mantle' and somehow things were never quite the same. More and more, the Electronic side took over; it was profitable, and despite increasing competition from others, Comptons raced ahead for new models were introduced. Demand had fallen in the pipe organ division, and so the Board of Directors decided to dispose of this to Rushworth & Dreaper Ltd. in 1964. It was a great shock to the organ world when the advertisement appeared in *Musical Opinion* for May of that year.

This side of the business could not have gone to a better firm, but there was much sadness that after just over sixty years of organ building, the 'Compton sound' would be heard no more.

In the September 1964 issue of *Musical Opinion*, there was a note stating that Mr Michael Foley, Organist and Master of the Choristers of St Alban's Church, Holborn, was to join the reconstituted business. 'It is expected that his wide experience in the field of church music will be of invaluable assistance to the company, now that they are concentrating their entire resources on the production of electric [sic] organs.'

The John Compton Organ Co. was wound up about 1965, and for a tme it operated under a receiver and manager. The magazine *Music Industry* for July 1967 featured an article: 'Compton re-born' from which we learn that the company had been acquired by Hirel Electronic Developments Ltd. who moved their head-quarters to the Chase Road premises. Headed by Col. F. R. Peathey-Johns, Comptons were re-named Compton Organs Ltd., with the Colonel as managing director and Leslie G. Milson as marketing manager. Unfortunately, the new company was not a success and in June 1971, *Musical Opinion* featured a full-page advertisement which announced: 'As Compton Organs Ltd. will shortly be ceasing all business activities, to ensure continuity of servicing organs, all existing maintenance contracts are being transferred to The Compton Organ Maintenance Co. Ltd. which is in the process of being taken over by Mr Gerald Carrington of Great Munden, Ware, Herts, who is well known in the trade, and was for many years voicer and tonal finisher [Electronic] for the John Compton Organ Co. Ltd'.

Meanwhile, in 1971, Mr J. R. M. Pilling, the well-known Lancashire musician and business man, bought on behalf of his family company, the stock, plus tools and engaged four of the principal men, among whom was Wally Fair, who had worked with Leslie Bourn (John Compton's associate in the electronic field for many years). His objective was to build only quality instruments and to quote him; 'which Compton Organs built for me in 1969 and which had acceptable reeds as well as flues—it was a multi generator organ'. The business started in a small way in Rochdale under the name of J. J. Makin Organs Ltd. and their first important instrument was at Christchurch Priory.

On the sale of the old established family business, the organ division moved to Oldham where it was known as Makin Organs Ltd.

A fine factory and showrooms became available and were known as Compton House, Franklin Street, and with an enthusiastic and talented staff under Mr J. R. M. Pilling and Mr David Clegg, tremendous strides have been made in recent years, resulting in the firm becoming a leading one in its own specialised field, with many important installations to their credit, not only in this country but overseas too. John Compton would be proud of his successors. It seems very appropriate therefore that a small example of their work has joined his magnificent creation in Downside Abbey, where it is used to accompany the daily offices of the monks in choir. Installed in 1987, it has the following two-manual tonal scheme, played from one keyboard with stop-key control—enclosed in a neat oak case. Two very large, but unobtrusive, speakers are high up in one of the arches, each side of the chancel.

Great division.—	Open Diapason 8ft, Stopped Diapason 8ft, Principal 4ft
	Nazard 2⅔ft, Fifteenth 2ft
Swell division.—	Hohl Flute 8ft, Dulciana 8ft, Voix Celestes 8ft,Gemshorn 4ft
	Mixture IV rks, Fagotto 16ft, Trumpet 8ft
	Auto Pedal, Super Octave, Great Enclosed
	Great On, Swell on, Swell and Great On—by pistons
	Transposer, Balanced swell pedal.

I first heard this particular instrument, with its own self-contained speakers and simple but neat casework, in a very fascinating visit to Makin's factory in 1986. Its tone, together with that of one or two larger two-manual and pedal instruments, was a revelation, for it was my first acquaintance with the work of a leading manufacturer who had succeeded in producing (for the most part) organ tone of near authenticity. I was particularly interested to find that in the tonal finishing, the 'voicer' was able to regulate not only the octaves, but individual notes too. On my visit to examine the Compton organ in Downside Abbey, I heard the Makin *in situ*, for I had a few minutes to explore its possibilities in a situation quite different from the showroom. Its tone was very convincing and altogether it could be described as a little gem. Finally, during 1993, I had the moving experience of hearing it from the nave in Compline; the rise and fall of the voices and the quiet, but varied organ accompaniment, was another facet of the 'Downside Experience' which I shall never forget. Of this, I am certain—no one hearing it would have the slightest idea that anything other than pipes had produced such tone. One must of course take into account the perfect acoustics and the very large speakers for such a small instrument.

In Liverpool Anglican Cathedral is a large three-manual Makin, the speakers of which are on the bridge, with the console down below. This proves very effective for special occasions held at that end of the nave from time to time. I'm told that it gets on very well with its huge relative in the Choir! for concerts embracing both have been held from time to time, which have been a great success.

The old electrostatic system lasted until 1980, when the firm changed to a new digitally controlled analogue system of their own design, which was used for the aforementioned instruments producing vastly improved tone than that of the pre-1980s. It is now succeeded by a totally digital system. One cannot foretell the future of this. I am sure, however, the expertise of this dedicated band of specialists, who 'like John Compton are church organists and pipe organ lovers' will be devoted towards seeking perfection, ever 'exploring the possibilities of producing the same sounds by less expensive methods'.

The debate on 'Pipes versus Electronics' goes on and generates much heat; technology also moves at a very rapid pace, but I am convinced that the pipe organ is here to stay. It is not without interest to learn that Makins manufacture and engrave stop-keys for pipe organ builders, whilst the latter manufacture handsome oak consoles for special custom-built electronic installations, when the situation arises in this very busy firm

John Compton 1874–1957

above
John Compton's birthplace at Newton
Burgoland, near Measham, Leics.
The shop sign reads:
John Compton & Son, Grocers & Drapers.
Courtesy of Ivor Norridge

above
J. I. Taylor

below
St Mary Magdelene Church,
Hucknall Torkard

below
Shakespeare Street Methodist Church,
Nottingham. Photo by the Author

above
Chamber organ for A. H. Midgley, 1922. On its
eventual removal, some of the pipework was included in
the organ built for St Luke's Church, Chelsea

right
A group of Cube Basses (Compton Patent)

below
Shepherd's Bush Pavilion. Considered by many to be
Compton's finest cinema organ.
Photo by G. C. Crispin, Whetstone

above
Downside Abbey. Photo by the Author
right
Downside Abbey: a close-up of the organ chamber
below
Downside Abbey: the blowing apparatus

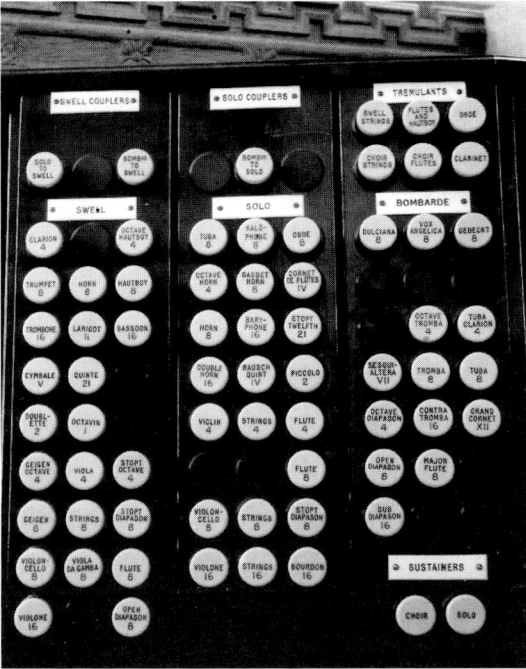

left
Downside Abbey:
Swell/Solo horn.
(Note the pyramid
capped resonators; this
stop is actually a
French Horn in
timbre)

below left
Downside Abbey:
independent mixture
ranks, Great Organ.
(Note swell shutters in
roof of chamber)
Photos by the Author

above
The Compton Unit Organ in St George's Hall,
Langham Place, London

above right
A logo used by The John Compton
Organ Co. in post-war years,
taken from a leaflet

left
Hull City Hall, showing the original
Forster & Andrews console

below
J. I. Taylor at the console of the
BBC Concert Hall organ

right
St Luke's Church, Chelsea.
Photo by Gilbert Benham

below right
St Luke's Church, Chelsea:
the console. Photo by
Gilbert Benham

below
St Swithin's, Lincoln.
Photo by the Author

above
St Bride's, Fleet Street, London.
The unenclosed Positiv Organ
with the Choir Organ box in
the background

left
St Bride's, Fleet Street, London.
The console

CHAPTER III

William Cyples Jones 1874–1967

A LEGEND IN HIS LIFETIME

T O be known as a legend in his lifetime is an honour given to few celebrities in any walk of life. Sir George Thalben-Ball was thus described by the officiating cleric on the occasion of his memorable recital at St Paul's Cathedral on 23rd October, 1980, at the age of 84. A congregation which filled the vast building greeted this acclamation by giving their hero a standing ovation which moved him deeply, for he was the most modest of men.

It can be said in all truth that in the world of organ building, no one deserved this honour more than 'Billy' Jones, as he was known to all his friends. As I have mixed with organ builders and organists in the course of my long life, the more I have realised the tremendous contribution he made to the creation of beauty in organ tone, particularly in reed work, combined with a constant aim for perfection in the end result. Inevitably, a generation of young organ builders is growing up not all of whom have heard of his name, which at first I found surprising. Yet on reflection one must remember that he was born in the age of Queen Victoria and at the time of writing it is now over thirty years since he was voicing for the trade. It is my hope therefore that this account of his work will adequately portray for posterity something of the devotion and expertise which he gave to the art of organ building, which happily has influenced those who were fortunate enough to be taught his methods. That G.T.B. and W.C.J. knew one another is more than likely for their paths would cross in the course of the tonal finishing of important instruments and opening recitals; they had so much in common: modesty, friendliness and a desire to achieve perfection in their own particular calling.

My first acquaintance with his reeds was as a lad of sixteen when I was allowed to play R. Spurden Rutt's superb rebuild of the Hunter organ at Christ Church, Beckenham, completed in 1929. I remember clearly what an impression they made on me, for my experience hitherto had been listening to the superlative reeds of the Father Willis organ at Lincoln Cathedral, and more recent work by one or two provincial firms which had not impressed me. Not long afterwards, Gilbert Benham took me under his wing and I was able to meet his friend 'Billy' Jones at several meetings of the Organ Club, visit his home and see him at work at Walker's factory, Ruislip. Then came World War II and afterwards, in 1948, we met again in St Martin's Church, Lincoln, where he was re-voicing the reeds on behalf of Comptons, of the three-manual Abbott & Smith organ there. Thus commenced a close friendship which continued until his death on 16th January, 1967, in his ninety-third year. His visits to Lincoln until the late 1950s where he voiced reeds from time to time for the firm of Cousans gave him immense pleasure. He held in high regard the then principal of the firm, R. A. Cousans, and his nephew, J. W. Tye, who succeeded him, and he soon became close to our little family: Judith, aged eight and Andrew aged two, who greatly intrigued him by rocking to and fro in his high chair at tea time! We had many conversations about organ building and I was able to watch him at work at the Cousans factory and learn much about his methods. When increasing age made further visits to Lincoln impossible, we corresponded regularly; every letter was kept and the information they contained (as well as those to my friend J. W. Tye) has been invaluable in recording his life story. On his ninetieth birthday a family luncheon was held at a Worthing hotel, for by then he was residing in a flat in that resort. My invitation was kept secret and I shall always remember the smile of affection and surprise that greeted me when we met. It was a long journey to Worthing in a day, but one of the most worthwhile events of my life.

The son of Samuel and Frances Elizabeth Jones, William Cyples (it is not known from whom he derived his second name) was born in Birkenhead in December 1874. His father, a printer compositor by trade, was partner in a Liverpool printing firm; his mother was very musical and frequently attended the Liverpool Philharmonic Orchestra concerts. Young William was a chorister in the choir at St John's Church, Birkenhead where Robert Hope-Jones was organist and choirmaster and at the age of sixteen was apprenticed to him in his newly formed business at Birkenhead. Here he spent several years in the console and action departments, during which he worked on the action of the Worcester Cathedral organ during its installation in 1896. Hope-Jones had a large and fully equipped factory and had built up a skilled staff of 100 men. An article contributed by 'C.V.' in *The Organist and Choirmaster* for January 15th, 1896, gives a fascinating account of each department of the factory. The section devoted to the manufacture of pipework is relevant to our story:

> 'The metal shop and pipe-making departments proved very interesting. The familiar patterns of pipes seem largely to have been departed from. We saw Lieblich Gedacts with curious conical growths above the stoppers. Pipes made of polished brass a quarter of an inch in diameter and eight feet in length. Pipes made of a curious looking dark metal with a dull, velvety surface, designated "spotted metal" beside large numbers of unusually shaped pipes of pure tin. Mr Hope-Jones uses very little spotted metal. For the lighter toned stops, pure tin of great thickness is used, while for the heavier stops he employs "special metal" of great weight. We chanced to see the pipes for the small (Great Organ) diapason for the new organ at Worcester Cathedral, brought into the stores from the metal shop. The eight foot C pipe weighed 68 pounds and the whole stop 609½ pounds. With these pipes before us we could not help wondering what his *large* diapason for this same organ would be like, and were inclined to take him seriously when he said that this latter stop would surpass in power any six diapasons ever made. In speaking of these diapasons, Mr Hope-Jones said: "The fashion of the day has changed. The old mellow diapason with its musical quality of tone, is discredited and well nigh forgotten in favour of the far more powerful but infinitely less beautiful stop. My chief pride is the restoration of the old soft musical quality of Father Smith and its combinations, with twice the modern power.'

This is not the place to comment on the tonal ideals of Hope-Jones; sufficient to say that he had four first-class voicers in J. W. Whiteley (head), Franklin Lloyd (reeds), J. B. Blossom (strings) and W. Beech ("the big stuff"!). W. C. Jones was taught reed voicing by Lloyd and flues by Whiteley, who had done some fine work for Jardine & Co. before joining Hope-Jones. These two skilled craftsmen gave him first class training in their art and at the conclusion of his apprenticeship he was ready for anything! Hope-Jones realised his potential and at the conclusion of his apprenticeship presented him with a silver watch engraved: W. C. Jones, from his friend R. H. J., 27.5.95, and this he used to the end of his life. I am proud to have inherited it. Three important organs on which he worked were Worcester Cathedral (where he spent two months), St George's, Hanover Square, London, and the McEwan Hall, Edinburgh. During Lloyd's serious illness during the building of this instrument, he completed the reeds and fine finished them in the hall; they were so successful that he was appointed reed voicer to the company on Lloyd's retirement. It is not generally known that Billy Jones was a horn player and played tenor horn in the Hope-Jones works band. His colleagues in those days were men who came from Denman of York, Forster & Andrews, Hull, and Jardine of Manchester who all settled in Birkenhead for a few years until the Hope-Jones firm broke up. 'Everything seemed to fall to pieces in the Hope-Jones' latter days.' His business failed and his patents were purchased by Norman & Beard whose flourishing business in Norwich employed upwards of 300 men at its peak. Billy Jones was transferred to the Norwich firm where he spent about eighteen months as a voicer; Hope-Jones went too for a time, before departing for America in the Spring of 1903.

The experience gained in Norman and Beard's highly organised factory where much fine work was being turned out was of great value. In a letter to me dated 26th June, 1944, Mr Herbert Norman had this to say: 'The Norwich organ factory was reputed to be the most up-to-date and best organised and it was claimed that 1,000 new organs were built in the period seventeen years prior to 1914. The electric action being used by Norman & Beard was basically the Hope-Jones system with the important difference that every effort was made to enable contacts, magnets and switch-gear to be quickly repaired by easily replaceable parts'.

W. C. Jones was never one to stand still (the spirit of adventure remained with him right to the end of his long life), with the result that he made the decision to set up in business as a flue and reed voicer to the trade in his home town, Birkenhead. He was married at the Parish Church of Morton, Cheshire, on 3rd June, 1903, and in due course, two children, Dorothy and Winifred, were born. Happily, at the time of writing, both are still alive and have taken the closest interest in the compilation of this chapter. His business soon became known to organ building firms throughout the country, one of whom was Arthur Harrison who eventually persuaded him to join him at Durham, to be responsible for reed voicing, Arthur himself being responsible for much of the flue work. Both men were drawn to one another by reason of their common aim—perfection in all aspects of their work. Belfast, Durham, Carlisle, Wells and Ely Cathedrals, St Luke's Church, Harrogate, St Martin's Birmingham, All Saints' Church, Tooting Graveney and West London Synagogue were some of the important instruments where the reed work passed through his hands. At Durham he designed and made a reed curving machine for the basses of large reeds; it is still there and in use. The collaboration of Arthur Harrison and Billy Jones in the fine tonal finishing of every instrument which left the Durham works, set a standard which soon brought the firm fame and since then it has never deviated from this policy. Such meticulous work cost time and money but this did not prevent the two men working very late hours at times, and Arthur continued to do so right to the end of his life, much to the chagrin of his assistants at times.

At Harrisons, the conditions necessary to his work were present to a marked degree; meticulous in every aspect of his craft he was insistent that the utmost co-operation from soundboard maker, action hand and pipemaker were essential to the success of his work. Each pipe was a carefully engineered item and he gave great care to the fitting of the spring, wedge and shallot. He was very particular about the choice of shallot scaling and that of the resonator too, as well as the correct length of the latter while the regulating slot was always carefully adjusted. The size of the footholes in the sockets was graded with care and sharp edges were always removed. The precise thickness and curvature of the tongue and its loading with felt and metal rather than brass, helped to give the timbre required. It is amusing to recall that he was criticised by some for his use of felt loading instead of the Willis method of brass loads screwed on the reed. His critics did not say that they too were adopting this method. Wherever possible he was adamant about finishing the reeds himself in the church, for he always maintained that if these conditions were fulfilled they would stand in perfect condition for many years provided they were properly tuned. This is borne out by the many superlative reeds in Harrison organs built over eighty years ago which still speak as of old. When the organ at All Saints', Tooting Graveney, was restored by the Durham firm in 1992, their voicer, Peter Hopps, described them to me as 'being characters in themselves and a joy to work on'. He has told me just one of what must have been other interesting facets of Billy Jones' methods to achieve the high standards he set in every aspect of his work there. Before commencing the voicing of a reed he was meticulous in ensuring that no dust came into contact with tongues or shallots. To this end he insisted on the benches being covered with brown paper and glue sized to ensure a smooth, clean surface. All his scales have been preserved and are still in use, being modified only where the type of instrument requires a different approach to reed tone. The W. C. Jones tradition has been handed down through Fred Howe, and the late Leslie Rowland to Peter Hopps, who proudly comments: 'The spirit of W. C. Jones and his successors runs through the veins of Harrison and Harrison to this day'.

Early in 1908, W. C. Jones felt the need to re-open his own business, much to the disappointment of Arthur Harrison. He did, however, retain the services of his friend during his free-lance years, reeds being supplied and finished on location from time to time. In 1922, when the Royal Albert Hall organ was being rebuilt, he was consulted about the re-voicing of the reeds and visited Durham to 'set the Cs of a number of stops' in collaboration with Fred Howe. It is no secret that at the time the Harrison firm was re-building the Westminster Abbey organ, Arthur tried to prevail upon him to return to Durham, but without success.

London became his base, and as far as can be ascertained, his first address was in Stoke Newington; he advertised in *Musical Opinion* and the issue dated May 1st, 1910, had this advertisement which possibly had been running for some time:

W. C. JONES, late Richardson

ORGAN PIPE MAKER AND VOICER

Church Path, Stoke Newington Green, London N.

SPECIALITIES IN SMOOTH TONE REED VOICING

A month later he announced that: Owing to the increasing demand for my pipework, I am removing to more commodious premises as under:

ORGAN PIPE WORKS, KNOTT'S GREEN, LEYTON, LONDON E.

At Leyton, Robert Spurden Rutt, who had established his business there in 1899, began a business association with W. C. Jones, their collaboration lasting until the outbreak of war in 1914. Their friendship was lifelong and Billy voiced reeds for a number of Rutt's finest instruments.

During the time that W. C. Jones was at Knott's Green, Leyton, his former colleague at Hope-Jones, J. B. Blossom, apparently was in partnership with him for a time, being responsible for flue voicing. When Casavant Frerès Limiteé of Saint Hyacinthe, Canada, built the new organ for St Paul's Church, Toronto, in 1914, they consulted Lieut. Col. George Dixon as to who should be responsible for the voicing of the reeds. His reply was immediate—W. C. Jones. Casavant's records show that he supplied the following stops, the voicing of which made a tremendous impression when they were first heard:

Pedal	Bombardon 32, 16, 8 ft unit
Great	Trombas 16, 8, 4 ft
Swell	Trumpets 16, 8, 4 ft
Solo	Tuba Sonora 8 ft
	Quint Trombone 5⅓ ft

In the course of time, reeds made and voiced from his works spread his fame to Australia and New Zealand. Unfortunately in our conversations together I never got round to ask him for whom he supplied reeds and flue work in this country. What I do know however is that he voiced a number of reeds for his friends Taylors of Leicester, whilst I recall taking him to West Parade Methodist Church, Lincoln on one of his visits to the city where there is a very delightful two-manual instrument by Rest Cartwright, c1909. His face lit up with pleasure for he recalled voicing the whole of the pipework there; from that experience alone I realised that his skill as a flue voicer equalled that of his reeds. I acted as deputy organist there at times over a number of years; no wonder this gave me such pleasure. Rest Cartwright established his business at West Green, London, N. in 1897; when the Methodist Conference was held in Lincoln during 1909, he placed an advertisement in the hand book which stated that thirty-four church organs had been built during the last five years. It also included the following testimonial from the West Parade Chapel: 'Yours was not by any means the largest specification, but the tone of your organs has been so highly spoken of, it is on this ground entirely that the Committee decided to give you the order'. I have a shrewd idea that W. C. Jones carried out other voicing for Rest Cartwright in those early days.

I had always been under the impression that he remained in London until his move to Worcester in 1921 but a fortunate purchase of a run of bound volumes of *Musical Opinion* as this chapter was being written revealed that he returned to his old home at Birkenhead, for the November 1917 issue contained the following advertisement:

W. C. JONES & GRIFFITHS

ORGAN BUILDERS, VOICERS AND TUNERS

104 Maybank Road, Birkenhead

ESTABLISHED IN LONDON 1908

Liverpool branch, *30 Ling Street, Kensington*

Specifications and estimates for new organs, renovations or tunings, submitted free.
Artistic voicing, superiority of workmanship and best materials only used.

ORGAN METAL PIPE MANUFACTURERS AND VOICERS TO THE TRADE

I know nothing of Griffiths, nor why a partnership with him was formed, or for how long; be that as it may, in 1921 he received an invitation from Nicholson & Co. of Worcester to join them as voicer and director and this he gladly accepted. Thus began a more settled period in his life; later he recalled his Worcester years with much pleasure and in a congenial environment he made a number of friends in the musical world. Moreover, he enjoyed the freedom of being able to voice reeds for the trade as and when the work could be fitted in with that of the firm and some magnificent examples of his work went from the Nicholson works to various organs in Britain.

At Worcester, W. C. J. developed his low pressure reed work which, as it became known in such instruments as Leominster Priory, Birmingham Cathedral and The Church of the Messiah in that city, to name but three, increased his already high reputation and brought fame to the Worcester firm. He produced brilliance and fire which was musical in tone and blended perfectly with the flue work; I shall never forget the impact made on me by those at The Church of the Messiah, nor Gilbert Mills' pride in the glorious sound they made. His admiration for his friend knew no bounds and he never ceased to pay him tribute. Here are some extracts from his appreciation quoted from letters to me over the years. 'Bill always kept a strict eye on action, soundboards and wind supply; everything had to be perfect before he allowed his reeds to go in. They were indeed 'his children' and on every one he bestowed boundless care and love.' 'I recall when his tuba was added to the "Messiah" organ about 1933, the case of pipes duly arrived and dear old West (Nicholson's tuner, a highly respected gent) came to help installation. Billy came in a bit late and found he had already got the tubas out without his supervision. Laurence—he went through us both 'like a dose of salts', we had committed the unforgiveable sin of handling his handiwork! Well, it was duly in and tuned by Billy and when I tried it out and pronounced my sincere admiration in un-mistakable terms, all was forgiven! I well recall his flue voicing and here again he was a great artist and a very kind "Doctor" to ailing ranks; I remember his transformation of the Nicholson in the Birmingham and Midland Institute about 1923.'

A further move came in 1931 when Walkers purchased the Nicholson firm and asked Billy to join their staff in London as reed voicer where he remained for the next ten years until he joined The John Compton Organ Co. in 1940, where he stayed until his 'official' retirement in 1945. The Walker organs of the thirties show the unmistakable mark of his work which was greatly valued by the Walker family.

The majority of the staff at Compton's were either called up or working on munitions, so that Billy was a valued member of the small team who were engaged in the very limited amount of organ work (mainly restorations) possible at this time. I recall him telling me that he did some work on the Derby Cathedral organ which Compton's had rebuilt. He described it as 'some tidying up', but actually it was some fine tonal finishing which greatly improved its effect.

When in 1945 he decided to leave Compton's, he was then an active and lively seventy-one, but felt the need to take life a little more quietly; the war years had been extremely difficult and he had worrying problems to sort out regarding his own home which took some time to finalise. Organ building was in his blood however, and so he decided to work free-lance, partly at home, at 8 Pasture Close, North

Wembley, and for a time had facilities at J. Fonseca's premises at 20 Torbay Street, Camden Town, London, who was a well known reed voicer to the trade. His old friend Spurden Rutt was quick to take advantage of his services and engaged him to re-voice the reeds at the Church of St Magnus the Martyr, London, the organ of which he was thoroughly reconditioning in 1950. He also renewed his association with his friends the Taylor family of Leicester for whom he had supplied reeds before the war, while Bishop & Son also engaged him, St Mary's, Kilburn showing some unmistakable marks of his skill. At times he was overwhelmed by orders, some of which caused problems. Nicholsons were anxious that he should rejoin them on a permanent basis; Stanley Lambert offered him a seat on the Board of Directors, 'a position which you used to occupy' and take over the tonal side of the business which was extremely busy. It was Billy Jones' dearest wish that this should become possible and was a great disappointment that the inability to obtain a suitable house in the area prevented it being realised.

During the next few years, Billy was able to voice or re-voice reeds for Nicholsons in a number of important instruments; these included a new double trumpet and clarion for Leominster Priory, in 1950, to complete the tonal scheme he had worked on in 1924; the restoration of the reeds he had voiced for the Birmingham and Midland Institute in 1924; St Nicholas, Hereford, and Hagley Parish Church in 1950. Acoustically this was a dead building and the organ was built in a chamber. The reeds were to be on 6 ins. wind, and in a letter written by Stanley Lambert on 8th June, 1950, to W. C. J. he said: 'Although we shall want to get quite a lot out of the reeds, they will at the same time require to be (like most of your reeds)—a refined blaze'. This was an apt description, but they must be heard to appreciate their superlative effect and perfect balance with the flue work. During those post war years, the use of 4 ins. for the reeds, generally speaking was the norm used by Billy Jones for Nicholsons.

Just after World War II, in a free-lance capacity for Comptons, he revoiced the five chorus reeds in the Abbott & Smith organ in St Martin's Church, Lincoln. They completely transformed the instrument, to the great delight of Ernest Pullein, the organist and choirmaster. It was while working in the church that he met R. A. Cousans, head of the Lincoln firm of organ builders and so commenced a close friendship between the two, for they shared similar ideals in organ building.

W. C. Jones' work for the Cousans firm at Lincoln has been fully documented in my book: *Family Enterprise; The Story of Some North Country Organ Builders* (1986). Looking back on those days I am amazed at what he accomplished for them, Nicholsons, and other firms under the difficulty of travelling, the transportation of his tools, the lack of a fully equipped workshop and having to leave his wife at home. Mrs Jones did not always enjoy the best of health, while he himself had several problems which made life trying. After completing a reed he invariably commented: 'this is not representative of my best work owing to the lack of proper facilities.' Ever a perfectionist, he could look back on the days when all the conditions he required were available. I could only say that no one but himself could possibly tell the difference between his current work and that of years gone by, but he knew better! I was able to watch him at work on the voicing machine and finishing reeds on site and I remember the care he gave to the magnificent Henry Willis II reeds at All Saints' Church, Lincoln, which he restored to their former glory. He greatly admired them, though his own preference was for reeds with a little less 'sting' than the Willis type.

In re-reading his correspondence to me and that to Mr Stanley Lambert, it has given me particular pleasure to recall his tribute to my lifelong friend, the late J. Wyndham Tye, nephew of R. A. Cousans and governing director of the Cousans firm from 1958 until its closure in 1974. He was a most accomplished flue and reed voicer and in a letter from W. C. J. to Stanley Lambert during 1953, this comment appears: 'You may not know Mr Tye personally, but I think he is a very good man and one of our best mechanics; there are not many of them, I know but a few like yourself'. Billy was able to visit Holy Trinity Church, Bramley, near Guildford, in 1964, where the Speechley/Lewis organ had been rebuilt by the Cousans firm, the reeds being re-voiced by J. W. T. The instrument was given the most stringent tests and he expressed his great delight with all he heard. In a letter to me dated 28th July, 1964, he had this to say of J. W. Tye's work: 'I did my best to let him know how much I admired him and his fine effort and owing to his great ability and courage he had produced a standard very much beyond the ordinary level and created something which is of the best'.

During the 1950s, W. C. J. was in great demand from old customers to supply them with reeds. In January 1952 he wrote to Stanley Lambert: 'I am being pushed by all and sundry for voicing, so for the time being I am as busy as ever'. When he had no workshop facilities and was compelled to work from home, his methods of working show the unerring skill of this remarkable man. I quote in all cases the letters to Stanley Lambert of Nicholsons and J. W. Tye of Cousans, Lincoln. 'What I can do quite well is to prepare and curve tongues for any stop or pressure and face shallots after they have been fitted in… Generally the result is very good as practically 95% of the tongues do not require adjustment and only one here and there require a touch either to increase curve slightly or reduce.' I had personal experience of this at the Lincoln works when a meticulously packed parcel arrived from him and the stops were placed on the voicing machine.

In summation of his tonal ideals it may be said that his chorus reeds had a refined brilliance which is easily recognisable today and when conditions warranted it, he could produce all the flair and 'devil' that was necessary. His low pressure chorus reeds were of distinctive quality and his work in that direction at The Church of the Messiah, Birmingham, and others while he was with Nicholsons, will always be a memorial to his genius. His quiet orchestral reeds were of exceptional beauty, particularly his Swell oboes, which are haunting in tone. His double clarinets too, the tone of which veered towards that of a corno di bassetto, were immensely effective as a Swell double reed, one of which may be heard at St John's Church, Weymouth (Harrison, 1927), which I first heard two years later.

Unlike some voicers of the past who were very reluctant to pass on their knowledge to others, W. C. J. was ever ready to pass on his methods to those who genuinely wanted to work on lines which would achieve the finest results possible. At Durham he founded a school of reed voicing which still is very much in evidence and of which the firm is proud, for it is now over eighty years since he worked there. Whilst at Walkers he passed on his knowledge to Walter Goodey who became an outstanding voicer, making a great contribution to the Walker organ. Arthur Jones, reed voicer to the present firm of Nicholson of Malvern is another who came under the influence of his namesake, while A. M. Parkinson of Eastbourne, a one time voicer to the trade, was taught by Billy at Harrisons.

There must have been others too, but W. C. J. was a modest man who rarely spoke of his achievements. It was with great difficulty that I persuaded him to set down in correspondence something about his activities for a future biographical sketch. In one letter to me, he had this to say: 'During those long periods I generally spent as a free-lance giving sundry firms assistance in many directions with their tonal problems and often giving also information to beginners, many of whom have done well in the voicing craft…' His was a well-known name overseas, for he had voiced reeds for organ builders in Canada, Australia and New Zealand. Thirty years or so ago, Edwin D. Northrup of Casavant Freres Limitée of Saint Hyacinthe, Canada visited England to view the organ scene. In a letter to me dated 12th December 1962, he had this to say: 'On a trip which I made in 1957 and again in November 1961, I was trying to locate Jones and finally did so through Walter Goodey last May. He is 88 today and living in Worthing; quite as bright and interesting as anyone I have seen. My purpose was to learn if he had any pupils who might be interested in coming out to Canada. Fred Howe of course considers himself too old to come back to the States (Fred Howe left Harrisons in 1912 to work for Hope-Jones in the USA, but due to the latter's difficulties, the job did not materialise and he eventually returned to this country). I enjoy his work very much and he has the greatest capacity of anyone I know in England'. He also spoke highly of Walter Goodey, saying 'We should like to have either one of them or both, but their situation is an enviable one. Jones felt that he was a bit out of the picture now and could only suggest one man who was at Comptons'. There was tremendous scope at Casavant Freres for highly skilled voicers and remuneration was high, but Northrup returned home without accomplishing his mission. He was disappointed, for at that time his firm had no less than thirty pipe makers and only half that number of voicers! '…we need a man who can handle pipes in all of the situations that arise, who can scale and carry through to an artistic conclusion.'

In retirement at Worthing, such contacts gave W. C. J. much pleasure, for his work had been his hobby. He missed the meetings of The Organ Club where he had many friends; in a letter to Stanley Lambert on 9th October, 1951, he said: 'Organ Club dinner Saturday evening, quite interesting; Henry (Willis) was there in good form, J. I. Taylor and Herbert Norman also spoke'. He retained his enthusiasm to the very end; in a letter to me in a firm hand a year or so before he died in his ninety-third year, he had this to say: 'I am now well on, soon be 92, wish I could go into action again and do the wonders which I think I could do now. I feel like emigrating to Lincoln, I can see you smile, eh Laurie!'

His tools are still in use in the voicing shop of Nicholsons at Malvern. They had been purchased by Stanley Lambert in 1958, who wrote to him: 'I do feel it is a privilege to have your equipment with which you have done so much wonderful work and I hope you will feel they are in good hands, for it is hard to part with tools you have used for so many years'. Sadly, many of his length rods and scales went in a flood at Comptons, but happily, his scales used at Durham remain with Harrison & Harrison.

Let Gilbert Mills have the last word: 'Billy Jones was loved and respected by young and old alike. He was a great Christian gentleman and one of those rare beings who made a lasting impact on the lives of those who knew him well'. For myself, I count it as a great privilege to have been amongst that select number. His place in history is assured as being one of the greatest voicers of all time.

W. C. Jones. A photo taken by the Author in 1950

Durham Cathedral: the organ. Photo by C. R. A. Davies

above right
Durham Cathedral. A favourite view of
W. C. Jones. Photo by the Author

above left
W. C. Jones. A photograph taken in 1950

below
W. C. Jones' reed curving machine in the voicing room,
Harrison & Harrison. Peter Hopps curving a reed tongue.
Photo by C. R. A. Davies

CHAPTER IV

Bath and Bristol

WILLIAM SWEETLAND EST. *c.*1849

GRIFFEN AND STROUD EST. 1892

JOHN AND JAMES CLARK *c.*1849–92

I N 1855, the Trustees of Wesley Chapel, Lincoln, an imposing edifice in the classical style, erected in 1836, decided to abolish their violins and bass viol which had led the singing for almost twenty years, and passed a resolution that: 'the musical instruments in Wesley Chapel, the property of the Trustees be sold, the amount to be given towards the expense of the organ'. One wonders if there was opposition from the instrumentalists at the passing of their orchestra or whether it had become difficult to find players. Be that as it may, it was decided to go as far afield as Bath, where William Sweetland was then well established as an organ builder. No record exists as to who advised them to choose a builder so far away when there were well-known firms nearer at hand, particularly in Yorkshire. The long and difficult journey from Bath would add to the cost and maintenance would have been difficult, but they took such things in their stride in those days and so they placed an order for a three-manual instrument for the sum of £250. The following specification is as correct as one can ascertain, for T. H. Nicholson of Lincoln carried out certain improvements in 1874 while further changes were made by Forster & Andrews when they carried out renovation work in 1889, 1891 and 1903. The charming case, classical in design with three main towers and two flats, was painted white and gold while the front pipes were decorated in gold and colours, the whole fitting perfectly into the style of the building.

WESLEY CHAPEL, LINCOLN 1855

3 Manuals: CC to G, 56 notes   Pedal: CCC to F, 30 notes

GREAT ORGAN	ft		
Open Diapason	8	Double Trumpet	16
Stopped Diapason	8	Horn	8
Principal	4	Oboe	8
Harmonic Flute	4	*Tremulant*	
Twelfth	2⅔		
Fifteenth	2	CHOIR ORGAN	
Posaune	8	Stopped Diapason	8
		Lieblich Flute	4
SWELL ORGAN		Piccolo	2
		Clarinet	8
Bourdon	16		
Open Diapason	8	PEDAL ORGAN	
Rohr Flute	8		
Salicional	8	Open Diapason	16
Celeste	8	Bourdon	16
Principal	4		
Piccolo	2	5 Couplers 6 Composition Pedals	
Mixture	III	Sloping stop jambs	

In 1924, it was decided to install an entirely new instrument to a scheme drawn up by the then organist, John R. Bee (later of cinema organ fame). I well remember my old friend R. A. Cousans, the Lincoln organ builder, telling me that he had attended the evening service when the announcement was to be made as to who was to build the new organ. His firm had submitted an estimate to rebuild the Sweetland instrument in its charming case; to his great disappointment, Abbott & Smith were engaged to build an entirely new organ with oak case extending almost the whole width of the chapel. Nothing daunted however, he purchased the old one, for he realised its value; it was rebuilt with tubular-pneumatic action for Zion Methodist Church, Longton, Staffordshire. Later it became necessary to move it to Bourne Methodist Church, Longton, and here, electro-pneumatic action and a detached console were added. It was a fine instrument in every way and I helped to tune it on one or two visits to Longton which gave me the opportunity to study Sweetland's stops which had not been re-voiced. In the November 1940 issue of *Musical Opinion* it was reported that 'the instrument had been wantonly and severely damaged; pipes valued at £2,000 having been torn away and thrown from the balcony into the church, by, it was believed, a gang of boys'. Many years later, holidays in the Bristol area with relatives enabled me to study other examples of this builder's work as well as that of Vowles of Bristol. When this book was planned I was determined to give a brief account of both, and with the ever ready help of Revd. B. B. Edmonds, together with a visit to Bath library, this has been possible. Griffen & Stroud of Bath was another fine builder of years gone by, a number of whose organs I had studied in Cornwall in the early 1960s so that their history too finds a place here.

William Sweetland was born in Devizes and worked for a time with George Sherborne, organ builder of 3 Half Moon Street, and later 13 Walcot Buildings, Bath. Sherborne advertised in the *Bath Annual Directory and Almanack*, 1849, as follows: 'GEORGE SHERBORNE & CO., 13 Walcot Buildings, Bath. Several fine toned organs of various sizes, for Chamber or Church, upon the most approved principles. Organs taken in exchange, repaired or tuned'.

It is understood that Sherborne moved to Sunderland about 1857 where he built a number of important organs. Among his grandchildren were Mr H. Sherborne Vincent, organ builder of Sunderland, Mr G. F. Vincent, organist of St Michael's, Cornhill, and Dr. Charles Vincent, one of the editors of *The Organist and Choirmaster*.

Directory entries cannot be relied upon for exact dates of businesses—but it would appear that Sweetland opened his own business about 1849, working from 21 Vineyards, remaining there until *c*.1859 when he removed to 7 Somerset Buildings. By 1872, he was listed in the *Bath Directory* at 4 Cleveland Place West which he occupied until 1902 when he sold the business and it was reconstituted as The Sweetland Organ Co. at the same address, with Harold E. Leach at the helm. After the take-over, Leach wrote to the musical press: 'We found amongst his papers, drawings of double-touch stop keys and various other modern improvements, all worked out long before Mr Hope-Jones or Mr Casson thought anything about organs'. (The source of this report is not known). The Revd. B. B. Edmonds informs me that an organ with some of his inventions stood in Grittleton House (built in *c*.1880) when he inspected it in 1948. These included patent stop-keys and the swell box could be opened by the player's wrist. Frank W. Haycraft, F.S.A. (Scot.) in his booklet *The Organs of Bath and District* (1932) has this to say: 'An interesting stop to be found in four organs of the city and in one outside (Corsham Parish Church) is the 'Euphonium' said to have been invented by the late Wm. Sweetland. It is something of the nature of a horn diapason, but it has a slight element of string quality, which is distinctly pleasing to the ear. Specimens are at Argyle (Congregational), 1888; Unitarian, 1876; Baptist, Manvers Street (*c*.1888); New Church, Henry Street (1886) and Hay Hill. The Argyle Euphonium is on the Great and is almost as powerful as the open diapason'.

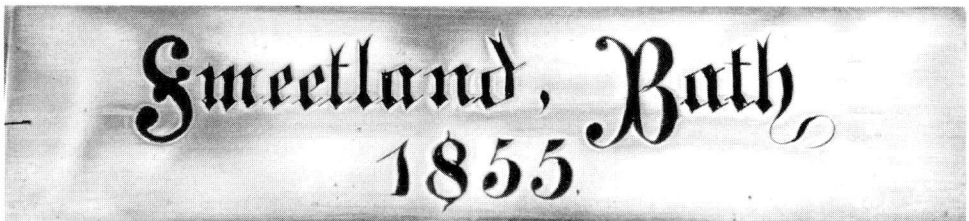

A brass name plate

GRIFFEN & STROUD,

Telephone 305.   ORGAN BUILDERS.

Church, Chapel, Concert Hall, and Chamber Organs built
to any design, and fitted on the most modern principles.
ORGANS REBUILT, ENLARGED, REVOICED OR REPAIRED.
Tuning by yearly contract or otherwise.

HEDGEMEAD PARK WORKS, BATH.

(Opposite Walcot Parish Church).

From *Dictionary of Organs & Organists* 1912

Musical Opinion for May 1st, 1882, advertised: 'Sweetland's Patent Vox Humana Stop (being the nearest approach to a choir yet produced)'. It was also stated that he was able to supply the trade.

William Sweetland died in 1910 in his ninetieth year. In his obituary (*Organist and Choirmaster* 15th November, 1910) he was described as 'one of the oldest organ builders in the country. As a mechanic he was exceedingly clever and carried out many improvements in organ construction. It was not until he reached the age of 82 that he handed over his business as a company... as a boy he showed much mechanical skill... Mr Sweetland was considered one of the finest voicers and tuners in the Kingdom'.

William Sweetland built or rebuilt at least thirty organs in Bath and district as well as beyond—as far apart as Brighton, Shrewsbury, Devonport and Newport. They were well placed to build small organs for country churches replacing their village orchestras, by some kind of wind instrument—either barrel, small one-manual organ or harmonium. As far as can be ascertained they did not manufacture barrel organs. Dorset, the Thomas Hardy country, is rich in lore relating to village church music of long ago.

I was able to acquaint myself with two examples of the Sweetland Organ Co's work during holidays spent in St Ives, Cornwall during 1959. The organ in Bedford Road Methodist Church (1936) incorporated a number of pipes from a two-manual organ by Ingram, and was a four-manual, to the following specification:

BEDFORD ROAD METHODIST CHURCH 1936

4 Manuals: CC to A, 58 notes   Pedal: CCC to F, 30 notes

GREAT ORGAN	*ft*		
Open Diapason No. 1	8	Oboe	8
Open Diapason No. 2	8	Cornopean	8
Clarabella	8	*Tremulant*	
Principal	4	CHOIR ORGAN	
Harmonic Flute	4		
Twelfth	2⅔	Open Diapason	8
Fifteenth	2	Rohr Flute	8
Trumpet	8	Dulciana	8
Clarion	4	Gemshorn	4
		Nazard	2⅔
SWELL ORGAN		Tierce	1⅗
Lieblich Bourdon	16	Clarinet	8
Violin Diapason	8	SOLO ORGAN	
Gedact	8		
Salicional	8	Viol d'Orchestre	8
Voix Celestes	8	Stopped Diapason	8
Principal	4	Waldflute	4
Jubal Flute	4	Quintadena	4
Quint	2⅔	Solo Horn	8
Piccolo	2	Cor Anglais	8

Vox Humana	8	Violone	16
Tremulant		Bass Flute	8
Trumpet (from Great)	8	Echo Flute	8
Clarion (from Great)	4	Violoncello	8
		Trombone	16

PEDAL ORGAN

		Tromba	8
Open Diapason	16		
Bourdon	16	17 Couplers 20 Pistons	
Echo Bourdon	16	Pneumatic Action Discus blowing	

I recall its number of interesting tonal colours, particularly the Solo quintadena and the lovely Choir division with its restful diapason, gemshorn and the two piquant mutations, together with the many and varied types of flutes, all of great beauty of tone.

Wesley Church, an austere, rectangular building in granite, of the old meeting house type, had a new organ by the Sweetland firm in the same year as that at Bedford Road. A large three-manual of 34 speaking stops, it has an open position on the gallery and needs handling with care, partly due to the very large Great open diapason No.1. Here again are some beautifully voiced quiet stops; both instruments are examples of high quality organ building of their time. The company was taken over by Rushworth & Dreaper Ltd. in the early 1960s.

Another Bath organ builder was John Clark who was listed in the *Bath Annual Directory and Almanack* for 1849 as occupying premises at 30 Dafford Street. By 1854, he was at Weymouth Street; then, in 1866, he had a workshop at 3 Albion Place; the last reference to him being in 1872 when he was on the Upper Bristol Road.

JOHN CLARK,
(*Sole Proprietor,*)
ORGAN BUILDER AND TUNER,
WEYMOUTH STREET,
WALCOT BUILDINGS, BATH,

In returning his sincere thanks for the distinguished patronage he has received, begs to inform the Public that he continues to produce Organs, which, for general excellence in quality and tone, cannot be surpassed. J. C. having a perfect knowledge of the different branches of the Trade, and having every part manufactured on the Premises, under his immediate inspection, is able to produce Organs which cannot fail in giving satisfaction to all who may honour him with their patronage.

N.B. ORGANS REPAIRED AND TUNED BY THE YEAR.
The Trade supplied with Organ Metal Pipes.
⁕9†

From *Bath Directory*, 1858–59

James Clark, his brother, appears in 1858 at 14 Axford Buildings; by 1868 he was at 24 Paragon, then in 1876 at 15 Vineyards; 1878, Somerset Buildings and finally by 1892, which was the last entry, 17 Portland Place. In Frank Haycraft's book, *The Organs of Bath and District*, John Clark is credited with an organ at the Catholic Apostolic Church, Bath; the Penitentiary Chapel, Bath; the Primitive Methodist Chapel, Westgate (J. Clark & Son, *c.*1881); Primitive Methodist, Claremont (Swell by Wm. Sweetland); St Thomas' Widcombe; United Methodist Chapel, Beechen Cliff; Wesleyan Chapel, New King Street (1858); Workhouse Chapel, and five others in the surrounding district. There is no mention of James Clark; it is possible that he carried out tuning and maintenance only and may have supplied the trade.

The last work of importance by the Sweetland Organ Co. that I am aware of, was a large three-manual for the Chapel Street Methodist Church, Penzance, in 1952. It incorporated a two-manual Walker of 1864 which was rebuilt by Hele of Plymouth in 1893, and a magnificent three-manual Bryceson organ of 1867, which had once stood in St John's Hall, Penzance, and had been purchased by the Chapel Street organist, Mr Hugh Branwell, with a view to using the best of the pipework there in a projected new organ. W. T. Best had been consulted as to its design and some of the most important organists of the day, including Best, gave recitals at Bryceson's factory, Brooke Street, Euston Road. Norman & Beard carried out some reconstruction and made one or two alterations to the tonal scheme in 1905.

It was decided to divide the new organ on each side of the gallery with a detached console in the centre of the choir seats. This necessitated the use of electro-pneumatic action and two new, well-designed cases executed by the builders. Dr. Harold Darke gave the opening recital on 1st February, 1952.

CHAPEL STREET METHODIST CHURCH, PENZANCE 1952

3 Manuals: CC to C, 61 notes   Pedal: CCC to F, 30 notes

GREAT ORGAN

	ft
Double Open Diapason	16
Open Diapason No. 1	8
Open Diapason No. 2	8
Open Diapason No. 3	8
Stopped Diapason	8
Clarabel	8
Dulciana	8
Quint	5⅓
Principal No. 1	4
Principal No. 2	4
Harmonic Flute	4
Twelfth	2⅔
Fifteenth	2
Mixture	III
Trumpet	8
Clarion	4

SWELL ORGAN

Double Open Diapason	16
Open Diapason	8
Lieblich Gedacht	8
Echo Gamba	8
Voix Celeste	8
Principal	4
Fifteenth	2
Mixture	III
Double Trumpet	16
Oboe	8
Cornopean	8
Clarion	4

CHOIR ORGAN

Double Stopped Diapason	16
Open Diapason	8
Dulciana	8
Rohr Flute	8
Stopped Diapason	8
Viola	8
Principal	4
Lieblich Flute	4
Piccolo	2
Clarinet	8
Trumpet (from Great)	8
Tuba (prepared for)	8

PEDAL ORGAN

Open Diapason	16
Bourdon	16
Violone (from Great)	16
Double Diapason (from Choir)	16
Quint	10⅔
Violoncello (ext. violone)	8
Principal (ext. diapason)	8
Bass Flute (ext. bourdon)	8
Tenor Flute (ext.)	4
Double Trumpet (from Swell)	16
Trombone	16
Trumpet	8

ACCESSORIES

11 Couplers and Tremulant
28 adjustable pistons
Balanced pedals to Swell and Choir Organs

Sweetlands entered upon this project with great enthusiasm and skill. I contributed an article on this organ to *The Choir* for January 1962. After a long absence, I was thrilled to hear its magnificent ensemble on a *Songs of Praise* programme a year or so ago. The quiet effects are almost endless, from the variety of tonal colours available. The Sweetland Organ Co. had every reason to be proud of their work in 1952 which was in the fine tradition of this grand old firm.

GRIFFEN AND STROUD

In 1892 two former employees of Sweetland—H. J. Griffen and one William Stroud—joined forces to found a company which built a number of fine instruments, not only in Bath and district, but well beyond. In the 1896 *Directory of Bath*, they advertised as 'Organ Builders, Voicers and Tuners, Bath Organ Works, 24 Somerset Buildings. Church, Chapel and Chamber Organs built to any design and fitted with either Electric, Tubular Pneumatic, Pneumatic Lever or Improved Tracker actions. Gas or hydraulic engines for blowing. Organs rebuilt, revoiced, enlarged or repaired. Tunings undertaken casually or by the year. Charges moderate, references given if required'. These were the early days of electric action and one is led to wonder whether they fell under the spell of Hope-Jones and used his action under licence. By 1920 they were based at London Street and by then had been taken over by the well-known music firm of Duck, Son & Pinker Ltd. (1918); a further move took place to Bridge Street *c.*1933; then, during World War II, organ building finally ceased. A pamphlet entitled *One Hundred Years of Music: a short history of Duck, Son & Pinker*, published in 1948, records 'Griffen & Stroud. The company unfortunately had to dispose of the pipe organ branch of their business (formerly Griffen and Stroud), owing to the sudden death during the war of Mr H. J. Griffen. His son, Mr L. Griffen, was in the army and there was no one left to carry on this fine old business, all the pipe organ staff, with the exception of two, being in the Forces'.

TELEPHONE 305.

GRIFFEN & STROUD
Organ Builders,
VOICERS AND TUNERS.

**CHURCH, CHAPEL, CONCERT HALL
AND CHAMBER ORGANS**

built to any design and fitted with either
Tubular Pneumatic, Pneumatic Lever or
Improved Tracker Actions,
on modern principles.

ORGANS REBUILT,
ENLARGED, REVOICED
or REPAIRED.

ELECTRIC, GAS or
HYDRAULIC
INSTALLATIONS,
for Blowing.

ESTIMATES FREE.
TUNING BY YEARLY CONTRACT OR OTHERWISE.

Hedgemead Park Organ Works

(Opposite Walcot Parish Church),

LONDON STREET, BATH.

From *Directory of Bath*, 1910

I first made the acquaintance with the work of Griffen & Stroud at the Methodist Church, Newquay, in 1938, and was very impressed by what I found. Tradition has it that it was built originally by John Snetzler for Andover Parish Church in 1772. Various work was carried out over the years by Gray & Davison (1862), Bevington (1872), and it is said that Dr. S. S. Wesley greatly admired the tone of the Choir Organ and other stops. When the time came for a new organ at Andover, Hele & Co. removed the instrument to Newquay where they rebuilt it for its new position. By 1937 it was completely worn out and Griffen & Stroud were commissioned to rebuild it with new tubular-pneumatic action, a modern console together with new casework to the chancel front, the old aisle case and pipes happily being preserved. The old flue work was carefully restored, great care being taken to preserve the original tone, whilst the new work was voiced to blend with the old, yet augment it to provide greater power for modern requirements. The new console and the interior workmanship is of the finest. The flutes, which are typical of Snetzler's work both in tone and construction are very beautiful; no wonder S. S. Wesley admired them. I quote from my article on this organ in *The Choir* for January 1939: 'The new work is entirely in keeping with the old, the reeds have not been overdone and the whole instrument is a testimony to the artistic work of the builders, who merit the utmost praise for preserving and at the same time adding to the old glory of this historic instrument'.

METHODIST CHURCH, NEWQUAY 1938

3 manuals: CC to C, 61 notes   Pedal: CCC to F, 30 notes

GREAT ORGAN

		ft
Double Diapason	old Open Nº 1	16
Open Diapason No. 1	new	8
†Open Diapason No. 2	old	8
†Stopped Diapason	old	8
Harmonic Flute	new	8
†Principal	old	4
†Twelfth	old	2⅔
†Fifteenth	old	2
†Mixture	old	III
Tromba	new	8

SWELL ORGAN

Bourdon	old	16
Open Diapason	old	8
Echo Gamba	new	8
Voix Celestes	new	8
Lieblich Gedacht	old	8
†Gemshorn	old	4
Fifteenth	old	2
†Mixture	old	II
Horn	old, with new harmonic trebles	8
Oboe	old	8
Tremulant	new	

CHOIR ORGAN

Gamba	new	8
Dulciana	old	8
Rohr Flute	old	8
Lieblich Flute	old	4
Piccolo	new	2
Clarinet	new	8
Tromba	from Great	8

PEDAL ORGAN

		ft
Open Diapason	old	16
Bourdon	*old*	16
Octave (extension)	new top octave	8
Bass Flute (extension)	new top octave	8
Trombone (extension from Great)		16

COUPLERS

Swell to Great   Swell Octave
Swell Sub-octave   Swell Unison Off
Swell to Choir   Swell to Pedal
Great to Pedal   Choir to Pedal
Choir Sub-octave
Great Pistons to Pedal Pistons

ACCESSORIES

4 Thumb & Toe Pistons to Swell Organ
4 Thumb & Toe Pistons to Great Organ
3 Thumb Pistons to Choir Organ
4 Toe Pistons to Pedal Organ
1 Toe Piston Great to Pedal
1 Thumb Piston Swell to Great
Balanced Pedals to Swell and Choir boxes
Discus Electric Blowing
Tubular-pneumatic Action

WIND PRESSURES

Great and Choir 3½ ins.
Pedal 3½ and 4½ ins.
Swell 4 ins.
Great and Pedal Reeds 7 ins.

† Pipework thought to be by Snetzler

Griffen and Stroud had a good connection, Cornwall particularly, amongst the Methodists. Wesley Chapel Camborne was rebuilt by them in 1938; it had started life as a two-manual in 1845, the last rebuild being the third in its long history. G. D. Cunningham gave the opening recital.

WESLEY CHAPEL, CAMBORNE 1845, 1938

3 manuals: CC to A, 58 notes   Pedal: CCC to F, 30 notes

GREAT ORGAN

	ft
Double Diapason	16
Open Diapason No. 1	8
Open Diapason No. 2	8
Stopped Diapason	8
Clarabella	8
Principal	4
Harmonic Flute	4
Fifteenth	2
Mixture	II
Tromba (high pressure)	8

SWELL ORGAN

Bourdon	16
Open Diapason	8
Stopped Diapason	8
Keraulophon	8
Voix Céleste	8
Principal	4
Fifteenth	2
Mixture	II
Oboe	8
Cornopean	8
Tremulant	

CHOIR ORGAN

Gamba	8
Dulciana	8
Rohrflöte	8
Waldflöte	4
Piccolo	2
Clarinet	8
Tromba (from Great)	8

PEDAL ORGAN

Open Diapason	16
Bourdon	16
Octave Diapason	8
Bass Flute	8
'Cello	8
Trombone (high pressure)	16

COUPLERS

Swell to Pedal   Great to Pedal   Choir to Pedal
Swell to Great   Choir to Great   Swell to Choir
Swell Suboctave   Swell Superoctave
Swell Unison Off   Choir Suboctave

ACCESSORIES

Thumb Pistons: 4 Great, 4 Swell, 3 Choir
Toe Pistons: 4 Pedal, 4 dup. Swell
Reversible Thumb Piston, Swell to Great
Reversible Toe Piston, Great to Pedal
Balanced Swell Pedal.   Rockingham Blower

W. G. VOWLES EST. 1858

The history of the Vowles firm is a fascinating one: they always advertised as having been established in 1814, but strictly speaking their establishment may be traced back to Brice Seede, c.1760, when he commenced organ building in Bristol. He soon became recognised for the quality of his work, with a result that the business flourished for some twenty-seven years until 1787, when his son Richard carried on for a further twenty-three years. Meanwhile, in Bath, John Smith had opened a workshop in 1815 where he remained for three years and then moved to Bristol, where it is said he married into the Seede family and eventually took over their business in 1823. To Smith belongs the credit of being one of the first to make 32ft Pedal stops in English organs and it is also said that he introduced (or invented) the octave coupler and first applied it to the organ of St James, Bristol, in 1824.

To quote from *Working Bristol: A series of sketches of the chief manufactories in the city*, reprinted from the *Bristol Times and Mirror* (1883), Smith was 'a man of genius, of large capacity, inventive turn of mind, of indomitable will, and withal a gentleman in the true sense of the term... He was a good amateur musician and early displayed a taste for the King of instruments'. Working under Brice and Richard Seede gave him excellent experience, and so with confidence he was able to branch out on his own at 69 Castle Street in 1814. 'He developed his business considerably for his organs were instruments of worth in regard to construction, quality and tone. The last member of the Seede family becoming too old to properly attend to his work, Mr Smith finished many of his instruments for him, and when, a few years after, Mr Seede purchased part of his plant and with the tools, ultimately followed the business… This employment although assiduously followed, was not enough for Mr Smith, for he turned his attention to many other matters. He it was who built the first steamboat in Bristol on the premises in Castle Street. She was called "The Bristol". She ran many pleasure trips between Bristol and Bath, carrying merchandise as well. She flied to and from Gloucester and Worcester and was ultimately sold to Spain… Another invention of his was the life-saving rocket apparatus used at all the coastguard stations… The last, and perhaps not least, of his productions was a road cleansing machine worked by horse-power… Mr Smith built the organ in the chapel of The Countess of Huntingdon, Lodge Street, which he himself played for many years. Many organs in the city were built by Mr Smith amongst which are those in St Nicholas' Church, The Moravian Chapel and the Mayor's Chapel. He also constructed the fine old organ in Bath Abbey.' (This cost; just under £1,000 in 1835; it was a three-manual instrument with pedals, couplers and composition pedals and like its predecessor stood on the screen dividing choir from nave.)

Smith flourished until 1848 when his step-son, Joseph Monday, took over the firm and carried on under his own name at 69 Castle Street until 1858 when W. G. Vowles, his son-in-law, took over the business and he too ran it under his own name. One wonders why he gave the date of the establishment of the Vowles firm as 1814; business research has taught me that such early dates cannot always be trusted. To be established as far back as the late eighteenth or early nineteenth century gave them prestige so that as far as Vowles is concerned this may be the date he commenced working for Smith. With the absence of records there are many questions which will never be answered.

For several years after W. G. Vowles succeeded to the business, he continued working from the Castle Street premises, but this building proving insufficient for his requirements he removed to St James's Square and here it remained until the present century. The increased work load meant additions being made to the building; likewise, there was a gradual increase in staff, which by 1883 numbered almost fifty. Tremendous progress had been made over the years, the hallmark of their success being the use of fine quality materials, first-class workmanship and a high standard of voicing. There was a circular saw, planing machine and other machinery driven by a gas engine. To quote from *Working Bristol* once again: 'They have built or rebuilt nearly all the organs in the city (including those of the Cathedral, Redcliffe Church and the Grammar School), have erected instruments in about fifty churches and other places in the vicinity of Bristol, have done considerable work in South Wales, extending to Pembroke, and their instruments are to be met with in Gloucester, Somersetshire, Wiltshire, Devonshire, Cheshire, Dorsetshire, Fifeshire, Herefordshire, Northamptonshire, Oxfordshire (in Oxford city), Worcestershire and Shropshire. They have also sent organs to Calcutta and several places in the West Indies, and are now engaged upon several orders, among which are organs for St Stephen's Church, Bath; All Saints' and St John's churches, in this city; Chew Stoke Church; Marshfield Church, near Newport; Keynsham Church and others. Besides building, Messrs. Vowles do an extensive business in tuning. They keep in repair and tune as many as two-hundred instruments in various parts of the country, one being situated at St Andrew's, Scotland, and another at Penzance'.

Vowles does not appear to have advertised to any extent; a search at Bath Library revealed an advertisement in *The Bristol Times and Mirror* sometime during 1883.

In *Musical Opinion* dated 1st March, 1892, it was announced that: 'The firm of W. G. Vowles are adopting the new Hope-Jones electric system for the reconstruction and enlargement of the organ at All Saints' Church, Bristol. This system admits of the Great and Swell with Pedal open being placed under the tower and the Choir and Pedal bourdon in the chancel, the organist sitting in such a position that he can hear both parts of the instrument and his choir equally'. These were early days for Hope-Jones 'electrics' and one wonders how successful this was.

Between 1958–59, I was able to examine four instruments by Vowles representing different periods of his firm's work. Buckingham Baptist Church, Bristol, proved to be a most interesting example of mid-nineteenth-century organ building which had been preserved with great care throughout the years, and apart from a new pedal board and additional bourdon pipes to extend the original one octave and two notes, it was exactly the same as when it was built.

BUCKINGHAM BAPTIST CHURCH, BRISTOL

2 manuals: CCC to F, 66 notes   Pedal: CCC to F, 30 notes

GREAT ORGAN	ft	SWELL ORGAN	
Open Diapason	8	Open Diapason	8
Stopped Diapason Bafs	8	Stopped Diapason	8
Clarabella	8	Salicional	8
Viol de Gamba	8	Principal	4
Principal	4	Tierce	1⅗
Flute	4	Fifteenth	2
Dulciana	8	Trumpet	8
Tremulant		Hautboy	8
Spare knob		Pedal Pipes	
		Bourdon Pedals	16

Couplers (operated by brass knobs working in a slot):
Pedal Octave   Swell to Great   Swell to Great Octaves   Great Organ to Pedals
Electric Blowing   Gothic casework

I was intrigued to find that the pipework of the Great Organ extended downwards to the normal CC, but the keyboard went down to CCC, the bottom octave of keys playing the pedal pipes. The Swell pipework went as far as tenor C, the next octave playing the pedal pipes, but beyond that the keys did not operate. The tone throughout was of the greatest charm and gentle intonation as a result of using very low wind pressure. I must confess that at first I was disconcerted by the long manual compass and the playing of the Pedal pipes thereon. However, it must have been a boon to players who could not use a pedal board. The effect would sound most unsatisfactory to us today, but bunches of notes in the right hand and a single bass note in the left was the technique of many amateur players in 1858. At the time of writing, I learn with sadness that the future of this fine old instrument is very much in doubt. I hope that it can be saved.

Arley Congregational Church, Bristol (now URC), at the junction of Arley Hill and Cheltenham Road, a building in the Italian style and with a fine organ case to match its surroundings, was built about the same time as that at Buckingham Baptist Chapel, but it had been rebuilt in 1938 with pneumatic action to manuals and pedal; a Pedal bass flute and voix celeste were also added and the reeds revoiced. With a 56 note compass and 30 note pedal board, it proved much more manageable than the Baptist organ. With a 9 stop Great, 8 stop Swell and 3 stop Pedal, it also gave greater output of tone than that at Buckingham Baptist Chapel, but the refreshing, old-fashioned tone and the clear ensemble of impeccable blend proved to be a great delight and I found it difficult to leave. The absence of a mixture was made up for by the strong and sparkling trebles. Clearly, W. G. Vowles was a man to be reckoned with and so I was led to examine a third example of his work at the great Lewins Mead Unitarian Chapel, Bristol.

I shall always recall entering this magnificent building with its three galleries, a superbly moulded coffered ceiling and rich mahogany pulpit complete with canopy. One could feel the atmosphere of the past when great preachers, particularly Lant Carpenter (1780–1840) drew congregations which filled the chapel and there were others too, into the present century, for Bristol and district has always been a stronghold of nonconformity. It was with sadness therefore that I heard of its closure in 1985 when the dwindling congregation moved to a smaller building in Brunswick Square. All was not lost however, for as a Grade 2 listed building, steps were taken to preserve it in some form and it is now secure, for in 1986 it was purchased by the Business Design Group, and to quote from their informative and attractively produced booklet, they 'appointed architects Fielden Clegg Design to convert it into a design studio and showroom. Because of the building's historical importance, the architects were required to work within strict guidelines when refurbishing the building and great care was to be taken to retain the form of the building and many of its original fittings' which include handsome memorial plaques to Lant Carpenter and others. 'The overall form of the building has been kept as a single large space. The mahogany pulpit and some pews have been retained… and some screens added in the 19th century were removed to restore the building to its near original form. Recent decoration (up to 100 years old!) has been removed as its decorative nature was not original. The large windows contained added stained glass which has been removed to give a wonderful transparency to the walls which they otherwise lacked. The remaining stained glass windows were a later addition and as such have been retained… Though the exact original decoration is not known, its new treatment is likely to be similar, providing a clear, neutral background to the modern furnishings.' My son, Andrew, who paid a visit to the Business Design Group Centre on my behalf, came away full of enthusiasm for what he had seen. This impressive suite of premises is open to the public twenty-eight days per year, by appointment.

What of the organ, built by Vowles sometime in the last century and housed in a fine classical case to match its surroundings? It was rebuilt by the same firm about 1951–52 with electro-pneumatic action to the manuals and pedal, the mechanical stop action being retained. When the building was closed, the pipework was acquired by Anthony Causton, who used some stops to add to the existing organ in the Priory Church of St Swithin, Leonard Stanley, near Stroud. The remainder of the instrument was scrapped. It contained the following stops:

LEWINS MEAD UNITARIAN CHAPEL, BRISTOL

2 manuals: CC to G, 56 notes   Pedal: CCC to F, 30 notes

GREAT ORGAN

	ft		
Open Diapason	8	Wald Flute	4
Clarabella	8	Principal	4
Dulciana	8	Fifteenth	2
Viola (formerly Trumpet)	8	Mixture 17·19·22	III
Flute	4	Horn	8
Gemshorn	4	Oboe	8
Clarinet (formerly Piccolo)	8	Clarion	4

SWELL ORGAN / PEDAL ORGAN

Double Diapason	16	Open Diapason	16
Open Diapason	8	Bourdon	16
Keraulophon	8	Lieblich Gedackt	16
Stopped Diapason	8		
Salicional	8	4 Couplers, 4 Composition Pedals	
Vox Angelica	8	Balanced Swell Pedal Angle Stop jambs	

To quote from my article on this organ which appered in *The Choir* for July 1963, it displayed a natural, unforced style of voicing, together with the correct harmonic development of each rank which is so characteristic of the best nineteenth-century work. The Swell Organ with its glittering upper work and fiery reeds of superb quality was most thrilling and effective and of typical nineteenth-century colour, while the quiet stops were all very lovely. 'An organ of modest resources, but a joy to player and listener alike.' What a disappointment the instrument was not retained as a whole and erected after restoration elsewhere. This is easier said than done, however, for with the ever-increasing number of redundant churches of all denominations, it gets more and more difficult to place organs in a new home.

I became intrigued by the work of this once notable Bristol firm and my pilgrimage led me to the Whitefield Memorial Tabernacle, Horfield, a church erected in 1960 as a memorial to Whitefield's Tabernacle which was a short distance away from Wesley's 'New Room' in the city centre. Founded in 1753, this historic building was closed in 1958 and later demolished, the pulpit, pews and organ being incorporated in the new church designed by Eustace H. Button of Bristol. The organ, with its superb case of Spanish mahogany, with three capped towers and two flats and gilded pipe fronts, bears a plate on its console inscribed: JOHN SMITH, BRISTOL, FECIT 1815; imagine my delight at discovering an organ by one of the founding fathers of the Vowles firm! It was rebuilt and improved by W. G. V. in 1881 and reconstructed for its present position by Daniel of Clevedon in 1960. It required a new Great windchest, electric action, stop-key control, with pistons and a radiating and concave pedal board. The old pipework was retained, the reeds were revoiced and the only addition was a Pedal bass flute. It has a 9 stop Great, 10 stop Swell and 3 stop Pedal, and can be described as a thrilling old organ of typically nineteenth-century character and beauty in its quiet effects. Messrs. Percy Daniel & Co. took great care to preserve the original character of the voicing, including the reeds, where no attempt was made to modernise the tone.

Finally, I was determined to find a larger and later example of Vowles' work and the opportunity presented itself to examine the 1891 Vowles organ at The Ebenezer Methodist Church, Bedminster, an instrument built on a generous scale in a lofty and spacious alcove in the choir gallery behind the pulpit. With mechanical action to manuals and drawstops, after a re-opening recital in 1932 to celebrate a general overhaul and the installation of electric blowing, Mr Ralph Morgan, organist of St Mary Redcliffe Church, Bristol, found the action and cumbersome controls very trying, for it is understood that afterwards he complained that he never had to work so hard in his life!

In 1959, when the Methodist Conference met in Wesley's great West Country Centre, Ebenezer Chapel was used for the Ordination Service. It was then decided to reconstruct the organ with electro-pneumatic manual and pedal action, together with the provision of new keyboards, pedal board and balanced Swell pedal. The reeds were also revoiced without losing their old Victorian 'devil and splash'.

W. G. Vowles built some fine low pressure organs in the last century and this is one of the firm's finest creations. One's immediate reaction on playing it is a feeling of immense satisfaction which quickly becomes charged with excitement as the chorus work builds up to the climax of full organ. The Great Organ in particular is nothing short of monumental in its whole conception. For sheer beauty of voicing, the typical Victorian Choir Organ would be difficult to surpass; indeed, all the quiet stops are of the same high standard.

From the tonal standpoint, this is a big organ, but all the pipework speaks naturally and there is no heavy pressure for either flues or reeds. It is built in 'the grand style' so typical of the Victorian organ at its best, with ample room on spacious soundboards for each pipe to speak. What a joy it is to find it preserved.

METHODIST CHURCH, BEDMINSTER

GREAT ORGAN

	ft
Double Open Diapason	16
Open Diapason	8
Horn Diapason	8
Clarabella	8
Harmonic Flute	8
Principal	4
Harmonic Flute	4
Twelfth	2⅔
Fifteenth	2
Mixture	III
Trumpet (revoiced, new harmonic trebles)	8

SWELL ORGAN

	ft
Open Diapason	8
Stopped Diapason	8
Dulciana	8
Vox Angelica	8
Principal	4
Wald Flute	4
Piccolo	2
Oboe (revoiced)	8
Cornopean (revoiced, new harmonic trebles)	8
Clarion	4
Tremulant	

CHOIR ORGAN

	ft
Gamba	8
Lieblich Gedacht	8
Dulciana	8
Flute	4
Harmonic Piccolo	2
Clarinet	8

PEDAL ORGAN

	ft
Open Diapason	16
Bourdon	16
Bass Flute	8
Cello	8

COUPLERS

Choir to Pedal   Great to Pedal   Swell to Pedal
Swell to Great   Swell to Choir

New Radiating and Concave Pedal Board
New Manual Keys
Balanced Pedal to Swell Organ
New electro-pneumatic action to manuals,
pedals, coupling action.

Usual complement of composition pedals

Since my pilgrimage in Bristol, thirty years or so ago, conversations with several West Country organ builders who have had Vowles instruments through their hands, have without exception spoken in glowing terms of their work and the pleasure they have experienced in either restoring or rebuilding them. In their day, they undoubtedly led the way in West Country organ building. A catalogue (undated, but possibly c.1908) is handsomely illustrated, has testimonials received between 1858–1907 and a list of some 511 organs built throughout England and Wales as well as the Colonies. In Bristol alone, they were responsible for either new organs or rebuilds in no less than 107 churches, including the Cathedral and St Mary Redcliffe.

At Bristol Cathedral we learn from the Revd. Andrew Freeman's article on the organs there (*The Organ*, October 1922), that in 1821, John Smith added an octave and a half of pedal 'pull downs'. 'He also added the missing pipes to the lowest octaves of Great and Choir, and a new bellows with five feeders. The last named were operated by a wheel and crank... There were no separate pedal pipes till 1838, in which year Joseph Monday added eleven open pedal pipes and new pedals capped with brass, as well as two couplers, Swell to Great and Swell to Choir.'

W. G. Vowles came upon the scene in 1860 when he rebuilt and enlarged the instrument, removing it from the screen to the north side of the quire in the third bay east of the tower. The consultant was Sir F. A. Gore Ouseley and the organist was J. D. Corfe. Some old pipes were retained, but a number of additions were made and the action was entirely new. Vowles' catalogue contains the following testimonial from Corfe:

May 1861

"I have much pleasure in bearing testimony to the beautiful tone and excellent workmanship of several of Mr Vowles' organs. He is now completing the erection of the organ in Bristol Cathedral and I feel confident the instrument will do him infinite credit."

The specification of the organ at this time, which remained unaltered until 1907, was as follows. It should be mentioned however, that it was tuned to unequal temperament until 1867, and in 1882 Vowles added pneumatic lever to the Great and its couplers. When Walkers built the present magnificent instrument in 1906, the Great Organ soundboard was retained, as were a good number of original pipes.

BRISTOL CATHEDRAL 1860

3 manuals: Great & Choir, GG to G, 61 notes   Pedal: CCC to F, 30 notes
Swell, gamut G to G, 49 notes (keys to GG, acting on the Choir)

GREAT ORGAN

	ft
Open Diapason No. 1	8
Open Diapason No. 2	8
Stopped Diapason	8
Clarabella (gamut G)	8
Principal No. 1	4
Principal No. 2	4
Twelfth	2⅔
Fifteenth	2
Sesqualtera	IV
Mixture	II
Trumpet (CC)	8
Clarion (CC)	4

SWELL ORGAN

Double Diapason	16
Open Diapason	8
Stopped Diapason	8
Principal	4
Harmonic Flute	4
Twelfth	2⅔

Fifteenth	2
Mixture	II
Cornopean	8
Trumpet	8
Hautboy	8

CHOIR ORGAN

Stopped Diapason (bass)	8
Stopped Diapason (treble)	8
Dulciana (gamut G)	8
Viol di Gamba (gamut G)	8
Principal	4
Flute	4
Piccolo	2
Clarinet (tenor C)	8

PEDAL ORGAN

Open Diapason	16
Bourdon	16
Principal	8

<table>
<tr><td>COUPLERS</td><td>ACCESSORIES</td></tr>
</table>

COUPLERS	ACCESSORIES
Swell to Great Swell Octave to Great	3 Composition Pedals to Great Organ
Swell to Choir Swell to Pedals Great to Pedals	3 Composition Pedals to Swell Organ
Choir to Pedals Pedal Octave	2 Composition Pedals for Great to Pedals

That other great Bristol church, St Mary Redcliffe, known and loved for its musical tradition and truly glorious organ which Arthur Harrison always regarded as one of his very finest creations, also had connections with Smith and Vowles in the last century. Huskisson Stubington, in his informative article on the history of the organs there, in *The Organ*, July 1935, tells us that John Smith carried out a complete restoration in 1829, the re-opening recitals on October 1st of that year creating tremendous attention, for they were given by Samuel Wesley (born in Bristol and son of Revd. Charles Wesley) assisted by his twenty year old son, Samuel Sebastian. It would appear from newspaper reports that the two together extemporised a duet in the form of a fugue, for a writer in *The Bristol Mirror* of Saturday October 3rd, 1829, spoke of "the stupendous powers of the magnificent instrument, upon which the father and the son were exerting, but evidently not exhausting, their talents…"! Stubington tells us that probably about this time Smith introduced a single polyphonic pedal pipe that has been described by the late Dr. C. W. Pearce and whose words I will quote (from *Musical Opinion*, September 1926, p.1215):

> "This clever attempt to obtain several sounds in succession from a single pedal pipe by boring holes in it—as a penny whistle—and by stopping these holes with *gigantic mechanical fingers* apparently never got beyond its initial experimental stage. John Smith, organ builder of Bristol, made one such pipe, which produced, in the manner described, the four sounds C, C sharp, D and D sharp… Probably the mechanism was found to be too costly; and what was even worse, the proper scale proportion of the pipe was too much disturbed thereby."

In 1866 the organ was completely rebuilt and divided each side of the chancel, not an easy task in those days, with tracker action. Vowles carried out the work most successfully and after giving the opening recital on July 30th, 1867, Sir John Stainer sent the following testimonial to the Bristol organ builder:

Mag. Col. January 24th, 1868

'I most willingly bear testimony to the excellence of your work as an Organ Builder. I have seen many instruments which have been built or repaired by you, but the best proof of your skill is the restoration of the old St Mary Redcliffe Organ. When I had the honour of presiding at its re-opening, I was very much pleased with the thorough goodness of your work, and I must say I think you deserve the highest credit, not only for the general design and arrangement of the mechanism, but also for the great care with which the smallest detail has been finished.'

ST MARY REDCLIFFE, BRISTOL 1867

3 manuals, 35 speaking stops, 2198 pipes

GREAT ORGAN	ft	SWELL ORGAN	
		Lieblich Gedacht	16
Open Diapason	16	Open Diapason	8
Large Open Diapason	8	Stopped Diapason	8
Small Open Diapason	8	Dulciana	8
Stopped Diapason	8	Vox Angelica	8
Flauto Traverso	4	Principal	4
Principal	4	Fifteenth	2
Twelfth	2⅔	Mixture	IV
Fifteenth	2	Double Bassoon	16
Sesquialtera	IV	Cornopean	8
Trumpet	8	Hautboy	8
Clarion	4	Clarion	4

CHOIR ORGAN		PEDAL ORGAN	
Open Diapason	8	Open Diapason (wood)	16
Stopped Diapason	8	Open Diapason (metal)	16
Viol-de-gamba	8	Bourdon	16
Harmonic Flute	4	Principal (metal)	8
Flûte-à-cheminée	4	Trombone	16
Gemshorn Piccolo	2		
Cremona	8		

COUPLERS

Swell to Great   Swell to Pedal   Choir to Great
Great to Pedal   Swell to Choir   Choir to Pedal

Whilst on the subject of testimonials from organists of importance, that from George Riseley, Organist of the Cathedral, Bristol (1876–99), is of considerable interest.

January 16th, 1874

'I have much pleasure in bearing testimony to your well known skill in organ building. During the past ten years, the numerous orders you have executed for me (some of them very intricate and requiring great thought and mechanical contrivance) have been carried out to my entire satisfaction. There is no need of my mentioning any particular organ, but the contract at All Saints' Church, Clifton, reflects the greatest credit on your mechanical knowledge. It always gives me great pleasure to recommend you whenever I have the opportunity, as I feel that the work will be done in a thoroughly conscientious manner and the fact of my placing the organ in the west of England (Colston Hall Organ) under your charge, is, I think, sufficient proof of the good opinion I have of your abilities.'

The organ in question was Father Willis's four-manual organ built for the Colston Hall in 1870 and opened by W. T. Best. Unfortunately it was destroyed by fire on 1st September, 1898; due to the generosity of Sir William Henry Wills (of tobacco fame), Willis built a second four-manual instrument which was completed in 1903.

The decision to place this organ's maintenance in Vowles' hands was no reflection whatsoever on Willis's work. It was purely a matter of expediency; the organ was in constant use for concerts and recitals which meant frequent maintenance by someone close at hand. It is believed Vowles carried out some West Country tunings for the Willis firm over the years. It is not uncommon to contract out tunings today where a firm has no representative nearby, and such collaborations are usually most happy ones.

With some 107 instruments built for Bristol places of worship up to c.1907, those at the Lord Mayor's Chapel; Christ Church (City); St James's and St George's, Brandon Hill, are worthy of mention.

John Smith built a new two-manual organ at the Lord Mayor's Chapel in 1830 which was replaced by a new one by W. G. Vowles in 1888. A two-manual of 24 speaking stops, it included a horn diapason as the second open on the Great. They were a speciality of Vowles and were of beautiful tonality. This organ was renovated and some other work carried out by J. W. Walker & Sons Ltd. after the war, and eventually rebuilt by them in 1962.

At Christ Church (City), John Smith rebuilt the organ in 1826; then in 1869, his successor, W. G. Vowles, modernised it at a cost of £198-15-0 and twenty years later added a Choir horn diapason, Swell voix celeste, a lower octave to the Swell, new swell box, action and bellows. Angle stop jambs were also fitted and all in all, the cost was £175, the re-opening taking place on November 1st, 1891. Walkers came upon the scene in 1925 to add an electric blower, echo gamba and octave couplers to the Swell organ together with tubular-pneumatic action to that department. Just before the war, W. G. Vowles & Co. added electric action to the Pedal Organ, a derived acoustic bass and a concave and radiating pedal board, after which the instrument comprised three manuals and 31 speaking stops.

Charles Wesley, brother of John, lived in the parish of St James, Bristol, and his son Samuel, born on 24th February, 1766, was baptised in the parish church. In a letter to his brother Charles in 1773 he said: 'Last Sunday I played a psalm at St James's Church'. The ailing Renatus Harris organ was extensively repaired by John Smith in 1824 and at intervals during the next few years, until W. G. Vowles carried out a thorough rebuild between 1872–73. At that time, the fine old case unfortunately was replaced by a new one. There were then four manuals and forty-four speaking stops. In 1931, W. G. Vowles Ltd. moved the organ to the east end of the north aisle and carried out a complete rebuild and modernisation to the following specification which was drawn up by the organist, Mr B. G. T. Wright, and Dr. Hubert Hunt, organist of Bristol Cathedral. After the war, the BBC (who considered it ideal for broadcasting) frequently made use of it.

ST JAMES'S CHURCH, BRISTOL 1931

3 manuals, 31 speaking stops, 11 couplers

GREAT ORGAN

		ft
Double Open Diapason	m	16
Large Open Diapason	m	8
Medium Open Diapason	m	8
Small Open Diapason	m	8
Clarabella	w	8
Stopped Diapason	w	8
Principal	m	4
Suabe Flute	w	4
Twelfth	m	2⅔
Fifteenth	m	2
Mixture	m	IV
Trumpet	m	8
Clarion	m	4

SWELL ORGAN

Lieblich Bourdon	w	16
Open Diapason	m	8
Stopped Diapason	w	8
Salicional	m	8
Vox Angelica	m	8
Viol d'orchestre	m	8
Principal	m	4
Flute	m	4
Twelfth	m	2⅔
Fifteenth	m	2
Mixture	m	III
Contra Fagotto	m	16
Cornopean	m	8
Hautboy	m	8
Clarion	m	4
Tremulant		

CHOIR ORGAN *unenclosed*

Stopped Diapason	w	8
Dulciana	m	8
Viol da Gamba	m	8
Flute	m	4
Harmonic Flute	m	4
Flageolet	w	2
Clarinet	m	8

PEDAL ORGAN

Acoustic Bass	w	32
Open Diapason (from Great)	m	16
Open Diapason	w	16
Bourdon	w	16
Violon	w	16
Echo Bourdon (from Swell)	w	16
Flute	w	8
Principal	m	8
Fagotto (from Swell)	m	16
Trombone	m	16

COUPLERS

Swell to Great   Swell to Great Sub
Swell to Great Super   Choir to Great   Swell Sub
Swell Super   Swell to Choir   Swell to Pedal
Great Pistons to Pedal Studs
Great to Pedal   Choir to Pedal

ACCESSORIES

5 Pistons each to Great and Swell Organs
3 Pistons to Choir Organ   5 Studs to Pedal stops
5 Studs duplicating Swell Pistons   1 Reversible Great
to Pedal Stud.   Balanced pedal to Swell Organ

The ubiquitous John Smith who never seemed short of work, built a new organ for St George's Church, Brandon Hill, Bristol in 1854 from his workshop at 91, Stoke's Croft, Bristol. Costing £500 it was a two-manual with a tenor C Swell and occupied the gallery at the back of the church. Vowles carried out a rebuild in 1874 and some repairs in 1907, when a testimonial was sent to him 'for the satisfactory way the work was carried out'.

For further reading about these interesting instruments, readers are referred to *The Organ* Vol. LII, No. 205 (article by Graham Hooper); Vol. XXVII, No. 105 (Esmond H. L. Roden); Vol. XXVIII, No. 110 (J. Graham Hooper) and Vol. XXXII, No. 127 (Edward G. Caple), to which I am indebted for certain information.

By 1930 the firm had become a Limited Company; they were active during the 1930s and advertised in *Musical Opinion* in December 1936:

W. G. Vowles Ltd. merged with that of J. W. Walker & Sons Ltd. *c.*1958, and continued to trade under its own name into the late 1960s, when it became wholly part of the parent company.

The Music Pocket Trades Directory for 1884 records another organ builder in Bristol: Jones & Co., est. 1858, of Broad Plain to Bread Street. They advertised as 'Organ Builders (by machinery) and manufact-urers of specialities in American Organs and Harmoniums, for home and export'. They were also metal pipe makers to the trade.

A brass name plate

173

above
The Sweetland organ, Wesley Chapel, Lincoln

above right
An early engraving of Wesley Chapel, Lincoln

right
J. R. Bee at the console of the Sweetland organ,
Wesley Chapel, Lincoln. He later became a well
known cinema organist

left
Chapel Street
Methodist Church,
Penzance. Photo
by the Author

above
Newquay Methodist Church.
Photo by the Author
below
Buckingham Baptist Church, Bristol.
Photo by the Author

above
Arley United Reformed Church, Bristol.
Photo by the Author

below
St James' Church, Bath

above left
St Mary Redcliffe Church, Bristol.
The Vowles organ

above right
Bedminster Methodist Church, Bristol.
Photo by the Author

below left
Lewins Mead Unitarian Chapel.
Photo by the Author

below right
The former Lewins Mead Unitarian Chapel,
Bristol. Photo by A. J. Elvin

CHAPTER V

Birmingham and District

JOHN BANFIELD 1833–1924

JOHN BANFIELD began his organ building career with J. C. Bishop in the autumn of 1825 when he was recorded in the wages list in September at 2/– per week. Here, he not only received excellent training, but made good progress, and six years later was earning £1–5–6 per week. If extra time was worked this was increased to £1–17–9. It has not been possible to ascertain from the firm's records when he left Bishop, but it is said that he remained in Birmingham after erecting an organ there and commenced his own business. In later years, his advertising gave the date of establishment as 1833. Doubtless Banfield saw the potential in the growing city of Birmingham; his policy in advertising appears to have been a simple statement that he was in business, as the following extract which appeared in *Musical Opinion* on 1st October, 1885—some fifty-two years after he had commenced work—shows: J.C. BANFIELD, ORGAN BUILDER 13,15 SOHO HILL, BIRMINGHAM. ESTABLISHED 1833. By this time the son had joined his father.

For many years the firm occupied premises at Soho Hill; it was carried on by his son after his father's death with the title, J. C. Banfield of Branston Street, Birmingham. He was listed in *The Music Trade Directory* for 1920, and four years later the business ceased to trade. J. C. Banfield died at Sutton Coldfield in his nineties *circa* 1944.

Three organs of 1878 are not without interest: St George's Church, Redditch; St John's Church, Brockmore; and the Parish Church, Handsworth, described respectively in *The Choir* for 27th July, 2nd March and 16th November, 1878.

REDDITCH.— On Friday last, Mr A. R. Gaul, B.M., of Birmingham, opened a new organ in St George's Church, which has been built by Messrs. J. Banfield & Son, of Birmingham. The instrument is enclosed in a very handsome case of pitch pine, chosen to match the choir stalls, &c., and is handsomely decorated and very carefully made and finished. It has given the very greatest satisfaction to the professional gentlemen who have tried it and to all who had the good fortune to hear the recitals given by Mr Gaul after the afternoon and evening services. The *timbre* of the different stops is exceedingly good, every stop having its own distinctive character, and the variety and purity of tone are such as to delight every hearer. The instrument reflects the highest credit upon the builders, who have spared neither skill nor expense in producing a really beautiful organ. The specification is as follows:—

GREAT ORGAN

	ft
Open Diapason	8
Stopped Diapason and Clarabella	8
Keraulophon	8
Harmonic Flute	4
Principal	4
Fifteenth	2
Mixture	III
Trumpet	8

Principal	4
Piccolo	2
Hautboy	8
Cornopean	8
Quintadena	4

PEDAL ORGAN

Grand Open Diapason	16
Bourdon (large scale)	16

SWELL ORGAN

Bourdon	16
Open Diapason	8
Lieblich Gedact	8

COUPLERS

Great to Pedal   Swell to Pedal   Swell to Great
3 composition pedals to Great Organ
and 2 to the Swell Organ

177

BROCKMOOR.— The following is a specification of a new organ, consisting of two complete manuals and independent pedal, which has been erected in St John's Church, Brockmoor… The bellows are made horizontal, with double feeders and double leathered, with concussion valves to steady the wind; the tables and upper boards of sound boards are of mahogany; the sliders of Riga oak; the swell-box has a double thickness, filled in with red deal sawdust. The case is of red deal, stained and varnished, and speaking front pipes decorated. The above organ, which has been built by Messrs. J. Banfield & Sons, Soho Hill, Birmingham, has so many excellent qualities that it is difficult to particularize its specialities. The diapasons are decided and round in quality of tone, and several other stops might be mentioned as possessing great beauty; the vox angelica, especially, is a stop of exquisite softness and delicacy of tone. The solid workmanship, the simplicity of construction, the delicate and careful voicing, the evenness of tone, and the charming variety of combinations that the instrument is capable of, are apparent to all who are capable of testing its merits. The authorities of St John's have shown good judgement in selecting the best possible position for their organ.

GREAT ORGAN

	ft
Open Diapason	8
Rohr Gedact	8
Dulciana (tenor C)	8
Harmonic Flute	4
Principal	4
Twelfth	2⅔
Fifteenth	2
Spare slide	

SWELL ORGAN

Violin Diapason	8
Lieblich Gedact	8

Vox Angelica	8
Salicet	4
Full Mixture	III
Trumpet	8
Oboe	8

PEDAL ORGAN

Bourdon (large scale)	16
Violoncello	8

COUPLERS

Great to Pedal   Swell to Pedal   Swell to Great
3 composition pedals

HANDSWORTH, BIRMINGHAM.— The organ at the Parish Church, which was originally built by Messrs. Bishop & Starr, of London, and has now been entirely re-built and enlarged by Messrs. Banfield & Son, Birmingham, was opened by Dr. Belcher, organist of the church, on the 28th ult. The following is a description of the organ. The stops marked † are new:—

GREAT ORGAN

	ft
Open Diapason	8
†Keraulophon (tenor C)	8
Stopped Diapason	8
Clarabella	8
Principal	4
†Harmonic Flute	4
Twelfth	2⅔
Fifteenth	2
Sesquialtera	III
Trumpet	8

SWELL ORGAN

Double Diapason (tenor C)	16
Open Diapason	8
Clarinette (flute)	8
Principal	4
Fifteenth	2
Mixture	III
Cornopean	8
Hautboy	8

CHOIR ORGAN

Dulciana (from Great)	8
†Voix Angelica	8
†Salicional	8
†Gedact	8
Flute (from Great)	4
†Clarinette (tenor C)	8

PEDAL ORGAN

Double Open Wood	16
Bourdon	16

COUPLERS

Swell to Choir   Swell to Great   Swell to Pedal
Great to Pedal   Great to Pedal Super Octave
Choir to Pedal   Sub Octave on Swell
Super Octave on Swell
(all the above couplers are new)

3 composition pedals to Great Organ
and 3 to Swell Organ

What possibly was Banfield's largest organ was that built for St Thomas's Church, Lancaster. Its specification appears in Hopkins & Rimbault (3rd edn., 1877) but no date of installation is given. In a note to *Musical Opinion* for June 1959, the Revd. Bernard Edmonds stated that this instrument still existed there and was 'not too drastically altered from the contents given in H & R... Further Banfield organs which occur to me are Yoxall (1868); Sacred Heart, Hanley (1891); the midget at St Kenelm's, Romsley; a large one, recently destroyed, at St Matthias, Ladywood; and St Michael, Boldmere'.

ST THOMAS'S CHURCH, LANCASTER

The organ in St Thomas's Church, Lancaster, was the noble gift of the Revd. Colin Campbell to his church and congregation. It was built by Banfield, of Birmingham, and is an extensive instrument, consisting of 35 sounding stops, comprising 3 complete Manuals, and an independent Pedal of 4 stops. The organ is enclosed in a very beautiful case of oak, made by Hatch, of Lancaster, from a design by Messrs. Sharpe & Paley, the architects.

The Pedal clavier is made on the radiating principle; and the doors which close up the organ are furnished with plate-glass panels. The specification of the above-named organ is as follows:—

GREAT ORGAN

	ft
Open Diapason	8
Open Diapason	8
Clarabella	8
Stopped Diapason	8
Principal	4
Twelfth	2⅔
Fifteenth	2
Sesquialtera	III
Mixture	II
Trumpet	8
Clarion	4

SWELL ORGAN

Double Diapason	16
Open Diapason	8
Stopped Diapason	8
Principal	4
Twelfth	2⅔
Fifteenth	2
Mixture	III
Horn	8
Trumpet	8
Hautboy	8
Clarion	4

CHOIR ORGAN

Dulciana	8
Keraulophon	8
Stopped Diapason, treble	8
Stopped Diapason, bass	8
Principal	4
Celestiana	4
Flute	4
Ottevena	2
Cremona	8

PEDAL ORGAN

Grand Open Diapason	16
Grand Bourdon	16
Grand Principal	8
Grand Mixture	III

COUPLERS

Great to Pedal   Swell to Pedal   Choir to Pedal
Pedal Organ in Octaves   Swell to Great
Swell to Choir   Swell and Choir to Great
Great to Swell Sub Octave
Great to Choir Sub Octave

Total number of pipes.— 2,033

Banfield built an organ in 1892 for Richard Cadbury, of chocolate fame, who resided at Moseley Hall, to the following specification:

LOWER MANUAL

	ft
Lieblich Gedackt	8
Dulciana (tenor C)	8
Lieblich Flute	4
Fifteenth	2

PEDALS

Bourdon	16

UPPER MANUAL

	ft
Open Diapason	8
Stopped Diapason	8
Principal	4
Mixture	II

COUPLERS

Upper manual to lower   Lower manual to Pedal
Upper manual to Pedal

E. J. BOSSWARD EST. 1847

The completion of the Hill organ in Birmingham Town Hall, during 1834, was not only a notable event in the history of organ building, but to the musical life of the city it was of the greatest importance. This vast instrument must have been a problem to William Hill as far as tuning and maintenance was concerned; today, it is difficult to realise the difficulties of travelling around Britain by stage coach, but as there was no other quicker nor comfortable mode of public transport, the folk of those days took it all in their stride. Since then, each age has taken the prevailing conditions for granted and accomplished marvels—what shall we be doing in 2,050? The coming of railways was a tremendous step forward; a network of lines gradually grew throughout the country so that travel and transport generally was transformed. Small towns and villages proved trying until railways reached many of them, but even so, a large number were left out. One has only to travel through the vastness of Lincolnshire to realise that in remote parts life must have been difficult until the coming of the motor car. As far as organ building was concerned, there was usually someone available to meet a train at the nearest station and take him to his destination by pony and trap, while hospitality would sometimes be provided by the more prosperous villagers.

Back to Birmingham Town Hall however. One of Hill's workmen, E. J. Bossward, who had worked on the erection of the instrument, was sent to reside there to be on hand for tuning and maintenance of this important organ which needed to be in pristine condition for the great musical events held there. It is understood that he was allowed the opportunity of taking private contracts when time permitted. Eventually he set up in business on his own in 1847 at 38 Oliver Road, but continued to look after the Town Hall organ as well as acting as Hill's agent. He advertised in the 1855 edn. of Hopkins & Rimbault, *The Organ, its History and Construction*, as follows:

EDWARD JAMES BOSSWARD,

Organ Builder, Birmingham,

(From Mr. Hill's, London),

Tuner of the Organ in the Birmingham Town Hall.

Organs of every description tuned and repaired in any part of the United Kingdom.

Bossward built a number of good organs, including one or two for overseas. Eventually, he took his two sons into partnership; they advertised in *The Musical Standard* as follows:

ESTABLISHED 1847.

E. J. BOSSWARD & SONS,

Organ Builders,

VOICERS & TUNERS,

38, Oliver Road, Birmingham.

Celebrated for beautiful quality of tone, simplicity combined with durability of mechanism, and general excellence of workmanship, materials, and finish.

Tunings in all parts of the Kingdom.

ESTIMATES FOR EVERY DESCRIPTION OF FIRST-CLASS ORGAN WORK.

Tuners of the renowned Birmingham Town Hall Organ.

The Music Trades Pocket Directory for 1894 records J. T. Bossward (one of his two sons), working from 80 Alston Street, Ladywood. W. J. Bird, who was one of the firm's apprentices, eventually took over the business.

Raymond D. Smith, in a letter to the Editor of *Musical Opinion* for July 1959, drew attention to E. J. Bossward having supplied an organ to Pear Tree Parish Church, Southampton, between 1866–67. His estimate, written on a sheet of foolscap, has been preserved and reads as follows:

> 'An estimate from Edward J. Bossward for an organ of the First Class. To consist of two full rows of Manuals, Two-and-a-Half octaves of German Pedals, Three Composition Pedals, Two couplers and the Following Stops of Pipes.—
>
> GREAT ORGAN, cc to f in alt.— Open Diapason, metal, 54 pipes. Stopd. Diapason, wood, 54 pipes. Principal, metal, 54 pipes. Twelfth, metal, 54 pipes. Fifteenth, metal, 54 pipes. Sesquialtera and Trumpet prepared for.
> SWELL ORGAN, cc to f in alt.— Open Diapason, metal, tenor C, 42 pipes. Stopd. Diapason, wood, 54 pipes. Principal, metal, 54 pipes. Dulciana, metal, tenor C, 42 pipes. Oboe, metal, tenor C, 42 pipes.
> PEDAL ORGAN.— Bourdon, 16 feet tone, 29 pipes.
>
> Total number of pipes.— 533
>
> Coupler, Swell to Great. Coupler, Great to Pedal. A neat case of Pine, Stained and Varnished and surmounted by speaking Front Pipes, Neatly Diapered. The organ to be of the Best Materials and Superior Workmanship. The draw-stops to Work in Cloth. The Bellows to be fitted with Concussion Valves and all Newest Improvements. The Organ to be Erected and Completed in the Church, Subject to the Inspection of any Competent person, with every Expense except Carriage from Birmingham. For £175.
>
> (signed)   Edward Jas Bossward
>
> Nov. 21st, 1865
>
> Written underneath the estimate is a note agreeing to pay the cost of carriage from Birmingham for the sum of £5, making a total of £180 altogether, and this is dated 30th January, 1866. Bossward's address is given as 229 Ladywood Lane, Birmingham. The organ seems to have lasted until the turn of the century when Gray & Davison either rebuilt it as a three-manual or supplied a completely new instrument'.

According to James Stimpson, organist at the Town Hall, Birmingham, from 1842–86, Bossward carried out several alterations to the organ there, including the fitting of a specially designed balanced swell pedal. He built a number of good organs including one or two for overseas. As a former apprentice to J. C. Bishop, it can be imagined that his standards were high.

W. J. Bird, who had rescued the remains of Bossward's business in 1888, had works in Latimer Street and did some excellent work, but according to the Revd. B. B. Edmonds, 'tended to undercharge'. *Musical Opinion* for December 1934 reported that a new private company, Walter James Bird & Sons Ltd., was formed with a capital of £1,000. The first director was Walter J. Bird, Selly Park, Birmingham. The firm was eventually bought by L. R. Fleming, who worked from Harborne and later traded for a time as W. J. Bird & Son (L. R. Fleming). Later, Nicholsons of Worcester took it over, leaving L. R. F. to manage it, but he left after some years to reside on the south coast to run a hotel.

There were several small firms working in Birmingham over the years, but their tenure is very difficult to trace. Adams of Hockley Hill was recorded in the *Music Trade Directories* for 1883 and 1894. J. Dresser of 181 Albert Road, Aston, was established in 1872; in 1881 he was at Perry Bank, Birmingham. A. Noble of 360 Coventry Road, Smallheath (1881) had moved to 11 Erasmus Road, Camp Hill, by 1894, while H. Stevenson, 8 Upper Highgate Street, Moseley Road (Est. 1880), 'Organ Builder & Automatic Organ Maker' (Est. 1880), was there in 1894.

J. HALMSHAW

Just when J. Halmshaw commenced business in Birmingham is not at all clear, but I would suggest sometime either in the late 1840s or early 1850s is about right, for neither Trade Directories nor advertisements give us a clue. I first came across him in an advertisement in *The Lincolnshire Chronicle* for early August 1858, when searching for something entirely unrelated to organs! I was intrigued to find the intimation that Newland Chapel, Lincoln [Congregational], was to have a concert of Sacred Music to celebrate the opening of their new organ:

GRAND ORGAN OPENING.
NEWLAND CHAPEL, LINCOLN.
On FRIDAY Evening, AUGUST 6, 1858, at 8 o'clock, A Selection of SACRED MUSIC will be performed on a splendid NEW ORGAN, (built by Messrs. Halmshaw, of Birmingham, containing upwards of 1000 pipes), by WM. MASON, jun., Organist, Southwell.—Admission by Ticket, Six-pence each.—The bellows of the Organ are to be worked by one of Messrs. Joy and Holt's Patent Hydraulic Engines. On LORD'S DAY, AUGUST 8th, the Rev. S. MC'ALL will preach Morning and Evening; Service commencing at 10.30 and 6.—Collections after each Service. On MONDAY Evening, AUGUST 9th, there will be a Public Tea Meeting in the School-room, and in a spacious Marquee in the Chapel Grounds, at 5 o'clock.—At Six o'clock there will be a Grand Selection of Sacred Music, Vocal and Instrumental.—Addresses will be delivered by the Rev. S. MC'ALL and other Ministers. Tickets for the Tea and Musical Service, 1s. each, or the Musical Service alone, 6d. each, to be had of Messrs. Grantham and Roome, and Caswell, High-street; of Messrs. Pennell and Gadsby, Silver-street; of Mr. Mason, Guildhall-street; and of Mr. Akrill, bookseller, High-street, where also Tickets for the Organ Performance on FRIDAY Evening may be had.

Being interested in the history of Lincoln music sellers, the advertisement below this notice was informative, for Wm. Mason Snr., of Guildhall Street, sold pianofortes, harmoniums and other musical instruments, together with sheet music. Moreover, he was a teacher of the pianoforte and singing while his son was an organist at Southwell, Nottinghamshire. At that time he was Lincoln's most prominent music dealer and remained so for many years.

The choice of the Birmingham builder suggests that Mason, who was well known in the music trade throughout the country, had been recommended by a fellow music trader in Birmingham. It was not uncommon for such firms to act as agents for reputable organ builders. In this case it could have been Sames of Birmingham (est. 1855) who did a large trade for many years in American organs, harmoniums and pianofortes. In later years, the well-known firm of Dale, Forty & Co. Ltd., of 83 New Street, Birmingham, with branches at Leamington, Cheltenham and Cardiff, acted in this way in collaboration with Bishop & Son in London.

The use of Joy and Holt's hydraulic blower, which had only been patented two years previously, will be noted. The opening was quite an event for the city, and the chapel must have been packed for the occasion.

No specification of this instrument is available, but *The Lincolnshire Chronicle* summarised its contents in their issue for 30th July, 1858; it had 25 stops and a 'splendid case of Gothic design'. The same newspaper, dated 6th August, reporting on the opening celebrations, provided a eulogistical account which gives one the impression that it may have been contributed by a local musician with knowledge of the organ.

'The organ, which contains 990 pipes, answers every expectation, and for brilliancy of tone, immensity of power and general variety, will rank equal to any in the city. The full Great Organ and the full Choir are exceedingly complete and satisfying. In the former, there is brilliancy without scream , breadth without undue heaviness and point without thinness, while the stops individually demand a particularisation which our space really does not admit of our giving in the present notice. The musical performance on Friday night, by Mr William Mason jun., was in every respect first-rate and it must have been highly gratifying to the young musician to have some of his pieces rapturously encored...' Another musical service in which Mr Mason took part was held on the Monday evening following, after a public tea was held in the schoolroom and in a spacious marquee in the chapel grounds, to which 'upwards of 600 persons including all sects and denominations sat down'. [How the Victorians enjoyed themselves on these notable occasions!] 'After the evening concert, Wm. Mason Snr. was presented by the organ committee with a valuable 8 day timepiece, under a glass shade, in token of their appreciation of his great labour and exertions, as well as good taste in the selection of so noble an instrument'.

This, the first Newland Chapel, was built in 1840 and when the fine new Gothic building with tower and spire was erected in 1876, the Halmshaw instrument was erected there until Jardine and Co. built a magnificent three-manual organ; where the one by Halmshaw went is not known.

It is important to record that Joseph Ruston (1835–1897), the world-famous engineer and founder in 1857 of Ruston & Proctor, later known as Ruston & Hornsby, and in more recent years, Ruston Gas Turbines Ltd. and now European Gas Turbines, was a member of Newland Church to which he was a generous benefactor. Dr. G. J. Bennett, the distinguished Organist and Master of The Choristers, Lincoln Cathedral from 1895–1930, was son-in-law of Joe Ruston (as he was affectionately known by all his workmen). Olive, his daughter, married Col. Riggall, sometime Chairman and Managing Director of Ruston & Hornsby. She was a pianist in her own right, having trained with her father and in London. Her intense love of Cathedral music remained with her right to the end of her life; her death in 1992 at the age of 85 was a great loss to the musical life of the city.

On the first of May 1873, the new Church of St Martin (replacing a much older building on another site) was opened. A harmonium (no doubt on loan from Mr Mason) was used until the pipe organ was ready, this having been ordered from Messrs. Halmshaw on the advice of Mason. The Parish Magazine for August 1873 stated: 'Mr Mason has made a visit to the manufactory and reports that the organ is in a fair state of progress and that there is every prospect of it being placed in the church during this month'.

The opening was fixed for Thursday, 23rd October, with a full choral service at 11 a.m., together with Holy Communion. The preacher was to be the Rt. Revd. The Lord Bishop of Lincoln, and in the evening a full choral service would be held at 7 p.m. preceded by a public tea in St Martin's School at 5.30 p.m. *The Lincolnshire Chronicle* gave no specification, but reported that the Great Organ would have 11 stops and 616 pipes; the Swell 11 stops, 580 pipes; Choir 6 stops, 244 pipes and Pedal 4 stops, 120 pipes and with 7 couplers making a grand total of 39 stops and 1,560 pipes. According to *The Chronicle* of 24th October, 1873 'Everyone in the church was eminently satisfied with its power and tone under the hands of Mr Mason'. St Martin's was always noted for its musical tradition so that by 1902 it was felt necessary to have a larger and more powerful instrument, the contract being given to Abbot & Smith of Leeds.

Halmshaw's work in the city established a connection with several villages in the vicinity. Coleby, a one-manual, was built in 1875, South Hykeham (n.d., one-manual, 9 stops) and Waddington Church, 1895—which was destroyed when the village was bombed during World War II. Coleby gives forth a very pleasant sound, but now requires restoration. South Hykeham was restored in 1993 by Cousans Organs.

The only alteration was the spraying with gold paint of the front pipes which were formerly diapered. It contains the following stops, which are all enclosed, except the diapason. 56 note compass; open diapason, treble (to tenor C); open diapason, bass; gamba 8; rohr flute 8; stopped diapason (lowest octave); principal 4; fifteenth 2. Pedal, bourdon. Pedal coupler. A 29–note straight pedal board, trigger swell pedal. No composition pedals. Electric blowing. A brass name-plate is engraved 'HALMSHAW, ORGAN BUILDERS, BIRMINGHAM'. It is a delightful little instrument and the thoroughness of the conservation work carried out should ensure a further long life.

Two early Halmshaw organs are mentioned in *The Musical Standard*. The issue dated 20th April 1867 records the opening of a new organ at Upper Hanley:

> On Tuesday evening, the 9th inst., a new organ provided for Providence Chapel, Upper Hanley (Co. Stafford), was opened by Mr Stimpson, of Birmingham. It has been built by Messrs. J. Halmshaw & Sons, of Birmingham, at a cost of £180. The following is a synopsis of the instrument… it contains two full sets of keys. Compass, CC to F in alt.—

GREAT ORGAN	ft	SWELL ORGAN	
Open Diapason	8	Open Diapason	8
Stopped Diapason and Clarabella	8	Gedact	8
Dulciana	8	Principal	4
Wald Flute	4	Cornopean	8
Principal	4	Oboe	8
Fifteenth	2	PEDAL ORGAN	
Mixture	II	Bourdon	16

Two years later, on 25th December, 1869, there is further news of the firm's work:

> BIRMINGHAM.— An organ has been built by Halmshaw & Sons, from the specification of Mr J. J. Mathews, of Cotes Hall, for St Nicholas' Free and Open Church. Our correspondent describes the tone of the instrument as "very satisfactory".—

GREAT ORGAN	ft		
Open Diapason	8	Principal	4
Claribel	8	Oboe	8
Dulciana (lower octave from Claribel)	8	PEDAL ORGAN	
Wald Flute	4	Bourdon	16
Principal	4		
Fifteenth	2	COUPLERS	
SWELL ORGAN		Great to Pedal Swell to Pedal Swell to Great	
Open Diapason	8	3 combination pedals	
Stopped Diapason	8		

Their successful work in Lincolnshire led them to advertise in *The Lincoln Diocesan Calendar* for 1888, and is reproduced on the facing page. The John Compton Organ Co. Ltd., who had knowledge of Halmshaw's work from their founder, wrote to *Musical Opinion* for April 1950 as follows:

> 'The Halmshaw firm built a good number of organs in several Yorkshire towns. Some were fairly large. Those in the Birmingham district were mostly smaller and of no particular merit. There was, however, one (at King's Norton perhaps) that Henry Halmshaw, son of the founder of the firm, built for his own use about seventy or eighty years ago. It had only one pedal stop of large-scaled, open pipes, lightly blown but very effective. The swell had nothing but a couple of 8fts, 4ft, mixture and two or three reeds; but the Great was dignified and impressive, having a 16 ft metal open, two 8 fts, 4ft, 2ft, four-rank mixture and one or two reeds. In later

years he built a more pretentious organ of four manuals at Sparkhill, but it was not more worthy than much of his earlier work; and at Edgbaston he made sparing use of extension and tubular-pneumatic action. The business changed hands at the close of the century, but a nephew continued to operate as a metal pipe-maker at another address for several years'.

Referring to Yorkshire, they built a three-manual instrument in 1881 for St James's Church, Halifax, with thirty speaking stops, and back to Birmingham, the predecessor of the Nicholson organ in The Church of The Messiah, was by Halmshaw, 1862. They built one organ for overseas: Christchurch R.C. Cathedral, New Zealand, ordered a small three-manual, with tracker action and wind pressure of 3¼ ins.

The Revd. B. B. Edmonds, in a letter to me, described the organ at Sparkhill Primitive Methodist Church (1896) as the firm's *magnum opus*. By then it had become J. Halmshaw & Sons. The following, taken from *The Musical Standard*, 1897, was its specification:

PRIMITIVE METHODIST CHURCH, SPARKHILL 1896

SPARKHILL.— Dr. T. W. Dodds, at opening of new organ in the Primitive Methodist Church, Feb. 17th.— Grand Sonata in G minor, Op. 11 (Otto Dienel); Pastorale in A major (Guilmant); Fugue in D major (Bach); Andante in G (Batiste); Festive March (Smart); Grand fantasia, "The Storm" (Lemmens); Offertoire in F minor (Batiste); Flute Concerto in F (Rink); Postlude in D (Lemmens). The following is the synopsis of the organ, built by Messrs. Halmshaw and Sons, Camp Hill, Birmingham.—

GREAT ORGAN	ft	SWELL ORGAN	
		Bourdon	16
Double Open Diapason	16	Open Diapason	8
Open Diapason	8	Lieblich Gedact	8
Stop Diapason and Clarabel	8	Salicional	8
Principal	4	Vox Celeste	8
Wald Flute	4	Principal	4
Fifteenth	2	Harmonic Flute	4
Mixture	IV	Mixture, various	II
Trumpet	8	Cornopean	8
		Hautboy	8

CHOIR ORGAN		COUPLERS
Dolce	8	Swell to Great Choir to Great Solo to Great
Clarabella	8	Sub Octave Great to Pedals Swell to Pedals
Gemshorn	4	Choir to Pedals Solo to Pedals
Clarionet Flute	4	
Piccolo	2	ACCESSORIES
Cremona and Bassoon	8	3 composition pedals to Great Organs stops
SOLO ORGAN		3 pneumatic pistons to Swell Organ
Orchestral Oboe	8	1 pneumatic piston to Tuba
Flute Harmonique	4	1 pedal for Swell Organ
Tuba	8	1 pedal for Solo Organ
PEDAL ORGAN		SUMMARY
Open Diapason	16	The organ has four manuals, with 40 Stops,
Bourdon	16	containing 1,874 Pipes. 4 Bellows supply wind to
Violoncello	8	each Organ. The Solo Organ and Pedal Organ are
Quint	10⅔	worked upon an Improved System of Tubular
Flute Bass	8	Pneumatics throughout. Solo on 10 ins. wind.

Their work, I gather, was quite prolific, some of it 'quite good, some pedestrian'. The business was purchased by F. W. Ebral *c.*1902 who ran it under his own name from 193–4 Camp Hill, Birmingham. It ceased (like several others) just after the end of World War I.

Two other members of the Halmshaw family were pipe makers and voicers. They advertised in *Musical Opinion* in the late 1890s and early 1900s as follows. It is not known just when they ceased to trade.

HAWKINS (ORGAN BUILDERS) LTD.

Formerly of Walsall Wood, now at Lichfield   Est. 1913

This firm can boast a direct connection with Charles Henry Nicholson, founder of Nicholson & Lord, for W. Hawkins was foreman of that firm until his retirement, *c.*1910–12. His eldest son, Ernest, worked for Nicholson & Lord until the business began to decline, when he left to join the staff of Rogers at Stoke-on-Trent in the Potteries, before returning to Walsall to establish his own firm in 1913, which was known as W. Hawkins & Son. Then came along T. Benyon, who, after serving his apprenticeship with Whiteleys of Chester, moved to Nicholson & Lord as an improver at the age of twenty. He lodged with the Hawkins family, and being of the same age as Ernest, the two became close friends. In 1913, he was appointed works foreman at Norman & Beard's in Norwich until war service cut short his career for a time. On the amalgamation of Norman & Beard with Wm. Hill & Son at London, Benyon became Midland Representative for the firm and once again resided in Walsall where he resumed his friendship with Ernest Hawkins. Eventually, they agreed to become partners and operated from Paddock Lane for a time, followed by Dudley Street and finally to John Street, until a further move in 1946 to Walsall Wood. At the close of World War II, F. H. Hawkins, grandson of W. H., who had worked for a time with his uncle E. H. H., rejoined the firm as voicer and tuner as well as having experience in general organ building. An excellent management team was thus built up.

H. A. Benyon joined the firm in 1929, much to his father's disappointment, but he was determined to become an organ builder when he left school and after seven years at Walsall decided to gain further experience with Osmonds of Taunton. Here, discipline was good and working conditions were excellent; there was no 'slacking' as everyone was under the watchful eye of Herbert Watts! His stay there was only for a year after which he returned to Hawkins, who by that time had secured the sub-contract work at Walsall Town Hall, when The John Compton Organ Co. rebuilt the organ.

World War II caused further disruption, for H. A. Benyon joined the RAF serving two years in this country and a further four in the Western Desert. Back home in 1947 and with no intention of returning to organ building, he had only been home for a day, when E. H. Hawkins (who felt the need for retirement) asked if he would become a partner with F. H. H. He agreed, for there was a strong wish that the long association of the two families should continue. Walsall Wood became their base until 1980 when the business removed to its present home in Lichfield, and at this time H. A. Benyon decided to retire.

I first became acquainted with Hawkins' work after they had restored the magnificent three-manual Father Willis (1877) organ at All Saints' Church, Hastings, in the late 1960s. This was a very thorough restoration, replacing all tracker wires, buttons and felts, re-centering of lever beams and re-bushing of roller boards etc. Great care was taken with the pipework to ensure that it remained 'Father Willis'; it was all carefully regulated and I was most impressed by Hawkins' skilled attention to the whole organ.

In 1980 I was called in to advise the parochial church council of St Bartholomew's Church, Wednesbury, regarding the replacement of their organ. An excellent organ, built by Peter Conacher in 1876 and later rebuilt by Nicholson & Lord, in the redundant Church of Christ Church, West Bromwich, was available for disposal and I was able to hear it before dismantling commenced. It was a fine instrument and ideal for rebuilding with a detached console in its proposed situation at St Bartholomew's. Hawkins, then of Walsall Wood, were most helpful; the organ was temporarily stored and only a short time afterwards, Christ Church was burned down by vandals. Had there been any delay in making a decision about the instrument's future, it too would have gone up in flames. As in all their work, the firm took great pride in carrying out this contract on home ground. The handsome detached console of English oak with black panels and ivory headed drawstops enables the player to hear and see what is going on in this church with its strong musical traditions. There was some tonal re-modelling and provision made for several additional stops. The opening recital on 23rd September, 1980, was given by Harold Britton, Borough Organist to the Walsall Corporation from 1957. His recitals on the Town Hall instrument are an important feature of the town, as were T. W. North's before him. He is also in great demand elsewhere as a recitalist, including St Paul's Cathedral; Birmingham Town Hall; All Souls', Langham Place, London and with Carlo Curley on his electronic organ at the Alexandra Palace, to name but a few in recent years.

ST BARTHOLOMEW'S CHURCH, WEDNESBURY 1980

3 manuals: CC to G, 56 notes   Pedal: CCC to F, 30 notes

GREAT ORGAN	ft		
Bourdon	16	Principal	4
Open Diapason	8	Rohr Flute	4
Stopped Diapason	8	Mixture	II
Principal	4	Horn	8
Fifteenth	2	Oboe	8
Mixture	III		
Trumpet	8	CHOIR ORGAN	
		Dulciana	8
SWELL ORGAN		Gedact	8
		Flute	4
Hohl Flute	8	Piccolo	2
Salicional	8	Cremona	8
Voix Celeste	8		

PEDAL ORGAN		ACCESSORIES
Open Diapason	16	13 thumb pistons 9 toe pistons
Sub Bass	16	10 couplers
Bourdon (from Great)	16	Electro-pneumatic action, detached console
Principal	8	
Bass Flute	8	
Fifteenth (ext. Principal)	4	
Mixture	III	
Trombone	16	
Trumpet	8	

The new instrument was a great success and fully bore out Gilbert Mills' claim in a letter to me some years ago: 'Hawkins carry on the old traditions of Nicholson & Lord and have done much work for me with all satisfaction'.

A fine rebuild of the two-manual Walker organ in All Saints' Parish Church, Claverley, in the Diocese of Hereford, was carried out by Hawkins, in consultation with Roger Fisher, then Assistant Organist at Hereford Cathedral, now at Chester Cathedral. In the extending of the Great chorus work, the new was carefully blended with the original Walker flue work, to produce a clear and balanced ensemble. The new console and action is electro-pneumatic. The specification of this fine and versatile instrument is as follows:

ALL SAINTS' PARISH CHURCH, CLAVERLEY

2 manuals: CC to A, 58 notes   Pedal: CCC to F, 30 notes

GREAT ORGAN	ft		
Bourdon	16	Mixture	III
Open Diapason	8	Double Trumpet	16
Dulciana	8	Tromba	8
Wald Flute	8	Trumpet	8
Principal	4	Clarion	4
Flute	4	Octave Tromba	4
Twelfth	2⅔		
Fifteenth	2	PEDAL ORGAN	
Mixture	II	Acoustic Bass	32
Tromba	8	Violone	16
Octave Tromba	4	Bourdon	16
		Violoncello	8
SWELL ORGAN		Bass Flute	8
		Superoctave	4
Stopped Diapason	8	Flute	4
Gamba	8	Octavin	2
Voix Celeste	8	Trombone	16
Principal	4	Tromba	8
Spitzflute	4	Octave Tromba	4

The business continues successfully from Lichfield. Its reputation for thoroughness is evidenced by its large tuning connection—some 300–400 instruments—in various parts of the country.

The Town Hall, Birmingham, as it appeared in 1934.
From *The Birmingham Town Hall 1834–1934*

above
An early engraving of the interior of Birmingham Town
Hall, taken from *The Birmingham Town Hall 1834–1934*.
Architect: Joseph Aloysius Hanson, 1803–1882

below left
The Parish Church, Dudley. Rebuilt by Hawkins & Son

below right
Coleby Church, Lincs. Organ by
Halmshaw. I am a great admirer of the
Victorian organs, but a number of organ
builders were responsible for ugly 'pipe
racks' which hardly could be called
cases. This example (which stands out
into the chancel of this lovely church) is
one of the worst examples known to
me. Photo by the Author, 1992

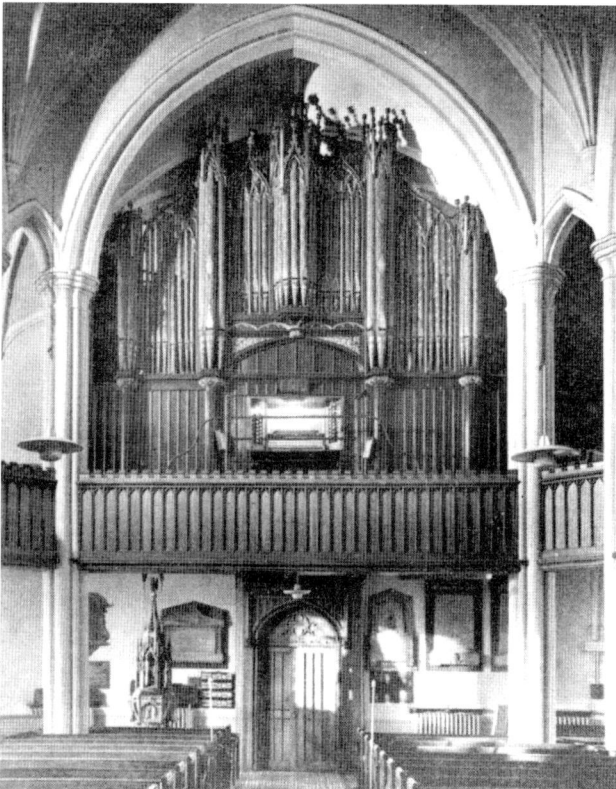

CHAPTER VI

Walsall

NICHOLSON AND LORD 1816–c.1950

IN about 1862, Maria Nicholson and her son, Charles Henry, moved the family organ building business at Rochdale, founded by her husband Richard (born c.1791, died c.1861), to the rapidly growing town of Walsall in the West Midlands. Maria was Richard's second wife, and had been a great help to her husband running the firm which he founded at Rochdale in 1816. She felt so confident in seeking pastures new that she and her able young son, who then was twenty-one, could make a success of the business to which she gave the name Nicholson & Son. She was quite correct in her surmise and from the commencement of the new enterprise which combined the sale of pianofortes, harmoniums and sheet music with organ building, it never looked back. Trading from The Bridge, Walsall, by 1869, they advertised locally as follows:

THE BRIDGE, WALSALL.

NICHOLSON & SON,
ORGAN BUILDERS,
Pianoforte and Harmonium Dealers,
AND GENERAL MUSIC SELLERS,

Take this opportunity of thanking their friends and the public for the very liberal patronage they have received, and to inform them that they have just fitted up a commodious SHOW ROOM, which enables them to display a larger and more varied Stock of Instruments than they have hitherto done. Having a practical knowledge of Muscial Instruments (the result of many years' experience in the Manufacture of Organs, &c.,) they are in a position to select the choicest of Instruments by the best makers.

NEW PIANOFORTES by the best London makers, from Twenty Guineas.

NEW HARMONIUMS by Alexandre, Cæsarini, and the best English Makers, from Six Guineas.

Second-hand PIANOS and HARMONIUMS, at all prices.

PIANOFORTES and HARMONIUMS FOR HIRE, on reasonable terms; also Tuned and Repaired.

N. and Son beg to call attention to the

SHEET MUSIC DEPARTMENT,

which is always kept fresh with the latest novelties. Above Ten Thousand Pieces to select from at half-price; and for some of the Non-Copyright Pieces a discount of 10 per cent. will be taken off, half-price for cash payment. Music sent out for selection.

N. and Son beg to add that they have engaged the services of a first-class Pianoforte Tuner (from one of the largest manufactories), who will visit periodically the out-lying districts of Bloxwich, Cannock, Hednesford, Pelsall, Great Barr, &c., and the towns of Wednesbury, Willenhall, Darlaston, &c.

ORGANS BUILT, REPAIRED, AND TUNED.
A List of more than 250 Organs already erected, with Testimonials annexed, sent post free.
Specifications and Estimates forwarded on application.

The list of course would mainly be concerned with organs built at Rochdale. The four brothers: Charles Henry at Walsall, John at Bradford, Thomas Haigh at Lincoln and James at Newcastle-upon-Tyne, all combined the sale of musical instruments and sheet music with organ building in their early days; other examples could be cited elsewhere for it undoubtedly provided a steady income whilst endeavouring to make a name for themselves in the organ building world. A further advertisement appeared in *The Walsall Red Book* for 1873:

NICHOLSON & SON,

ORGAN BUILDERS, PIANO-FORTE DEALERS,

AND GENERAL MUSIC SELLERS,

beg to call attention to their stock of Piano-fortes and Harmoniums, by *Broadwood, Collard, Alexandre, &c.*, and all the first class London makers.

NEW PIANO-FORTES, from Twenty Guineas.

NEW HARMONIUMS, by *Alexandre, Cœsarini, &c.*, from Six Guineas,

SECOND-HAND PIANOS & HARMONIUMS.

PIANO-FORTES FOR HIRE. TUNED, & REPAIRED,

Piano-Fortes and Harmoniums on the 3 years system.

NEW MUSIC,—HALF-PRICE.

Violins, Bows, Strings, English & German Concertinas, Guitars, &c., and all kinds of Musical Instruments.

Organs Built, Enlarged, Repaired, and Tuned.

NICHOLSON & SON having manufactured more than 250 Organs for different parts of the country, can with confidence recommend their instruments to be equal to any in London.

The following are a few of the numerous Organs built by them during the years 1871-72.

St. John's Church, Lichfield.
Hanford Church, near Stoke-on-Trent.
Trent Vale Church,   ditto
Christ Church, Wolverhampton.
St. John's Church, Swindon.
St. Thomas's Church, Glasgow.
St. Barnabas' Church, Birmingham (re-built)
Gedling Church, near Nottingham, (re-built)
Keele Church, near Newcastle.
All Saints' Church, Denstone, Ashbourne.
Newberries Hall, Watford.
Wesleyan Chapel, Kirkby-Stephen, Westmorland.
Oakland's Chapel, Shepherd's Bush, London.
Wesleyan Chapel, Oldbury. &c.,

References and Testimonials from clergymen in all parts of the country; also from Dr. Stainer, Organist of St. Paul's, London, and Sir G. Elvey, Organist to Her Majesty, Windsor, and other leading professors.

SPECIFICATIONS & ESTIMATES.

Observe: NICHOLSON & SON, Music Saloon, The Bridge;
Organ Manufactory,—Bradford St. and Newport St., Walsall.

It is clear that the firm had made an impact not only in Staffordshire, but far beyond and they must have felt very satisfied at their progress; certainly from that time onwards they did not look back. They had commenced work in small premises off Ablewell Street, then moved to more spacious workshops in Bradford Street, and later Vicarage Place, where they remained until well into the present century.

The year 1873 also marked the transference of the musical instrument and sheet music to H. Taylor & Son who continued to trade there for many years. This advertisement from *The Walsall Red Book* shows the extent of their business:

A further milestone in the history of the firm came in 1874 when Edmund Lord, who had been works foreman for twenty-five years, was taken into partnership and henceforth the firm was known as Nicholson & Lord. The Lord family is an interesting one, but the exact relationship of those concerned with organ building is not at all clear. In *Musical Opinion* for February 1930 there is a short article entitled 'An Old-Time Organist' from which I quote:

'In 1877 the sexton of Whitworth Church (Lancs.) was Edmund Lord, a name well known amongst organ builders. As was usual in other days, the man who performed the duties of sexton usually combined other occupations with the office. Thus Edmund Lord taught singing and also officiated at burials before the ground was consecrated, for the visits of the Bishops happened only at remote intervals. John Lord, whose portrait we reproduce, was the son of Edmund Lord. He was born in 1800 and became the organist of Whitworth Church at the age of eleven. At twenty-one he was appointed organist at St James' Rochdale and the portrait is from an oil painting presented to him at the age of twenty-eight by the congregation of St James' Rochdale. The organ at St James was a three-manual built by Richard Nicholson of Rochdale… John Lord was a pupil of Mendelssohn. He received lessons on the violin, organ and piano at John Broadwood's, London, and Mendelssohn's fee for three lessons was twenty-five pounds. The coach expenses from Rochdale to London and back cost another twenty-five pounds.'

This account was contributed by Mr Sam Lord of Walsall, and in 1977 the portrait was in the possession of his daughter, but it has been impossible to trace its present whereabouts at the time of writing this book. Sam, of 63 Vicarage Street, Walsall, was in business for many years as a reed and flue voicer as well as a piano and instrument dealer. He had spent twenty-five years with Nicholson & Lord until he decided to branch out on his own. An advertisement in Cope's *Walsall Blue Book and Directory* for 1895 describes him as an 'Organ and Piano Tuner and Dealer in Pianos, American Organs etc' at 63 Vicarage Street, Walsall. He was listed in Rudall, Carte & Co.'s *Musical Directory* for 1930, but just when he ceased to trade is not known. John William Lord, who worked on the instrument built by the firm for Walsall Town Hall in 1908, and who was in charge of the installation of this and other organs built for various parts of the country, was a cousin of Sam.

The various members of the Lord family were all musicians. John William, who died in 1941 at the age of 85, and his son Isaac Wolstenholme Lord (who was in business as a painter and decorator, died in 1972 at the age of 94), both played in a Silver Prize Band, while John William also played the double bass.

After the death of Edmund Lord, his grandson H. J. Lord carried on the business which prospered; early in the first decade of the present century they issued a brochure which listed instruments built county by county as well as overseas which totalled some 469 installations. Contracts abroad comprised 7 in France, 1 in the English Church, Moscow, 6 in Australia, 4 in New Zealand and 2 in South America. In 1902 they had a branch at 748 Great George Street, Sydney, but for how long it was open is not known. In England their work is to be found as far north as the county of Durham. Each page featured a logo consisting of a seal imprinted with the words 'Nicholson & Lord, Organ Builders, Walsall' and this has a short ribbon running through the back. They claimed that their factory was 'the largest in the Midlands, covering a large area of space and is fitted up with the modern machinery and every facility for carrying on the various branches of the art of Organ Building. A large and efficient staff of workmen are employed and the whole of the many parts of the instruments are manufactured on the premises, separate departments and staff controlling the interior mechanism and action, metal and zinc pipe making, wood pipe making, voicing and tuning, case making, decorating etc etc. The metal for the pipes is mixed and cast on the premises and, in fact the whole process from the designing and setting out to the tuning and finishing of the completed instrument is executed in the factory. A large stock of the best selected timber is kept on the premises where there is ample accommodation for drying and seasoning'. During World War I they were engaged on war work, making wooden shell cases; afterwards things were never the same again and work gradually declined, both order-wise and in importance. It became a limited company known as Nicholson & Lord (Walsall) Ltd. in about 1922, and about ten years later, with one or two exceptions, little else was done except tunings and overhauls. It gave up its factory sometime during the Second World War. About 1950, it was taken over by W. J. Bird & Son of Birmingham, then owned by L. R. Fleming who eventually sold out to Nicholsons of Worcester. So, after almost ninety years of service, this once important firm ceased to exist.

Mr R. F. Miner recalls that his father joined Nicholson & Lord as an apprentice in 1884, which was for a period of five years. His weekly wage was 4/− during the first year, followed by 5/−, 7/−, 9/−, 11/− and finally 13/−. One week's expenses working out of town comprised rail fares 2/9, candles 5d, drayman 3d, solder 3½d, 1 gross of screws 9d, tape 1d, white spirit 1d and sandpaper 1½d.

Two comments on the standard of their work are interesting. In a letter to me dated 29th August, 1976, from Mr Herbert Norman, he has this to say: 'The few N. & L. tubular-pneumatics that came our way for various attentions (Hill, Norman & Beard Ltd.) were thought to be crude and 5th rate—but not so a couple of older tracker jobs of 70–80s period. These were memorable for sound, simple, durable construction and a bright gentle singing tone in the choruses'. Mr H. A. Benyon, in 1976, when he was partner in W. Hawkins & Son, commented in a letter to me dated 19th October of that year: 'It is my humble opinion that Nicholson & Lord were one of the most under-rated firms in this country; their diapasons equal to the best that I have heard and their tracker and composition actions of impeccable design and construction... The pneumatic side of the business was not so successful except for a short period just before the first World War when a Mr Dunn was the manager—some of whose work was first class'. In one of his many letters to me, dated 10th August, 1976, Gilbert Mills had this to say of their work: 'Nicholson & Lord I knew as a young man; they built many fine organs, in fact I used to sit with my uncle Tom Mills, as a lad, when he played at Bloomfield Wesley Chapel, Tipton, Staffordshire. It was built like a battleship—cut off the joint and two veg job!—and contained much excellent tonal work'.

Their *magnum opus* was the four-manual instrument at Walsall Town Hall, built in 1908 to the design of C. W. Perkins, Organist of Birmingham Town Hall, and was opened by him on October 1st of that year. Erected in memory of Queen Victoria, it has a finely carved case of walnut, with gilded front pipes.

WALSALL TOWN HALL 1908

4 manuals: CC to C, 61 notes   Pedal: CCC to G, 32 notes

GREAT ORGAN

		ft	pipes
Double Open Diapason	m & z	16	61
Large Open Diapason	m & z	8	61
Small Open Diapason	m & z	8	61
Hohl Flöte	w	8	61
Gamba	m	8	61
Harmonic Flute	m & z	8	61
Harmonic Flute	m	4	61
Principal	m	4	61
Fifteenth	sptd. m	2	61
Mixture	sptd. m	IV	244
Trumpet	m	8	61
Clarion	sptd. m	4	61

SWELL ORGAN

		ft	pipes
Contra Gamba	m & w	16	61
Horn Diapason	m	8	61
Rohr Flöte	w & m	8	61
Viol d'Orchestre	m (sptd. to ten. c)	8	61
Voix Célestes	m (sptd. to ten. c)	8	52
Geigen Principal	m	4	61
Flageolet	w	2	61
Mixture	sptd. m	III	183
Contra Fagotto	m	16	61
Horn	m	8	61
Oboe	sptd. m	8	61
Clarion	sptd. m	4	61
Vox Humana	m	8	61
Tremulant to heavy wind			
Tremulant to light wind			

CHOIR ORGAN *enclosed*

Lieblich Bourdon	w & m	16	61
Violin Diapason	m	8	61
Lieblich Gedackt	w & m	8	61
Dulciana	m	8	61
Salicional	m (sptd. to ten. c)	8	61
Voix Célestes	sptd. m	8	49
Flauto Traverso	w	4	61
Piccolo	sptd. m	2	61
Clarinet	sptd. m	8	61
Tremulant			

SOLO ORGAN *enclosed*

String Gamba	pure tin (zinc bass)	8	61
Orchestral Flute	w	4	61
Orchestral Oboe	m	8	61
Tuba	m	8	61

PEDAL ORGAN

Contra Bourdon	w	[32]	32
Open Diapason	w	16	32
Violone	m	16	32
Subbass	w	16	32
Bourdon	w	16	32
Violoncello	m	8	32
Flute Bass		8	12
(12 notes by transmission from Subbass)			
Octave	m	4	32
Trombone	m & z	16	32
Trumpet		8	12
(20 notes by transmission from Trombone)			

ACCESSORIES	COUPLERS
5 combination thumb pistons to Great	Swell to Great (2 knobs, 1 on each side)
5 combination thumb pistons to Swell	Swell Octave
4 combination thumb pistons to Choir	Swell Sub-octave
5 composition pedals to Pedal	Swell to Choir
1 knob to connect Pedal to Great pistons	Choir to Great
1 reversible pedal for Great to Pedal coupler	Solo to Great
1 reversible pedal for Swell to Great coupler	Solo to Choir
1 reversible pedal giving Full Organ without	Choir Sub-octave
moving drawstops	Swell to Pedal
1 balanced crescendo pedal to Swell	Great to Pedal
1 balanced crescendo pedal to Choir	Choir to Pedal
1 balanced crescendo pedal to Solo	Solo to Pedal

T. W. North in his article in *The Organ*, for October 1941, said this: 'It was a really well-built instrument, containing the very finest material which is just as excellent today; it was undoubtedly the most outstanding work the firm had ever produced—tubular-pneumatic action throughout'.

T. W. North ('Tommy' to his friends) was Walsall's first and only civic organist, having held that position for no less than 46 years. *Musical Opinion* in its obituary notice in the December 1955 issue paid this tribute to his life and work: 'One of the most popular men in the musical life of the Midlands, Mr T. W. North died recently... He was a pupil of Mr C. W. Perkins, a former Birmingham City Organist and became organist of Dudley Parish Church in 1908. He conducted Dudley Choral Society. He accompanied at four of the Birmingham Triennial Festivals under Hans Richter... His knowledge of organ building brought involvement in organ schemes throughout the Midlands and beyond and the collaboration of his close friend, Gilbert Mills, in some of them, always gave him pleasure and resulted in some fine work being done. It can be said that both were "household names" in the area'.

An advertisement from *The Walsall Red Book*, 1929–31

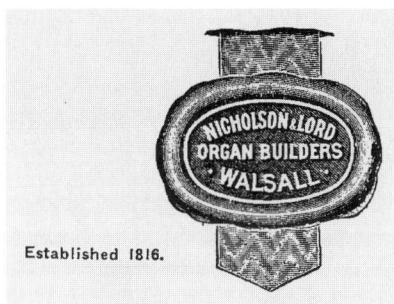

The firm's Seal.
Their registered Trade Mark was a shield—inset a knight mounted (with lance),
with the motto 'Challenger' above

SOME ORGANS BY NICHOLSON & LORD 1877–1930

RUSHALL CHURCH 1877

2 Manuals: CC to G, 56 notes   Pedal: CCC to E, 29 notes

'The organ has two fronts—one filling up the chancel arch and the other the transept arch—made of pitch pine, varnished, from a neat and chaste design; and the front pipes are plain gilt. The whole of the instrument is made of the very best materials and workmanship; and all the latest and best improvements have been added. The sound-boards are made of mahogany; all centres of the action are bushed with cloth, so that the action works easily and quietly. All the heavy machinery is made of iron or hard wood, and the roller-boards are fitted up with iron rollers. Pneumatic bellows have been added to play the bottom octave of the Swell, which makes the touch as light and as pleasant to play upon as a piano.'   [From *The Choir*, October 20th, 1877]

GREAT ORGAN

		ft	pipes
Open Diapason	m	8	56
Stopped Diapason	w	8	56
Clarabella (grooved into stopped bass)		8	44
Dulciana (to Gamut G)	m	8	49
Principal	m	4	56
Waldflute	w	4	56
Fifteenth	m	2	56
Sesquialtera	m	III	168

SWELL ORGAN

Bourdon	w	16	56
Open Diapason	m	8	56
Stopped Diapason	w	8	56
Dulciana (tenor C, bass grooved)	m	8	44
Principal (Geigen)	m	4	56

Piccolo	w	2	56
Fifteenth	m	2	56
Mixture	m	III	168
Cornopean	m	8	56
Trumpet	m	8	56
Hautboy	m	8	56

PEDAL ORGAN

Double Open Diapason	w	16	29
Bourdon	w	16	29

COUPLERS

Swell to Great   Swell to Pedals   Great to Pedals

Clochette   3 Composition Pedals

WESLEY CHAPEL, WILLENHALL 1877

2 Manuals: CC to G, 56 notes   Pedal: CCC to E, 29 notes

'On Tuesday evening, September 25th, a grand organ recital was given in the Wesley Chapel, Willenhall, by Mr Stimpson, organist of the Town Hall, Birmingham. The following was the programme: Opening Hymn and Prayer; Offertoire in C major (Wèly); Larghetto (Batiste); Grand Sonata (Mendelssohn); Andante (Stimpson); Fugue in D major (J. S. Bach); Andante (Haydn); Grand Offertoire (Batiste); March, from *Eli,* (Costa); Largo Appassionate (Beethoven); Wedding March (Mendelssohn); Grand Double Chorus, "The Horse and his Rider" (Handel); Concluding Hymn and Benediction. The description of the organ, which was built by Messrs. Nicholson & Lord, Walsall, is as follows: [From *The Choir*, October 20th, 1877]

GREAT ORGAN

		ft	pipes
Open Diapason	m	8	56
Stopped Diapason and Clarabella		8	56
Dulciana	m	8	56
Viol da Gamba (tenor C)	m	8	44
Principal	m	4	56
Waldflute	w	4	56
Fifteenth	m	2	56
Sesquialtera	m	III	168
Trumpet	m	8	56
Spare slide for Cremona			

PEDAL ORGAN

Double Open Diapason	w	16	29

SWELL ORGAN

Bourdon	w	16	56
Open Diapason (grooved bass)	m	8	49
Stopped Diapason	w	8	56
Geigen Principal	m	4	56
Harmonic Piccolo	m	2	56
Mixture	m	III	168
Keraulophon (tenor C)	m	8	44
Cornopean	m	8	56
Hautboy (tenor C)	m	8	44

COUPLERS

Swell to Great   Swell to Pedals   Great to Pedals

5 Composition Pedals: 3 to Great, 2 to Swell

LONGTON PARISH CHURCH, STAFFORDSHIRE 1878

3 Manuals: CC to G, 56 notes   Pedal: CCC to F, 30 notes

'The following is the programme of an organ recital given by Mr G. H. Gregory, Mus. Bac., Oxon., on the occasion of the opening of a new organ in Longton Parish Church: Overture to "Sampson" (Handel); Andante in F sharp minor (S. S. Wesley); Barcarolle, 4th Concerto (Bennett); Song for Tenor (Smart); Sonata in A, Nᵒ 3 (Mendelssohn); Toccata and Fugue in D Minor (Bach). The organ, which was built by Messrs. Nicholson and Lord, of Walsall is blown by Lea's "Climax" water motor, and cost £600. The Specification is as follows:'   [From *The Musical Standard*, May 18th, 1878]

GREAT ORGAN	ft		
Open Diapason	8	Mixture	III
Dulciana	8	Hautboy (orchestral)	8
Viol di Gamba	8	Cornopean	8
Stopped Diapason	8	**CHOIR ORGAN**	
Octave	4		
Super Octave	2	Dulciana	8
Sesquialtera	III	Stopped Diapason Clarabella	8
Trumpet	8	Harmonic Flute	4
		Waldflute	4
SWELL ORGAN		Flauto Traverso (prepared)	
Bourdon	16	Cremona	8
Open Diapason	8		
Gedact	8	**PEDAL ORGAN**	
Keraulophon (prepared)	–	Open Diapason	16
Geigen Principal	4	Bourdon	16
Harmonic Piccolo	2	Violoncello (prepared)	

ST PAUL'S CHURCH, WALSALL 1895

3 Manuals: CC to A, 58 notes   Pedal: CCC to F, 30 notes

GREAT ORGAN	ft	pipes			
†Bourdon	16		Lieblich Gedact	8	58
Open Diapason (large)	8	58	Salicional (grooved bass from Gedact)	8	46
Open Diapason (small)	8	58	Flute	4	58
Stop Diapason	8	58	Piccolo	2	58
†Gamba	8		Clarionet	8	46
Clarabella	8	46			
Principal	4	58	**PEDAL ORGAN**		
Fifteenth	2	58			
Mixture	III	174	Open Diapason	16	42
Trumpet	8	58	Bourdon	16	42
			Violoncello (18 from Open Diapason)	8	
SWELL ORGAN			Bass Flute (18 from Bourdon)	8	
Bourdon	16	58	†Trombone	16	
Open Diapason	8	58	†Posaune	8	
Stop Diapason	8	58	**COUPLERS**		
Viol d'Amour (to gamut G)	8	51			
Voix Celeste (to tenor C)	8	46	Swell to Great Swell to Choir Choir to Great		
Principal	4	58	Swell Octave to Great Swell to Pedal		
†Mixture	III		Choir to Pedal Great to Pedal *Tremulant* to Swell		
Trumpet	8	58	**ACCESSORIES**		
Hautboy	8	58			
†Clarion	4		4 Composition Pedals for Great & Pedal Organs		
			3 Composition Pedals for Swell Organ		
CHOIR ORGAN			1 Double-acting Pedal for Great to Pedal coupler		
			1 Composition Pedal for Choir *Open Diapason* and		
†Open Diapason	8		*Piccolo* (reversible) 1 ordinary Swell Pedal		
Dulciana	8	58	1 extra Swell Pedal for *Clarionet* (Choir)		
			† Stops which are only prepared for		

CONGREGATIONAL CHURCH, HIGH TOWN, CREWE 1897

2 Manuals: CC to A, 58 notes   Pedal: CCC to F, 30 notes

'The instrument is constructed with the Tubular-pneumatic Action throughout upon the latest scientific principles. The Couplers are constructed with Air Chambers, so that when all are in use the weight of the touch is not increased in the slightest degree. The Sforzando Pedal works in thirteen gradations, putting on the full power of the Instrument gradually or all at once, and reducing in the same way, without taking the hands off the keys'.   [From *The Organist and Choirmaster,* 1897]

GREAT ORGAN

		ft	pipes
Open Diapason (large)	m	8	58
Open Diapason (small)	m	8	58
Clarabella (with Stopt Bass)	w	8	58
Gamba	m	8	58
Dulciana	m	8	58
Principal	m	4	58
Harmonic Flute	m	4	58
Fifteenth	m	2	58
Clarionet (to tenor C)	m	8	46

SWELL ORGAN

Lieblich Bourdon	w & m	16	58
Open Diapason	m	8	58
Lieblich Gedact	w & m	8	58
Viol d'Amour	w & m	8	58
Voix Céleste (to tenor C)	m	8	46
Gemshorn	m	4	58
Mixture	m	III	174

Cornopean	m	8	58
Oboe	m	8	58
Tremulant			

PEDAL ORGAN

Open Diapason	w	16	30
Bourdon	w	16	30

COUPLERS

Swell to Great   Swell to Pedals   Swell Octave
Swell Sub-Octave   Great to Pedals

ACCESSORIES

3 Double Acting Combination Thumb Pistons
and Composition Pedals to Great Organ
3 Composition Pedals to Swell Organ
1 Reversible Pedal for "Great to Pedals" on and off
One Sforzando Pedal   Patent Pneumatic Swell Pedal

BAPTIST CHAPEL, STAFFORD STREET, WALSALL 1899

2 Manuals: CC to G, 56 notes   Pedal: CCC to F, 30 notes

GREAT ORGAN

		ft	pipes
Open Diapason	m	8	56
Clarabella (with Stopt Bass)	w	8	56
Dulciana	m	8	56
Gamba	m	8	56
Principal	m	4	56
Harmonic Flute	m	4	56
Fifteenth	m	2	56
Trumpet (spare slider)			

SWELL ORGAN

Lieblich Bourdon	w	16	56
Open Diapason	m	8	56
Viol D'Amour	w & m	8	56
Voix Celeste (to tenor C)	m	8	44
Lieblich Gedact	w & m	8	56
Gemshorn	m	4	56
Mixture	m	III	168
Cornopean	m	8	56
Oboe	m	8	56

PEDAL ORGAN

Open Diapason	w	16	30
Bourdon	w	16	30
Lieblich Bourdon (from Swell)		16	
Bass Flute (18 from Pedal Bourdon)		8	12

COUPLERS

Swell to Great   Swell Super Octave
Swell to Pedals   Great to Pedals
Tremulant to Swell

ACCESSORIES

3 Combination Thumb Pistons to Great Organ
3 Combination thumb Pistons to Swell Organ
1 Double-acting Pedal for "Great to Pedals"
Sforzando Pedal

Total number of pipes 1,068

[From *The Nonconformist Musical Journal*, April 1899]

Note: In examining a number of specifications of two-manual organs of larger size than the above, it is noticeable that Nicholson & Lord frequently included a Swell clarion.

ST PAUL'S CHURCH, WALSALL, REBUILT 1926

3 Manuals: CC to C, 61 notes   Pedal: CCC to G, 32 notes

GREAT ORGAN	*ft*
Double Open Diapason (metal)	16
Large Open Diapason	8
Small Open Diapason	8
Clarabella	8
Stopped Diapason	8
Salicional	8
Principal	4
Fifteenth	2
Mixture	III
Trumpet	8

SWELL ORGAN	
Lieblich Bourdon	16
Open Diapason	8
Stopped Diapason	8
Viol d'Amour	8
Voix Celestes	8
Principal	4
Mixture	III
Hautboy	8
Cornopean	8
Clarion	4

CHOIR ORGAN	
Lieblich Gedact	8
Viol d'Orchestre	8
Dulciana	8
Flute	4
Piccolo	2
Clarionet	8
Tremulant	
Contra Tuba	16
Tuba	8

PEDAL ORGAN	
Open Diapason (from Great)	16
Open Diapason (wood)	16
Bourdon	16
Lieblich Bourdon (from Swell)	16
Octave (from Open Wood)	8
Bass Flute (from Bourdon)	8
Bombarde (from Contra Tuba)	16
Tuba (from Choir)	8

16 Couplers

The instrument was later rebuilt with tonal additions, new electro-pneumatic action and drawstop console, by R. H. Walker & Son (Organ Builders) Ltd.

NEW METHODIST CENTRAL HALL, WALSALL 1930

3 Manuals: CC to C, 61 notes   Pedal: CCC to F, 30 notes

GREAT ORGAN	*ft*
Open Diapason	16
Large Open Diapason	8
Small Open Diapason	8
Clarabella	8
Salicional	8
Flute	4
Principal	4
Fifteenth	2
Mixture	III
Tromba	8

SWELL ORGAN	
Lieblich Bourdon	16
Horn Diapason	8
Gedact	8
Viol d'Orchestre	8
Voix Celeste (tenor C)	8
Gemshorn	4
Fifteenth	2
Horn	8
Oboe	8
Clarion	4
Tremulant	

CHOIR ORGAN	
Violin Diapason	8
Stop Diapason	8
Dulciana	8
Gamba (tenor C)	8
Suabe Flute	4
Piccolo	2
Clarinet	8
Tremulant	

PEDAL ORGAN	
Acoustic Bass	32
Open Diapason	16
Open Diapason	16
Bourdon	16
Violoncello	8
Trombone	16

11 Couplers and all essential accessories.

Pneumatic action; electric blowing.

To descend to the basics in organ design we have a Scudamore type of instrument in the church of South Carlton, Lincoln. It was not built for this building; where it came from, or when, I have been unable to ascertain, but I have known it for many years and can only say that its four stops tell us in no uncertain way of the excellence in voicing that made the name of Nicholson & Lord famous in its day. It has these stops: Compass CC–G, 56 notes, 2 octaves of pedal pull-downs, open diapason (tenor C), stopped diapason bass, stopped diapason treble (from tenor C), dulciana, principal; Electric blowing, but bellows handle preserved at the side. The stained deal case is attractive, as will be seen from the illustration. This little gem provides real atmosphere in accompanying the worship; there is a very lovely and quiet dulciana, a full but bright-toned stopped diapason with a touch of 'chiff' together with a diapason and principal with a slight edge, most satisfying in tone and power and providing a remarkable sense of bigness.

Nicholson & Lord—a grand old firm with many examples of their work (particularly in Staffordshire) still extant. What a pity that it had to share the fate of a number of firms in the 1930s when dwindling orders resulted in eventual closure.

T. W. North *left*, and at the console, Walsall Town Hall, *right*
From *The Organ*, January 1932

left
South Carlton Church, near Lincoln. Scudamore type organ by Nicholson & Lord.
Photo by the Author

above
A typical Nicholson & Lord case design at St Thomas' Church, Framfield, Sussex, 1900

below
Nicholson & Lord. The staff, early 1900's

202

CHAPTER VII

Derby and Newark

J. H. ADKINS 1898–1958

JOHN Housley Adkins, born in Derby on 28th December, 1869, became interested in pianos and organs as a boy and eventually became a competent player. After attending Derby Grammar School he started work at a local organ builders, one John Mitchell Grunwell, an ex-Hill employee who had commenced his own business. On 29th July, 1884, his father Joseph Adkins indentured him to Grunwell for seven years; for the first year he was paid four shillings per week, rising each year by two shillings. In 1887, by mutual consent, these indentures were cancelled and young Adkins went to Grantham to work for White & Sentance where he gained experience on pianos and to a lesser extent on organs, for the business was mainly concerned with pianos and reed organs.

Married at Brook Street Methodist Church, Derby, in 1892, the young couple settled in Grantham for a short time; one of Adkins' colleagues was an Arthur Spencer who later had a large piano showroom in Chippenham. He also took in organ repairs and from time to time called upon Adkins to assist on some of the more specialised work. Around 1893–94, Adkins moved to work for Denning of Stamford who had both a piano and organ connection. There is a Denning organ in Trussley Parish Church, Derbyshire, which was installed by his former employee in 1949.

Between 1897–98, Adkins returned to Derby and commenced business on his own in 1898. In order to supplement his income, piano tuning and repairs were also carried out, the first job being a 3/6d tuning! For a time the old Wesleyan Chapel, built in 1765 in St Michael's Lane, was rented and later purchased. As he grew in experience, the young builder became well known; his connections grew and he obtained orders beyond the confines of Derby. The year 1903 seems to have been the turning point in his career and as the years went by organs were built for churches as far afield as Stewerton (Scotland), Chippenham, Oldham, Luton and Kilburn, London, with one being exported to a Methodist Church in Durban, South Africa. During his lifetime some nineteen organs were built or rebuilt in Derby. During the period between the two wars there was a regular staff of a dozen or so workmen. Two particular stalwarts were the foreman, Harold Sheraton, who was related to the famous cabinet maker of that name, and Charles Bamberger, who shared the voicing with Adkins and was, it is believed, trained at Speechley's in London. During this period Reginald J. Poyser became manager and the firm entered its busiest period. When the Second World War came, he, together with most of the staff, were compelled to join the forces and like others, the firm carried on under difficulties in a somewhat reduced form.

After the war it was difficult to obtain staff and at the age of 78 J. H. Adkins passed away in 1947. His grandson, J. H. Poyser, had assisted him in various ways from an early age during school holidays and on leaving school in 1949 he joined the firm. Staff difficulties continued for a number of years and in 1958 the business was taken over by J. W. Walker & Sons Ltd., Poyser becoming their Derbyshire representative under Arthur Cooper at Leicester, who later became North Midlands area manager. All this was valuable experience and when Walkers were taken over in 1975 and moved to Brandon, J. H. Poyser decided to place his trust in the customers whom he had served for many years and started his own business. To use his own words: 'I am pleased to say that their support and that of clients gained since that time have resulted in it being a successful venture'. He now trades as J. H. Poyser, M.I.S.O.B., Organ Builder, 19 Derwent Drive, Stenson Fields, Sinfin, Derby DE2 3AQ, offering Overhauls, Restorations, Rebuilds, New Organs, Tuning and Maintenance.

THE JOHNSON ORGAN CO.

Founded by Alan S. Johnson in 1954, who had worked for J. H. Adkins between 1946–52, he was later joined by his son Paul, the firm trading under the name of The Johnson Organ Co., of Gosforth Road, Osmaston Industrial Estate, Derby. Equipped to carry out rebuilds, restorations and new organs either with electric or tracker action, the firm is particularly proud of their rebuild of the fine Father Willis organ in St John's, Bridge Street, Derby, for its centenary in 1975. Another centenary was celebrated as far away as Stornaway, Isle of Lewis, when the two-manual Bevington organ in St Peter's Episcopal Church there, built in 1885, was rebuilt in 1985. As a result, Johnsons maintain the three organs which are the sum total of pipe organs in the Outer Hebrides. Since 1966 the firm has featured what is known as The Johnson Minor Pipe Organ on an additive basis, so that a base unit of one stop may be purchased and as further funds become available, additions may be made until the instrument is complete to the following specification:

> Open diapason 8ft, dulciana 8ft (tenor C), flute 4ft, twelfth 2⅔ft (extension from fifteenth), fifteenth 2ft. The Pedal bourdon and bass flute are produced electronically through a 12 inch speaker; control is by stop-keys and the simple casework can be supplied in light or dark oak or sapele. A silent electric blower is enclosed within the case. This organ has successfully filled a need where space and cost are limited.

Thirty-eight years have gone by since Alan Johnson founded his business which latterly was now managed by his son Paul, a member of the Federation of Master Organ Builders. Like a number of small firms today run by fully trained organ builders, it had worked quietly on, giving a service throughout Derbyshire and beyond at the lowest possible prices without sacrificing quality. As this chapter was being written, Alan Johnson died suddenly while tuning in Scotland. In 1994, the business was purchased by Henry Groves & Son, Nottingham, and Paul became a member of the staff there.

Mr Poyser informs me that the firm of Noble & Co. were in existence towards the end of the last century and for the first part of this, 'and produced an unremarkable but solid job'. Middleton by Wirksworth Methodist Church was built by them, while rebuilds were carried out at Christ Church, Derby (two-manual), Dale Road Methodist Church, Derby (two-manual), Barrow-on-Trent Methodist Church (one-manual) and Shirley Parish Church (two-manual).

Another firm, John Stacey of Derby, was engaged in organ building about that time; their work was limited, but in 1896 at Tansley Parish Church they rebuilt the Forster & Andrews barrel organ which was brought from South Elkington in 1848. Stacey's name-plate also appeared on the two-manual organ at Greenhill Central Methodist Church, Derby, Junction Street Baptist Church in the same city (two-manual) and Alvaston Baptist Church (one-manual).

J. F. HARSTON, LATER HARSTON AND SON 1835–c.1912

The name Harston is rarely heard of in the organ world; the firm was well known to me in Lincoln for many years where it was a 'household name' in the city centre as a prestigious music shop. It was not until after the war, when walks in the immediate countryside took my wife and I to the lovely church of St Peter, Doddington, which stands adjacent to the Elizabethan mansion, Doddington Hall, that I made an interesting discovery. There I found a delightful one-manual organ (showing signs of its age) by J. F. Harston of Newark, which greatly intrigued me for it bore a strange resemblance to the tone of Forster & Andrews' work, *circa* 1860s. When, in later years, the Forster & Andrews Order Books came into my hands on permanent loan, I found the following entry in their ledger commencing November 16th, 1844:

Courcelle must have been making pipes in London for Forster & Andrews at this time, for they had only been established in Hull for a year. Moreover, it shows that Harston had either built or obtained a barrel organ, the barrel of which required tunes being set. There is no other entry for Courcelle in Forster & Andrews' three early ledgers, nor is there any mention of another trade pipe-maker being employed, so it can only be assumed that a metal hand was on the staff of the firm within a year or so of their opening their business in Charlotte Street, Hull. This entry creates a problem regarding Courcelle, for in 1847 he was working for J. C. Bishop and did not leave his employment to found his own business as an organ builder and pipe-maker to the trade until 1853. His brother George also worked at Bishops until 1845, after which I have been unable to trace him. Was it he who made the pipes for Harston's order, or did brother John do some pipe-making 'on the side' to supplement his income, for the family was poor (as will be seen from my book, *Bishop and Son, Organ Builders*). We shall never know the circumstances behind this entry. It is believed however that Forster & Andrews made and voiced some pipework for Harston on occasions during the early part of his career, although there is no firm evidence to support this. His later work does not show the same marked characteristics.

The name Harston abounded in Nottinghamshire villages and can be traced as far back as *c*.1652. John Harston established an engraving business in Stodman Street, Newark, in 1806, and it seems very likely that this included the engraving of music. By 1835, it had developed into a flourishing music warehouse at 40 Stodman Street, a three-storeyed building which extended a considerable distance to the rear. In the mid 1840s, on leaving school, his son Joseph Frearson Harston joined the business and before long became involved in every aspect of music selling, musical instruments of all kinds and a limited amount of organ building, tuning and maintenance. This work was carried on at the back of the shop and several journeyman organ builders were employed, working under the direction of J. F. Harston whose name appeared on the handful of organs I have examined or been able to trace. In 1880, the firm built a two-manual organ for Christ Church, Newark (which formed the basis for the present organ by Cousans of Lincoln, in 1958). Two years later, J. F. Harston died in the fiftieth year of his age. He was highly thought of in both business and social circles, and on the Sunday after his death, the *Dead March in Saul* was performed on the organs of the Parish Church, Christ Church and St Leonard's Church, as a mark of respect, and an obituary notice appeared in *The Newark Advertiser* for 1st March, 1882. His widow lost no time in placing a business advertisement in *The Advertiser* for 8th March, which reads as follows:

MUSIC WAREHOUSE, 40 STODMAN STREET, NEWARK

MRS J. F. HARSTON

Begs to announce that owing to the lamented death of her late husband, she and her eldest son have entered into partnership for the purpose of carrying on the business for the benefits of the large family left dependent upon the successful continuance of the various branches to which the deceased gave such careful and energetic attention. She sincerely thanks all those who have hitherto given them patronage, and hopes that in the future, with the assistance of her eldest sons and thoroughly experienced workmen, the business may be conducted entirely to the satisfaction of all customers. The trade will be carried on as heretofore in the name of

HARSTON & SON

J. J. HARSTON, in entering into partnership with his mother as above announced, most respect-fully invites the support of his friends and the public in undertaking a heavy responsibility as eldest son of a large family so unexpectedly bereaved, and he hopes by a diligent and careful attention to all orders to merit an extended share of public support. Careful personal attention will be given to the Tuning departments. the important orders for Organ building lately received will be promptly and efficiently carried out.

PIANOS, HARMONIUMS AND ORGANS TUNED BY THE YEAR

ESTIMATES GIVEN FOR ORGAN BUILDING AND REPAIRS

Depot for New Sheet and Church Music

Every possible advantage will be given to cash purchasers of Pianos and other instruments. Also on the one, two, or three years' system.

All communications to be addressed

HARSTON & SON, 40, STODMAN STREET, NEWARK

Various publications appeared during the last century advertising the merits of every conceivable type of business and some entries make amusing reading today. In *The Industries of Nottinghamshire* (1899) Harstons had a column 3 ins. deep:

HARSTON & SON, MUSIC WAREHOUSE, 40, STODMAN STREET. There can be no question regarding the eminent standing of Messrs. Harston & Son in the music trade, for they are both dealers in and manufacturers of instruments, and are "highly recommended by Messrs. Broadwood & Sons". They commenced business in Newark in 1835, and during the whole of its existence their house has held a leading and influential position in the town. It is now one of the most popular among the highest and most desirable circles of patronage in the town and district. The premises utilized at No. 40, Stodman Street, possess a good three-storied frontage, and extend a considerable distance to the rear, comprising show, stock, and workrooms, which are very conveniently arranged and equipped in the best style. In the showroom a fine display is made of pianofortes by the best known English and Continental makers; American organs, harmoniums, harps, violins, cellos, accordions, and, in fact, every description of brass and string instruments and fittings. Messrs. Harston & Son are noted organ builders, and no better proof of the thoroughly first-class character of the instruments made by them could be given

206

than the fact that their trade in this particular department is steadily increasing. They employ an efficient number of skilled workmen, and are prepared to execute all orders in the shortest possible time. They also make a speciality of pianoforte and organ tuning and regulating, guaranteeing thorough efficiency and lowest charges. In all their dealings Messrs. Harston & Son will be found exceedingly liberal, prompt, and courteous, to which they no doubt owe much of their success. At the present time the business is being conducted with rare energy and ability, and it is sure to continue in its prosperous career.'

In the same issue we find another branch of the family, J. & J. Harston, advertising as 'Painters, Decorators, Picture Frame Makers, Paper-hangers, etc, of 10 and 11 Lombard Street'. This firm was established by Robert Harston in 1784 and was still in existence in 1947, when it advertised in the town's official guide published in that year. By then it had a branch at Buxton.

In 1897, whoever was in control of the music business decided to establish a branch in Lincoln. This was a bold move, for already there were four well-known firms operating very successfully: Charles Hannam, Silver Street; Charles Harrison, 362 High Street; W. Mason & Son, 6 Guildhall Street and E. S. Rose, 347–8 High Street. Harston & Son first occupied a shop in Corporation Street, but two years later they had the most prominent premises in the city at 228 High Street, with the large drapery store of Mawer & Collingham next door on their north side and the high-class grocery, provision and wine and spirit shop of H. Beaumont on the south side.

The Lincoln branch of the business attracted the notice of the reviewer employed by *Musical Opinion* to visit and report on music dealers' activities. A two-column contribution on Lincoln music shops appeared in *Musical Opinion* for December 1903. Headed—'A look at Lincoln'—Harstons received the maximum coverage:

'At the warehouse of Messrs. Harston & Son, High Street, brightness and business were the order. It was a pleasure to meet with so extensive and well-stocked a warehouse looking so cheerful at the close of a day which had not been favourable for business. The highly polished instruments and fittings seen in the beams of the electric light presented a very bright and attractive appearance and suggesting prosperity. I was glad to accept an invitation to view the premises, and thereupon proceeded to inspect "The Lincoln Piano and Organ Depot" as Messrs. Harston & Sons establishment is designated. The rooms on three extensive upper floors are devoted to the purposes of the business. On the first floor, at the front, a very tastefully furnished room is used as the showroom for high grade pianos. Here I viewed some beautiful instruments, judiciously displayed so that the individuality of each might be maintained. There was variety without embarrassment and quality in design and tone to meet the fancy of the most exacting. On the second floor I found well-stocked organ and harmonium showrooms, with some of the newer models of both instruments. Some very chaste Estey, Bell and Mason & Hamlin organs were well displayed in these rooms. A useful and daintily cased instrument, Harston's Academy organ, made for the firm, was pointed out to me as their speciality "line" in organs. It was a pretty instrument with ten stops and a low top, in a new and artistic design with a bevelled semi-circular mirror in the centre. In the harmonium room I was pleased to find two Cristophe & Etienne instruments which were shown as offering large stop and tone value at moderate prices. Each harmonium was in plain light oak unvarnished; the cases being left in the "white" suggesting the desire that the instruments should be closely inspected by intending purchasers. The showrooms were lighted by electricity throughout; thus, as far as light was concerned, enabling the instruments to be seen to good advantage after nightfall. This firm holds a large stock of sheet and book music and have an extensive tuning connection. Their business now ranks with the oldest in that part of the United Kingdom.'

The Newark business closed down *circa* 1912, and as far as can be ascertained, no organ building had been carried on since towards the end of the 1800s. At Lincoln, Mawer & Collingham purchased Harstons (possibly at the same time) but the name was retained until just before the outbreak of war, when trading ceased to allow the shop to be absorbed into the rapidly growing store of Mawer & Collingham Ltd. (now Binns—a branch of The House of Fraser group).

To revert to organ building at Newark, the checking of various country-wide lists, county by county, and the exchange of information with others, suggests that the output of new organs was limited. I have traced and examined four in Lincolnshire, while Colin Menzies has kindly notified me of two in Scotland.

CHRIST CHURCH, NEWARK 1881

Manual compass CC to G 56 notes: Pedal Organ CCC to F, 30 notes

GREAT ORGAN	ft	SWELL ORGAN	
		Bourdon	16
Open Diapason	8	Open Diapason	8
Dulciana	8	Gedact	8
Gamba	8	Salicional	8
Stopped Diapason	8	Principal	4
Principal	4	Mixture	II
Harmonic Flute	4	Cornopean	8
Twelfth	2⅔	Oboe	8
Fifteenth	2	PEDAL ORGAN	
Clarinet	8	Bourdon	16
		Open Diapason	16

The Cousans firm, when rebuilding and enlarging this instrument with electro-pneumatic action for the new Christ Church, built in 1958 for the rapidly growing estate of Hawtonville and the surrounding area, expressed their pleasure at working with the old pipework. Together with their additions, they created an extremely fine and resourceful instrument which received the highest praise from a number of well-known authorities when it was completed in time for the dedication by the Lord Bishop of Southwell on the 15th March, 1958.

At Marston Parish Church near Grantham, Harstons built a slightly larger two-manual instrument at the west end of this beautiful church, but the date of installation is not known. It bears an ivory name-plate engraved J. F. HARSTON, ORGAN BUILDER, NEWARK; whether it was completed before his death or after that date (in which case his name-plate continued to be used) is not known, but I am fairly certain that it was no later than the early 1880s. The case is simple; it has an oak frame with pine panels, and silvered front pipes, which must have been done much later.

MARSTON PARISH CHURCH, GRANTHAM *c*.1880

Manual compass CC to G 56 notes: Pedal Organ CCC to F, 30 notes

GREAT ORGAN	ft	SWELL ORGAN	ft
Open Diapason	8	Lieblich Bourdon	16
Stopped Diapason	8	Lieblich Gedacht	8
Dulciana (tenor C)	8	Open Diapason	8
Gamba	8	Vox Angelica	8
Principal	4	Principal	4
Flute	4	Flute Harmonique (engraved 8ft)	4
Twelfth	2⅔	Piccolo Harmonique (engraved 4ft)	2
Fifteenth	2	Horn	8
Cremona	8	Hautbois	8

PEDAL ORGAN		3 Composition Pedals Balanced Swell Pedal in the
	ft	corner replacing the original trigger pedal
Bourdon	16	K.C. Electric Blower Horizontal stop jambs
Open Diapason	16	Ivory keys and curved key cheeks in the Willis style

Julian Paul, organ builder of Ingham, near Lincoln, has carried out restoration work in many stages as and when funds have permitted. This has included the replacement of the very indifferent original Swell reeds, by stops from a redundant Lloyd organ in New Basford, Nottingham, which are most effective, together with a radiating and concave pedal board. The final stages of the work comprised the electrification of the Pedal stops together with the extension of the bourdon to 8, 4 and 5⅓ pitches and the open diapason to 8ft. The stops of the Pedal Organ are now operated by stop-keys over the Swell manual. A tremulant was also added (by drawstop) and the balanced swell pedal moved to a central position. The whole organ is now in excellent condition—a state it has not enjoyed for many years.

Music can be made upon this organ; there are some lovely flutes, while the splendid chorus work is much more effective heard down the church than at the console. The church is fortunate in having a very capable organist—Douglas Pearman—whose interest in restoring this fine old organ (which was not in a good state when I heard it years ago) has been invaluable. It is well worth hearing, but it should not be judged in its entirety from the console.

The two Harston organs in Scotland discovered by Colin Menzies are Newton Stewart Episcopal Church in the south-west, together with the main Presbyterian Church in the same town. In the Episcopal Church, the two-manual instrument occupies a chamber on the north side of the chancel, the pipes being decorated by blue and gold stencils, or diaper work, as it was known when this was fashionable in the last century. As either the Patron, or the first Rector, had connections with Newark and was acquainted with Harston's work, the contract was placed with him, possibly *circa* 1875. On the strength of his work there, shortly afterwards he obtained the contract to build a substantial organ on the west gallery of the quite large and imposing Presbyterian Church. This would be about 1878; it was re-actioned by Hill, Norman & Beard Ltd. in 1962, the console being retained.

The three small organs in Lincolnshire—all one-manuals—are at Owmby, Osbournby and Doddington churches. No dates are known for the last two, but when the soundboard of the Owmby organ was opened up in 1991, the year 1898 was written inside. Its original location is not known, but J. L. Taylor, successor to Walker & Taylor of Lincoln, renovated it in 1948 for Normanby Methodist Church, who donated it to their friends at Owmby-by-Spital Parish Church, when the Methodists closed their place of worship in 1991. It was then meticulously restored by the young grandson of the founder of Henry Groves & Son of Nottingham—Jonathan Wallace—who now directs the firm.

OWMBY–BY–SPITAL (1898)

Manual compass CC to F 54 notes: 1½ octaves of pedals

LEFT–HAND JAMB	RIGHT–HAND JAMB
Bourdon	Gamba
Stopped Bass	Open Diapason
Dulciana	Principal
Clarabella	Diocton

3 Composition Pedals   Sloping stop jambs, ivory keys   Electric Blowing
Ratchet Swell pedal – all enclosed except bottom octave of the Open Diapason

The console bears a large brass name-plate: HARSTON AND SON, NEWARK & LINCOLN. The use of square drawstop rods and the nomenclature 'diocton' for the octave coupler, as late as 1898, is puzzling; could it have been an earlier Harston, given a new name-plate that year?

The organ was dedicated by the Bishop of Lincoln on 15th September, 1991, when Colin Walsh, Organist and Master of the Choristers, Lincoln Cathedral, gave a recital. He expressed his pleasure at the completion of the restoration of this modest little instrument. By the time this chapter is in print, a two-rank mixture and small trompette will have been added.

The Osbournby organ is virtually 'Scudamore' in design and is situated on the north side of the chancel; it has a 54-note compass and one octave of pedals. The case is of pine and the console of walnut, with celuloid keys; all stops stand on an open soundboard and are as follows: open diapason, principal, stopped bass, claribel, dulciana, bourdon. K.C. Electric blower. It gives forth a pleasant sound, but is quite inadequate for this large church; it is hoped to move it to a small church in the neighbourhood and replace it with a larger instrument when funds permit. It bears a label HARSTON AND SON, NEWARK; the date is unknown, but at a guess I would place it in the 1860–70s period.

Finally, we come back to the organ in Doddington Church, which sparked off the research into this rather elusive firm, which I suspect derived most of its income from the selling of music, together with pianos, reed organs and their maintenance, rather than from organ building. Over the years it has become an old friend! It fits unobtrusively into the chancel of this beautiful old church, being placed in a chamber on the south side. It has a stained pine case and a diapered pipe front which has become faded and generally shabby with paint peeling here and there, yet viewed from the nave it is hardly noticeable. The action rattles away merrily and it is not easy to achieve clean playing. The interior is very dirty while tuning is infrequent to say the least. Yet with a good, sympathetic player, it makes music and creates atmosphere. Major conservation would work wonders, but unfortunately this is most unlikely, as only one or two services are held annually, for the village is very small. However, the church is lovingly maintained by someone, but what of its future, for structural repairs are necessary.

The console is of mahogany with sloping stop jambs, key cheeks curved very much in the Willis style and an ivory label engraved J. F. HARSTON, ORGAN BUILDER, NEWARK—its date?— c.1860-70s at a guess. There are the following stops (rosewood with ivory labels on square rods). Right-hand side: stopped diapason bass, dulciana, claribel, gamba, open diapason. Left-hand side: diaocton (octave coupler), bourdon, principal, flute 4ft, trumpet bass, hautbois. All enclosed, except bourdon and bottom octave of the diapason which forms part of the pipe front. 1½ octaves of pedals, 2 composition pedals (originally there were three), ratchet swell pedal (very awkward!), electric blowing.

With the box open, the diapason and principal provide a strong, bright lead; the flutes have character, but the gamba is rather too keen in tone. Why the reed was so named is strange, for it is a trumpet throughout. Fiery and now rough in tone—it could be improved!

Harston & Son—only one of a number of small firms of the last century who combined the selling of sheet music and musical instruments with organ building, but well worth researching further.

From *Musical Opinion*, January 1st, 1894

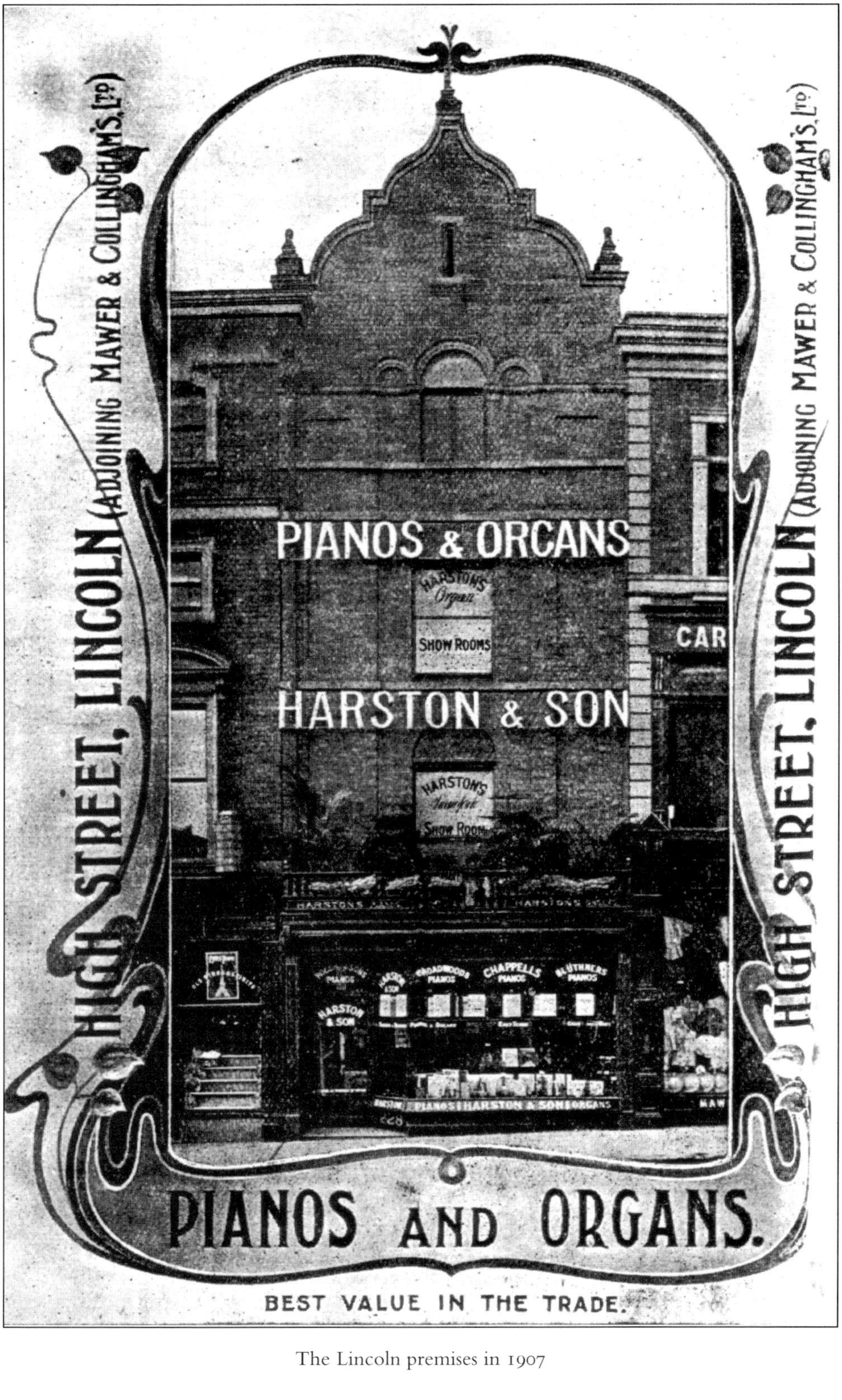

The Lincoln premises in 1907

Victoria Street Congregational Church, Derby. Three-manual organ by Forster & Andrews, 1896, rebuilt by Adkins with detached console, c.1920s.   Photo by the Author

Owmby-by-Spital Church, Lincs.
Organ by Harston.
Photo by Jonathan Wallace

Marston Church, Lincs.
Organ by Harston.
Photo by the Author

Doddington Church, near Lincoln
Organ by Harston.
Photo by the Author

CHAPTER VIII

Leicester and Melton Mowbray

S. TAYLOR AND SON 1866–1965

FOR many years, Leicester was the home of two highly regarded provincial organ builders: Stephen Taylor & Son and J. Porritt & Son. Stephen Taylor, son of a bootmaker and grandson of a Baptist Minister, was born in 1838 and apprenticed to a joiner in Sileby, Leicestershire, then moved to Worcester to learn the art of organ building with John Nicholson. How long he remained there is not known; what is certain however is that he would receive first-class training in a shop where standards of workmanship were high and the use of first-class materials paramount. In commencing his own business in Leicester in 1866, at the age of twenty-eight, with the aid of an interest free loan of £100 from the Thomas White Charity of Leicester, he was determined to follow the high standards he had known at Worcester and these were maintained by each member of the Taylor family as time went on. As a result, the newly-formed firm flourished and quickly made a name for itself in Leicester and beyond. Stephen was a versatile man; he played the violin at Sileby Church as a member of the Church band before it had an organ; when this was installed it was built by Holdich, but Stephen Taylor & Son rebuilt it in 1931. The first workshop was in Albion Street; two or three years later it moved to Erskine Street for a similar brief stay, finally moving to Nelson Street where it remained until the business closed in 1965.

Quiet but steady progress was made in the 1860s to early '70s and by the end of the decade the firm had built or rebuilt a number of large instruments in Leicester and beyond. The *Musical Standard* for 13th January, 1877, contains the following account of the organ in the Victoria Road Church, Leicester:

VICTORIA ROAD CHURCH, LEICESTER 1877

Dr. Spark, organist to the Leeds Corporation, re-opened the organ at Victoria-road Church, on Thursday night, by giving a grand recital. The instrument has undergone important improvements, including the addition of a new choir organ. The work has been executed by Mr Taylor, Leicester, and the cost of the repairs and additions has been about £210; £160 of which has already been subscribed by the congregation and friends. The organ contains the following stops:—

GREAT ORGAN

	ft
Large Open Diapason	8
Small ditto	8
Stopt ditto (treble)	8
Stopt ditto (bass)	8
Viol di Gamba	8
Principal	4
Suabe Flute	4
Rohr Flute	4
Grave Mixture	II
Mixture	III
Trumpet	8
Clarion	4

SWELL ORGAN

Bourdon	16
Open Diapason	8
Stopt ditto	8

Bell ditto	8
Harmonic Flute	4
Principal	4
Piccolo	2
Cornopean	8
Hautboy	8

CHOIR ORGAN

Open Diapason	8
Dulciana	8
Viol d'Amour	8
Voix Céleste	8
Lieblich Gedact	8
Gemshorn	4
Lieblich Flute	4
Flautina	2
Cremona	8
Bassoon	8

PEDAL ORGAN		COUPLERS
Grand Open Diapason	16	Swell to Great Choir to Great
Grand Bourdon	16	Great to Pedals Swell to Pedals Choir to Pedals
Grand Principal	8	Swell Octave Pedal Octave
		3 Composition pedals to Great and Swell
		2 Composition pedals to Choir

The recital afforded to those who listened to Dr. Spark's remarkable execution, masterly style and correct interpretation of the pieces performed, a treat to lovers of music rarely surpassed in Leicester. There was a very large attendance. The following was the programme:—

Organ Concerto, G minor (Handel), Larghetto e staccato—Allegro—Adagio—Andante; Introduction and Air (varied), G Major (Haydn); March for Organ, B flat major (Silas); "Jerusalem the golden", with variations and finale (W. Spark); Andante, G major, "The Pilgrim's song of hope" (Batiste); Extemporaneous Introduction and Grand Fugue, D minor (Bach); Fantasia on Two Christmas Carols, B flat major (Guilmant); Hallelujah Chorus (Messiah), Finale (Handel).

In the above selection every variety of organ tone was displayed, and the instrument was proved to possess a beauty and special character not often surpassed in much larger and more pretentious organs.

Perhaps it is not generally known that Stephen Taylor carried out work on the Ripon Cathedral organ during 1874. Edwin J. Crow, MUS. DOC., CANTAB, Organist, wrote to him from Ripon on 7th July, 1874: 'I have pleasure in stating that the tuning of the organ in this Cathedral to equal temperament and certain changes in the action, have been most satisfactorily carried out by Mr Stephen Taylor of Leicester'.

By 1884, Stephen Taylor had a number of prestigious contracts to his credit to which he drew the attention of the public in a full-page advertisement in Wright's *Leicester Directory* of 1884 (opposite). Two years later, he was able to draw attention to his latest achievements in Wright's *Directory*:

STEPHEN TAYLOR, ORGAN BUILDER,
NELSON STREET, LONDON ROAD, LEICESTER.

Most Perfect Organs in England.   Oldest established Organ Builder and Voicer in Leicester.

The new Organs built for the Churches of S. John the Baptist, S. Saviour's, All Saints, S. Leonard's, Christ Church, and St. Michael's, Leicester, are pronounced to be unsurpassed in this country for beauty of tone and high-class workmanship. An inspection and trial is solicited.

Organs built to any design or dimensions, and constructed so as to suit any position. Organs which have been tampered with by unskilful tuners thoroughly restored. Repairs promptly executed. Tunings, &c., by yearly contract. Tunings personally effected. Tubular pneumatic "noiseless" applied to all organs now.

The following are a few of the Organs built by S. Taylor:—

S. Saviour's, Leicester.	Wesleyan Chapel, Burton.	St. Margaret's, Leicester (now
S. Leonard's, Leicester.	T. F. Henley, Esq., London.	building).
Christ Church, Leicester.	Hoby Church, Leicestershire.	Quorndon Church.
S. John the Baptist, Leicester.	Bond Street Congregational Church,	Leire Church.
Victoria Road Church, Leicester.	Leicester.	All Saints', Wellingore, Grantham.
Knighton Church, Leicester.	Thurmaston Church, Leicester.	Syston Church, Leicester.
Thurnby Church, Leicester.	Wigston Church, Leicester.	Thrussington Church, Leicester.
Emanuel Church, Loughborough.	Swadlincote Church, Burton.	Staverton Church, Daventry.
Billesdon Church.	Thringstone Church.	Gresley Church, Burton.
Asfordby Church.	All Saints', Leicester.	All Saints', Hawley, Hants.
Owston Church.	St. Michael's, Leicester.	

From G. A. LOHR, Esq., Leicester.   (*Unsolicited*).   LEICESTER, *8th November,* 1877.

DEAR SIR,—I wish to express my great satisfaction in playing the Organ (built by you for St. Leonard's Church) at the Consecration Service, and my entire satisfaction with the tone of the Instrument throughout, also the excellent workmanship of the mechanical parts. Without going into the merits of each stop, I must say the charming quality of the Open Diapasons and the perfect clearness of the delicate stops seem to be all that can be possibly wished for. The *Reed* is particularly free and of full round quality.
Yours truly, G. A. LOHR.

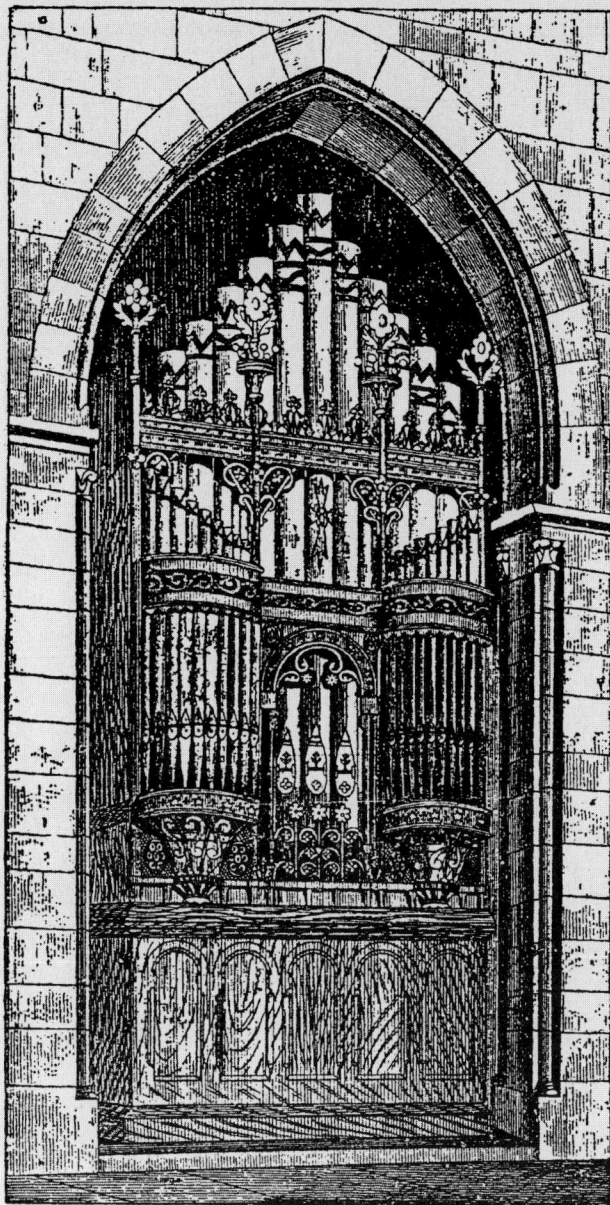

In the 1890s, Stephen Taylor was a prolific advertiser both in *Musical Opinion* and local directories, for he was determined to bring his firm to the notice of as many people as possible. There is no doubt that this policy was fully justified, for some important work came his way which in itself was a splendid recommendation for quality and artistry in tone. Three advertisements are full of interest, the first being taken from *Musical Opinion* for July 1st, 1890:

MOST PERFECT AND SUBSTANTIAL ORGANS IN ENGLAND.

STEPHEN TAYLOR, Organ Builder,

Established 1866.]   **LEICESTER.**   [Established 1866.

BUILDER OF HIGH CLASS ORGANS ONLY, AND AT PRICES PAID TO COMMON BUILDERS.
The important Organs built for Leicester are pronounced (by the greatest Organists of the day) to stand unsurpassed for every excellence by any known maker.   All the Voicing is personally effected by S. TAYLOR, who is recognized as the most skilful Voicer in the Kingdom.
THE SUCCESSFUL SPECIFICATIONS PREPARED FOR EVERY KIND OF BUILDING (avoiding unnecessary stops and outlay) is attributable to S. TAYLOR & SON's long experience as Church Organists.
Tunings and Repairs effected in any part of the Kingdom in the most careful manner.
TUBULAR PNEUMATIC AND OTHER MODERN ACTIONS.   TUNINGS BY YEARLY CONTRACT OR OTHERWISE.
VOICING TO THE TRADE.
☛ *Everyone should have one of S. Taylor's "Student's Practice Organs."* ☚
SEND FOR PROSPECTUS.
Leicester Organs built by S. Taylor: St. Saviour's, St. Leonard's, St. John the Baptist, All Saints', Christ Church
Bond Street Church, &c.

Wright's *Directory of Leicester* for 1892 informs us that Taylor too had joined the 'band wagon' of organ builders who were anxious to embrace the newly invented Hope-Jones electric action on licence. As far as is known, no organs were built on this system.

STEPHEN TAYLOR,
ORGAN BUILDER AND TUNER,
NELSON ST., LONDON RD., LEICESTER.

ANNUAL CONTRACTS FOR KEEPING INSTRUMENTS IN REPAIR AND TUNE.

SPECIFICATIONS AND ESTIMATES ON APPLICATION.

OLDEST ESTABLISHED ORGAN BUILDER AND VOICER IN LEICESTER.

Organs built to any design or dimensions, and constructed to suit any position.
Tubular pneumatic noiseless applied to all organs.
LICENSEE FOR USING R. HOPE JONES' PATENT NEW ELECTRIC PNEUMATIC ACTION.

THE FOLLOWING ARE A FEW OF THE

ORGANS BUILT BY S. TAYLOR:

LEICESTER AND DISTRICT.—St. Saviour's, St. Leonard's, Christ Church, St. John the Baptist, All Saints', St. Michael's, Knighton, Wigston, Thurnby, Thurmaston, Syston, Thrussington, Bond Street Congregational Church ; also, Emanuel Church, Loughborough, Billesdon, Asfordby, Hoby, Owston, Swadlincote, Thringstone, Wesleyan Chapel, Burton, All Saints', Wellingore (Grantham), Staverton (Daventry), Gresley (Burton), Newhall Catholic (Burton), All Saints', Hawley (Hants).   Hallaton, Shepshed, and others building.

The earliest Taylor organ known to me is in the Parish Church of Wellingore, some ten miles south of Lincoln. Situated at the east end of the north aisle, it has a simple case with a partly diapered pipe front and was built in 1886 to the following specification:

WELLINGORE PARISH CHURCH 1886

2 manuals: CC to G, 56 notes   Pedal: CCC to F, 30 notes

GREAT ORGAN

	ft
Open Diapason	8
Geigen	8
Dulciana	8
Rohr Flute	8
Principal	4

SWELL ORGAN

Open Diapason	8
Salicional	8
Lieblich Gedacht	8

Geigen Principal	4
Horn	8

PEDAL ORGAN

Open Diapason	16

COUPLERS

Swell to Great   Great to Pedals   Swell to Pedals
2 Composition pedals to Great
Electric blowing

Cost: £240 (just under £22 per speaking stop)

On January 6th, 1887, Mr F. Dunkerton, assistant organist of Lincoln Cathedral, examined the new organ. John Thomas, the Churchwarden, passed on his comments to Stephen Taylor:

'Your organ is worth ten of our box of whistles put in the nave of our Cathedral [a temporary organ for nave services]. Yours has a beautifully grand, full, pure, pervading tone, resembling very much our old organ in the Choir of the Cathedral; besides, you have such a splendid selection of stops, and I must congratulate you on meeting with so good a builder.' With its bold and quite brilliant ensemble it is very reminiscent of Father Willis's work of that period and with a fiery, splashy horn as the only reed. Readers are referred to Chapter XIV for further details of this instrument.

At the other end of the scale, I was taken by Billy Jones in the 1950s to hear their instrument at the De Montford Hall, Leicester, built in 1914, when the firm was Stephen Taylor & Sons. It was the gift to the city of Mr Alfred Corah and the opening recital was given by Sir Walter Parratt. Our visit included a call at the works where a warm welcome was extended to me, for W. C. Jones had carried out voicing for them for many years and had become a close friend of the family. The hall possesses considerable resonance and the organ stands in a fine open position at the back of the platform, enclosed by a case of mahogany. The console arrangements are not unlike those found in some of Norman & Beard's consoles in the early 1900s, the miniature drawstops only ¾ inch in diameter and having but a ⁵⁄₁₆ inch draw are placed in a single row over the Swell manual and extending to each angle jamb. The pistons are adjustable and are set by rows of knobs which are fixed to stout wires, each knob operating the drawstop in front of it. When the knob is in the down position, the piston pulls out the drawstop knob; when the knob is in the up position, the drawstop is pushed in by the action of the piston. The row of knobs which belong to each piston is parallel to the drawstops, so that it is a simple matter to set the combination desired from behind the panels on each jamb at the rear of the music desk. This system is perhaps unique in being entirely mechanical; that is, there is no pneumatic or electric action employed. I cannot say, however, that the system of miniature drawstops appeals to me.

The interior of the instrument is a sheer joy, being well planned with ample speaking room for each pipe and the workmanship is of the very highest order. The majority of the pipes are cone tuned.

Tonally, it is quite impossible to do justice here to the magnificence of the ensemble and the outstanding beauty of the quiet effects; it is a romantic concert hall organ of the very highest order, with superlative tone and tonal finishing throughout. After I had contributed an article to *The Choir*, I was amused to have this comment in a letter from Henry Willis III. 'Your article on De Montford Hall organ—it only goes to show how opinions on organs can differ'!

DE MONTFORD HALL, LEICESTER 1914

3 manuals: CC to C, 61 notes   Pedal: CCC to F, 30 notes

GREAT ORGAN

	ft
Double Open Diapason	16
Open Diapason	8
Large Open Diapason	8
Dulciana	8
Claribel Flute	8
Principal	4
Flute Harmonique	4
Grave Mixture 12·15	II
Full Mixture 17·19·22	III
Trombone (10 ins w.p.)	16
Tromba (ditto)	8
Clarion (ditto)	4

SWELL ORGAN

Contra Gamba (open through)	16
Open Diapason	8
Violin Diapason	8
Stopped Diapason	8
Salicional	8
Voix Celeste	8
Principal	4
Lieblich Flute	4
Fifteenth	2
Mixture 12·17·19·22	IV
Double Trumpet (10 ins w.p.)	16
Horn (ditto)	8
Hautboy	8

SOLO ORGAN

Violin Diapason	8
Lieblich Gedact	8
Viol d'Orchestre	8
Concert Flute	4
Orchestral Oboe	8

Corno di Bassetto	8
Tuba Mirabilis (15 ins w.p.)	8
Great Organ Reeds (unenclosed)	
Trombone	16
Tromba	8
Clarion	4

PEDAL ORGAN

Double Open Diapason	32
Open Diapason (wood)	16
Open Diapason (metal)	16
Bourdon	16
Viol di Gamba (enclosed in swell box)	16
Octave Diapason	8
Bass Flute	8
Double Trombone (15 ins w.pr.)	32
Bombarde (ditto)	16
Trumpet (ditto)	8

COUPLERS

Swell to Great Unison   Swell to Great Sub Octave
Swell to Great Octave   Swell Octave   Swell to Solo
Solo to Great   Solo to Pedals   Great to Pedals
Swell to Pedals   *Tremulant* to Solo
Tremulant to Swell

4 Pistons to Great   4 Pistons to Swell
3 Pistons to Solo   1 Piston to Great "Off"
5 Composition Pedals to Pedal Organ

Wind Pressures: 3½ to 15 ins
Tubular pneumatic action throughout

Blown by two — J. H. Taylor's Rotary Blowers,
driven by 8 h.p. electric motor

Testimonials were received about the De Montford Hall organ from the following distinguished recitalists, all of whom had performed there after the official opening: H. L. Balfour, G. D. Cunningham (then organist at the Alexandra Palace), Reginald Goss Custard, C. W. Perkins, J. A. Meale, Alfred Hollins, Bernard Johnson and Edwin H. Lemare. What a galaxy of players, and each one spoke in glowing terms of every facet of what was a magnificent conception of a concert hall organ which was worthy to take its place with any in the country.

A private recital before the opening of the organ was given on the evening of Wednesday, February 18th, 1914, by Mr Cardinal Taylor MUS. BAC., F.R.C.O. The donor, Alfred Corah, who had taken the greatest interest in every stage of its construction and installation, accompanied Mrs Reg. Corah in the opening solo after the National Anthem, and Mr Charles Hancock, MUS. BAC. F.R.C.O. (who had undertaken to act as Hon. Adviser pending the appointment of an organist by the Corporation) played one of his own compositions—a Postlude in B♭. No city organist has ever been appointed and the instrument has been used more for accompanimental purpose than for recitals.

A year after L. B. and R. A. Cousans of Lincoln had launched their newly invented electric blower, using fans in series, under the name 'Kinetic', John Henry Taylor (1862–1938) brought out a very efficient fan blower which became most successful. In *Musical Opinion* during 1908 he drew attention to his 'Electro-Fan Organ Blower. Simple—Reliable—Absolutely Silent. Special pneumatic control from console.

No complicated starters'. He had been trained in his father's firm as an organ builder and then ran his own company from Severn Street until 1916, when he was absorbed by Stephen Taylor & Son, who continued to make blowers which were a major part of the firm's output until they were taken over by Walkers. An early catalogue featured twelve models of one, two, or three fans ranging from ¾ h.p. to 6 h.p. and supplying wind from 400 c.f.m. to 1900 c.f.m. at pressures ranging from 3 to 12½ inches. After about 1934, mainly single-stage blowers were manufactured, over three thousand being made during the firm's existence—a no mean achievement. The following advertisement from *The Organist and Choirmaster* for August 8th, 1913, was typical of those published at that time. Their patent pneumatic starter was an ordinary drawstop connected by a pneumatic tube to the motor, thus 'danger of fire was absolutely minimised'. This tube, ⁵⁄₁₆ of an inch in diameter, closed the electric circuit, when the motor was then brought up to speed automatically.

The blowing installation at the De Montford Hall consisted of 'five organ blowing rotors running in series and in separate chambers'. These developed pressures of wind varying from 3½ to 15 inches. The blower was driven by an 8 horse power motor, the current being supplied from the Corporation lighting mains. It still works efficiently, the only alteration having been the conversion of the original leather belts on crowned cork pulleys to v-belt drive.

Stephen Taylor (1838–1920) had five children, three of whom were male, John Henry (1862–1938) the blowing engineer; Stephen Oliver Taylor (1870–1953) worked closely with his father and it was during these years that the firm was so very successful. Cardinal Taylor (1872–1943) trained as an organ builder, but became an outstanding professional musician, gaining his MUS. BAC. at Durham and the Fellowship of the Royal College of Organists. For twenty-five years he was Organist and Choirmaster at St Stephen's Presbyterian Church, Leicester. Once established in his musical career, he played no further part in the business.

Jeffrey Lewin Taylor B.SC. (1907–1975), the younger son of Oliver, trained and worked in the business until the second World War, spending much time with J. H. T. on the blowing side. He was responsible for the design of the later blowers which were very successful up to the mid 1950s. He rejoined the family firm in 1949 as partner when it became a limited company. Stephen Arthur Taylor (1897–1954), the eldest son of Oliver, trained and worked all his life in the firm until tragically killed in a car crash. He was joint partner with his brother at the time of his death. The deaths of Oliver and Stephen in one financial year put a tremendous strain on Jeffrey Taylor. He continued to run the business on his own, building three new electric action organs for Hucknall Notts., Oadby, Leics., and Carley Street Baptist Church, Leicester, during this time. In 1965 he sold the tuning round and work in hand to Walkers, but not the

company. Thus, this grand old firm failed to reach its centenary by just one year. He worked on his own making parts for Walkers and Hill, Norman & Beard until his death.

Taylor organs were noted for their spacious lay-outs with everything accessible; they were famous for their highly effective wooden Violones and ingenious exhaust-pneumatic actions; sometimes pressure and exhaust were combined. In later years they brought out their electro-pneumatic actions (Free Masons' Temple, London Road, Leicester, 1948) the rebuild of a Gern organ at Lutterworth Parish Church, then later on, one or two direct electric actions, one of the last being Carley Baptist Church, Leicester (recently replaced with Solid State by Roy Young). At their peak they employed some fifteen men; they made all their wood pipes, but those of metal were supplied by the trade. All flue voicing was done by succeeding members of the family—but reeds were the work of specialists in the trade, particularly W. C. Jones, who voiced for them over a period of many years. At the turn of the century and for some years afterwards, when some firms emasculated the upper work of their flue choruses, Taylors did not conform to the prevailing pattern. Some found their mixtures a little too bold, although I would venture to say that their output is modest compared to what one hears today in some quarters. All in all they were noted for their fine, virile and cohesive ensembles.

In addition to the De Montford Hall organ, Taylors built three other four-manual instruments in Leicester—a no mean achievement—which possibly was the cause of jealousy on the part of some London and Provincial firms over the years from the 1930s, who, I am reliably informed, decried the work of the Leicester firm. St Peter's (1910), to the following specification, has survived—but only just—and this has been due to the loving care of Roy Young who has done his utmost to keep it going. It has been described as 'an organ of considerable splendour' and one wonders if it will survive in these difficult times of depleted congregations and eventual closure of churches:

ST PETER'S CHURCH, LEICESTER 1910

The Organ has been built by Messrs. S. Taylor & Son, of Leicester, to the following specification drawn up by the builders in consultation with W. J. Bunney, Esq., F.R.C.O., Organist and Choirmaster of the church. It contains Four Manuals, CC to C, 61 notes; and a Pedal Organ CCC to F, 30 notes. Pedal board radiating and concave. There are 45 speaking stops and 13 couplers, making a total of 58 drawstops. The whole Organ is on the builder's Tubular Pneumatic System.

GREAT ORGAN

	ft		
Double Open Diapason	16	Harmonic Flute	4
Large Open Diapason	8	Grave Mixture	II
Small Open Diapason	8	Full Mixture	III
Claribel Flute	8	Tromba (10 ins. w.p.)	8
Principal	4	Clarion (ditto)	4

SWELL ORGAN

	ft
Violon	16
Open Diapason	8
Violin Diapason	8
Stopped Diapason	8
Viol d'Amour	8
Voix Celestes	8
Principal	4
Flute	4
Fifteenth	2
Mixture	III
Double Trumpet (6 ins w.p.)	16
Horn (ditto)	8
Oboe (ditto)	8

CHOIR ORGAN

Open Diapason (unenclosed)	8
Lieblich Gedact	8
Dulciana (unenclosed)	8
Viol	8
Salicet	4
Flauto Traverso	4
Piccolo	2
Clarinet	8

SOLO ORGAN

Horn Diapason	8
Hohl Flute	8
Viol d'Orchestre	8
Concert Flute	4
Quintaton	8
Orchestral Oboe	8
Tuba	8

PEDAL ORGAN

Contra Violon	32
Open Diapason	16
Violon	16
Bourdon	16
Octave Diapason	8
Flute	8
Trombone (10 ins w.p.)	16

COUPLERS

Swell to Great Unison   Swell to Great Octave
Swell in Octaves   Swell to Choir   Solo to Great
Solo in Octaves   Great Unison Off
Choir to Pedals   Great to Pedals   Swell to Pedals
Solo to Pedals   *Tremulant* to Flue work
Tremulant to Swell Reeds

ACCESSORIES

3 Pistons each to Choir and Solo Organs
4 Pistons each to Great and Swell Organs
3 Composition Pedals to Pedal Organ
1 Composition Pedal to Great to Pedal Coupler

WIND PRESSURES

Flue Work: 3¼ ins   Swell Reeds: 6 ins.
Great and Pedal Reeds: 10 ins.
Action: 5—13 ins.
Blown by J. H. Taylor's Rotary Blower (4–stage)
and 5 h.p. Electric Motor

The Contra Violon (wood) is a remarkable stop and
very prompt in speech. Taylors were famous for their
16 and 8ft wood string basses.

St John the Baptist, Leicester (1896), had a conventional drawstop console; it was rebuilt in 1964 by Walkers, who reduced it to three manuals:

ST JOHN THE BAPTIST, LEICESTER 1896

GREAT ORGAN

	ft
Bourdon	16
Open Diapason	8
Open Diapason	8
Stopped Diapason	8
Hohl Flute	8
Principal	4
Harmonic Flute	4
Twelfth	2⅔
Fifteenth	2
Mixture	III
Trumpet	8

SWELL ORGAN

Lieblich Bourdon	16
Open Diapason	8
Wald Flute	8
Principal	4
Twelfth	2⅔
Fifteenth	2
Mixture	III

Double Trumpet	16
Horn	8
Oboe	8
Clarion	4
Tremulant	

CHOIR ORGAN

Dulciana	8
Viola	8
Claribel Flute	8
Lieblich Flute	4
Piccolo	2

ECHO ORGAN

Dulciana	8
Lieblich Gedact	8
Vox Celeste	8
Clarinet	8
Vox Humana	8
Tremulant	

PEDAL ORGAN	
Open Diapason	16
Bourdon	16
Open Diapason	8
Flute	8
Trombone (6 ins w.p.)	16

COUPLERS

Swell to Great Unison Swell to Great Octave
Swell to Great Sub Octave Swell to Choir

Choir to Great Sub Octave Swell to Echo
Choir to Pedals Great to Pedals
Swell to Pedals Echo to Pedals
Great to Pedals—off and on—by popjoy

4 Thumb Pistons each to Great and Swell Organs
3 Thumb Pistons each to Choir and Echo Organs

Tubular-pneumatic action throughout

Blown by J. H. Taylor's Rotary Blower (3–stage),
and driven by a 4 h.p. Electric Motor

St John the Divine, Leicester (1904), had a Solo Organ prepared for, but the stops were never inserted. When the church closed some years ago, the organ was vandalised. J. H. Taylor was organist here for a number of years:

ST JOHN THE DIVINE, LEICESTER 1904

GREAT ORGAN	ft
Open Diapason	16
Open Diapason	8
Small Open Diapason	8
Claribel Flute	8
Principal	4
Twelfth	2⅔
Fifteenth	2
Mixture	III
Trumpet	8

SWELL ORGAN	
Double Dulciana	16
Open Diapason	8
Stopped Diapason	8
Keraulophon	8
Celeste	8
Principal	4
Flute	4
Grave Mixture	II
Cornopean	8
Oboe	8

CHOIR ORGAN	
Dulciana	8
Viol	8
Gedact	8
Harmonic Flute	4
Clarinet	8

SOLO ORGAN	
Viol di Orchestre	8
Solo Flute	8
Solo Flute	4
Trumpet	16
Orchestral Oboe	8
Tuba	8
Clarion	4

PEDAL ORGAN	
Contra Violon	32
Open Diapason	16
Violon	16
Bourdon	16
Principal	8
Flute	8
Trombone	16
Trumpet	8

COUPLERS

Swell to Great Unison
Swell to Great Octave
Swell to Great Sub Octave
Swell to Choir Solo to Great
Solo to Swell Solo Octave
Choir to Pedal Great to Pedal
Swell to Pedal Solo to Pedal

Taylors designed a small four-stop Portative organ; several were built, but the exact number is not known. I gather that the firm was more concerned with the production of fine organs rather than keeping records about them! The estimated total number of organs built throughout its existence is approximately 300. The *Dictionary of Organs and Organists* (1921 edn.) lists 24 instruments built or rebuilt by them in the city of Leicester.

I always regard S. Taylor & Son as the third member of the trilogy of organ builders—Vowles of Bristol and Wilkinson of Kendal—serving strategic parts of the country, and working to the highest ideals, producing instruments which will last well into the future if given expert care and maintenance. Care is the responsibility of the church; maintenance must be carried out with skill and sympathy by a builder who is committed to conservation.

left
De Montford Hall, Leicester.
The console

right
Taylor organ at
Wellingore Church, Lincs.
The author at the console.
Photo: Jonathan Wallace

below
Portative organ by Taylor

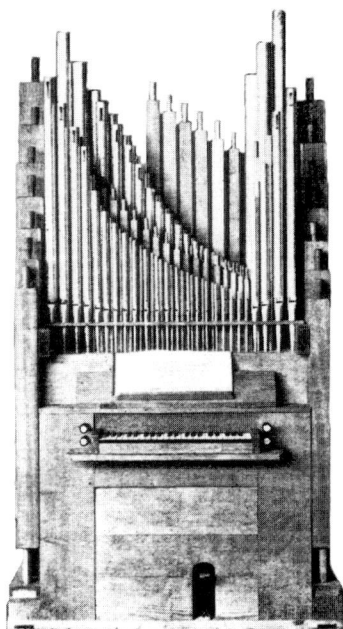

J. PORRITT & SON 1867–1965

The firm of Porritt was somewhat overshadowed by that of Taylor; nevertheless, they did some good solid work which has endured over the years. They had a wide connection in the Midland counties as well as in Yorkshire and as far south as Surrey. Joshua Porritt commenced organ building on his own account a year after Stephen Taylor established his business. He had gained experience with several North Country firms, most important of which were Forster & Andrews, where he rose to become voicer, finisher and tuner. In 1867, he decided to commence in business for himself, removing to Leicester, where, after several removals, including a number of years at 64½ and 66 London Road, he altered a large joinery works at 84 London Road in order to meet his requirements.

By 1871, Porritt had become well known beyond Leicestershire, for he was chosen to rebuild the organ at Holy Trinity Church, Coventry, to the following specification, which appeared in *The Musical Standard* for 16th December, 1871. The cost of the work was £1,500.

HOLY TRINITY CHURCH, COVENTRY 1871

3 manuals: CC to G, 56 notes   Pedal: CCC to F, 42 notes

GREAT ORGAN

	ft
Bourdon	16
Double Open Diapason	16
Open Diapason	8
Horn Diapason	8
Stop Diapason	8
Principal	4
Wald Flute	4
Twelfth	2⅔
Fifteenth	2
Full Mixture	IV
Sharp Mixture	III
Posaune	8
Solo Trumpet	8
Clarion	4

SWELL ORGAN

Sub Bass	16
Double Diapason	16
Open Diapason	8
Stop Diapason	8
German Gamba	8
Principal	4
Fifteenth	2
Piccolo	2
Full Mixture	III
Contra Fagotto	16
Cornopean	8
Oboe	8
Clarion	4
Tremulant	

CHOIR ORGAN

Dulciana Bass	8
Dulciana Treble	8
Viola de Gamba	8
Stop Diapason	8
Gemshorn	4
Rohr Flote	4
Fifteenth	2
Dulciana Mixture	III
Krummhorn	8
Bassoon	8

PEDAL ORGAN

Grand Double Open Diapason	16
Bourdon	16
Violon, Principal	8
Fifteenth	4
Trombone	16
Coupler in Octaves various	

COUPLERS

Great to Pedals   Choir to Pedals   Swell to Pedals
Swell to Great   Swell Super Octave to Great
Choir to Great   Swell to Choir

4 Composition Pedals to Great Organ
2 Composition Pedals to Swell Organ

The extension of the Pedal Organ to a compass of 42 notes, to take the octave coupler, will be noticed.

In 1878, their work became known in Liverpool where they obtained the contract for a new organ for St Mary's Church, Prescot. The following details are taken from *The Choir* for 11th May, 1878:

> PRESCOT, NEAR LIVERPOOL:— The following is the specification of a new organ recently built for the parish church of St Mary, at Prescot. The instrument has three complete manuals, compass CC to G in alt., pedals from CCC to F, thirty notes, and containing the following stops, &c:—

GREAT ORGAN

	ft
Lieblich Bourdon	16
Open Diapason	8
Viola	8
Stopped Diapason & Clarabella	8
Principal	4
Flute Harmonique	4
Twelfth	2⅔
Fifteenth	2
Mixture	III
Posaune	8

SWELL ORGAN

Lieblich Bourdon	16
Open Diapason	8
Lieblich Gedact	8
Viol d'Amour	8
Principal	4
Flageolet	2
Mixture	III
Contra Fagotto (tenor C)	16
Cornopean	8
Oboe	8

CHOIR ORGAN

Dulciana	8
Lieblich Gedact	8
Voix Céleste	8
Gemshorn	4
Wald Flute	4
Flautino	2
Clarionet & Bassoon	8

PEDAL ORGAN

Grand Open Diapason	16
Grand Bourdon	16
Violoncello	8
Spare slice	–

The pedals are radiating and concave, and all the metal pipes are of fine spotted metal, built in a chamber on the north side of the chancel, with frontages to chancel and north aisle. There is a handsome carved oak case. The builder is Mr Joshua Porritt, of Leicester, and the cost is about £1,000. It was opened on Sunday the 5th of May, by Mr W. Amps, organist of St Peter's College, Cambridge, and there was a service and recital on Wednesday, the 8th, for which Mr W. H. Jude was engaged. On that occasion the fine choir of St Nicholas's Parish Church, Liverpool, officiated.

What possibly was the largest instrument built by Joshua Porritt was that for St Mary's Church, Leicester, in 1880. The following details are taken from *The Musical Standard* for June 5th, 1880:

ST MARY'S CHURCH, LEICESTER 1880

GREAT ORGAN

	ft
Large Open Diapason	16
Open Diapason	8
Stop Diapason	8
Principal	4
Flute Harmonique	4
Twelfth	2⅔
Fifteenth	2
Mixture	III
Trumpet	8

SWELL ORGAN

Lieblich and Bourdon	16
Open Diapason	8
Gamba	8
Vox Angelica	8
Lieblich Gedact	8
Principal	4
Lieblich Flöte	4
Fifteenth	2
Mixture	III
Cornopean	8
Oboe	8
Clarion	4

CHOIR ORGAN

Dulciana	8
Keraulophon	8
Lieblich Gedact	8
Wald Flute	4
Gemshorn	4
Fifteenth	2
Bassoon and Cremona	8

PEDAL ORGAN

Open Diapason	16
Bourdon	16
Violoncello	8
Flute	8
Contra Fagotto	16

COUPLERS

Swell to Great   Swell to Choir   Swell to Pedals
Great to Pedals   Choir to Pedals
Swell Octave to Great   Swell Sub Octave to Great

3 Composition Pedals each to Great & Swell Organs
1 Horse-shoe Pedal—on and off—Great to Pedals
1 Horse-shoe Pedal—on and off—all Pedal stops,
excepting Bourdon

The organ is divided and built in such a form as not to interfere with the beautiful large stained glass window, with which the east end of the church is adorned. The case of the organ, designed by Mr Shenton, Architect, Leicester, is of selected Memel oak, very ornamental, and richly carved, and in character with the 12th-century screen in the chancel, and of which the organ case may be almost said to form a part; its total length, including screen, is forty feet, height twenty-eight feet.

In my own county of Lincolnshire there are three examples of the founder's work of the last century: Grantham United Reformed Church (formerly Congregational) built in 1887; Grantham Catholic Church and Folkingham Parish Church. The first instrument came to my notice in the early 1980s and I was struck by its fine quality of tone, although the action was in need of a thorough reconditioning. The church records of 1887 reveal considerable discussion as to the choice of builder; Forster & Andrews were considered, for they had been responsible for five instruments in the town, including the Parish Church (1851, 1869), the Wesleyan Chapel (1857), St John's Church, Spittlegate (1871), the Independent Chapel (being the forerunner of the present United Reformed Church) and a residence organ for a Mr Richard Short in 1851. A Bristol firm (possibly Vowles) had submitted a tender, but after careful consideration of the various proposals, and taking into consideration the most suitable position, on the advice of a Mr Dickinson, Porritts were ordered to build a two-manual instrument in the north-east corner of this Gothic church. There were four special services during February and March 1888, and on 23rd February there was a special tea costing one shilling, followed by an organ recital by Mr Dickinson. They never did anything by halves in those days!

In 1985-6 Henry Groves & Son Ltd. of Nottingham carried out a comprehensive restoration. The re-opening recital was given by Noel Cox who spoke most highly of the instrument. His playing displayed all the facets of this fine Victorian organ and it is now in first-class condition and with almost a century of service, ready for many more years to come. Its splendid quality of tone has that extra 'something' to which a player immediately responds—need one say more.

UNITED REFORMED CHURCH, GRANTHAM 1887

2 manuals: CC to G, 56 notes   Pedal: CCC to F, 30 notes

GREAT ORGAN

	ft		
Open Diapason	8	Gemshorn	4
Geigen Principal	8	Piccolo	2
Dulciana	8	Horn	8
Stopped Diapason	8	Oboe	8
Principal	4	*Tremulant*	
Wald Flute	4		
Fifteenth	2	PEDAL ORGAN	
Mixture 19·22	II	Sub Bass	16
		Violoncello	8

SWELL ORGAN

		COUPLERS	
Lieblich Bourdon	16		
Open Diapason	8	Swell to Great Swell to Pedals Great to Pedals	
Viol d'Amour	8	Balanced Swell Pedal	
Voix Celestes	8	Tracker action to manuals; pneumatic to Pedals	
Lieblich Gedacht	8		

By 1897, Porritt had every reason to be satisfied with his progress and no doubt with some pride advertised in *The Organist and Choirmaster* (overleaf). Joshua Porritt retired in 1904 and was succeeded by his son, Walter Samuel Lord Porritt, who was born in Leicester in 1873 and entered the business at the age of 14, where he gained a thorough knowledge of general organ building in the workshops as well as the large tuning and repairing connection, while he specialised in voicing. He was go-ahead, and believed in advertising; the following is taken from *Kelly's Directory of Leicestershire* for 1908:

ESTABLISHED 1867.

J. PORRITT,

ORGAN BUILDER, VOICER, TUNER, &c.

MIDLAND COUNTIES ORGAN MANUFACTORY,

66 & 64½, LONDON ROAD, LEICESTER.

The most extensive Organ Works in the Midlands, covering an area of 6,400 feet.

The following are a few Extracts from Testimonials received :—

SIR GEORGE ELVEY, Mus. Doc. Oxon., late Organist of the Chapel Royal, Windsor, says :—" I can confidently recommend Mr. Porritt as a Builder of Organs that will prove eminently satisfactory to all lovers of true organ tone."

C. W. PERKINS, Organist of the Town Hall, Birmingham, says :—" It is always a pleasure to play on your organs, as I always find them particularly ' honest,' which is a quality sadly lacking in many organs. I have no hesitation in expressing my unqualified approval of the *tone and workmanship of these excellent instruments.*"

Several really good Second-hand Organs for Sale, very cheap.

ESTABLISHED 1867.

J. PORRITT & SON,

Midland Counties . .

Organ Manufactory, .

LEICESTER,

Invite Correspondence on all matters relative to Organs or Organ Building.

Diapason, Flute, String, and Reed Tones of great individuality.
A Pneumatic System, durable, prompt, and perfect in repetition.
Wind supply by Electric, Gas and Hydraulic Power.
Cases to harmonize with any building or to Architect's designs.

The Workshops and Instruments in Leicester are always open to Inspection.

References and Testimonials free on application.

Taylor and Porritt were in competition in Loughborough, where the latter had a branch factory in later years. In 1908, Porritts built a three-manual organ for Baxter Gate Baptist Church which was given publicity in that year.

> LOUGHBOROUGH.— The dedication of the new organ at Baxter Gate Baptist Church took place on October 14th, when Mr C. W. Perkins gave a recital, the programme including Best's Fantasia in F, Bach's Prelude and Fugue in C, Spohr's Andante in F, Faulk's Toccata in D minor, Tschaikovsky's Prelude, Elegy and Finale on a Russian Air, Mendelssohn's Andante in E and Wagner's Overture to "Tannhauser". The organ is the work of Messrs. J Porritt & Son and is blown by an electric motor and fan placed in a chamber behind the school room at the rear of the chapel. The specification of the organ follows:—

GREAT ORGAN

	ft
Violone	16
Diapason major	8
Open Diapason	8
Hohlflöte	8
Principal	4
Waldflöte	4
Fifteenth	2
Tuba minor	8

SWELL ORGAN

Lieblich bordun	16
Open Diapason	8
Viole d'orchestre	8
Voix Célestes (tenor C)	8
Lieblich Gedackt	8
Gemshorn	4
Lieblich Flöte	4
Flautina	2
Mixture	III
Horn	8
Oboe	8
Tremulant	

CHOIR ORGAN

Gamba	8
Stopped Diapason	8
Dulciana	8
Gambette	4
Harmonic Flute	4
Corno di Bassetto	8

PEDAL ORGAN

Acoustic Bass	32
Open Diapason	16
Sub Bass	16
Lieblich Bordun	16
Violoncello	8
Stopped Flute	8

COUPLERS

Swell to Great   Swell to Choir   Swell to Pedal
Great to Pedal   Choir to Pedal

3 combination pedals to Great, Swell & Pedal Organs
Great to Pedal by pedal
2 balanced crescendo pedals
Tubular-pneumatic and tracker action

Seven years later, Porritt commenced what proved to be a frustrating connection with Loughborough Parish Church. W. L. Sumner tells the story in an article in *Musical Opinion* for June 1946, from which we learn that the Ingram & Hope-Jones Company built a large four-manual instrument with a detached console in 1901. Unfortunately, it was not noted for its reliability and within ten years became unplayable. At the commencement of World War I, Dr. Alan Gray of Trinity College, Cambridge, was consulted and plans were drawn up for a complete rebuild on a single site in a chamber on the north side of the chancel. Previously, the departments had been split up in four different positions in typical Hope-Jones fashion. Tonally this must have been most unsatisfactory and there is little wonder that it failed to work efficiently. A large draw-stop console was made and a divided Choir Organ with three pedal stops became playable as a temporary measure. The years went by and nothing further was done, to the intense frustration of a very musical vicar and the excellent musicians who served this important church over the years. In 1946, Dr. Sumner commented that the action was working remarkably well; eventually, by 1966, this long suffering church was able to acquire the Binns organ from Bridgway Hall Methodist Mission, Nottingham (which had closed), and Henry Willis & Sons Ltd rebuilt it to the delight of all concerned.

LOUGHBOROUGH PARISH CHURCH: PORRITT'S SCHEME 1915

GREAT ORGAN

	ft
Double Open	16
Large Open	8
Geigen	8
Dolce	8
Hohl Flöte	8
Octave	4
Waldflöte	4
Twelfth	2⅔
Super Octave	2
Mixture	III
Enclosed section (heavy wind)	
Diapason Phonon	8
Harmonic Claribel	8
Harmonic Tromba	8

SWELL ORGAN

Lieblich bourdon	16
Open Diapason	8
Dulciana	8
Quintaton	8
Lieblich Gedacht	8
Viol d'Orchestre	8
Viol Céleste (tenor C)	8
Suabe Flöte	4
Octave	4
Super Octave	2
Mixture	III
Oboe	8
Contra Posaune (heavy wind)	16
Cornopean (ditto)	8
Clarion (ditto)	4

CHOIR ORGAN		Enclosed	
		Contra Gamba	16
Unenclosed		Harmonic Flute	8
Open Diapason	8	'Cello	8
Stopped Diapason	8	Viole d'Orchestre	8
Phoneuma	8	Orchestral Flute	4
Gedacht	8	Octave Viol	4
Salicional	8	Cor Anglais	16
Harmonic Flute	4	Orchestral Oboe	8
Principal	4	Clarinet	8
Harmonic Piccolo	2	Horn	8

According to that invaluable source of information, the Revd. B. B. Edmonds, the tone of Porritt's work in the early years of the present century tended to be 'Hope-Jonesey' at times, while their tubular-pneumatic action was sometimes rather slow (despite their advertisement in 1908!).

The presence of tibia plena on the Great Organ of the instrument built for Chipping Norton Parish Church in 1912, will be noted. Situated at the east end of the north aisle, it had a detached console, with tubular-pneumatic action. It had a very comprehensive scheme which remained intact until 1952 when Rushworth & Dreaper replaced the tibia plena by a stopped diapason when they overhauled the instrument.

CHIPPING NORTON PARISH CHURCH 1912

GREAT ORGAN			
	ft	Clarabella	8
		Gemshorn	4
Bourdon	16	*Enclosed section*	
Diapason Major	8	Viole d'orchestre	8
Diapason Minor	8	Dolce	8
Tibia Plena	8	Flauto Magico	4
Dulciana	8	Harmonic Piccolo	2
Octave Diapason	4	Clarinet	8
Hohlflute	4	Vox Humana	8
Twelfth	2⅔		
Fifteenth	2	PEDAL ORGAN	
Trumpet	8	Double Open Diapason	16
		Open Diapason	16
SWELL ORGAN		Violone	16
		Sub Bass	16
Lieblich Bourdon	16	Echo Bass	16
Open Diapason	8	Violoncello	8
Lieblich Gedact	8	Flute Bass	8
Viole di Gamba	8	COUPLERS	
Vox Angelica	8		
Voix Celestes	8	*Over Swell keys:* Swell Octave Choir Octave	
Geigen Principal	4	*Left jamb:* Pedal couplers	
Wald Flute	4	*By 'on–off' pistons, no other control:*	
Harmonic Gemshorn	2	Swell to Choir Choir to Great Swell to Great	
Mixture	III		
Cornopean	8	9 Combination pedals	
Oboe	8	Reversible Combination pedal: Great to Pedal	
CHOIR ORGAN		*Tablets below Choir manual:*	
		Unenclosed Choir off—on Enclosed Choir on–off	
Open Diapason	8	Bartouch to *Tremulant*	
Viola	8		

Under Walter Porritt's direction, the firm continued to progress; he was an accomplished pianist and organist and a competent cellist. In his youth, before business responsibilities became too great, he took a leading part in the musical life of Leicester. He was a member of the Federation of Master Organ Builders from its inception in 1913, and did valuable work for it for many years. His death in 1953, his eightieth year, was a great loss to the family firm to whom his long experience of the industry was invaluable.

William Henry Porritt, his son, was at that time a science Master at Downside Abbey School. It was his intention to return to Leicester on retirement at sixty and take over the business, but he died suddenly in 1956 at the age of 56. Meanwhile, H. Walmsley was appointed manager and carried on the direction of the firm, known as Porritt & Son (Organ Builders) Ltd., until his retirement in 1965, when Rushworth & Dreaper Ltd. (his former employers for about thirty-five years) took over most of the tuning contracts. Thus, yet another family business which was highly thought of in its day ceased trading after failing to make its centenary by only two years.

Grantham United Reformed Church
Organ by Porritt. Photo by the Author

RUGBY: ROY YOUNG EST. 1973

Roy Young not only is a skilled organ builder devoted to his craft, but an enthusiastic preservationist too, of good historic work, and above all that of Taylor of Leicester whom he admires so much, for it was there that he come into daily contact with all that is best in organ building. It is understandable, therefore, that Leicester City Council placed the De Montford Hall organ in his care from 1975, and the ongoing restoration of this magnificent instrument is a matter of great pride to Roy and his son Keith. The work (not yet completed) is being carried out in stages when funds permit. He was an indentured apprentice to Taylors between 1948–54. Here he was involved not only in general organ building but in the blowing department too, assisting in some of the sheet metal work and silencing boxes, not to mention installation in some very difficult sites. After completing his National Service, he gained valuable experience as a draughtsman in an engineering works, did some part-time work as an organ builder and eventually started his own business in 1973. He works from a 200 year old building with storage room in the galleries and ample workshop space down below. Originally he had an apprentice and a small staff; now he and his son Keith work closely together, sharing the same enthusiasm and he has extra assistance where there is heavy lifting to be done. He is responsible for all his own flue voicing and is fully experienced in the use of Solid State. When time permits, he is fortunate to have some assistance from the last of the Taylors—Stephen (J. S. G. Taylor)—who, although an Experimental Officer in the department of Physics, Leicester University, has organ building in his blood and is a mine of information about the family firm.

A sample of some of the interesting contracts he has carried out since 1973 includes the rebuild of an 1863 Bevington organ at Attleborough Church, Nuneaton (c.1973), the electrification of the three-manual Nicholson & Lord organ in the Baptist Church, Rugby (1976) and the restoration as it was of the one-manual Lincoln organ of 1806 in the Baptist Church, Studley.

In 1980, he built a new two-manual organ with electric action (which included some pipes from the former Forster & Andrews organ in Holy Trinity Church, Rugby) for St George's Church in that town. The year 1989 saw the restoration of the Speechley organ in Launde Abbey, Leics. Roy Young is an organist too and leads an extremely busy life enjoying to the full his main interest—organ building.

PETER COLLINS, MELTON MOWBRAY

One of the leading exponents of the neo-classical organ, Peter Collins, has occupied his splendid purpose-built factory since June 1989. A modern unit on an industrial estate on the outskirts of the town, it has an area of almost 6,000 square feet, with a maximum height of thirty feet in one section, enabling jobs to be completely assembled. There is a separate woodworking mill at one end.

He has been involved with organs since his schooldays, acting as 'Keyholder' for the tuners of Bishop & Son, London, to whom he was later apprenticed. With them he worked on the restoration and rebuilding of many different organs with various types of actions and voicing styles which gave him valuable experience. The opportunity to meet Continental organ builders when The International Society of Organ Builders met in London during 1962 gave him the opportunity to meet Josef von Glatter-Gotz, from Reiger Orgelbau of Austria, with whom he worked in Austria and Germany during 1954 and 1965. He then established his own firm at 88 Park Street Village, St Albans, later moving to Redbourn, Herts. He was determined to concentrate on building new tracker organs and this he has done, almost without exception since 1970, with some ninety organs, ranging from one stop to fifty-five, to his credit. In recent years, he has constructed several instruments is historic case styles. His export work has included ten instruments for Australia, two for Eire and one each to Switzerland, Canada and Norway. To celebrate twenty-five years of organ building on his own account, he branched out into the compact disc market in 1990, and in his letter to me dated 12th February, 1991, he spoke of three of his instruments having been recorded: St Peter Mancroft, Norwich (1984, John Scott), International Organ Festival organ, St Saviour's, St Albans (1989, Peter Hurford), and a two-manual house organ at Kew, built in 1984 (Margaret Phillips).

Some interesting examples of his work of recent years may be heard at St Oswald's Church, Durham, St Mary's on Paddington Green, London (two-manual), Manchester Grammar School (two-manual) and St Mary's Church, Barnes, London (two-manual). Their cases have been designed and made to complement the buildings in which they are placed. Not only are they impressive in design, but in workmanship too. In this work he has been fortunate in having the services of Siegfried Pietzch of Redbourn.

The facilities at their splendidly equipped workshops enable them to carry out all the cabinet work for consoles and cases in the finest seasoned timber, as well as windchests and other working parts. Visitors, who are always welcome by appointment, have spoken to me of how impressed they have been by what they have seen, together with the splendid organisation behind it all. I have yet to pay a visit there. In June 1992, they held an Open Day which featured demonstrations of pipe making, reed and flue pipe voicing, and displays of work, at the close of which was a short concert by Douglas Hollick. It was so successful that 'Workshop in a Workshop' followed on 19th September, held specially for those interested in the art of tuning pipes.

In addition to their larger instruments, the firm's three-stop box organs are in demand, either for use in small churches or for hirings and recordings, both in this country and abroad. A complete restoration and tuning service, as well as high quality reconstruction work, is available as well as the construction of entirely new organs.

Peter Collins looks back with pride at his many achievements, and it has all evolved from being a tuner's boy—not too many years ago.

CHAPTER IX

Nottingham and District

C. LLOYD & CO. 1859–1928

NOTTINGHAM has been the home of no less than seven organ builders since 1859, when Charles Lloyd, together with his partner Lorenzo Valentine, established a workshop in Bilbie Street. Lloyd had been voicer and tuner for the previous ten years with Samuel Groves of London; he had trained under John Gray of New Road, Fitzroy Square, London, who in 1838 took as partner Frederick Davison, thus founding the firm of Gray & Davison. Amongst a number of other contracts, Groves built organs for St Paul's, Cambridge, St Julian's, Shrewsbury, St Margaret's, Leicester, Holy Trinity, Dorchester, together with repairs and alterations to the organ at St Mary Woolnoth, London, between 1850–51. In 1853 he was introduced to the committee of the Mechanics Institute, Nottingham, where there was a large three-manual instrument in the great hall built in 1849 by Bevington to a scheme drawn up by Dr. Gauntlett. The permanent organist was Mr W. Shelmerdine and it was he who within the organisation of the Institute, founded the still flourishing Nottingham Harmonic Society. In 1853, Shelmerdine induced the committee to embark on a large scheme of reconstruction to the organ which unfortunately the financial position of the Institute did not justify. He introduced Groves who undertook at a cost of £100 to add eight new stops and remove the Choir and Swell Organs from inside the case to anterooms underneath the orchestra. When the account was presented, however, it was found to be more than double the original amount.

An advertisement by Groves will be found in Hopkins & Rimbault, *The Organ*, 1855 edn., which reads as follows:

SAMUEL GROVES, ORGAN BUILDER,

Inventor and Provisional Patentee of Rotary Pneumatic Apparatus for pumping or forcing air, whereby an Organ of any dimensions may be supplied with wind by machinery instead of manual labour, at a comparatively small expense. DIRECT ACTION, which, in an Organ of 3 rows of keys, causes upwards of 600 centres to be dispensed with; LEVER VALVE, which so thoroughly resists the pressure of air as to render the touch of a large Organ most agreeable (equally light to that of a grand piano of the first maker), and admits a full supply of wind to the pipes. 7, Great Marlborough-street; Manufactory, 11, Little Marlborough-street, Regent-street, London.

Sadly, in 1867 the Mechanics Hall and organ were destroyed by a disastrous fire. When the new hall was opened in 1869, a fund was commenced for a new organ and this was built by Hill & Son. Between 1890–94 a series of Saturday afternoon recitals which attracted large audiences were given by Edwin H. Lemare. The Lincoln firm of Cousans Sons & Co. restored the instrument and constructed an entirely new console with angle jambs in 1896, and Lemare re-opened it. Gradually the popularity of the hall decreased; eventually it was leased as a cinema, but hall and organ have long since gone.

It seems more than likely that Charles Lloyd, after working with his master at the Mechanics Hall in 1853 and paying subsequent visits to tune it, felt that the rapidly growing city of Nottingham had great potential for an organ building business. By 1859 he decided to become his own master and with his partner Lorenzo Valentine, commenced work from a building in Bilbie Street. The partnership was short-lived however, and by 1862 the firm was known as Lloyd & Dudgeon, operating from Union Road. From the outset a regular advertising policy appears to have been formulated and in 1868 the following advertisement appeared in *Wright's Directory of Nottinghamshire* and it was followed by many others during the life of the firm.

LLOYD & DUDGEON,
ORGAN BUILDERS,
UNION ROAD, NOTTINGHAM,

Organs of every size Built, Repaired, Revoiced & Tuned

ON THE MOST REASONABLE TERMS.

SCUDAMORE AND ST. CECILIA ORGANS, FROM £25 UPWARDS.

Annual Contracts for maintaining Organs in Order and Tune.

N.B.—C. L. was for Ten Years Voicer and Tuner to the late S. GROVES, London.

MESSRS LLOYD & DUDGEON REFER WITH PLEASURE TO SOME OF THE PRINCIPAL ORGANS
BUILT BY THEM.

Nottingham and Neighbourhood.

All Saints' Church, new organ.
St. Ann's Church, new organ.
St. John's Church, new organ.
St. Luke's, new organ.
St. Peter's Church, enlarged and revoiced throughout.
St. Mary's Church, enlarged and revoiced.
St. James's Church, revoiced throughout.
St. Nicholas' Church, revoiced throughout.
Catholic Apostolic, enlarged and revoiced.
Alfred St. Methodist Free Church, new organ.
Hyson Green Church, new organ.
De Ligne Street Wesleyan Chapel, new organ.
Shireoaks Church, new organ.
Dunham Church, new organ.
Lowdham Church, new organ.
W. Wells, Esq., Nottingham, new organ.
Southwell Wesleyan Chapel, new organ.
Holme Pierrepont Church, new organ.
Epperstone Church, new organ.
Kirkby Woodhouse Church, new organ.

Orston Church, enlarged and revoiced.
Bulcote Church.

Derby and Neighbourhood.

St. John's Church, enlarged and revoiced.
Wesleyan Chapel, new organ.
Belper Wesleyan Chapel, new organ.
P. Nuttall, Esq., Burton-on-Trent, new organ.
Cromford Church, enlarged and revoiced.
Ripley Church, new organ.
Ripley Wesleyan Methodist Chapel, new organ.
Riddings Wesleyan Chapel, new organ.
Riddings Baptist Chapel, new organ.
Pinxton Church, new organ.
West Hallam Church, new organ.

Leicester.

St. George's Church, enlarged and revoiced throughout.
Ratcliffe College, new organ.
Twyford Church, new organ.
Scalford Church, new organ.
Melton Mowbray Chapel, new organ.
Loughborough Church, enlarged and revoiced.

Bridgnorth Catholic Apostolic, new organ.

It will be noted that Lloyds (as the firm was always referred to in Nottingham), in common with Henry Willis, were already building Scudamore organs as first introduced by the Revd. John Baron of Upton Scudamore, at the General Architectural Congress at Oxford on June 9th, 1858. The 'St Cecilia' was of a different pattern; both are fully described in Willis's prospectus which appeared in: *Scudamore Organs, or Practical Hints respecting Organs for Village Churches and small Chancels, on Improved Principles, by the Revd. J. Baron, Rector of Upton Scudamore, with Designs by G. E. Street, F.S.A., and Suggestive Ancient Examples*: Second edition, revised and enlarged, Bell & Daldy, 1862. There was a wide difference in price between the two firms. Willis' basic model was £35–40; that of Lloyd—£25!

In 1867, the partners carried out alterations to the Snetzler organ of 1776, with a Pedal open diapason added by Buckingham *c.*1820, in St Mary's Church, Nottingham, and this prolonged its life until 1871 when Bishop & Starr built a new instrument. They had successfully enlarged the 1770 Green organ in the city centre church of St Peter in 1863 and built a new one for St Ann's church two years later, so they had already gained a high reputation for quality workmanship in the city and beyond.

One of the many nonconformist chapels which once stood in the centre of Nottingham was that of the Armenian Baptists, which was a large building in Broad Street, erected in 1818 by a number of members, who, with their Pastor, separated from the General Baptist Chapel in Park Street which dated back to 1799. *The Musical Standard* dated August 28th, 1869, included the following paragraph regarding the installation of an organ there.

BAPTIST CHAPEL, BROAD STREET, NOTTINGHAM 1869

GREAT ORGAN	ft	SWELL ORGAN	
		Double Diapason	16
Open Diapason	8	Open Diapason	8
Stopped Diapason	8	Stopped Diapason	8
Clarabella	8	Principal	4
Keraulophon	8	Fifteenth	2
Dulciana	8	Cornopean	8
Principal	4	Oboe	8
Flute	4	PEDAL ORGAN	
Fifteenth	2		
Sesquialtera	III	Bourdon	16
Spare slide for Trumpet	—		

3 couplers   3 composition pedals

In the 1860s and '70s, Lloyd & Dudgeon built a number of small one-manual organs for village churches and chapels. *The Musical Standard* dated 28th September, 1872, reported that at Great Ponton, 'Lloyd & Dudgeon have erected a small but good toned instrument in the Parish Church'. Its specification was: CC–G compass—open diapason, stopped bass, stopped treble, keraulophon (tenor C), principal, fifteenth. Enclosed in general swell. Pedal CCC–G, 20 notes, grand bourdon, Pedals to Great.

In travelling around one comes across examples of such instruments in poor condition, by a variety of builders. If well built by a reputable firm and have been carefully maintained, they give forth a pleasant sound, which is adequate to accompany the small number who gather together (not always Sunday by Sunday, for churches more often than not are in a group). It is a sad state of affairs to find that they are regarded as out of date and thus worthless by some church councils who express a wish to replace them with cheap electronics. In fairness to them, many rural communities are desperately short of funds, have fabric problems and Diocesan Quotas to pay; the position is serious in such cases and the threat of redundancy faces them.

It was not long before their work was known in the neighbouring county of Derbyshire and in *The Musical Standard* for January 7th, 1871, this note appeared:

MACKWORTH.— The new organ built by Messrs. Lloyd & Dudgeon, of Nottingham, was opened last week. The sermons were preached by the Rev. W. Gilder, vicar of Mackworth. The organ is the gift of W. Munday, Esq., J.P., of Markeaton Hall, and was presided at by Mr W. H. Orme, organist of the church. The instrument is very fine in quality, and gives the greatest satisfaction. The front pipes are richly decorated, and the case stained and varnished. The following are the contents of the instrument:—

GREAT ORGAN.— Open diapason (metal), 8 feet, 56 pipes; stopped diapason (wood), 8 feet, 12 pipes; clarabella (wood), 8 feet, 44 pipes; principal (metal), 4 feet, 56 pipes; fifteenth (metal), 56 pipes; two spare slides.

SWELL ORGAN.— Open diapason (metal and wood), 56 pipes; stopped diapason (wood), 56 pipes; principal (metal), 56 pipes; three spare slides.

PEDAL ORGAN.— Grand bourdon, 16 feet, 25 notes.

couplers.—Pedals to great, swell to great.

Price £130, fixed complete... This is the fourth organ they have erected in Derby within a short space of time.

By 1876, the partnership had been dissolved and the business became known as C. Lloyd & Co. In *Musical Opinion* for June 1878, they advertised:

ORGAN.—CC, four stops, open metal, stop bass, stop treble, principal (metal), one octave and a half of pedals, case painted mahogany, gilt pipes, &c. Price £15.—C. LLOYD & Co., Organ Builders, Nottingham.

What happened to Alfred Dudgeon is not known, but it is believed that Lloyd's son, Charles Frederick, had joined his father by this time.

Some of Lloyd's early pipework was imported ready voiced from Laukhuff of Germany, but by 1876 they were advertising in various publications as: 'Organ metal pipe makers, price lists forwarded on receipt of penny stamp'. Even so, when very busy they continued to deal with Laukhuff until well into the 1900s, with Alfred Palmer (successor to John Courcelle) of 12 Sandringham Road, Kingsland, London, supplying the reeds.

It is interesting to compare their prices in the 1890s with those of Alfred Palmer of 12 Sandringham Road, Kingsland, London W., who was one of the leading suppliers in the country.

	Lloyd	Palmer
Open Diapason 8ft (56 notes)	£11–0–0	£11–7–0
Voicing	£1–10–0	£1–5–0
Principal 4ft	£3–0–0	£3–7–6
Voicing	13–0	11–6
Cornopean	£8–0–0	£8–6–0
Voicing	£2–10–0	£2–15–0

It became clear that the volume of work undertaken necessitated a capacious and well-organised factory, with a result that by 1881, the business had moved to what appears to have been a purpose-built premises in Brighton Street, Peas Hill Road, and here the largest contracts could be dealt with, while there was ample space in the yard for the seasoning of timber. It was a two-storeyed building with steam-driven machinery and must have been the envy of some of their competitors. The firm used the following advertisement for several years in local directories and musical journals such as *Musical Opinion*, *Musical Standard* and *The Organist & Choirmaster*.

Prize Medal, Class 1, with Certificate of Merit, awarded to C. LLOYD & CO., for Excellence of Tone and Superiority of Workmanship.

CHARLES LLOYD & CO.

Organ Builders,

Works: Brighton Street, Peas Hill Road,

NOTTINGHAM.

(ADJOINING ROBIN HOOD'S CHASE.)

Annual Contracts for keeping Organs in Order and Tune.

ORGAN METAL PIPE MAKERS AND VOICERS.

Price Lists forwarded on application.

Formerly of London.   *Established 1859.*

The Prize Medal and Certificate of Merit was awarded at The Midland Counties Exhibition held in 1865. The organ exhibited there found a home at Holme Pierrepont Church, Notts.

By 1905, their advertisements were updated, as will be seen in the following extract from *Wright's Directory*, 1905–6:

In 1885, Lloyds built a two-manual organ for Addison Street Congregational Church, Nottingham, to a specification drawn up by a Mr S. D. Major, organist of Percy Chapel, Bath.

ADDISON STREET CONGREGATIONAL CHURCH 1885

2 manuals: CC to G, 56 notes   Pedal: CCC to F, 30 notes

GREAT ORGAN	ft	SWELL ORGAN	
Open Diapason (large, full scale)	8	Bourdon	16
Dulciana	8	Open Diapason	8
Stopped Diapason Treble (tenor C)	8	Viol di Gamba	8
Stopped Diapason Bass (to CC)	8	Lieblich Gedact	8
Principal	4	Gemshorn	4
Harmonic Piccolo	2	Voix Celeste	8
Keraulophon	8	Mixture	IV
German Flute	4	Horn	8
Clarionet	8	Oboe	8
		PEDAL ORGAN	
		Open Diapason	16
		Bourdon	16

The organ was opened on Thursday, 5th February, 1885, when a recital was given by H. S. Irons who was then organist of St Andrew's Church, Nottingham. Born at Canterbury on January 19th, 1834, he became a chorister there, of which his father was a Lay Vicar. He became an organ pupil of Dr. Stephen Elvey at Oxford, and for a year, from 1856, was organist and Precentor of St Columba's College, Rathfarnham, until his appointment as Rector Chori (Organist and Choirmaster) of Southwell Minster in 1857. He moved to Chester Cathedral to become assistant there in 1873, and three years later he settled in Nottingham, where he became Organist of St Andrew's Church. He was a composer of church and organ music and is remembered for his fine tune, *Southwell*, which appears in most hymn books.

At West Bridgford Parish Church, in 1899, Lloyds built a large two-manual instrument with a Choir Organ prepared for at a cost of £300. This was completely rebuilt and enlarged by Henry Willis & Sons Ltd. in 1952.

In *The Choir and Musical Journal* for June 1952, I contributed an article on the organ built by Lloyd for Albion Congregational Church, Sneinton, Nottingham (now no longer a place of worship). The organ had a fine Classical case and originally was a two-manual, which Lloyd rebuilt and enlarged to three manuals in 1904–5. This was one of the largest and most ambitious works of the Nottingham firm. The action was tubular-pneumatic; the stops were operated by stop-keys, while combination key-touches, similar to the T. C. Lewis type, took the place of the usual pistons. Each manual was provided with an adjustable combination touch set by means of small buttons below the stop-keys. Tonally, the organ was a 'mixed bag' of good, fair and in one or two cases, indifferent tone—the latter referring to some of the reeds which more than likely came from the old organ, the builder of which is not known. Roger Yates found from Lloyd's records which stops were supplied by Laukhuff; these are marked † in the following specification.

ALBION CONGREGATIONAL CHURCH, SNEINTON 1904–5

GREAT ORGAN	ft	CHOIR ORGAN	ft
†Contra Viola	16	†Quintaton	16
Open Diapason (large, heavy metal, leathered)	8	Violin Diapason	8
Open Diapason (small)	8	Lieblich Gedact	8
Clarabella	8	Dulciana	8
Keraulophon	8	†Flauto Traverso (wood)	4
Principal	4	Piccolo	2
Flute	4	Clarinet	8
Fifteenth	2		
Trumpet	8	PEDAL ORGAN	
Clarion	4	Harmonic Bass	32
		Open Diapason	16
SWELL ORGAN		Sub Bass	16
		Echo Bourdon	16
Lieblich Bourdon	16	Violone (from Great)	16
Open Diapason	8	Violoncello	8
Stopped Diapason	8	Bass Flute	8
†Viol de Gamba	8		
†Salicional	8	9 couplers 10 combination touches	
†Celestes	8		
Voix Celeste	8	Trigger swell pedal Tubular-pneumatic action	
Gemshorn	4	Reeds voiced or revoiced by Alfred Palmer, London.	
Mixture	III		
Cornopean	8		
Oboe	8		
Vox Humana	8		
Tremulant			

The May 1907 issue of *Musical Opinion* contains the specification of the new organ at Canaan Primitive Methodist Church, Nottingham.

NOTTINGHAM.— The opening of the new organ at Canaan Primitive Methodist Church was marked by a series of recitals, the performers being Mr Norman Hibbert, Mr F. Wyatt and Mr T. H. Bennett. The new organ was built by Messrs. C. Lloyd & Co., and the action throughout is tubular-pneumatic and the stops are operated by stop-keys placed immediately over the upper manual. Each manual is provided with key touches, and a special feature is their free combination touches, which enable the organist to fix and refix his combinations as often as desired, even while playing; in addition to which the combinations as set for the time being are plainly visible. The specification is as follows:—

GREAT.— Bourdon, open diapason, dulciana, hohl flöte, principal, harmonic flute, piccolo, clarionet, trumpet.

SWELL.—Lieblich bourdon, horn diapason, lieblich gedackt, echo gamba, voix celestes, geigen principal, cornopean, oboe.

PEDAL.— Open diapason, bourdon, echo bourdon, bass flute.

COUPLERS.— Swell octave, swell sub octave, swell to great sub octave, swell to great, great to pedal, swell to pedal, swell tremulant. Reversible pedal for great to pedal.

3 double-action combinations pistons each to great and swell.

Roger Yates once told me that their pneumatic actions were not altogether successful, but their tracker work was excellent.

A well-known Nottingham musician, J. T. Masser, who was organist at Addison Street Congregational Church for many years, had a residence organ at his home at 32 Mapperley Road, built in 1848 by John Nicholson of Bradford. Lloyds rebuilt it in 1908 with tubular-pneumatic action, but according to a letter from Roger Yates to me, dated 8th June, 1952, Masser made Lloyd 'take it all out and replace it with tracker'! This seems to suggest that it was not particularly successful. Both instruments had a peculiar style of music desk which Masser liked. When he moved to The Croft, Alexandra Park, he engaged Yates (who by then had established a business in Nottingham, having taken over Lloyd's premises) to move his historic organ when a new violin diapason was added; sadly, when Masser died, the organ was broken up.

In the April 1909 issue of *Musical Opinion* appeared this announcement: 'Mr C. F. Lloyd writes: I beg to inform you that the organ building business carried on by my late father in Nottingham, for the last forty-nine years, has now been acquired by me and will be continued under the style of C. Lloyd & Co. as heretofore'. C. F. Lloyd was a musician of ability and was organist at St Ann's Church, Nottingham. The firm carried on until 1928 when it was purchased by Roger Yates. He considered the 1880s–1890s as being the best period of Lloyd's work, with excellent pipework and a liberal use of spotted metal. Two such examples were well known to me some forty years or so ago: The Friary Congregational Church, West Bridgford (1884), and West Bridgford Parish Church (1899).

West Bridgford, Nottingham, has three lively Free Churches: Musters Road Methodist, Baptist and the Friary United Reformed Church (previously Congregational). The organ here is a fine example of Lloyd's work of 1884 which was originally built for the old Friar Lane Chapel in the heart of the city. It was a large and handsome Gothic building in the decorated Early English style, erected in 1828, to seat 800 persons. Underneath the chapel were catacombs for 500 bodies and a novel feature of the two towers at the main entrance, containing staircases to the galleries, was a ventilator in the centre part of one of the catacombs, and in the other, a chimney for the furnace that warmed the chapel! This building has long since suffered the fate of several large dissenting places of worship in the city centre which have been demolished or used for other purposes over the years.

Lloyds were very fond of the keraulophon which they included in their Swell or Great Organs during the last century. Invented by Gray & Davison and first used in their organ for St Paul's, Knightsbridge, London, in 1843, it is described in J. I. Wedgwood's *Dictionary of Organ Stops* as 'of large dulciana scale, the peculiar feature of the pipes being a round hole or slot of fair size in the pipe about one diameter from the top. It is tuned with a slide, through which the hole sometimes extends. The keraulophon emits a peculiar soft and muffled tone, though some builders erroneously make it as loud as a powerful gamba'. Lloyd voiced them as very delicate, stringy salicionals, and their instrument at Friary United Reformed Church contains a delightful example.

This instrument was a splendid example of Lloyd's work at its best; much of the pipework was of spotted metal, resulting in a diapason chorus of natural, bright, singing tone of perfect blending properties. The chorus reeds had the typical nineteenth-century freedom and clang, while all the quiet stops were colourful and distinctive in tone. Since I was acquainted with the organ in the 1950s it has been given a new lease of life on two occasions; J. W. Walker & Sons Ltd. cleaned and overhauled it in 1960 when the Swell oboe was converted into a contra oboe 16ft (tenor C only); pneumatic action replaced the tracker action to the Pedal Organ which gained by the addition of a new radiating and concave pedal board and the octave coupler to this department was removed and a bass flute and octave 8ft added. Leonard Reeves of Stoke-on-Trent (now Cartwright & Cartwright) carried out a further clean and overhaul in 1980 when they re-covered the bellows, converted the contra oboe back to 8ft pitch and replaced the original swell shutters by a secondhand set, resulting in a much more effective box.

Lloyds had a large tuning connection which covered a wide area and this kept them going when business was slack. In common with other firms after the war, life was difficult, and by 1928, when Roger Yates purchased the business, after seventy years of service, an entirely new outlook was required. The firm had every reason to be proud of its contribution in the world of local organ building, particularly during the reign of Queen Victoria, and anyone rebuilding one of their instruments of that period, has a sound basis to work upon.

ROGER YATES 1905–1975

Born in 1905, and baptised at the Parish Church, Solihull (where I was married in 1938), Roger Yates received his education at Tonbridge School. He spent his boyhood until 1918 at Beckenham, Kent, where his father was Commissioner for Boy Scouts. In a letter to me dated 26th December, 1968, he had this to say: 'I can remember quite clearly hearing my first organ about 1910 when I was five, at a big Scouts Service—the Forster & Andrews in St George's. My parents took me there several times before the 1914 war and though mysterious to me as it was then, sound coming down as it seemed from the roof, made a lasting impression on me. When I went to Willis's as a boy in 1922, I used to go into St Andrew's, Ashley Gardens, under the lea of Westminster Cathedral and hear the F. & A. there. Even under the Willis influence I used to think this was a fine old organ. It had tracker action and sloping jambs'. This letter was in acknowledgement of my first book *Forster & Andrews, Organ Builders 1843–1926*, which had been given him by his wife as a Christmas present. In 1922, he became a premium apprentice of Henry Willis & Sons Ltd., Brixton. Here he went through every department of this flourishing and highly organised firm and had first-hand experience of some of the prestigious instruments being built at that time as well as the great instruments at St Paul's Cathedral and those newly built at Westminster Cathedral and Liverpool Cathedral. He became Junior Voicer and was quick to show his talent in this field, a love for which remained all his life. Henry Willis gave the young Yates every encouragement, and in turn, Roger absorbed the Willis methods of tone production which was very much in evidence when he voiced his own pipework.

At the age of twenty-three he was ready to commence business on his own, and with the backing of his parents, purchased the business of Charles Lloyd & Co., Nottingham, which by then was ready for rejuvenation and it was not long before the young organ builder was making his mark in Nottingham and beyond. W. L. Sumner became a close friend; they had similar ideals and both had opportunities to travel abroad and absorb some of the finest instruments in Austria, France and Germany. Roger Yates also visited the USA to see and hear what was going on there.

It was during his time at Willis's that he became acquainted with Marcel Dupré and thus began a friendship which Roger greatly valued. It is perhaps not generally known that at the early recording of the Allegro from Widor's 6th Symphony on the Alexandra Palace organ, he sat at the console with Dupré and gave occasional assistance with stops. To quote the late John Holmes of Monasterevan, Ireland: 'At one point, on side A of the record, the 32ft reed comes on. Yates told me that he drew that stop for Dupré'.

Whilst on the subject of Dupré, it is perhaps not generally known that he played for the wedding ceremony of the Duke of Windsor and Mrs Simpson at the Chateau Condé, France. Its wealthy owner, M. Bedaux, had installed a fine chamber organ and as Dupré had inaugurated it, he was invited to play on this important occasion. Mrs A. M. Henderson, in her article 'Marcel Dupré at home' in *Musical Opinion* (June 1938) tells us that it was 'intended by M. Bedaux that this should be regarded by Dupré as a professional engagement; but with the perfect taste of the great artist, Dupré asked that he might be permitted to render a little service to one who was at that time, "the guest of France" and who represented a country which had always treated him with the greatest kindness.' Dupré gave a recital at Lincoln Cathedral to a vast congregation during 1924, to which I was taken as a boy of eleven.

The Lloyd/Yates works were sited near the top of Brighton Street in the St Ann's district of Nottingham, adjacent to the tree-lined walkway known as Robin Hood Chase. They were spacious premises; machinery consisted of a circular saw, surface planing machine, self-feed planing machine, small engineer's lathe, wood-turning lathe, screw-threading machine, and of course, a voicing machine in its own separate room.

Let H. W. Hinton (who joined the firm at the age of fourteen on leaving school) take up the story: 'The staff consisted of Bill Latham (foreman), Wilfred Henson, Reg. Rowberry, Albert Wilkins, Arthur Bailey and myself on the shop floor. Miss Muriel Handley was the one and only member of the office staff. I would mention that at busy times, forty-year old George Leigh was called in from his native Lancashire; he was a bachelor and thus something of a free spirit, always apparently available when required and able to tackle any job he was given. Ronald Cleaver, whom I came to know well, had completed his 'time' with Yates, but then was promptly dismissed by Mr Latham, so the story went. Ronald was an irrepressible character who cared not a jot for authority and perhaps Latham was pleased to see the back of him. However, he started his own one-man business as a piano and organ tuner and repairer and occasionally did outdoor work for Roger Yates at busy times. It was well known that Mr Yates had a private income and did not rely on profit from organ building for a living. He also had a liking for big transatlantic cars and I recall such makes as Buick, Chrysler, Essex, Humber and Oldsmobile being owned at one time or another. Eley's garage in St Mark's Street specialised in used Canadian and American cars and Mr Yates was a valued customer. Mrs Yates had a 'Bullnose' Morris Cowley open tourer which was kept in very nice condition, and, unlike her husband's various cars, wasn't exchanged for anything else so far as I can recollect'.

In the early 1930s, Roger Yates gave considerable thought to the design of a rotary blower. Experiments were carried out and the first installation was at his new organ for The Church of The Good Shepherd, Collier Row, Romford, Essex, in 1935. Bill Latham enthused over its performance and a second installation in the following year was for the rebuild of the Brindley & Foster organ in Ruddington Parish Church, Notts. Yates, ever a perfectionist, did not consider that they matched up to the design and performance of the famous 'Discus' blower, manufactured by Watkins & Watson, and thereafter used this make wherever a blower was required. In common with other organ builders at the time, he was kept busy with the installation of new blowers and he fitted machines by other makers in various parts of the country.

Roger Yates designed a very compact all-electric stop-key console for two-manual instruments, measuring 4ft 7ins. long, 4ft 3ins. deep and 3ft 8ins. high. The entire mechanism, operating couplers, stop-key combination action, magnets and solenoids, was manufactured and assembled on the premises. Both the keyboards and pedal board could be raised for inspection and adjustment when necessary. His thorough training with Henry Willis enabled him to carry out all the flue and reed voicing and he was meticulous in the final tonal finishing in the church.

Working drawings were always laid out on thin, smooth, top quality plywood boards, and it was H. W. Hinton's job to visit a local timber yard from time to time to purchase these.

In *Musical Opinion* for June 1936, it was reported that: 'Members of the Nottingham and District Society of Organists witnessed at University College Buildings an interesting lecture on the practical voicing of organ pipes given by Mr Roger Yates of Nottingham. The President, Mr L. Gordon Thorp was in the chair and Mr W. L. Sumner, a University College Lecturer and an acknowledged expert on organ matters, was present. Mr Yates demonstrated his lecture with the aid of voicing machine and an assortment of organ pipes. Some of the pipes displayed were made by Vincent Willis, one of the sons of the late Henry Willis. The lecturer voiced several pipes and explained the processes used in connection with this branch of organ building'. No date of this meeting was given.

At the Annual Dinner of the Nottingham Society of Organists (in 1935), Mr Henry Willis was the principal guest, and in his speech said that it might be of interest to Nottingham music lovers that the four-manual organ built by his firm for the Elite Cinema, Nottingham 'had now gone to the magnificent new Brangwyn Civic Hall at Swansea where, under the direction of Sir Walford Davies, it was able to obtain a hearing under ideal conditions'. This was not a cinema organ, but a very comprehensive concert organ which I had the privilege of playing after a dance in the Elite Ballroom in 1934. It has since been restored in stages by Henry Willis IV who also removed the old Echo Organ and replaced it by a new Positif division. Mr Willis spoke of 'the necessity for a broad international outlook in organ building with respect to the tonal structure and he suggested that an organ music society might be formed in Nottingham. Mr Roger Yates also spoke, and in thanking Mr Willis, said: 'that he had been a pupil at the Willis works and he traced the history of that firm through three generations and said that the name of Willis stood for the best in organ building'. Mr W. L. Sumner, of University College, also spoke. This dinner was fully reported in the January 1936 issue of *Musical Opinion*.

In 1934, there was a staff of six, of whom Reg Rowberry later managed the Nottingham branch of Henry Willis & Sons Ltd. Arthur Bailey, who later joined Henry Groves & Son as a partner, and H. W. Hinton, whose memories of those days have been invaluable in writing this account of the Yates firm. Life in the organ building trade is never without its moments of humour and with one or two characters on the firm's staff, life was far from dull. H. W. Hinton recalls assisting Bill Latham, the foreman, in a general tuning of the organ in Belgrave Square Church, Nottingham. In those days tuners used candles in metal holders for illumination inside the instrument. As the two men were walking across the town at the bottom of Brighton Street, 'Latham stopped in his tracks and asked, have we brought the candle with us? He received a reply in the affirmative, and then told the young Hinton to open the tool bag and make sure, saying: 'If I've left it in the organ that _ _ _ job will go up in smoke'! I can recall the days when I 'held down the notes' for R. A. Cousans in tuning country church organs before the advent of electricity into the villages by Grid—and what a hazard the candle illumination was, as well as inefficient. Bill Latham was Branch Secretary of The Organ Builders' and Musical Instrument Makers' Trade Society, as far back as 1920, and possibly earlier.

The monthly report for February 1920 stated: 'In the organ building section—despite a little slackness at Dundee and Walsall—most firms have orders booked which will keep them busy for some considerable time to come… The following O.B. firms are in need of men: Messrs Andrews & Sons, Bradford; P. Conacher & Co., Huddersfield; Osmond, Taunton; Walker & Sons, London; R. S. Rutt & Co., Leyton… and four firms who hide their identity by using Box Nos. respectively… at "*The Musical Opinion*", Chichester Chambers, London WC2. In other districts, where trade is reported good, there are openings for O.B.s… Wage Rates… the rates at Lincoln (Cousans) and Worcester (Nicholsons) we find, have been advanced to 1s. 11d. and 1s. 9½d. per hour respectively. At the latter place the advance was secured after a two days' strike'.

Yates advertised in *Musical Opinion* from time to time: the following is an example from the early 1930s.

ROGER YATES, Organ Builder

Telephone: Nottingham 2374   *Successor to C. LLOYD & CO.*   Telegrams: "Organs, Nottingham"

79, Brighton Street, NOTTINGHAM

ORGANS BUILT WITH ELECTRIC OR PNEUMATIC ACTIONS

for Churches, Concert Halls or Cinemas

Also with Player Action taking Standard 65 or 88-note Rolls, suitable for Private Residences.

Estimates and Advice free and without obligation.   *Tuning Contracts arranged.*   *Enquiries welcomed*

The rebuilding of Lloyd's organ in Addison Street Congregational Church, Nottingham, in 1930, must have been one of the first jobs of importance. It gave him much pleasure to work on this instrument for there was a considerable amount of spotted metal of excellent quality. He re-designed the tonal scheme, added a new Choir Organ and replaced the action by electric, with a detached all-electric stop-key console. The specification stood as follows:

ADDISON STREET CONGREGATIONAL CHURCH 1930

GREAT ORGAN

	ft
Gontra Geigen (lowest 12 stopped wood)	16
Open Diapason No. 1	8
Open Diapason No. 2 (ext. Contra Geigen)	8
Open Diapason No. 3	8
Flute Couverte	4
Octave	4
Principal (ext. Contra Geigen)	4
Nason Flute	4
Fifteenth	2

SWELL ORGAN

Lieblich Bourdon	16
Open Diapason	8
Lieblich Gedacht	8
Viole de Gamba	8
Voix Celestes	8
Gemshorn	4
Mixture	IV

Cornopean	8
Hautboy	8

CHOIR ORGAN

Violoncello	8
Concert Flute	8
Dulciana	8
Flute Ouverte	4
Clarinet	8

PEDAL ORGAN

Resultant Bass	32
Open Bass	16
Bourdon	16
Octave	8
Principal (from Great Open No. 2)	8
Flute (from Bourdon)	8

The detached console had solid ivory stop-keys which were varied in colour for the various categories of stops. When I visited the organ in order to write an article for *The Choir and Musical Journal* for December 1953, I felt that this performed no useful function, while it detracted from the appearance of the console. This was realised by Roger Yates at a later date, when he discontinued the practice. His use of extension, limited though it was, certainly was not influenced by his experience gained at the Willis firm, but the liveliness of the flue chorus and brilliance of the very fine reeds, was decidedly 'Willis' in effect. The action was by lever magnets, which together with the solenoids operating the couplers, were made and wound in the Yates factory. Roger Yates informed me that he felt the lever magnets were not altogether satisfactory and he did not repeat the experiment. Alas, church and organ are now but a memory amongst non-conformity in Nottingham, for worship ceased there in 1966, when the organ was sold.

An entirely new two-manual organ of the same date may still be heard in the smaller room of the Masonic Temple in Goldsmith Street, Nottingham. It has a curious specification and it is difficult to see the reasoning behind the design of the Swell department, in view of the enclosed Solo.

MASONIC TEMPLE, GOLDSMITH STREET 1930

GREAT ORGAN

	ft
Open Diapason No. 1	8
Open Diapason No. 2	8
Principal	4

SWELL ORGAN

Salicional	8
Vox Angelica	8
Gedacht	8
Flute Ouverte	4

SOLO ORGAN

Hohl Flute	8
Dulciana	8
Flute Harmonique	4
Oboe	8
Clarinet	8

PEDAL ORGAN

Resultant Bass	32
Bourdon	16
Flute	8

13 couplers including Tremulant   12 pistons
One stop-key 'Solo on and off'
2 balanced crescendo pedals

All the quiet stops are of charming tonality, while the bold and brilliant Great division is so skilfully voiced that greater resources are suggested.

My interest in Yates' work took me to Park Hill Congregational Church, Nottingham, where in 1934, he had rebuilt the Bishop organ of 1884 to the following specification:

PARK HILL CONGREGATIONAL CHURCH 1934

2 manuals: CC to C, 61 notes   Pedal: CCC to F, 30 notes

GREAT ORGAN

	ft
Lieblich Bourdon	16
Open Diapason	8
Flute Couverte	8
Dulciana	8
Principal	4
Flute Octaviante	4
Fifteenth	2
Cornet 12·17	II
†Trompette Harmonique	8
†Clarion (ext.)	4

SWELL ORGAN

Geigen	8
Lieblich Gedacht	8
Salicional	8
Vox Angelica	8
Geigen Octave	4
Lieblich Flute	4
Trompette (harmonic trebles)	8
Hautbois	8

PEDAL ORGAN

Resultant Bass	32
Open Wood	16
Bourdon	16
Lieblich Bourdon	16
Octave	8
Flute	8
Octave Flute	4
†Bombarde (from Great)	16
†Trompette (from Great)	8
†Clarion (from Great)	4

WIND PRESSURES

Great: 3½ ins., reeds 7 ins.
Swell and Pedal: 3½ ins.

9 couplers and tremolo   16 pistons
Detached oak console with interior fittings of
ebony and ivory tilting tablets.

† prepared for

The instrument was opened on October 22nd, 1934, by M. Marcel Dupré. The former Swell mixture and harmonc piccolo were removed—possibly due to overcrowding—but rather to the detriment of the Swell chorus. Much of the old pipework was used again after revoicing, the trebles of all stops being entirely new. Tonally, the Great Organ was supreme, the Swell Organ sounding very retiring against it. Great to fifteenth was a bright, ringing ensemble of the greatest clarity, but to the writer's ears, the cornet was keen and too assertive. All the quiet stops were of great beauty. The organ could be summed up as an example of the brilliant school of voicing and marked individuality of tone.

The church is now Greek Orthodox, having ceased to be a United Reformed Church (formerly Congregational) in 1985. The organ is still there.

Roger Yates, in later years, was very critical of his early work and once told me that he preferred to forget it! He certainly had not the slightest reason to feel so—but, knowing him as I did, he could perhaps best be described as an 'ultra-perfectionist' ever seeking for what he considered to be the absolute truth in tonal design and the end result. As this chapter unfolds, it will be seen that his pilgrimage led him gradually to the European concept; had he lived longer, one can but conjecture whether he would have opted to build organs only in this tradition.

A two-manual organ for the Church of The Good Shepherd, Collier Row, Romford, Essex, brought him a letter from Harry Goss Custard, Organist of Liverpool Cathedral, which must have given him great encouragement.

'I would like to tell you again how much I enjoyed playing on the organ. It is certainly one of the most beautiful small organs I ever touched and I congratulate you heartily on a great achievement.'

Goss Custard too, was a perfectionist; he measured everything by the tremendously high standard of his beloved Cathedral organ—so that a letter such as this was high praise indeed.

In addition to this, H. W. Hinton has recalled that a letter from 'the Henry Willis management' (presumably from H. W. himself) was circulated amongst the Brighton Street staff, complimenting Yates on the excellence of the electro-pneumatic action, and in particular, its quickness of response. The Romford specification was as follows:

CHURCH OF THE GOOD SHEPHERD, ROMFORD

GREAT ORGAN

	ft
Open Diapason	8
Flûte Couverte	8
Dulciana	8
Principal	4
Flûte Octaviante	4
Double Trumpet (from Swell)	16
Trumpet (from Swell)	8
Clarion (from Swell)	4

SWELL ORGAN

Geigen Diapason	8
Lieblich Gedeckt	8
Salicional	8
Vox Angelica (tenor C)	8
Geigen Octave	4
Super Octave	2
Cornet 12·17	II

Double Trumpet	16
Trumpet (harmonic trebles)	8
Clarion	4

PEDAL ORGAN

Resultant Bass	32
Contra Bass	16
Bourdon	16
Octave	8
Flute	8
Octave Flute	4
Double Trumpet (from Swell)	16
Trumpet (from Swell)	8
Clarion (from Swell)	4

10 couplers and usual complement of pistons etc.
Pitch: French diapason normal C = 517.3

In 1931, on the advice of Mr L. Henniker, MUS. BAC., F.R.C.O., A.R.C.M. (organist of St Andrew's Church, Nottingham), Yates was selected to build a new organ for Church Drive Methodist Church, Nottingham. I reviewed this organ in the May 1952 issue of *The Choir and Musical Journal*. Typically Yates in tonal quality, it was most versatile, but one missed the 8ft salicional and Swell geigen diapason and whether they were ever inserted I do not know. The two mutations were kept very quiet in order not to overbalance the aeoline and cor de nuit, with a result that when the superb trumpet made its appearance, the ensemble was all reed; what a thrill it provided—in the true Willis tradition!

At the Parish Church, Ilkeston, rebuilt by Yates in 1931, he found a conglomerate of work by Brindley & Foster and Adkins of Derby, based upon a J. C. Bishop organ of 1831 which was built for St John's, Paddington, London, in 1831, and removed to Ilkeston in 1866. According to an article by W. L. Sumner in *The Organ*, October 1934, 'it collapsed entirely in 1931' and Yates rebuilt it with a detached stop-key console to the following scheme:

THE PARISH CHURCH, ILKESTON 1931

GREAT ORGAN

	ft
Lieblich Bourdon	16
Open Diapason No. 1	8
Open Diapason No. 2	8
Flûte Couverte	8
Octave	4
Principal	4
Twelfth	2⅔
Fifteenth	2
Cymbal 19·22	II
Tuba	8
Octave Tuba	4

SWELL ORGAN

Open Diapason	8
Lieblich Gedacht	8
Salicional	8
Vox Angelica	8
Principal	4
Lieblich Flöte	4
Plein Jeu 12·15·17	III
Hautboy	8
Double trumpet	16
Trumpet	8
Clarion	4
Tremolo (to light wind)	

CHOIR ORGAN
enclosed

Viola	8
Claribel Flute	8
Dulciana	8
Hohl Flöte	4
Nasard	2⅔
Piccolo	2
Tierce	1⅗
Clarinet	8
Tuba (from Great)	8
Tremolo	

PEDAL ORGAN

Resultant Bass	32
Open Bass	16

Bourdon	16
Lieblich Bourdon	16
Octave	8
Flute	8
Bass Tuba	16
Tuba	8
Octave Tuba	4

WIND PRESSURES

Great: 3¾ ins., tubas 12 ins.
Swell: flues and hautboy, 3¾ ins.,
reeds and plein jeu 7 ins.
Choir: flues and clarinet 4¼ ins.
Pedal: 3¾ ins., 4¼ ins. and 12 ins.

19 couplers and 25 combination pistons

Marcel Dupré wrote to Yates: 'Congratulations on a magnificent organ'. W. L. Sumner contributed an article to the October 1934 issue of *The Organ*; he described it as 'probably the finest organ in the large diocese. The whole organ shows the influence of the ideals of the Willis firm to which Mr Yates was indebted for some of his training. Nevertheless, the true artist does more than copy the work of another and this builder has many ideas of his own'. H. Goss Custard, Organist of Liverpool Cathedral, who gave a recital there, wrote: 'You have done wonders with the old pipework and the whole instrument pleased me greatly. The action was splendid. It responded to every demand I made upon it throughout the evening. My sincere congratulations on a most excellent job. I do hope I may have the opportunity of playing on another organ of yours before long and I shall certainly welcome any opportunity I may have of recommending you highly. Very kind wishes'.

This instrument was rebuilt in 1992 by another firm, in collaboration with a consultant, as a two-manual with Great and an enclosed Choir division, together with mechanical action throughout. One can but conjecture what the three aforementioned eminent authorities would have to say today.

An organ which stands out in my memory as one of the very finest examples of Yates' work was that in the residence of Mr A. E. Allen (who had the controlling interest in 'Aristoc', the manufacturers of ladies' stockings), 'Meadowcroft', Radcliffe on Trent, which due to his kindness I was able to thoroughly examine in 1944. Although at the time he was a very sick man, his enthusiasm knew no bounds and he obviously gained great pleasure from showing every facet of his remarkable instrument with a keen musical ear; he was a violinist of no mean ability and an organist—for he regarded the organ as 'the King of Instruments'. Shortly after my most enjoyable visit to his home, I was posted in the RAF to India and it was with great sadness that I heard of his death. Completed in 1936, except for one or two additions during the following year, this was the specification:

A. E. ALLEN'S RESIDENCE, RADCLIFFE ON TRENT 1936

2 manuals: CC to C, 61 notes   Pedal: CCC to G, 32 notes

GREAT ORGAN

	ft
Violone	16
Open Diapason	8
Claribel Flute	8
Dulciana	8
Principal	4
Viola	8
Double Trumpet (from Swell)	16
Trompette (from Swell)	8
Clarion (from Swell)	4

SWELL ORGAN

Geigen	8
Bourdon	8
Salicional	8
Vox Angelica (tenor C)	8
Flûte Ouverte	4
Octavin	2
Cornet 17·22	II
Double Trumpet	16
Trompette (harmonic from mid. C)	8
Clarion	4

PEDAL ORGAN		WIND PRESSURES
Sub Bass	16	Manual flue work and viola: 3½ ins.
Violone	16	Pedal flue work: 4¼ ins.
Gross Quint	10⅔	Chorus reeds: 5 ins.
Flute	8	Action: 6½ ins.
Octave Flute	4	
Cornet 5·8·10	III	There are 28 speaking stops, 12 couplers etc.,
Double Trumpet (from Swell)	16	and one Tremolo, making a total of 41 registers.
Trompette (from Swell)	8	
Clarion (from Swell)	4	Pitch: New Philharmonic, C = 522

How the instrument came to be built is interesting. Let the late John Holmes, of Monasterevan, a close friend of Roger Yates, take up the story. 'Dupré, who had given a recital at Park Hill Congregational Church, Nottingham, in 1934, was absolutely delighted with the organ and decided to give an expanded improvisation of a four movement symphony to conclude his programme. Mr Allen was approached to entertain Dupré for the night and readily agreed. He had a good Brindley & Foster organ in his music room and was only delighted to invite some of the church folk and organist friends to dinner, after which Dupré was invited to play. To poor Mr Allen's acute embarrassment, the organ cyphered badly and generally seems to have misbehaved. Next day, Roger received instructions to put in hand a completely new organ of the finest quality. I do not know if Dupré ever paid a return visit to 'Meadowcourt', but I have a hazy recollection of hearing somewhere that he was invited back to inaugurate the new treasure.'

The organ was totally enclosed and was situated in a chamber occupying almost the whole of one side of the room and extending backwards into the room beyond. The case was of teak with an imposing pipe front of pure tin, while the console, which was built out from the casework, was beautifully designed, with key fittings, music desk and stop jambs of highly polished mahogany, keys of thick ivory and solid ivory stop knobs and pistons. The interior was a marvel of planning and every available inch of space was utilised. The expression chambers enclosing the Swell, Great and Pedal departments opened into an ingeniously constructed mixing chamber so that each department was perfectly balanced. The tone of the chorus work , in common with all the work of this builder, was a perfectly balanced, scintillating brilliance of the greatest artistry; it had a real sense of 'bigness' which was exactly right for the size of the room. The atmosphere and feeling of distance created by the very beautiful quiet registers was another feature and the regulation of the pipework—impeccable. It was one of those rare instruments that was completely absorbing and it was with difficulty that one tore oneself away from it. It was a revelation to the writer and all who heard it, and formed the subject of an article in the May/June issue of *The Choir and Musical Journal*, which I eventually received with great delight, whilst serving with the RAF on the outskirts of Burma. Such interests as mine, kept one sane in those very difficult days.

In 1949, the organ was purchased by the church of St John, Carrington, Nottingham, where Roger Yates rebuilt it. In the opening programme he stated that 'as the designer and voicer of the original organ, I would like to make it quite clear that the tone of the organ is exactly as it was in 'Meadowourt'; no revoicing or increasing of the wind pressures has been attempted. The only tonal alterations are the re-arrangement of the reed stop so that it is not duplexed on both keyboards'. In a letter to me he stated that all the work had been done by himself; later on I had the pleasure of hearing it and in a building with such fine acoustics, the effect was thrilling in the extreme.

A point of interest is that, like the first organ to be built in 'Meadowcourt' some seven years earlier by another firm, it was dedicated to the memory of Mr Allen's father and the music desk was inscribed IN MEMORIAM PATRIS AMATISSIMI. This music desk now forms part of a memorial in Radcliffe-on-Trent Church, and a new one, made from pieces of walnut saved from the console of the first organ, takes its place, so making a visible link between the two organs.

I heard this organ in its new surroundings, in the company of Roger Yates, soon after its installation; I can only say that I was tremendously thrilled by what I heard, and my immediate reaction was that it would certainly meet with the full approval of its first proud owner. The slightly revised specification was as follows:

ST JOHN, CARRINGTON, NOTTINGHAM 1949

2 manuals: CC to C, 61 notes   Pedal: CCC to G, 32 notes

GREAT ORGAN

	ft
Violone	16
Open Diapason	8
Claribel Flute	8
Dulciana	8
Principal	4
Viola	8

SWELL ORGAN

Geigen	8
Bourdon (stopped metal throughout)	8
Salicional	8
Vox Angelica (tenor C)	8

Flûte Ouverte	4
Octavin	2
Sesquialtera 12·17	II
Trompette	8

PEDAL ORGAN

Sub Bass	16
Violone	16
Gross Quint	10⅔
Flute	8
Octave Flute	4
Mixture	III
Double Trumpet (from Swell)	16

W. H. Gabb, Sub-Organist of St Paul's Cathedral, gave the opening recital on Wednesday, 23rd February, 1949.

By 1991, the action was showing signs of wear and tear, and so this was replaced by Wood of Huddersfield, who carried out the following tonal modifications: Great; dulciana discarded, new fifteenth and mixture 19·22·26. Great to Swell coupler discarded. Pedal; gross quint and mixture discarded, new principal and fifteenth. 5 adjustable general pistons added.

At the Parish Church, Oakham, Yates built what probably was the most comprehensive of his three-manual schemes; this was in 1937. At the time of proofing this chapter, it was announced that it was to be replaced by a new two-manual instrument by Kenneth Tickell.

THE PARISH CHURCH, OAKHAM, RUTLAND 1937

3 manuals: CC to C, 61 notes   Pedal: CCC to G, 32 notes

GREAT ORGAN

	ft
Violone	16
Principal	8
Viola	8
Hohl Flöte	8
Quint	5⅓
Octave	4
Flöte	4
Quint	2⅔
Super Octave	2
Sesquialtera	II
Cymbale	IV
Posaune	8

SWELL ORGAN

Principal	8
Gedeckt	8
Salicional	8
Unda Maris (tenor C)	8
Octave	4
Gedeckt Flöte	4
Cornet	III
Fagott	16
Trompet	8

Oboe	8
Clarion	4

CHOIR ORGAN
enclosed

Viola da Gamba	8
Gross Gedeckt	8
Dulciana	8
Wald Flöte	4
Nasat	2⅔
Octavin	2
Terz	1⅗
Schalmey	8
Posaune (from Great)	8
Glockenspiel	8

PEDAL ORGAN

Principal Bass	16
Violone	16
Sub Bass	16
Gross Quint	10⅔
Principal	8
Flöten Bass	8
Nachthorn	4
Schweigel	2

Cornet	III	Schalmey (from Choir)	4
Posaune Bass (partly from Great)	16		
Fagott (from Swell)	16	There are 17 couplers etc., 2 Tremolos and	
Posaune (from Great)	8	Glockenspiel, making a total of 65 registers.	

I think it is fair comment to say that this instrument, to a limited extent, for the first time shows the influence of the Continental tonal design which absorbed Yates more and more as time went by.

A paragraph in *Musical Opinion* for November 1938, regarding this organ, tells us that 'the specification was worked out by the builder and Mr W. L. Sumner, who was adviser to the organ committee. The design is intended to be eclectic, with a strong bias to the German type (*c*.1700) as regards the Great, Choir and Pedal Organs. The Swell Organ shows English influence, as well as French and German. The original instrument was built by Brindley of Sheffield in 1872'.

Another instrument opened in 1937 was that for East Bridgford Parish Church, Notts., to the following specification:

EAST BRIDGFORD PARISH CHURCH, NOTTS. 1937

GREAT ORGAN

	ft		
Open Diapason	8	Flûte Harmonique	4
Principal	4	Octavin	2
Bourdon (from Swell)	8	Cornet 12·17	II
Salicional (from Swell)	8	Trompette	8
Flûte Harmonique (from Swell)	4		

PEDAL ORGAN

		Resultant Bass	32
		Sub Bass	16

SWELL ORGAN

		Flute	8
Viola (prepared for)	8	Octave Flute	4
Bourdon	8		
Salicional	8		
Vox Angelica (tenor C)	8		

At the other end of the tonal scale, the Parish Church of Glapthorne, Northants., has a most effective Yates organ of one manual and seven speaking stops to this design:

MANUAL.— Bourdon (partly from pedal, stopped wood and metal); open diapason, 8; flute couverte, 8; aeoline (tenor C), 8; principal, 4; plein jeu (12·15·17), III; octave coupler.
PEDALE.— Bourdon, 16. Manual to pedale. Wind pressure, 3¼ ins. throughout.

A variant on this scheme was built for Wysall Methodist Church, Notts., in the early 1930s, and proved to be immensely versatile for such a small scheme. On paper there seems but little, but an imaginative player can do wonders with just a handful of stops.

MANUAL.— Open diapason, 8; gedeckt bass, 8; gedeckt treble, 8; aeoline, 8; principal, 4; flute ouverte, 4; fifteenth, 2;
PEDALE.— Bourdon, 16. Manual to pedal coupler.

Before he left Nottingham, Yates was called in by the two most important churches in the city— St Mary's and St Andrew's. At the former, in 1936, he cleaned the four-manual Walker of 1916 and re-voiced the Great large and medium diapasons, principal and fifteenth, while the Swell mixture was re-cast and re-voiced as 12·15, the 17th rank being supplied by Yates. I have happy memories of fine singing by the choir and the accompaniments of the then organist and choirmaster, H. O. Hodgson, who at one time was assistant organist to Dr. G. J. Bennett at Lincoln Cathedral. It was a very impressive example of Walker's work of that period and I was deeply shocked when I heard of its removal from St Mary's. A tuba on 15ins. wind was added by Yates to the St Andrew's organ; in a note to me (undated) he said 'I hate tubas in any organ'!

After the rebuild of the three-manual Brindley organ in Ruddington Church in 1937, with electric action and a detached stop-key console, a rather quiet time followed and one or two staff left. Roger Yates spent a good deal of time in the West Country, for he was greatly attracted to this lovely part of the world. By the late 1930s, he decided to sell the Nottingham premises and move to Bodmin, and in *Musical Opinion* for August 1937, he announced his new location:

ROGER YATES

ORGAN BUILDER

MAKER AND RESTORER OF HARPSICHORDS

AN ILLUSTRATED BROCHURE DEALING WITH TONAL MATTERS, RECENTLY COMPLETED WORK, OLD ORGANS AND HARPSICHORDS, IS IN COURSE OF PREPARATION, AND A COPY WILL BE SENT TO ANYONE WHO IS INTERESTED

Office and Works :
85 Fore Street
BODMIN, Cornwall
Telephone : BODMIN 214

For Nottingham and Midlands :
105 Clumber Avenue, Mapperley
NOTTINGHAM
Telephone : ARNOLD 68637

Organs recently Completed and in Course of Construction :—

RUDDINGTON, NOTTS.
THE PARISH CHURCH
3 manual. Electric

MEADOWCOURT, RADCLIFFE - ON - TRENT, NOTTS.
RESIDENCE OF A. E. ALLEN, Esq.
2 manual. Electric

EAST BRIDGFORD, NOTTS.
THE PARISH CHURCH
2 manual. Electric

OAKHAM, RUTLAND
THE PARISH CHURCH
3 manual. Electric

He took three of his staff with him, leaving Reg Rowberry to carry out tuning and repair work on Yates' Nottingham circuit. Eventually, this was taken over by Henry Willis & Sons Ltd., with Rowberry as manager. Some old church premises in Fore Street, Bodmin, were taken over, which were an improvement on the old Lloyd workshops. Electrically driven woodworking machinery was installed, together with other plant, and the erecting room was lofty with good acoustical properties. Visitors were welcome and all seemed set for another fruitful era in the realm of organ building and in the making and restoration of harpsichords, for this had always interested him. At the time his handbook was compiled, which was a handsome and informative publication (now a collector's item), he had in his possession several of these, including a fine double Kirkman harpsichord and a spinet in a walnut case, made in 1731, as well as a modern harpsichord which was illustrated. He offered his services as a lecturer on such instruments, illustrated by a considerable number of lantern slides. He also gave personal attention to the restoration of organs of historic interest and restored a small bureau organ built by John Snetzler in 1764; this found a home with Arnold Dolmetsch of Haslemere, who wrote to him: 'The organ is a treasure, I get wonderful effects out of it'. Work went on quietly as he described it (even so, every day was full of activity until late in the evening!), until war broke out in September 1939. He then suspended his business and joined the Royal Navy, becoming a torpedo expert with the rank of Chief Petty Officer. After the cessation of hostilities, he acquired Michaelstowe Old Rectory and resumed his business in a workshop in the grounds. Many famous organ builders and organists, both English and from overseas, were visitors to his home, while Roger Yates and his wife made many visits to the Continent examining a wide variety of organs, compiling a most comprehensive collection of photographs and details of each instrument. These visits undoubtedly influenced his thinking as far as tonal design in organ building was concerned, as I learned from our several conversations together. He was a most accomplished photographer and examples of his work may be seen in *The Rotunda*, the house magazine of Henry Willis & Sons Ltd.

At Michaelstowe, he worked single-handed with occasional assistance from his sons Tom and James and devoted wife Emmie, who was a most accomplished pianist. He also kept in touch with his work in Nottingham; all in all he worked very long hours, and in looking back, and with what knowledge I have gained since of his multifarious activities, I do not know how he kept going, but it was sheer will-power and a love of his craft which refused to allow him to let go. He once said that he preferred to work on his own, because he was unable to find anyone to come up to his exceedingly high standards.

The rebuild, with some additions, of the very beautiful Gern chamber organ from Tockington Manor, near Bristol, for St Catherine's Church, Nottingham, in 1948, gave Roger Yates particular pleasure. It stood in the entrance hall of this fine Georgian House and was probably built in about 1870; the case in which it stands is of English workmanship *c.*1760. The Revd. Andrew Freeman, the greatest authority of his time on organ cases, described it as 'one of the best examples of its period and an ornament to any church'. The old console was retained, except for for the additional stop knobs and a new pedal board. Its original specification is as follows:

ORGAN BY AUGUST GERN, TOCKINGTON MANOR, BRISTOL

GREAT ORGAN

	ft
Open Diapason	8
Lieblich Gedackt	8
Vox Angelica	8
Geigen Principal	4
Lieblich Flöete	4
Octavin	2

SWELL ORGAN

Lieblich Bordun	16
Flûte Harmonique	8
Viole de Gambe	8

Voix Célestes	8
Gemshorn	4
Basson Dessus }	16
Basson Basse	
Trompette	8

PEDAL ORGAN

Bourdon	16
Viola	8

Tracker action to manuals, pneumatic to pedals. Wind Pressure: $2\frac{5}{8}$ ins. throughout.   Hand blowing.

ST CATHERINE'S CHURCH, NOTTINGHAM 1948

GREAT ORGAN

	ft
Lieblich Bordun	16
Open Diapason	8
Lieblich Gedackt	8
Vox Angelica (bass from Gedackt)	8
Geigen Principal	4
Lieblich Flöte	4
Doublette	2

SWELL ORGAN

Flute Harmonique	8
Viole de Gambe	8
Voix Célestes	8
Gemshorn	4

Fourniture	II–V
Basson	16
Trompette	8

PEDAL ORGAN

Bourdon	16
Lieblich Bordun (from Great)	16
Quint (from Great Bordun)	$10\frac{2}{3}$
Viola (open wood)	8
Quintade (stopped metal)	4
Basson (from Swell)	16

Pipework: $2\frac{5}{8}$ ins.

His best known work in the West Country was the restoration of the historic organ at Kirkhampton Parish Church, in 1958, and the Father Willis organ at St John's Church, Taunton (1964), with some additions. At Newquay Parish Church, in 1962, he collaborated with John Dykes Bower in drawing up the specification for a new organ built by Nicholson of Malvern. Not only did he superintend its erection for his friend Stanley Lambert, managing director of Nicholsons, but he was also responsible for much of the voicing and tonal finishing of this truly magnificent instrument. It was a great shock to hear of its destruction by fire (caused by vandalism) as this chapter was being written. He also carried out much of the voicing for the organ in King Street Methodist Church, Plymouth, in 1959.

In the midst of this very taxing lifestyle, he was ever ready to welcome visitors (and never failed to answer serious letters of enquiry). Turning to his original home ground in the Nottingham area, he constructed and voiced, single-handed, a remarkable new organ for Kegworth Parish Church, Notts., in 1954, which I had the pleasure of reviewing for *The Choir* (May 1956).

KEGWORTH PARISH CHURCH 1954

2 manuals: CC to C, 61 notes   Pedal: CCC to G, 32 notes

GREAT ORGAN

	ft
Principal	8
Holzflöte	8
Octav	4
Rauschquint	II
Grossgedackt (from Swell)	8
Salicional (from Swell)	8

SWELL ORGAN

Grossgedackt	8
Salicional	8
Flöte	4

Superoctav	2
Sesquialta	II
Trompete	8

PEDAL ORGAN

Principal Bass (prepared for)	16
Subbass	16
Flotenbass (ext.)	8
Quintade	8
Trompetenbass (ext. Swell)	16

It should be made clear just what building this instrument 'single-handed' entailed. To quote from his letter to me dated 31st August, 1955: 'I made the whole thing myself, and alone, from the building frame to the cornices, including the whole of the console and its case, tilting tablet action, key contact action, coupler switches and combination actions (these last two are pneumatically operated, there is wind in the console), all the soundboards, duplexing relay actions, swell box, swell front and so on; the only trade parts are the chest magnets, ivory work, metal and wood pipes, and four sets of small motors Mr Fleming made for me in return for some voicing. All the soundboard puffers and the under actions are a peculiar arrangement of my own and I would not do it quite the same again. I nearly wore out my drilling machine and used dozens of split pins… The case is of my own design, the idea was taken from the Martinskirche in Basel…'.

In a further letter to me, dated 27th October, 1955, he wrote: 'About my tonal ideals. I really do not know if I have any in the accepted sense. Before I do any organ work, I think about it for a long time and picture or imagine to myself what sort of sound the full organ will make when heard in the church and then, when voicing cannot be delayed any longer, I do it as quickly as I possibly can, deliberately working to make the tonal effect imagined beforehand, for the ensemble and nothing else. The tone of all the stops is really governed by this and I do not make any conscious effort to make them interesting individually—this just comes automatically. As far as Kegworth is concerned, I must say I knew before-hand exactly what it was going to sound like and I made the ensemble very brilliant because it was a dead sort of building (not only tonally), and needed a lively organ to wake it up! However, I had been in Austria, Germany, Italy, Holland, France and so on before and while I was working at Kegworth I tried to give the impression of the thrilling ensembles one hears there from the handful of stops available, not nesessarily powerful out in the church. In other words, the whole thing is thoroughly bad—much out of little!' Such was the modesty of the man.

The instrument was dedicated on 29th May, 1954, when a recital was given by Harry Gabb, the Sub Organist of St Paul's Cathedral. Almost two years later, on 7th February, 1956, F. G. Ormond, B.A. (OXON) Organist and Master of the Choristers, Truro Cathedral, made the long journey from Cornwall and gave a memorable recital.

On a personal note, I heard this organ in 1956, later, in July of that year contributing an article for *The Choir*. The materials are of the finest, with much spotted metal pipework and the workmanship of every part is an example of real craftsmanship. Its great brilliance produces a really 'big' organ effect that is entirely unforced and most striking; moreover, it is a musical sound and I venture to say that is more than can be said of *some* modern instruments one hears today. At Kegworth, one finds great clarity and vitality; no matter what music is performed, every note can be heard clearly. At the time it was built it created much discussion and not everyone could appreciate its tonal 'message'; times have changed since then, however, and one wonders how we could live with some of the dull and oppressive work of the 1920s and 30s in particular. Kegworth was a *multum in parvo* instrument and Roger Yates will always be remembered for his forward looking thinking as long as the Kegworth organ remains unaltered.

It was here that the late John Holmes and I met, both of us becoming friends of Roger Yates and admirers of his work. An enquiry from the former regarding a Bishop & Starr organ in Ireland, was the means of us getting in touch with one another some thirty-eight years later, resulting in information which has been of the greatest value in the writing of this study.

In a note to me (undated) written in the mid-1950s, Roger Yates commented: 'If I had my time over again I would never consider anything else but slider chests and I think the best arrangement for a modern organ is tracker manuals and pedals and electro-pneumatic stop action so that the console can be arranged with English type combination movements. But the location of English organs rarely lends itself to the 'block' construction needed for a good simple tracker setting out'.

Prophetic words indeed—for at Dartington College he was given the opportunity to build such an instrument during 1969. *The Dartington Hall News* for 10th October, 1969, gives an account of this, for the organ was due to be inaugurated on 12th October. Situated in the Round Room of the Music School, his commission was for an organ 'suitable for teaching as well as for recitals'. He described it as follows: 'This is a traditional English type of tone. It owes nothing to the heavy and obscure tone which was popular in the early years of this century, up to 1930 or so. It isn't slavish imitation, but it has been built in the spirit of the reform movement which has grown up in America and certain European countries and is now coming to this country. I have tried to make it an up-to-date instrument, and also to give it something of my own'. There are two manuals and pedal with eleven speaking stops and three couplers. The case is of oak and the naturals of the keyboards are of boxwood, with the sharps of ebony. The stop handles are also of boxwood. Roger Yates made them out of skittles which his son tracked down in a club which had no further use for them. Some were too battered for use. All of them showed signs of honourable wear. But out of two sets of nine, eleven were good enough to turn into stops. The display pipes are 85% tin and 15% lead, those inside are 50/50%.

THE MUSIC SCHOOL, DARTINGTON COLLEGE 1969

MANUAL ONE	ft		PEDAL ORGAN	
Gedackt	8		Pommer	16
Principal	4		Quintade	4
Flageolet	2		Dulzian	16
Mixture 22·26·29·33	IV			
			3 couplers by hitch-down pedals	

MANUAL TWO	
Nason	4
Principal	2
Quint	1⅓
Regal	8

'The clear, bright tone of the Dartington organ is a part of its nature as a teaching instrument. Playing it will be a challenge to think' said Roger Yates, illustrating this point by quoting a friend's criticism of a similar organ as being 'one he couldn't doodle on! He wanted an organ on which he could pull out all the sugary stops and improvise in a vaguely Wagnerian manner'. 'This is a serious instrument, for serious playing. It isn't a toy. You wouldn't expect to get the best out of a high-powered sports car if you didn't appreciate the difference between driving with the throttle half-way down and the throttle full on. You would never have a full sense of control, and it is the same with an organ like this one'. (It is perhaps not generally known that he once had a reputation as a racing motor-cyclist.) Since then, the organ has been re-sited within the college by Michael Farley of Budleigh Salterton.

Nottingham was never far from his thoughts, and he certainly was not forgotten there. In 1967, he restored the two-manual August Gern organ in St Paul's Church, Daybrook, Nottingham, built originally in 1890. Repairs and some re-voicing were carried out by him in 1950, but the work done in 1967 included moving the whole structure of the organ to allow more room for access, the provision of a new main wind reservoir, new electric action, new console and a complete tonal revision with several new stops. Peter Hurford gave the re-opening recital on 18th May, 1967. Roger Yates had a great respect for Gern's work and always referred to him as a very great tonal expert. 'He was an Alsatian with a good knowledge of German organ building and later became foreman to Aristide Cavaillé-Coll, the greatest of 19th century European organ builders. He supervised the erection of several organs Cavaillé-Coll built in England and owing to the mid-nineteenth century decline in French organ building decided to establish himself in this country, which he did in 1866. He modelled his tonal schemes very largely on Cavaillé-Coll's work, relying to a large extent on reeds for effect, but unfortunately had a predeliction for long distance and complicated tubular-pneumatic actions, Daybrook organ being an example of this kind of work. Otherwise his workmanship was good and he made many house organs for the "Nobility and Gentry" to quote the words of one of his advertisements. He was supported by the Douglas-Home family in Scotland, where he made many organs. By 1902 he had built at least 52 organs including several of four manuals.'

ST PAUL'S CHURCH, DAYBROOK 1967

GREAT ORGAN

	ft
Open Diapason	8
Gedackt	8
Dulciana	8
Principal	4
Gedackt (ext.)	4
Twelfth	2⅔
Fifteenth	2
Mixture	IV
Trumpet	8
Clarion	4

SWELL ORGAN

Hohlflöte	8
Viole de Gamba	8
Voix Céleste	8
Principal	4
Octave (ext.)	2
Cymbale	III
Basson	16
Trompette	8

Hautbois (ext.)	8
Clairon (ext.)	4

PEDAL ORGAN

Open Diapason	16
Bourdon	16
Quint	10⅔
Principal	8
Flute (ext.)	8
Fifteenth (ext.)	4
Basson (from Swell)	16
Trumpet (from Great)	8
Clairon (from Great)	4

WIND PRESSURES

Great: 3 ins. Swell: 3¼ ins. Pedal: 3¾ ins.

4 couplers and 17 pistons

On 27th October, 1963, he wrote to John Holmes of Monasterevan: 'I have made a little extension organ in Kent. Basic ranks are gedackt 8ft, gemshorn 8ft with stopped bass, principal 4ft, mixture 1ft, all independent ranks and sesquialtera 2½ft from mid C up, both ranks independent. These extended to 14 stops on two manuals and pedal, no couplers nor pistons, drawstop knob console. It was very successful, in fact still is (!) but I think a small tracker organ with the same contents would have been less complicated. Still, it was a very interesting try out'. This was in 1962, and due to the kindness of the organist at Ulcombe, Mr David de la Rue, I have been able to ascertain how the ranks have been extended:

MANUAL ONE.— Gemshorn, 8; gedackt, 8; principal, 4; gemshorn, 4; mixture 22.26, II.
MANUAL TWO.— Gemshorn, 8; gedacht, 8; gedacht, 4; principal, 2; sesquialtera 12.17, 2⅔.
PEDAL ORGAN.— Sub bass, 16; gedackt, 8; principal, 4; mixture 22.26, II.
The whole of the organ is enclosed. Full organ by hitch-down pedal.

It should be noted that in his extraordinarily busy life he found time to act as consultant for the rebuild by the Willis firm of the Father Willis organ at Truro Cathedral. No tonal alterations were made.

In a letter to me dated 10th April, 1966, Roger Yates mentioned the Ulcombe organ: 'The Rector says if he leaves Ulcombe he will have another organ exactly like it and I notice one or two other people have taken up the same idea. It was thought out a good time before it was made in 1961'.

He worked quietly on but purposely also, at Michaelstowe, and churches in a wide area have cause to be thankful for his ministrations. Many famous organists and organ builders, both English and from abroad, were frequent visitors to his home. To my great regret, family commitments prevented me from accepting an invitation to examine his Lloyd records which were packed away in tin trunks. Had I been able to make the long journey there, without a car, it is very likely that the Lloyd section of this chapter would have been much more complete.

The organ in the church of Stogursey, Somerset, was in course of construction when illness prevented Roger Yates from completing it. His friend Bill Drake, of Buckfastleigh, took over and carried out the necessary work of completion. Some tuning and maintenance contracts went to him and in the course of time, Lance Foy of Truro found himself looking after most of Yates' local jobs.

The last year or two of his life were sadly marred by a severe stroke; he was then living at Thurnby, Leicester, where he died in hospital on 2nd September, 1975, within a few days of his 70th birthday. So passed a most remarkable man, modest in character and in the output of his work, but a truly great organ builder who was once described as 'years ahead of his time'. John Holmes commented: 'He was held in highest regard by distinguished organists such as Dupré, Germani, Sir John Dykes-Bower, Ralph Downes, Sir George Thalben-Ball and organ builders von Beckerath, Flentrop, Donald Harrison and Victor Gonzales'.

I am proud to have known him and been able to record some of his many achievements. It is my fervent hope that some of his finest work will escape the whims and fancies that beset organ building in some quarters today, when it becomes necessary to give them attention.

HENRY GROVES & SON

Alvin Henry Groves commenced his training at Henry Willis & Sons' Nottingham branch, under the supervision of Reg Rowberry, where he gained useful experience of a variety of builders' work in a wide area of Nottinghamshire and beyond. By 1957, he decided to commence business on his own; it was a bold move, for his only capital was payment in advance for his first job. In November of that year he rented premises in Edwin Street, formerly used as a lace works, and about the same time, his close friend Arthur Bailey (who had been with him on the Willis staff) joined him and thus began a very successful partnership.

Concentrating on rebuilding quality organs and on cleaning and overhauling, they soon began to be known for their splendid craftsmanship and fair business dealings which brought them to the notice of Dr. W. L. Sumner. Their first rebuild from Edwin Street was a two-manual Hardy of Stockport; this had been inspected by Dr. Sumner and was sold to Pleasley Hill Parish Church, Mansfield, for the moderate sum, even then, of £800. It was the first of many such jobs from the workshop in Edwin Street and sold nationwide as far as Carlisle in the north and Sussex in the south.

In 1969, the firm of E. Wragg & Son, Nottingham (Est. 1894), was purchased on the death of its owner and thus was provided a better workshop; the staff was retained and their large tuning round was taken over. Here they remained for the next ten years during which a steady business was done with a wide variety of work.

In 1979, the City Council required the land on which the premises stood, for road improvements. The workshop was demolished and the firm was found new premises of similar size at Swinburne Street. A former school, these are still in use. Arthur Bailey retired some years ago and has since died; Alvin Groves retired in 1991 when his grandson, Jonathan Wallace (who had been with him since leaving school in 1985), took over the direction of the family firm. The constant and lively progress made since then is continued in Chapter XIV.

In looking back over the years, one is impressed by the wide variety of work carried out by the principal and his small staff, which is quite remarkable. It was not accomplished without the 'burning of midnight oil' and eventual and complete retirement was certainly timely. The firm's advertisement in *Musical Opinion* in September 1972 lists a number of contracts in hand or recently completed, the most important of which were as follows. Holy Trinity Church, Paisley, electrification, detached console, tonal additions. Whitefield Memorial Church, Tottenham Court Road, new installation with electric action. Bingham Parish Church, Notts., electrification with detached console. The contract which gave the firm particular cause for pride was the rebuild, with electrification, of the four-manual 1897 Hill organ in the Parish Church, Buxton, in 1974. In those days, the tuning contracts extended right down to the Isle of Wight, but eventually a pruning became necessary due to distance and the high cost of servicing, with the result that the organ in Brook Parish Church, on the Island, was passed to other hands.

My own personal recollection of Groves' work goes back some twenty years or so. In the county of Lincolnshire they have been involved with some twelve contracts, ranging from restorations, rebuilds with electrification and new organs incorporating some pipework from elsewhere, as well as new. All show the care and attention to detail which has been a feature of their work and which was noticed by W. L. Sumner during his lifetime, resulting in his recommendation in a number of instances.

Three instruments have particularly impressed me: St Nicholas' Church, Lincoln (1983), St Hugh's R. C. Church, Lincoln (1974 and 1988), and Uffington Parish Church (1989).

St Nicholas was a complete rebuild with Solid State action, together with the addition of a Swell mixture, of the Nicholson of Lincoln organ of 1868, which had been rebuilt by Cousans of Lincoln in 1930. The re-opening recital was given by Jennifer Bate, who went through every stop in the afternoon and made some highly complimentary remarks to Alvin Groves regarding the splendid regulation. This was well merited, for some of the old Nicholson pipework had required much patient work to bring it up to scratch. A brilliant recital displayed this magnificent instrument to the full, to which Nicholson, Cousans and Groves have all contributed their skill, aided by superb acoustics. After an interval of some years, I recently made its acquaintance once again and it gave me the usual thrill. I was particularly pleased to come across the metal trebles of the bass flute which I remember voicing when I was but seventeen: and I was quite delighted to find them satisfactory!

St Hugh's Roman Catholic Church, Lincoln, was the possessor of a three-manual organ by Jackson of Lincoln shortly after the church was consecrated in 1893. By 1976, the organ was in urgent need of a very thorough rehabilitation throughout, and this was most successfully carried out; the very poorly designed tracker action was re-planned where possible, the reeds were revoiced and all the flue work re-balanced. Two additions were made—a trumpet to the Great and a larigot to the Choir. Alas, all this good work was undone by water entering the chamber some years later, on two occasions. The latter was so serious that a new organ was imperative. In 1988, this became possible when a splendid two-manual organ by Rushworth & Dreaper was installed by Groves, sited in a gallery on the west side of the chancel (the church stands north to south) with a detached console below, so that at long last this fine building has a truly worthy instrument to accompany its worship.

The organ came from Egremont Baptist Church and had tubular-pneumatic action. It was rebuilt with Solid State and four stops were added: principal and fifteenth (a 73 note extension unit), together with trumpet to the Great, and a Swell mixture in place of the former voix celestes.

ST HUGH'S ROMAN CATHOLIC CHURCH, LINCOLN 1988

GREAT ORGAN	*ft*	SWELL ORGAN	
Open Diapason	8	Echo Gamba	8
Dulciana	8	Lieblich Gedact	8
Hohl Flute	8	Salicet	4
Flauto Traverso	8	Mixture	III
Principal	4	Cornopean	8
Fifteenth	2	PEDAL ORGAN	
Trumpet	8	Sub Bass	16
		Bass Flute	8

At Uffington Parish Church, South Lincolnshire, stood a fine old Walker organ of 1867, which was badly in need of rehabilitation. Wire work was rusty, action uneven and extremely noisy—in fact, there was much to be done. The tone was what one would expect from Walker, but it spoke with an uncertain speech. When all was completed, the church could not believe that it possessed such a beautiful instrument. The result was a triumph for the skill and patience of the Nottingham firm, which has not gone un-noticed by several authorities who have examined it. The instrument has been turned round at some time during its history; the pipe front now faces south in the chamber, which reduces its carrying power, but funds were simply not available to remedy this.

UFFINGTON PARISH CHURCH, LINCOLNSHIRE
ORGAN BY J. W. WALKER 1867

GREAT ORGAN

	ft		
Open Diapason	8	Gamba	4
Stopped Diapason	8	Oboe	8
Dulciana	8		
Principal	4	PEDAL ORGAN	
Flute	4	Bourdon	16
Fifteenth	2		
Mixture	III	COUPLERS	
Spare slide	—		

Swell to Great   Great to Pedals

SWELL ORGAN

Swell Organ from tenor C.
Mechanical action throughout.

Double Open Diapason (wood)	16	
Horn Diapason	8	
Lieblich Gedacht	8	

Oak casework with spotted metal pipe front.

Amongst the variety of organ builders represented in the firm's extensive tuning round, Alvin Groves has always had an affinity with the work of Forster & Andrews, several of whose organs he has maintained over the years. One of these is a particularly fine example—that at St Peter's Parish Church, Sturton-le-Steeple, Notts., built in 1903, about a year before James Forster retired, leaving the firm in the sole ownership of Philip H. Selfe, who had been manager since 1897. In 1972, the Nottingham firm cleaned and overhauled the instrument and at the same time added a balanced swell pedal and radiating and concave pedal board. It is still in their care; moreover, the organist, Mr J. H. Tuddenham, has held the post with distinction for no less than fifty-three years.

MIDLAND ORGAN BUILDERS

A firm which became notable for their specialisation in the restoration of fairground organs in addition to the rebuilding, restoration and tuning of church organs, was the partnership of Roger Bassett, M.I.S.O.B. and Tony Cragg, known as Midland Organ Builders of Nottingham. The partnership was formed in 1970 by Roger Bassett, who commenced his career as an apprentice with Cedric Arnold in his home village of Thaxted, Essex, later working for Henry Willis & Sons at their Nottingham branch, and finally became Nottingham representative for J. W. Walker & Sons Ltd. Tony Cragg was another member of the Willis Nottingham branch from 1957. Preservation of steam locos, vintage vehicles and the like flourishes as never before, and fairground organs create enormous interest wherever they can be heard. Tony Cragg can frequently be seen with his small fairground organ at Steam Rallies. This Nottingham firm has played an important part in the restoration of these fine old instruments built purely for entertainment and have dealt with many example of the work of Gavioli, Chiappa, Hooguys, Verbeeke, Limonaire, Marenghi and Bruder, which have passed through their works. Another feature of their work was the tuning of some of the few remaining Wurlitzer and Compton cinema organs. The partnership was dissolved in 1988 and the two men continued working happily but separately in their own names in a quiet way. The firm then became known as Bassett Organ Builders (Midland), Pipe Organ Specialists. It ceased on the retirement of Roger Bassett in 1991, when it was purchased by Anthony Herrod of Skegby, Notts., who had established his business in 1985. Some of the instruments with which he has been involved are: The Old Meeting House, Mansfield (rebuild with direct electric action of the organ by Cousans and Sons & Co., of Lincoln), Greasley, St Mary's Church, Notts., rebuild of the 1910 Lloyd organ with electric action, St Wilfrid's Parish Church, Kirkby-in-Ashfield, overhauling an 1888 Banfield organ, including electrification of, and the addition of, two stops to the Pedal Organ, and numerous jobs requiring cleaning and general overhaul.

MARTIN GOETZE & DOMINIC GWYNN
5 THE TAN GALLOP, WELBECK

At Welbeck, in the heart of the Dukeries, is the workshop of two specialist craftsmen, a partnership of two young men devoted to the reviving of 'the classical tradition of English organ building and to raise the level of interest in old English organs'. Partly with the assistance of the Harley Foundation, who have provided them with a subsidised workshop, working amongst other craftsmen, their situation in the beautiful countryside in which Welbeck Abbey stands could not be more ideal. The Tan Gallop was a glass-roofed riding school built for the 5th Duke of Portland, known for his underground buildings which included a ballroom connected to many other rooms by tunnels, and a miniature underground railway. The Tan Gallop has disappeared but the name remains. A profile of Dominic Gwynn appeared in *The Journal of the International Society of Organ Builders* for Summer 1991, but the firm has kindly provided me with a summary of their history. Martin worked with Grant, Degens & Bradbeer from 1967–77 when he joined the staff of Gabriel Kney in Canada. Dominic Gwynn left Oxford University in 1974 with a degree in history and after spending a year at joinery classes in The Worshipful Company of Carpenters' Building Crafts Training School, worked with H. K. Bruggencate for four years. Their first work was carried out from a small workshop in Northampton; after five years there, they moved to their present address. Here they were joined by another ex-employee of Grant Degens & Bradbeer, who before joining the team at Welbeck, had worked with Hradetzky in Austria and had worked as a voicer on the Sydney Opera House organ for a year. Their first apprentice, Stuart Dobbs, joined them in 1989 and a year later their staff was increased by the entry of Tudor Roberts, a young German organ builder who had gained experience in Johannes Rohlf's workshop in the Black Forest.

The firm's training had been in the modern neo-classical tradition, but their growing interest in the historic English organ led them to build instruments whose sound and construction was based on old ones, their particular interest being those of the seventeenth and eighteenth centuries.

This has meant much detailed study and as a result, the manufacture of *all* parts, except blowers, is carried out in their workshops. Restoration of early organs is also an important part of their work and in this they have been very successful. This has included work for The National Trust, Burghley House, The Victoria and Albert Museum and private individuals. They have been particularly proud to have gained contracts for overseas, including Germany, The Eastman School of Music, Rochester, USA, Vancouver and The Hague. Those for St Andrew's Wesley Church, Vancouver (one-manual) and St John's and St Philip's den Hague (two-manual) were both new.

Underlying all their activities is their desire to revive the classical tradition of English organ building and to encourage the level of interest in old *English* organs and this I find most laudable.

The start of their tenth year in partnership saw their first new church organ in Britain, that for the church of St John the Baptist, Marldon, Devon. It occupies an ideal position on a purpose-built west gallery in the tower arch. This is the third organ they have built in the style of Richard Bridge; the following is its specification.

ST JOHN THE BAPTIST, MARLDON, DEVON

GREAT ORGAN		SWELL ORGAN	
	ft	Stop'd Diapason	8
Open Diapason	8	Principal	4
Stop't Diapason	8	Fifteenth	2
Principal	4	Cornet	II
Flute	4	Hautboy	8
Fifteenth	2		
Sesquialtera	IV	PEDAL ORGAN	
Trumpet	8	Bourdon	16
		Bass Flute	8

There are the usual couplers and a balanced swell pedal. The sesquialtera has a double draw, so that it can be used without the tierce rank. The longest pipe in the front is the open diapason G, C to F sharp being supplied by the stopped diapason and independent helpers. The bass flute is an extension of the bourdon.

The pitch is A = 440. The tuning is that known as Young's, with six tempered fifths and six pure fifths, in which all the keys can be used, with C the best major key and F sharp the worst.

The wind system is based closely on that in the Snetzler organ at Cobham Hall in Kent, with two 6 by 3 single fold wedge bellows providing a pressure of 64 mm. They can be operated manually, though normally only the lower bellows is used, fed by an electric blower.

The *Organ Club Journal* (No. 1, 1994) announced that Martin Goetze and Dominic Gwynn had just installed a new organ for St Matthew's Church, Carver Street, Sheffield: 'an organ that Bernard Smith might have made at the time he arrived in England'. It has been influenced by a number of English, Dutch and North German organs which include examples of Smith's work at Edam and Walton-on-Thames, together with organs at Noorwolde, Eenum and Adlington Hall. There are two manuals on one soundboard and the following is the specification.

UPPER KEYBOARD.— Prestant, 8; holpyp, 8 †; octaaf, 4; sexqualter, I–II; mixtur, III; trompet bas, 8 †; trompet disc, 8 †.
LOWER KEYBOARD.— Quintadeen, 8; roefluit, 4; octaaf, 2 †;
PEDAL.— Bourdon, 16; fluit, 8.
Stops marked † are available on either manual

To quote the note in the *Journal*: 'The voicing, sound and temperament is ideal for music of the sixteenth and seventeenth centuries and those exploring music from this wonderful repertoire will learn a lot from playing or listening to this organ. It is an important addition to Britain's gradually increasing number of historically inspired organs'.

This small firm deserve congratulations on their high ideals and I wish them well.

An early name-plate in brass

above
An early name-plate in brass

left
Dudley Wesley Chapel: C. Lloyd & Co

below left
Albion Congregational Church,
Sneinton, Nottingham, 1904–5

below
St Peter's Parish Church,
Sturton-le-Steeple.
Photo: Jonathan Wallace

above left
Ilkeston Parish Church. From the collection of the late Dr. W. L. Sumner

above right
The Yates organ at Oakham Church. Photo, the Author, 1991

below
A. E. Allen's Chamber Organ, erected in Roger Yates' factory, August 1936

262

To Mr and Mrs Roger Yates
In pleasant memory of my visit in Nottingham
Marcel Dupré
25 October 1934

top
Saint Sulpice, Paris. Marcel Dupré (1888–1971).
Signed photo of the composer, seated at the console.
Courtesy of Tom Yates

above
Roger Yates' Organ Works, Bodmin.
Courtesy of Tom Yates

left
Anglican Church of St Nicholas, Yonago, Japan.
Martin Goetze and Dominic Gwynn.
Courtesy of the firm

CHAPTER X

Huddersfield

PETER CONACHER & CO. LTD. EST. 1854

JAMES CONACHER & SON EST. 1879

WOOD OF HUDDERSFIELD EST. 1966

IN the December 1954 issue of *Musical Opinion*, Peter Conacher & Co. Ltd. of Springwood Organ Works, Huddersfield, proudly announced the centenary of their establishment, during which time nearly 2,000 instruments had been installed. They were recipient of 'sincere congratulations' from the editor in the Minor Notes column, who stated that: 'During that time they have built and despatched to all parts of the world, some 1,800 organs'. These included two five-manuals; Calne Parish Church, Wilts., and the other in the residence of H. G. Harris, J.P., of Calne. Today, despite some vicissitudes along the way, they are still in existence which is no mean achievement when a number of old established firms (particularly in Yorkshire) have long since disappeared.

My experience over the years of Conacher's work of the last century has been a mixed one—perhaps it has been fair to say—a 'love hate' relationship which has varied as a result of the quality of the particular instrument I have come across. There have been many, for note holding on their tuning round for Cousans of Lincoln, in my younger days brought me into contact with a mixed bag of organs by various builders which included a fair sprinkling of Conachers of various dates.

My first experience was not a happy one; I had lessons on a three-manual of 1875 vintage at Hannah Memorial Methodist Church, Lincoln, the best feature of which was a fine pitch pine case to a classical design of their standard pattern of which there were one or two variants. It had a very unpleasant tracker action which made playing extremely hard work when Swell and Great were coupled; the drawstops of rosewood had china engraved labels and there was an uncomfortable pedal board and ratchet swell pedal. The pipework by Zimmerman of France was thin and of average quality, giving forth a colourless sound as far as the chorus work was concerned, while the reeds were brassy and rough. To be fair, there were some pleasant flutes! I disliked it intensely, yet about a mile down High Street I loved the Forster & Andrews organ in St Catherine's Methodist Church, which made a deep impression on me even at the age of fourteen.

After the War, Comptons paid a visit to 'Hannah' and spent some time on renovation and revoicing the pipework; it emerged an entirely different instrument. The money had been wisely spent, but it was not for long that its sound was heard, for the church was demolished in the '60s and the organ sold. A very different instrument is to be found in the magnificent parish church of Navenby, some nine miles from Lincoln. It must have been built in two stages, for the Great Organ stops have china labels and those on the Swell, ivory. It gives forth a fine sound and is a pleasure to play. After studying many examples of their work over many years, I have come to the conclusion that in the last century they were willing to 'tailor' a job according to financial resources of the church placing an order. That Conachers built some fine instruments at that time is indisputable; their list of organs published as a booklet shows some important contracts, and it must not be forgotten that Hanley Town Hall formed the basis for the magnificent Henry Willis III instrument of 1922. Nottingham has always been a happy hunting ground for interesting organs ever since my 'teenage years (alas—a number have now gone) and the discovery of a four-manual in Derby Road Baptist Church in the late 1930s and a three-manual in Parliament Street Methodist Church in the city centre, quickened my interest in the firm and so I set about acquiring their catalogues and other literature and delving into their history. A close friendship with their former manager, Philip Wood, now running his own business with distinction, taught me much about the Conacher family and the firm, which has enabled me to write this brief sketch. It is but a 'taster' for a much more thorough account which he hopes to publish when time permits. I can only express my gratitude for his generosity in sharing readily with me the results of his research, which has been carried out with expertise and enthusiasm. It will certainly rank as the definitive work of an interesting family, and that of their successors.

Born at Brookfoot, Perthshire, in 1823, Peter Conacher as a boy was interested in music and after serving an apprenticeship in Glasgow and Edinburgh c.1836–42, he journeyed to Liepzig where he worked as an artisan organ builder learning in particular the art of German voicing.

On returning to England he spent some time working for Hill and Walker. His aim in life was to become a master organ builder and whilst taking part in the erection of a large instrument Walkers had built for Highfield Chapel, Huddersfield, he could see the great potential for business in that rapidly growing city and district and so decided to stay and try his luck. It proved to be a wise move; in December 1854 he took small premises with a fellow workman named Martin, who did not stay long.

MESSRS. MARTIN AND CONACHER (from LONDON), ORGAN BUILDERS, beg most respectfully to inform the Nobility, Clergy, and Gentry of Huddersfield and vicinity, that they have commenced business in White Lion Yard, Cross Church-street, Huddersfield, where they hope, by care and attention to business, to merit a share of public support. Messrs. M. & C., after having had many years' experience in the first Establishments of the Metropolis, and in different parts of Germany, feel confident that they are qualified to execute any orders which may be entrusted to them in a superior manner. Amongst the Mechanical Improvements which Messrs. M. and C. are prepared to attach to new and old Organs, may be mentioned the following, viz.—

The *Pneumatic Lever* to Manuals, which lightens the touch of the largest Organ, equal to that of a Piano-forte, the couplers drawn making no difference.
The *Pneumatic Lever* to draw stops and couplers, which eases them to any extent required.
The *Pneumatic Composition Keys*, which are very short sharps placed in the spaces between B and C and E and F. They require no composition Pedals, and give the Organist full command over the whole Organ.
The *Diagonal Action*, enabling the performer to read the draw stops without altering his position.
The *Improved German Trembulant*, for Church and Chamber Organs, performing a shake, giving the Organ a peculiar effect.
Also, the *Grand Tuba Ophicleide*, a powerful reed stop, giving weight and power to the whole organ equal to six stops of common reeds.

Organs of every description Built and Re-Constructed with all the recent Improvements. Flue and Reed Pipes re-voiced on an Improved Principle, causing the lower notes of the reeds to speak with the greatest rapidity. Organs carefully Cleaned and Tuned, yearly or singly, on moderate terms.   Private Residence — No. 33, St Paul's Street.

[from *The Huddersfield Chronicle*, 2nd December, 1854]

Martin was replaced by another named Brown and all seemed set for a successful partnership. An advertisement was placed in the Leeds newspaper for October 18th, 1856, drawing attention to their work, which reads as follows:

CONACHER AND BROWN (from LONDON), ORGAN BUILDERS, HUDDERSFIELD, return their grateful Acknowledgements to the Musical Public for the Patronage hitherto bestowed upon them, and beg to inform their Friends that having recently made considerable additions to their Premises, they have now one of the Largest Establishments in the Provinces, and are prepared to build ORGANS of every description, from the Chamber to the Cathedral Organ, the tone and workmanship of which they guarantee to be such as cannot be surpassed by any house in the kingdom.

C. and B. call especial notice to their REEDS, which they furnish in every variety, and which are unrivalled for power, brilliancy, and standing in tune.

C. and B. have just completed an extensive alteration in the large Organ in the Parish Church of Leeds, to which instrument they invite attention. References given to some of the first Professors in the Kingdom.

1 & 7, Upperhead Row, Huddersfield.

Their collaboration did not last long however, and Peter was left on his own; he was not downhearted for he had confidence in his abilities and there was much work to be done. He was fortunate in attracting a local gentleman and lover of music—Mr Joseph H. Hebblethwaite—who provided much needed capital and so the firm was re-named Messrs. P. Conacher & Co. Real progress was made at last and having outgrown the old premises, in 1859 they had a handsome new building in the Gothic style erected in George Street, installed a small steam engine and their first machine, a small circular saw. As organs were completed they organised recitals by well-known players, including Peace and Parratt. The latter was born at Huddersfield in 1841, was organist at St Paul's Church there for seven years and in 1882 succeeded Sir George Elvey at St George's Chapel, Windsor Castle. He was made a Knight Bachelor in 1892.

Such recitals proved extremely popular and undoubtedly brought business to the firm. Amongst a number of references received during the 1860s, those from S. S. Wesley and T. W. Spark were particularly helpful:

From Dr Wesley, Organist of Winchester Cathedral (who designed and superintended the erection of the Organ in St George's Hall, Liverpool)

"The Organs lately erected by Messrs. Conacher & Co., which I have seen, entitle their builders, in my opinion, to great respect and confidence. These Instruments, in some of the most essential particulars, are as perfectly sound as any Organs I am acquainted with, and the tone is powerful, melodious, and of true organ quality. I paid their manufactory at Huddersfield a visit, and with much pleasure observed their spacious premises, and the ample stock of well seasoned, and expensive materials which they retained for business uses. I am happy to be able to add that, from my personal knowledge of Messrs. Conacher and Co., I consider them to be influenced in the conducting and arrangement of their business affairs by motives and intentions as creditable to themselves as beneficial to those who employ their services in the building of Organs.   S. S. WESLEY"

From Dr. Spark, Organist to the Town Hall and St George's Church, Leeds

"The Organs of Messrs. Conacher & Co., Huddersfield, can be highly recommended on the general grounds of utility, excellence, and cheapness. Their large stock of well-seasoned wood, extensive factory, and special resources, enable them to compete with any builders in price, and I am confident that when a fair sum is given for an Organ, Messrs. Conacher & Co. will produce a fine Instrument, good in workmanship, large and varied in tone, and containing the best materials, both in metal and wood.   WILLIAM SPARK, MUS. DOC."

On the death of Joseph Hebblethwaite, Peter Conacher was joined by his brother James, their first great enterprise being the erection of a large organ for the Yorkshire Exhibition held in York in 1866. This was awarded a gold medal and was sold to Huddersfield Parish Church where Mr H. Parratt was organist.

ORGAN IN THE YORKSHIRE FINE ART AND INDUSTRIAL EXHIBITION.— On the 24th ult., the exhibition at York was opened by his Grace the Archbishop, and the new organ, built by Messrs. Conacher, of Huddersfield, was prominently brought into use on the occasion by the splendid and skilful performance of Mr William Rea, of Newcastle-upon-Tyne, whose playing was of the very highest order. In the course of the ceremony the following selection of music was performed, the vocal portions being under the direction of Dr. E. G. Monk, organist of York Minster: — Chorus, "Hailstone," Handel. Chorus, "Long Live the King," Handel. The Hundredth Psalm, old version. Chorus, "Achieved is the Glorious Work," Haydn. Chorus, "Hallelujah" (Messiah), Handel. "The National Anthem." Subsequently, Mr Rea treated the audience to a magnificent performance of Meyerbeer's grand march from "Le Prophete," and Rossini's overture to "William Tell."

Description of the Organ.— The instrument measures 20 feet in frontage, 10 feet in depth, and about 22 feet in height. The draw-stops act diagonally, and the keys have sparrow-beaked fronts. The jambs and music-desk are of polished walnut. The Pneumatic action has been applied to the great organ and couplers. The bellows are worked by a wheel and cranks, having four different pressures of wind. The levers, rods, and fittings throughout are of polished walnut and mahogany. All the trundles, squares, shafts, composition pedals, and fans, are of patent flexible cast iron, which gives a lightness, combined with stability, to the mechanism of the instrument. The upper portion of the organ is without a case, so that all the pipes are exposed. The lower parts are protected by open framing, filled in with glass, showing the working of the pneumatic machine, and all the movements. The reeds and mixtures are placed upon separate chests. The sound boards are double palleted throughout.

THE YORKSHIRE EXHIBITION 1866

3 manuals: CC to G, 56 notes   Pedal: CCC to F, 30 notes

GREAT ORGAN

		ft
Tenoroon Diapason	bright burnished & sptd. m	16
Large Open Diapason	bright burnished m	8
Open Diapason	bright burnished m	8
Stopped Diapason	w	8
Principal	bright m	4
Harmonic Flute	bright m	4
Twelfth	bright m	2⅔
Fifteenth	bright m	2
Sesquialtera	bright m	IV
Trumpet	sptd. m	8
Trumpet	sptd. m	4

SWELL ORGAN

		ft
Double Diapason	w	16
Open Diapason	bright m	8
Stopped Diapason	w	8
Salicional	sptd. m	8
Gemshorn	bright m	4
Fifteenth	bright m	2
Mixture	bright m	III
Horn	sptd. m	8
Oboe	sptd. m	8
Clarion	sptd. m	4
Tremulant		

CHOIR ORGAN

		ft
Lieblich Gedact	w	16
Gedact	w	8
Dulciana	sptd. m	8
Viol-de-Gamba	sptd. m	8
Flauto Traverso	w	8
Gemshorn	bright m	4
Stopped Flute	sptd. m	4
Piccolo	w	2
Clarionet	sptd. m	8

PEDAL ORGAN

Double Open Diapason	w	16
Principal	m	8
Trombone	w	16

COUPLERS

Octave   Swell to Great
Swell to Pedals   Great to Pedals
Choir to Great   Choir to Pedals

7 Composition pedals
Radiated pedals, 30 notes

This instrument has been very highly spoken of by local judges, and appears to have given the utmost satisfaction to the executive committee, for at the banquet held subsequently to the opening the vice-chairman in proposing the health of Mr Conacher, the builder, alluded to it in the most complimentary and flattering manner.   [From *The Organist*, 1866, pp 74–75]

Thereafter, business increased rapidly with a result that the factory proved too small and so an entirely new one was built in 1873 in Water Street, Springwood, which soon became known as one of the largest and most complete of its kind in the country. Its machinery, which included a planing machine, was steam-driven and for the first time there was a metal pipe-making department.

The 1873 factory, used as their letter-heading as late as 1912

James Conacher eventually left the firm with his three sons to found his own company which was in business at Bath Buildings, Bath Street, by 1880. His place was taken by Peter Conacher's son, Joseph Hebblethwaite Conacher, who then was twenty-three years of age. The partnership continued until the beginning of 1898 when father sold his share to his son who then changed the name of the firm to Peter Conacher & Co. Ltd. Two months later, in April, Peter Conacher died at the age of 71; he had contemplated retiring at Lytham, but illness intervened. He was known as a very genial man with a generous disposition; he had served the city council and was in office for nine years; he had also been churchwarden at Huddersfield Parish Church, despite the fact that he had been brought up a Presbyterian. He had also been a Freemason for about thirty years.

Joseph Conacher directed the company until his death in April 1913, at the early age of 57. During his career he had spent some time in Paris where he studied the French system of organ building. He brought home with him several French workmen to introduce the French system of voicing reeds and gambas and the construction of French metal pipes. The organ in Huddersfield Parish Church was one of a number of important instruments built under his direction in 1908; it was opened by Sir Walter Parratt. He too had been a churchwarden there; he was a man with wide interests, and in his younger days was widely known for his prowess as an athlete and rugby footballer, playing for Yorkshire County at the age of seventeen. Like his father before him, he had been a Freemason. He inherited his father's genial disposition, strict integrity and generosity.

An advertisement in *Musical Opinion* during the 1890s

269

The specification of the Huddersfield Parish Church organ was drawn up by Dr. A. Eaglefield Hull, F.R.C.O., the then organist of the church, in conjunction with the builders. The 'Chromo-Digit' Board appears to have been a row of stop-keys above the Solo division, and were rather tightly placed. The cost of the instrument was £1,200.

HUDDERSFIELD PARISH CHURCH 1908

4 manuals: CC to C, 61 notes   Pedal: CCC to G, 32 notes

GREAT ORGAN

		ft	pipes
Double Open Diapason	m	16	61
Large Open Diapason	m	8	61
Small Open Diapason	m	8	61
Dolce	m	8	61
Clarabella	m	8	61
Principal	m	4	61
Harmonic Flute	m	4	61
Fifteenth	m	2	61
Trumpet	m	8	61
Clarion	m	4	61
Mixture	sptd. m	III	183

SOLO ORGAN

		ft	pipes
Concert Flute (Harmonic)	m	8	61
Tuba (Harmonic)	m	8	61

SWELL ORGAN

		ft	pipes
Lieblich Bourdon	w	16	61
Open Diapason	m & w	8	61
Viola	m & w	8	61
Rohr Flote	m & w	8	61
Salicional	m	8	61
Voix Celestes	m	8	49
Gemshorn	m	4	61
Spare slide for 8ft Flute			
Piccolo	m	2	61
Sharp Mixture	sptd. m	III	183
Contra Fagotta	m	16	61
Cornopean	m	8	61
Oboe	sptd. m	8	61
Vox Humana	m	8	61
Tremulant			

CHOIR ORGAN

		ft	pipes
Violin Diapason	m & w	8	61
Echo Dulciana	m	8	61
Flauto Traverso	w	8	61
Unda Maris	w	8	49
Flute	w	4	61
Flautina	w & m	2	61
Clarinet	m	8	61
Orchestral Oboe	sptd. m	8	61
Viol d'Orchestre	pure tin	8	61
Tremulant			

PEDAL ORGAN

		ft
Harmonic Bass	w	32
Open Diapason (large scale)	w	16
Violone	w	16
Bourdon	w	16
Lieblich Bourdon	w	16
Octave Bass	w	8
Flute Bass	w	8
Ophicleide	m & w	16
Tromba	m	8

COUPLERS

Swell Octave   Swell Sub Octave   Swell to Great
Swell Octave to Great   Swell Sub Octave to Great
Swell to Choir   Swell to Pedal   Great to Pedal
Choir to Pedal   Solo to Pedal   Solo to Great
Solo Sub Octave   Choir Sub Octave

ACCESSORIES

4 Composition Pedals to Great Organ
4 Composition Pedals to Swell Organ
3 Composition Pedals to Choir Organ
4 Combination Pistons to Great Organ
4 Combination Pistons to Swell Organ
3 Combination Pistons to Choir Organ
Piston to add Pedal Organ to Great Compositions
1 Reversible Pedal for Great to Pedal Coupler

The Choir Organ is placed in a Box.
The Solo Organ is elevated over the Great Organ.

The Action is Tubular Pneumatic throughout.
The Console is away from the instrument,
and is arranged in a position giving the Organist
full view of the Choir.

The "Chromo Digit" Board, which takes the place
of Draw Stops, was specially designed by Dr. Hull.

Case of Oak. Front Pipes Silvered (Aluminium).

The wind is generated by special feeders, worked by
two of Calvert's Hydraulic Engines, placed in the
Crypt. There are several Reservoirs in the Organ
supplying wind at various pressures to the
different departments.

Joseph Conacher's death was a great blow to the company for it was then at the height of its powers and had a world-wide connection with some 1,500 organs to their credit. The cause of Joseph's death was a heart attack and it seems very likely that the destruction by fire of the firm's factory on 23rd July, 1910, may have contributed to it, for undoubtedly there was a great strain and stress in the efforts to maintain production as well as to supervise the erection of a new building and equip it with the latest machinery. Built on the former site, it was a large three-storeyed building with basement, to a more modern design than the old one, which was attractive in the use of Gothic for its frontage, in the taste of its time. It was described as the largest organ factory in the country and it was fitted with the most labour-saving machinery then available, some of which remains to this day.

When Joseph Conacher died, his son Philip Gordon Conacher, who was then only nineteen years of age, and had little experience of organ building, was unable to carry on and so the firm was directed by James Stott who had a number of years management experience with Joseph Conacher, having joined the company at the age of fourteen in 1900. Having been Organist and Choirmaster of St Thomas' Church, Huddersfield since 1910, where he presided at a three-manual Conacher organ installed in 1915, he had the great advantage of understanding the instrument and its requirements from the practical point of view of the player. After serving throughout the Great War, Philip Conacher became titular head of the company which was owned by his mother, but unfortunately took little interest in it; he died in 1952, and thus ended the family's direction of the firm for two years short of a century. Very often the third generation of a business loses interest; hence the old Lancashire saying: 'Clogs to clogs in three generations'. In this instance, it proved to be the fourth.

A full description of the new factory appeared in the firm's brochure *Conacher Organs*; this was produced by James Stott whose portrait appears therein. It is handsomely produced with fine illustrations of cases, consoles, together with views of the exterior of the factory and four of its most important workshops. From it we learn that:

> 'To a special degree the works are self contained. Very little indeed is done outside. In the basement hard zinc sheets are rolled into pipes without softening. On the first floor you find the offices, together with the case-making department and machine shops... We do practically all our own machining down to threading and milling screws for Conacher components... On the second floor, soundboards, bellows, action and other components are made. We have benches here for 40 workmen. The outstanding room however, is the erecting shop—over 30ft high, where 8 or 10 organs can be built together. On the top floor and separated by double partitions are the voicing rooms... the foundries, blacksmith's shop and pipe-making department are all in a separate building behind. We regularly employ about 80 people in all.
>
> Conacher's is fast becoming a show place. Universities, Works, Schools, Rotary Clubs and other organisations constantly visit us. We have much to show them and all are welcome at any time by arrangement. The plant is worth seeing, and the use we make of it is a musical revelation.'

This great building was solidly built of stone in the style of a Yorkshire woollen mill; there was a tall chimney at the back which leads one to believe that in those days, the machinery was driven by a steam engine. The days of these vast works are gone; those of Conachers and Harrison & Harrison at Durham must be the last to remain; they have an atmosphere all their own and long may they continue.

It was due to the initiative of Stott that the firm embarked on the building of cinema organs during the 1930s and were fortunate enough to secure the services of Reginald Foort as technical adviser and designer. Their brochure, *Notes on the Conacher Theatre Organ* makes interesting reading today.

They enlarged and modernised the factory at a cost of over £5,000, installed the most up-to-date machinery and plant as well as engaging an additional staff of experts in all the various branches of theatre organ design, construction, electric action and voicing. While the boom in the demand for cinema organs lasted they shared to a limited extent in the great number of contracts awarded to British firms in the 1930s, but in all they built only eight instruments.

An attractive brochure entitled *Organs of Intimate Charm*, by Peter Conacher & Co. Ltd., was compiled by Stott, a copy of which is in my possession. From it we learn that their magnets (except for the Bakelite pressings) were manufactured in their own electrical engineering shop. It includes case and console illustrations, the former featuring double-touch pistons, adjustable from switch boards, cancellers to each department, electrically controlled swell pedals and a general crescendo pedal. Extension was featured with sample specifications of instruments using this system.

271

James Stott died in 1957 and was succeeded by his son, Ronald, a Dewsbury solicitor, who appointed Leonard E. Bartram (manager of Conacher's Dublin branch, for they had a wide connection in Ireland), as general manager, with Maurice Milnes as works manager. Thereafter, there were unfortunate difficulties at the Springfield works; in October 1964, Philip Wood was recalled from his post as a manager in Ireland to take over as general manager at Huddersfield, but after twenty-two months there left to found his own business which opened on 1st October, 1966. He had served his apprenticeship at Peter Conacher & Co. from September 1947, gaining valuable experience there. After two years National Service he returned to his old firm being appointed Northern Ireland representative at Belfast in March 1954, and then in 1963 he was promoted manager in Ireland.

Eventually it became necessary to sell the business which included the premises at Huddersfield. Organ builders were circularised and I recall sitting in Cuthbert Harrison's office discussing the production of the first edition of *The Harrison Story* and at the same time conjecturing who would purchase Conachers! In 1972 it was announced that Henry Willis & Sons Ltd. had taken it over as a tuning and maintenance base for Yorkshire and the north. During the 1970s, Springwood Organ Works were used mainly for the storage of stock, also as a pipe making, voicing and console shop and to store parts from the ill-fated Alexandra Palace organ. The staff continued with not only their own work but were also sub-contractors for the owners.

In 1988, John Sinclair Willis, second son of Henry IV, purchased from his father the business of Peter Conacher & Co. Ltd. and moved to Huddersfield (where he had served part of his apprenticeship) to put his own stamp on the 'old firm' as it had been known in its heyday. He was interested in the work of the founders and was anxious to engage in restorations when they arose, as well as instruments of worth by other builders, of any age. Harmoniums and reed organs had intrigued him since the age of sixteen, when on recovering from illness his father placed a harmonium in his care for rehabilitation. He had not intended to become an organ builder—but eventually the family tradition entered his blood, and he has never looked back. He decided therefore to offer conservation service for reed organs, for there has been a renewal of interest in them during recent years. It is interesting to record that Cavaillè-Coll and Father Willis both had a training on reed organs and harmoniums. It would appear to have been a somewhat daunting task to take over this huge factory which had become a 'time warp', with benches, tools, machinery etc left just as they were when the business was active. John Sinclair not only has great ability but is endowed with an infectious enthusiasm too. He made it known that the 'time warp' would be retained and that visitors would be welcome. It has proved so successful that visits by individuals or parties now have to be restricted to weekends, in order to avoid interruption to work in progress by his staff. A recent visit there was a fascinating experience. The firm has been included on the Conservation Register maintained by the Conservation Unit of the Museums and Galleries Commission, who recognise their integrity in restoration by strictly avoiding putting their own imprint on any such work carried out. This is carefully documented and is done strictly to the original pattern—the old parts also being left and labelled for posterity. The firm also carries out sub-contract work for others, so that tunings, repairs, conservation work, as well as dealing with visitors (parties of which vary from 5 to 40), John Sinclair and his staff have brought the old Springwood works to life once again. He has also rented spare space to craftsmen musical instrument makers—thus forming a busy community.

He is well known as a highly-skilled reed voicer, in true Willis tradition, and since removing to Hudders-field has also become involved with the Petersfield works on such work; he thoroughly enjoys reed voicing, while father specialises in flue work. As this chapter is being written, John informs me that three second-hand organs have been shipped to Australia where, after erection, he is to follow in order to carry out the tonal finishing. John Sinclair Willis is a Fellow of the Institute of Musical Instrument Technology, a Fellow of the Incorporated Society of Organ Builders and a Fellow of the Royal Society of Arts, as well as a Freeman of the City of London and a Liveryman of the Worshipful Company of Musicians.

It has always intrigued me as to how John received his second name. I can recall a member of the Sinclair family (who can trace their origins back to the 1200s) being Secretary to the Willis firm for many years. I now learn that Henry Willis III married Clara Sinclair, while her brother married Henry Willis's sister and as there is no direct descendant from this family—the name happily goes on via John.

In *The Daily Telegraph* dated 13th August, 1992, 'Peterborough' in his daily column reported that John's son, Duncan Sinclair Willis, aged ten (one of the youngest people in the country in possession of a shotgun certificate), spoke on Radio 4's 'Today' programme at 6.00 a.m. the day before, 'to justify the 1968 Firearms Act which sets no minimum age for children holding shotgun certificates'. Peterborough went on to say: 'He carried it off with aplomb, overcoming some bluster from Alan Milburn MP that children and shotguns are a "potentially lethal cocktail". In fact he was more lucid than many of the politicians who usually fill Today…'

Duncan's ambition is to shoot at the Olympic Games; he shares his great interest with his father and by the time these words will have appeared in type, they will have enjoyed grouse shooting together in Scotland. He is a keen tennis player, loves the family farm which is run by his mother Ruth, who is a director with her husband, of the Conacher firm. Peterborough's notes were accompanied by a splendid photograph of Duncan and his dog amongst the hilly countryside. Will he carry on the family craft of organ building I wonder?—whatever he decides to do, I am certain there is a splendid future ahead of him. His great great great grandfather, Father Willis, would approve—for his love apart from organ building was yachting.

One of the pleasures in the writing of this book has been to make interesting discoveries; the John Sinclair Willis family and their work has been one of several and I heartily wish them every success in their future endeavours.

SOME CONACHER ORGANS

In 1873, Peter Conacher & Co. were called in at Derby Road Baptist Church, Nottingham, to build a new organ in collaboration with the organist, W. Shelmerdine (who had been appointed organist at the Mechanics Hall, Nottingham, by competition) and John Rogers. Both were experts in organ building, Shelmerdine having spent some time in the factory of Gray & Davison. Rogers, who had travelled extensively abroad and had become friendly with Schulze—which of the brothers Edmund (who died in 1865) or Edward, we are not sure—decided to include some German and French voiced stops in the instrument and Rogers' own words show what these were:

SCHULZE— Stopped diapason 8ft, Great organ, oak; Suabe flöte 4ft, Choir organ, pine, triangular, introverted mouth; Flauto traverso 8ft, Choir organ, pear tree, triangular; Nason 4ft, Choir organ, oak [this was a copy of the Father Smith stop of that name in the Temple Church organ]; Wald flöte, Swell Organ, pear tree, triangular, introverted mouth. These stops were voiced by Edward Schulze.

CAVAILLÉ-COLL— Harmonic Flute 4ft, Great organ, spotted metal

M. ZIMMERMAN— Horn diapason 8ft, Great organ, spotted metal; Principal 4ft, Great Organ, spotted metal; Piccolo 2ft, Choir Organ, spotted metal; Salicional 8ft, Swell Organ, spotted metal.

3 manuals: CC to G, 56 notes   Pedal: CCC to D, 27 notes

GREAT ORGAN	ft	SWELL ORGAN	ft
Open Diapason	8	Lieblich Gedackt	16
Horn Diapason	8	Open Diapason	8
Stopped Diapason Bass	8	Salicional	8
Clarabella Treble	8	Rohr Flute	8
Principal	4	Principal	4
Harmonic Flute	4	Waldflote	4
Fifteenth	2	Fifteenth	2
Sesquialtera	III	Mixture	III
Trumpet	8	Cornopean	8
		Orchestral Oboe	8
		Clarion	4
		Tremulant	

CHOIR ORGAN		PEDAL ORGAN	
	ft	Double Open Diapason	16
Dulciana	8	Bourdon	16
Keraulophon	8	Violoncello	8
Flauto Traverso	8		
Suabe Flote	4	COUPLERS	
Piccolo	2	Swell to Great Great to Pedal Swell to Pedal	
Clarinet	8	Choir to Pedal Swell to Choir	

This instrument stood behind a carved oak screen, there being no exterior show pipes; the tone was considered to be very fine, the French and German stops being especially beautiful.

The organ, together with the roof and interior of the church, was destroyed by fire in 1893 and Conachers were given the contract to build another instrument for the restored church. Shelmerdine having passed away some time previously, the responsibility for its design rested with John Rogers. At first it appeared that it would not be possible to reproduce the outstanding beauty of Schulze's stops as well as those of the French voicing, for Cavaillé-Coll and his voicer M. Reinburg, were advanced in years. Fortunately it was found that Schulze's business was still carried on in Paulinzelle where the original records were still available, while after much negotiation, the services of Cavaillé-Coll and his voicer were engaged, much to the delight of John Rogers.

From the Rogers' notes it was clear that he was anxious to include a soft Pedal 32ft and a 16ft reed in the instrument, but room was not available. Two other interesting facts also emerged—the original use of the stop named Evacuant and the actual inventor of the flute couverte on the Solo Organ. The former was a copy of the stop of that name in the organ at Vienna Cathedral; it enabled the organist to empty the reserve of wind in the bellows (which, in the Derby Road organ, was more generous than usually provided) when not required, without the slightest noise. It was out of action when I visited the organ in 1935. In Wedgewood's *Dictionary of Organ Stops*, Conachers were credited with the invention of the flute couverte, but it was actually made by them to Rogers' design.

John Rogers undoubtedly was a perfectionist; he spent three months in the Huddersfield factory following the work through stage by stage. No amount of money was spared in order to obtain the finest materials and workmanship and to this end Mr Rogers devoted much of his time, valuable knowledge and money while Conachers gave of their very best. This was very much in evidence when I heard the instrument. It was, however, in need of a thorough clean and overhaul which had not been carried out for many years. Mr Rogers was not alive to generate the necessary interest, but after my visit and enthusiastic comments about the organ, his daughter, Miss Ida Rogers, initiated a fund for the work to be done, but whether this was carried out I do not know. I have very pleasant recollections of a kind and charming lady, who showed me her father's extensive library in the large Victorian house in Tennyson Street, where she presented me with a number of his books on organ building, including one of his note books, for she was anxious that they should go to a good home and not be sold. I have treasured them to this day, for they have been of the utmost value in my research over the years.

The organ was not ideally placed, for it was in a chamber in the chancel of this fine Gothic building, with a case of richly carved oak to match the handsome choir stalls and altar. The pipes to the chancel front were of burnished tin with French mouths; those of the Great violone facing the aisle were of rich spotted metal with English mouths. The fine polished oak console had large ivory stop knobs arranged in vertical rows on angled jambs.

I recall the fine, virile ensemble of the Great chorus, the delightful sparkle and mystery of that on the Swell and the fine old reeds which were needing careful cleaning and regulation. All the quiet stops were beautifully voiced, particularly the lovely collection of flutes on the Choir Organ and the luscious Cavaillé-Coll harmonic flute. The quiet effects were innumerable despite the lack of enclosure of the Solo Organ, while the general effect of the ensemble down the church was exceedingly fine. I had high hopes that a major restoration would be carried out when sufficient funds became available, but it was not to be.

The church had a fine musical tradition; the chanting of the psalms had been introduced as far back as 1850, but not without opposition. In 1940 and 1945, when I contributed articles to *Musical Opinion*, together with one in *The Choir* (March–April 1943), psalms and canticles found a regular place in the services, with an anthem sung both morning and evening. Mr L. A. Pattison, A.R.C.O., A.R.C.M., had held the appointment of organist and choirmaster with great distinction for some ten years and even at that difficult time in our history, the very capable choir was about twenty strong, including four professional singers. Special musical services, with orchestral accompaniment, were held from time to time; altogether the pattern of worship was almost unique for a non-conformist church, reminding me of The Church of the Messiah, Birmingham (Unitarian) where a similar pattern prevailed under Gilbert Mills which was one of the highlights of church life in the city centre. It is worthy of recording that Miss Ida Rogers was still a member of the choir in 1943, having completed no less than fifty-five years' service.

DERBY ROAD CHAPEL, NOTTINGHAM

4 manuals: CC to G, 56 notes   Pedal: CCC to F, 30 notes

GREAT ORGAN

		ft	pipes
Violone	sptd. m	16	56

(26 pipes on Great soundboard & 30 on Pedal soundboard)

Large Open Diapason	m	8	56

(heavy metal, full scale, of plump round tone peculiar to English diapasons)

Horn Diapason	sptd. m	8	56
Stopped Diapason	w	8	56

(made in Germany of Wainscot Oak)

Principal	sptd. m	4	56

(full scale, best Parisian make)

Harmonic Flute	sptd. m	4	56

(Cavaillé-Coll's make, CC to BB, 12 pipes of ordinary speaking length. Tenor C and all pipes above of double speaking length and blown the octave)

Fifteenth	sptd. m	2	56
Sesquialtera	sptd. m	III	168
Trumpet	sptd. m	8	56

(true Trumpet tone, good enough to use for a Trumpet solo or combine with Cornopean or Clarion)

Twelfth	sptd. m	2⅔	56

SOLO ORGAN

Viola	burnished tin	8	56

(stringed toned, best Parisian make, with distinctive French mouths)

Flute Harmonique	sptd. m	8	56

(Cavaillé-Coll's make, details of scale to be arranged later)

Cor Anglais	sptd. m	8	56

(French reeds suitable for Solo)

Vox Humana	sptd. m	8	56

(to be boxed with Tremulant to Mr Conacher's instructions)

Flute Couvert	tin	8	56

SWELL ORGAN

Lieblich Gedackt	w	16	56
Open Diapason	m	8	56
Salicional	sptd. m	8	56

(the finest Parisian make, say Gustave Masure)

Rohr Flote	m & w	8	56

(metal to Tenor C, 12 pipes, wood to CC)

Principal	m	4	56

Wald Flute	w	4	56
Fifteenth	sptd. m	2	56
Mixture	sptd. m	III	168
Cornopean	sptd. m	8	56

(a close imitation of the instrument)

Orchestral Oboe	sptd. m	8	56
Clarion	sptd. m	4	56

(clear and bright)

Tremulant

CHOIR ORGAN

Dulciana	m	8	56
Keraulophon	sptd. m	8	56

(as made by Gray)

Gamba Frein Harmonique	tin	8	56

(the cylindrical string toned Gamba)

Flauto Traverso	pear tree wood	8	56

(the peculiar make of Herr Schulze, triangular pipes of German pear tree wood)

Suabe Flote	pine	4	56

(introverted mouth, but distinct from Wald Flute)

Nason	oak	4	56

(made in Germany of Wainscot Oak)

Gemshorn	tin	4	56

(tone clear, German make. The pipe at cc key to 6/8, Tenor C 4/8, Mid C 3/8 Mouth CC 2¾, Tenor C 1½, Treble C 1)

Piccolo	sptd. m	2	56

(Parisian make, tone of Boehm Flute)

Clarionet	sptd. m	8	56

(tone of instrument)

PEDAL ORGAN

Open Diapason	w	16	30
Bourdon	w	16	30
Violone	sptd. m	16	(30)
Octave	w	8	(12)
Bass Flute	w	8	(12)

(Numbers 1 and 4 equal 42 pipes; numbers 2 and 5 equal 42 pipes; number 3 equals 30 pipes on this soundboard)

COUPLERS

Swell to Great   Choir to Great   Solo to Great
Great to Pedal   Swell to Pedal   Choir to Pedal
Swell to Choir   Solo to Swell
8 Composition Pedals

It was with sadness that I heard of the closure of the church and the removal of the organ by Martin Renshaw to Gresham's School, Holt, Norfolk, in 1965, where it was re-erected. In 1970, Nicholson & Co. reduced it to three manuals, the Great Organ being raised to where the Solo Organ stood and this gave greater tonal egress to support congregational singing. Michael Allard, M.A., MUS.B., F.R.C.O., who retired in 1993 from full-time work at the school after thirty-five years' service, informed me that the organ has given him great delight.

In Parliament Street Methodist Church, Nottingham, a fine building in the Gothic style erected in 1874, stands a Peter Conacher three-manual organ built during the latter part of the last century, which gives forth a splendid sound. When it received a major overhaul a number of years ago by Henry Willis & Sons Ltd., the work included some revoicing and re-balancing, to which it responded well. Dr. W. L. Sumner acted as consultant and after its completion I spent a most enjoyable half hour there. Now that the Albert Hall is not in Methodist hands, Parliament Street Church is headquarters of the Nottingham City Mission.

The specification of the organ built by the firm in 1888 for the Victoria Hall, Hanley, shows the firm's tonal thinking for a four-manual concert hall organ at that time.

VICTORIA HALL, HANLEY 1888

4 manuals: CC to C, 61 notes   Pedal: CCC to F, 30 notes

GREAT ORGAN	*ft*	CHOIR ORGAN	
Double Open Diapason	16	Violin Diapason	8
Open Diapason No.1	8	Dulciana	8
Open Diapason No. 2	8	Clarabella	8
Hohl Flute	8	Lieblich Flute	4
Principal	4	Clarionet	8
Harmonic Flute	4	SOLO ORGAN	
Fifteenth	2	Harmonic Flute	8
Mixture	III	String Gamba	8
Trumpet	8	Orchestral Oboe	8
SWELL ORGAN		Tuba	8
Lieblich Bourdon	16	PEDAL ORGAN	
Open Diapason	8	Open Diapason	16
Stopped Diapason	8	Bourdon	16
Vox Angelica	8	Quint	10⅔
Voix Celestes	8	Violoncello	8
Rohr Flute	8	Trombone	16
Principal	4	COUPLERS	
Piccolo	2	Swell to Pedals Swell to Choir Choir to Pedals	
Mixture	III	Solo to Great Great to Pedals Solo to Pedals	
Contra Fagotto	16	Swell to Great Tremulant to Solo by piston	
Cornopean	8	and drawstop 4 Composition pedals to Great,	
Oboe	8	Swell and Solo Reversible piston Great to Pedals	
Clarion	4	Pneumatic action to Great Organ	

King Street Methodist Church, Derby, is one of Methodism's most historic instruments and was built originally by Booth of Wakefield. In 1896 it was completely rebuilt by Peter Conacher & Co. The magnificent mahogany case with gilded front pipes, dominates this large building and very impressive it is, for it is one of the best examples of the period and certainly one of the finest to be found in a nonconformist church. When Conachers rebuilt the instrument in 1937 they placed a detached stop-key console (also of mahogany) immediately in front of the organ. James Stott, Managing Director of the firm, gave the opening recital on 6th September, 1937. To quote from my article in *The Choir* in July 1940: 'The builders have made no attempt to modernise the tone of the flue work. The diapason chorus is of old fashioned, light, singing tone that is quite ample for this large building. The chorus reeds are magnificent examples of modern reed tone and exhibit the highest degree of finish… many beautiful quiet effects are obtainable; the three stopped diapasons are the original Booth stops and are exquisite registers of true old fashioned flavour'. It is good to know that this instrument is still in existence.

KING STREET METHODIST CHURCH, DERBY 1896

3 manuals: CC to A, 58 notes   Pedal: CCC to F, 30 notes

GREAT ORGAN	
	ft
Double Open Diapason	16
Open Diapason	8
Stopped Diapason	8
Principal	4
Twelfth	2⅔
Fifteenth	2
Mixture	III
Trumpet treble	8
Trumpet bass	8

SWELL ORGAN	
Double Open Diapason	16
Open Diapason	8
Stopped Diapason	8
Viol D'Orchestre	8
Voix Celeste	8
Principal	4
Harmonic Piccolo	2
Mixture	III
Double Trumpet (prepared for)	16
Cornopean	8
Oboe	8
Vox Humana	8

CHOIR ORGAN	
Viola	8
Dulciana	8
Stopped Diapason	8
Principal	4
Flute	4
Clarinet Treble	8
Clarinet Bass	8

PEDAL ORGAN	
Open Diapason	16
Bourdon	16
Quint	10⅔
Principal	8
Flute	8
Trombone	16

COUPLERS

Swell to Great   Swell to Choir
Choir to Great   Swell Super Octave
Swell Tremulant   Swell to Pedals
Great to Pedals   Choir to Pedals

ACCESSORIES

4 Combination pedals to Great
3 Combination pedals to Swell
Reversible pedal Great to Pedal

1937

3 manuals: CC to C, 61 notes   Pedal: CCC to F, 30 notes

GREAT ORGAN	
	ft
Double Open Diapason	16
Large Open Diapason	8
Small Open Diapason	8
Stopped Diapason	8
Principal	4
Twelfth	2⅔
Fifteenth	2
Mixture	III
Trumpet	8

SWELL ORGAN	
Double Diapason	16
Open Diapason	8
Stopped Diapason	8
Viol D'Orchestre	8
Voix Celeste	8
Principal	4
Harmonic Piccolo	2
Mixture	III
Cornopean	8

Oboe	8
Vox Humana	8
Tremulant	

CHOIR ORGAN	
Viola	8
Dulciana	8
Stopped Diapason	8
Dulcet	4
Flute	4
Vox Humana	8
Clarinet	8
Trumpet	8
Tremulant	

PEDAL ORGAN	
Harmonic Bass	32
Open Diapason	16
Violone	16
Bourdon	16
Echo Bourdon	16

Quint	10⅔	
Octave	8	
Flute	8	
Trombone	16	
Trumpet	8	

COUPLERS

Swell to Great   Swell Octave to Great
Swell to Choir   Choir Sub Octave to Great
Swell to Great   Great to Pedal
Swell Sub Octave   Swell Sub Octave to Great
Choir to Great   Choir Sub Octave
Swell to Pedal   Choir to Pedal

ACCESSORIES

4 Thumb Pistons to Great Organ
4 Thumb Pistons to Swell Organ

4 Thumb Pistons to Choir Organ
4 Toe Pistons to Great & Pedal Organs
Thumb & Toe Pistons operating Great to Pedal "on
and off" (all pistons interchangeable)
Balanced crescendo pedals to Swell and Choir
Cancel Bars to each department

WIND PRESSURES

Great Flue Work 4½ ins.
Swell Flues and Reeds 6 ins.
Choir Organ 4 ins.   Great Reed 7 ins.
Pedal Flues 4½ ins.   Pedal Trombone 8 ins.

Electric Action throughout

Dermid Rotary Blower & Generator
(Messrs. J. H. Adkins)

One of the most important instruments to be built before the firm changed hands in 1972 was that for Belmont Presbyterian Church, Belfast, in 1964. It featured open plan pipework on a gallery instead of a normal case and the following specification which appeared in *Musical Opinion* for September 1964 shows how far the firm's tonal designs had advanced since the 1950s.

BELMONT PRESBYTERIAN CHURCH, BELFAST 1964

3 manuals: CC to C, 61 notes   Pedal: CCC to F, 30 notes

GREAT ORGAN

		ft	pipes
1	Sub Bass	16	61
2	Large Open Diapason	8	61
3	Small Open Diapason	8	61
4	Stopped Diapason	8	61
5	Hohl Flute	8	61
6	Principal	4	61
7	Harmonic Flute	4	61
8	Fifteenth	2	61
9	Mixture	III	183
10	Harmonic Trumpet	8	61
11	Harmonic Clarion (from 10)	4	12
12	*Swell to Great*		
13	*Swell Octave to Great*		
14	*Swell Sub Octave to Great*		
15	*Positive to Great*		

SWELL ORGAN

		ft	pipes
16	Geigen Diapason	8	61
17	Lieblich Gedact	8	61
18	Viol D'Orchestre	8	61
19	Voix Celeste (tenor C)	8	49
20	Salicet	4	61
21	Waldflute	4	61
22	Fifteenth	2	61
23	Mixture 19·22·26	III	183
24	Contra Fagotto	16	61
25	Harmonic Cornopean	8	61
26	Oboe	8	61
27	Harmonic Clarion	4	61
28	*Swell Octave*		
29	*Swell Sub Octave*		
30	*Tremulant*		

POSITIVE ORGAN

		ft	pipes
31	Principal	8	61
32	Rohr Flöte	8	61
33	Octave	4	61
34	Wald Flute	4	61
35	Nazard	2⅔	61
36	Block Flute	2	61
37	Tierce	1⅗	61
38	Larigot	1⅓	61
39	Cymbel 29·33·36	III	183
40	Trompette	8	61
41	Trumpet (from Great)	8	ext
42	*Swell to Positive*		

PEDAL ORGAN

		ft	pipes
43	Acoustic Bass	32	ext
44	Open Diapason (wood)	16	42
45	Open Diapason (metal)	16	54
46	Bourdon	16	42
47	Echo Bourdon (from Great)	16	ext
48	Octave (from 44)	8	ext
49	Principal (from 45)	8	ext
50	Bass Flute (from 46)	8	ext
51	Flute (from 47)	8	ext
52	Fifteenth (from 45)	4	ext
53	Trombone (from Great)	16	12
54	Contra Fagotto (from Swell)	16	ext
55	Trumpet (from 53)	8	ext
56	*Swell to Pedal*		
57	*Great to Pedal*		
58	*Positive to Pedal*		

ACCESSORIES

5 Double Touch Thumb Pistons to Great Organ
adding suitable Pedal on second touch
5 Double Touch Thumb Pistons to Swell Organ
adding suitable Pedal on second touch
5 Single Touch Thumb Pistons to Positive Organ
5 Toe Pistons to Great & Pedal Organs ⎱ *6 settings on*
5 Toe Pistons to Swell & Pedal Organs ⎰ *piston board*
Reversible Thumb & Toe Pistons to Great to Pedal
Reversible Thumb & Toe Pistons to Swell to Great
Duplicate Reversible Toe Pistons for Swell to Great
and Great to Pedal couplers at both sides of Console

Conveniently placed switchboards for changing piston
settings at the Console
Canceller Name Plates to the stops of each section —
Swell, Great, Positive & Pedal
Detached Drawstop Console with balanced Swell Pedal
in centre of kneeboard
Our latest design Console Stop-key Lighting
for Couplers only
Signal light for Blower — *Green*
Signal light for Minister, Weddings, etc — *Red*
'Discus' Electric Blowing Plant & Rectifier Equipment

JAMES CONACHER & SONS

James Conacher (1821–86) and his three sons: John (1841–1902), James II (1845–1932) and Peter II (1849–1921), all of whom had worked at Peter Conacher & Co.'s factory, left to found an independent company: Jas. Conacher & Sons at Bath Buildings, Huddersfield, in the year 1879. Whether it was the result of a family feud is not known, but these were not uncommon in the Victorian era while Yorkshiremen could be very stubborn and outspoken at times! *The Yorkshire Musician* during 1888 gave an effusive account of the new firm's work and were rather coy about revealing the family relationship with Peter Conacher & Co., for they stated that James, the founder of the business in 1879, 'had previously been a partner in another noted organ building firm in Huddersfield. In the management of the business and the supervision of the industry, Mr John Conacher, the present head of the firm, has the assistance of two brothers, all of whom are thoroughly practical men, and under this proprietary, the house has steadily pursued its way to high repute and sound prosperity'. It went on to say: 'Messrs. James Conacher & Sons' premises constitute a practically perfect organ factory, being equipped in the best and most complete manner… they are in a position to complete in first-class style one organ per month all the year round… Messrs. James Conacher & Sons have identified their name with many invaluable inventions that have become widely known and esteemed in the organ world… in 1886 they perfected and patented a 'Light Wind Tubular Pneumatic Action' which is acknowledged to be unsurpassed in perfect repetition and reliability… The gold medal of the Bradford Exhibition of 1882 is held by Messrs. James Conacher & Sons as an evidence of the success they have achieved and in many parts of the United Kingdom the organs in important churches, chapels and public buildings, bear witness to their constructive capability. Among the many organs built by this firm in the past ten years, the following fine instruments are prominent, viz: those in Christ Church, Bradford; the Parish Church, Cross Stone; the Baptist Chapel, New North Road, Huddersfield; the Moldgreen Congregational Chapel, Huddersfield; Milton Church, Huddersfield—the first organ built in Great Britain with the new system of electro-pneumatic action; the Public Hall, Rochdale—a particularly handsome and effective organ with three manuals and 46 registers; St Mary's Cathedral, Aberdeen; Christ Church, Glanogwen, Bangor; and numerous others, including organs for many private gentlemen and large instruments for South Africa etc… Messrs. Conacher hold a host of testimonials commending their work as organ builders and among the well-known names appended to these letters are those of many organists of high ability and position. Altogether, this house affords very worthy and skillful representation of a great art industry'.

In the April issue of *Musical Opinion* for 1890, the firm drew attention to their work in this advertisement:

279

In the same issue is a note to say that 'organs on the Hope-Jones system are to be built for Longwood Church, Huddersfield (by Messrs. James Conacher & Sons)' so it can be presumed that the electric action and other features were used under licence from Hope-Jones.

Just when the business ceased is not clear, but there are no entries in the 1909 *Directory of Huddersfield* so that it would seem closure took place sometime between the entry for 1900 and 1909.

P. CONACHER, VOICER TO THE TRADE

Peter Conacher II was highly respected in Huddersfield. He decided to set up in business for himself after voicing for the business founded by his father James. The exact year is not known, but it would possibly be in the early 1890s; he advertised in *Musical Opinion* during 1896:

ORGAN PIPE VOICING AND TUNING

P. CONACHER

VOICER AND TUNER TO THE TRADE
Formerly with Conacher & Co., and late Head Voicer with Jas. Conacher & Sons

Voicing undertaken in all its Branches

Speciality: REED WORK (Purity of Tone, and Guaranteed to Stand in Tune). Yearly Tunings or Singly.
Organs Repaired, Cleaned, and Revoiced on Reasonable Terms.

Address: P. CONACHER, 23 Arnold Street, Birkby, HUDDERSFIELD

Peter Conacher was advertising as an organ pipe-maker and voicer in *The Music Trade Directory* for 1920, from 62 Arnold Street, Birkby; it would appear that he ceased to trade sometime during the 1920s, for there is no entry for him in the 1930 edition and he died in 1932.

Finally, Herbert Conacher, son of James II; on the breaking up of Jas. Conacher & Sons, for a short time he was in partnership with P. H. Sheffield, trading as Conacher Sheffield & Co. Ltd., organ builders of Harborne.

All in all, the Conacher family were quite remarkable. Like all such dynasties there comes a time when there is no remaining member left to carry on a business. Due to the foresight and enterprise of Henry Willis IV together with his son John Sinclair, the name lives on and long may it continue.

The firm's logo which appeared on their correspondence for many years
since the management of James Stott

WOOD OF HUDDERSFIELD EST. 1966

A firm which has two Cathedral organ rebuilds to its credit, together with a goodly number of contracts of importance, is no mean achievement in just under 30 years of organ building. The secret of their success is that Philip Wood and his son and co-director, David, are what may be termed born organ builders, combining skill, enthusiasm and a 'feel' for fine instruments of the past, particularly those by the grand old Yorkshire firms: Forster & Andrews, J. J. Binns, Peter Conacher, Abbott & Smith, William Andrews, Brindley and others. They are fortunate too in having a splendid team of craftsmen who share their ideals.

I first met Philip Wood in the late 1970s when lecturing to the Huddersfield and District Association of Organists. This visit provided an opportunity to visit the works where several model organs were in production. These impressed me by their splendid workmanship as did their three-manual concert organ in Huddersfield Polytechnic (now the University). Although I am not a devotee of the neo-classical organ, its fine quality was very evident. It was clear that here was a builder to be reckoned with, and so began an association which developed into close friendship with father and son, as the years went by.

HUDDERSFIELD POLYTECHNIC 1977, 1991

3 manuals: CC to C, 61 notes   Pedal: CCC to G, 32 notes

MANUAL I

	ft
Gedact	8
Praestant	4
Rohrflöte	4
Principal	2
Quint	1⅓
Octave	1
Sesquialtera II	2⅔
Cymbel III	½
Cromorne	8
Tremulant	
Cymbelstern	
III – I	
I on Pedal pistons	

MANUAL II

Gedacktpommer	16
Principal	8
Rohrflöte	8
Octave	4
Spitzflöte	4
Gemshorn	2
Mixture V–VI	2
Scharf IV	1
Trompete	16
Trompete	8
Tremulant	
III – II	
I – II	
II and Pedal combinations	

MANUAL III *(enclosed)*

Cèleste (tenor C)	8
Spitzgamba	8
Holz Gedackt	8
Principal	4
Koppelflöte	4
Nazard	2⅔
Waldflöte	2
Tierce	1⅗
Scharf IV	2
Basson-Hautbois	16
Trompette	8
Tremulant	
III on Pedal pistons	

PEDAL

Principal	16
Subbass	16
Octave	8
Rohr Gedackt	8
Octave	4
Nachthorn	2
Mixture	2⅔
Contra Posaune	32
Posaune	16
Trompete	8
Schalmei	4
Tremulant	
III – Pedal	
II – Pedal	
I – Pedal	

TONAL CHANGES 1977–1991

1980 – Manual III, Tierce 1⅗ new stop.
1984 – Manual II, Mixture 2 revised to V–VI ranks with 12th entering c13.
1986 – Pedal, Contra Posaune 32, new stop. ½ length resonators. Mahogany.
1990 – Manual II, Trompete 8, new stop. Trompete 16, revision. c25–g56 Pedal Schalmei (Trompete)

replaced existing pipework. Pedal Schalmei 4, now consists of Manual II Trompete 16 (c25–g56) fitted with French Shallots. Manual III, Scharf IV, revised to Scharf IV, 2 (15·22·26·29).

Mechanical key and pedal action   Electric stop action
Tremulants adjustable for speed and depth

The case was designed by David Graebe, and the tonal design was a result of the collaboration of Keith Jarvis (Polytechnic Organist) and Philip Wood.

Our paths crossed again at St Mary's Church, Long Sutton, Lincs., where, as Diocesan Organ Adviser, I was able to gain first-hand knowledge in observing the skill and sensitivity of the restoration with slight additions, of the historic instrument in this magnificent church which retains some particularly fine Norman work within. Built by William Allen of London, in 1827, it is significant that he had built a new instrument for Lincoln Cathedral in 1826 in accordance with a specification drawn up by Samuel Wesley. Pigot's *Directory of London and its suburbs* for 1839 lists his son Charles as occupying premises at 11 Sutton Street, Soho, and it was he who enlarged and improved the Lincoln organ in 1851.

Henry Willis & Sons Ltd. carried out some work to the Long Sutton organ during 1926 and the following extract from Wood's leaflet shows the extent of their work in 1981:

ST MARY'S CHURCH, LONG SUTTON 1981

A fine example of early nineteenth-century organ building, the organ is notable for the clarity and beauty of both individual stops and the complete ensemble. The flutes in particular have a delightful piquancy of tone and there is a splendid fiery trumpet which adds a distinctive colour to the whole.

The work carried out by us in 1981 comprised the rehabilitation of the action, windchests and other parts, the careful restoration of the pipework to its former glory, the replacement of the Swell oboe by a mixture and the addition of a bourdon in 16, 8 and 4ft pitches to the Pedal division. The keys were re-covered in ivory and Allen's original console has been retained, the new drawstop knobs having been made and engraved to match the originals. The oak case was cleaned and polished and the front pipes re-gilded in gold leaf.

The manual compass originally extended to GG and the keyboards remain unaltered, although the pipes extend from CC to F, 54 notes. The compass of the Pedal Organ is CCC to F, 30 notes.

GREAT ORGAN	ft	pipes
Open Diapason	8	54
Stop Diapason	8	54
Dulciana	8	54
Principal	4	54
Flute Ouverte	4	54
Fifteenth	2	54
Sesquialtera (17·19·22)	III	162
		486

SWELL ORGAN		
Open Diapason	8	54
Stop Diapason	8	54
Principal	4	54
Mixture (15·19·22)	III	162
Trumpet	8	54
		378

PEDAL ORGAN		
Open Diapason	16	30
Bourdon	16	30
Bass Flute (ext. Bourdon)	8	12
Flute (ext. Bass Flute)	4	12
		84

COUPLERS

Great to Pedal
Swell to Pedal
Swell to Great

ACCESSORIES

3 Composition Pedals to Great Organ
Balanced Swell pedal

Wind Pressure 2⅛ ins.

The action to manuals, drawstops and Pedal open diapason is mechanical; Solid State is used for the new bourdon unit. The pedal board is radiating and concave and the wind is supplied by a "K.C." electric blower. The total number of pipes is 948.

A similar restoration carried out with great thoroughness at Ewerby Church, Lincs., in 1984, brought the Hill organ of 1870 (which was in an appalling state) to full working order and what a delightful sound was heard when all was fine finished. It started life as a barrel and finger organ by Gray, *c*.1830.

Back to 1981 when the Parish Church of St Laurence, Skellingthorpe, but 2½ miles from my home, was requiring an organ, but had limited funds available. Philip Wood was able to construct a delightful one-manual in a simple, but effective painted case, using some good second-hand pipework and this enabled the church to become the proud possessor of an organ of real quality at long last. It consists of the following stops: open diapason (unenclosed), lieblich gedacht, salicional, principal, fifteenth, mixture II ranks—all enclosed. Pedal, bourdon. Mechanical action. In all three instruments I was able to participate in the final regulation of the pipework, sitting at the keys, which gave me immense pleasure for throughout my life I have been absorbed with 'pipes' rather than 'actions'! The Skellingthorpe organ is a little gem; it provides a tonal effect which makes one play and is adequate in every way for village church worship.

Since the days of the firm's establishment, it has come very much to the fore; there has been overseas work as well as in the Isle of Man and the Channel Islands. Four new organs were built in 1968 and since then, in addition to rebuilds, cleanings and overhauls over a very wide area, the following contracts of special interest have been carried out. Rotherham Parish Church (1971), reconstruction of the historic Snetzler/Abbott & Smith organ; Huddersfield Parish Church (1983), rebuild and enlargement of the four-manual organ of 1908, said to be one of P. Conacher & Co.'s finest. Cathedral Church of All Saints', Wakefield (1985), extensive reconstruction including new Solid State note switching system and capture system piston action (eight levels); restoration of the Choir Organ to the Pearson case and some tonal revision of the Compton organ. The Parish Church of Our Lady and All Saints', Chesterfield (1988), rebuild and enlargement of the Lewis/Henry Willis III organ (1963)—now a four-manual with the latest Solid State transmission system. With its splendid Lewis pipework, together with Henry Willis's contribution and finally that of the Huddersfield firm, an outstanding instrument has resulted, with a most impressive and lively ensemble that is truly musical in effect.

CHESTERFIELD PARISH CHURCH 1988

GREAT ORGAN

	ft
Double Open Diapason	16
Open Diapason No. 1	8
Open Diapason No. 2	8
Stopped Diapason	8
Principal	4
Gemshorn	4
Stopped Flute	4
Twelfth	2⅔
Fifteenth	2
Mixture (19·22·26·29)	IV
Cornet (tenor C 1·8·12·15·17)	V
Posaune	8
Clarion	4
Swell to Great	
Choir to Great	
Solo to Great	

SWELL ORGAN

Bourdon	16
Open Diapason	8
Rohrflöte	8
Viol de Gambe	8
Voix Celeste (tenor C)	8
Geigen Principal	4
Flute	4
Fifteenth	2
Mixture (12·15·19·22)	IV
Sesquialtera (12·17)	II
Contra Fagotto	16
Horn	8
Oboe	8

Clarion	4
Tremulant	
Swell Octave	
Swell Unison Off	

CHOIR ORGAN *unenclosed*

Lieblich Bourdon	16
Stopped Diapason (Snetzler)	8
Open Diapason	8
Octave	4
Flute (Snetzler)	4
Fifteenth (Snetzler)	2
Mixture (22·26·29)	III
Trompette	8
Tremulant	
Solo to Choir	
Swell to Choir	

SOLO ORGAN *enclosed*

Contra Tromba	16
Tromba	8
Tromba Clarion	4
Harmonic Flute	8
Dolce (Snetzler)	8
Unda Maris (undulating)	8
Flauto Traverso	4
Piccolo	2
Orchestral Oboe	8
Vox Humana	8
Clarinet	8
Tremulant	
Solo Octave	

PEDAL ORGAN

Sub Bourdon (to EEEE)	32
Great Bass (wood)	16
Open Diapason (metal, from Great)	16
Violone	16
Bourdon	16
Lieblich Bourdon (Choir)	16
Octave (wood)	8
Octave (metal)	8
Violoncello	8
Bass Flute	8
Super Octave	4
Flute	4
Mixture (19·22·26·29)	IV
Contra Trombone	32
Trombone	16
Trumpet	8
Solo to Pedal	
Swell to Pedal	

Great to Pedal
Choir to Pedal
Great & Pedal combinations coupled

ACCESSORIES

Manual cancels, 12 reversible pistons, 8 general pistons
8 adjustables to Great & Swell, 6 to Choir & Solo,
by setter piston (8 level memory).
Balanced expression pedals to Swell and Solo.
Trombas under expression on Solo pedal by switch
(Trombas are on high pressure)
Detached Solid State electric console, 4 manuals.
Solid State note switching system.
Electro-pneumatic action.
62 stops, 3 tremulants, 12 couplers,
2 combination couplers = 79 drawstops.
Total number of pipes = 3864

Each of these contracts received universal acclaim by those competent to judge, with a result that one led to the other, leading up to the most prestigious of them all—a nave organ for Southwell Minster—completed in 1992. Paul Hale (Rector-Chori), or in modern parlance, Organist and Master of the Choristers, was anxious to install an organ in the south triforium to accompany nave services, and for concert use. It so happened that a particularly fine J. J. Binns organ of 1904 was available from the Upper Independent Chapel at Heckmondwike, Yorks., a large and fine chapel which, like others of its size throughout the land, had been compelled to close due to dwindling congregations. Paul Hale greeted the idea of its purchase with enthusiasm, for he was quick to realise that the bold tone of the chorus work together with the varied and beautiful quiet tonal colours would be ideal for the purpose he had in mind. Thus, a magnificent example of Binns' work was preserved and on its completion, Philip Wood had this to say: 'It gives us a great sense of satisfaction and pride. J. J. Binns didn't manage to build a Cathedral organ— but we've achieved it for him!' It has already been greeted with enthusiasm in organ circles, after the series of recitals held between 1992–93, while the Minster authorities are delighted, and in particular, their Rector Chori. I was able to hear it in July 1994, and too was impressed.

The great span of the Norman arches of the triforium and the ample roof height enable the tone to reach the nave with ease. The handsome drawstop console is fully mobile and the connection from keys to pipes is by a computerised data transmission system, manufactured and installed by Jeffery Heard of Steeton, Keighley, West Yorkshire. The hundreds of connections are made through just two twisted pairs of wire and to quote Philip Wood: 'Even the signal lights for weddings are operated through the same wires'!

Most of the Binns pipework appears again in the scheme drawn up by Paul Hale in collaboration with the builders. This reads as follows:

SOUTHWELL MINSTER, THE NAVE ORGAN 1992

GREAT ORGAN

		ft			
Double Open Diapason (on chest)	J.J.B.	16	Twelfth	J.J.B.	2⅔
Open Diapason No. 1	J.J.B.	8	Fifteenth	J.J.B.	2
Open Diapason No. 2	J.J.B.	8	Mixture (15·19·22·26)	new	IV
Gamba	J.J.B.	8	Mixture (26·29·33)	re-composed J.J.B.	III
Hohl Flute	J.J.B.	8	Posaune	new	8
Rohr Flute	J.J.B.	8	Clarion	new	4
Principal	J.J.B.	4	*Tremulant*		
Gemshorn	new	4	*Swell to Great*		
Harmonic Flute	J.J.B.	4	*Solo to Great*		

SWELL ORGAN

Bourdon	J.J.B.	16
Open Diapason	J.J.B.	8
Gedackt	J.J.B.	8
Salicional	J.J.B.	8
Voix Celeste (tenor C)	J.J.B.	8
Geigen Principal	J.J.B.	4
Flauto Traverso	J.J.B.	4
Fifteenth	J.J.B.	2
Piccolo	J.J.B.	2
Mixture (15·19·22)	re-composed J.J.B.	III
Sesquialtera (12·17)	new	II
Oboe	J.J.B.	8
Contra Fagotto	J.J.B.	16
Trumpet	J.J.B.	8
Clarion	stock	4
Tremulant		
Swell Octave		
Swell Unison Off		

SOLO ORGAN

Tuba	Southwell (chest)	8
Clarion	Southwell (ext. Tuba)	4
Clarinet	J.J.B.	8

PEDAL ORGAN

Open Diapason (wood)	J.J.B.	16
Open Diapason (metal, Great No.1)	J.J.B.	16
Bourdon	J.J.B.	16
Octave	J.J.B.	8
Bass Flute (from Bourdon)		8
Fifteenth (from Octave)		4
Stopped Flute (from Bass Flute)		4
Trombone	J.J.B.	16
Trumpet (from Trombone)		8
Swell to Pedal		
Great to Pedal		
Solo to Pedal		

ACCESSORIES

8 Generals   8 Pistons each to Great, Swell and
Pedal Organs   2 Pistons to Solo Organ
8 Piston Memories   Swell to Great   Solo to Great
Swell to Pedal Great to Pedal Solo to Pedal
Great & Pedal Combinations Coupled   Generals on
Swell Toe Pistons Setter Piston General Cancel Piston

WIND PRESSURES

Pedal Flues 4¼ ins., Reeds 6½ ins.   Swell 3¾ ins.
Great 4 ins.   Tuba 16 ins.

Small organs of various types have been developed over the years, with mechanical or electric action, straight or extended pipework (unenclosed or partially enclosed), classical or English voicing, console attached or detached. They have been very successful in difficult sites where ingenuity has been called for in several instances where the situation seemed almost impossible. Interesting examples may be heard at St Edmund's Church, Allestree, Derby; Emmanuel Church, Anglican Chaplaincy, Leeds University; the Parish Church at Barwick-in-Elmet, near Leeds; the Parish Church of Little Bowden near Market Harborough; Trinity Methodist Church, Bradford; St Aidan's Church, Buttershaw, Bradford; and one of the latest at Armitage Bridge Parish Church, Huddersfield (1987), to the following specification:

ARMITAGE BRIDGE PARISH CHURCH 1987

2 manuals: CC to A, 58 notes   Pedal: CCC to F, 30 notes

MANUAL I	*ft*	MANUAL II	
Open Diapason	8	Stopped Diapason	8
†Chimney Flute	8	**PEDAL**	
†Principal	4	Bourdon	16
†Fifteenth	2		
†Mixture (19·22·26)	III	I – Pedal II – Pedal	
†Trumpet	8	Mechanical Action Ash Case † enclosed stops	

The functional pipe lay-out of the two-manual, four-rank, classically designed organ at Leeds University is supported on a 10 × 12 ins. steel column, the blower being housed within the organ. It is played from a detached console which is situated near to the choir stalls. The inaugural recital, given by Dr. Francis Jackson when he was at York Minster, was broadcast on the BBC Radio 3.

In June 1994, the reconstruction as a four-manual of the organ at Grantham Parish Church was completed and the next work of importance is to be the rebuild of the organ in Beverley Minster.

Philip Wood, founder of this go-ahead business which has come to the fore in such a short time, looks forward with confidence to the future, for he knows that in his son David it will be in excellent hands when he is compelled to retire. It is hoped and is more than likely that this will not be for many years to come, for his father was active until the age of ninety!

above
Peter Conacher. The original portrait is
in the office.
Courtesy of John Sinclair Willis

right
Conacher & Co., an entry from their
ledger, September 1870.
Courtesy of John Sinclair Willis

left
For Methodist Chapels in particular,
in the last century, Conachers
frequently supplied cases of Classical
design, to match the style of the
building. That at Hannah Memorial
Wesleyan Chapel, Lincoln (1875),
was a typical example of pitch pine,
with a mahogany console

right
King Street Methodist
Church, Derby
Photo by the Author

below
A typical and good example of
simple casework at Navenby
Church, near Lincoln.
Photo by the Author

The works of Peter Conacher & Co., 1994
The adjoining house was the Conacher residence.
Photo by the Author

above
The works of Peter Conacher & Co. One of the workshops,
showing the original steam-driven machinery.
Courtesy of John Sinclair Willis
right
Part of the Conacher workshop, 1994.
Courtesy of John Sinclair Willis
below
Skellingthorpe Church, near Lincoln.
Organ by Wood of Huddersfield.
Photo by the Author

above
Southwell Minster. The Great Organ in the triforium
Courtesy of Wood of Huddersfield
right
Long Sutton Parish Church, Lincs.
Photo by the Author
below
Southwell Minster. The mobile nave console.
Photo by the Author

The Polytechnic of Huddersfield: St Paul's Hall.
Organ by Wood of Huddersfield, 1977–1991. Case designed by David Graebe

CHAPTER XI

Liverpool

THERE are records of organ builders in Liverpool as early as 1820, to my knowledge, although research by others may have unearthed information before then. Nicholas Thistlethwaite, in his monumental work, *The Making of the Victorian Organ*, tells us that the firm of Bewsher & Fleetwood was formed in 1821, and records organs built for Wrexham Parish Church in 1827, St George's, Everton (1845) and St Paul's, Toxteth Park, Liverpool (1847). The Revd. Andrew Freeman, in a letter to *Musical Opinion* (n.d.) recorded that Pedal pipes were added to the organ in St Patrick's Cathedral, Dublin, *c.*1826. New organs were built for Wrexham Abbey in 1827 and St Paul's, Burslem (three-manual). W. A. Roberts, in his article on the Rushworth & Dreaper organ in The Philharmonic Hall, Liverpool (*The Organ*, January 1931), mentions the old organ there as being the work of this firm 'who did good work in the old fashioned way; not adventurous but very enduring... It was on a Bewsher organ in Pembroke Chapel that Best, as a boy in his 'teens, practised...'. Another organ in Liverpool was at Great Homer Street Wesleyan Chapel, 1839. At Kendal Parish Church in 1824 they added Pedal pipes and renewed the bellows. Their business and factory in Bronté Street was taken over by Gray & Davison, probably *c.*1840, and they retained their base at Liverpool for many years. They had several moves during that time; by 1862 they were at 9 Russell Street; by 1881 they had moved to Colquitt Street; 1894, 30 Upper Stanhope Street (Geo. Nicholson being the manager); 1915, 272 Upper Parliament Street, but by 1920 in *The Musical Trade Directory*, there is no further record of them. *The Organist & Choirmaster* for August 15th, 1906, records the death of 'Charles Davison, senior member of Gray & Davison of London, Liverpool and Oxford, at Cromer, on 8th July. He was many years manager at the Liverpool branch and in 1889 took over the management at London. He secured the friendship of many organists of his day'.

Jackson of Liverpool and Bolton has been documented by David C. Wickens in *The British Institute of Organ Studies Reporter* (Vol. 17, No. 1, January 1993). Sufficient to say here that Richard Jackson was born in Rochdale about 1807. A xerox copy, in my possession, of a scrap book made up by Forster & Andrews, of cuttings relating not only to their own work, but others too, has this advertisement from a newspaper, presumably published in Liverpool.

R. JACKSON & SON, ORGAN BUILDERS, 28 SPRINGFIELD, LIVERPOOL, and 13 & 14 CROWN STREET, BOLTON.— beg most respectfully to call the attention of the nobility, gentry and clergy of Lancashire and the adjacent counties, to their manufactories at the above towns, and to inform them that they are now able to undertake the most extensive and elaborate orders, to give the highest satisfaction to their employers, and thus fearlessly place themselves in competition with any house in the trade, London or provincial.

Every improvement in Organ Building up to the present period is carried out by them to the fullest extent; and far from remaining satisfied with what has already been done, they are determined to emulate the advancing spirit of the age, and, by the adaptation of mechanical science, do all that is possible to enhance the weight, character, and brilliance of tone in their instruments.

R. JACKSON & SON have the greatest pleasure in referring all parties to the Organs they have already erected; but without reverting to upwards of a hundred that are scattered over every part of the Empire, they content themselves with placing before the public those which have been manufactured by them and opened during the present year.

Grand Organ at the Collegiate Institution, Liverpool. Organ at Bootle Church. Organ at New Church, Whitworth, near Rochdale. Organ at Preston Parish Church. Organ at Walmsley School, near Bolton. Organ at Hope Chapel, Wigan. Organ at Parish Church, Wigan (in course of erection). Organ at Elton Church, near Bury. Organ at St Catherine's Church,

Wigan. Organ at Warrington Diocesan School. Organ at St Paul's, Warrington (enlarged). Organ at Stanley Church, near Liverpool. Organ at Witton Church, near Blackburn.

In addition to the foregoing, R. JACKSON & SON beg to call the attention of parties residing in Liverpool to the Organs erected by them at Birkenhead, one at St John's, Grange-lane, and one at St Werberg's Catholic Chapel.

In conclusion, they feel assured that their instruments have only to be heard for their superiority to be felt; and where funds are not available for the purpose of purchasing an addition to the services of the Church, they will be most happy to give every facility in their power.

N.B.— Organs tuned and repaired by contract. In any part of the United Kingdom.— Liverpool, Sept. 23, 1850.

Jackson built an organ with a very comprehensive tonal scheme for the Collegiate Institution, Liverpool, in 1850, the following specification being taken from Hopkins & Rimbault, *The Organ, Its History and Construction*, 1st Edn., 1855. The instrument was opened by Henry Smart.

THE COLLEGIATE INSTITUTION, LIVERPOOL 1850

GREAT ORGAN		CHOIR ORGAN	
	ft	Open Diapason	8
Tenoroon	16	Stopped Diapason	8
Bourdon	16	Claribella	8
Great Open Diapason	8	Keraulophon	8
Small Open Diapason	8	Dulciana	8
Stopped Diapason	8	Principal	4
Principal	4	Flute	4
Twelfth	2⅔	Piccolo	2
Fifteenth	2	Bassoon	8
Sesquialtera	III	Clarionet	8
Mixture	III		
Sharp Twentieth		PEDAL ORGAN	
Trumpet	8	Great Open Diapason	16
Clarion	4	Bourdon	16
		Principal	8
SWELL ORGAN		Twelfth	5⅓
Double Diapason	16	Fifteenth	4
Open Diapason	8	Grand Mixture	VI
Stopped Diapason	8	Posaune	16
Principal	4		
Fifteenth	2	ACCESSORY STOPS, MOVEMENTS &C.	
Echo Dulciana Cornet	III		
Cornopean	8	Great to Pedal Swell to Pedal Choir to Pedal	
Oboe	8	Swell to Great Choir to Swell	
Clarion	4	Sub Octave Choir to Great Super Octave to Pedals	
		Six Composition Pedals	

A further addition to the list of organs built by this firm was that at Union Chapel, Queen's Park, Liverpool, built in 1853. Its specification after repair and enlargement by Alex Young & Son appeared in *Musical Opinion* dated March 1906. It was a two-manual of 19 speaking stops.

Wickens tells us in his contribution to *BIOS Reporter* that Richard Jackson's eldest son William was included in the firm's title in 'Slater's Directory for 1851 (albeit in Bolton)' and that 'Richard Jackson disappears from view after 1857. Rumour has it that he went to India and/or the Isle of Man'.

As this chapter was being finalised for the printer, in searching for other information, I came across this paragraph in *The Church Choirmaster and Organist* for 1868. I can but surmise that P. W. Jackson was a printer's error in respect of the first initial, which should have been R and that Richard's eldest son, William, was actually R. W., Richard or Robert. Be that as it may, it is worth recording and following up in case of any doubt in the mind of David Wickens. Such research involves much time and 'deadlines' have to be kept in the preparation of a book such as this.

'On Thursday the 19th ult., a very fine organ, built by Mr F. W. Jackson, and presented to the Church of St Thomas, Bury, by Mr Oliver Ormrod Openshaw, was opened by Dr. Wesley. As the instrument is of somewhat unusual completeness, we subjoin the following description.—

GREAT ORGAN

	ft
Double Open Diapason	16
Open Diapason	8
Gamba	8
Clarabella	8
Principal	4
Harmonic Flute	4
Twelfth	2⅔
Fifteenth	2
Full Mixture	IV
Sharp Mixture	IV
Posaune	8
Clarion	4

SWELL ORGAN

Lieblich Bourdon	16
Spitz Flote	8
Lieblich Gedackt	8
Hohl Flote	8
Gemshorn	4
Gedackt Flote	4
Fifteenth	2
Twenty Second	1
Cornopean	8
Oboe	8
Clarion	4

CHOIR ORGAN

Open Diapason	8
Dulciana	8
Viola da Gamba	8
Voix Celeste	8
Stopped Diapason	8
Geigen Principal	4
Wald Flute	4
Geigen Fifteenth	2
Clarionet	8

PEDAL ORGAN

Open Diapason	16
Bourdon	16
Principal	8
Stopped Diapason	8

COUPLERS

Swell to Great   Choir to Great Sub Octave
Swell to Pedal   Great to Pedal   Choir to Pedal

Great Organ: compass CC–G, 936 pipes
Swell Organ: compass CC–G, 604 pipes
Choir Organ: compass CC–G, 480 pipes
Pedal Organ: compass CCC–F, 120 pipes

The total number of pipes is 2,140. There are four double-action combination pedals acting on the stops of the Great Organ, two on those on the Swell Organ, and two on the coupler stops. The movements are on the "simplification system". The soundboards are of such amplitude that every pipe is placed over the channel from which it is supplied with wind, thus securing for it a full tone and prompt intonation. The instrument is tuned on the "unequal" temperament, by the special request of the donor. For the supply of the manual and pedal organs there are two bellows with double feeders, and concussion valves to equalise the wind pressure. The pedals are concave and radiating. At the opening, the *Manchester Courier* tells us, musical men mustered in great force to hear Dr. Wesley, who, says that paper, "seems to be the connecting link between the old and new schools of the organ, possessing as he does the peculiar close touch of the old school with the elasticity and freedom of the new." In extemporaneous performance Dr. Wesley gave ample proof of his powers by his introductory movements and a fugue, the subject of which was dotted down only a minute or two before performance.'

Other firms who had branches in Liverpool during the first two decades or so were Ingram & Co. of 194 Phythian Street in 1915 (later incorporated with Rushworth & Dreaper), Lewis & Co. Ltd., 2 Empress Road, Kensington (and at 234 Ferndale Road, Brixton, London)—1915 and 1920 *Music Trades Directory*— together with Nicholson & Co. of 30 Ling Street, Kensington (1920 M.T.D.). As Lewis & Co. were incorporated into Henry Willis & Co. Ltd. in 1918, the necessary alteration as far as Liverpool was concerned could not have been made in time for the publication of the M.T.D. In using these, I have found several discrepancies over the years, whilst locally I have found that some city and county directories have gone to press just ahead of the year concerned!

Franklin Lloyd, the eminent reed voicer, who had worked for Robert Hope-Jones at Birkenhead, spent the greater part of his life in business for himself at Liverpool. His death at the age of 76 was reported in *Musical Opinion* in June 1932, where it was stated that: 'for some years he had been retired from business'.

RUSHWORTH & DREAPER LTD.

Organ building is notable for its long family connections and in Liverpool we have two great firms in Rushworth & Dreaper and Henry Willis & Sons, still in family ownership, the former holding the record, with 165 years of service since 1828, the close runner-up being Willis with 149 years. In an age of closures or take-overs, this is quite remarkable and both are naturally extremely proud of their longevity as well as their artistic achievements through a period of tonal change and technical development. Neither of the two firm's founders could possibly envisage such a future and there seems to be no reason why both will not operate well into the next century.

William Rushworth, the founder, started the organ building business in Mill Lane, Liverpool, in the year 1828. Shortly afterwards, his two sons, Edwin and Walter, were taken into partnership and about the same time the manufacture of pianos was commenced, with a subsequent growth of this young and energetic firm. The obituary of Walter Rushworth in *Musical Opinion* for September 1903, tells us that 'on the death of Mr William Rushworth, the sons (Edwin and Walter) continued the business and carried on the two branches (organ building and piano making and selling) jointly. In 1870, a division of the business and a dissolution of the partnership were decided upon. Mr Walter Rushworth tool over the organ building branch and Mr Edwin took charge of the piano, harmonium and small instrument branch. In the process of time Mr Edwin Rushworth retired from the pianoforte business, leaving his three sons to carry it on, Mr William Rushworth acting as general manager.

Meanwhile, Mr Walter Rushworth developed the organ building branch and a wide church connection was formed. The deceased gentleman was greatly devoted to the art of constructing and tuning organs. He was very affable and would talk with much animation of matters pertaining to organ construction.

The writer enjoyed many a pleasant talk with him in the upper rooms of the old organ works in Mill Lane and in the office near the works when Mr Rushworth was tuning or engaged with the affairs of the business. One of the quietest and most unassertive of men and of kindly disposition, he endeared himself even to those whose intercourse with him was of a purely business kind. He was known and respected over a wide area in the north of England and his works survive him in the organs which he made for many churches'.

The adjoining illustration shows the music warehouse of Rushworth and Sons, with residence above, in Islington Terrace, during the last century. It was also the home of a gifted musical family, whose drawing room was an open salon to friends who gathered regularly

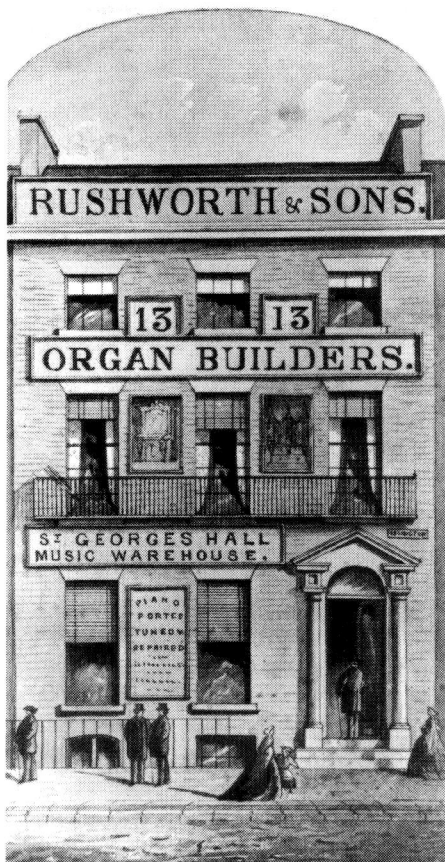

together to make music. It was not unusual for crowds to gather outside and 'listen in rapt delight'.

Walter Rushworth was followed by his sons Harry and Maynard, who, with their cousin, William II as a director, opened the extensive organ works in Great George Street in 1911. Maynard Rushworth was an organist and a note in *Musical Opinion* for July 1907 informs us that he gave a recital at St James' Church, Liverpool at the dedication of the new organ built by Rushworth & Sons. Maynard's daughter, May, who shared his interest in organs avidly, attended his many recitals and travelled to many organist's congresses, died only last year (1993) in her nineties. The current generation of Alastair J. Maynard Rushworth was named after his great uncle. There was never actually a Dreaper in the firm; the name was included in the title by reason of William Rushworth II taking over the piano and music business of the Dreaper Bros., in Bold Street, on their retirement.

In checking old musical periodicals for examples of the firm's early work, I came across this small organ, built in 1867 for Ellastone Church, near Ashbourne, Derbyshire:

Compass CC–F, 54 notes. Open Diapason, 8 (wood bass). Stopped Diapason treble, Stopped Diapason Bass, 8. Dulciana, 8 (tenor C). Principal, 4. Wald Flute, 4 (tenor C). Horn Diapason, 8 (tenor C). Fifteenth, 2.

Composition of Pedal Clavier, CCC–C, 25 notes. Bourdon Diapason, 16. Manual to pedals. Two composition pedals, general swell. Number of pipes, 362.

'In its quality of tone, the instrument is said to be very satisfactory. The horn diapason is also mentioned as being most effective, possessing the scale of an open diapason with the distinctive pungency of a free reed. This stop, little known in England at present, we believe is a valuable substitute for an oboe where a tuner is not always at hand.'

This letterhead tells us something about the activities of the firm before its incorporation as Rushworth & Dreaper Ltd.—this being announced in small type at the bottom of the subject matter.

It will be noted from the above letterhead that 1839 was given as the date of establishment, but this was incorrect. Advertising matter at the side of this letter stated that: 'Recent extensions and a greatly increased plant of modern machinery places W. R. & Sons in a more favourable position than ever to undertake contracts for the building and rebuilding of pipe organs. Tuning and repairs by a special staff of experts under close personal supervision. Tuning connection includes the more important churches and chapels in and around Liverpool for a radius of 100 miles, many organs having been in our charge for unbroken periods of 40, 50 and 60 years… Now associated with the firm of Rushworth & Dreaper, Piano, Military Band Instrument, and Music Warehouse, Concert Bureau, 11 and 18 Islington'.

The firm's records of organs built only go back to 1913. The following is fairly typical of their small two-manual schemes of that period on 3½ or 4 ins. wind. The inclusion of a second diapason on the Great Organ, when there is a lack of upper work, will be noted.

DURN BAPTIST CHURCH, LITTLEBOROUGH

2 manuals: CC to G, 56 notes   Pedal: CCC to F, 30 notes

GREAT ORGAN

	ft
Large Open Diapason	8
Open Diapason	8
Dulciana	8
Clarabella	8
Principal	4

SWELL ORGAN

Open Diapason	8
Lieblich Gedackt	8
Salicional	8
Gemshorn	4
Cornopean	8
Oboe	8
Tremulant	

PEDAL ORGAN

Sub Bass	16
Bass Flute	8

COUPLERS

Swell to Great   Swell Octave   Swell Sub Octave
Swell to Pedal   Great to Pedal

4 double acting composition pedals to each manual department

Case of prime figured Oak. Front pipes of the best hard rolled V.M. zinc, silvered. Tubular-pneumatic action. Console case and fittings to be of prime figured oak, doors enclosing keys to be fitted with glass panels

From 1908, the firm continued growing, establishing organ works branches in London, Edinburgh and Bristol in the 1920s, with retail branches in Chester in 1945, Birkenhead in 1949 and Southport in 1973. The Edinburgh workshop is managed by Mr Ivor Norridge, who joined the firm from Comptons. His experience is wide and he still looks after several Compton organs, taking pleasure in keeping them in good order.

The list of companies taken over is an impressive one and comprises Joynsons of Bristol (1955), Ingrams of Edinburgh (1956), Inglis of Glasgow (1959), Wilkinson & Co. of Kendal (1957), The John Compton Organ Co. Pipe Organs (1964), Binns, Fitton and Haley (Leeds 1963), Hall & Broadfield of Hull (1965), Porritt of Leicester (1966), Kingsgate Davidson, London (1966), Rothwell of Harrow (1960) and Sweetland of Bath (1962). Their records form one of the most extensive archives of any organ builder in this country and are of course of the utmost value.

The firm has always been mindful of friendly staff relations. From the March 1975 issue of *Musical Opinion* we read of the annual directors' dinner party, 'when Mrs James Rushworth, the wife of the Chairman and Managing Director… made presentations to seven long serving members of the staff. An inscribed silver ash tray and cheque for £50 to Mr R. J. Barnett, the organ works production manager for 50 years' service, and engraved clocks with twenty-five years' service Rushworth tie, to the following: F. Joynson, organ works, Bristol, branch manager, K. Springer, organ works estimating department manager, W. Hunter, polishing and repair workshop foreman, H. Barnes, radio and electronic engineer, A. Thomas, organ works storekeeper'. Some of these relate to the music branch of the company which for many years has been situated in Whitechapel, Liverpool. That is almost twenty years ago, but I am well aware of the happy staff relations which still prevail under the management of Alastair Rushworth. There are still two 60 year serving members, namely Jack Jones, works foreman, and Colin Evans, electric chargehand, together with a number of the earlier mentioned 25 year presentees. Staff now numbers 55 nationwide and the number of tuning contracts are almost 2,500.

My first encounter with an organ by Rushworth & Dreaper occurred in 1930 when I was but seventeen years of age. I had been invited to take tea with J. B. Jamison, then of the Estey Organ Co., USA, one Sunday in London. We had been together a few days previously at Ely Cathedral in company with Gilbert Benham and Lynwood Farnum, the distinguished American recitalist, who gave us a private recital on that gorgeous Harrison organ. Afterwards, J. B. Jamison took me all over the instrument with which he was tremendously impressed. He pointed out many things of interest, which taught me much and the whole day there was a great experience.

During tea at The Strand Palace Hotel, he told me many facets of modern organ building here in England and in the USA; moreover, he wrote to me from the States from time to time and I never cease to wonder how much pleasure it appeared to give him to pass on the benefit of his experience to a mere lad of seventeen. He was anxious to take me along to hear the recently built organ by Rushworth & Dreaper at St Mark's, North Audley Street, which had made a great impression in London musical circles. Maurice Vinden was the organist and demonstrated the organ in a masterly manner; he was tremendously proud of it and so was the large congregation which attended Sunday by Sunday, for those were the days of full churches. Sadly, this fine church closed some years ago, but the organ may still be heard at the Church of the Holy Trinity, Brompton.

As I remember it, the tone was magnificent—the power of the chorus work, however, was rather on the big side, on which Gilbert Benham agreed in his article in *The Organ* (No. 37). It is possible that Vinden specified this, for it was a fashionable church and a strong lead was required in hymn singing. We were given a warm welcome and I was able to play the instrument myself. There was so much to explore and a seemingly endless supply of beautiful quiet effects from superbly voiced stops. I was also impressed by the handsome console and commented that the drawstop bushes were similar in pattern to those used by Norman & Beard: ie. a combination of ivory and ebony which looked quite distinctive. Commenting on this I learned that the instrument had been designed and built in collaboration with Mr Llewellyn Simon, of Rushworths. The name meant nothing to me at the time, but as this chapter was being written, Mr Herbert Norman, who at the age of ninety is blessed with a remarkable memory, put me in the picture. When Norman & Beard of Norwich went into liquidation in 1916, it meant the end of an era of fine organ building from a very large factory. Two of their leading executives went to Rushworth & Dreaper: Llewellyn Simon, Company Secretary and a very able salesman, together with the head draughtsman—one Parker, as well as voicing staff, namely the Cahill family, Rackham and a number of experienced organ builders. Under the direction of Simon, Parker and William C. Cooper, manager (with thirty years' experience in the firm of Cooper, Gill & Tomkins of Cape Town), Rushworths too, became a modern, well-equipped factory, highly organised and with splendid staff. They soon achieved national esteem for their design, innovative outlook and fine tone. Standards were set in those days from which they have never departed and over the years some superb instruments have emanated from Great George Street, and since 1974, at 72 St Anne Street. Here there is a large timber mill, metal and pipemaking shops, voicing shop, consoles and soundboards, general construction and erecting shop (the latter with ample space above and around for the largest instrument) together with drawing and administration offices. They have the advantage of being able to acquire fine timber of all kinds, for there is a constant supply entering Liverpool Docks.

The fourth generation of the family—Mr James Rushworth, O.B.E., M.A., J.P., held in great affection by all who know him—is now in retirement; his son Alastair, F.S.I.O.B., F.I.M.I.T., is now Chairman and Managing Director, proudly representing the fifth generation of a remarkable family. After leaving Wrekin College in 1964, his early training took him through all the departments of the factory, after which he gained similar experience with the firm of Flentrop of Holland, who are considered leading exponents in the use of mechanical action. Here, Alastair ended up in design and tone production under the present director of the firm, Hans Steketee. Whilst at Flentrops, he carried out study tours in Germany, Scandinavia, France, Italy, Portugal and Spain—all of which proved of the greatest value. After his Dutch training, he studied under another internationally famous organ builder, Larry Phelps, at Casavants in Canada. They are one of the largest organ builders in the world with a fine reputation for building organs on the North European principles, which enabled him to take advantage of the managerial aspects of a very large company. On his return to England, Rushworths developed an entirely new department for instruments with mechanical action and this has meant re-training staff right through from the drawing board, through the mill and into the workshop, which required a great deal of re-tooling.

Alastair is also very archive-minded; when The John Compton Organ Co. was taken over in 1964, not only was all their stock, materials, tuning and organ building contracts and some stock organs taken over, but also some of the staff, and what was particularly important, drawings, patents, files and many records of jobs built, which of course are of great historic value.

Not long after hearing the St Mark's, North Audley Street organ, I journeyed to Scotland as far as Oban on a tuning round with my friend, R. A. Cousans, head of Cousans Sons & Co., of Lincoln, to whom I owe so much in gaining some practical experience in organ building. I was able to play a delightful small two-manual R. & D. at Dollar Parish Church, but the highlight (apart from the very beautiful Harrison organ in St Mary's Cathedral, Edinburgh) was the R. & D. rebuild of a two-manual organ by Lewis & Co. (1897) in St George's West Church, Edinburgh, which had been electrified by Norman & Beard in 1907, and again in 1919. In 1930, Dr. Alfred Hollins drew up a scheme to rebuild and enlarge the instrument by the addition of a Choir/Solo Organ and several other stops to add to the ensemble, for although the original organ was described after its erection in *The Organist and Choirmaster* as 'admirable in every way' it was not sufficient for the church with its large congregations, and 'also unworthy of Mr Hollins' distinguished powers, whose services the committee have had the good fortune to secure as their regular organist'. Since my visit some sixty-three years ago, Rushworths have modified the design of the Choir Organ, as well as the Swell and Great, together with the conversion of the action to Solid-State. A brighter and more versatile organ has emerged. The organ was re-dedicated at a special morning service on Palm Sunday, 12th April, 1981. It now has the following specification.

ST GEORGE'S WEST CHURCH, EDINBURGH 1981

GREAT ORGAN

	ft
Open Diapason I	8
Open Diapason II	8
Hohl Flute	8
Principal	4
Lieblich Flute	4
Fifteenth	2
Larigot	1⅓
Mixture	IV
Tromba	8
Clarion	4

SWELL ORGAN

Geigen Principal	8
Cor de Nuit	8
Salicional	8
Octave Geigen	4
Fifteenth	2
Mixture	II
Oboe	8

Cornopean	8
Tromba (from Great)	8

CHOIR ORGAN

Stopped Diapason	8
Principal	4
Flauto Traverso	4
Nazard	2⅔
Flageolet	2
Clarinet	8
Tromba (from Great)	8

PEDAL ORGAN

Great Bass	16
Sub Bass	16
Octave	8
Bass Flute	8
Trombone	16
Tromba	8

To hear Dr. Hollins' masterly accompaniment to the service was an experience in itself, with an added bonus of meeting him afterwards in the vestry, where R. A. Cousans greeted him as follows. 'Do you remember me Dr. Hollins?', which brought an immediate reply: 'Well it's Mr Cousans of Lincoln'. What a remarkable memory, for they had not met for a number of years! For me it is one of the highlights of a life rich in musical experiences and later, as a result of this meeting, I became the proud possessor of a signed copy of Dr. Hollins' book, *A blind musician looks back*, together with an interesting and immaculately typed letter accompanying his gift. The works of Alfred Hollins were very popular in recital programmes in my youth, then they went out of fashion. When he was at Lincoln Cathedral, Dr. Philip Marshall played one or two of his works; now, Thomas Trotter and Ian Tracey have included them in their programmes and instead of a small audience, large crowds are becoming the norm, where interesting programmes are given by master players.

So—I had been introduced to the work of Rushworth & Dreaper before I was twenty, and interested I was! I collected specifications of their organs, which has gone on to this day, and on the death of my friend, Dr. W. L. Sumner, became the possessor of a bound volume of these—for he was an expert book-binder. All these have contributed towards giving this all too brief account of their contribution to organ building in this country as well as overseas during the last sixty years. In addition, I have had first-hand experience of their work, which has resulted in a number of articles in the now defunct journal, *The Choir*.

In London, in addition the fine instrument in St Michael's Church, Cornhill (1925 and 1975), made famous by that great musician, Dr. Harold Darke, to which Rushworths have devoted their care and attention since they first rebuilt it, they are represented by such prestigious instruments as those in St Paul's Church, Knightsbridge, St Mary le Bow, rebuild at Westminster Chapel, Buckingham Gate, the Methodist Central Hall, Westminster and in 1974, a new two-manual organ with mechanical action at Ealing Abbey, to replace the Compton organ which was destroyed in the blitz. Built on Classical lines, the twenty-six stops were selected to 'cover the widest range of musical resources under the circumstances'. The stop action is electric.

Four-manual instruments such as Guildford Cathedral, St Andrew's Church, Plymouth, Church of the Holy Rood, Stirling (restored in 1993 with the most up-to-date Solid State key and stop actions), Malvern Priory, King George's Hall, Blackburn, and the fine five-manual at Christ's Hospital, Horsham (the largest private school organ in the world), bear the hallmark of Rushworth quality, to which may be added the rebuilds at Chester Cathedral, Derby Cathedral, Hull City Hall, Llandaff Cathedral, St David's Cathedral, Dyfed, McEwan Hall, Edinburgh, Stowe School, Fort Augustus Abbey, Perth City Hall and Liverpool Philharmonic Hall. I have always regarded that at Malvern Priory particularly beautiful; the work was carried out during 1927 and the console is similar in design to the North Audley Street instrument. Later on, the design changed and more often than not, the drawstops were splayed on panels—that at Guildford Cathedral being a handsome example of this style.

Overseas, work has included six new organs for Nigeria of various size, not forgetting St Mary's Cathedral, Johannesburg, South Africa. Over many years, the firm have built a number of Model Organs, to various designs with one or two manuals and using extended ranks. These have been very popular and have been marketed under the names of 'Ardeton', 'Cappella', 'Miniatura' and 'Polyphonic'.

At SS. Peter and Paul's Church, Teddington, is a new two-manual organ with seven speaking stops with the whole of the mechanical action contained within the manual soundboard, which is no greater than keyscale. Thus it is economical from the point of view of action, space and finance. It has been specifically designed to meet the needs of small modern churches.

In the 1992 bomb damage in the City of London, the historic organ in the church of St Mary Axe, London, going back to Renatus Harris, 1696, suffered damage and this has now been restored by Rushworths. During 1993, when this chapter was commenced, the Brindley & Foster organ of 1880 in St Mary's Church, Nantwich, had been rebuilt together with St Paul's and St George's Episcopal Church, Edinburgh, and in 1994 as this book approaches completion, the following contracts are in hand. The Royal Military Academy, rebuild; The Cathedral Church of St Peter, Abeokuta, Nigeria, new three-manual; the Church of St Thomas à Becket, Wandsworth, rebuild of the 1929 Willis, and St Mary Immaculate Church (Refuge of Sinners), Dublin, professional restoration to the original, built by White of Dublin in 1857.

It is interesting to place on record that Rushworths built a two-manual organ for the new chapel of Gordonstoun School, where H. R. H. The Prince of Wales received his education. To me, it represents an ideal scheme for an organ of its size; one has the best of both worlds, ie. a chorus in the Classical style with sufficient quiet stops of a romantic nature so that organ music of all periods can adequately be performed. In short, a splendid 'middle of the road' outlook which I have always felt to be most important in this present day and age when extremes have taken over in many instances.

GORDONSTOUN SCHOOL CHAPEL, MORAYSHIRE 1966

GREAT ORGAN

	ft
Bourdon	16
Open Diapason	8
Gedeckt	8
Octave	4
Chimney Flute	4
Blockflöte	2
Sesquialtera 12·17	II
Mixture 22·26·29·33	IV

SWELL ORGAN

Rohrflöte	8
Viola	8
Viole Celestes	8

Spitzflöte	4
Principal	4
Gemshorn	2
Larigot	1⅓
Cimbel 29·33·36	III
Bassoon	16
Trumpet	8
Tremulant	

PEDAL ORGAN

Principal	16
Sub Bass	16
Octave	8
Flöte (from Sub Bass)	8
Nachthorn	4
Mixture 15·19·22	III

Posaune	16
Schalmei	4

COUPLERS

Great to Pedal   Swell to Pedal   Swell to Great

ACCESSORIES

10 thumb pistons and 3 reversible thumb pistons
10 toe pistons and 2 reversible toe pistons
Combinations set by switchboard and protected by
an independent lock

WIND PRESSURES

Great: 2¼ ins. Swell: 2¾ ins. Pedal: 2½ ins

This chapter began with the very enlightened tonal scheme of the St Mark's, North Audley Street organ of 1929, and it is deemed suitable to close it with the very comprehensive specification of Guildford Cathedral organ, 1961. We all have different views, and rightly so, yet I find it most encouraging that many of us see eye to eye! On paper it looks fascinating—to hear it in the Cathedral is an inspiration, while it broadcasts exceedingly well. I feel sure that its builders regard it with great pride.

GUILDFORD CATHEDRAL 1961
4 manuals: CC to C, 61 notes   Pedal: CCC to G, 32 notes

GREAT ORGAN

	ft
Double Diapason	16
Open Diapason I	8
Open Diapason II	8
Open Diapason III	8
Waldflöte	8
Stopped Diapason	8
Octave Diapason	4
Principal	4
Stopped Flute	4
Twelfth	2⅔
Fifteenth	2
Mixture (revoiced 1993)	IV
Trombone	16
Trumpet	8
Clarion	4

SWELL ORGAN

Contra Salicional	16
Geigen Diapason	8
Rohrflöte	8
Salicional	8
Vox Angelica (tenor C)	8
Principal	4
Koppelflöte	4
Fifteenth	2
Sesquialtera	II
Mixture (revoiced 1993)	IV
Oboe	8
Tremulant	
Contra Fagotto	16
Cornopean	8
Clarion	4

CHOIR ORGAN

Bourdon	16
Open Diapason	8
Dulciana	8
Stopped Diapason	8
Gemshorn	4
Suabe Flute	4
Nazard	2⅔
Flageolet	2
Mixture	III
Trombone (from Great)	16
Trumpet (from Great)	8
Clarion (from Great)	4

POSITIVE ORGAN

Gemshorn	8
Rohrgedackt	8
Spitzflöte	4
Principal (1993)	4
Nazard	2⅔
Blockflöte	2
Tierce	1⅗
Larigot	1⅓
Fourniture	III

SOLO ORGAN

Viole d'orchestre	8
Viole céleste (tenor C)	8
Hohlflöte	8
Concert Flute	4
Piccolo	2
Orchestral Oboe	8
Clarinet	8
Tuba	8
Tremulant	

PEDAL ORGAN

Sub Bass	32
Open Wood	16
Open Metal (from Great)	16
Violone	16
Bourdon	16
Salicional (from Swell)	16
Quintatön (from Positive)	16
Octave Wood	8
Principal	8
Bass Flute	8
Fifteenth	4
Octave Flute	4
Mixture	IV
Contra Trombone	32
Ophicleide	16
Posaune	8
Clarion	4

COUPLERS

Positive to Great   Choir to Great   Swell to Great
Solo to Great   Positive to Swell   Solo to Swell
Positive to Choir   Swell to Choir   Solo to Choir
Positive to Pedal   Choir to Pedal   Great to Pedal
Swell to Pedal   Solo to Pedal

WIND PRESSURES

Great Organ: flue work 3 ins., reeds 6 ins.
Swell Organ: flue work and oboe 4 ins.,
chorus reeds 6 ins.
Choir Organ: flue work 3 ins.
Positive Organ: 2¼ ins.
Solo Organ: tuba 15 ins., remainder 4½ ins.
Pedal Organ: flue work 5 ins.,
ophicleide unit 7 ins.

Total number of pipes, 4,400

Entirely new eight-level capture system and solid state coupling system, 1993,
and new detached mobile choir console for Positive Organ.

The 150 years celebration of this family company was held in 1978. It consisted of a concert in the Blue Coat Chambers on Wednesday, 11th October, the programme consisting of early nineteenth-century music carried out in the dress of that period, using the Rushworth 1820 Vertigrand upright piano from their permanent collection of antique musical instruments. This collection was created during the 1920s by William Rushworth and was on permanent display at the firm's huge showrooms in Islington, Liverpool, until 1960, when the building was demolished to make way for road development. The collection was bought for Liverpool Museum in 1967. Also, on Monday, 6th November, a service of Thanksgiving was held at Liverpool Parish Church of Our Lady and St Nicholas.

It is only some thirty-four years to the '200th'—during that time there are bound to be further developments in technology which never stands still. The age old craft of producing beautiful sounds from pipes will continue however, and with the present young and energetic management, a successful future is assured. It is very much hoped by the author of this very inadequate history, that a future celebration will be graced by an adequate account of "Two Centuries' Achievement".

DAVID WELLS ORGAN BUILDERS

I first met David Wells at Lincoln Cathedral in the organ loft, where I was showing a friend our glorious Father Willis of 1898, reconstructed by Harrisons in 1960. David, who had just turned up to tune, was then working for Harrisons; this was in 1977 during the tenure of Dr. Philip Marshall, who is now living in retirement in a quiet village near Lincoln. He is busily engaged in composition, for his organ and choral music is much sought after. He has also found time to assist occasionally at St Peter-at-Gowt's Church, Lincoln, and Branston Church, where his accompaniments light up the worship.

Back to David Wells however; we soon found that we shared enthusiasm for the work of Father Willis and looking after the Lincoln organ gave him particular pleasure. His connection with it later ceased, and in 1981 he took the bold step of leaving H. & H. to commence his own business. From man and boy he now has a team of ten. Although we had corresponded, our paths did not cross again until the Anniversary Recital of the Liverpool Cathedral Organ in October 1993, after which a member of his staff gave my son and me a conducted tour of this great instrument, climbing perilously to the very top of each chamber, and somehow photographing as we went—an experience we shall never forget!

David commenced his organ building career as an apprentice under Henry Willis IV in Easter 1959, when the overhauling and modernisation of the Cathedral organ was in progress, and so his association there stretches unbroken for some thirty-four years. He 'guards it like a treasure' and his enthusiasm for this wondrous instrument knows no bounds, regarding it as a great privilege to have it not only in his care, but in being largely responsible for the design and construction of the mobile console in the central space, and the re-modelling of that in the gallery, as well as alterations to the Lady Chapel organ.

The company's workshop, known as Cathedral Works, is situated in the highly successful Brunswick Business Park, where some forty hectares of derelict dockside buildings have been re-furbished to provide industrial and commercial accommodation for some 120 companies, including the BBC, whose TV Studio was opened by Prince Edward. During her Premiership, Mrs Margaret Thatcher saw some of the work in progress at David Wells' establishment during 1989. An illustration appeared in *Merseyside Task Force* for Spring of that year, and is reproduced in this chapter.

Four years after his establishment, David Wells was able to announce in the columns of *Musical Opinion* for October 1985 details of work in progress. This included the Birkenhead School Chapel organ—cleaning and overhauling together with the provision of a Great open diapason and Swell tierce. St Luke's Church, Orrell, near Wigan—installation of new Solid State coupler action with modified Swell and Great key action, this being the first stage of major work to the two-manual Wilkinson organ rebuilt by Gray & Davison in the early 1960s. Bebington, St Andrew's Parish Church—after a recent clean and overhaul of the 1962 Henry Willis IV instrument, the trumpet to the Swell was to be added, thus completing the organ as its builder envisaged. Since then, his order book has been full.

The sheer enthusiasm for whatever work David is undertaking is a great asset in his business life. The work of Willis and Harrison is 'in his blood', but he is equally keen to undertake conservation of any worthwhile instrument. This is becoming an encouraging feature of the organ building world of today, whereas not so long ago, organs would be rebuilt and in so doing, take on a new personality which was not always the best.

In 1993, the 1895 Forster & Andrews organ in St Peter's Parish Church, Woolton, Liverpool (rebuilt by Rushworth & Dreaper c.1947) received a grand overhaul which included glue flooding of the Great soundboards and changing the mechanism to electro-pneumatic with a modern console, but no tonal changes were made. Another F. & A. instrument to receive careful conservation during the same years was that at Norcliffe Chapel, Styal. The soundboards were restored some years ago, but the mechanical actions became rather desperate and so they have been back to the works for restoration. Two fine Harrison organs to receive attention during 1993 were in Leigh Parish Church, which was cleaned, leaving work on the mechanism hopefully planned for the future to bring a good and lasting result. At the Parish Church of St Helen, St Helens, the organ received some of the prepared for pipework, while that at the Parish Church, Ormskirk (a very fine Rushworth & Dreaper c.1927), following recent cleaning, is having electro-pneumatic action added.

When the Woolton organ was dismantled, a copy in pristine condition of *The Eastern Morning News and Hull Advertiser* for 13th June, 1895, was found inside the Great soundboard. In those days and for many years into the present century, local newspapers had a host of advertisements and public notices occupying the front page. In this issue there are many to engage our interest; for example, 'Best Selected House Coal' was only 15/6d per ton, Hull Bon Marche were advertising Ladies' Costumes, Complete at 27/6d, while under Shipping Notices, the Hull Steam Company's First Class Fast Steamer Norwood steamed from Hull to Aberdeen on Saturdays (returning Tuesdays) at a single fare 'First Cabin 15/–, Second Cabin 10/–, with return tickets lasting three months—First Cabin 22/6d, Second Cabin 15/–. 'Liquors at moderate rates, Electric light throughout'.

The firm's two major contracts at Liverpool Cathedral and St George's Hall, Liverpool, will go down to posterity in company with Henry Willis & Sons; David's great pride in making his own important contribution to both instruments is fully justified and they are tended with loving care by him and his enthusiastic staff.

By 1991, work on the St George's Hall organ became essential, but funds were limited and so it was decided to carry out the work in stages, the wind supply and alterations to the couplers were dealt with initially, leaving the soundboards and re-leathering of the reservoirs to be done when money becomes available. The new blowers supplying wind at 6,000 cfm and 500 cfm were supplied by Meidinger of Switzerland. The tilting coupler tablets were replaced by drawstops, thus requiring the re-modelling of one of the jambs. The consultant was Professor Ian Tracey, who gave the opening recital on 25th May, 1992. In view of the past uncertainties regarding the use of the Hall, it is good to know that the organ is being used once more for recitals which are proving very popular, and it is the earnest hope of all that funds will soon become available for the complete re-habilitation of this magnificent instrument.

Some seven concerts featuring the organ were held during 1993, our own Cathedral organist at Lincoln, Colin Walsh, described as 'one of the finest players of the younger generation and a specialist in French Romantic music', gave the recital on Saturday, 23rd October. A most popular event first started in 1992, 'St George's Family Carols' was held on Saturday 11th and Sunday 12th December, 1993. It had been completely sold out in August, the year before, and patrons were advised to book early. In addition to the organ, the St George's Singers 'Close Harmony' (the local King's Singers group) appeared with Ken Dodd as compère. St George's Hall has come into its own again and now I hear that Ian Tracey opened the 1994 season on 2nd May with an entertaining Bank Holiday special request programme.

Let David Wells relate how he first became connected with the Liverpool Cathedral organ.

'It was in April 1959 that I first encountered the Grand Organ of Liverpool Cathedral. I was a boy of 15; Mr Willis jnr. (Henry IV, as he was then) took me on that short trip up the hill from his works to Liverpool Cathedral organ. To him this was another of his inspection visits to the restoration work in progress at that time, but to me it was a whole new world. Since that day I have retraced my steps many times whilst tuning and caring for this very special instrument.'

Apart from fortnightly tunings of sections of the organ, followed by two full tunings a year, David's first major work was the construction and installation of the mobile console in the central space in 1989. It was made possible by the generosity of Victor Hutson CBE, who had flown over 7,000 miles from Malaysia every year for the anniversary recital for the last forty-two years. Ian Tracey, in his article in *The Organ*, October 1989, had this to say: 'It has been his dream to 'see the organist entertain' and this year the dream became a reality, thus giving generations of music lovers at Liverpool tangible proof of his dedication to, and love of, music making in the Cathedral'. As a result, organ recitals have become more alive than ever (though they have never been dull in this Cathedral) and the great crowd who attend the anniversary recital each October, together with celebrity recitals held from time to time, are now able to participate. There is always competition to get the best vantage point—how very different from listening to a recital by someone hidden away in an organ loft. As long as I can remember, Liverpool Cathedral has been alive with ideas in the presentation of its message—and warmly welcoming—which is apparent as soon as one enters the building.

The design of the new console was the result of collaboration between David Wells, the Cathedral's organ builder and curator, Ian Tracey and Keith Scott OBE, the consultant architect to the Cathedral. Its superb craftsmanship is apparent in every way, with its fine hand-engraved drawstop heads, bone covered keys and beautifully crafted woodwork, all built in the Liverpool factory, except for the console electronics which were designed and made by Alan Taylor of A. J. & L. Taylor Ltd., of Ramsbottom, Lancs.

The console, which, except for a few modifications, additions and minor improvements, follows the same pattern as its fellow up on the organ gallery. The Willis III 'Infinite Speed and Gradation' swell pedals have been retained on both consoles, for they have been favoured by the succession of Cathedral organists at Liverpool—others elsewhere have discarded them—so Liverpool is unique in their retention. This vast console is connected by micro-computer to the organ by a thin cable which is hardly noticeable— such is the wizardry of modern technology. Ian Tracey contributed a most informative article to *The Organ* for October 1989.

Finally, the gallery console was re-modelled in time for Christmas 1991; gone are the luminous stop heads (I have never been able to understand why Willis used them!) and the general layout returns to that of the original console, except there are more accessories. It is tremendously impressive and despite its great size—the acme of comfort. To watch Ian Tracey accompanying Evensong is an experience; delicate and varied tone colours in the psalms come and go, disappearing into the stonework, while in the Magnificat, Nunc Dimittis and Anthem, there is great scope for 'word painting' and all is done so effortlessly. I shall never forget the Anniversary Evensong for 1993, at which Herbert Howells' *Gloucester Service* was superbly sung. I can only sum it up that Choir, Organ and Organist, not forgetting the Choir Conductor, all combine to create 'the Liverpool sound' which is a deeply moving experience.

One must not forget the organ in the Lady Chapel, for here again David Wells has made his contribution to the two-manual Willis of 1910 (rebuilt in 1973 by Hill, Norman & Beard) which I had the joy of playing during the 1950s. A fine and typical Willis of its period, the tone was altered in 1973. The work carried out by David Wells in 1992 consisted of restoring the manual slider soundboards, replacing the transmission, together with manual and pedal keyboards and a new piston system; several additional couplers and a new half-length 32ft contra fagotto 'to gently underpin the foundation a little' were added.

As this chapter is being written, work in hand includes the overhauling of the organ from St Mary's Parish Church, Hucknall (a Nigel Church organ *c.*1976) for installation in Sedbergh School.

David Wells has come a long way in some twelve years as a master organ builder. He has reached the ultimate in being appointed curator of the organs in St George's Hall, the Anglican Cathedral and the Metropolitan Cathedral, with its fine Walker organ, of which he is justly proud. With his ability and dedication to all he undertakes, I predict with confidence a great future ahead.

HENRY WILLIS & SONS LTD.

Henry Willis & Sons have maintained a presence in Liverpool since 1853, when it was necessary to have a working base in the city during the building of the organ at St George's Hall, commenced in that year and completed by 1855. It then served as a tuning and maintenance shop for the Hall organ and others in the district, but by 1865 it was enlarged to become a fully equipped factory for the building of organs, with a steam-driven plant and facilities for pipe making. Vincent Willis (the eldest son of the founder), who inherited his father's gifts as a voicer as well as a most able general organ builder, was in charge, and under his direction a large number of two- and three-manual organs were built. I am indebted to Mr Bruce Buchanan for the following information about Vincent.

'Born in 1848, the elder of Father Willis' two sons, he was educated at the Merchant Taylors' School, then in the City, and was thereafter apprenticed to his father's firm which had just moved to its most famous address, the Rotunda Works, Camden Town. Whilst in Liverpool, Vincent met and married his wife who bore him two sons and three daughters.

Vincent Willis had an extremely ingenious mind and he set himself to improve and advance not only the mechanical but also the tonal aspects of the organ. In 1894, he left the firm to set up on his own as an inventor, taking for the purpose a disused Free Church in Brentford. Room forbids a complete catalogue of his patents, but they include the reed curving machine, two of which exist and are in use today, the improved Barker Lever, known as the Floating Lever of 1884, and the improved Pneumatic Lever of 1889. His tonal devices included the double languid pipe and the extraordinary attenuated air organ in which the pipes were placed in a chamber at lower than atmospheric pressure. When the pallets, placed on the outside, were opened, air was sucked through the pipes. One example was made and installed in a house in Bournemouth before the Great War.

Vincent Willis was in many ways an architypal inventor with a brilliantly imaginative mind and a curious disregard for the everyday practicalities of money. Of his two sons, one was killed in the Great War whilst the other, Henry Vincent, survived and emigrated to America where he worked as a voicer, most notably on the Atlantic City Organ where there are a great number of double languid pipes... Vincent Willis died at Ealing in 1928.'

In 1882, his place was taken by his brother, Henry II, who was in charge for almost twenty years and was responsible for the partial renovation and modernisation of the St George's Hall organ from the Liverpool works. Both brothers had been made partners in the firm in 1876. In the *Music Trades Pocket Directory* for 1894, the firm is recorded as occupying premises at 2 May Street, Mount Pleasant. Here, there was a full manufacturing facility as well as a metal pipe making shop.

Henry Willis III, in his house journal *The Rotunda*, Vol. II, No. 1, September 1925, had this to say in his introduction, titled 'Intentions'. 'My father, the 2nd Henry Willis, was a great voicer and a great artist, who, following his more famous father, was perhaps "unheralded and unsung", and so to myself a mere organ builder, trained and instructed as such.' I understand that Henry Willis II was a Classical scholar, being interested in Latin verse. His ivory name plates bore this latin inscription: HOC ORGANUM AEDIFICATION EST PER HENRY WILLIS AND SONS. PER AURES AD ANIMAM. Translated, it reads: this organ is built by Henry Willis and Sons. Through the ears to the soul.

> 'My earliest practical experiences were of acting as tuner's boy to my father, whose great hobby it was to go to organs on Saturday afternoons and tune them *perfectly*. A good organ tuner will always give of his best and in the hands of an artist-tuner, superb results can be attained. Under the tuition of my father I learnt to be dissatisfied with any but the most perfect results. I well remember an occasion, it was at St James' Church, Waterfoot (Lancs.), in 1906, where I was entrusted with the 'finishing' of the new organ. It was opened amid general plaudits and I felt that all was well! My father came down later to see that everything was right and to give the finishing touches. I shall never forget the organist's remarks two days later, "Well Mr Willis, I thought the organ was perfect, but now its a different instrument, it's simply wonderful" the result being of course, due to very "close" tuning and regulation.' Henry III was to instil the importance of fine tuning to his tuners throughout his life, as one well known to me (who was given the care of St Paul's Cathedral and Westminster Cathedral organs as a young man) has told me.'

After the death of Father Willis in 1901, Henry II moved to London and took charge of the firm. At this point, A. E. Temple was appointed as Liverpool director, and by 1929 had been with the firm for over forty years without any absence due to sickness, even for a single day. His death, in 1938, was a great loss for he was a most able organ builder with a friendly personality which endeared him to everyone. If he had lived until November 1939, he would have completed fifty years' service with the firm. He was greatly involved with the installation of the Liverpool Cathedral organ and the restoration and modernisation of the St George's Hall organ.

Henry Willis III (born in 1889) was proud of the fact that he was Liverpool born and bred; he was educated at Liverpool College Upper School. Even as a boy, the young Henry helped in any work that was being done at St George's Hall and was present at the re-opening at the major rebuild of 1898. Nine years later at the age of 18, during the illness of the regular tuner, he was placed in charge of the weekly tuning for the Saturday afternoon and evening recitals.

In a letter dated 15th March, 1943, from the Territorial Hall, Taunton, where he was serving as a Captain, he reminded me that as a youngster he tuned the Lincoln Cathedral organ on one or two occasions. He stayed with the Cathedral Organist, Dr. G. J. Bennett 'who was always delightful to me— I well remember one evening playing dummy dummy bridge with him for three solid hours'!

On entering the firm he went through all the departments of organ building the hard way, working alongside several members of the staff who had actually worked with Father Willis and had lived in the neighbourhood all their lives. The oldest of these was Joseph Green, who had been with the firm for no less than fifty-nine years, having started as a tuner's note holder in 1870, and to quote *The Rotunda*: 'Still able to put up an excellent show against the youngsters'. He was then over seventy years of age—organ builders have often found it hard to retire.

During the management of Henry II, more than 30% of the firm's total reed work was made and voiced at Liverpool and much of this was done by him. The ill-health of Henry Willis II led to the practical control of the firm devolving on his son, who left the Liverpool branch in the care of A. E. Temple during 1910, and it was not long before it was caught up with the constructional work for the Liverpool Cathedral organ, the design for which had been the responsibility of Henry III. In a letter to me dated 22nd March, 1936, Mr Henry Willis informed me that his father 'was personally responsible for much of the reed work from 1875 onwards and trained Wesson, who became reed voicer in 1882, and after that year my father personally voiced many reed stops etc. as our records show'.

My first knowledge of the importance of the Liverpool branch came from R. A. Cousans, organ builder and head of the firm of Cousans Sons & Co., when I first met him in 1928. For some time, I had been given the freedom of the beautiful two-manual Father Willis instrument in Branston Parish Church, near Lincoln, built in 1893; it was a gem, typical of its builder and I learned that it had been built at Liverpool, as had a two-manual chamber organ for A. H. Leslie Melville in Branston Hall, where R. A. Cousans played from time to time, for he was organist at the church for some years when a young man. The Hall organ was a two-manual instrument with 10 speaking stops, an oak case, and cost £300, which worked out at £30 per speaking stop.

During 1940, I did my pre-service training in the RAF (commonly known as square bashing!) at Blackpool, where I had the opportunity in spare time to examine several fine instruments by Harrison, Nicholson & Co., Binns and Willis, the latter being at St John's Parish Church, built in 1915 as a three-manual with a total of 49 stops. It was opened by Herbert F. Ellingford, MUS. BAC. OXON, organist of St George's Hall, Liverpool, on 3rd February, 1915. It was a typical Willis of that period, of great magnificence; with a variety of quiet tonal colours of outstanding beauty. Much, or all of this, was probably built at Liverpool and more than likely Henry III was responsible for the voicing at the London works. In the actual tonal scheme, I detected several tone colours such as flute ouverte and aeoline, which in name were a departure from the traditions of the past, but found in the tonal schemes of the firm from that time onwards. There were foot pistons too, instead of composition pedals and adjustable pistons; the Willis firm was certainly moving ahead under its third generation owner—but much more was to come.

It is time to take a look at the head office and works at Ferndale Road, Brixton, 'The Rotunda Organ Works', previously the home of T. C. Lewis & Co. Ltd., which was incorporated with Henry Willis & Sons in 1918. At the early age of fifteen, I was given an introduction to Henry Willis by Gilbert Benham and at the Rotunda Works I received a warm welcome by that very busy man and thus commenced a friendship which lasted until his death. I was given to understand that I could spend a whole day there if I wished and from that time onwards until I left school at the age of seventeen, I availed myself of the opportunity. It should be explained that holidays were spent with relatives at Beckenham and that was the base from which I visited countless organs by various builders in the vicinity. From time to time I was thrilled by the regular recitals on the organ at the Crystal Palace, attended Evensong at St Paul's Cathedral and Westminster Abbey, knew almost every church in the City of London and the works of all the organ builders of note in London—all most valuable experience, for organ building was in my blood and those who share this experience never lose it.

The Rotunda Works was a spacious, tall building of yellow brick, darkened by London's 'smog'. There was a private house built on to it, occupied by the firm's stores superintendent, one Jones, with thirty years' service, a great character and kindly disposed to an enthusiastic lad. His memory went back to the days of Father Willis, for whom he worked as well as being a personal friend. Many an anecdote was told me, often with a laugh or a roguish smile, and it was clear that there had been a close friendship between the two. A collection of Father Willis stop knobs was soon built up, through his interest in my activities, with the essential blessing of 'the guvnor'!

Other senior members of staff in those days, some of whom I recall, were: Mr Daykin, works manager, Aubrey Thompson-Allen, research etc., Mr George Sinclair, secretary, Mr North, chief console expert (35 years' service), Mr Jackson, metal shop foreman (17 years' service), Mr Hulbert, senior action hand (40 years' service), Mr Rashbrook, action hand (over 50 years' service) and Mr D. Batigan Verne, publicity etc. Their portraits, together with Mr Henry Willis, are featured in *The Rotunda*, Vol. 3, No. 1, September 1929.

What made the greatest impression on me was the spacious and very tall erecting shop where the largest instrument could be built up. There was a very busy metal casting and pipe making shop and long workshops devoted to action work, console assembly, soundboard construction, miscellaneous wood working and the like. There was, of course, a saw mill and a yard where timber was stored under cover for seasoning. It was a highly organised works with a large staff; each bench had a card, clipped showing the work in hand, so that in his daily tour, H. W. could see at a glance what was going on. He rarely spoke, except to the foreman concerned. The drawing office I never saw and only caught glimpses of his private office on the walls of which were framed portraits of Dupré and others, together with famous Willis organs. He was always extremely busy, but had a friendly word, and looking back over the years, I feel that I was highly favoured. When I commenced writing articles at the age of nineteen, he showed the greatest interest in my work and always found time, right to the end of his life, to give me the fullest information possible about a Father Willis organ and comment with appreciation on my writings on the work of his grandfather as well as the work of other firms, even when he did not always see eye to eye with my comments! I treasure a letter from him relating to the fine Taylor organ in the De Montford Hall, Leicester, which I reviewed for *The Choir and Musical Record*. It was not his idea of a concert organ and read: 'Dear Elvin, your article: De Montford Hall Organ. It only goes to show how opinions on organs can differ. Yours Sincerely, Henry Willis'.

There were two voicing shops, with George Deekes in charge of reeds and Dick Piper, flues. He later left the firm to join Austins in America, to be in charge of tonal matters. Henry Willis set the Cs and each day checked the work in progress—notebook and silver pencil in hand. I recall the rapport between master and the two men, particularly with Deekes, who was always addressed as George. There was a friendly and easy atmosphere which one did not always sense in the main shops, when the 'guvnor' was about. Voicing and tonal finishing was Henry Willis' great forté and every aspect of the flues and reeds was thoroughly worked out and then presented on instruction sheets to both voicers who closely followed them. I learned much from the hours I spent watching progress there.

When the great instrument in the Alexandra Palace was in course of restoration during 1929, Felix Aprahamian and myself were granted permission to wander inside at will when everything had been stripped down. I was able to take photographs of progress from the passage boards and when all was completed, was completely stunned by the magnificent blaze of sound from this great instrument at the opening recital by G. D. Cunningham, and the regular Sunday afternoon recitals by the official organist, Reginald Goss-Custard.

During visits to the Alexandra Palace, I was introduced to Sydney J. Ambler, a well-known organ expert of his day and a highly skilled craftsman. He was a character, inclined to be 'prickly' and needed to be handled with care but when he realised that you had a genuine and intelligent interest in his work, was soon helpful and friendly. His great practical knowledge caused him to be in demand as an organ consultant and he was called in at St Martin-in-the-Fields to collaborate with R. Spurden Rutt when he rebuilt the organ there. His base was a fully equipped workshop, meticulously laid out within the spacious interior of the Father Willis organ in Park Chapel (Congregational), Crouch End. Henry Willis III rebuilt it with a modern console at which Dr. Eric Thiman then presided with great distinction. Ambler was curator of the organ and added a number of pistons at the request of Thiman, with complete professional skill. He kept it in perfect tune and his honorary maintenance and additional work did not endear himself to Willis!

G. D. Cunningham had his first lessons at Park Chapel from Josiah Booth under whom he made such rapid progress that a member of the chapel offered to send him to the Royal Academy of Music and here he studied the organ with Dr. Charles Steggall. The rest of his remarkable career is well known, for like Sir George Thalben-Ball, he became a 'legend in his lifetime'. The young G. T. B. was one of G. D. C.s many students. Cunningham was organist at The Alexandra Palace from 1902–1914 and during that time gave over 1,000 recitals. He was appointed organist at Birmingham Town Hall in 1924 where he remained until his death in 1948, when he was succeeded by his former pupil, G. T. B. Willis rebuilt the Town Hall organ in 1933 with the enthusiastic co-operation of Cunningham.

Marriage and six years war service curtailed my London visits, but afterwards, the occasional holiday enabled me to renew old contacts and make fresh ones, but it was a very different London from that of my teenage years, and many fine instruments had gone. I was able to hear the post war Willis rebuild of

1951 at All Souls' Church, Langham Place. In its enlarged form, Willis had created a fine, bold and lively ensemble on typical 'Willis' lines, while retaining the beauty of Hunter's fine voicing, particularly the quiet registers. His director, H. P. Hamblen, demonstrated it most ably and I was then given the freedom of the console.

One night's raid during the blitz had destroyed the Ferndale Road works, which was a tremendous blow to Henry Willis who, during the war years, was a reserve Captain in the army. What upset him most was the destruction of some of the valuable records, including scales and voicing details of many organs for which he had been responsible. He carried on with great courage however, his able assistant, Aubrey Thompson Allen, being responsible for day to day correspondence etc from a house at Beulah Hill, London.

After the war, premises at Marlborough Grove, Old Kent Road, were purchased and opened in 1946; they were bigger than those at Ferndale Road and proved ideal in every way. Willis and his staff set about the necessary re-organisation; men returned from the forces and it was not long before the factory was a hive of activity once again. I am privileged to be able to print the following description of these premises, written by one who was employed there for some two years prior to 1953.

'I can remember a row of grey terraced houses and then came the entrance to the factory, with its own drive in. The house at the entrance served as the front office with Henry Willis and Aubrey Thompson Allen in offices on the ground floor, with all the other normal administrative staffs spread accordingly. Going down the drive, past an empty space on the right, brought one to a large yard, with two extensive buildings with large sliding doors for easy access. On the right hand side of the building comprised the erecting shop on the ground floor, in which a large three-manual could be erected with ample space above and around it. On the left was the stores and at the back of the left wall was the staircase (very steep!) up to the console shop with about six or seven benches. Each bench had at its end an elevated board to which was pinned a description of the job being done, with its location and job number. This enabled any of the management to pass down the shop and see at a glance what job was being done by each man. At the very end of the console gallery behind a glass partition with its own door, stood the reed voicing shop, the domain of George Deekes senior (his son was a tuner for the firm). As G. D. was a staff member, his hours did not start before nine in the morning, while the rest of the employees began at eight. I served as his assistant for a short time. G. D. was an absolute martinet, a stickler for tidyness and efficiency and extremely good at his job, with years behind him at Ferndale Road. At ten each morning, H. W. (senior) could be seen making his way down the console shop gradually, en route to his customary visit to the reed voicing shop. Invariably, he would have his hat on, and sometimes his overcoat as well. He would rarely comment on what he saw and rarely spoke to the men, and then only to ask a pertinent question. (I have reason to know that his eagle eye never missed a thing and an inquest would sometimes be held in the privacy of the office if something caught his eye with which he was not altogether satisfied.) Eventually he would reach the voicing shop, usually opening the proceedings with "Good morning, George, what have we here?" Often on one of the two reed voicing machines would be a reed already set up for him to try. Sometimes, though, all that would be in place would be the five Cs of, say, an 8ft oboe or trumpet. It was normal for H. W. to set the Cs as to power and tone, as a guide for Deekes to work on (often the sixth C—the bottom one—would be standing against the wall). I can recall one occasion when a contra oboe was being voiced for somewhere. G. D. had much trouble getting the stop as he wanted it, with much swearing and cursing throughout the day. In the morning, H. W. came in at ten, and with G. D. looking on, tried the stop. "Hmm" said H. W. "It's those damned half-length basses sir—that's the trouble" complained G. D. with not a little bitterness. Almost like a father, H. W. said quietly "I know, I know, I know (with emphasis on the 'I'), we'll just have to do the best we can…' He tried the stop and played a few chords. Invariably he would twist his head suddenly in order to change his direction of hearing. Playing a note, he would jerk his head to stare, seemingly at the ceiling or at the side wall. Then, picking up a reed knife and staring at the pipe through the very bottom of his glasses, would tap gently (rather more than G. D.!) at the spring to adjust the regulation. At the end of this exercise there was another "Hmm". He then said to G. D. "a little more colour in the tenor octave George and then we can let it go". And with that he was gone. He would then go across the yard, into the other large building wherein was the flue voicing shop with Dick Piper in charge. This building on the left of the yard contained on its ground floor, a huge room for storing new wood. A brick wall at the rear separated the metal shop, with benches set out as indicated previously. A smaller room at the rear of this housed the metal casting shop. (To the uninitiated, this contained a long, covered table. When the time came for the hot liquid metal to be poured, a ladle was dipped into the melting pot, and two men, working quickly, would then pour it into the runner. This was parked atop the flat table at one end. Once the pouring had been done, the men almost ran the runner along the table. The hot, liquid metal ran out through a gap in the bottom of the runner, and when all went well, a long sheet of pipe metal would be spread out on the top of the table. Both men inspected this closely for any flaws and, if any were found, did the whole run again with a new ladle of metal). There was a pipe making department as well as shops devoted to the construction of windchests, reservoirs, swell boxes, building frames etc. An amusing recollection is the the regulating of a 32ft reed standing on the floor of the erecting shop. H. W. came in one morning to regulate the bottom octave; an apprentice had to lie on his back to push through the armatures to operate the notes (they had their own starters). H. W. would start with tenor C and with a left flick of his hand, would indicate that the next note down should be played. First C, then B, then A sharp—then Willis did a right flick of his hand indicating that the lad should go back one and play the note before. The lad did as he was told, but the only sound that came out was a hiss. H. W. then shouted out with some power: "Oh these God-damned starters". Someone fixed the trouble and the audition went on as before!'

The handsome Willis consoles, fully equipped with every modern accessory are too familiar to warrant discussion here. I must confess that I never felt at home with the Infinite Gradation swell pedal, while tablets for couplers over the top manual did not feel so convenient as drawstops placed with the departments they augment, while I was sorry to see the earlier console fittings of mahogany or rosewood replaced by an ebonised finish. I shall never forget the sight of the first console at Liverpool Cathedral with its rosewood jambs, music desk etc; it had such distinction and I could never understand the change to black. It is all a matter of taste however.

In the correspondence columns of *Musical Opinion* during the 1930s, letters (sometimes lengthy) appeared from H. Willis from time to time if he disagreed with opinions by others; his chief hobby horse was of course manual extension and total enclosure, to which he was strongly opposed. He never unbent on the former , except, as far as I know, at St Jude's Church, Thornton Heath (1930) where he extended the Swell oboe down to 16ft and actually totally enclosed manual and pedal divisions. At the conclusion of his article on this instrument in *The Rotunda*, Vol. 3, No. 3, September 1930, he commented: 'My own feeling is that although this is the first 'Willis' organ to have an enclosed Great, it will not be the last'! As far as duplexing was concerned, he did not unbend until a "New Model" No. 1 two-manual organ partially "Duplexed" was introduced in 1930. It had thirteen speaking stops, eleven couplers and a full complement of accessories. Three quiet stops from the Swell were also playable from the Great (which had but a diapason and principal); the cost ex works and without case was £1,000.

Henry Willis' other bone of contention was the rebuild by others of his grandfather's organs and it was usually clear to whom he was referring. Yet he was on the friendliest terms with his contemporaries at the meetings of the Federation of Master Organ Builders and the Incorporated Society of Organ Builders, where he was greatly esteemed for the Papers he read to the Society and was equally appreciative of the scholarship of his contemporaries.

I count myself fortunate in having heard and in some cases examined some of Henry Willis's most important work both pre and post war up to the mid 1950s. I shall never forget hearing the Liverpool Cathedral organ for the first time in 1929 at a service of The Friends of the Cathedral and then a look at the mighty console. Tonally, it proved an emotional experience even to a youngster of sixteen and it remains so today. Here I met Edgar Robinson (Choirmaster), who was a former pupil of Dr. G. J. Bennett at Lincoln Cathedral. After the war, that great and kindly man, Harry Goss Custard, gave of his valuable time to demonstrate some of the facets of the organ he loved so much. I can remember very clearly him telling me that he asked Henry Willis not to give him what he considered the rather excessive brilliance of the Westminster Cathedral organ, and this was readily agreed. What Willis did give him was an instrument of unparalleled grandeur, generally acknowledged to be without equal the world over. I loved the small Willis in the Lady Chapel built by Henry III in 1910 and which reminded me of his father's work at All Saints' Church, Lincoln, for I had the freedom of the console on more than one occasion. It has since been rebuilt by Hill, Norman & Beard, with further work by David Wells of Liverpool in 1992. I can but wish that tonally it had been allowed to remain, for Henry Willis II was so impressed by his son's first instrument that he made him junior partner at the age of twenty-one.

LIVERPOOL ANGLICAN CATHEDRAL
THE LADY CHAPEL ORGAN 1910

2 manuals: CC to C, 61 notes   Pedal: CCC to F, 30 notes

GREAT ORGAN	ft		
Lieblich Bourdon	16	Hautboy	8
Open Diapason I	8	*Tremulant*	
Open Diapason II	8	**PEDAL ORGAN**	
Claribel	8	Acoustic Bass	32
Dulciana	8	Open Diapason	16
Harmonic Flute	4	Violone	16
Principal	4	Bourdon (from Great)	16
Fifteenth	2	Octave (partially derived)	8
Harmonic Trumpet	8	Bass Flute (from Great)	8

SWELL ORGAN		COUPLERS	
Geigen Diapason	8	Swell Octave Swell Sub Octave Swell Unison Off	
Lieblich Gedackt	8	Swell to Pedal Swell to Great Unison	
Salicional	8	Swell to Great Super Swell to Great Sub	
Vox Angelica	8	Great to Pedal	
Gambette	4	4 adjustable pistons to Great and Pedal, 3 to Swell,	
Echo Mixture 17·19·22	III	dulpicated by toe pistons.	
Cornopean	8	Great to Pedal piston	

The blaze and brilliance of the Westminster Cathedral organ, which I heard for the first time at High Mass in 1928, overwhelmed me in an extremely different way; it was tremendously exciting. Marcel Dupré loved it, as did other recitalists—others were less enthusiastic. One of the encouraging features of organ building today is the respect given to masterpieces of the past, by organ builders with a different outlook from the original creator. A striking example of this was the restoration of the Westminster Cathedral organ by Harrison & Harrison, under the enthusiastic direction of Mark Venning, their Managing Director. I cannot do better than quote his remarks in the programme, *Westminster Cathedral Grand Organ Recital Series 1985*, where he commented on its 'blazing grandeur… the voicing reflects what we know of the builder himself—incisive, extrovert and completely without compromise, compelling attention by sheer force of personality'.

The new organ for Sheffield City Hall, built in 1932 and opened by Sir Edward Bairstow, Organist and Master of the Choristers at York Minster, came over the radio as rather 'hard and brittle', but here

Henry Willis had a building entirely devoid of resonance—or as it was once described, as being as 'dead as a door nail'! It was a great disappointment to him; at the time it was hoped to remedy this as far as possible, at some future date, but whether this was ever done, I do not know. It is good to hear that the instrument is in working order (although requiring a clean and overhaul) and used from time to time throughout the year, usually as part of selected Philharmonic Concerts. The Willis rebuild of the Conacher organ of 1888 at Victoria Hall, Hanley, in 1922, was a truly magnificent example of the firm's work of that period. It was demonstrated to R. A. Cousans, organ builder of Lincoln, and myself, one evening by the City Organist, Dr. Sydney H. Wealé, F.R.C.O., who held the appointment with great distinction from 1919 until his lamented death in 1943. He was a fine recitalist and extremely popular in the Potteries where his distinguished playing and friendly personality were held in great esteem. He had drawn up the specification in collaboration with the builders; he loved his organ (and rightly so) and I have memories of a delightful evening in his company when the many interesting features of the instrument were superbly displayed; his enthusiasm for it was infectious and we came away thrilled by its magnificent ensembles and the innumerable quiet effects which were of great beauty. It survived the war and in 1987–88, Hill, Norman & Beard Ltd. carried out a thorough restoration and installed a modern Solid State electric transmission.

I also recall with pleasure the organ in Bradford on Avon Parish Church (1926)—a lovely and most satisfying sound of moderate brilliance, and St John's, Eden Park, not far from Beckenham, Kent.

In 1954, Henry Willis IV (or 4 as he prefers to be known) went to Liverpool to manage the firm's branch there. Three years later, he was responsible, together with his father, for directing the restoration of the organ in St George's Hall, which had remained silent since war damage on December 21st, 1940. He was largely concerned with the tonal finishing, for he inherited his father's great interest in tonal matters. In the month of June of that year, no less than seven distinguished recitalists were heard: Fernando Germani (who opened the organ on 17th June), Jean Demessieux, Dr. George Thalben-Ball, Dr. Caleb Jarvis, Noel Rawsthorne, Marcel Dupré and Pierre Cochereau.

Between 1958–60, a major overhaul of the Liverpool Cathedral organ took place. The choir console, originally built with pneumatic action, was rebuilt with all electric action, while the unenclosed Choir Organ section was replaced by a new Positive division. A new humidifying system was also introduced in both organ chambers and in the blowing room. In March 1965, a mobile two-manual tilting tablet console was designed by Henry Willis IV, with casework designed by George G. Pace. Controlling thirty-two speaking stops from the Swell, Great, Bombarde and Pedal, and mounted on an oak platform with rubber-covered wheels, with sixty feet of spare cable, it was low enough for the organist to have an unimpaired view of the congregation and choir. It could be played from the Memorial Chapel, the central space, or near to the choir. This replaced the large five-manual console placed at the north-east side of the central space with luminous stop heads attached to the music desk to control couplers, which was installed in 1940. It provided for three additional sections: Corona, to be placed in the Corona or tower for etherial and antiphonal effects. The West End Section, to be placed at the west end of the central space, for the accompaniment of large congregations, and the Central Space Accompanimental Section, for the accompaniment of the choir when services were held in the central space. The Corona and West End Section were under construction in September 1939, while the former was completed in the factory in 1940, but never installed due to the violent enemy action over Liverpool. Sadly, the entire section was destroyed at the Rotunda Works, London, in 1941, and the project has never been revived.

In 1958, Henry Willis IV designed a small organ known as his 'Junior Development Plan' where the basic one-manual instrument could also be the Great Organ of a two-manual, which might be developed at a later date. The basic specification consisted of a klein gedackt 8ft and gemshorn 4ft, with tremolo. The action was electric and the stop control was by tilting tablets. There were optional extras ie. a detached console together with additional stops such as dulciana, flageolet and a pedal board with manual to pedal coupler. Further extras comprised Pedal gedackts in 16, 8 and 4ft pitches, while variants of the basic scheme, with optional extras, were also available. The pipework was exposed. The following list shows the locations of these small organs which were mostly manufactured (up to number 55) in the Liverpool works.

1	Flint, Convent of Our Lady of the Taper	Sept. 1958
2	Walberswick, see Opus 7 St Andrew's Church (1st part)	Jan. 1960
3	Liverpool, Eldon Place, St Mary's Church	Apr. 1960
4	Aberdare, St Joseph's Catholic Church	Aug. 1960
5	Sheffield University, Firth Hall (To Sheffield Cathedral)	Nov. 1960
6	Wigan, St Joseph's Catholic Church	Dec. 1960
7	Walberswick, St Andrew's Church (2nd part)	May 1961
8	Belfast, Saintfield Rd. Presbyterian Church	Nov. 1961
9	Lancaster, Quernmore Parish Church (1st stage)	Nov. 1961
10	Savernake, St Katharine's Church	Nov. 1961
11	Yeading, St Raphael's Catholic Church	Nov. 1961
12	Witham, Guithavon Valley Evangelical Church	Feb. 1962
13	Belfast, Donegal Pass Presbyterian Church	Apr. 1962
14	Dublin, Cappagh, St Mary's Hospital Chapel	Apr. 1962
15	Cranleigh, Junior School Chapel	Apr. 1962
16	Ruthin, Llanelidan Church	May 1962
17	East Wittering, St Anne's Church	Aug. 1962
18	Paisley, Glenburn Church	Sept. 1962
19	Bebbington, St Andrew's Parish Church	Sept 1962
20	Cumbernauld, Kildrum Church	Nov. 1962
21	Dundee, Menzieshill Church	Dec. 1962
22	London, Camberwell, St Philip's Church	Jan. 1963
23	Grangemouth, Kirk of the Holy Rood	Jun. 1963
24	Co. Dublin, Balheary, Christian Brothers Novitiate	Aug. 1963
25	Whitsbury, St Leonard's Church	Nov. 1963
26	Sutton, St Barnabas Church	Dec. 1963
27	Portsmouth, Milton, St Mary's Hospital Chapel	Dec. 1963
28	Preston, Fulwood, St Cuthbert's Church	Mar. 1964
29	Liverpool, Knotty Ash, St Margaret Mary's Church	May 1964
30	Liverpool, Litherland, St Paul's Church	Jun. 1964
31	Hendon, Hendon College of Technology	Aug. 1964
32	Glasgow, Colston Milton Church	Sept. 1964
33	Corringham, Essex, St John's Church	Sept. 1964
34	Muirhouse Parish Church, Edinburgh	Dec. 1964
35	Lady Margaret House, Cambridge	Dec. 1964
36	Nelson, St Joseph's Catholic Church	Dec. 1964
37	Musselburgh, St Ninian's Parish Church	Feb. 1965
38	Streatham, London, Bishop Thomas Grant School	Feb. 1965
39	Helsby, Cheshire, Methodist Church	Apr. 1965
40	Litherland, Liverpool, Our Lady Queen of Peace	Apr. 1965
41	Isleworth, Campion House, Osterley	May 1965
42	St Jude's RC Church, Poolstock, Wigan	Jul. 1965
43	Ipswich, Ince Residence Organ	Oct. 1965
44	St Oswald's Church, Tile Hill North, Coventry	Dec. 1965
45	St Mary's Church, Atte-Bow, London	Dec. 1965
46	Countess of Huntingdon Mission, Waterloo, Sierra Leone	Dec. 1965
47	"Loan Organ" Label Opus 47. To Jamaica House, London	Jan. 1966
48	Goddard Residence Organ	Mar. 1966
49	Knebworth, St Martin's Church	Dec. 1965
50	Royal Academy of Music, London	Jun. 1966
51	Ballingry Parish Church, Lochgelly	Nov. 1966
52	Wyggeston Hospital Chapel, Fosse Rd. South, Leicester	Dec. 1966
53	Scone, Old Parish Church, Perthshire	Dec. 1966
54	Crosby Merchant Taylors' School	Apr. 1967
55	Corby, St Ninian's Church	Aug. 1967
56	Tregaron, Eglwys Sant Caron	Jul. 1968
57	Laleham Abbey (1st manual)	Nov. 1968
58	Torbain Parish Church, Kirkcaldy	May 1969
59	St Michael & All Angels, West Meads, Bognor Regis, West Sussex	May 1970
60	St Mary's Parish Church, Compton, Chichester	Nov. 1970
61	All Saints' Church, Royal School of Signals, Blandford Forum	Jan. 1971
62	St Peter's Church, Ravenshead, Notts	1971
63	Ashford School, Kent	Apr. 1972
64	Folkestone, Pugh Residence	Dec. 1973
65	Tonypandy, St Gabriel and St Raphael's Catholic Church	1975
66	Corpus Christi Catholic Church, Sturges Rd., Wokingham	1984

The prices in April 1965 of the Junior Development Plan organs are interesting. The basic one-manual with two speaking stops and tremolo, but no Pedal division, £750 ex works. The oak finish console's music desk folded down over the manual keys. Optional extras were: dulciana (bass from klein gedackt), £240; flageolet 2ft, £125; concave and radiating pedal board, 32 notes with manual to pedal coupler, £320; Pedal gedackt 16ft (12 pipes from manual), £285.

One-manual and Pedal organ, six speaking stops, 1 coupler and tremolo, ie. klein gedackt 8, dulciana 8, gemshorn 4. Pedal: gedackt 8, gedackt flute 4, klein gedackt 2. Manual to pedal coupler, £1410 ex works. Extras as basic model. Detached console, 20 feet of cable, £35. Exposed pipework in both cases, and electric blower included.

In pre-war days before inflation, the Willis Plainsong Model 1B, consisting of diapason, bourdon 8, salicional, gemshorn, plein jeu (12·15), all enclosed, sub bass 16, manual to pedal coupler and tremolo, with plain wood enclosure and console fittings of ebonised wood, was £545 ex works. The new 'Willis No. 1 Model Organ' (partially duplexed) with ten speaking stops, plus 3 Great ranks duplexed from the Swell, 11 couplers, 11 pistons, general crescendo pedal, detached console in oak, £1,000 ex works.

In all cases, electric action and blowing plant. Breaking down the prices is revealing: pre-war, approx. cost per rank of Model B, £90; post-war, basic one-manual without pedals, £375; with pedal board, gedackt 16ft and coupler, approx. £451. The cost today can be imagined.

Henry Willis III died at his home in Streatham on 27th April, 1966, in his seventy-seventh year; he had been suffering from ill-health for some time and had struggled against it, for his whole life was concerned with organ building, whilst he attained the highest offices in various musical associations and companies.

The Incorporated Society of Organ Builders was founded in 1947 and its first President was Henry Willis. He contributed a number of learned Papers to the Society which were of the greatest value; reading through them again as I write this chapter, I realise the scholarship and depth of thinking born out of travel on the Continent and the USA, where he met other organ builders and heard some of the historic instruments which have been landmarks in organ building during two centuries. He will go down in history as a great organ builder—the organ in Liverpool Cathedral will always be a monument to his genius. Harry Goss Custard had this to say in a booklet on the organ, which he autographed for me in 1953. 'Surely never was a Cathedral more truly endowed with its fit and proper voice than Liverpool. Majesty and dignity are pre-eminently the characteristics of Cathedral and organ alike... The result secured proves how wisely the specification was planned and with what artistry the scaling and voicing was carried out.'

Henry Willis was a great traveller, both on the Continent and in the USA, where he made many friends amongst distinguished organists and organ builders. Vierne, Karg-Elert and Dupré and others dedicated works to him. He was a great innovator, being very much to the fore in console and electric action development, his consoles not only being handsome in design, but the acme of comfort. His great interest was in tonal matters and readers are strongly recommended to read *The American Classic Organ, a History in Letters*, by Charles Callahan (The Organ Historical Society, Richmond, Va., USA) which is a fascinating account of his correspondence to and from noted organ builders and others. To quote from the section: Henry Willis III, 1889–1966. 'His concept of the ideal organ varied only slightly over the years.'

Henry Willis IV returned to London in 1965; two years later, the Marlborough Grove premises were sold and the firm moved to The New Rotunda Organ Works, 87–91 Rushes Road, Petersfield, Hampshire, a large modern building with every facility. After the death of his father, Henry Willis IV became Managing Director. His eldest son, Henry, after working in the firm for some ten years, decided that organ building was not his calling, found his true vocation as a Pastor in a church in South Africa. His brother, John Sinclair Willis, is still a director of the family business, together with his mother, Mrs Barbara J. Willis and Mr P. Cobon, whose long and practical association with the business is valuable. It incorporates the former firms of Lewis & Co., A. Hunter & Sons, Scovell & Co., Ivimey and Cooper, Ingram & Co. (Hereford) and Brook & Co. and others, while there are branches or tuning representatives at Glasgow, Edinburgh, Huddersfield, Liverpool, Sheffield, Hereford, Nottingham and London. In all, some twenty-five organ builders are employed throughout the organisation.

Amongst the contracts of various kinds carried out under the direction of Henry Willis from Petersfield, including restorations and rebuilds of Willis, Lewis and instruments by other builders, one instrument I am sure must have given him particular pleasure. This is the Brangwyn Hall organ at Swansea, which is the former Willis III instrument built originally for the Elite Cinema, Nottingham, in 1921, which I had the pleasure of playing many years ago. A brochure at the time described it as 'specially designed for this Theatre at almost fabulous cost'. It was claimed to be 'the largest organ ever to have been built for a British cinema'. The placement of all but the Echo Organ was in chambers on each side of the screen, with the Echo Organ in the roof of the cinema, the tone entering the building through a concealed grill in the ceiling. The console was in the orchestra pit. Its original cost was just over £9,540: it had four manuals and a very comprehensive specification. By the late 1920s, the cinema had declined; it was decided to sell the organ to the Willis firm in 1929 who stored it in their Liverpool works. Eventually it was sold to the Brangwyn Hall, Swansea, where the opening recital was given by Dr. W. H. Harris on 23rd October, 1934. Since then, from 1971 onwards, major work has been carried out by the Willis firm, which has included tonal revision and it is now a most versatile instrument.

It is perhaps not generally known that the Willis firm were concerned, to a limited degree, with cinema organs at this time. The booklet *The Brangwyn Hall Organ*, by J. R. Alban and J. M. Fussell, records that circulars were sent to a number of cinema companies by Henry Willis III 'outlining the services the firm could provide' and 'among the cinemas which actually received Willis organs were The Elite at Kingston upon Thames, a cinema at East Sheen, the Palais de Luxe at Liverpool and the Whitechapel Rivoli'. They were, of course, concert organs and not of the cinema organ type.

The undertaking of the restoration of the Alexandra Palace organ has been a matter of great pride to Henry Willis IV, but it has been fraught with one difficulty after another during the past twenty-four years, and looking back to 1970, when Willis's first estimate was sent in, the refusal of the GLC to entertain any work being done, and the subsequent sale of the organ to Henry Willis IV in order to prevent it being broken up, and thus preserve it for the nation, it is a miracle that it now speaks again. As much as possible was removed to Willis's workshops for safe keeping, leaving the case, building frame and the 'shell', together with the huge 32ft pipes on the front. Then, in 1980, the west and central parts of the Palace, including the Great Hall and organ case etc., were destroyed in a disastrous fire. It was thought that this really was the end, but the Palace itself was rebuilt and a public appeal launched in 1982 by Yehudi Menuhin. Sufficient money was raised by 1985 to make a start on restoration work at the Petersfield Works and five years later the partly rebuilt organ was heard again. Costs, of course, had escalated; it has been the wish of Henry Willis that the organ could have been rebuilt as a whole, with a subsequent saving in cost, but this has been impossible and so parts of the Great, Swell, Pedal and Solo Organ, housed in temporary casework, were heard again on 19th August, 1990, to the great interest and delight of a large audience. The organ now stands on a gallery; there is no vast 'orchestra' to seat a choir and orchestra; when this is needed, temporary staging has to be hired and erected. When the fund is closed—which means that the organ is completed—Henry Willis will have designed a case, as far as possible in the style of the original one, and a diapered front with suitable colours to match this magnificent hall, which in itself is a triumph for the Alexandra Palace Trustees. It is constant use for one event or another and on the day of my visit during October 1993, there was an air of great liveliness throughout the Palace, which was most encouraging. I was not able to hear the organ, for the Hall was in use for a Needlework Exhibition; I understand, however, that it makes a most thrilling sound. The difficulties suffered by Henry Willis and his staff can be imagined, when I say that shortly after the addition of further stops to the Choir Organ in the Autumn of 1993, torrential rain entered the building through the roof immediately above the organ, resulting in the dismantling of the Choir division for treatment and the replacement of the newly installed pipework, which comprised the dulciana, viola 4, nason flute, nazard, piccolo, tierce, mixture 17·19·22, trumpet, clarion—all unenclosed. As this chapter is being completed, work is being started on the provision of five more stops to this division and due to a grant, it is expected that the completion of the remainder will have been achieved by the end of 1994. The present appeal committee Secretary, Dr. G. G. Wyld, with great drive and enthusiasm, is exploring every avenue for grants and is hoping that all organ lovers will contribute something, *no matter how small*, so that once more, we may hear in all its glory, what was described by Marcel Dupré as 'the finest Concert Organ in Europe'.

At the time of writing, the organ comprises the specification overleaf, played from the 1929 console in front of the organ on the gallery.

When complete, the Choir Organ will consist of those stops already mentioned as being playable, together with those projected, which are: contra viole, viole da gamba, viola celestes, claribel flute, lieblich gedackt, gemshorn, corno di bassetto, cor anglais, tremolo on light wind. There still remains the completion of the Great, Swell, Solo and Pedal Organs, as well as the provision of a case—a formidable task indeed, which Henry Willis dearly wishes to accomplish, but it is not an impossible one if support is forthcoming.

In a leaflet, Henry Willis has this to say: 'The Father Willis organ in St George's Hall, Liverpool, which I restored to my father's specification and with his guidance and help, was a great apprenticeship for the work on the Ally Pally. Much of that pipework too was severely mutilated and its restoration was of particular interest to me, especially as I was dealing with my father's pristine pipework in Liverpool Cathedral as well'. It is important therefore to record the 1929 specification—*it must be re-created!*

THE ALEXANDRA PALACE, LONDON 1994

GREAT ORGAN

	ft
Open Diapason No. 1	8
Open Diapason No. 2	8
Clarabella	8
Quint	5⅓
Octave No. 1	4
Octave No. 2	4
Flute Couverte	4
Octave Quint	2⅔
Super Octave	2
Mixture 24·26·29	III

SWELL ORGAN

Rohr Flöte	8
Salicional	8
Principal	4
Flauto Traverso	4
Twelfth	2⅔
Fifteenth	2
Sesquialtera 17·19·22	III

Cornopean	8
Clarion	4

SOLO ORGAN

Contra Tromba	16
Tromba Harmonic	8
Tuba Harmonic	8
Clarion Harmonic	4

PEDAL ORGAN

Open Bass No. 2	16
Bourdon	16
Principal	8
Flute	8
Super Octave	4
Octave Flute	4
Bombarde	32
Trombone	16
Octaves on Pedal Chorus	

THE ALEXANDRA PALACE 1929

GREAT ORGAN

	ft
Double Open Diapason	16
Bourdon	16
Open Diapason No. 1	8
Open Diapason No. 2	8
Open Diapason No. 3	8
Clarabella	8
Quint	5⅓
Octave 1	4
Octave 2	4
Flute Couverte	4
Octave Quint	2⅔
Super Octave	2
Seventeenth	1⅗
Furniture	II
Sesquialtera	III
Mixture	III
Double Trumpet	16
Trumpet-harmonic	8
Trumpet	8
Posaune	8
Clarion	4

SWELL ORGAN

Double Open Diapason	16
Lieblich Bourdon	16
Open Diapason No. 1	8
Open Diapason No. 2	8
Flute Couverte	8
Rohr Flute	8
Salicional	8
Vox Angelica (tenor C)	8
Principal	4
Flauto Traverso	4
Twelfth	2⅔

Fifteenth	2
Furniture	II
Sesquialtera	III
Mixture	III
Waldhorn	16
Cornopean	8
Hautboy	8
Vox Humana	8
Contra Posaune	16
Trumpet	8
Tremulant	

CHOIR ORGAN

Contra Viola	16
Viola da Gamba	8
Viola Célestes (tenor C)	8
Claribel Flute	8
Lieblich Gedackt	8
Dulciana	8
Gemshorn	4
Viola	4
Nason Flute	4
Nazard	2⅔
Piccolo	2
Tierce	1⅗
Mixture	III
Corno di Bassetto	8
Cor Anglais	8
Trumpet	8
Clarion	4
Tremulant	

SOLO ORGAN

Violoncello	8
Tibia	8

Viole d'Orchestre	8	Octave Viola	4
Violes Celestes (bb)	8	Octave Flute	4
Flute-harmonique	8	Sesquialtera	III
Octave 'Cello	4	Mixture (2)	III
Concert Flute	4	Bombarde (1)	32
Solo Nazard	2⅔	Trombone (1)	16
Piccolo-harmonique	2	Ophicleide (2)	16
Bassoon	8	Clarion (2)	8
Orchestral Oboe	8	Octaves on Pedal Chorus (1)	–
Orchestral Clarinet	8	Octaves on Pedal Chorus (2)	–
Contra Tromba	16
Tromba-harmonic	8
Tuba-harmonic	8
Clarion-harmonic	4
Tubular Bells (20 notes)	–
Tremulant	–

PEDAL ORGAN

Double Open Bass	32
Double Open Diapason	32
Sub Bass	16
Open Bass No. 1	16
Open Bass No. 2	16
Contra Basso	16
Bourdon	16
Bass Viola	16
Octave	8
Principal (1)	8
Viola	8
Flute	8
Super Octave (1)	4

ACCESSORIES

8 adjustable combination pistons to each department
8 general pistons to the whole organ
8 reversible pistons to couplers
1 locking piston for the adjustment of pistons
1 cancel to each department   1 general cancel
"Doubles Off" by tilting tablet in Swell key slip
"Pedal Stops Off" by tilting tablet in Great key slip
3 balanced swell pedals   General crescendo pedal
"Full Organ" toe piston, with indicator
Swell pedal switch plate
Electro-pneumatic action   Electric rotary blower

WIND PRESSURES

Great: flue work 5 ins. and 6 ins., reeds 5–15 ins.
Swell: flue work 5–6 ins., reeds 6–20 ins.
Choir: 6 ins. throughout
Solo: light pressure 10 ins., reeds 15–25 ins.
Pedal: flue work various, reeds 15–30 ins.

Contracts completed and in hand at the same time as the prolonged work at the Alexandra Palace comprises some interesting and important commissions. The Henry Willis III organ at St Magnus' Cathedral, Kirkwall, has undergone major work, including new electronic systems. The Lewis organ at St Mary the Virgin, Beddington, has been restored and electrified and the organ at St Michael in the Northgate, Oxford, has had a new Positif Organ as well as other work of importance throughout. The Brangwyn Hall organ is being rebuilt in stages, the most recent work being the rebuilding of the under Pedal bellows, the Positive drawstop machine and the central stack of three bellows. The beautiful Hunter organ at Hertford College, Oxford, has undergone major conservation with de-humidifying apparatus installed; St Peter's Church, Easton, Portland is now undergoing conservation work as well as having a de-humidifier fitted to reduce the damp from the church, while St Paul's Church, Finnart, Greenock, has had the leather motors restored and the rest of the organ cleaned and overhauled. Henry Willis (like his father before him) is particularly interested in tone production and a lot of tonal alterations and additions have been done here and there, including work such as a new trompette 8ft at All Saints' Church, Southampton.

Henry Willis & Sons Ltd. have been working from Brecon to Giffnock, Bucknell to Cusop, Twickenham to Dundee, Abergavenny to Kinnoull, moving organs, reconstructing them, cleaning, re-leathering and generally restoring instruments throughout the land.

Henry Willis IV has all the vigour and imagination of his father and illustrious great-grandfather before him, but the opportunities presented to him have not been so great. His achievements, therefore, have mostly been in connection with reconstructions, as well as the difficult task of running a national tuning and repair service. He takes pride in being very much a working organ builder, specialising in flue voicing and tonal finishing; being 'chair bound' in the office does not appeal to him. He is a great character with a unique sense of humour. He is an active Vice-President as well as Treasurer of the Federation of Master Organ Builders, is President and Honorary Treasurer of the Incorporated Society of Organ Builders, was Master of the Worshipful Company of Musicians between 1991–92 and is still a member of the Court of that Company.

above
The works of Rushworth & Dreaper in Mill Lane, Islington, Liverpool; an early photograph. It is thought that Walter Rushworth is standing at the bench in the immediate foreground.
Courtesy of Alastair Rushworth
right
Malvern Priory, organ by Rushworth & Dreaper
below
William Rushworth, founder of the firm, with his sons Alfred, Edwin and Walter.
Courtesy of Alastair Rushworth

left
Dr. Alfred Hollins at the console of the
organ of St George's West, Edinburgh.
From a photo given to the Author
by Dr. Hollins

above
The Rushworth & Dreaper console,
Hull City Hall. Photo by Nigel Rhodes

below left
St Mary-le-Bow, London.
Photo by Stewart Bate Ltd., Liverpool

below
Guildford Cathedral: the console.
Courtesy of Alastair Rushworth

top left
Rushworth & Dreaper: logo style
in current use

above
Gray & Davison name-plate, 'Branch House,
9 Russell Street, Liverpool'

above right
Alastair Rushworth

below
The present factory of Henry Willis &
Sons, Petersfield, Hants. Photo by
W. Davies Owens, 1994

Father Henry Willis (1821–1901)
He is seated at the console of the organ in Blenheim Palace in 1891, where he was engaged in
tonal finishing. The mount is signed and dated by the Duke of Marlborough. Courtesy of Bruce Buchanan

above
Henry Willis II

below
Henry Willis IV.
Photo by Ian M. Frost, 1954

above
Vincent Willis (1848–1928)
as a young man. Courtesy of
Bruce Buchanan

below
John Sinclair Willis.
A photograph taken at the
Conacher works in 1994

centre
Henry Willis III.
Photo by Ian M. Frost, 1954

above "Willis" sliderless chest in course of construction, Ferndale Road Works, London. *The Rotunda*, April 1927. Courtesy of the firm.

below The Ferndale Road Works, London, in the 1920s. Courtesy of Bruce Buchanan

above
Reed voicing machine,
Ferndale Road works *c*.1929.
Photo by the Author

below
The main hall, the Willis works
at Liverpool, *c*.1929. Courtesy
of Henry Willis & Sons Ltd

centre
George Deeks, reed voicer,
Henry Willis & Sons Ltd.
From *The Rotunda*, September
1929. Courtesy of the firm

right
Richard J. Piper, flue voicer
c.1929. He later left the firm
and became Vice-President and
tonal director of Austin Organs,
Inc. He died in 1978 at the age
of 74. Photo by the Author

above
St George's Hall, Liverpool.
Photo, Gilbert Benham in the late 1920s

Herbert F. Ellingford

below left
Herbert F. Ellingford at the Father Willis console, St George's Hall, Liverpool. Photo by Gilbert Benham

below
War damage to the interior of the organ, St George's Hall, Liverpool.
Courtesy of Henry Willis IV

above
Former Prime Minister, Lady Thatcher, talking to
David Wells in his workshop, Brunswick Business
Park, Liverpool, 1989.
By kind permission of Margaret Robinson
Photography and Merseyside Task Force

left
St George's Hall, Liverpool, the console,
after re-modelling by David Wells in 1991.
Photo by David Wells

below left
The Alexandra Palace, with the
Father Willis console intact

below
The Alexandra Palace, showing the Father
Willis console, from a photograph taken by
the Author, shortly before the restoration
commenced in 1929

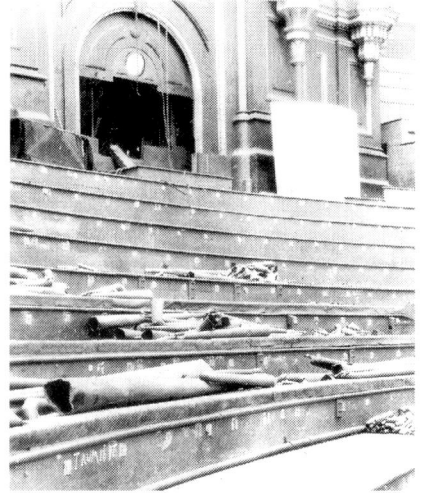

above and right
The Alexandra Palace: first stages of the restoration
in 1929. Photos by the Author

centre left and right
An ivory pass given to Father Willis by the Trustees of
The Alexandra Palace. Courtesy of Bruce Buchanan

left
Henry Willis III
console, The Alexandra
Palace. Photo by
Gilbert Benham

A contrast.—

left: Winthorpe Church, near Skegness. Scudamore type organ by Father Willis. Photo by the Author

above: The Junior Development Plan Organ, Opus 1, Convent of Our Lady of the Taper, Flint, 1958

below left
Damaged pipework from the Alexandra Palace, in store at Conacher's factory. Photo by the Author, 1994

below right
This distinctive logo has been used by the house of Willis for many years, to my knowledge, certainly as far back as the late 1920s

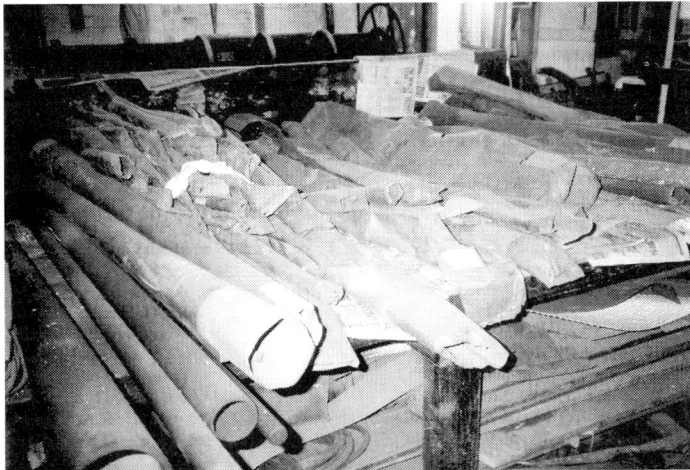

above
Liverpool Cathedral: north casework.
Photo by Valentines, 1930s

above right
Liverpool Cathedral: the original
console. Photo by Gilbert Benham

below right
Liverpool Cathedral: the new mobile
nave console. Courtesy of David Wells

below
Harry Goss Custard at the re-modelled
console (1958–60) by Willis.
Photo by Gilbert Benham

above
Liverpool Cathedral:
the 32ft Contra Bombarde.
Photo by the Author, 1993

below
Liverpool Cathedral:
part of the Positive Organ.
Photo by the Author, 1993

above and below
Liverpool Cathedral: gallery console, right
and left jambs, as re-modelled in 1991.
Photo by the Author, 1993

left
Liverpool Cathedral. The Lady Chapel organ

above
Liverpool Cathedral. Mobile nave console
designed by Henry Willis IV, 1965, now
preserved in the blowing chamber.
Photo by the Author, 1994

below
Liverpool Cathedral. Main blowers (1 & 2).
Photo by the Author, 1994

CHAPTER XII

The Whiteley Family of Chester and Chislehurst

THE firm of C. and J. Whiteley of Chester was formed in 1869 by Charles Hickson Whiteley (born 1835 in Salford) and his brother, John Handforth (born 1838 in Manchester). Charles served his apprenticeship with Jackson of Liverpool and from there went to Gray & Davison at their Liverpool branch. About 1862, he moved to Leeds where he looked after the organ in Leeds Town Hall. By 1869, he felt it was the right time to establish his own business, and so with his brother John (who had trained, presumably, with Gray & Davison), they commenced trading from premises at 1 City Walls (North), Northgate, Chester, which they occupied until 1872 when they moved to Victoria Road. By the turn of the century a further move had been made to Crane Bank. The firm was then known as Charles H. Whiteley, for brother John had died in 1874.

As far as can be ascertained, the firm did little advertising in those days, but The Cheshire County Library has been able to trace the following brief notice in the *Chester Directory* for 1870.

C. & J. WHITELEY,
Organ Builders,
CITY WALLS, NORTHGATE, CHESTER.
Tuners of the Cathedral Organ.
TESTIMONIALS ON APPLICATION.

A small three-manual organ, the specification of which appeared in *The Choir* for 26th August, 1876, gives us an idea of the type of instrument of this size being built at that time.

> The new organ in the church of "All Hallows," Allerton, which has just been opened, although (as usual with organ builders), "not quite finished," has been built by Messrs. Whiteley, of Chester, and its cost has been defrayed by a number of residents in the neighbourhood. It is a three-manual and pedal organ, the following being the specification.—
>
> GREAT ORGAN.— Open diapason, 8 feet; gamba, 8 feet; clarabella, 8 feet; principal, 4 feet; harmonic flute, 4 feet; twelfth, 2⅔ feet; fifteenth, 2 feet; mixture, 3 ranks; trumpet, 8 feet.
>
> SWELL ORGAN.— Bourdon, 16 feet; open diapason, 8 feet; salicional, 8 feet; stopped diapason, 8 feet; gemshorn, 4 feet; doublette, 2 ranks; cornopean, 8 feet; oboe, 8 feet; clarion, 4 feet; and tremulant.
>
> CHOIR ORGAN.— Dulciana, 8 feet; pierced gamba, 8 feet; lieblich gedacht, 4 feet; and stopped flöte, 4 feet.
>
> PEDAL ORGAN.— Open diapason, 16 feet; violone, 16 feet; and violoncello, 8 feet.
>
> There are also the usual couplers and composition pedals, and the organ is blown by hydraulic pressure.

In *The Musical Standard* for 14th February, 1880, it was reported that 'an organ recital was given by Mr Minshall of the City Temple, London, on the organ in Chester Street Congregational Church, Wrexham, on Wednesday, 4th February, on an organ recently erected by Whiteley of Chester. There was a large and appreciative audience'.

The firm built an organ at Eaton Hall, for the Duke of Westminster, together with many instruments in Cheshire, the North of England, North Wales, the Midlands and beyond. Their work was of a high quality and deserves a study in greater depth than is possible here.

Only seven years after their establishment, the Chester Cathedral authorities then had sufficient confidence in their work to commission them to completely rebuild the Gray & Davison organ of 1844, which was then the largest Cathedral organ in England, with the exception of that at York; its cost was £1,400—a goodly sum of money in those days. Whiteley's organ was situated at the entrance to the north transept on a loft, and with a case designed by Sir George Gilbert Scott. Five stops of the Choir Organ had to be accommodated in a small case designed by Scott on his new wooden screen dividing quire and nave. The cost of this work was £2,000 and a very fine instrument resulted.

The specification appeared in *The Choir* for July 29th, 1876, and differs slightly from that in John T. Belcher's attractive booklet, *The Organs of Chester Cathedral*.

> The following is the specification of the organ in Chester Cathedral, as re-constructed by Messrs. Whiteley, of Chester:—
>
> ECHO AND SOLO ORGAN.— Lieblich bourdon, 16 feet; viola, 8; lieblich gedacht, 8; vox angelica, tenor C, 8; lieblich flute, 4; flautina, 2; vox humana, 8. [These stops are enclosed in a swell-box, and voiced to a very light pressure of wind.] Diapason harmonic, 8; harmonic flute, 4; tromba, 8. [Borrowed from great organ.] Orchestral trumpet, 8; tuba mirabilis, 8.
>
> SWELL ORGAN.— Bourdon, 16 feet; open diapason, 8; viola di gamba, 8; stopped diapason, 8; suabe flute, 4; principal, 4; fifteenth, 2; mixture, 4 and 5 ranks, various; contra fagotto, 16 feet; cornopean, 8; trumpet, 8; oboe, 8; clarion, 4.
>
> GREAT ORGAN.— Double open diapason, 16 feet; contra gamba, 16; bourdon, 16; open diapason, major, 8; open diapason, minor, 8; flute-à-pavilion, 8; stopped diapason, 8; harmonic flute, 8; principal, 4; harmonic flute, 4; twelfth, 2⅔; fifteenth, 2; fourniture, 5 ranks, various; mixture, 4 ranks, various; contra posaune, 16 feet; tromba, 8; clarion, 4.
>
> CHOIR ORGAN.— Double dulciana, 16 feet; open diapason, 8; pierced gamba, tenor C, 8; salicional, 8; clarabella, 8; stopped diapason, 8; principal, 4; stopped flute, 4; piccolo, 2; clarinet, 8.
>
> PEDAL ORGAN.— Double open diapason, 32 feet; open diapason, 16; violon, 16; sub-bass, 16; octave, 8; violoncello, 8; quint, 10⅔; fifteenth, 4; trombone, 16; bombarde, 8.
>
> ACCESSORY STOPS, &c.— Swell octave; swell sub-octave; swell to great; swell to choir; solo sub-octave; solo to great; solo to pedal; swell to pedal; great to pedal; choir to pedal.
>
> Compass of manuals, CC to A, 58 notes; ditto of pedals, CCC to F, 30 notes.
>
> Five composition pedals to the great organ to act also on the pedal stops. Four composition pedals to the swell. Pedal to bring on and take off the octave couplers to the swell organ. The stops to draw at an angle of about forty degrees. The couplers to be arranged in a row over the upper manual. Separate wind reservoirs, with different pressures to each manual. The bellows are to be blown by hydraulic power. The pneumatic lever to be applied to the great, swell, and pedal organs, and also to the drawing of the stops.

It will be noted that hydraulic power was to be used for blowing, whereas the booklet states that a 6 h.p. steam engine was employed and remained in use until 1910, when Hill & Son rebuilt the organ.

This is explained by the fact that there were difficulties with the hydraulic blower from the very beginning, and several experts were called in. There is no record of the maker; at that time there were several hydraulic engines on the market made by highly reputable firms. However, the situation may be summed up by a letter in *The Chester Chronicle* of 19th August, 1876, from Dean Howson, an extract from which reads: 'Finally, I must mention the apparatus for blowing the organ which must be made perfect without delay. Hydraulic pressure has been found inapplicable to the case; we have been disappointed in the attempt to use a gas engine and we are now having recourse to steam'. The inconvenience of such a method in a busy Cathedral with services, rehearsals and recitals, can be imagined. There were one or two stop discrepancies too: Echo and Solo Organs—no mention of the tromba 8ft (borrowed from the Great). An orchestral oboe was placed on the orchestral trumpet slide by Gray & Davison in 1895, when one or two other alterations were made. Great Organ: original contra gamba 16ft replaced by gamba 8ft by Gray & Davison. Choir Organ: dulciana 8ft in booklet instead of salicional, gemshorn 4ft and hohlflute 4ft additional to those published in *The Choir*. A two rank mixture replaced the original Pedal quint in the 1895 work by Gray & Davison.

The booklet gives other details: tremulant to Swell reeds and to Echo Organ; the Echo and screen division of the Choir Organ, on tubular-pneumatic action with separate reservoirs for each manual, ranging in pressures from 2¼ ins. to 7 ins. It would appear that plans were changed somewhat after the specification appeared in *The Choir*.

This was a most comprehensive and imaginative tonal scheme; with the liberal use of spotted metal and skilful voicing, the instrument made a great impression in the district and beyond. To quote the Revd. B. B. Edmonds: 'There was hostility in the trade that such a new firm should secure the important Chester Cathedral contract over the "big boys" in London. Some of the other firms tried to nobble them by tempting their men away with higher wages, but because they were a family firm, they were able to complete the job'. He also quotes the Revd. Andrew Freeman: "They were strongly recommended for the job by the late Dr. Audsley and the event proved that they were fully capable of turning out a very fine organ". Although J. H. Whiteley had died in 1874, the other two brothers, Reginald Heber (1844–1918) and Henry Shilton Whiteley (1846–1905) were working in the firm at that time and this would be a great help in the carrying out of the Cathedral contract. They remained until 1893 when they parted company with Charles for some unknown reason, and founded their own business known as H. & H. Whiteley.

C. H. Whiteley died in 1913 when the firm passed to two sons, John Henry (born 1862) and Samuel Charles (born 1876). J. H. W. retired in 1939 and died in 1942, leaving S. C. W. as sole proprietor until his death in 1966, when Hill, Norman & Beard took control. The firm was active in the early 1960s, for *Musical Opinion* reported that the Bishop of Stockport had dedicated a new two-manual organ installed by Charles Whiteley & Co. Ltd. of Chester, in the chapel of the Deva Hospital, Chester. Other work at that time included the rebuilding of the organ which was in Holy Trinity Church, Chester, prior to the closing of the church and which was being installed in the new church of Holy Trinity-without-the-Walls at Blacon, Chester. It had three manuals, forty-three drawstops and a detached console. Work on the very fine Brindley & Foster in Christ Church, Chester, had been completed, and a recital given by Malcolm Boyle, B.MUS., Organist of Chester Cathedral from 1942–49.

H. & H. WHITELEY

A break away firm from the Charles Whiteley was that of H. & H. Whiteley, founded in 1893 by Reginald Heber and Henry Shilton, brothers of Charles; it can only be assumed that a rift had occurred in the family for reasons unknown.

After H. S. Whiteley's death in 1905, his brother ran the business from Garden Lane, Chester, but the workshops remained in Saltney until 1919 when they were transferred to Sandy Lane, Boughton, Chester. Under the name as used hitherto, 'Cathedral Organ Works', Saltney workshops were retained as a warehouse until the mid-1930s. When Thomas Arthur Shilton Whiteley died on 13th October, 1927, Colin Robert Whiteley (1888–1914), son of H. S. W., became sole proprietor. He did much to expand the business at this time. In particular, he extended greatly the tuning and maintenance connections in South Wales and built some new organs in the area. As well as consolidating the firm's presence in North and Mid Wales, Cheshire and Lancashire, he found new business in the Midlands. On his death, Mrs Elizabeth Whiteley became the owner, the practical side of the firm being the responsibility of Francis John Richard Whiteley (1894–1953), brother of Colin. He was the last of the Whiteleys running that business and so the goodwill

H. & H. WHITELEY,

ORGAN BUILDERS,

121, GARDEN LANE, CHESTER.

Works: SALTNEY.

Tuners of the Eaton Hall Organs.
ORGANS REBUILT, ENLARGED & RE-VOICED.
Tunings and Repairs a speciality.

was purchased by Charles Whiteley & Co., the premises being sold to a woodworking company. Unfortunately, I have no record of their work.

I understand that the existence of two separate firms of organ builders in Chester, of the same name, caused confusion amongst potential customers. There was also tension between the two firms when enquiries for the one went to the other.

HENRY POYSER

When the Chester Cathedral organ was rebuilt by William Hill & Son in 1910, their foreman was Thomas Poyser, who had working with him his brother, Henry, who had been employed by Gray & Davison for some twenty-five years. About 1912, the Hill firm had many tuning and maintenance contracts in the area. They therefore came to an agreement with Henry Poyser for him to live in Chester and take over on his own account these contracts as well as establishing his own business. His works, office and home were at 34 Nicholas Street, and for a time in the 1930s there were workshops in Lower Bridge Street. The firm had the tuning and maintenance contract at the Cathedral for over forty years. He advertised as 'Specialist in Touch and Tone.' Henry Poyser died before the outbreak of World War II, but his son, Henry Eaton Poyser, continued the business until his retirement in about 1955.

J. W. WHITELEY, CHISLEHURST

My first acquaintance with J. W. Whiteley was at his works in Chislehurst during school holidays spent at Beckenham during 1929. I knew nothing of his history, but on realising my interest in his work, his rather gruff manner relaxed and I gleaned much information which has taken some sixty-five years to put fully into print! When he told me that he had done some voicing for Jardine of Manchester, his face lit up with pride when I mentioned the three-manual Jardine organ of 1891 in Newland Congregational Church, Lincoln, for he had been responsible for the voicing of much of the flue work there for the firm. A warm friendship developed between us and he corresponded with me for many years, almost up to the time of his death on 23rd May, 1940. Organ building completely absorbed him and looking back, it seems to me that he felt I was a kindred spirit.

Born in Liverpool in 1865, he was a chorister of Chester Cathedral and probably took part in the opening ceremony of the rebuild of the organ there in 1876. He served his apprenticeship under C. H. Whiteley at Chester; thereafter he worked as a voicer for Jardine & Co. for a time, then at the newly-formed Robert Hope-Jones Electric Organ Co., where he became head voicer, being personally responsible for all the string toned stops and flutes. Here, he taught W. C. Jones flue voicing and I can but regret that I never got round to discussing him with 'Billy' Jones during our conversations at Lincoln.

His connection with Jardine & Co. resulted in the Newland Congregational Church, Lincoln, becoming the fortunate possessor of an outstanding instrument during 1891. The specification was:

NEWLAND CONGREGATIONAL CHURCH, LINCOLN 1891

3 manuals: CC to G, 56 notes   Pedal: CCC to F, 30 notes

Photo by the Author

GREAT ORGAN	ft	SWELL ORGAN	
		Double Diapason	16
Double Open Diapason	16	Open Diapason	8
Open Diapason	8	Salicional	8
Gamba	8	Voix Célestes	8
Clarabella	8	Rohr Gedacht	8
Principal	4	Gemshorn	4
Harmonic Flute	4	Harmonic Piccolo	2
Twelfth	2⅔	Mixture 17·19·22	III
Fifteenth	2	Cornopean	8
Trumpet	8	Oboe	8
		Tremulant	

CHOIR ORGAN	
Dulciana	8
Lieblich Gedacht	8
Wald Flute	4
Clarinet	8
Vox Humana	8
Tremulant	

PEDAL ORGAN

Open Diapason	16
Bourdon	16
Bass Flute	8

COUPLERS

Swell to Great   Swell to Choir   Choir to Great
Swell Octave   Swell Sub Octave   Swell to Pedal
Great to Pedal   Choir to Pedal

ACCESSORIES

4 composition pedals each to Great, Swell & Pedal
Balanced swell pedal to Swell Organ
Lever pedal to box enclosing Choir reeds
3 reservoirs to Swell, Great and Pedal, and Choir

WIND PRESSURES

Great, Pedal: 3½ ins. Swell: 3¼ ins. Choir: 2¾ ins.

Tracker-pneumatic action to Swell and Great Organs
Tracker action to Choir Organ
Tubular-pneumatic action to Pedal Organ

Kinetic Blower

The cost of the organ was £753, with the addition of
£19 for decorating the pipes, and £85 for the case.

I contributed a detailed article on this superb example of Victorian organ building in *Musical Opinion* for May 1956, where I had this to say: 'The chorus work has real personality, with clarity in individual ranks and ensemble resulting from the skilful voicing of well made pipes of first class metal, well scaled and on low wind, with an eye not only to quality of tone, but the perfect blend of each rank with its fellow.' From a chorus point of view, the outstanding feature of the instrument was the Great Organ flue work which was complete from an open metal double to twelfth and fifteenth.

This instrument received the highest praise from some of our most distinguished organists who gave a number of recitals in its later years. When the congregation moved to St Andrew's Presbyterian Church, becoming 'St Andrew's with Newland' in 1973, the fine old Gothic building was eventually purchased by another denomination who had no use for the organ and it remained silent from then onwards. When urgent restoration was necessary, involving the foundations and the roof of the building in 1992, the organ was scrapped and the interior re-modelled. My reactions, as well as those of others (far and wide), may be imagined. For myself, I had known and loved the organ since the age of nineteen, and had on occasions deputised as organist. I was able to save, however, the first Kinetic Fan Blower which was made by the Cousans brothers in Lincoln in 1902, and installed at Newland on loan for a period and then purchased. A number of organ builders examined it there, including Robert Hope-Jones, who used a large installation at Worcester Cathedral. Thus was born the Kinetic Co., the first to use fans in series, and it was not long before blowers found their way to various parts of the world. Their prototype at Newland happily is now exhibited at the Museum of Lincolnshire Life, Lincoln, where it will remain for posterity.

After spending some time with Hope-Jones, it would seem that Whiteley could see 'the writing on the wall' as far as security of employment was concerned, for he moved to join the staff of Casson's Patent Organ Co. Ltd. (late Michell & Thynne) which did not last long, for it was re-named Beale & Thynne, trading from Woodstock Road, Shepherds Bush, by May 1894, when they advertised in *Musical Opinion*. This business ceased about 1902, when it was forced into bankruptcy. Thynne had died previously and for the last remaining years, Whiteley was designer and voicer, having received valuable experience with that 'master voicer' William Thynne, who was well known as a great artist, not only in this country, but in the USA, where he worked for a time.

He voiced a number of organs built by the firm, including that in the concert hall of the Battersea Polytechnic and St Stephen's, Wandsworth. Gilbert Benham reviewed the latter instrument in *The Organ*, No. 41, July 1931. The Wandsworth organ started life as a Bevington chamber organ; it was enlarged and revoiced in 1900 for St Stephen's and officially was the work of Beale & Thynne—in effect it was designed, voiced and finished by Whiteley. Six years later, when he was in business for himself, he revised the wind pressures, with the consequent revoicing of the pipework, at the same time adding new drawstop action, piston control machines etc. Gilbert Benham described the Great diapason chorus as 'glorious';

the viole de salon on the Choir was 'beyond his powers of description without seeming extravagant', while the Swell viole d'orchestre was 'one of the most sublime stops imaginable... all the string work prompts the fanciful thoughts that the pipes must be silver'.

ST STEPHEN'S CHURCH, WANDSWORTH 1900

GREAT ORGAN

	ft
Double Open	16
Open Diapason (large)	8
Open Diapason (small)	8
Bell Diapason	8
Major Flute	8
Claribel	8
Rohr Flöte	8
Dulciana	8
Principal	4
Harmonic Flute	4
Twelfth	2⅔
Fifteenth	2
Full Mixture	IV
Double Trumpet (ext.)	16
Trumpet (harmonic)	8
Clarion (ext., harmonic)	4

SWELL ORGAN

Bourdon	16
Geigen	8
Lieblich Gedackt	8
Viole d'orchestre	8
Violon Célestes (flat)	8
Viole Célestes (sharp)	8
Echo Salicional	8
Principal	4
Wald Flöte	4
Flautina	2
Mixture	III
Contra fagotto	16
Cornopean	8
Clarion (harmonic trebles)	4
Oboe	8
Vox Humana	8

CHOIR ORGAN

Open Diapason	8
Stopped Diapason	8
Viole de salon	8
Dolce	8
Unda Maris	8
Suabe Flöte	4
Piccolo	2

Orchestral Oboe	8
Clarinet	8

PEDAL ORGAN

Harmonic Bass	32
Open Wood	16
Open Metal (from Great)	16
Grand Bourdon	16
Bourdon (from Swell)	16
Octave Diapason	8
Violone	8
Flute	8
Ophicleide	16
Trumpet (from Great)	16
Tromba (ext. Ophicleide)	8

COUPLERS

Choir to Great   Swell to Great   Swell to Choir
Swell to Great Sub   Swell to Great Super
Swell Sub Octave   Swell Super Octave
Swell to Pedal   Great to Pedal   Choir to Pedal
Great pistons to pedals

ACCESSORIES

5 pistons each to Great and Swell, 3 to Choir
2 pistons for couplers
1 piston on each manual reducing pedal to Bourdon
3 pedals to Pedal Organ
Reversible pedal to Great to Pedal
Ventil pedal giving diapasons and unison couplers
Ventil pedal for full organ and unison couplers
Tremulants to Swell (low and high wind)
Choir tremulant

WIND PRESSURES

Great: flues, 5 ins.; major flute and reeds, 8 ins.
Swell: flue and quiet reeds, 5 ins.;
chorus and viole, 8 ins.
Choir: all 3½ ins.
Pedal: flue, 5 ins.; reeds, 12 ins.
Coupler action: 12½ ins.; pistons etc., 18½ ins.

Discus 7½ h.p. motor

Whiteley founded his own business in London in 1902, but at what address I have not been able to ascertain. From there he was invited by the Los Angeles Art Organ Co. to voice the organ exhibited by them for the 1903–4 Great Exhibition, St Louis, Missouri, later installed in the Kansas City Hall. This later formed the foundation of the celebrated organ in the Wanamaker Store, Philadelphia. In a note contributed to *Musical Opinion* for February 1913, Whiteley had this to say: 'Whilst I did not voice every pipe, I voiced by far the greater portion and finished and adapted the remainder in accord with what I considered to be the most satisfactory result possible within the limits of the conditions and the time at my disposal. I personally feel grateful to Mr Wanamaker for his enterprise in finding a permanent home for this instrument; also, I extend my congratulations to the craftsmen who have been engaged upon the repair and re-erection'. Whilst in the States, he carried out voicing on some other instruments for the same company. His voicing was awarded the 'Grand Prize, St Louis, 1904'.

That great authority on W. T. Best, J. Mewburn Levien, in a letter to *Musical Opinion* dated August 1st, 1940, spoke of Whiteley's appreciation of Best, regarding him as "the greatest master of the organ"; he once said that in his young days he had never missed an opportunity of hearing Best play. On one occasion he was in charge of an organ on which Best was to give a recital. 'The combination pedal mechanism did not work accurately and there was no time to put it right. Best, coming early for his all-day practice (as was his wont), began testing the mechanism and pushed down a combination pedal. Whiteley, before Best could give utterance to the disapproval his countenance showed in a instant, said "I will make that all right tonight Mr Best". "How will you do that?" asked Best. Whiteley replied "I shall be inside the organ all through the recital and will steady the mechanism with my hands". So, when the time came, into the organ went Whiteley and lying face downwards and stretching his arms out above his head, controlled the mechanism all the time with his hands. He could hear Best, he said, chuckling to himself as he gave a few more pushes to the combination pedals than he would otherwise have done, just to keep Whiteley busy. But a good tip was forthcoming as soon as Whiteley emerged from the interior of the organ.'

On Whiteley's return from the USA, he was engaged by E. G. Meers to rebuild and enlarge the residence organ in his home at Chislehurst, where Whiteley eventually settled when he left London. Dr. W. L. Sumner knew this organ well and was greatly impressed by it. Quoting from his letter to *Musical Opinion* in October 1964, he said 'I went to see it and was impressed by its quality. The voicing was superb. I can remember the wealth of spotted metal, even the 32ft reed. The soft strings were gorgeous. This was in 1921 at Chislehurst'. Eight years later, Whiteley went to Sydney, New South Wales, to superintend the erection of this organ which had been sold to the Chapter of St Andrew's Cathedral there, of which it has been said 'that it was one of the most massive and beautiful ecclesiastical instruments in Australia'. Here is the specification of the instrument.

ST ANDREW'S CATHEDRAL, SYDNEY, N.S.W. 1929

GREAT ORGAN

	ft
Violone	16
Open Diapason I	8
Open Diapason II	8
Open Diapason III	8
Clarabella	8
Dulciana	8
Octave Diapason	4
Principal	4
Flute	4
Mixture	II & III
Sesquialtera (without break)	III
Trumpet	8

SWELL ORGAN

Quintaton	16
Diapason Phonon	8
Salicional	8
Lieblich Gedackt	8
Unda Maris	II
Principal	4
Mixture	III
Cymbal	III
Double Trumpet	16
Cornopean	8
Oboe	8
Vox Humana	8

Clarion	4
Tremulant	

SOLO-CHOIR ORGAN

Contra Viola	16
Horn Diapason	8
Hohl Flute	8
Violin II ranks to CC	8
Violin *pp* II ranks to B flat	8
Hohl Flute	4
Piccolo	2
Clarionet	8
Orchestral Oboe	8
Tuba	8

PEDAL ORGAN

Contra Bourdon	32
Great Bass (wood)	16
Open Diapason (wood)	16
Violone (metal)	16
Contra Viola (from Solo)	16
Bourdon	16
Octave (from Open Wood)	8
Flute (from Bourdon)	8
Contra Trombone	32
Ophicleide	16
Tromba (from Ophicleide)	8

It has been said that the mechanism of Whiteley's organs were never one of their best features. Frank Uppington, who had been organist of St Stephen's, Wandsworth, for sixteen years, in a letter to *Musical Opinion* in October 1964, comments: 'Whiteley was a great and artistic voicer and his personality likeable once his gruff exterior was penetrated. The best way to do that was to evince a real interest in the organ and then you were his friend. He had odd ideas about advertising his work and for this reason he probably never achieved the reputation which his work merited'. We learn from Alan A. New (who served his apprenticeship with him), in a letter to *Musical Opinion* for December 1964, that J. W. W. had a 'fiery temper that cared not one "jot" for anybody, but with it all he was the kindest person imaginable and in those days looked after me like a father. His business acumen was completely nil, he did not know whether he was making either profit or loss, but owing to the inordinate time he took to complete an organ, I should say it was mostly loss. On the death of Mr E. G. Meers, his patronage came to an end and very little work of importance took place after, except perhaps the organ in St John's, Cowley Road, Oxford, which instrument I played possibly ten to fifteen years ago and thought it the most ethereally beautiful I had ever heard'. Another was at All Saints' Church, Maidstone.

After his death on 23rd May, 1940, at the age of seventy-five, his business was carried on for some years by J. W. Wallace, twenty years with the late John Whiteley. In his advertisement in *Musical Opinion* for October 1945, he offered 'Tunings, renovations, blowing plants installed, electric action, war damage work undertaken. Organ Works, Old Hill, Chislehurst, Kent'.

I count it a privilege to have known John W. Whiteley. The last letter I had from him on his official notepaper (on which he was described as 'Specialist and Expert in Organ Design and Voicing for Church, Chamber and Concert') spoke of difficulties at work, illness at home and an accident to himself. I fear that his last four years were fraught with some difficulties.

After his death, F. Webb, in his letter to *Musical Opinion*, said: 'The passing of such an artist in voicing is greatly to be regretted and is a loss to the organ building world. Those who are the fortunate possessors of pipework voiced by John W. Whiteley should treasure them as records of artistic craftsmanship not easily replaced'. In Lincoln, due to circumstances beyond our control, we have seen such pipework disappear for ever, which to the few of us who realise its value, is a matter for great concern.

The first Kinetic blower (1902) in the former
Newland Congregational Church, Lincoln. Photo by the Author

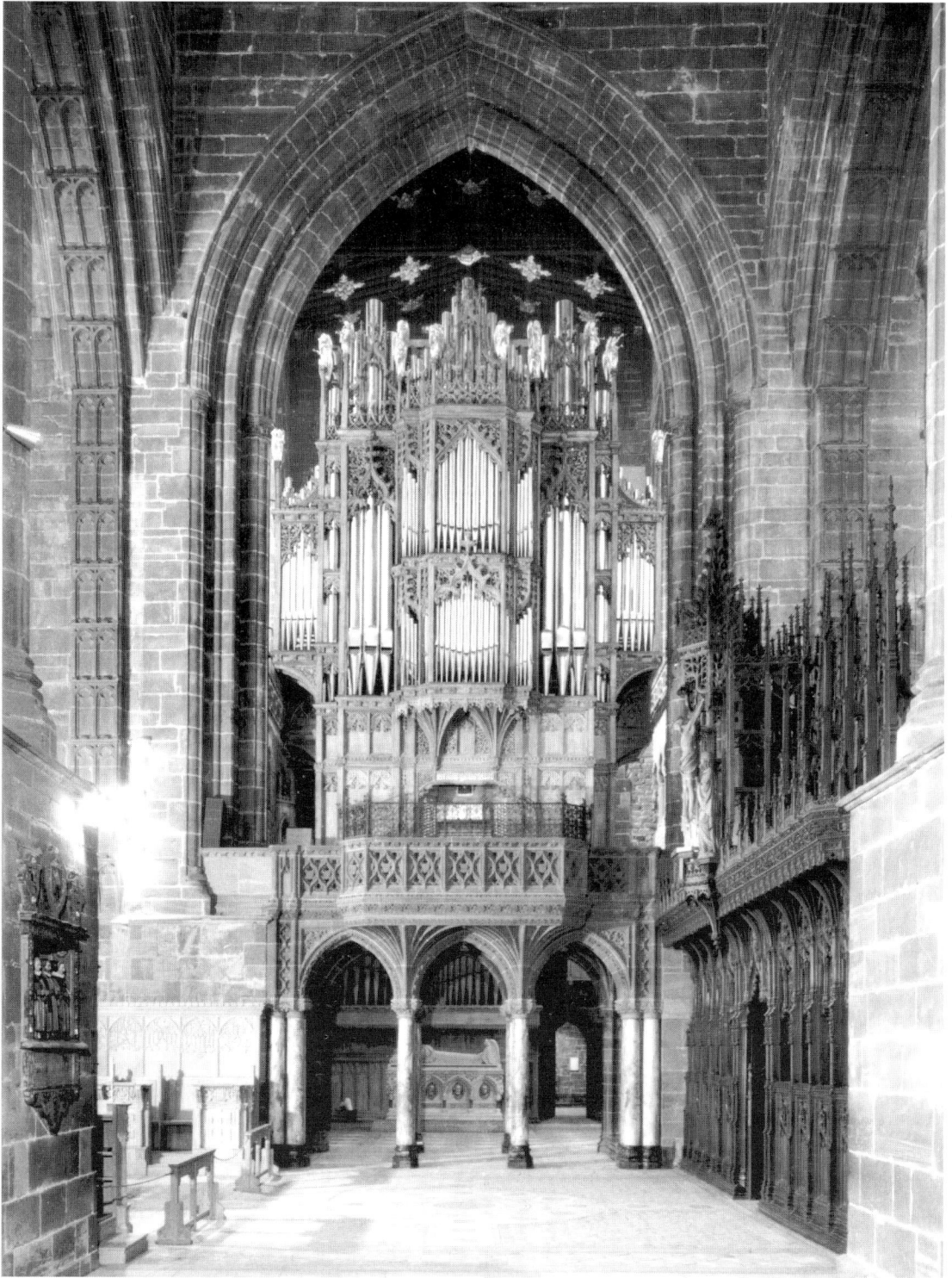

The Gilbert Scott case in Chester Cathedral. Courtesy of Rushworth & Dreaper Ltd

CHAPTER XIII

Kendal

WILKINSON & SONS EST. 1829

THE firm of Wilkinson of Kendal and Vowles of Bristol were notable in their day for fine tone and workmanship; they led the way in the north-west and west country respectively gaining a high reputation which brought them many orders. In both cases it is still possible to hear Victorian examples of their work which speak with their original voice, and how satisfying they sound. Neither was concerned with achieving fame but worked quietly on to produce a truly 'musical' instrument whether it be for a humble village church or a larger place of worship or public hall. In the prevailing climate of preservation in the organ world, we must treat them with respect and ensure that the hands of the 'rebuilder' does not attempt to update their tone by revoicing. In a letter to me dated 4th May, 1966, Miss Margaret Wilkinson had this to say: 'Like many families, mine never considered their work would one day be of interest and much which would now have been historically valuable data they carried in their heads!... so much of the craftsmanship of those times was so excellent and so lasting. In this connection it is perhaps of interest to tell you that last Autumn I was invited to a service in a small village church near here to commemorate the centenary of the organ which was built by my great-grandfather one hundred years ago and is still going and giving useful service. Incidentally, we still tune it!'

Founded in 1829 by William Wilkinson, who was a nephew of the well-known organ builder Thomas Greenwood (a partner in Greenwood Bros. of Halifax), Thomas was a cousin of John Greenwood, the celebrated musician who played before the Royal Family before he was fifteen years of age and was appointed organist of Leeds Parish Church in July 1821 'with all the excitement and expense of a contested Parliamentary Election.' No less than sixteen booths had to be erected for the convenience of the Clerks of the poll, when 'with native wit, each voter carried over his head a green bough, making the mass seem a moving grove and conveying to the initiated the intimation they they were all in favour of *Green-wood*.' Simon Lindley in his booklet, *The Organs, Organists & Choir of Leeds Parish Church* (1976) tells us: 'There were three candidates for the post (salary £50) and a three days' poll of the "parishioner lay-payers of the township of Leeds and the villages within the parish" was demanded. No fewer than 4089 Leeds folk were sufficiently interested to vote and John Greenwood was elected' (with a majority of 1107 over his two opponents). He held the post until 1828 and thirteen years later the organ was rebuilt by Messrs. Greenwood Bros.

Back to the Wilkinson family; William, who 'was a man of remarkable repartee and geniality of disposition possessed strong inventive powers.' He was a friend of William Sturgeon, the pioneer electrician who invented the electro-magnet and between them they carried out some of the earliest experiments in its application to organ action. Wilkinson commenced business in a small way in Kirkland, Kendal, near the Ring O' Bells Inn, but the workshop proved to be insufficient after a few years, necessitating larger premises and these were found in Stramongate, where work was carried on for a considerable time.

In 1856, William's son Thomas, who was a trained musician and scientist, was taken into partnership although he never intended to enter the business. Two years previously he had been appointed organist of Ambleside Parish Church, a position which he held with great distinction for thirty-five years. He found that he thoroughly enjoyed the craft of organ building; moreover, he liked to open his finished products too. At one such opening it is recorded that 'the large and commodious building was filled by a most respectable assemblage'. Thomas made a great contribution to the work of the firm by introducing improved methods in pipe-scaling and voicing. In what spare time he had was devoted to lecturing to learned societies where he was in great demand.

The specification of the organ in Ulverston Parish Church built in 1866 shows an imaginative tonal design for its period. Its price at £1050 worked out at almost £26 per speaking stop compared with just over £23 for a similar sized instrument by Forster & Andrews.

The Parish Church, Ulverston.

Description of the large Organ,

BUILT BY

Wilkinson & Sons,

NORTHERN COUNTIES'
ORGAN MANUFACTORY,

(One of the oldest Established Organ Firms
in the Kingdom.) KENDAL.

This Instrument contains four complete Manuals, the Compass extending from CC to G, 56 Notes each. The Pedal Organ extends from CCC to F, 30 Notes.

GREAT ORGAN.

		FEET.		PIPES.
1 Double Open Diapason	CC	16	metal	56
2 Open Diapason	CC	8	,,	56
3 Violon Diapason (South Front)	CC	8	,,	56
4 Hohl-Flöte	CC	8	wood	56
5 Stopped Diapason	CC	8	wood & metal	56
6 Wald-Flöte	CC	4	wood	56
7 Principal	CC	4	metal	56
8 Twelfth	CC	2⅔	.,	56
9 Fifteenth	CC	2	,,	56
10 Sesquialtera } (4 ranks)	CC	various	,,	224
11 Cornet				
12 Mixture (2 ranks)	CC	various	,,	112
13 Trombóne	CC	8	,,	56
14 Clarion	CC	4	,,	56

SWELL ORGAN.

		FEET.		PIPES
15 Bourdon	CC	16	wood	56
16 Open Diapason	CC	8	metal	56
17 Keraulophon	CC	8	,,	56
18 Stopped Diapason	CC	8	wood & metal	56
19 Principal	CC	4	metal	56
20 Fifteenth	CC	2	,,	56
21 Sesquialtera (2 ranks)	CC	various	,,	112
22 Mixture (2 ranks)	CC	,,	,,	112
23 Double Trumpet	CC	16	,,	56
24 Cornopean	CC	8	,,	56
25 Oboe	CC	8	,,	56
26 Clarion	CC	4	,,	56

£1050

CHOIR ORGAN.

			FEET.		PIPES.
27	Dulciana	CC	8	metal	56
28	Voix Céleste	C	8	,,	44
29	Gedacht-Bass				
30	Gedacht-Treble	CC	8	wood & metal	56
31	Viol-di-Gamba	C	8	metal	44
32	Principal	CC	4	,,	56
33	Flute	CC	4	wood & metal	56
34	Flageolet	CC	2	,,	56
35	Clarionet				
	and	CC	8	metal	56
36	Bassoon				

PEDAL ORGAN.

			FEET.		PIPES.
37	Open Diapason	CCC	16	wood	30
38	Bourdon	CCC	16	,,	30
39	Principal	CCC	8	metal	30
40	Trombone	CCC	16	,,	30
41	Trumpet	CCC	8	,,	30

COUPLERS, &c.

42 Swell to Great.   47 Choir to Pedals.
43 Choir to Great.   48 Pedal Organ Attachment.
44 Swell to Choir.   49 Tremulant.
45 Swell to Pedals.   50 Clochette.
46 Great to Pedals.

ACCESSORIES.

4 Composition Pedals to Great Organ.
2   ,,   ,,   Swell   ,,
2 Swell Pedals acting upon Horizontal Shutters.
2½ Octaves of German Pedals.

GENERAL SUMMARY.

	STOPS.	PIPES.
Great Organ	14	952
Swell ,,	12	784
Choir ,,	10	424
Pedal ,,	5	150
Couplers	9	

Total 50 Stops.   Total 2310 Pipes.

There are two Metal Fronts to this Instrument (facing west and south) the Pipes of which are from Stops No. 1 to 3. The Casing about the Book-Board and Draw-Stops is of polished black Bog Oak, which, in contrast with the white Ivory Keys and Draw-Knobs, presents a very beautiful effect. The Wind is supplied by a pair of Hydraulic Engines.

Eminent musicians were quick to perceive the many improvements introduced to the organs of the firm as the years went by and agreed that 'their organs were scientifically conceived and carried out'. Orders were received for churches as far afield as Weston Super-Mare, South Wales and of course nearer home—in Lancashire.

To the regret of all who knew him, William Wilkinson died in 1870 from a severe attack of sciatica which left his son Thomas in sole charge. In 1880, Thomas took his son William Greenwood Wilkinson into the business and three years later his other son Croft; both had been indentured apprentices. The former was organist at Kendal Wesleyan Chapel for twenty-five years where the firm had built a two-manual instrument in 1865. The introduction of young blood into the business brought 'enterprise, energy, mechanical and musical skill as well as architectural knowledge'. Thus, a new era commenced which lasted for just over half a century—William Greenwood dying in 1927 and Croft in 1935.

The year 1880 was a milestone in the firm's history; the order was received to build a four-manual organ for the new Public Hall, Preston, the gift to the Corporation of J. Dewhurst. The following specification is taken from the firm's booklet.

Description of the Grand Organ

(PRESENTED BY J. DEWHURST, Esq., to the CORPORATION OF PRESTON,

FOR THE

NEW PUBLIC HALL.)

BUILT BY

WILKINSON & SONS,

NORTHERN COUNTIES' ORGAN MANUFACTORY,

KENDAL.

(One of the largest Organ Works in England).

———◆———

This Instrument contains Four Complete Manuals, the Compass extending from CC to C, 61 Notes each. The Pedal Organ extends from CCC to F, 30 Notes.

———◆———

GREAT ORGAN.

		FEET.		PIPES.
1 Double Open Diapason	CC	16	metal	61
2 Open Diapason	CC	8	,,	61
3 Horn Diapason	CC	8	,,	61
4 Hohl-Flöte	CC	8	wood	61
5 Gamba	CC	8	metal	61
6 Principal	CC	4	,,	61
7 Wald-Flöte	CC	4	wood	61
8 Twelfth	CC	2⅔	metal	61
9 Fifteenth	CC	2	,,	61
10 Sifflet	CC	2	wood	61
11 Sesquialtera (4 ranks)	CC	various	metal	244
12 Mixture (3 ranks)	CC	various	,,	183
13 Trumpet	CC	8	,,	61
14 Clarion	CC	4	,,	61

SWELL ORGAN.

			FEET.			PIPES.
15	Double Diapason	CC	16	wood		61
16	Violon Diapason	CC	8	metal		61
17	Claribel	CC	8	wood		61
18	Salicional	CC	8	metal		61
19	Voix Céleste	C	8	,,		49
20	Octave Violon	CC	4	,,		61
21	Viole d'Amour	CC	4	,,		61
22	Flageolet	CC	2	wood & metal		61
23	Larigot	CC	1⅓	metal		61
24	Rossignol	CC	1	,,		61
25	Mixture (3 ranks)	CC	various	,,		183
26	Sharp Mixture (4 ranks)	CC	various	,,		244
27	Contra Fagotto	CC	16	,,		61
28	Cornopean	CC	8	,,		61
29	Oboe	CC	8	,,		61
30	Clarion	CC	4	,,		61

CHOIR ORGAN.

			FEET.			PIPES.
31	Lieblich Bourdon	CC	16	wood		61
32	Lieblich-Gedacht	CC	8	wood & metal		61
33	Dulciana	CC	8	metal		61
34	Spitz-Flöte	CC	8	,,		61
35	Rohr-Gedacht	CC	4	wood & metal		61
36	Celestina	CC	4	metal		61
37	Gemshorn	CC	4	,,		61
38	Flautina	CC	2	,,		61
39	Clarionet and Bassoon	CC	8	,,		61

SOLO ORGAN.

(Enclosed in a Swell-box).

			FEET.			PIPES.
40	Flûte Harmonique	CC	8	metal		61
41	Concert Flute	CC	4	,,		61
42	Piccolo Harmonique	CC	2	wood & metal		61
43	Tromba	CC	8	metal		61
44	Orchestral Oboe	CC	8	,,		61
45	Vox Humana	CC	8	,,		61

PEDAL ORGAN.

			FEET.			PIPES.
46	Contra Básso	CCC	32	metal		30
47	Open Bass	CCC	16	wood		30
48	Sub-Bass	CCC	16	,,		30
49	Flute-Bass	CCC	8	,,		30
50	Violoncello	CCC	8	metal		30
51	Super-Octave	CCC	4	,,		30
52	Mixture (3 ranks)	CCC	various	,,		90
53	Posaune	CCC	16	,,		30
54	Trumpet	CCC	8	,,		30

All the most modern improvements are adopted. The Resolutions and Recommendations contained in the Report of the Conferences on Organ-building, held by the Council of the College of Organists, have been carefully kept in view in the design of the Instrument. The finest spotted metal is largely employed for the Metal Pipes, prepared zinc being used for the Pipes of the Pedal Contra-Básso (46) which, forming the Front Screen, are artistically illuminated. Every Pipe in the Instrument, with the exception of those in the Front Screen, stands upon its own wind. The Pneumatic Lever action is applied to both the Great and Swell Organ Manuals, and all the Couplers connecting those Claviers with any other act without adding weight to the touch. Three Pallets are allotted to each Note in the Great and Swell Organs, while six Reservoirs supply them with six separate pressures of wind. The Choir Organ has one Pallet to each Note, and a single reservoir giving a light and delicate wind-pressure. The Solo Organ has two Pallets to each Note, and two Reservoirs. The wind-pressure throughout the Instrument ranges from two and a-half to twelve inches, and is supplied by three powerful Hydraulic Engines.

COUPLERS.

55 Solo to Great.	61 Solo to Pedals.
56 Swell to Great, Super-Octave.	62 Swell to Pedals.
57 Swell to Great Unison.	63 Great to Pedals (left hand).
58 Swell to Great Sub-Octave.	64 Great to Pedals (right hand).
59 Choir to Great.	65 Choir to Pedals.
60 Swell to Choir.	66 Pedal Ventils PP.

ACCESSORY MOVEMENTS.

4 Combination Pedals, acting upon the Stops of the Great Organ, each effecting a proportionate and simultaneous combination of Stops upon the Pedal Organ.

1 Double-acting Horse-shoe Pedal acting upon Ventils, by which all the Pedal Organ Stops can be cut off except the Sub-Bass (48), equivalent to Draw-knob (66), and causing the Great Organ Combination Pedals to become inoperative as regards the Pedal Organ.

    3 Combination Pedals acting upon the Swell Organ.
    2 Combination Pedals acting upon the Solo Organ.
    2 Combination Pedals acting upon the Pedal Organ.
    1 Pedal acting upon the Tremulant to the Solo Organ.
    1 Double-acting Horse-shoe Pedal acting upon Coupler (57).
    1 Pedal acting upon the Shutters of the Swell Organ.
    1 Pedal acting upon the Shutters of the Solo Organ.
    2½ Octaves of Parallel and Concave German Pedals.

GENERAL SUMMARY.

	STOPS.	PIPES.
Great Organ	14	1159
Swell Organ	16	1269
Choir Organ	9	549
Solo Organ	6	366
Pedal Organ	9	330
Couplers	12 Draw-knobs	
	Total 66 Draw-knobs.	Total 8673 Pipes.

The long drawn out saga about the future of this notable instrument is too well known to repeat here; sufficient to say that it is now stored in the Church of All Souls, Halifax, to await—what?—it is impossible to say.

In 1880, a most informative booklet of 84 pages was published. It commenced with 'Some Notes Upon Organs' followed by '*Names of Organ Stops*', 'Specifications of Organs of Various Sizes, with explanatory remarks', some being suggested schemes and others those of contracts actually carried out. Some bear snippets of information such as 'The first in England to use Steam-power in The Manufacture of Organs'; 'One of the largest Organ Works in England.' 'One of the oldest Established Organ Firms in the Kingdom' (Floor Space of Works—10,000 feet sq.). In the printed notes at the end, it is made clear that 'the purchasers are required to pay the carriage of the organ from the works at Kendal to the destination of the instrument.' This booklet was advertised in *Reeves' Musical Directory* for 1881:

T. WILKINSON & SON,

ORGAN BUILDERS, STRAMONGATE, KENDAL

POSTAL ADDRESS.—LAKE VIEW, AMBLESIDE (ESTABLISHED 1829)

Just Published, "SOME NOTES UPON ORGANS," price 1s., or post free for Twelve Stamps.
This Pamphlet will be found most useful to Clergymen, Organists, Churchwardens, Organ Committees, Dealers in Musical Instruments, and others who are contemplating the erection of an Instrument, and who may wish to be enabled to form some opinion as to the merits of a Specification.

During this period the works were in Stramongate, Kendal, with a Postal Address: Lake View, Ambleside and replaced in handwriting: Castle Street, Kendal. The booklet was printed by J. Skelton, "Herald Office", Church Street, Ambleside, 1880. The specifications bear handwritten notes of prices etc, together with the information: 'The prices on these leaflets were sent to Mr W. J. Burton, South Wales Domestic Supply Association, Albany Buildings, Gower Street, Swansea, 24th April, 1885'. All in all it is a fascinating publication.

Some outstanding instruments were built in the run up to 1880 and in the next decade. These included a two-manual for St Thomas' Church, Kendal with very complete tonal schemes for Swell and Great (26 speaking stops in all); and St George's Church, Kendal (1883), a three-manual of 31 speaking stops.

St. Thomas' Church, Kendal.

SYNOPSIS OF THE ORGAN,

BUILT BY

WILKINSON & SONS,

NORTHERN COUNTIES'
ORGAN MANUFACTORY,

KENDAL.

The first in England to use Steam-power in the
Manurfacture of Organs!)

This Organ contains two Complete Manuals, the Compass extending from CC to G, 56 Notes each. The Pedal Organ extends from CCC to F, 30 Notes.

GREAT ORGAN.

		FEET.		PIPES.
1 Double Open Diapason	CC	16	metal	76
2 Open Diapason	CC	8	,,	56
3 Dulciana	CC	8	,,	56
4 Gamba (grooved)	CC	8	,,	44
5 Claribel	CC	8	wood	56
6 Harmonic Flute	C	4	metal	44
7 Principal	CC	4	,,	56
8 Twelfth	CC	2⅔	,,	56
9 Fifteenth	CC	2	,,	56
10 Mixture (3 ranks)	CC	various	,,	168
11 Trumpet	CC	8	,,	56
12 Clarionet	C	8	,,	44
13 Clarion		spare slider.		

SWELL ORGAN.

			FEET.			PIPES.
14 Bourdon ...	...	.. CC	.. 16	...	wood ...	... 56
15 Open Diapason...	...	... CC	... 8	...	metal...	.. 56
16 Stopped Diapason	...	... CC	... 8	...	wood and metal	56
17 Keraulophon ..	...	... C	... 8	...	metal...	.. 44
18 Principal	...	... CC	.. 4	...	,, ...	... 56
19 Fifteenth ..	...	... CC	... 2	...	,, ...	... 56
20 Mixture (3 ranks)	...	... CC	various	...	,, ...	... 168
21 Contra Fagótta	...	spare slider.				
22 Cornopean	..	... CC	... 8	...	,, ...	... 56
23 Oboe ...	...	... CC	... 8	...	,, ...	... 56
24 Clarion ...	...	.. CC	... 4	...	,, ...	... 56

PEDAL ORGAN.

			FEET.			PIPES.
25 Open Diapason	...	... CCC	... 16	...	wood ...	... 30
26 Sub-Bass	...	.. CCC	... 16	..	,, ...	... 30

COUPLERS, ETC.

27 Swell to Great.
28 Swell to Pedals.
29 Great to Pedals.
30 Pedal Organ Attachment.
31 Tremolo.

ACCESSORIES.

4 Composition Pedals to Great Organ.
2 ,, ,, Swell ,,
1 Swell Pedal.
2½ Octaves of radiating German Pedals.

GENERAL SUMMARY.

	STOPS.		PIPES.
Great Organ...	... 13 ...		... 760
Swell ,,	... 11 ...	...	... 660
Pedal ,, ...	... 2 ...	..	... 60
Couplers	... 5		
Total ... 31 stops.		Total ...1480 pipes.	

The Pipes forming the Front and Side Screens are of Burnished Metal, and belong mostly to Stop No. 1.

With the exception of these, every pipe in the organ is over its own wind.

The Swell-box is five inches in thickness.

In connection with the Bellows is a special device for securing steadiness of wind,

Other interesting instruments at this time were St Michael and All Angels' Church, Wigan (three-manuals, 30 speaking stops), 1883, and what must have been a charming small two-manual chamber organ for the Earl of Lathom. The specification is again reproduced from the firm's booklet and bears a hand-written price as built, with pure tin pipes working out at approximately £33 per speaking stop and if the usual materials were used—at £29 per speaking stop.

It is interesting to note that the Wigan organ had Great and Swell divisions on tracker action, but the Choir, which was situated in a chamber above the vestry, was operated by electro-pneumatic action successfully for many years; this was the invention of William Greenwood and Croft Wilkinson. The frequent use of spotted metal is noticeable at this period of the firm's history and continued whenever the price of the job made it possible.

DESCRIPTION OF THE ORGAN

BUILT FOR

The Right Hon. The Earl of Lathom,

AND ERECTED IN THE

PRIVATE CHAPEL, LATHOM PARK,

BY

MESSRS. WILKINSON & SONS,

ORGAN BUILDERS,

AYNAM WORKS, KENDAL.

———o———

" (One of the largest Factories of its kind in England.)"

———o———

This Instrument consists of Two Complete Manuals, the Compass extending on the Manuals from CC to C, 61 Notes, and on the Pedal Organ from CCC to F, 30 Notes.

GREAT ORGAN, CC TO C, 61 NOTES.

1 Open Diapason.................CC...8 feet.........tin ....61 Pipes.
2 Lieblich-Gedacht ....CC...8 feet tone...wood & tin...61 ,,
3 Salicional ....CC...8 feet.........tin ....61 ,,
4 Octave ....CC...4 feet.........tin ....61 ,,

244 Pipes.

SWELL ORGAN, CC TO C, 61 NOTES.

5 Viola-di-Gamba ....CC...8 feet.........tin ....61 Pipes.
6 Rohr-Flöte ....CC...8 feet tone...wood & tin...61 ,,
7 Voix Celeste...................CC...8 feet.........tin ....49 ,,
8 FlûteOctaviante HarmoniqueCC...4 feet.........tin ....61 ,,
9 Horn ....CC ..8 feet.........tin ....61 ,,

293 Pipes.

[handwritten annotations in right margin:] £ 360 £ 320 this instrument with ... pipes Cole ... pine ... was £ 360 £ 320 first Class ... with wood Cole and ... for ...

PEDAL ORGAN, CCC TO F, 30 NOTES.

10 Bourdon ....CCC......16 feet tone......wood......30 Pipes.
11 Flute-Bass ....CCC...... 8 feet tone......wood......30 ,,

60 Pipes.

COUPLERS.

12 Swell to Great   15 Swell to Pedals.
13 Sub-Octave Swell to Great   16 Great to Pedals.
14 Great Super Octave (on its
     own Manual.)

ACCESSORY MOVEMENTS.

2 Combination Pedals to Great Organ.
2 Combination Pedals to Swell Organ.
1 Balance Pedal to Great Organ Vertical Swell Shutters.
1 Balance Pedal to Swell Organ Vertical Swell Shutters.
1 Horse-shoe Pedal acting upon No. 12.
1 Horse-shoe Pedal acting upon No. 16.
$2\frac{1}{2}$ Octaves Parallel and Concave German Pedals.

GENERAL SUMMARY.

Great Organ.................4 Stops.................244 Pipes.
Swell Organ ....5 ,, ...293 ,,
Pedal Organ ....2 ,, ... 60 ,,
Couplers ....5 Draw-knobs. ....

16 Draw-knobs.   597 Pipes.

The whole of the Metal Pipes in this Instrument are made of tin, those which form the Screens being burnished. All the Pipes belonging to the Manuals stand upon their own wind. The whole of the Swell Organ Stops are enclosed in their Swell-box, the Great Organ Stops being in a separate Swell-box. The Case is of carved oak, the Parallel and Concave Pedals are of Dantzic oak, having the Sharps tipped with ebony, while the ... after the example of some of the old English Organs, ...als made of ebony and the Sharps of ivory.

For the Inventions Exhibition held in London during 1885, Miss Wilkinson informs me that it was their intention to exhibit an organ, and she always understood they had one ready but at the last minute it could not be exhibited. A leaflet amongst the firm's records states: 'Originally it was the intention of Messrs. Wilkinson & Sons to exhibit one of their organs, but owing to the very small space at their disposal, only a few of their numerous inventions and improvements which they adopt in their instruments can here be shown'. These inventions referred to included their 'Patent Adjustable Composition Action', 'Improved Check Swell Pedal' and 'Anti-Friction Blowing Apparatus'. There was an acute shortage of space and a number of exhibitors unfortunately were crowded out which caused great dissatisfaction. Wilkinsons were listed as exhibiting in Division 2, Group 32, No. 3525; this information together with a highly laudatory article appeared in an article: Messrs. Wilkinson & Sons' Organs. 'Patent Adjustable Composition Action etc' in *The Railway Supplies Journal* of September 1st, 1885.

It became quite clear that the number of contracts being received, some of which were of large scale, made the building of a new factory essential and so a handsome two-storeyed limestone building was erected in Aynam Road, during 1885–1886. The frontage included a dwelling house, was 150 feet in length and there was a floor space of some 10,000 square feet. It had every facility for the construction and setting up of organs as well as a showroom for the display of pianos, the sale of which Wilkinsons were also engaged. A writer of 1908, referring to these premises, said: "they suggest the atmosphere of Euterpe and Clio—music and history—for in front is the noble parish church of Kendal and behind is the picturesque remnant of Kendal Castle, where the last wife of that wretched character Henry VIII, was born". The *Cambridge Encyclopedia* defines Euterpe: 'In Greek mythology one of the Muses, usually associated with flute playing and Clio, the Muse of history and of lyre playing.'

MESSRS. WILKINSON & SONS' ORGANS.
PATENT "ADJUSTABLE" COMPOSITION ACTION, &c.

The following article is reprinted from "Railway Supplies' Journal" of September 1, 1885:—

Immense as is the area covered by the International Inventions Exhibition, it is scarcely a tithe of what it would have been had each exhibitor been allotted the space which he desired to have. The task of the committee to whom the duty of allotment was entrusted must have been an extremely difficult one, and even more difficult the task which the exhibitors had before them of bringing within their narrow limits any sufficient exemplifications of the inventions which they desired to introduce to public notice. Indeed, it seems to us that their inventiveness was in some instances more strikingly illustrated in the success with which they contended with this problem than in the exhibits themselves, clever and surprising as these undoubtedly are. We certainly wonder that many exhibitors have been able to furnish any intelligible exposition of their specialities, particularly in such cases as that of Messrs. Wilkinson and Sons. Their organs are some of the finest instruments to be seen in the world, and no adequate idea of what they are could possibly be formed by looking at some isolated portion of so complex a structure. An expert osteologist can, we all know, build up a skeleton of an animal if you give him a single bone, but an architect who had

WILKINSON & SONS' NORTHERN COUNTIES ORGAN MANUFACTORY, KENDAL.
The Largest Organ Manufactory in England. Floor Space 10,000 feet.

never seen St. Paul's would make a poor attempt at giving an outline of the building if he had nothing to guide him but a pillar, a window, or even a sketch of the dome. In like manner it would be impossible to conceive what one of Messrs. Wilkinson and Sons' organs may be from any of their exhibits ; but, nevertheless, as one examining a drawing of the dome of St. Paul's would conclude that the architect who designed it must certainly have produced a magnificent building, so anyone who understands these matters at all has only to look at the specimen of inventions and improvements in organ building shewn at South Kensington by this renowned firm to see at once that their complete organs must be of a very high order of excellence. Take for instance the first of these exhibits, viz., what is called the " Adjustable" Composition Action (the two left hand pedals). This is one of the most ingenious and useful inventions which has ever been seen in connection with organ building. The pedals, which act pneumatically can be instantaneously adjusted by the performer to act upon any combination of stops, couplers, &c., throughout the instrument, without the aid of additional mechanical appliances or movements in front, such as Hitching Pedals, Helping Pedals, Rocking Levers, turning round of Draw-knobs, &c. All previous attempts in this direction have been marred by the necessity for having these auxiliary appliances or mechanical movements in front, to the perplexity of the performer. Another advantage of this invention is that the pedals or buttons will act if required, upon all the stops and couplers throughout the organ by one and the same movement. The old form of composition pedals gives but one combination each, but by this arrangement millions of different combinations may be obtained from even a small organ, whilst the number of combinations which one " Adjustable " pedal will command upon an instrument containing 52 stops is 29, 057, 566, 289, 639, 762, 787, 920, 280,000. It is not necessary to specially construct an organ for this "Adjustable"Composition Action, as it can be inserted in existing instruments, and made to work in conjunction with the old form of composition pedals if desired. It should also be stated that suitable combinations of stops may be prepared before commencing on a piece of music, or the combinations may be varied during the performance of such piece. More-over, the principle upon which the pedals work might be applied to numerous purposes.

Another of Messrs. Wilkinson's inventions is the " Improved Check Swell Pedal " (right hand pedal). This pedal may be used in the ordinary way, or can be left to remain in any position on withdrawing the pressure of the foot. The device here adopted prevents the possibility of injury from accidental slamming of the louvres, and also enables the performer to leave the swell doors at any degree of *crescendo* or *diminuendo*. A very useful appliance is the " Anti-Friction Blowing Apparatus," which works upon hardened steel points, and is constructed with a view to permanent silence and durability. Provision is made for retaining oil or other lubricant at both ends of the lifting-rods, and the invention is in every particular an admirable and perfect device.

Messrs. Wilkinson and Sons have earned the thanks of all who are interested in organs and organ construction by these improvements which they have designed, and not by these only, but by the efforts which they have so successfully made to perfect this noble instrument. Their manufactory is, we believe, the largest in England, having a floor-space of 10,000 superficial feet, and as they are themselves practical organ builders, and personally superintend every part of the work, bringing vast experience and the highest skill to bear upon every detail, we do not wonder at the reputation which they have gained. There is scarcely a town in the kingdom where their organs are not to be found, and the highest testimonials from the most notable authorities affirm the superior quality of the instruments sent out from their manufactory. To all who are thinking of purchasing an organ, we not only heartily commend this firm in the sincere conviction that we shall be doing good service to the public, but we would also say, procure and read their excellent pamphlet, entitled " Some Notes upon Organs." It is a capital little *brochure*, which may be had for a shilling; and which, by the valuable information it contains, may lead to the saving of many pounds. We ought to say that the exhibits to which we have called attention are to be found at the Inventions Exhibition, Division 2, Group 32, No. 3525. The manufactory of the firm is at Kendal, and their London address, 39, Charington-street, Oakley-square, N.W.

Constant developments took place under Thomas Wilkinson but he could not go on for ever. However, he worked on up to his death in 1917; thereupon his two sons became joint proprietors until the death of William Greenwood Wilkinson in 1927. Two years later Austin Jones, who had served his apprenticeship with Wilkinsons, and then left to join Harrison & Harrison, was asked to return to his old firm at Kendal, where Croft was delighted to engage him as Works Manager. His experience gained at Harrisons was valuable, for he had supervised the erection of the new organ for Shanghai Cathedral in 1925 and had been in charge of such important instruments as Manchester Cathedral (in which city he later became tuning representative for the area), as well as the Cathedrals of St Mary, Glasgow, Belfast and Downpatrick. His brother, D. A. Jones, who had accompanied him to Shanghai, decided to join Wilkinsons (where he had also learned his trade) in 1929; thus the firm gained two first class men, so their tradition for fine quality work happily was maintained.

Victorian businesses were very adept at calling attention to their many excellences, as in the following advertisement:

ORGANS BUILT

On the most Approved Principles

Finished with the greatest nicety of detail
BY THE AID OF STEAM POWER
and constructed to suit any position

ORGANS FITTED

WITH HYDRAULIC, GAS, STEAM, OR HOT AIR ENGINES

Together with

SPECIAL CONCUSSION VALVES & AIR RESERVOIRS
For rendering the wind free from unsteadiness

ORGANS RE-BUILT

ENLARGED, RE-VOICED, NEW STOPS ADDED

and the Instruments otherwise Restored and Converted
to suit Modern Requirements

TUNINGS BY YEARLY CONTRACT

OR OTHERWISE.

In the 1890s in *Musical Opinion* they were content to draw attention to the fact that they possessed 'The largest church organ manufactory in England.' By 1921, when the second edition of *The Dictionary of Organs and Organists* was published, their reputation was so well established that they merely drew attention to the fact that they were still active.

Established 1829.

WILKINSON & SONS,

Organ Builders,

KENDAL.

Just before Croft Wilkinson's death in 1935, he persuaded his daughter Margaret to become the firm's Secretary, a position which she held with distinction for some thirty-three years. Thereafter, with the family in control (Mrs Wilkinson being sole owner until her death in 1954), the firm made further progress and expanded. They produced a very reliable electro-pneumatic action which was complemented by fine tonal work gaining them high praise from a number of notable organists. In addition, they manufactured an extremely quiet and efficient fan blower of their own design.

In common with many early Victorian organ builders, they dealt in pianos and such was the skill of the Wilkinson founders that they manufactured their own until 1870 when this ceased except for tuning and servicing. When D. A. Jones joined the company he took over the direction of renovation of pianos of all makes. This department built up a large connection, and tuning and servicing were associated with a particular school in the district for almost 100 years.

Mrs Wilkinson died in 1954 after which a company was formed and with a works manager, Miss Margaret Wilkinson carried on until 1958 when the business was incorporated with Rushworth & Dreaper Ltd. with M. L. Wilkinson, W. J. L. Rushworth, G. Hutchence and C. Lythgoe as the directors. This proved a very happy association and it became a tuning and maintenance unit covering an area from north of Preston to approximately the Scottish Border. Miss Wilkinson remained to manage this with a staff of organ tuners, but only minor organ repair work was carried out. The piano business continued as before. In 1968, Rushworth & Dreaper decided to close down several of their local offices and concentrate them at Liverpool. Thereupon, Miss Wilkinson took well-earned retirement. A tuning representative was stationed in the area to carry on the organ tuning, while the piano tuning connection was divided between the remaining tuners who started off on their own with very happy results.

From an article by A. G. Matthew on The Organs of Zion Chapel, Kendal, in *The Organ* for July 1946, it is interesting to note that Sydney J. Ambler, whom I knew well in my teenage years, came north from London in 1936 to act as consultant in collaboration with Wilkinsons, to rebuild and enlarge the Thomas Wilkinson organ of 1874 in Zion Chapel, Kendal. Some of the former pipework was included together with several stops from a Hill organ that one time stood in Park Chapel, Crouch End, London. S. J. A. was a great acquirer and hoarder; his pipework was very useful in this instance—the rest of it was new. There were 'money and spatial limitations' but due to Ambler's enterprise and Wilkinson's skill a most versatile and effective organ was created to the following specification:

ZION CHAPEL, KENDAL 1874, 1936

GREAT ORGAN

	ft
Unenclosed	
Open Diapason No. 1	8
Open Diapason No. 2	8
Principal	4
Twelfth	2⅔
Fifteenth	2
Enclosed	
Dulciana	8
Clarabella	8
Viol	8
Clarinet (tenor C)	8
Posaune	8
On Unit Chest	
Bourdon	16
Stopped Diapason	8
Great to Pedal	

SWELL ORGAN

Salicional	8
Celeste	8
Lieblich	8
Geigen Diapason	8
Principal	4
Fifteenth	2
Oboe	8
Trumpet	8
Swell to Great	
Swell to Pedal	
Swell Octave	
Swell Sub-octave	
Tremulant	

PEDAL ORGAN

Bourdon minor (from Unit Chest)	16
Bourdon major	16
Bass Flute	8
Major Bass	16
Octave (from Major Bass)	8

PISTONS *(Exhaust Pneumatic)*

4 to Swell Organ
7 to Great Organ
3 Toe Pistons to Pedal Organ
2 reversible pistons: Great to Pedal, Swell to Great
All pistons adjustable at the console
Detached Console   Electro-pneumatic Action

The whole of the factory is now divided into seventeen flats. The house adjoining was used by the family until Miss Wilkinson's grandfather died. To quote her: 'It had many bedrooms, I think it was eight, because each member still at home then—four sons and two daughters—preferred single rooms. There was one huge attic room, with windows out to the side rear, which they used as a billiard room. After Grandfather died, Greenwood Wilkinson, his wife and two children lived there very briefly, after which it was tenanted for many years by succeeding tenants and finally sold with the premises. These have been most skilfully converted; the interior retains its special features such as the panelled pitch pine doors, the extremely wide shallowed stepped pitch pine staircase and the granite pillars either side of the front porch in both house and factory vestibule entrances. The lower section on the left of the porch was originally used as a family music room on the ground floor; this later became the piano showroom'. The architect—Eli Cox—was a friend of Thomas Wilkinson and he designed some excellent buildings in Kendal. The small houses south of the organ works are Almshouses and Cox saw to it that the design of these harmonised with the organ works and house. At the time, one of grandfather Wilkinson's sons was articled to Eli Cox and although he became an architect, he did not follow the profession for long.

As far as I am aware, Miss Margaret L. Wilkinson, together with the late Miss H. M. Suggate (owner of Bishop & Son of London & Ipswich), shared the honour of being the only two ladies at the head of an organ building firm in the country. Both were extremely capable and as far as the subject of this account is concerned, was well known in the area not only for her business acumen, but for her kindly personality and desire to be of service wherever the opportunity arose. In her retirement she has continued to lead a busy life in the community, particularly with the Parish Church and Civic Society. For no less than 42 years, until 1990, she was Honorary Local Representative for the Associated Board, Royal Schools of Music, London, and apart from one other, was the longest serving member holding this office. She greatly enjoys travel, particularly her visits to Australia to stay with an old friend and loves the life there and its climate; may she long continue to do so.

After this chapter had been typeset, the second issue of the *Journal of the Incorporated Society of Organ Builders* (June 1951) came into my hands. This contained a most detailed and interesting article, complete with drawings, entitled 'Electrical Organ Mechanisms Past, Present and Future' by J. I. Taylor. In it he says 'The invention or the discovery of the electro-magnet must be attributed to William Sturgeon, who was born in 1783 at Whittington near Kirkby Lonsdale. Sturgeon was by trade a shoemaker and served for eighteen years as a private soldier in the Royal Artillery. He was entirely self-taught, an enthusiastic experimenter with electricity and he described his first electro-magnet in a communication to the Society of Arts in 1825. Wilkinson, the Kendal organ builder and a friend of Sturgeon, was one of the first to see the possibilities of the magnet as applied to organ action and commenced to experiment, but there is no record of him achieving practical results…'.

An agreement signed by Thomas Wilkinson and John Dewhurst (the donor)
to build the new organ for the Corn Exchange (Public Hall), Preston

left
Thomas Wilkinson.
Courtesy of Miss M. L. Wilkinson

above right
Miss Margaret Wilkinson.
Photo by the Author, 1994

below
The former works in Aynam Road, Kendal.
Photo by the Author, 1994

The Wilkinson organ in the Corn Exchange (latterly the Public Hall), Preston.
A photograph taken in the late 1890s. Courtesy of Everson Whittle

above left
Wilkinson organ at the Convent of the
Holy Child Jesus, Winckley Square,
Preston, late 1939

above right
Organ at the Ripley Hospital Church,
Lancaster, 1893

right
Zion Chapel, Kendal 1936

CHAPTER XIV

Youthful Enterprise
Three Master Organ Builders

MICHAEL FARLEY, BUDLEIGH SALTERTON, DEVON

GRIFFITHS & COOPER, SOUTHSEA, HAMPSHIRE

JONATHAN M. WALLACE (HENRY GROVES & SON), NOTTINGHAM

"Enthusiasm finds the opportunities and energy makes the most of them."
Anonymous   (Henry S. Haskins)

ONE of our up-and-coming young organ builders, Michael Farley, of Budleigh Salterton, was apprenticed to the firm of Eustace & Aldridge of Exeter in 1974, at the time when they were working on the rebuild of the Walker organ in Portsmouth Cathedral. Eustace was the organ builder of the partnership; he was apprenticed to Hele & Co. (the old firm) and then spent some time with Henry Willis & Sons Ltd. Aldridge, a joiner, left the partnership not long after it was formed in 1969, leaving his former partner to carry on alone, which he did for some ten years, after which he ceased to trade. Most of his tuning and maintenance contracts passed to Michael Farley when he started business under his own name in 1984, since when it has trebled in size, with a total of four full-time and three part-time members of staff.

Since its establishment ten years ago, the business has grown steadily, for Michael has become well known for his artistry, sound craftsmanship and imaginative approach to all classes of work. Moreover, he is endowed with an infectious enthusiasm and is a musician in his own right, having given two recitals at Liverpool Cathedral—an experience he will never forget. He is currently organist at Ottery St Mary Parish Church, a position which he has held since 1985.

As tuners of over 180 organs throughout Devon, Dorset, Somerset, Avon, Wiltshire and the Isle of Wight, this has brought the firm to the notice of many discerning musicians, as evidenced by the long list of important contracts undertaken, numbering some seventy instruments during the past few years. They include major rebuilds, tonal additions and improvements, installation of the latest Solid State action, restorations (including several historical instruments) and major overhauls with improvements.

Major rebuilds include: St John's Church, Bathwick, Bath, with a new three-manual drawstop console; Barnstaple Parish Church, in conjunction with Lance Foy of Truro; Budleigh Salterton Parish Church (incorporating the former nave organ by Harrison & Harrison from Worcester Cathedral and with a new three-manual mobile drawstop console); St James', Exeter—provision of a third manual, Solid State action and capture system; Dartmouth Royal Naval College, three manuals with five extended ranks; Sidmouth Parish Church, tonal additions, new action and console re-designed on a new mobile platform; Christ Church, Totland and Freshwater Parish Church, Isle of Wight. The first stage carried out at Freshwater in 1986 comprised a new multiplexing system to replace the ageing electrical switches and the provision of a new mixture for the Swell Organ. In 1992, the pipework was cleaned and the Great mixture re-modelled with new pipework. Here, a mobile platform was provided, enabling the console to be easily moved. Due to the enterprise of Arthur Starke, Freshwater Parish Church has a long tradition of organ recitals and concerts by well-known choirs during the summer season, which are well supported by visitors. Amongst those who attracted considerable interest during 1993 included Professor Ian Tracey, Organist and Master of the Choristers, Liverpool Cathedral, and the choir of Jesus College, Cambridge.

Budleigh Salterton was an interesting contract which was carried out during 1991–92 and was finally completed with the addition of the 32ft Pedal reed (half length)—one of only two such stops west of Bristol. It was made of wood by Michael Farley and the voicing was the work of Keith Bance of Harrow, who, together with Roger Box of Plymouth and F. Booth & Sons of Leeds (who made the new pipework), were responsible for the remainder of the voicing. The original organ was the work of Hele of Plymouth and the scheme for the rebuilding and amalgamation of this and the portable Harrison organ from Worcester Cathedral was drawn up by Roger Fisher, Organist and Master of the Choristers, Chester Cathedral, in consultation with John Fear, the organist and choirmaster of St Peter's Church, together with Michael Farley. The Harrison & Harrison ten stop instrument from Worcester Cathedral was built in 1973 to accompany nave services and concerts, including the Three Choirs Festivals. It consisted of two portable sections, comprising a Swell Organ, made from a 1911 Harrison organ which once stood in St Basil's Church, Deritend, Birmingham, and a Positive division made new in 1973. This department had five stops, using open foot voicing; on the Pedal there was a bourdon and a bass flute. In 1989, this instrument was offered for sale due to the pending restoration of the building, and I was delighted to learn that it had found a home at Budleigh Salterton, for there was competition for its purchase as far away as Dallas, Texas. Roger Fisher and Professor Ian Tracey gave recitals to mark the completion of the project.

It can only be said that Christ Church, Totland, and Arthur Starke are inseparable. For many years he has been organist and choirmaster there, playing a two-manual organ by Norman & Beard (1911) of good tone, but with limited resources. With a three-manual Harrison organ in his own home, which is well known to many distinguished musicians who have enjoyed his hospitality over the years, he has worked and planned for a rebuild of the Totland organ to a comprehensive tonal scheme. In 1991, his dream was realised when sufficient funds became available for Michael Farley to carry out a rebuild in consultation with Philip Drew, the Diocesan Organ Adviser, and Arthur Starke. From the outset, it was agreed that the Norman & Beard pipework should remain unaltered; the new work has been skilfully voiced and finished to enhance it, with a result that I heard an outstanding instrument during the summer of 1992, when my wife and I paid our twenty-seventh visit to Freshwater. Here we have become steeped in Tennyson and that great Victorian photographer, Julia Margaret Cameron, both of whom resided there and were close friends. One of the rewarding results of our long connection with that lovely part of the world, has been the friendship of Arthur as he is known to his countless friends, and through him my knowledge of a number of fine organs on the Island has been made possible. We enthused over the remarkable transformation of the Totland organ, in which Ian Tracey and other distinguished players have joined. Funds were not then available however, to add the Great mixture and the Positive Organ. Nothing daunted, however, Arthur campaigned for their inclusion, with the encouragement of the then vicar, the Revd. Ken White, and by 1993, as a result of a generous gift from a benefactor of the church, and the efforts of the congregation, this became possible. As this chapter is being written, the work is in hand, and by the time of publication I shall have heard the completed instrument. I have little doubt that we shall have a small celebration—a toast to the newly completed organ and the publication of the result, almost three years' research and compilation of this, my last book.

The specification of the organ as completed in 1991, is as follows, together with the additions now in hand. The Positive Organ is on a mobile platform which normally forms part of the original case and organ, but capable of being moved for special events.

CHRIST CHURCH, TOTLAND 1991

GREAT ORGAN	ft	SWELL ORGAN	
Open Diapason	8	Open Diapason	8
Clarabel	8	Rohr Gedact	8
Dulciana	8	Viola da Gamba	8
Principal	4	Celeste	8
Fifteenth	2	Geigen Principal	4
Mixture 19·22·26	III	Fifteenth	2
Trompette	8	Mixture 22·26·29	III
		Horn	8

Double Trumpet	16	Octave Quint	$5\frac{1}{3}$
Trumpet	8	Fifteenth	4
Clarion	4	Bombarde	16
		Trompette	8

POSITIVE ORGAN

		Double Trumpet	16
Chimney Flute	8	Trumpet	8
Flute	4	Clarion	4
Nazard	$2\frac{2}{3}$		
Principal	2		
Tierce	$1\frac{3}{5}$		
Larigot	$1\frac{1}{3}$		
Sifflote	1		
Clarinet	8		
Cymbal Mixture 29·33·36	III		
Tremulant			

COUPLERS

Swell to Pedal   Swell to Pedal 4   Great to Pedal
Positive to Pedal   Swell to Great 16
Swell to Great   Swell to Great 4
Swell to Positive   Positive to Great
Positive to Great 4   Positive flues on Great
Great and Pedal Combinations Coupled

PEDAL ORGAN

Acoustic Bass	32
Violone	16
Bourdon	16
Principal	8
Bass Flute	8

ACCESSORIES

8 thumb pistons to each manual division
8 toe pistons each to Swell and Pedal
64-level capture system
15-stage general crescendo pedal

A feature of the Totland organ which is so important to any organist is that not only is the console handsome in appearance, but it is so very comfortable to play.

This brief account of Michael Farley's work would not be complete without mentioning his very imaginative scheme for the rebuild of the Hill/Hele organ in Sidmouth Parish Church, completed in 1992. Much of the pipework is original Hill of 1882 with a little of the Hele of 1949; the new stops are the work of Don Wherly and F. Booth & Son of Leeds. I heard this instrument some years ago at a recital; although it contained some good work, there was a decided lack of brilliance, which was all the more apparent to me as only two or three days earlier I had been listening to a recital on the Father Willis organ at Lincoln Cathedral. I was delighted therefore, to learn during 1991 that it was to be rebuilt by Michael Farley.

SIDMOUTH PARISH CHURCH 1992

GREAT ORGAN

	ft		
		Vox Humana	8
Violone	16	Clarion	4
Open Diapason	8	*Tremulant*	
Hohl Flute	8		
Principal	4		

POSITIVE ORGAN

Wald Flute	4	Lieblich Gedact	8
Twelfth	$2\frac{2}{3}$	Spitz Flute	4
Fifteenth	2	Nazard	$2\frac{2}{3}$
Piccolo	2	Principal	2
Tierce	$1\frac{3}{5}$	Larigot	$1\frac{1}{3}$
Mixture 19·22·26·29	IV	Tierce	$1\frac{3}{5}$
Trumpet	8	Cymbal 33·36	II
		Clarinet	8

SWELL ORGAN

		Tuba	8
		Trumpet	8
Lieblich Gedact	8	*Tremulant*	
Gamba	8		
Voix Celeste (tenor C)	8		

PEDAL ORGAN

Flute	4		
Principal	4	†Subbass	32
Fifteenth	2	†Open Wood	16
Mixture 22·26·29	III	Violone	16
Contra Fagotto	16	Bourdon	16
Cornopean	8	Octave	8
Oboe	8	Bass Flute	8

361

Fifteenth	4
Open Flute	4
Mixture 19·22·26·29	IV
†Sackbut	32
Trombone	16
Contra Fagotto (from Swell)	16
Trumpet (from Positive)	8

†Electronic stops

ACCESSORIES

8 thumb pistons to each manual division
10 general pistons 1 general cancel
Reversers to all unison couplers, trombone,
sackbut and subbass
8 toe pistons each to Swell and Pedal
6 reversible toe pistons
Generals on Swell toe pistons
Great and Pedal pistons coupled
64 levels of memory with lock
General crescendo pedal (30 stages) with indicator

Three-manual drawstop console on a mobile
platform with adjustable bench.

COUPLERS

Swell to Great   Swell to Positive   Positive to Great
Swell Octave   Swell Sub Octave   Positive Octave
Positive Sub Octave   Swell to Pedal
Great to Pedal   Positive to Pedal

It is not Michael Farley's usual practice to use electronic stops, but their use is justified here due to lack of space; they have proved to be most convincing and certainly add to the resources of the Pedal Organ. After all—Comptons used some electronic stops at Church House, Westminster, as far back as 1939!

An interesting collaboration with the organ builder Lance Foy, of Porth Kea, Truro, was the restoration in 1992 of the John Crang organ, built in 1764, in Barnstaple Parish Church. Since then, several unfortunate rebuilds had taken place and the aim of the two builders in the work of 1992 has been to remove the worst excesses and to preserve the tonal structure of the original work, with judicious additions and a new console.

As this chapter was being written in January 1994, major rebuilding work will have commenced on the old Gray & Davison organ in Mattock Parish Church, near Yeovil. The original character will be preserved, but there will be some tonal improvements, together with new electro-pneumatic action.

Michael Farley is fortunate in having a skilled and dedicated staff who share his enthusiasm; they are— William Creasey, John Few, Howard Foreman and Charles Gailor. This regular team is supplemented by other part-time folk when necessary, and these include some excellent Trade Suppliers.

Michael Farley's achievements in ten years as a master organ builder are quite remarkable; he is utterly dedicated to his craft and I predict a great future for him.

GRIFFITHS & COOPER, SOUTHSEA, HAMPSHIRE

One of my customers, when my first book *Forster & Andrews, Organ Builders 1843–1956*, was published in 1968, was Andrew Cooper, then a schoolboy. This gave me great pleasure, for I was absorbed by organs at the same age and hoped to be an organ builder when I left school, but this was not to be and perhaps just as well! Since then I have followed Andrew's career with interest and was delighted to hear that he had joined Henry Willis & Sons Ltd. at Petersfield, to pursue his chosen profession. Here he gained experience of a variety of work over a wide area, including the Isle of Wight, where he lived. By 1988, at the age of twenty-six, he felt the need to start his own company, and joined Geoffrey Griffiths, with whom he formed a partnership, with a workshop at Southsea, and an Isle of Wight office at his home in Ryde. Possessing enthusiasm with a natural ability, he found an ideal partner in Geoffrey Griffiths—a clever engineer by trade, who has made a most useful contribution to a number of instruments on a tuning round through four counties in the south of England, the Isle of Wight and Channel Islands. Of some twenty-eight overhauls, three electrifications and other work carried out between 1988–1993, the following are of particular interest.

Southsea, St Swithin (1989). Two manuals and pedal by James Ivimey, electrified by Comptons in 1947, with a detached stop-key console. In addition to overhauling, the tonal scheme was recast to provide a specification of greater utility. A new Multiplex system was installed.

ST SWITHIN'S CHURCH, SOUTHSEA 1989

GREAT ORGAN

	ft
Open Diapason	8
Gedackt	8
Principal	4
Flute	4
Gemshorn	2
Sext 12·17 (new)	II
Mixture 19·22·26 (new)	III
Tremulant	

SWELL ORGAN

Rohr Flute	8
Viola	8
Koppel Flute (new)	4
Principal	2

Larigot	1⅓
Trumpet	8
Tremulant	

PEDAL ORGAN

Acoustic Bass	32
Bourdon	16
Bass Flute	8
Fifteenth	4

COUPLERS

Swell to Great   Swell Octave to Great
Swell Sub Octave   Swell Octave
Swell Unison Off   Great to Pedal
Swell Octave to Pedal   Swell to Pedal

At St Barnabas' Church, Southampton (1989), some tonal alterations have been carried out in 1971 to the two-manual electro-pneumatic Willis organ of 1957. In addition to a general overhaul and new multiplex action, further tonal alterations and additions were made in 1989, including the provision of a new Swell mixture, Swell and Pedal reeds. A Pedal major bass 16ft was also added, utilising the Pedal open wood from the ill-fated Willis organ at Kingston upon Thames.

An interesting contract in 1992 was that at St Thomas' Church, Lymington, where the three-manual organ by Brindley & Foster of 1910, with pneumatic action, was electrified, and at the request of the church and Diocesan Adviser, the Brindley console was retained complete with its transformers and other gadgets, which are now operated electronically.

At Odiham All Saints (1993), a two-manual Bryceson organ with tracker action was reputed to have originally stood in St James' Hall, Piccadilly. It had been much altered over the years; the pedal action had been converted to pneumatic and some curious additions made to this department. These were removed and the bottom six notes of the Pedal open wood re-sited to encourage greater tonal egress into the nave. A new west case was designed to match the existing casework. As there was a spare slide on the Great, a trumpet was fitted here.

To revert to 1990, at Barton Church, near Newport, Isle of Wight, there is a fine three-manual organ by Forster & Andrews, built in 1894, with additions in 1904. Local folklore has it that this was partly the gift of Queen Victoria, on account of Barton being daughter church of St Mildred's Church, Whippingham, where the Queen worshipped during her long stays at Osborne.

The organ is well laid out, but there is no room for any more additions to the Pedal Organ. The original specification was as follows.

BARTON CHURCH, NEWPORT, ISLE OF WIGHT

3 manuals: CC to G, 56 notes   Pedal: CCC to F, 30 notes

GREAT ORGAN

	ft
Open Diapason	8
Clarabella (added 1904)	8
Principal	4
Suabe Flute	4
Twelfth	2⅔
Fifteenth	2
Mixture 19·22 (added on a clamp 1904)	II

SWELL ORGAN

Double Diapason	16
Open Diapason	8
Hohlflöte	8
Salicional (spotted metal)	8
Voix Celestes (tenor C)	8
Principal	4
Piccolo	2
Mixture 12·15·19·22·26	V

363

Double Trumpet	16		PEDAL ORGAN	
Horn	8			
Oboe (spotted metal)	8	Violone		16
Orchestral Oboe (tenor C)	8	Bourdon (from Swell)		16
Vox Humana	8			
Clarion	4		ACCESSORIES	

CHOIR ORGAN

Dulciana	8
Lieblich Gedact	8
Flauto Traverso	4
Flautino	2
Clarinet (tenor C)	8

ACCESSORIES

6 couplers 5 composition pedals
Balanced pedals to Swell and Choir Organs
Choir, Swell flues and Great flues, tracker action
Great and Swell reeds on pneumatic chest
Pedal action tubular-pneumatic

Cost of the organ: £722

Some years ago, in company with Arthur Starke, organist at Christ Church, Totland, and a prominent Isle of Wight musician, I had ample opportunity to hear this instrument, for we were marooned for some time due to an extremely heavy thunderstorm. It was clear that renovation was needed and Griffiths & Cooper were the obvious choice, owing to their enthusiasm for the Hull firm's work. It is now in first class condition; in addition to the normal clean and overhaul, the Great, Choir and Pedal pneumatics were re-leathered, the reeds revoiced and a new mixture 19·22 added to the Great in place of a hohl flute 8ft, which had displaced a mixture of the same composition some years previously. The fine casework was refurbished and the diapered front pipes sprayed gold. The church has every reason to be proud of its organ, which has now reached its hundredth birthday. A salutary thought to those contemplating the installation of an electronic organ in place of what they consider to be their worn out instrument.

As there is a keen interest in the work of the Hull firm, the original specification from their order book is reproduced opposite. In the main, they were immaculately written out, but this one was the result of second thoughts and is rather untidy.

James Forster II would be actively engaged with this instrument in 1894; he was a man of wide interests and about 1904 decided to retire at the early age of fifty-seven, when he sold the business to his manager, Philip H. Selfe. He retired to Scarborough, where he resided for some years and here he took a great interest in church life, for he was a staunch Anglican. His knowledge of German enabled him to act as a censor at the War Office during the 1914–18 war. After the cessation of hostilities he moved to Ryde, Isle of Wight, where he died in 1925 at the age of seventy-seven. Andrew Cooper has been engaged on research and has found this entry in the *Isle of Wight County Press* for January 14th, 1925.

FORSTER.— On the 9th inst., at Hollington, Swanmore Road, Ryde, Major James Forster J.P., late R. E. (Militia) late of Welton Garth, East Yorks. and Scarborough, aged 77 years.

He was buried on January 14th, the service being conducted by the Revd. Hugh Le Fleming, Vicar of All Saints, Ryde. His wife, Elizabeth, lived for another fourteen years; she was buried on January 13th, 1939, aged 87 years. Both are buried in an unmarked grave in Ryde Cemetery, and I find it very sad that a man of such distinction, as well as his wife, should have no headstone to their memory.

With only six years experience as master organ builders, the partnership has gained a reputation for first class work and what is more, a real enthusiasm for whatever contract comes their way. In company with the other two firms mentioned in this chapter, they are committed craftsmen who will go to endless trouble to ensure the best possible result. I look forward to hearing of their progress in future years.

Barton Church near Newport
1144

(Box) GREAT. (III.)

1	Open Diap (low oct ff pipes)	56
2	~~Lieblich Gedact~~ Suabeflote 4'	56
3	~~Dulciana~~ S.B. Principal 4	56
4	~~Flauto Traverso~~ Twelfth	56
5	~~Suab flute~~ Fifteenth 2'	56
6	~~Principal~~ CHOIR IN A BOX	

CHOIR IN A BOX

1	~~Twelfth~~ Lieblich Gedact 8	56
2	~~Fifteenth~~ Dulciana S.B. 8	56
3	~~Clarinet~~ Flauto Trav. 4	56
4	Flautino 2	56
5	~~Flautina~~ Clarinet 8	44
		548

COUPLERS

1 Great to Pedals
2 Swell to Pedals
3 Swell to Great
4 Swell Octave
5 Swell Tremulant
6 Choir Tremulant

(Box) SWELL (III.)

1	Double Diap. S.W.	16	56
2	Open Diap. .W.	8	56
3	Hohlflöte S.B.W.	8	56
4	Salicional S.B.M. sord.	8	56
5	Voix Célestes spotted	8	44
6	Principal	4	56
7	Piccolo .M.	2	56
8	Mixture 5 ranks		280
9	Double Trumpet	16	56
10	Horn	8	56
11	Oboe spot.	8	56
12	Orchestral Oboe spot.	8	44
13	Vox Humana spot.	8	56
14	Clarion spot.	4	56
			984

PEDAL

1	~~Open Diapason~~ Violone .M. 16 feet Large scale		30
2	Sallot Bourdon (from Sw. Dble.) 16		
			30

Three Comp. Pedals to Swell. Two Comp. Peds. to ~~Choir~~ Great
Pitch pine Case. Impost high. Handsomely decorated front pipes
C. of C. Ped. & Bd. & Draw Stop arrangements
Balance Pedals to Choir & Swell, side by side, so as to be worked
by one foot. Swell Box 3 inches. Choir Box 2 inches
"Great to Pedals" by Pedal, on and off
Choir Organ Voiced as a Choir.

Rev. W. H. Nutter, M.A. St Paul's V. Barton. I. of W.

	£704	0	0
B. Nutter — Flautino	10	0	0
Oak Seat.	2	2	0
Double acting Pedal	10	0	0

From Forster & Andrew's Order Book

JONATHAN M. WALLACE (HENRY GROVES & SON), NOTTINGHAM

A master organ builder at the age of twenty-two is no mean achievement, but such is Jonathan Wallace, grandson of Alvin Groves, who was owner of H. Groves & Son of Nottingham until 1991, when the business was taken over by this young man. He can only be described as 'having organ building in his blood', for he was assisting his grandfather from the age of ten. At school he studied technical drawing and craft design technology; he was destined for the bank, but this was not to his liking and so, at the age of sixteen, he entered the firm where he quickly grasped all aspects of the work, including Solid State, which held no terrors for him! Not only does he possess technical ability, but he has great enthusiasm for his craft, a capacity for hard work and an attitude that can only be termed perfectionism, and to achieve this, time is no object. Little wonder that he has gained three important contracts within two years. When the new company was formed in 1991, the spacious works were retained while the staff and two part-time employees, together with the assistance from time to time of a third, has coped with a big work load. The office is at 44 Holkham Avenue, Chilwell, Beeston, Nottingham, where he has the invaluable help of his mother as secretary and father as accountant, thus leaving him in the main to work on the practical side. The first job to be undertaken was the clean and overhaul of the Cousans organ in St Paul's Church, Lenton Boulevard, Nottingham.

His successful restoration of the Harston organ at Owmby Church, Lincs., in 1991, led in 1993 to the firm obtaining the contract to carry out the thorough restoration of the two-manual Brindley & Foster organ in the church of St Helens, Willingham-by-Stow, Lincs., which included the provision of electric action to manuals and pedals, together with a new pedal board, and the revoicing of the Swell oboe. 'Conservation' is the term preferred by Jonathan to describe such work; no matter how small the organ, he is concerned to preserve its integrity wherever practical. Without exception, each job receives a coat of paint on the building frame, swell box etc., but other internal parts are varnished.

Thus, not only does the work look good, but keeping the woodwork in good condition for the future is ensured. The interior of some of our village organs has to be seen to be believed.

A contract that has given him particular pleasure was the renovation of a charming one-manual chamber organ, by Theodore Bates, in the Methodist Chapel at Glentham, not far from Owmby. Theodore Bates was established in 1812 and worked for a time from St John Street, Smithfield, London, and thereafter at 7 Jerusalem Passage, St John's Square, Smithfield (c.1813), 20 St John's Square (c.1814–1824) with additional premises at 18 Holywell Street, Strand (c.1820–22) and 490 Oxford Street (c.1822–24). He had a large business in the manufacture of barrel organs, which has been described by the late Lyndesay G. Langwill and Canon Noel Boston in *Church & Chamber Barrel Organs*, an invaluable work, now out of print. A partnership with G. Longman was formed from c.1824–33, working from 6 Ludgate Hill; Samuel Chappell joined them from 1829–c.1833 and on his death in 1834, Bates continued on his own at Ludgate Hill until 1847 when he was assisted by his son. The firm continued as T. C. Bates & Son (1847–59) as Bates & Son, Burdett Road, Stepney (1859–63) and 2 Little Bridge Street, for a further year when the business closed down. In their last advertisement in *The Daily Telegraph* for 1864, they were selling off 'secular organs from £2-2-0 and Church Organs @ £10'.

The Musical Standard dated 15th May, 1863, under Organ News had this to say:

> 'Mr Bates of Ludgate-Hill has just completed a pretty little organ of two manuals, having the following stops.—
> Upper manual: 1. Gamba, 2–3 Stopped Diapason Treble and Bass (sic) 4. Horn.
> Lower manual: 5–6 Open Diapason Treble and Bass, 7. Stop Diapason, 8. Clarabella, 9. Principal, 10. Flute, 11. Fifteenth, 12. Mixture.
> Pedale, 13 notes: Bourdon, 16 foot tone.
> Couplers: 14–15, Upper to Lower Manual. Manual to Pedal. Composition Pedals.

The whole is enclosed in a general Swell and furnishes a very effective instrument at a comparatively moderate cost. The reed of the upper manual is voiced sufficiently loud to make a very fair substitute for a trumpet on what would be in an ordinary organ, called the 'Great Organ'. The case is in ancient English (we hate the term) "Gothic" style and is neat'.

The charming mahogany case at Glentham (newly polished) fits snugly into this little Methodist Chapel, to which it adds a distinct atmosphere of the early 1800s. Until Jonathan Wallace examined it and assured the Trustees that it could be effectively restored, they were thinking of an electronic; now they are extremely proud of it, for not only is it a visual asset, but its charming tone is ideal to lead the congregation Sunday by Sunday. After examining every aspect of the work carried out, I can only say that it represents conservation at its best, for it was a labour of love on the part of Jonathan Wallace, who worked solely on it himself.

METHODIST CHAPEL, GLENTHAM 1993

1 manual: Gamut G to F

Open Diapason (from tenor G)	8	Dulciana (from tenor G, later addition)	8
Stopt Diapason Bafs	8	Principal (gamut G to top F, lowest 4 wood)	4
Stopt Diapason Treble (from tenor G)	8	Flute (from tenor G, later addition)	4

The keys slide into the case and swell shutters on the roof of the box, operated by a cord via a pulley to a pedal, are now permanently open. An ivory name-plate is inscribed: THEODORE E. BATES MANUFACTURER, 6 LUDGATE HILL, LONDON, which places its construction sometime between c.1824–33. The instrument was brought back into use during 1993.

It quickly became clear that the work of the firm was not to be confined to Lincolnshire and Notts., for during 1991, as a result of an advertisement in *The Church Times*, its young owner was approached by Brian J. Martin, F.R.C.O., A.R.C.M., L.R.A.M., of Barnet, with a view to installing a two-manual organ in his church at Monken Hadley, close to High Barnet. The instrument advertised had been purchased from St Mary the Virgin Parish Church, Church Fenton, and it was understood that it had been built originally by Forster & Andrews for a church in Hull which had been bombed during the war. I was approached in the hope that its specification and date built could be traced from the Forster & Andrews Order Books, but there was nothing that bore any resemblance to the specification. There was great disappointment on the part of us all that no firm proof could be found as to its origin. However, it was decided to purchase the organ, which was ideal in every way for its new situation. On examining this fine instrument in the Summer of 1993, I came to the conclusion that the parts of it bore a strong resemblance to the Forster & Andrews tonal policy in the 1860s, but there was nothing else to support this opinion. J. W. Walker & Sons Ltd., who installed the organ at Church Fenton in 1948 and added the trumpet, could find no trace in their records of its previous history. As the three of us concerned (B.J.M., J.M.W. and myself) are all admirers of the Hull firm's work, we have had to accept the fact that we had drawn a blank! but its tonal excellencies are such that its pedigree is of minor importance. It fits perfectly into the church, being situated at the far end of the north aisle; the charming Gothic case is painted 'scorched earth' in colour, with small carved work picked out in gold leaf, while the pipes are in antique silver. The console has sloping stop jambs: the pedal board is straight and slightly concave.

The organ gives forth a fine sound; quiet stops are of real beauty and one is thankful for its preservation and that it is greatly valued by the talented musician who plays it week by week. It was the stepping stone for greater things by the newly constituted Groves firm; Brian Martin spread the news of its success to others and as a result, St Andrew's United Reformed Church, Frognal, and St Peter's Church, Arkley, placed contracts for the rebuild of their instruments. The specification of the Monken Hadley organ must not be forgotten, and is described overleaf.

St Andrew's Church, Frognal, is a very fine example of Edwardian Gothic architecture, opened in 1903. The organ occupies a chamber each side of the chancel, with detached drawstop console (having typical Brindley 'pot' knobs of the period) behind the communion table, with the choir stalls adjoining. An oak reredos is behind the player, extending halfway up the chancel wall, with a stained glass window above; the pews are of oak and the nave windows are filled with stained glass.

MONKEN HADLEY CHURCH 1993

2 manuals: CC to F, 54 notes   Pedal: CCC to F, 30 notes

GREAT ORGAN

	ft
Large Open Diapason	16
Small Open Diapason	8
Stopped Diapason	8
Dulciana	8
Principal	4
Flute	4
Gemshorn	2
Twelfth	2⅔
Fifteenth	2
Sesquialtera	II
Trumpet	8

SWELL ORGAN

Open Diapason	8
Stopped Diapason	8
Principal	4
Cornopean	8
Hautboy	8

PEDAL ORGAN

Bourdon	16

COUPLERS

Swell to Great   Swell to Pedal   Great to Pedal
Balanced Swell pedal   3 composition pedals

Mechanical action throughout

Wind pressure: 3 ins.

ST ANDREW'S CHURCH, FROGNAL 1992

3 manuals: CC to C, 61 notes   Pedal: CCC to F, 30 notes

GREAT ORGAN

	ft
Double Stopped Diapason	16
Open Diapason Large	8
Open Diapason Small	8
Hohl Flute	8
Dulciana	8
Principal	4
Flute Ouverte	4
Fifteenth	2
Mixture	III
Trumpet	8

SWELL ORGAN

Geigen Principal	8
Stopped Diapason	8
Echo Diapason	8
Voix Celeste	8
Gemshorn	4
Flute	4
Mixture 15·19·22	III
Contra Oboe	16
Horn	8
Oboe	8
Clarinet	8

CHOIR ORGAN

Gedacht Flute	8
Salicional	8
Viol d'Orchestre	8
Clear Flute	4
Viole d'Amour	4
Piccolo	2
Cornet	III

PEDAL ORGAN

Open Diapason	16
Bourdon	16
Violoncello	8
Flute	8
Trombone	16

ACCESSORIES

11 couplers and Swell *Tremulant* by stop-keys
25 toe and thumb pistons, adjustable by switches

Balanced swell pedal

All soundboards are sliderless

Wind pressures 4 ins. throughout, except for
Pedal violoncello, 6 ins.

Various plates on the console indicate the organ's history. It was built by Brindley & Foster in 1903; Henry Willis & Sons improved it in 1926 and 1938, Rushworth & Dreaper 1949 and Henry Groves & Son, 1992–93. *Musical Opinion* for December 1938 records: 'This instrument first came into Mr Willis' hands in 1926, when it was overhauled and some important tonal revisions and revoicing undertaken. Now, new electro-pneumatic action has been fitted and further tonal improvements effected together with complete restoration of all parts and installation of new electric blowing plant'.

When Jonathan Wallace carried out his inspection, the organ was in extremely poor condition; indeed, much of it was unplayable. Apart from a very thorough clean and overhaul of all working parts, the main work was the provision of Solid State to replace multi-pallet action and this has been a great success—quick in response, silent and reliable. The very cramped conditions inside the organ made working very difficult; long hours and hard work were the order of the day as the transformation progressed. The reeds were revoiced and have responded well to the expert treatment they have received from F. J. Rogers Ltd., of Bramley, Leeds.

The detached console is in a most unfortunate position, for the sound from each chamber is directed down the church and misses the player, who has no idea what power is being used. In the body of the church, however, the ensemble is extremely fine and very virile, while the quiet stops are of considerable beauty of tone. The instrument is a real triumph for this young organ builder who devoted many hours to the final tonal regulation. The church has a high musical standard and everyone is very appreciative of the work that has been carried out.

The year 1993 saw the commencement of the replacement of the manual and pedal action of the Henry Speechley organ of *c*.1893 in the Parish Church of St Peter, Arkley, Herts., and the substitution of the Great clarinet by a fifteenth in spotted metal. This instrument, with its fine spotted metal front on the south side of the chancel, is a good example of the fine old firm of Henry Speechley & Son, who did much excellent work during its long existence. Henry Speechley worked for J. C. Bishop during the 1840s before he joined Father Willis, to whom he became foreman. When he opened his own business in 1860, he described himself as 'Nephew of the late J. C. Bishop'. About 1889, the firm was known as Henry Speechley & Sons, the two sons, Frank and Harry, having become partners with their father. The quality of their work brought them many orders and over the years they became an honoured name in organ building. The business continued until 1952 and after the death of Frank Speechley, in 1953 (Harry having died in the early 1940s), the business was taken over by Noel Mander, who had been a close friend for some years.

The Arkley organ was built originally with tracker action, later replaced by tubular-pneumatic. As completed by the Groves firm during the early part of 1994, the specification reads:

ST PETER'S CHURCH, ARKLEY, HERTS. 1994

GREAT ORGAN	*ft*		
Open Diapason No. 1	8	Flageolet	2
Open Diapason No. 2	8	Cornopean	8
Dulciana	8	Oboe	8
Clarabella	8	**PEDAL ORGAN**	
Principal	4	Bourdon	16
Flute	4		
Fifteenth	2	**ACCESSORIES**	

SWELL ORGAN

Violin Diapason	8	
Lieblich Gedact	8	
Gemshorn	4	

3 composition pedals each to Swell and Great Organs
5 couplers   Trigger swell pedal

The organ is cone-tuned throughout

Wind pressure: 3 ins.

An extremely busy year closed with the completion of the cleaning and overhauling of the fine two-manual Bishop organ (*c*.1905) in Barrow-on-Soar Parish Church, together with the addition of a fifteenth to the Great Organ.

As this chapter was being completed, in January 1994, the Johnson Organ Co. of Derby was purchased. The large tuning connection was included, while Paul R. Johnson was to join the staff in the Spring. I can but marvel at what has been achieved in so short a time by Jonathan Wallace, who, with great enthusiasm for organ building and a determination to achieve perfection in any work he undertakes, reviews his progress so far with justifiable pride, and looks forward to the future with confidence.

right
St Paul's Church,
Barton, Isle of
Wight. Photo by
Mike Smith

right
An early engraving
of Osborne House,
Isle of Wight

OSBORNE HOUSE, ISLE OF WIGHT.

above
St Andrew's Church, Frognal, London.
The right-hand side case. Photo by the
Author, 1993

left
Theodore Bates organ,
Methodist Chapel, Glentham, Lincs.
Photo by Jonathan Wallace

below
Portable organ, designed and built by
Jonathan Wallace

CHAPTER XV

Miscellaneous

I SUPPOSE that part of this chapter more correctly should be called 'Stop Press', for it contains information that has come in at the last minute which I feel is of value and interest. It was intended to be much smaller, but as this book neared completion, I have discovered certain items which have been amplified by the assistance of others, so that more space has had to be found!

THE CRYSTAL PALACE

In one of my bound volumes of organ builders' publicity material is a collection of Gray & Davison's specifications of the last century. On green paper, they are delightful examples of Victorian design and printing; one of them is the specification of the great organ built in 1851 for the Crystal Palace. It was a very important contract, built at a time when they were busily engaged on building fine organs at their factory, 370 Euston Road, with a branch at 9 Russell Street, Liverpool. Today, the 'Palace' is but a memory to those of my age; to most young people the name means nothing except to those interested in football, for the name is perpetuated by the Crystal Palace football team in the first division. When the Great Exhibition of 1851, in Hyde Park, closed its doors, Paxton's great building of cast iron and glass was moved and enlarged to the heights of Sydenham, where it could be seen for miles around. The Exhibition building had not been built without opposition however, mainly on the part of Col. Sibthorp, the eccentric Tory MP for Lincoln, who told Parliament that he had never been to the Crystal Palace 'and would not have gone had he been offered a thousand pounds... The very sight almost sickens me—stuffed with foreign fancy rubbish. The Crystal Palace is a transparent humbug... the sooner the thing is swept away the better'. Here Father Willis built his epoch making instrument which was his stepping stone to fame and led him to building the organ at St George's Hall, Liverpool, in 1855.

After two years hard work by no less than 5,000 workmen, it was opened on 10th June, 1854, by Queen Victoria, accompanied by Albert, the Prince Consort, their children and the King of Portugal. The whole building, in its extensive grounds, fascinated me as a lad (as it did Roger Yates), but the two great attractions were the weekly Thursday evening fireworks display (the like of which I have never seen since) and the daily organ recitals by Walter Hedgcock, who was organist and accompanist for many years. I was often to be found listening and gazing with rapt attention at the organ in the great concert hall which could accommodate a vast choir and audience of well over 4,000 for the great Handel Festivals held every three years. By then, the organ had been drastically rebuilt by J. W. Walker & Sons in 1920, to the following specification.

THE GRAND TRANSEPT ORGAN, CRYSTAL PALACE 1920

4 manuals: CC to C, 61 notes   Pedal: CCC to F, 30 notes

GREAT ORGAN

	ft		
Double Open Diapason	16	Flute	4
Open Diapason, Large	8	Twelfth	2⅔
Open Diapason, Medium	8	Fifteenth	2
Open Diapsaon, Small	8	Mixture	IV
Harmonic Flute	8	Double Trumpet	16
Wald Flute	8	Posaune	8
Quint	5⅓	Harmonic Trumpet	8
Principal	4	Clarion	4

SWELL ORGAN

Bourdon	16
Open Diapason	8
Gamba	8
Voix Celeste (tenor C)	8
Concert Flute	8
Octave	4
Flute	4
Twelfth	2⅔
Fifteenth	2
Flageolet Harmonic	2
Mixture	IV
Contra Fagotto	16
Cornopean	8
Oboe	8
Clarion	4
Vox Humana	8
Tremulant to stops on light wind	–

CHOIR ORGAN

Contra Gamba	16
Lieblich Bourdon	16
Gamba	8
Salicional	8
Vox Angelica (tenor C)	8
Clarinet Flute	8
Harmonic Flute	4
Claribel Flute	4
Octave Flute	2
Harmonic Piccolo	2
Clarinet	8
Orchestral Oboe	8
Tremulant	

SOLO ORGAN

Open Diapason, Large	8
Harmonic Flute	8
Harmonic Flute	4
Tromba	8
Clarion	4
Corno-di-Bassetto	8
Preparation made for Double Tromba 16ft	–

PEDAL ORGAN

Double Open Diapason	32
Open Diapason, wood	16
Open Diapason, metal	16
Bourdon	16
Gamba (from Choir)	16
Quint	10⅔
Principal	8
Violoncello	8
Octave	8
Flute	8
Contra Bombarde	32
Trombone, metal	16
Ophicleide, wood	16
Trumpet	8

COUPLERS

Choir to Pedal   Great to Pedal   Swell to Pedal
Solo to Pedal   Swell to Great   Swell to Choir
Solo to Great   Swell Octave   Swell Sub Octave
Swell Unison Off   Solo Octave
Solo Sub Octave   Solo Unison Off
Great Pistons to Pedal Combinations

ACCESSORIES ETC.

5 adjustable combination pistons each to Great and
Swell Organs; 3 each to Choir and Solo Organs
1 adjustable combination piston controlling
combinations over the whole organ
5 combination pedals each to Pedal and Swell Organs
2 double-acting pedals; Great to Pedal, Swell to Great
2 double-acting pistons;
Swell tremulant, Choir tremulant
Balanced swell pedal.
Ivory-headed drawstops arranged on fumed oak
panelled stop-jambs placed at 45 degrees.
Tubular-pneumatic action throughout.
Harmonic trebles to chorus reeds.
Wind at various pressures generated by "Discus"
blowing installation electrically driven.
The wind is distributed throughout the organ by
means of fourteen separate reservoirs.

The heyday of the Crystal Palace was in the Victorian and Edwardian eras, when it was tremendously important musically. August Manns (later Sir August), the German born conductor organising musical events between 1855–1901, invited the young George John Bennett (later to become distinguished Organist and Master of the Choristers at Lincoln Cathedral from 1895–1930) to contribute his Serenade and Overture (Jugendtraum) to a concert programme during 1887, when he was only twenty-four years of age. Manns wrote to young Bennett: 'I was glad to find that your new overture fulfilled my first views about its merits and that I was able to secure for it a fine performance… go on as you have begun'. We in Lincoln look back with pride at G. J. B.s era in the city, both at the Cathedral and as conductor of the Lincoln Musical Society and now named the Lincoln Choral Society.

The Crystal Palace was looking shabby when I knew it and much was required to be done and somehow it survived until the great fire on 30th November, 1936, which totally destroyed the building. It was regarded almost as a personal loss by countless numbers of people. For myself, I always eagerly looked forward to the first sight of this great 'glass house' on returning to Beckenham from one of my London jaunts; it seems but yesterday, but it is sixty-two years ago! Memories of the Crystal Palace are kept alive by The Crystal Palace Foundation, a lively and enthusiastic body engaged in research, holding lectures, exhibitions etc., and publishing a quarterly magazine.

THE ORGAN IN THE PALM COURT AT SELFRIDGES

The once flourishing and notable firm of Norman & Beard of Norwich has already been mentioned in connection with Rushworth & Dreaper of Liverpool. As this book was being finalised for the printer, I came across the leaflet describing the organ in the Palm Court, Selfridges, Oxford Street. It seems doubtful whether anyone today has any knowledge of the presence of an organ in this great store and it is appropriate therefore that some space should be allotted to it. The great organ in the Wanamaker store in the USA has achieved world fame, but as far as I am aware, there has been no record of this much smaller instrument in the heart of London's shopping centre. Selfridges' handsome shop was opened on 15th March, 1909. As Norman & Beard went into liquidation in 1916, it would be built between those years and more than likely ready to grace the beautiful Palm Court when it was opened. Many functions were held there when orchestras were engaged to play, and it is understood that selections of music were given during afternoon tea. During the Great War, *Rule Britannia* was played daily!

Although not a large instrument, it was considered to be a prestigious one by Norman & Beard. It is worthwhile briefly to consider the history of the firm which, before its closure, had arguably become the largest in the country.

Let Herbert Norman relate the story: 'William Norman (1830–1877) was a trained cabinet maker in Marylebone and did cabinet work for the nearby organ builder, J. W. Walker. In 1852 he built a one-manual organ in a piano case. It is still extant in private hands in Norfolk. His interest led him to join Walkers as a voicer and his eldest son, William, was apprenticed to them and was discharged for breach of his indentures by sitting on his bench idle because he wanted to be taught voicing! In 1873 he moved to stay with relatives in Diss, in Norfolk, where he commenced business as an organ tuner. His brother, Herbert John, then aged twelve (1861–1937), joined him there as an apprentice. By 1879 (he was eighteen), he was doing the tuning round with a Russian pony and trap, picking up key holders at the local school, for the master was often the parish organist. G. Wales Beard joined him as a fellow apprentice about 1875. Norman Bros. moved to Norwich sometime in the 1880s; here they built the Cathedral organ, under the name of Norman Bros. and Beard, in 1889. They became one of the first Limited Companies as Norman and Beard Ltd. and took possession of their large purpose-built works at St Stephen's Gate, Norwich, circa 1898. Hitherto, their works had been at Chapel Field Road, Norwich: in *Musical Opinion* for October 1st, 1889, they advertised: 'Organ Pedals, new method of attachment to Pianos by Tubular Pneumatic Action. Unsurpassed for prompt and organ-like touch'. Wales Beard became salesman based in the City of London, first in Poultry E.C., later Berners Street (near Selfridges)'.

Eventually they had a London factory in addition to that at Norwich; this was at 19 Ferdinand Street, Chalk Farm, N.W., which was part of Chappel's piano works. For a time it was under the joint management of T. C. Lewis and Herbert Davis who, for many years, was managing foreman to Messrs. Henry Willis and Sons. In 1899, Norman & Beard purchased the business of the Electric Organ Co. Ltd., founded by Robert Hope-Jones, and this they carried on in conjunction with their own.

The quality of their work rapidly became known, resulting in many important contracts being received; their works at Norwich was the largest in Britain and all in all there was a staff of 300 at the firm's peak. The timber yards, which were separated from the main works immediately opposite Victoria Station, covered a large acreage and contained over £1,000 of selected and well-seasoned timber of all kinds, in addition to which there were specially heated drying buildings for the treatment of timber required for instruments destined for extreme climates. At their busiest period they turned out one organ per week. It can be truly said that their factory was run with the same efficiency as that of the John Compton Organ Co. Ltd. in later years. Resident tuners were at Glasgow, Cambridge, Diss, Liverpool, Leeds, Nottingham, Birmingham, Bristol, Swansea and Belfast. Their quality of work was such that I have always felt that it was a great pity that it could not continue as an independent firm. It went into liquidation in 1916, after shipping the Johannesburg Town Hall organ to its destination, and joined with Wm. Hill & Son to become Hill, Norman & Beard Ltd. This four-manual instrument with 97 speaking stops was described by Dr. Alfred Hollins (who drew up the specification) as a 'great artistic triumph'. E. W. Norman designed the mechanism, which was tubular-pneumatic, and Mr Herbert Norman snr. closely supervised the whole project and carried out the tonal finishing in the hall. It became one of the great organs of the world and it is sad that it was the last to be built by this firm as an independent concern, which enjoyed phenomenal success for but a short period of time.

The young Herbert Norman, son of H. J. N., left Norwich in September 1916, aged twelve, for Great Yarmouth, where he was to study architecture. Together with his brother 'and a barrel of home-grown apples, he rode on Mr Moon's horse-drawn trolley—his last job for Norman & Beard'.

To return to the Palm Court organ at Selfridges. In 1918, at the age of sixteen, Herbert joined his father in the firm after studying at the Great Yarmouth College of Art, and with him visited the Selfridge Store where he saw the Palm Court organ being dismantled and packed on to a steam waggon belonging to Jones of Holloway. Two men were assisting—one of whom having the reputation of being the strongest man in the factory— he could carry anything, even a soundboard! The organ had been bought by Pardo Thomas, a shipping magnate of Newport, for his home, and for the young Herbert this was his first job with father in the newly created firm of H. N. B. Mr Herbert Norman (to whose kindness I am able to publish these reminiscences) has a phenomenal memory at the age of ninety, and tells me that the waggon narrowly missed over-turning at Chepstow, for it was not built to carry such a heavy load. The organ was duly erected in the music room of the Pardo residence; this was much smaller than its former home at the Palm Court, with a result that it proved too loud. So—Mr Herbert Norman snr. installed specially designed swell shutters of mahogany, which helped matters. The shutters in fact gave total enclosure, so the main Swell was affected and the strings and celeste ranks became almost inaudible when both were closed. This installation was valuable experience for his son for he was able to learn all about exhaust pneumatic action on the spot. He recalls sorting out the wood pipes and had a great difficulty in finding one—E sharp—luckily it eventually came to light! On the death of Pardo Thomas, the organ was left by him in his Will, to a church in the suburbs of Newport, Monmouth.

THE ORGAN IN THE PALM COURT AT SELFRIDGES c.1910

3 manuals: CC to C, 61 notes   Pedal: CCC to G, 32 notes

THE ORGAN IN THE PALM COURT AT SELFRIDGE'S

GREAT ORGAN

	ft
Open Diapason (large)	8
Open Diapason (small)	8
Claribel Flute	8
Dolce	8
Principal	4
Tromba	8
Swell Octave to Great	
Swell Sub Octave to Great	
Choir Sub Octave to Great	

SWELL ORGAN

Lieblich Bourdon	16
Geigen Principal	8
Lieblich Gedacht	8
Aeoline	8
Voix Celeste	8
Lieblich Flöte	4
Cornet d'Violes	III
Harmonic Horn	8
Tremulant	
Sub Octave	
Octave	
Choir Sub Octave to Swell	

CHOIR & ORCHESTRAL ORGAN

Hohl Flute	8
Viole d'Orchestre	8
Dulciana	8
Concert Flute	4
Orchestral Clarinet	8
Orchestral Oboe	8
Vox Humana	8
Tromba (from Great)	8
†Carillon	—
Tremulant	
Sub Octave	
Octave	
Unison Off	

PEDAL ORGAN

Open Diapason	16
Sub Bass	16
Lieblich Bordun	16
Bass Flute	8

UNISON COUPLERS

Swell to Great   Swell to Pedal   Swell to Choir
Great to Pedal   Choir to Great   Choir to Pedal

The organ is blown by an electric motor by
The Rotasphere Co.
The action is tubular-pneumatic throughout.

† The Carillon is a novelty and the first of its kind
to be installed in a Concert Organ.

The Palm Court was destroyed by enemy action on 10th May, 1941, having already been damaged in an air raid on 16th of the previous month. After the war, a restaurant took its place; canned music had come to stay and the age of Edwardian elegance is now but a memory.

SAXON ALDRED, REDBOURNE, HERTS.

In 1960, when Compton's pipe organ division had lost drive, Saxon Aldred joined the firm of Cooper, Gill and Tomkins, of Cape Town. So, after finishing all the drawings and preparatory arrangements for the installation of the new Compton organ at St Andrew's Church, Holborn, he packed his bags and flew to Cape Town. Both Cooper and Gill were former J. J. Binns men who had come out to erect organs in Cape Town and had decided to stay. Tomkins was a former Norman & Beard man who had come out with the last Norman & Beard job, and their biggest, for Johannesburg Town Hall in 1915. In 1968, Saxon met his wife, Bryony, and they were married in her home town of Padstow, Cornwall. They returned to South Africa and eventually came home for good in 1973, sailing on one of the last voyages of The Edinburgh Castle—a memorable trip. He obtained a post at the works of Peter Collins, Redbourne, and here he tells me that he learned more about organ building than in the thirteen years he had spent overseas. He worked on jobs in Brasenose College, Oxford, Worksop Priory and a number of others. In 1976, he decided to commence his own business and so began to be involved in restoring historically interesting organs, together with rebuilds, some maintenance, with new instruments from time to time. His policy has been 'to try and give all his work a freshness of tone and sensitivity of touch in order accurately to relay the feelings contained in the music through the organist to those listening'.

New organs have included some interesting one and two-manual and pedal schemes, which have been exhibited at the St Alban's International Organ Festivals. Two-manual instruments have included

St Mary's Church, Guildford, with 14 stops and suspended tracker action and St Mary's Parish Church, Battersea. This scheme is interesting and represents his current thinking for an organ of this size, on which all schools of music may be performed as well as its main purpose for liturgical use. It was built during 1991–92. There is some former pipework incorporated in the following specification.

ST MARY'S PARISH CHURCH, BATTERSEA 1992

2 manuals: CC to G, 56 notes   Pedal: CCC to F, 30 notes

Courtesy of Saxon Aldred

GREAT ORGAN

	ft
Open Diapason	8
new front pipes, with old Swell open	
Stopped Diapason	8
old Swell bourdon revoiced	
Bell Gamba (tenor C)	8
old, revoiced	
Principal	4
Old Swell principal revoiced	
Open Wood Flute	4
old, revoiced	
Gemshorn, *new 1:2 taper*	2
Nazard, *new 1:2 taper*	2⅔
Tierce, *new 1:2 taper*	1⅗
Fourniture	IV
Old Swell mixture plus second-hand	
pipes, 12·15·19·22	
Trumpet, *new 52% spotted metal*	8

SWELL ORGAN

Clarabella, *ex Great, revoiced*	8
Viol, *old, revoiced*	8
Principal, *old, revoiced*	4
Chimney Flute, *ex 8ft revoiced,*	4
plus 12 new top notes	
Fifteenth, *new spotted metal*	2
Larigot, *new, plain metal, 1:2 taper*	1⅓
Mixture, *new, spotted metal, 19·22·26·29*	IV
Fagotto, *ex oboe, with new bass*	16
Cornopean, *old, revoiced*	8
Cremona, *ex Great clarinet, revoiced*	8

PEDAL ORGAN

Bourdon, *old, revoiced*	16
Principal Bass, *old Great diapason, revoiced*	8
Gedackt Bass, *violone, stoppered*	8

Fifteenth, *old Great principal*	4
Posaune, *new, zinc and 52% spotted metal*	16

OTHER DETAILS ETC.

6 couplers and Tremulant   15 thumb and toe pistons

Suspended tracker action for manuals
Balanced tracker action for the pedals

Electric drawstops with Plug Link piston action.

Wind Pressures: Swell & Great, 3 ins., Pedal 3½ ins.

Manual keys covered with bone and ebony
Concave and radiating pedal board in oak
with ebony sharps.

'Ventus' organ blower.

Saxon Aldred makes a speciality of small instruments for private residences or small churches. Of either one or two manuals, they are voiced in the Early English style, the finest quality materials being used. His wife Bryony plays an important part in his business, designing and carving casework for any situation. Her work may be seen in the Battersea instrument, the architectural details here being by Frank Bradbeer (formerly with Grant, Degens & Bradbeer).

The ideals of Saxon Aldred are a far cry from the instruments he was helping to create for Comptons. His workshop at the Old Chapel, 6 Lydbury Lane, Redbourne, is the home of individual, high quality craftsmanship, backed by his expertise with many years of varied experience in all methods of organ building.

WILLIAM DRAKE, BUCKFASTLEIGH

'Bill' Drake, as he is known to his many friends, worked with Roger Yates on one or two occasions; his reminiscences of Roger and his work have been invaluable in the writing of this book, and it is only right that Drake's important contribution to organ building in an entirely different style, should be recorded here. He studied his craft in Austria and Germany, working in both countries with several firms and with a colleague he was responsible for the conservation of Italian organs in Yugoslavia. He obtained the German Master Organ Building Certificate and then settled in Buckfastleigh in 1974, opening a workshop with very definite ideas as to the style of work he wished to embark upon. He is a purist in outlook, with ability and patience to study in depth examples of eighteenth-century work before embarking on whatever project he undertakes. This, together with the use of the very finest materials and workmanship, have all contributed to make him an artist craftsman of the highest order. He is aided by three staff, including two Dutch organ builders.

In 1975, Bill Drake built a two-manual organ, tuned to an eighteenth-century tuning realised by Alexander Mackenzie of Ord (whom I met on several occasions when he was residing near Bristol in the heart of the surrounding countryside). This was for the John Loosemore Centre for Organ and Early Music Studies, Buckfastleigh, the intention being to build an instrument on which the sounds of the sixteenth- and seventeenth-century composers will sound as they did in the period before the present system of equal temperament was adopted. The centre takes its name from the famous seventeenth-century organ builder of Devon, and is housed in the former United Reformed Church, Buckfastleigh. The opening of this centre realised the vision of Mr Drake, John Willingham, organ teacher, and others. The instrument consisted of two manuals and pedal, together with eleven stops.

His work came very much to the fore in 1991, when he built a new instrument for Grosvenor Chapel, London. The decision to place the work with him was based on his fine instruments at Totnes, Stourport and Lulworth Castle; here he restored the eighteenth-century instrument in the chapel. The original case by Abraham Jordan at Grosvenor Chapel was restored by Drake, with pipe gilding by John Brennan. The new specification 'represents a typical eighteenth-century scheme, with the addition of a quint mixture on the Swell and a small Pedal Organ seen as an extension of the manual stops'.

THE GROSVENOR CHAPEL, LONDON 1992

GREAT ORGAN

	ft		
Open Diapason	8	Principal	4
Stopt Diapason	8	Fifteenth	2
Principal	4	Cornet Treble 12·15·17	III
Flute	4	Cornet Bass 17·19·22	III
Twelfth	2⅔	Mixture 22·26·29	III
Fifteenth	2	Trumpet	8
Sesquialtera 17·19·22	III	Hautboy	8
Furniture 19·22·26	III		
Cornet (from middle C) 1·8·12·15·17	V	**PEDAL ORGAN**	
Trumpet Treble	8	Stopt Diapason	16
Trumpet Bass	8	Principal	8
		Trumpet	16

SWELL ORGAN

Open Diapason	8	
Stopt Diapason	8	

3 couplers   Balanced swell pedal
Mechanical action to keys and drawstops

Completed in 1992, the organ has attracted many well-known recitalists and concerts have been given by the professional choir under the direction of the Director of Music, Richard Hobson. It will be seen that the organ has gone back to its eighteenth-century roots and William Drake has been described as 'a pioneer in the extent of its re-creation of the original'. At the time of writing, he was to build a chamber organ for Alfred Champness; he has built a practice organ for Thomas Trotter and in 1993 he installed an instrument in the nineteenth-century style in Jesus College, Oxford.

LANCE FOY, TRURO

A modest man, a Cornishman born and bred, and completely dedicated to his craft, Lance Foy's knowledge of organs in the county of Cornwall is encyclopaedic. This is not surprising since he has some 250 organs in the West Country and Isles of Scilly in his care. In a letter to me dated 10th February, 1991, giving me information regarding Roger Yates and replying to my request for details of his own activities, the letter concluded: 'I am not really a very interesting sort of fellow, so don't waste pen and ink on me'. A 'phone call in March of this year informing him that I *did* intend to waste *printer's* ink on him, brought a ready response and so, as often in contacts such as this, I learned much of value which is worth recording.

He is one of a small group of organ builders in the West Country who enjoys working with wood and metal to produce the best possible sounds they can—moreover, they gladly co-operate with one another from time to time and this I find most encouraging. It was Henry Willis IV, who, if I remember rightly, some years ago stated, that in his opinion, the future of organ building lay in small craft workshops. He has proved to be right, for apart from 'the big six' this book alone gives some idea of the excellent work being done by small firms, and there are others who go unrecorded.

Lance Foy was apprenticed to Hele of Plymouth (who were then consolidated with J. W. Walker & Sons Ltd.) where he worked as a journeyman until their Cornish representative retired, when he took over his post until 1974 on deciding to commence his own business. With a workshop at Truro and six staff, together with his wife, he has kept very busy and at the time of writing has work booked ahead to 1995. He describes himself as 'a general practitioner' equally interested in restorations or rebuilds with electric or mechanical action as well as tuning and maintenance. He is fortunate in having an excellent flue and reed voicer on his staff, Howard Bye, while there is a pipe-maker to the trade, close at hand, Don Wherly, at Pensilva near Liskeard on the edge of Bodmin Moor. Most of Roger Yates' work is in the care of Lance Foy and he derives particular satisfaction in keeping it in good trim. There are a number of Father Willis organs in the area and he takes great pride in their maintenance and conservation. Keeping Truro Cathedral's Father Willis (1887) up to scratch is a labour of love, for he assisted N. P. Mander Ltd. in their reconstruction of this lovely instrument during 1991. I have known the Truro organ for more years than I care to remember; in common with those at Lincoln and Salisbury Cathedrals (not forgetting Hereford too), one feels that there is nothing quite like them. In an article in *The Guardian* on 26th June, 1971, by Christopher Ford, entitled 'The Mersey Sound, the Willis Family, makers of romantic organs', he quotes Noel Rawsthorne (Organist at Liverpool Cathedral from 1955–1980); 'The first time I went into Truro Cathedral, it must be twenty-five years ago. I didn't know the organ at all… the organist was improvising quietly; it was a thrilling sound and I said at once, it must be a Willis'.

One of the finest Father Willis organs in the area, and an early one too (1864), was a large three-manual, originally built with Barker-Lever action and a very complete tonal scheme and altogether a real thriller, at the former Congregational Church (later URC), Sherwell, Plymouth. Henry Willis & Sons and Lewis & Co., as the firm was known in 1923, restored it in that year and in 1951 Hele & Co. installed electro-pneumatic action and a detached console, but it escaped any tonal alterations. In 1989, it became possible to purchase it and replace the organ in the Parish Church of St Michael and All Angels, Great Torrington, North Devon. Lance Foy carried out the work of re-furbishing and reconstruction for its new site, but no alterations were made to the tone. The few additions made are the result of extension or borrowing from the original ranks.

ST MICHAEL & ALL ANGELS, GREAT TORRINGTON 1989

GREAT ORGAN

	ft
Double Open Diapason	16
Open Diapason I	8
Open Diapason II	8
Stopped Diapason	8
Principal	4
Harmonic Flute	4
Twelfth	2⅔
Fifteenth	2
Mixture	III
Posaune	8
Clarion	4

SWELL ORGAN

Double Diapason	16
Open Diapason	8
Gedackt	8
Salicional	8
†Celeste	8
Principal	4
Piccolo	2
Mixture	III
Contra Fagotto	16
Cornopean	8
Oboe	8
†Vox Humana	8
Clarion	4
Tremulant	
Sub Octave	
Super Octave	
Unison Off	

CHOIR ORGAN

Open Diapason	8
Stopped Diapason	8
Dulciana	8
Viol d'Amour	8
Concert Flute	4
Harmonic Piccolo	2
Corno di Bassetto	8
Orchestral Oboe	8
Posaune (from Great)	8
Swell to Choir	
Sub Octave	
Super Octave	

PEDAL ORGAN

Open Diapason	16
Bourdon	16
Quint	10⅔
Violoncello	8
Flute	8
Octave Flute	4
Ophicleide	16
Posaune (from Great)	8
Clarion (from Great)	4
Swell to Pedal Great to Pedal Choir to Pedal	

ACCESSORIES

Usual complement of couplers etc., by means of 64-Channel Capture System with Setter Panel.

† Tucker of Plymouth (?1881) together with two pedal stops.

Another three-manual Father Willis organ I knew well, some thirty years or so ago (that at St Paul's Church, Bournemouth), was removed in 1984 when the church was made redundant, and stored until it was rebuilt with electric action and solid state switching, for All Hallows Church, St Kea, in 1989. Every effort was made to preserve the Willis pipework in its original condition, very little regulation and balancing being necessary for its new environment. It is interesting to record that the keyboards and some of the woodwork and the Willis name-plate are from the Truro Cathedral console prior to its rebuilding in 1963.

Restoration of historic instruments has included the two-manual Byfield organ in Truro Cathedral, the Avery organ in the Chapel of St Michael's Mount, and the Crang & Hancock organ in Barnstaple Parish Church (in collaboration with Michael Farley).

Recent major work includes the rebuild with tonal additions of the three-manual Hele organ in the Parish Church of St Ives (which I remember well when we spent some very happy holidays there a number of years ago), together with the rebuild of the instrument in Falmouth Parish Church, where Lance is assistant organist.

What has given me particular pleasure is to learn that one of the 'Premier Organs' (one-manual with automatic Pedal Bass) by Cousans, Sons & Co., of Lincoln, at Gwithian Church, has been restored by Lance Foy.

Truro was once the home of an organ builder by the name of W. J. Brewer of 97 Pydar Street, from c1883–1893, the latter date being the final entry in the *City of Truro Directory*. He was taken over by Heard & Sons, a very old established firm of instrument and music dealers who were established in 1810, and although the ownership changed over the years, they were advertising as instrument dealers and organ builders as late as 1920 in *The Music Trade Directory* for that year. Brewer worked for them for some time and many fine and solidly built tracker instruments, with excellent tonal qualities, were constructed both by Brewer on his own and on behalf of Heards. The work of both has responded successfully to restoration and this has given Lance Foy great satisfaction. A character and a man of many parts, he enjoys his work and the social contact with organists and other organ builders in the West Country, all of whom have one thing in common—the love of organs.

JARDINE & CO., MANCHESTER EST. 1889

In checking through a Manchester Telephone Directory during preparation of this book, I was delighted to find therein the entry of Jardine Organs of Old Trafford, Manchester, for I had been informed that this fine old firm had ceased to exist in 1976. This was a great disappointment to me for I had traced the long history of the Jardine family and their successors in my book, *Bishop and Son, Organ Builders*, while I had a lifelong connection with and admiration for the three-manual organ built in 1891 for Newland Congregational Church, Lincoln, which alas, is now no more.

The facts, as kindly related to me by Mr M. R. Denny are as follows: The firm of Jardine & Co. Ltd., whose managing director, Mr Dennis Walker, who had carried it on for some time, unfortunately found it necessary to go into voluntary liquidation in September 1976. Determined to keep the business alive, only one week later founded a new firm, Jardine pipe Organs Ltd., from his home, together with Mr M. R. Denny and two others, and with the support of old customers they were able to continue their tuning and maintenance together with cleanings and rebuilding. The latter was made possible by Longstaff & Jones of Dudley doing some of their bench work, Jardines reciprocating by assisting them on site when the occasion arose. Sadly, Dennis Walker died suddenly in June 1980. It was his wish that the honoured name of Jardine should continue, which it did effectively for some time until 1982, when re-organisation became necessary and Martin Denny, together with David Ginder, formed the present company. David Ginder was with the original firm of Jardine & Co. and rejoined Dennis Walker about 1978.

Premises in Silk Street, Salford, were in use for some two years, but due to compulsory purchase and later demolition, a move was made to their present premises at 43 Elsinore Road, Old Trafford, only a few yards from the original Jardine & Co. works, which still stand. The former Technical Director of

Jardines, Mr Harold Davies, J.P., F.I.S.O.B., F.I.M.I.T., although retired, is still active in the present firm as consultant and training officer for apprentices.

Tuning and maintenance is carried out as far afield as South Wales, Norfolk, Oxford, North Cumbria and Yorkshire, including Cathedral and City Hall contracts. They work on all types of actions, from mechanical to the latest multiplex and programmable piston action, and are always glad to be associated with restorations of historic instruments. It is to be hoped that the honoured name of Jardine, which has been associated with Manchester since 1848, will go forward successfully for many years to come under its present enthusiastic and go-ahead management.

ROGER TAYLOR, BURRINGTON, BRISTOL

Roger Taylor can be described as the Curator of the Downside Abbey organ, for he is very committed in keeping this *magnum opus* of John Compton in first class condition. His enthusiasm for its design and tonal qualities is infectious. He has other Compton organs in his care too, some of which he has up-dated with new solid state action, including St David's Catholic Cathedral, Cardiff, and Victoria Street Methodist Church, Weston-Super-Mare, where the console has been moved and new solid state action fitted; both are 'ten rankers'. I am delighted to learn that they have been given a new lease of life for many years to come, for adverse comment on Compton extension organs, from time to time in this so-called 'enlightened' age, disturb me, to put it mildly. Other Compton organs in his care are St Martin's Church, Roath, Cardiff (a rebuild of a three-manual Hill), Sketty Methodist Church, Swansea, a two-manual of four ranks, formerly in Townhill Methodist Church, Swansea, and St Mark's Methodist Church, Cheltenham (two manuals, four ranks).

A former employee of Rushworth & Dreaper, Roger Taylor established his business at Burrington, some fifteen miles outside of Bristol in 1982. He has the assistance of one man and leads a very busy life, which embraces tunings, repairs, overhauls, restorations and rebuilds, and he enjoys working on some fine instruments in the West Country by such builders as Vowles, Sweetland and Nicholson & Lord. Conservation work has been carried out to the 1884 Vowles organ at St Nicholas on the Mount, Without, at Bristol, while the former Vowles organ at Clifton Down United Reformed Church, Bristol, removed to St Mary's Church, Castle Street, Reading, has been re-trackered but no tonal alterations made. Dr. Christopher Kent was the consultant. At Minchinhampton Parish Church, Gloucs., a three-manual Nicholson & Lord/Hill, Norman & Beard, has been fully restored, while a Sweetland three-manual organ from Trinity Methodist Church, Risca Green, South Wales, has been electrified and moved to the Methodist Church, Aberdare. At the time of writing, a three-manual Norman & Beard organ in the Methodist Church, Penarth, is to be electrified and in 1995, a three-manual Binns of 1925 at St Alban's Church, Westbury Park, is to be electrified.

WORDSWORTH & MASKELL AND THEIR SUCCESSORS

Leeds has been the home of at least seven organ builders during almost two centuries; J. J. Binns, John Calvert, est. 1877, Wm. Holt & Co., est. 1830, Radcliffe & Sagar, est. 1861, Wordsworth & Maskell, later Wordsworth & Co., est. 1866, together with four pipemakers and voicers: F. Booth & Sons, Terry Davies, William Naylor (est. 1898) and F. J. Rogers, est. 1897.

Wordsworths had a large connection in the counties of Lancashire, Lincolnshire and Yorkshire; in Leeds alone they built over fifty new organs as well as rebuilding fifteen others. In all, Yorkshire accounted for over eighty instruments, Lancashire being a close runner up with sixty or so. They exported to Australia, India, Newfoundland, Russia, Victoria B.C., Canada and the West Indies. In attending the Methodist Church, Suddar Street, Calcutta, one Sunday whilst serving in the RAF in India, I found a pleasant Wordsworth two-manual organ, but I was not allowed to play it after service; that privilege was granted to no one! Their most prestigious instrument was the four-manual in Epping Parish Church, with its magnificent case; this was in 1895. At St Margaret's Church, Kings Lynn, in 1895, they rebuilt the historic organ, originally the work of Snetzler. Their other four-manual was at Rudstone Parish Church, Bridlington, in 1889, for Mr A. W. M. Bosville, who resided at Thorpe Hall, Bridlington. Now in the care of Peter Wood & Son, it had 68 stops, electro-pneumatic action and a detached console, 140 feet away! The original blowing apparatus consisted of a 2 h.p. electric motor acting on a quadruple crankshaft connected to four double-acting feeders, discharging air at about 800 cubic feet per minute, Mr Bosville supplying the electricity from his plant at the hall. He soon found that he did not have a sufficient supply for the motor, and so it was replaced in 1891 by an apparatus driven by a Priestman Oil Engine, designed by Mr Herbert Davis and Mr J. C. R. Okes, of London. This is fully described in Chapter VI of the writer's book, *Organ Blowing, its History and Development* (1971). This instrument was rebuilt as a two-manual by Rushworth & Dreaper in 1933.

At Lincoln Cathedral, J. M. W. Young, organist from 1850–95, was never very happy with the mechanism of the instrument, and so Wordsworth renewed much of it and transferred the keyboards from their original position between the two cases (on the Quire side) to the north side of the main case, thus making the instrument available for services in the nave as well as in the Quire. As far as can be ascertained, this was sometime during the 1880s. I treasure a drawstop from this console, given to me by the late Mrs Olive Riggall, daughter of the late Dr. G. J. Bennett.

The firm of Wordsworth & Maskell/Wordsworth & Co. built no less than twenty-three organs for Lincolnshire churches, being introduced to the county by Canon F. H. Sutton (author of *Some account of the medieval organ case still existing at Old Radnor, South Wales and Church Organs, their position and construction*. Canon Sutton was not only an authority on organs, but also a designer and maker of stained glass, which he carried out at his Rectory at Brant Broughton, near Lincoln. He designed the organ in his own church at Brant Broughton in 1888 and Leadenham Church, a little later, both being built by Wordsworth. Both are still in existence.

Sometime during the 1870s, John Edward Wood entered the firm and eventually rose to the position of foreman; during the next decade he was promoted to the status of partner and by 1922 the business became known as Wood, Wordsworth & Co. His son, John William Wood, followed in his father's footsteps and from the early 1920s the firm's output was mostly under his direction. In common with a number of other firms, they survived the Great War of 1914–18, with limited resources. His son Peter, born in 1931, entered the business at the age of fifteen, went through every department and succeeded his father as Managing Director in 1967. Like many other craftsmen in this trade, father did not retire, but continued working until his death in 1981 aged eighty-eight! Peter Wood, with a staff of up to twenty-four, carried on, carrying out mostly rebuilds around the country from Hampshire and Sussex up to Elgin in Scotland. The firm gained the contract to rebuild the Leeds Town Hall organ in the 1970s, reducing it from four manuals to three. Dennis Thurlow, who was responsible for the voicing and tonal finishing, went on long into the night to enable the work to be completed by the stipulated time. Work on Leeds Parish Church and Worcester Cathedral followed, but by 1981 the business was compelled to go into voluntary liquidation, which was a great blow to the Wood family. Happily however, it was possible to make a fresh start with Peter, his son Mark, and a staff of four, working in the most idylic setting—literally as a cottage industry. They have carried out a considerable number of rebuilds and electrifications over the years and have a particular interest in conservation. Their work covers a wide area and at the time of writing they are fully occupied for a year ahead.

F. J. ROGERS LTD., PIPE MAKERS & VOICERS, LEEDS

Modern technology plays such an important part in the world of organ building—even the 'computer draughtsman' is with us—that it was refreshing to pay a visit recently to see the age-old craft of pipe making being carried out in the largest establishment of its kind in England, that of F. J. Rogers Ltd., of Elmfield Works, Town End, Bramley, Leeds. Here there are eighteen members of staff together with three in the office, working to capacity, supplying pipes voiced and unvoiced for this country and as far away as Australia, Bermuda, Canada, France, Japan, New Zealand, South Africa, Tokyo and the USA. The firm was founded in 1897 by Frederick Rogers, a pipe-maker who had worked for J. J. Binns. The high quality of his work soon became known and by 1902 he purchased larger premises and took in two junior partners, bringing with them their expertise from local firms, and from that time onwards success was assured. Bob Buckle rose from the ranks to become managing director in 1959; his son Stephen (who became a director), was a fine voicer and his untimely death six years ago was a great blow to the family and the business. He contributed a very informative article on 'The casting of organ pipe metal, Lead/Tin Alloys, to *The Organbuilder*, Vol. 1, March 1983. Yorkshire folk have always been noted for their tenacity, and with great courage Mrs Elizabeth Buckle took over the management of the firm, aided by Mr & Mrs R. Buckle senr., who come in three days each (the latter being responsible for the book-keeping) so that it is still a family concern, and a very happy one too, which is evident as soon as one has been in the building for a short time. Mrs Buckle travels the world to discuss the requirements of leading organ builders, who appreciate her complete grasp of every facet of pipe scales, construction and voicing, and so interesting were her experiences that we could have outstayed her warm welcome. She proudly describes herself as a Scot/Yorkshirewoman!

It is many years since I saw metal being cast at the works of Cousans, Lincoln; on the morning of our visit, the molten metal was just right for pouring from the skilly into the gauge and then 'run' down the casting bench (which is of slate) and behold—a long sheet of fine metal was the result. The accompanying photograph was taken by the author just at the right moment.

Casting metal at the works of F. J. Rogers Ltd., Leeds 1994. Photo by the Author

The sight of gleaming pipes of metal, spotted metal and pure tin standing by the walls, after being meticulously crafted on the benches of men obviously dedicated to their trade, was most impressive, as were a number of packing cases awaiting despatch to their various destinations. Finally, we heard a superb trumpet on 2¼ ins. wind, voiced by Roger Penny, who has been with the firm for nineteen years. It had considerable brilliance and splash, without being brittle in tone—in short, a very impressive example of voicing.

This quotation from *Ecclesiasticus*, Ch. 38, in a brochure of the firm, aptly sums up the endeavours of those working at Elmfield Works: "All these rely on their hands and each is skilled in his own work...".

ROY YOUNG, RUGBY EST. 1973

Roy Young not only is a skilled organ builder devoted to his craft, but an enthusiastic preservationist too, of good historic work and above all that of Taylor of Leicester whom he admires so much, for it was there that he came into daily contact with all that is best in organ building. He was an indentured apprentice to Taylors between 1948–54. Here he was involved not only in general organ building but in the blowing department too, assisting in some of the sheet metal work and silencing boxes, not to mention installation in some very difficult sites. After completing his National Service, he gained valuable experience as a draughtsman in an engineering works, did some part-time work as an organ builder and eventually started his own business in 1973. He works from a two-hundred year old former Congregational Chapel at Stretton-under-Fosse, a splendid old building with storage room in the galleries and ample workshop space down below. Originally he had an apprentice and a small staff; now he and his son Keith work closely together, sharing the same enthusiasm and he has extra assistance where there is heavy lifting to be done. He is responsible for all his own flue voicing and is fully experienced in the use of solid state. When time permits, he is fortunate to have some assistance from the last of the Taylors, Stephen (J.S.G. Taylor), who, although an Experimental Officer in the Department of Physics, Leicester University, has organ building in his blood and is a mine of information about the family firm. It is understandable therefore, that Leicester City Council placed the De Montford Hall organ in his care from 1975, and the ongoing restoration of this magnificent instrument is a matter of great pride to him and his son Keith. The work (not yet completed) is being carried out in stages when funds permit.

A sample of some of the interesting contracts he has carried out since 1973 includes the rebuild of an 1863 Bevington organ at Attleborough Church, Nuneaton (*c*1973), the electrification of the three-manual Nicholson & Lord organ in the Baptist Church, Rugby (1976), and the restoration as it was of the one-manual Lincoln organ of 1806 in the Baptist Church, Studley.

In 1980, he built a new two-manual organ with electric action (which included some pipes from the former Forster & Andrews organ in Holy Trinity Church, Rugby) for St George's Church in that town. The year 1989 saw the restoration of the Speechley organ in Launde Abbey, Leics.

Roy Young is an organist too and leads an extremely busy life enjoying to the full his main interest—organ building.

CONSERVATION

The word conservation is becoming more frequently used in the 'topsy turvy' world of organ building today, for which I am truly thankful as long as it does not go to extremes, which is not unknown here and there. Valuable work in this direction has been done by Harrison & Harrison in restoring the sound of the Lewis organ of 1897 in Southwark Cathedral, the 1890 Lewis in St Paul's Cathedral, Melbourne, Australia, and their own instrument in the Caird Hall, Dundee, which retains its original pneumatic action of 1923, to quote but three. N. P. Mander Ltd. have done similar conservation work, retaining the original tone and pneumatic action at Bristol Cathedral and Eton College Chapel, while Henry Willis & Sons and Peter Conacher & Co., under the direction of John Sinclair Willis, together with other smaller firms, are showing great interest in such work.

The latest major work of this nature, carried out by Harrison & Harrison, was at the Albert Hall, Nottingham, where on 29th October, 1993, the Binns organ spoke once again in all its glory, to the great delight of a capacity audience of organists, organ lovers, organ builders and the general public. I cannot recall a more enthusiastic evening; Thomas Trotter electrified us all and the authentic Binns sound was heard again after a number of years of silence. After being undervalued by some who have described the Binns sound as 'plenty of roast beef, Yorkshire 'Pud' and two veg...', we can now rejoice in the vision that has been shown to re-create the sound that Binns originally created, for there have been alterations along the way, since he built it in 1909 for the then Albert Hall Methodist Mission, it being the gift to the City of Nottingham by Sir Jesse Boot, whose shopfitters made the fine walnut casework. Since the closure of the Hall on the cessation of its use by the Methodists, it had been out of use. It is now a conference centre, with a new floor inserted at gallery level, thus creating additional space downstairs, and here Harrisons had mounted an impressive display of their work.

No alterations have been made; the original tubular-pneumatic action has been meticulously restored and is absolutely silent; it should work efficiently for many years to come. Great care and skill on the part of Harrison's chief voicer, Peter Hopps, has restored the reeds to the tone intended by Binns and voiced for him by the celebrated voicer—Evenett of London. To this end, Binns' instructions to Evenett and his comments to Binns were helpful.

Bernard Johnson, City Organist from 1910–34, whose recitals I remember so well, would be overjoyed if he could hear his beloved organ today. For myself who knew the organ in his day and during the time of his successor, it was an exciting experience to hear its rich and noble ensemble and its wealth of quiet tonal colours of great beauty, displayed in his usual masterly manner by Thomas Trotter. May it be well used for many years to come. At Lincoln Cathedral we have built up attendances of up to 500 at the season of organ recitals by distinguished players during the Spring and Summer; it can be done at Nottingham, provided the authorities take courage in both hands and engage some of our leading players. There is a public within a wide area waiting to give support as was evident from the many conversations I had after the recital, before at long last the doors were closed!

Only a stone's throw or so away stands another untouched Binns at the former Castlegate Congregational Church, now the Congregational Centre. Here the gallery well has been filled in by a floor, thus creating room below and church above, which is also used as a concert hall. J. J. Binns' organ, built originally for the residence of G. E. Franklin of Derby in 1903, with a fine walnut case, four manuals and forty-five speaking stops. It was purchased by the Castlegate Church six years later, and opened by Bernard Johnson, then organist of Bridlington Priory Church. I have happy memories of this very fine instrument which I knew well in the days of my youth, and contributed an article on it and the Albert Hall organ for *The Choir.* I revisited the church in 1993 and was delighted to find that it had received conservation at the hands of an 'organisation of young musicians and trained organ builders'. Its handsome figured walnut console and solid ivory drawstops is a joy to behold. Tonally it possesses some exquisite quiet stops, while the flue ensemble is perhaps of a brighter texture than that at the Albert Hall.

J. J. Binns, who spent sixty-two years of his life in organ building, left school at the age of eleven and was apprenticed to Radcliffe & Sagar of Leeds, established by M. Sagar in 1861. Some seven years later, he joined Abbott & Co. (later Abbott & Smith) as a voicer and after five years' experience there, he set up in business on his own account. After several successful instruments had been erected, he built the fine premises at Bramley, Leeds, which he was to occupy until his death in 1929. As early as 1890, he was advertising in *Musical Opinion* as 'Inventor and Patentee of new Tubular Pneumatic and Electro-Pneumatic Actions which ensure a repetition and attack hitherto unattained by any other Pneumatic Actions. The voicing and regulating of *every* pipe used in the construction of organs at this factory are done personally by Mr Binns, which, coupled with exceeding care bestowed in the mechanism and other departments, give a most perfect result'. A disciple of Schulze, he was an idealist and a man of tireless energy; his instruments were noted for their fine craftsmanship, excellence of mechanical design and artistic tone. His work was the means of his gaining many important contracts and friendships of the leading organists of his day.

In an early Binns catalogue, Bernard Johnson summed up his testimonial on the Albert Hall organ by saying: 'The organ has been seen and heard by many of the first organists in this country and their invariable verdict has been "Magnificent" '. Today, Carlo Curley has described it as 'one of the finest concert organs in the world'.

THE ALBERT HALL, NOTTINGHAM 1909 & 1993
4 manuals: CC to C, 61 notes   Pedal: CCC to G, 32 notes

GREAT ORGAN

	ft
Double Open Diapason	16
Large Open Diapason	8
Medium Open Diapason	8
Small Open Diapason	8
Claribel Flute	8
Stop Diapason	8
Wald Flute	4
Octave	4
Dulciana Twelfth	2⅔
Fifteenth	2
Mixture	IV
Trombone	16
Tromba	8
Clarion	4

SWELL ORGAN

Contra Gamba	16
Quintaton	16
Open Diapason	8
Lieblich Gedact	8
Dolce	8
Viol d'Orchestre	8
Vox Angelica (originally Salicional)	8
Octave	4
Fifteenth	2
Mixture	III
Double Trumpet	16
Cornopean	8
Oboe	8
Clarion (originally Octave Oboe)	4
Tremulant	

CHOIR ORGAN

Lieblich Gedact	16
Lieblich Gedact	8
Hohl Flute	8
Dulciana	8

Viol de Gamba	8
Viole Céleste (originally Cor Anglais)	8
Harmonic Flute	4
Gemshorn	4
Flautina	2
Bassoon	16
Vox Humana	8
Tremulant	

SOLO ORGAN

Enclosed	
Harmonic Flute	8
Lieblich Gedact	8
Flauto Traverso	4
Piccolo	2
Bassoon (originally Violoncello)	8
Orchestral Oboe	8
Clarionet	8
Tremulant	
Unenclosed	
Tuba	8
Carillon (percussion, originally Reveille Bells)	–

PEDAL ORGAN

Double Open Diapason	32
Open Diapason	16
Contra Bass	16
Bourdon	16
Dulciana	16
Octave Diapason	8
Bass Flute	8
Dolce	8
Violoncello	8
Trombone	16
Euphonium	8

The Albert Hall, Nottingham, 1993. Photo by the Author

COUPLERS

Choir to Pedal   Great to Pedal   Swell to Pedal
Solo to Pedal   Swell to Choir   Solo to Choir
Choir to Great   Swell to Great   Solo to Great
Solo to Swell   Swell Octave   Swell Sub Octave
Swell to Great Octave   Swell to Great Sub Octave
Solo to Great Octave   Solo to Great Sub Octave
Solo Octave   Solo Sub Octave

ACCESSORIES

4 interchangeable combination pistons to Choir
4 interchangeable combination pistons to Great
and Pedal (duplicated by combination pedals)
1 fixed piston to Full Great and Pedal Organs
(duplicated by combination pedal)
4 interchangeable combination pistons to Swell
(duplicated by combination pedals)
1 fixed piston to Full Swell Organ
(duplicated by combination pedal)
4 interchangeable combination pistons to Solo

Reversible pedal to Great to Pedal
Balanced expression pedals to Choir, Swell and
Solo Organs.
Each interchangeable combination piston is adjustable
by a drawstop, on Binns' patent system

WIND PRESSURES

Pedal: Trombone, 8 ins.; Open Diapason, 6 ins.,
remainder, 4 ins.   Choir: 3¼ ins.
Great: reeds, Large Open Diapason & Octave, 6 ins.,
remainder, 4 ins.
Swell: reeds and Open Diapason, 6 ins.,
remainder, 3¾ ins.

The pitch is c = 517

Action: Binns' Patent Tubular-pneumatic System.

In 1992, I heard with pleasure of the restoration by Harrisons of the Father Willis organ of 1880 in Emmanuel United Reformed Church, Trumpington Street, Cambridge, which I was able to examine during the war on a quick visit to Cambridge for the RAF! It was rebuilt by Norman & Beard in 1911 who installed pneumatic actions and added a Choir Organ. Most of the Father Willis organ survived however, including the console, soundboards and pipework. In 1992, the additions were removed and the original two-manual specification re-instated; any changes to the voicing were reversed. New tracker actions for the manuals and couplers were made in the style of Father Willis; the Pedal Organ remains pneumatic, as originally, and a new independent Trombone has been added.

The specification is as follows, and I can assure readers that this exciting old instrument is well worth a journey to hear.

EMMANUEL UNITED REFORMED CHURCH, CAMBRIDGE 1992

GREAT ORGAN	ft		
Open Diapason	8	Salicional	8
Open Diapason	8	Vox Angelica (tenor C)	8
Claribel Flute	8	Gemshorn	4
Gamba	8	Flageolet	2
Dulciana	8	Mixture 17·19·22	III
Principal	4	Oboe	8
Harmonic Flute	4	Horn	8
Fifteenth	2		
Tromba	8	PEDAL ORGAN	
Clarinet	8	Open Diapason (wood)	16
		Bourdon	16
SWELL ORGAN		Trombone (new)	16
Lieblich Bourdon	16	COUPLERS	
Lieblich Gedact	8		
Open Diapason	8	Swell to Great Swell to Pedals Great to Pedals	

ST. BEES PRIORY CHURCH, CUMBRIA

As this book was being finalised in May 1994, a much needed holiday took my wife and I to the Lake District. As we had not visited the west coast of Cumbria before, we had a most pleasurable excursion to Silloth, overlooking the Solway Firth, through Whitehaven and thence to St Bees, with the hope of being fortunate enough to hear the famous Father Willis organ of 1899 in the Priory Church. It has become legendary in the organ world due to the publicity given it by Lieut. Col. George Dixon, M.A., T.D. (1870–1950), one of the leading authorities on British organ design in the first half of this century and author, with the late Cecil Clutton, of *The Organ, Its Tonal Structure and Registration*. A full obituary of this remarkable man will be found in *Musical Opinion* for Nov.–Dec. 1950. Col. Dixon took me under his wing when I met him in London in 1929 at the age of sixteen; thereafter he corresponded with me regularly and I have all his letters from which I learned much. He was the most kindly and forthright friend anyone could have; I particularly treasure a most informative letter sent to me whilst serving in a lonely RAF outpost not far from the Japanese troops in Burma. He was a close friend and constant visitor to the home of Arthur Harrison at Durham, where the three daughters, Dorothy, Elizabeth and Margaret were very fond of him; the late Lady Longland (known to all her friends as 'Peggy') once told me that he was known to them as 'Mr Punch'!

It has taken me some sixty-five years to hear the St Bees organ on a very rushed visit to the Priory Church, which was made possible through the kindness of Mr & Mrs G. Brightman, the former being assistant organist. I found the interest in the organ and Col. Dixon unabated, and it was a great tonic to hear this as well as to find literature available, a tape recording by Roger Fisher and details of organ recitals given or planned by our leading players. A visitors book, commenced by the Colonel in 1910, containing signatures of leading organists, organ builders, writers and others, was pressed into my hands and so another signature was added!

The earliest recorded visit to the organ in this little brown book is: 'Alfred Hollins gave recitals August 1906, July 1911' in Col. Dixon's own hand. Another reads 'Lieut. Col. Dixon, T.D., M.A., to whom the Priory organ owes its existence, died on 21st October, 1950, aged 80 years. The Funeral Service in the Priory was fully choral and the organist was Norman Cocker, Manchester Cathedral'. He was a frequent visitor to the organ.

It so happened that the pedal board was at Harrison's works for re-facing, together with restoration of the combination action, and so my playing and that of Mr Brightman was confined to the manuals only, while the swell pedal was not in use. The church gives no assistance acoustically but the organ is memorable for its tonal beauty, perfect balance and indeed, everything that makes a Father Willis instrument so unique in the emotional experience it provides. I was able to compare it with that at Lincoln Cathedral (built a year previous to St Bees) at masterly recitals by James O'Donnell of Westminster Cathedral, on 30th May, and Colin Walsh on 13th June, and can only say that I am always deeply moved by its wondrous beauty and majesty of tone. At Lincoln, both Swell and Great mixtures are 12·19·22; at St Bees, that on the Swell is of the same composition, but the Great is 17·19·22, which according to a letter to me dated 15th March, 1943, from Henry Willis III, 'was on Stainer's persuasion adopted by his grandfather and thereafter called "The Stainer Mixture", breaking to 15·19·22 and 8·12·15'.

The St Bees organ has a link with Lincoln Cathedral in that most of the Pedal open diapason wood 16ft consists of former pipes of William Allen's solitary pedal pipes in his instrument of 1826 as enlarged by his son Charles, in 1851. They have oak mouths and doubtless were discarded as being insufficient in scale for such a vast building as Lincoln.

Henry Willis, clad as always in his skull cap, personally supervised the construction and final tonal finishing and considered that the Swell contra posaune was the finest example that had emanated from his voicing shop. He inserted the stopped diapason which had originally been included in his first Cathedral organ at Gloucester in 1847—a lovely stop with historic associations. Despite the dull acoustics of the building, he was pleased to have the whole of the lofty space of the south transept to build in and how he needed it to accommodate the pneumatic tubing alone, together with the bulky apparatus for the adjustable pistons, similar to that at Lincoln Cathedral.

A very brief account of the development of this very important instrument is essential, for it shows the loving care that has been expended on it over some ninety-five years. F. J. Livesey (organist of the Priory 1887–1934) who, as a boy, was inspired by the playing of W. T. Best at St George's Hall, Liverpool, designed the tonal scheme and during his tenure of office, had the following work carried out.

> 1905.— W. C. Jones (then reed voicer at Harrisons) revoiced the Pedal ophicleide on 15 ins, its former pressure of 7 ins. proving inadequate for its use in the full organ. The brass-loaded reeds were retained and the tone was unaltered. The Great reeds received harmonic trebles while the clarinet and tuba were minutely regulated. The Great twelfth was re-scaled two pipes bigger and the Great cornet was inserted. The lowest thirty pipes of the Great double open diapason were placed on separate chests and borrowed on to the Pedal Organ.
>
> 1908.— The richly carved oak front, designed and executed by Ralph Hedley, R.A., of Newcastle-upon-Tyne, was added.
>
> 1931.— Clean and overhaul by Harrison & Harrison, when Livesey had the lowest five notes of the Pedal open diapason (wood) carried down to GGG 21⅓, to form a 32ft stop. The adjustable piston mechanism was also fully restored.
>
> 1949.— To celebrate the Golden Jubilee of the organ, the Pedal ophicleide was extended down to provide a 32ft reed. Presented by Col. Dixon, it was the sixteenth 32ft reed Harrisons had voiced or re-voiced.
>
> 1979–82.— This period marked the last major restoration when the remainder of the 1899 leatherwork was replaced.

ST BEES PRIORY 1899

3 manuals: CC to A, 58 notes   Pedal: CCC to F, 30 notes

GREAT ORGAN

	ft
Double Open Diapason	16
Stopped Diapason	8
Hohl Flute	8
Geigen Principal (prepared for)	8
Open Diapason No. 1	8
Wald Flute	4
Principal	4
Twelfth	2⅔
Fifteenth	2
Cornet 17·19·22	III
Tromba (harmonic trebles)	8
Clarion (harmonic trebles)	4

SWELL ORGAN

Lieblich Gedackt (prepared for)	8
Open Diapason	8
Gemshorn	4
Flageolet	2
Mixture 12·19·22	III
Vox Humana (prepared for)	8
Double Bassoon (prepared for)	16
Oboe	8
Contra Posaune	16
Cornopean	8
Clarion	4
Tremulant	

SOLO ORGAN

Enclosed

Contra Salicional (closed wood bass)	16
Viole d'Amour	8
Voix Celestes (tenor C)	8
Claribel Flute	8
Concert Flute	4
Harmonic Piccolo	2
Orchestral Clarinet	8
Sharp Mixture 22·29 (prepared for)	II

Unenclosed

Tuba Mirabilis	8

PEDAL ORGAN

Double Open Diapason (to GGG)	32
Bourdon	16
Open Diapason (metal)	16
Open Diapason (wood)	16
Bass Flute	8
Double Ophicleide	32
Ophicleide	16

WIND PRESSURES

Pedal: flue work, 3, 3½ and 4½ ins. reeds, 15 ins.
Manual flue work, with clarinet, vox humana
and double bassoon, 3½ ins.
Chorus reeds and oboe, 7 ins.
Action: 12 and 16 ins.
Tubular-pneumatic action, patented 1889.

OTHER DETAILS

14 couplers, 21 pistons and composition pedals.
Pistons adjustable from interior switchboard.
2 lever swell pedals with pneumatic locking
mechanism (Willis Patent N° 1244, 1890).
Solid ivory drawstops, the speaking stops being
lettered in black and the couplers in red.
The pistons are of engine-turned brass.

The Organists and Choirmasters at the Priory since F. J. Livesey (1887–1934) have been Andrew Pettigrew (1934–36); W. M. Coulthard (1936–1950); A. G. Matthew (1951–52); E. G. Whipp (previously deputy organist, then Organist and Choirmaster November 1952–58) and today's incumbent; Edward G. Robertson, appointed in July 1955.

In the vestry is an oak music cupboard with four finely carved medallions, each representing aspects of nineteenth-century organ music, in this order, right to left: head and shoulder portraits of H. Willis (organ building), W. T. Best (organ playing), H. Smart (organ music) and S. S. Wesley (choral music). No records exist as to who was responsible for these, but it is thought that F. J. Livesey had the cupboard made for his music and that Ralph Hedley made and carved it when he executed the case in 1908. It must be unique and the music staff of the Priory are justly proud of it. In thinking of W. T. Best, and his remarkable achievements, reminds me of a talk given by H. Goss Custard, that other great organist in the City of Liverpool. In December 1949, he spoke about his reminiscences to the Liverpool Organist's Association, the following extract being taken from *Musical Opinion* for February 1950. 'Regarding Sir John Stainer, he (Best) said that he had not heard his equal as an accompanist of a Cathedral Service. Dr. A. H. Mann, of King's College, Cambridge, probably came nearest in this respect. Stainer's accompaniment to Spohr's 'Last Judgement' (which was performed every Advent at St Paul's) was of such an order that W. T. Best frequently went to hear him.'

My visit to St Bees Priory will always remain a cherished memory; a glorious instrument and a warm welcome awaits the organ lover, while St Bees Head and the surrounding coastline provides relaxation; all in all it is a must! Detailed articles will be found in *The Organ* No. 43: 'St Bees Priory Church and its Organs', (George Dixon); No. 100, 'St Bees Revisited' (Cecil Clutton); No. 114 'The Golden Jubilee of a Celebrated Organ' (Reginald Whitworth). To sum up, the late Cecil Clutton wrote… 'It is the rigid economy of design for which the specification is most conspicuous, within thirty-five speaking stops have been compressed all the important effects to be looked for (but not always found) in a Cathedral organ'.

Our Father Willis organ at Lincoln Cathedral has received the same care and devotion during the past ninety-six years as that at St Bees. Dr. G. J. Bennett (Organist and Master of the Choristers, 1895–1930) designed the specification in collaboration with Willis and the stops, Pedal and Accompaniment to Solo Pistons and Pedal and Accompaniment to Choir Pistons were his brainchild. The idea was worked out at the London works and proved so successful that the former stop was included in the St Bees scheme. Dr. Bennett greatly loved his organ and throughout his career at Lincoln invited many famous recitalists to display its beauty.

Dr. Gordon Slater (1930–66), with his infectious enthusiasm, spread the fame of the organ far and wide and when the time came for a much needed rebuild in 1960, he was adamant that the original tone was preserved throughout, to which Harrisons were in full agreement.

Dr. Philip Marshall's magical accompaniments to the services and his masterly improvisations in his recitals showed every facet of the instrument, at which he presided with distinction from 1966–86. He ensured that it was kept in tip top condition and made its fame known throughout the land by the broadcast of Evensong and recordings of both choir and organ.

Our present Organist and Master of the Choristers, Colin Walsh, came to Lincoln with the sound of the earlier Father Willis organ in Salisbury Cathedral ringing in his ears. His enthusiasm for 'The Lincoln Sound' knows no bounds! A portrait of Father Willis hangs in the organ loft and he has gone to immense pains to find out everything he can about the instrument which he greatly treasures. He revels in making it known to a wider audience than that at Lincoln, by a number of magnificent recordings which have proved very popular, as have the annual celebrity organ recitals which attract large numbers. His own brilliant recitals reveal hidden beauties in this remarkable instrument and in acknowledging the applause at their conclusion, he invariably pays tribute to it as will be seen from this photograph taken by the author, on 13th June, 1994.

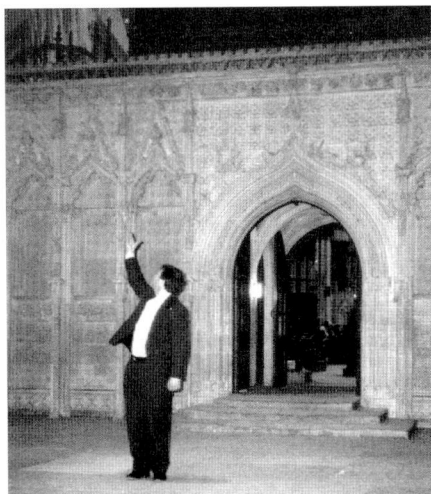

right
Lincoln Cathedral organ, the west front. Photo by the Author

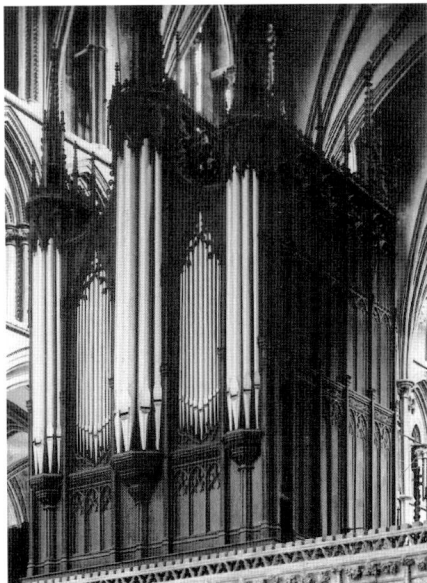

These last two illustrations certainly fall under the heading 'Stop Press', for they were discovered in checking some references during proof reading! The 'Kinetic' advertisement appeared in the handbook for The Wesleyan Methodist Conference, 1925, held at Lincoln. By then, the two Cousans brothers responsible for the invention of the blower, had severed their connection with the company. Sometime during 1910, L. B. Cousans started his own business: The Rotasphere Co. in London, where amongst other products he manufactured were motor generators for John Comptons's electric action during the early days of his firm in Nottingham. The business founded by L. B. Cousans was sold when he emigrated to Australia, soon after the first world war; it became G. R. Dain & Co., who named their blowers 'Duplex'. Finally, from about 1924–25, the firm became a subsidiary of Wm. Hill & Son and Norman & Beard Ltd. The Kinetic Company of Lincoln and London was eventually purchased by The Sturtevant Engineering Company Ltd.

The cartoon was specially drawn for *The Hull Daily Mail* in 1909. It bore this caption: WHEN (!) THE CITY HALL IS OPENED. Visitor to City Hall. "I did not know you had an aviary here". Attendant: "No Sir, we haven't, that's the organist practising".

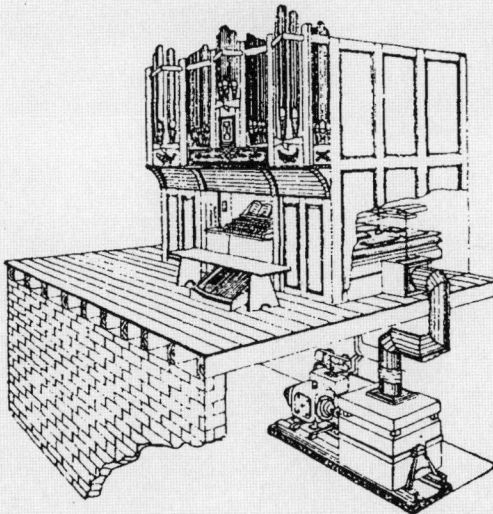

Office Entrance
St Stephens

above
Norman & Beard's factory
at Norwich. Taken from
their catalogue, 1912

left
The Crystal Palace

below left
The Grand Transept Organ,
Crystal Palace

above
Lincoln Cathedral. The Father Willis
console, 1898. Photo by the Author

right
Organ lovers often are devotees of steam
locomotives too. In the opinion of the
author, a Father Willis console and a
steam locomotive share a similar
grandeur. Pictured here is the G.W.R.
loco 'Clun Castle' at Rothley, on the
Great Central Line between
Loughborough and Leicester.
Photo by A. J. Elvin, 1993

left
St Bees Priory Church.
Photo by Roger Savage,
courtesy of D. R. Lane

below left and right
Priory Church of St Bees,
left- and right-hand stop
jambs. Photos by
the Author

398

Wood carvings on the music cupboard doors in the vestry at St Bees Priory.
Reproduced by the kind permission of Norman Parkinson, St Bees, Cumbria.
clockwise S. S. Wesley, Father Henry Willis, W. T. Best, H. Smart

above and below The Binns organ in The Congregational Centre, Nottingham. Photos by the Author, 1992

right
Had it not been for the
long friendship with
R. A. Cousans, organ
builder, of Lincoln,
and all he taught me, it
is doubtful whether this
book, together with the
previous ones, would
ever have been written

far right
A voicer's apprentice.
The Author at the age
of seventeen, voicing a
dulciana at the works of
Cousans Sons & Co.,
Lincoln

below
The premises and cars of the Kinetic-Swanton Co. Ltd., outside the works on Waterside North, Lincoln. Hugh
Swanton became a partner when R. A Cousans left the Kinetic Company, which he had founded with his brother
in 1902. They were co-patentees of the first organ blower using fans in series. Blowers went all over the world
and the firm eventually became known as The Kinetic Co. Ltd., of Lincoln and London

At the conclusion of three years' work on this book, it was inevitable that the vast accumulation of papers had to be tidied up and put away—a mammoth task which brought to light several treasures. Amongst them was this photograph of Herbert Hodge at the Father Willis console of 1871 of the Royal Albert Hall organ, which was given to me some years ago by the late Cuthbert Harrison. As it is very doubtful whether it has ever been published, it simply had to be included at the very last minute. Autographed at the foot of the photograph, it was the work of the well-known London photographers, J. Russell & Son, By Appointment To H. M. The King. Its date is not known.

In conversation with Henry Willis IV at the 68th anniversary organ recital at Liverpool Cathedral on 15th October, I mentioned its inclusion in my forthcoming book, saying how pleased Father Willis would have been if he knew. Henry Willis's reply was immediate—'So would Cuthbert too'!

It is good to be able to recall Cuthbert Harrison in this book; not only was he a distinguished organ builder, but was held in great esteem by all who knew him.

HERBERT HODGE.
AT THE
ROYAL ALBERT HALL. LONDON.

TRADE SUPPLIERS

During the long and detailed research which this book has entailed, further names of trade suppliers have come to light. In view of their importance to organ builders and historians not only today, but in the future, it has been decided to include this list, which is supplementary to that published in the author's book: *Family Enterprise, The Story of Some North Country Organ Builders* (1986).

The abbreviation OB refers to the journal: *The Organbuilder*

Keith S. Bance, Organ builder and voicing specialist. 72 Waverley Road, Harrow, Middx. (OB 1994).

Roger Box, voicing specialist. Plymouth. (1994)

Solid State Transmission. Christie Music Transmissions Ltd., 61 Magdalen Street, Colchester, Essex CO1 2JU. (current)

John R. Clough & Sons. Organ builders. Moorcroft Works, 80 Moorcroft Drive, Bradford. Top quality wooden pipes, bellows etc. (OB Sept. 1993).

G.P.S. Agencies. Sole suppliers of alternative ivory, CoL.849/TM, the only Cast Polyester with the characteristics of real ivory, also alternative grained or plain ivory and bone. Units 3 & 3a, Hambrook Business Centre, Cheesman's Lane, Hambrook, Chichester, West Sussex PO18 8XP. *The Organ*, April 1994.

David Graebe. Architect and designer of organ cases. Chant Stream Cottage, Kent Street, Sedlescombe, Battle, East Sussex. (OB 1991).

Richard Le Grice. Reed voicer, tonal finisher, general tuner. The Old Hart, Weston Longville, Norwich. (OB Sept. 1993).

David Hunt. Computerised engraving services. Specialist engraver of stop knobs, builder's name plates and console components etc. Curples Cottage, High Street, Fineham, King's Lynn, Norfolk. (OB Sept. 1993).

Jeffrey M. Heard. 83 Thornhill Road, Steeton, Keighley, West Yorkshire. Installation of Solid State and Electro-Mechanical systems. Consoles wired. Fault diagnosis and repairs. (*Organists' Review* 1991).

Lyndale Woodcarving Associates. Derek Riley and Keith German. Specialists in decorative carving for organbuilders, church work and carved lettering. (OB Sept. 1993).

Metra Non-Ferrous Metals Ltd. Zinc for organ pipes. Pindar Road, Hoddesdon, Herts. (OB 1991).

The Piano Warehouse. 30a Highgate Road, London NW5. Keyboard recovering and repair specialists. 50 years' experience (formerly Monington & Weston). (OB 1991).

Russell Fine Leathers. Great North Road, Wyboston, Bedfordshire. (OB Sept. 1993).

A. J. & L. Taylor Ltd., Thorp Street, Ramsbottom, Lancs. Suppliers of quality components, Mechanical or Microprocessor. Tradition or Technology. (OB Sept. 1993).

Don Wherly, Pipemaker. Liskeard, Cornwall. (current).

It is interesting to record that Henry Willis & Sons Ltd. had an Electrical Amplification Dept. at 234 Ferndale Road, London SW9, which was advertised in *The Rotunda* during 1934.

ADDENDA

Specialist books can never claim to be 100% complete. Personal experience and in particular, friendship with the late Sir Francis Hill (Lincoln's distinguished Historian and author of major works on the city's history), taught me the importance of knowing when to stop in compiling a book. Inevitably, facts from some source or other will come to light some time after publication, no matter how thorough the research has been. It is hoped that *Pipes and Actions* will stimulate someone in the future to bring forth much more information about the organ builders of this country.

Before this narrative went to press, an interesting and most informative conversation with Mr Michael Mason, who was with Comptons for some thirty-two years, gave me a genuine excuse for adding this paragraph. He informed me that the BBC concert organ and that at Maida Vale are kept in good order by B. C. Shepherd & Son of Edgware, Middx.

Michael Mason has St Bride's Church, Fleet Street and St Luke's Church, Chelsea, in his care. In both cases, Solid State has been introduced and other work—thus up-dating action which had given many years excellent service. The Chelsea instrument was originally only intended to be a 'six ranker'. The basic work comprised pipework from Midgeley's residence organ with additions; John Compton had carried out much of the voicing. Known to his staff as 'The Boss', he gave freedom to experiment for he regarded them as his family.

At Downside Abbey, the internal reservoirs were his idea, the practicalities being worked out by J. I. Taylor. Supplying individual pressure to each rank, they have one disadvantage. Mr Roger Taylor tells me that on the very rare occasions when they need attention, the whole soundboard has to be turned over to get at them—not any easy task within the very narrow confines of the chambers.

Several ranks of pipes were new to me when I examined the interior of the Downside organ; in particular were the small scale gedachts with an extremely high arched mouth similar to the pointed arch of a church. It was not easy to get a photograph to illustrate them here. They were known amongst the staff as the 'Mersey Tunnel' mouths! They certainly produced a piquant tone. The horn, which actually is a French horn in tone, has bigger tips that usual (which helped to give the orchestral 'bubble') and there are pyramid-shaped caps to the resonators. There is a similar stop at St Bride's, Fleet Street. They were voiced by George Farrer, who later went to Peter Conacher & Co. at Huddersfield. Much of the final tonal finishing of the entire instrument was carried out by John Compton. When Marcel Dupré first heard the organ, he could not believe it was built on the extension system!

'Of making many books there is no end...' *Ecclesiastes*. I realised this when the proofing of this work was almost over, for the organ recital by Ian Tracey, commemorating the 68th Anniversary of the opening of the Liverpool Cathedral organ, on 15th October, 1994, inspired additional photographs, for which, fortunately, there was room. It was a great occasion, for not only was present the usual large audience, but also the members of the Federation of Master Organ Builders and the Incorporated Society of Organ Builders. It was a great pleasure to meet old friends and for the first time, master organ builders who have made valuable contributions to this book. A breathless discussion with Henry Willis IV included the subject of the Alexandra Palace organ, to which he has given so much of his expertise in restoring it to its present state, but also considerable time in appealing for the necessary funds to complete this vast undertaking. Ian Tracey's masterly playing of an exciting programme included the first performance of Noel Rawsthorne's *Fantasie on B.A.C.H. for Pedals*. This was a veritable *tour de force*; in the words of the composer, it was written 'in order that I could come and watch my successor get his feet in a twist'! This did not happen, for Ian came down into the audience and shook hands with his predecessor amidst tumultuous applause after hearing thirteen movements of a brilliantly conceived work.

right
Henry Willis IV 'cut off in his prime' at the 68th Anniversary Recital, Liverpool Cathedral, 15th October, 1994, taken under great difficulties.
Photo by the Author

Index